Biology

Teacher Book

Muriel Claybrook, Keith Hirst, Sue Kearsey

with Rob Wensley

Series editor
Nigel English

www.pearsonschools.co.uk
✓ Free online support
✓ Useful weblinks
✓ 24 hour online ordering

0845 630 33 33

Part of Pearson

Longman is an imprint of Pearson Education Limited, Edinburgh Gate, Harlow, Essex, CM20 2JE.

www.pearsonschools.co.uk

Longman is a registered trademark of Pearson Education Limited

Typeset by Tech-Set Ltd, Gateshead

Cover photo: A succulent adapted to a dry environment, with spiny leaves to deter animals seeking food. © Corbis: Micha Pawlitski.

First published 2011

15 14 13 12 11

10 9 8 7 6 5 4 3 2 1

British Library Cataloguing in Publication Data

A catalogue record for this book is available from the British Library

ISBN 978 1 408 25375 5

Printed in Spain by Grafos SA.

Acknowledgements

Every effort has been made to contact copyright holders of material reproduced in this book. Any omissions will be rectified in subsequent printings if notice is given to the publishers.

Websites

Links to websites relevant to this book are available on our website at www.pearsonhotlinks.co.uk. Search for the title AQA GCSE Biology Teacher Pack or ISBN 978 1 408 25376 2.

Introduction and how to use this book

The aim of this Teacher Book is to give you an overview of the Longman AQA GCSE Biology resources published to support the teaching of the three Biology units: B1, B2 and B3. It is designed to make planning your teaching of the AQA GCSE Biology specification straightforward.

The book contains images of each spread in the Biology Student Book with text taken from the accompanying lesson guide (the full lesson guide is in the Biology Teacher and Technician Planning Pack) to give you an at-a-glance view of the suggested structure of each lesson.

This gives clear references to the AQA specification for the lesson. There are links to the main specification points, the suggested practical activities, how science works in terms of the skills, knowledge and understanding (SKU) bullets at the start of each section in the specification, and the controlled assessment (CA) specification points.

Links to useful websites/Internet sites are also included. They are in blue within the text. See the imprint page for details on how to access the websites.

These suggested activities are taken from the lesson guide and give you some ideas on how to structure the lesson. Worksheets, practical and teacher sheets available in the Teacher and Technician Planning Pack or Activity Pack are highlighted in bold.

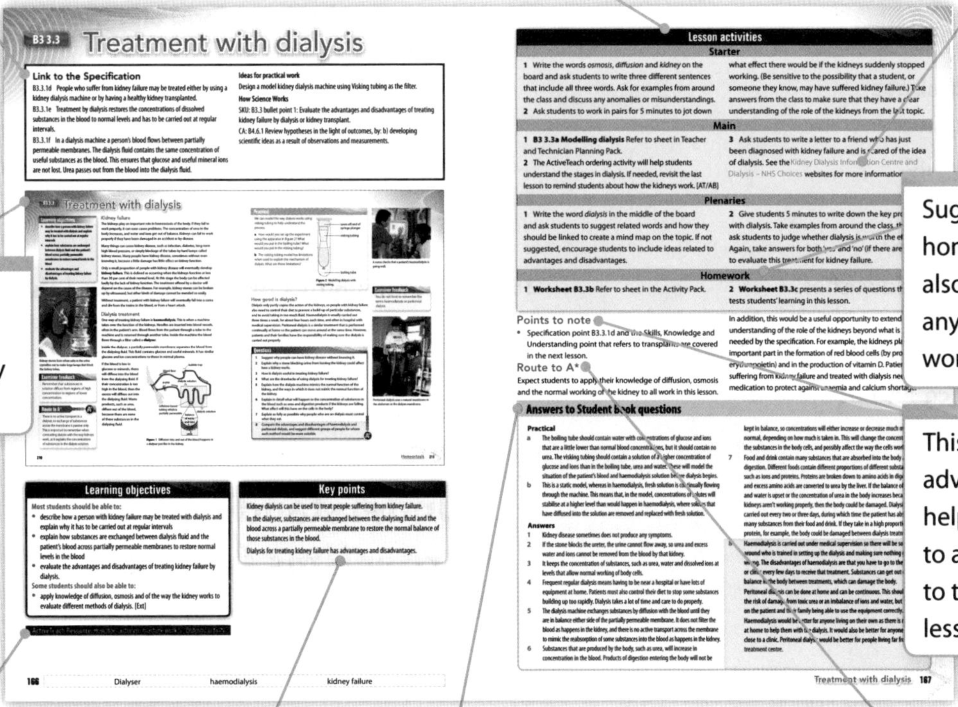

An image of the Student Book is included for easy reference.

Suggestions for homework are also given with any references to worksheets in bold.

This includes advice that will be helpful, particularly to a teacher new to teaching the lesson.

Key points are included as well as keywords and lesson objectives; they are focused on stretching the more able.

Suggestions are offered on how to extend the lesson to stretch the most able.

Where there is a digital asset on the Biology ActiveTeach disk, such as a video, interactive activity, animation or PowerPoint that supports the lesson, this is highlighted.

Answers to all questions on the main and ISA practice student book pages are included. The answers to the assess yourself questions and the examination style questions are in Word files on the Teacher and Technician Planning Pack CD-ROM so that they can be easily printed/photocopied to give to students, if required.

Contents

Researching, planning and carrying out an investigation

This lesson looks at how students can research a scenario and then develop a hypothesis that can be tested from research.

Link to the specification

Controlled assessment

- Stating the purpose of an investigation. [B4.1.1]
- Recognise significant variables in an investigation. [B4.1.1]
- Recognising a control variable in an investigation. [B4.1.1]
- Understanding the purpose of a control group. [B4.1.1]
- Identifying intervals in measurements. [B4.1.1]
- Understanding the meaning of the term hypothesis. [B4.1.2]
- Making a prediction about the outcome of an investigation, based on a hypothesis. [B4.1.2]
- Planning a fair test. [B4.1.2]

Presenting, analysing and evaluating results

Learning objectives

- describe how to report and process your experimental data
- evaluate the data collected, identifying errors
- analyse the evidence from your data and other data
- use research to confirm whether the findings are valid.

Processing your data

On the previous pages you looked at the hypothesis *Leaves in shade are larger to allow them to collect the same amount of energy from light as smaller leaves in direct sunlight*. To judge if the hypothesis is true or false, you need to process the data you have obtained, and look for patterns and trends in the data.

Sometimes you can spot a trend or pattern in a set of results from a table, but more likely you will need to see the data as a bar chart, if the independent variable is **categoric**, or as a line graph, for **continuous variables**.

When plotting a line graph you should first plot the points and then look for a pattern in the points. Draw the best-fit line or curve. Sometimes there are anomalous results, which show up as points that would not lie on your best-fit line or curve. Plot the line or curve leaving these points out.

The best-fit line or curve shows you the relationship between the two variables. Straight lines indicate a linear relationship. In Figure 1, the top graph shows a **positive linear** relationship, while the middle graph shows a **negative linear** relationship. If the line goes through the origin, where the axes meet, then the relationship may be **directly proportional**. This is only the case when the origin of the graph is truly zero on both axes.

Curved lines indicate a more complex relationship. Be aware that if a curved graph has a peak, it can be hard to predict where exactly the peak is for the data you have. You need to get more data from the part of the range where you think the peak is. This would be an improvement to your investigation.

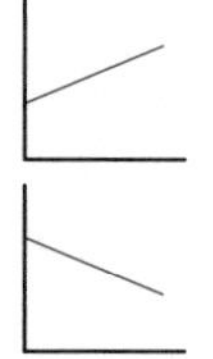

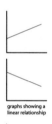

graphs showing a linear relationship

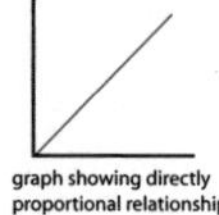

graph showing directly proportional relationship

Figure 1 Examples of line graphs.

Examiner feedback

In science you should only plot your line with the data you have. Unless you have a value for the origin, do not plot it or connect your line to it. Not all graphs meet the axes at the origin. For example, remember that in winter the temperature drops to less than 0°C. This means that 0°C is not zero for a temperature axis. In fact the lowest possible temperature, the true value for zero, is −273.15°C.

Examiner feedback

When asked for improvements to an investigation you should clearly identify what you want to change, with a clear reason for the change and how this will help to prove or disprove the hypothesis. For example, 'From my results I cannot be sure where the peak activity for an enzyme is in terms of the pH, so I need to obtain more values between pH 4 and 6.'

Analysing the evidence

Your conclusion must relate to the investigation. In our example of leaf area, you should clearly relate the light intensity to the area of the leaf, for example '*My graph shows that as the light intensity increases, the average leaf area decreases*.' You should also state whether this confirms or rejects the hypothesis.

x

Other people have also researched this type of problem. Football clubs find it difficult getting grass to grow on the pitch because of the shadows cast by the stands. Data from a study into grass-blade area in a football ground could provide data to back up your hypothesis. Look for ways that the data can confirm (or contradict) the trend you have observed. Remember the pattern is the important fact, not the actual figures.

Table 1 and Figure 2 contain more data about leaf area and growth rates. Try to identify which data would support the hypothesis and why.

How would you help this grass to grow evenly?

Questions

1 Look at the graph in Figure 2. Describe as fully as you can the relationship between the light intensity and the length of stalk.

2 Look at the data in Table 1. What evidence is there from Trial 1 to support the hypothesis?

Table 1 The area of hornbeam leaves against light intensity measured for different parts of a hedge.

Light intensity reading/mV	Area of each leaf/cm²			
	Trial 1	Trial 2	Trial 3	Mean area
195	26	28	22	25
408	19	19	22	20
598	14	27	16	19
812	12	8	10	10

3 Look at the data in Table 1 and Figure 2. Does the evidence here support the hypothesis?

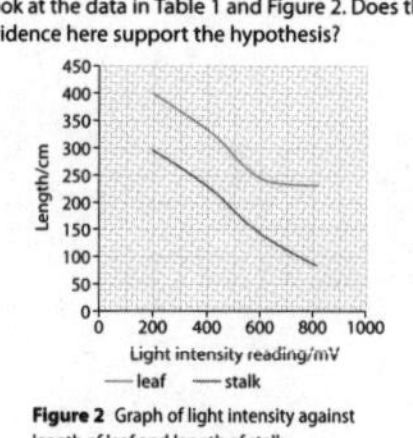

Figure 2 Graph of light intensity against length of leaf and length of stalk.

4 Critically evaluate the evidence from Tables 1 and 2 and Figure 2 and say whether you believe the hypothesis is proved.

Table 2 Light intensity on the pitch at Wembley at 6.00 pm.

Light intensity reading/mV	Position of grass in stadium
857	in front of North Stand
150	in front of West Stand
895	in front of East Stand
524	in front of South Stand

5 If you were to carry out this investigation, suggest improvements to the investigation in terms of measurements and techniques. You should also state any further work you might want to carry out to extend the investigation.

6 The head groundsman at Wembley would like your advice about how to make the blades of grass the same area across all the pitch. On the basis of the data and the investigation, what advice would you give him? Explain why you are giving that advice.

A*

How science works 1

Learning objectives

Most students should be able to:

- research and analyse scientific problems and develop hypotheses about these problems
- research and describe practical ways to investigate hypotheses. Explain the risks present in an experimental procedure and how to minimise them
- describe different types of variables and how to measure them.

Some students should also be able to:

- evaluate the different types of data available and judge which data is most likely to produce valid results.

Control variable categoric variable continuous variable control measure dependent variable hazards hypothesis independent variable observation prediction range repeatable reproducible research theory

Lesson activities

Starter

1 CAP (Consider All Possibilities) Give your students the statement 'The leaves on one side of my hedge are always bigger than the other.' Ask them to come up with as many possible reasons (possibilities) as they can for the observation. They may suggest it's to do with orientation of the hedge, amount of rain, buildings nearby, other plants, etc.

2 PMI (Plus, Minus, Interesting). 'The leaves on plants are all different sizes.' Students have to each suggest something positive about having different sized leaves, something negative and an interesting fact (which may be totally irrelevant) about leaf size, e.g. it's great to scuff through big leaves in the autumn.

Main

1 Students discuss what features of a habitat might affect the size of a leaf. They should also consider whether the time of day or weather has an impact on this.

2 Students should be encouraged to make a hypothesis about this, or weaker students could be given a hypothesis.

3 Students in small groups discuss how they can collect relevant data. They should find three or four sources of data.

4 Students should discuss what data they would need to obtain from one of the sources to allow them to test the hypothesis. They should also list those features that should be controlled. *Or* students could plan an investigation into the prediction that 'north facing leaves are larger than south facing leaves'.

5 Students should then carry out a risk assessment of the hazards of obtaining the data they need. They should mention the control measures they should use.

6 ***Alternative main task***. Split the class into groups. Give the groups the hypothesis from Starter task 1, then ask each group to carry out one of the Main tasks above, except for task 2. The most able group could be given the Route to A* task. Each group should produce a quick poster to meet the requirements of the task. After 30 minutes each group should present their findings to the whole class. (Use the order of the tasks for the presentations.)

Plenaries

1 Students produce a flow chart of the research, hypothesis and planning process they have carried out.

2 Give students a hypothesis, e.g. 'tall trees have bigger leaves than short trees'. Using 'show me boards', callout one variable at a time, and the students write if it is 'independent', 'control' or 'dependent'. Variables to use would include: height of tree, leaf size, soil nutrients, amount of water available.

Homework

1 Ask students to carry out the task 4 alternative they haven't done.

2 Students suggest places where they could find data to support the hypothesis 'living next to nuclear power stations causes more cancers in the population'. They should list the data they would need to collect to be able to prove or disprove the hypothesis.

Points to note

- The lesson is best conducted as a discussion lesson. Break the class into groups and review with a mini-plenary each of the tasks as they are done. You may need to set some ground rules for the lesson such as only one group can contribute at a time. Make it clear that criticism of data and methods is welcome so long as it is not personal.

Route to A*

Ask students to consider the sources of data about leaf size of plants that are not native to this country. They could suggest methods of gaining data other than the internet, e.g. visiting parks and gardens and finding non-native plants.

Answers to Student Book questions

1 A hypothesis is a general statement relating the known facts to a plausible explanation. A prediction is a statement that can be confirmed or disproved by an experiment, or collection of suitable data.

2 Take equal volumes of soil from the roots around each plant at the same time, record mass of wet soil, dry soil in oven and then re-weigh. Calculate percentage of water in soil sample, and divide leaf areas by the percentage.

3 Take samples of soil as in **2**, measure concentration of key elements (N, P, K) in each soil sample. Classify leaf sizes accordingly. Bearing in mind that leaf growth is most affected by nitrates, this would be best ion to test.

4 Average area of these leaves would be 1250 mm^2.

5 Hold leaf against each template in turn, and choose the template size for which the leaf fills the largest amount. Rules:
- set stalk of leaf against template stalk, so that leaf starts at same place as the template
- align leaf edges at one side of the template
- if leaf is just bigger than template, count it in that size if the excess amount is less than the unfilled amount of the larger template.

6 Students give a plan that allows a suitable number of leaves to be measured, and measures amount of light they each receive. They should seek to use mature leaves (leaves from low down a stem), and measure light intensity at the point from which the leaf is removed.

Presenting, analysing and evaluating results

This lesson looks at how to present data, analyse trends, evaluate a hypothesis, errors in data, and evaluating the evidence.

Link to the specification

Controlled assessment

- The mean (or average) of the data refers to the sum of all the measurements divided by the number of measurements taken. [B4.4.1]
- Line graphs can be used to display data in which both the independent and dependent variables are continuous. [B4.4.2]
- Patterns in tables and graphs can be used to identify anomalous data that require further consideration. [B4.5.2]
- A line of best fit can be used to illustrate the underlying relationship between variables. [B4.5.3]
- Conclusions must be limited by, and not go beyond, the data available. [B4.5.4]
- Evidence must be scrutinised for any potential bias of the experimenter, such as funding sources or allegiances. [B4.5.1]
- Evidence can be accorded undue weight, or dismissed too lightly, simply because of its political significance. If the consequences of the evidence could provoke public or political disquiet, the evidence may be downplayed. [B4.5.2]
- There are some questions that we cannot answer, maybe because we do not have enough reproducible, repeatable and valid evidence. [B4.5.4]

Presenting, analysing and evaluating results

Learning objectives

- describe how to report and process your experimental data
- evaluate the data collected, identifying errors
- analyse the evidence from your data and other data
- use research to confirm whether the findings are valid.

Processing your data

On the previous pages you looked at the hypothesis *Leaves in shade are larger to allow them to collect the same amount of energy from light as smaller leaves in direct sunlight*. To judge if the hypothesis is true or false, you need to process the data you have obtained, and look for patterns and trends in the data.

Sometimes you can spot a trend or pattern in a set of results from a table, but more likely you will need to see the data as a bar chart, if the independent variable is **categoric**, or as a line graph, for **continuous variables**.

When plotting a line graph you should first plot the points and then look for a pattern in the points. Draw the best-fit line or curve. Sometimes there are anomalous results, which show up as points that would not lie on your best-fit line or curve. Plot the line or curve leaving these points out.

The best-fit line or curve shows you the relationship between the two variables. Straight lines indicate a linear relationship. In Figure 1, the top graph shows a **positive linear** relationship, while the middle graph shows a **negative linear** relationship. If the line goes through the origin, where the axes meet, then the relationship may be **directly proportional**. This is only the case when the origin of the graph is truly zero on both axes.

Curved lines indicate a more complex relationship. Be aware that if a curved graph has a peak, it can be hard to predict where exactly the peak is for the data you have. You need to get more data from the part of the range where you think the peak is. This would be an improvement to your investigation.

graphs showing a linear relationship

graph showing directly proportional relationship

Figure 1 Examples of line graphs.

Examiner feedback

In science you should only plot your line with the data you have. Unless you have a value for the origin, do not plot it or connect your line to it. Not all graphs meet the axes at the origin. For example, remember that in winter the temperature drops to less than 0°C. This means that 0°C is not zero for a temperature axis. In fact the lowest possible temperature, the true value for zero, is −273.15°C.

Examiner feedback

When asked for improvements to an investigation you should clearly identify what you want to change, with a clear reason for the change and how this will help to prove or disprove the hypothesis. For example, 'From my results I cannot be sure where the peak activity for an enzyme is in terms of the pH, so I need to obtain more values between pH 4 and 6.'

Analysing the evidence

Your conclusion must relate to the investigation. In our example of leaf area, you should clearly relate the light intensity to the area of the leaf, for example '*My graph shows that as the light intensity increases, the average leaf area decreases.*' You should also state whether this confirms or rejects the hypothesis.

x

Other people have also researched this type of problem. Football clubs find it difficult getting grass to grow on the pitch because of the shadows cast by the stands. Data from a study into grass-blade area in a football ground could provide data to back up your hypothesis. Look for ways that the data can confirm (or contradict) the trend you have observed. Remember the pattern is the important fact, not the actual figures.

Table 1 and Figure 2 contain more data about leaf area and growth rates. Try to identify which data would support the hypothesis and why.

How would you help this grass to grow evenly?

Questions

1 Look at the graph in Figure 2. Describe as fully as you can the relationship between the light intensity and the length of stalk.

2 Look at the data in Table 1. What evidence is there from Trial 1 to support the hypothesis?

Table 1 The area of hornbeam leaves against light intensity measured for different parts of a hedge.

Light intensity reading/mV	Area of each leaf/cm²			
	Trial 1	Trial 2	Trial 3	Mean area
195	26	28	22	25
408	19	19	22	20
598	14	27	16	19
812	12	8	10	10

3 Look at the data in Table 1 and Figure 2. Does the evidence here support the hypothesis?

Figure 2 Graph of light intensity against length of leaf and length of stalk.

4 Critically evaluate the evidence from Tables 1 and 2 and Figure 2 and say whether you believe the hypothesis is proved.

Table 2 Light intensity on the pitch at Wembley at 6.00 pm.

Light intensity reading/mV	Position of grass in stadium
857	in front of North Stand
150	in front of West Stand
895	in front of East Stand
524	in front of South Stand

5 If you were to carry out this investigation, suggest improvements to the investigation in terms of measurements and techniques. You should also state any further work you might want to carry out to extend the investigation.

6 The head groundsman at Wembley would like your advice about how to make the blades of grass the same area across all the pitch. On the basis of the data and the investigation, what advice would you give him? Explain why you are giving that advice.

A*

How science works 1

Learning objectives

Most students should be able to:

- describe how to report and process experimental data
- evaluate the data collected, identifying errors
- analyse the evidence
- understand the terms repeatable, reproducible, resolution, calibration and uncertainty
- assess whether the findings are valid.

Some students should also be able to:

- describe the extent to which the evidence supports the hypothesis.

Anomalous result	calibration	errors	mean	random errors	repeatable
reproducible	systematic errors		uncertainty	validity	zero errors

Lesson activities

Starter

1 The time of day a leaf is exposed to light is an important factor in determining its size. Name the independent and dependent variables in the statement. List at least three control variables you should have in any investigation into the statement.

Main

1 Anomalous results and calculating means. Look at Table 1 in the Student Book. Ask students to identify the anomalous result in the data. Discuss how to calculate the mean of data, excluding any anomalous results. Students re-calculate the mean.

2 Plotting the graph. Students plot a graph of these results, i.e. light intensity against mean area of leaf.

3 Trends and patterns 1. Ask students to describe the results from their graph in terms of any trend they can spot. Does it confirm the hypothesis?

4 Trends and patterns 2. Ask students to use the data from Figure 2 in the book to make a conclusion about light intensity and length of the leaf stem.

5 Errors in data. Show your students this table of data.

Height of leaf above ground (cm)	Average size of 10 leaves (cm^2)	
	east side	west side
20	25	34
40	23	32
60	20	31
80	18	29
100	15	23

A group of students used the template method (Method B) from page ix of the Student Book to measure the size of the leaves on both sides of a hedge. The hedge had east and west facing sides. For this investigation two teams worked together, one on each side, and had separate templates. Tell them that the group measuring the leaves on the west side had a template that was wrong by 9 cm^2, so their results have an error (uncertainty). Discuss the ideas of zero errors, systematic errors, calibration, repeatable, reproducible, uncertainty using the data. Discuss how to remedy the error.

6 Validity and the hypothesis. Discuss if the results from Study 2:

- provide more evidence for the hypothesis
- are valid in terms of the hypothesis and investigation.

Students should see that the data does suggest that the higher the hedge leaf is, the smaller it is, and suggest this is because there is more light higher up. They should also point out that the (corrected) results show little difference between both sides.

Plenaries

1 Students make notes on the lesson keywords.

Homework

1 For students with weak graphing skills use data in part 6 to plot a graph.

2 Students should be asked to decide what type of relationship each of the graphs they have seen or drawn during the lesson shows, with reasons.

Points to note

The key points in the lesson include:

- producing a results table, and graph or bar chart
- examining data critically for errors and inconsistencies
- recognising that data is open to different interpretations.

Route to A*

Ask students to suggest reasons for the shape of the graph line on graph 1 for leaf size.

Answers to Student Book questions

1 The greater the light intensity the shorter the stalk. The relationship appears to be linear (within the limits of experimental variation).

2 The data support the hypothesis, as at a reading of 195 mV on the light meter the leaf area is 26 cm^2, and at 812 mV it is smaller, 12 cm^2.

3 Using the mean data from Table 1, and excluding the anomalous result at 598 mV, 27 cm^2, the data agrees with the hypothesis. While Figure 2 deals with stalk and leaf length, the fact that both are greater when the light levels are low supports the hypothesis as well.

4 Table 1 and Figure 2 strongly support the hypothesis; although in Figure 2 the type of leaf is not defined, a longer leaf will most likely have a greater area than a shorter leaf. The data in Table 2 has no relevance to the hypothesis, as it simply shows the light intensity at different parts of the pitch, and tells us nothing about the area of the blades of grass. It is also for a time of day when the sun is in the west, shading the grass in front of the West Stand more than it does during the rest of the day, and exposing the grass in the east to a higher reading than during the morning.

5 Improvements: Table 1 has too few results, so increase the sample size. Figure 2 measure the leaf area, and identify the type of plant. Improve the measurement of the area to mm^2 rather than cm^2. I would be interested to measure the size of the grass leaves in the different parts of Wembley (Table 2).

6 Ensure that all parts of the pitch receive the same amount of light each day; that way the leaves of the grass will be more likely to grow to be the same area. It would also make the grass stalks nearly the same length. (You could credit a suggestion to partially cover the stadium using the roof to ensure the same amount of light energy reaches the grass all over the pitch.)

B1 1.1 Diet and exercise

Link to the specification

B1.1.1a A healthy diet contains the right balance of the different foods you need and the right amount of energy. Carbohydrates, fats and proteins are used by the body to release energy and to build cells. Mineral ions and vitamins are needed in small amounts for healthy functioning of the body. A person is malnourished if their diet is not balanced. This may lead to a person being overweight or underweight. An unbalanced diet may also lead to deficiency diseases or conditions such as Type 2 diabetes.

B1.1.1c The rate at which all the chemical reactions in the cells of the body are carried out (the metabolic rate) varies with the amount of activity you do and the proportion of muscle to fat in your body. Metabolic rate may be affected by inherited factors.

B1.1.1d Inherited factors also affect our health; these include metabolic rate and cholesterol level.

B1.1.1e People who exercise regularly are usually healthier than people who take little exercise.

Ideas for practical work

Computer simulations to model the effect of: balanced and unbalanced diets and exercise.

How Science Works

SKU: B1.1 bullet 1: Candidates should use their skills, knowledge and understanding to evaluate information about the effect of food on health.

CA: B4.4.1a Appreciating when it is appropriate to calculate a mean; B4.4.1b Calculating the mean of a set of at least three results; B4.5.2a Identifying causes of variation in data; B4.5.2b Recognising and identifying the cause of random errors. When a data set contains random errors, repeating the readings and calculating a new mean can reduce their effect; B4.5.2c Recognising and identifying the cause of anomalous results; B4.5.2d Recognising and identifying the cause of systematic errors.

B1 1.1 Diet and exercise

Learning objectives

- explain why we need a healthy diet
- describe what is meant by metabolic rate
- interpret information about how metabolic rate and exercise are related to fitness
- explain how inherited factors affect our health
- evaluate information about the effect of food on health
- evaluate information about the effect of lifestyle on development of disease.

Changing lifestyles

The newspaper article in Figure 1 shows how medical experts are worried about the effects of poor diet and lack of exercise on young people. Experts are warning that many children are overweight or obese and therefore have more chance of developing serious health problems in later life.

Science skills

BRITISH CHILDREN TOP LEAGUE FOR UNHEALTHY LIVING

From our health correspondent.

The largest study of youth health reveals that British children live on sugary snacks and almost no fruit and vegetables.

The World Health Organisation report, based on surveys of more than 160 000 children in 35 countries, found that the dietary habits of Britain's young were among the worst.

Doctors recommend at least five portions of vegetables daily for a healthy diet. More than two-thirds of children aged 11–15 admitted that they did not eat even a single portion of vegetables a day. A third of 11-year-olds drank at least one sugary drink a day, as well as eating sweets and chocolate every day. Snacks and sugary drinks are high-energy foods.

Poor diet and increasingly inactive lifestyles are blamed for a massive increase in the number of people who are overweight.

Figure 1 Unhealthy children.

a Use information from the newspaper article to explain why poor diet and inactive lifestyles are blamed for the increase in obesity.

Taking it further

Insulin controls the amount of glucose in the blood. In one form of **diabetes**, type 2 diabetes, the body still makes insulin, but needs more than it produces, or cannot use insulin properly. Type 2 diabetes is much more common than type 1 diabetes (in which no insulin is produced). It usually develops in people over the age of 40. The risk of developing diabetes increases with body mass; it is three times more common in people who are 10 kg overweight. However, type 2 diabetes is now being reported in children, all of whom so far have been overweight.

You are what you eat

The amount and type of food that you eat has a major effect on your health. **Carbohydrates** and **fats** in your food provide the energy you need to stay alive and be active. Food also provides the **proteins**, **vitamins** and **minerals** your body uses to grow and to replace damaged cells and tissues. By eating a varied diet you are more likely to get everything you need to keep your body healthy.

Malnutrition happens when you eat the wrong amount of each type of **nutrient**; either too much or too little. **Deficiency diseases** can occur when the body doesn't get enough of a certain vitamin or mineral. These diseases are avoided by eating the right kinds of food. Figure 2 shows the types and proportions of different foods that make up a healthy **balanced diet**.

Figure 2 These are the proportions of different foods that make up a balanced diet. Does this match the food that you eat?

Metabolism

The more exercise you do, the more energy you need. Many chemical reactions take place in your body. These reactions release the energy from food. Your **metabolic rate** is the speed at which your body uses that energy.

Even when you are resting, you need energy to keep your heart beating and for breathing and digestion. The rate at which you use energy when you are resting is called your resting or basal metabolic rate.

The higher your metabolic rate, the more energy you use. As you exercise your body builds up muscle tissue. Regular exercise also increases your metabolic rate.

4

Your body uses some of its fat stores to replace the energy that it uses. Exercise increases the proportion of muscle to fat in the body, which in turn increases metabolic rate.

Everybody has a different metabolic rate. It depends on many factors including inheritance and how you live your life. Your metabolic rate decreases with age.

Science skills

b Medical experts recommend that young people carry out at least 60 minutes of moderate exercise every day. What percentage of 15-year-old boys achieve this recommendation?

c Suggest a reason for the change in activity levels among girls as they get older.

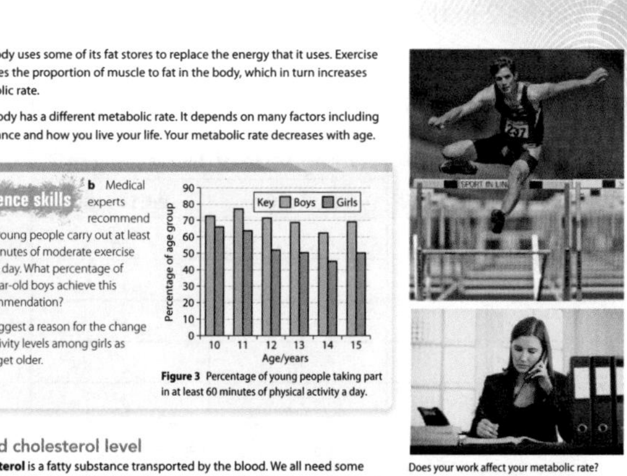

Figure 3 Percentage of young people taking part in at least 60 minutes of physical activity a day.

Does your work affect your metabolic rate?

Blood cholesterol level

Cholesterol is a fatty substance transported by the blood. We all need some cholesterol to keep our body cells functioning normally. Blood cholesterol level depends on the amount of fat in the diet. It is also affected by inheritance. People with high blood cholesterol levels are at increased risk of developing diseases of the heart and blood vessels.

Examiner feedback

Examination questions are likely to provide data that you will be asked to comment upon or evaluate.

Practical

You can compare the energy values of different foods by burning them under a beaker of water as shown in Figure 4. The rise in the temperature of the water is measured for each food. The greater the temperature rise, the greater the energy content of the food.

d Give two variables that should be controlled in this experiment.

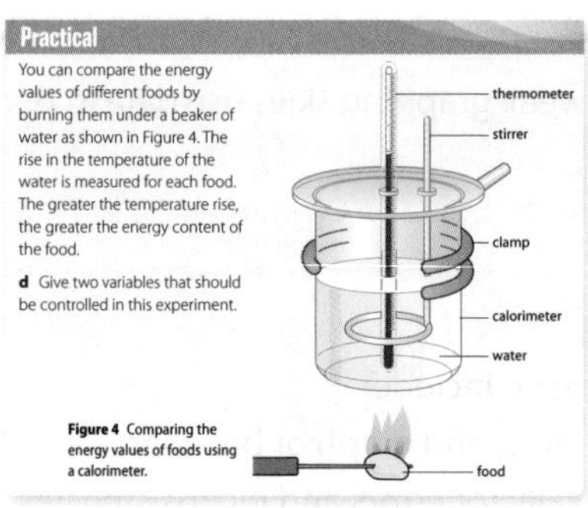

Figure 4 Comparing the energy values of foods using a calorimeter.

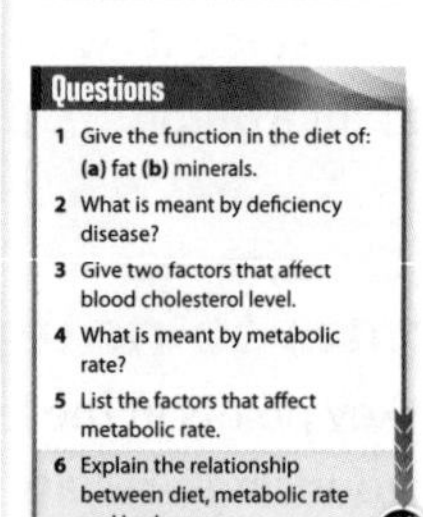

Questions

1. Give the function in the diet of: **(a)** fat **(b)** minerals.
2. What is meant by deficiency disease?
3. Give two factors that affect blood cholesterol level.
4. What is meant by metabolic rate?
5. List the factors that affect metabolic rate.
6. Explain the relationship between diet, metabolic rate and body mass.

Healthy bodies 5

Learning objectives

Students should be able to:

- explain why we need a healthy diet
- describe what is meant by metabolic rate
- interpret information about how metabolic rate and exercise are related to fitness
- explain how inherited factors affect our health.

ActiveTeach Resource: Diet definitions – *Matching game*

Key points

A balanced diet supplies the correct amount of energy and nutrients for a healthy body.

Metabolic rate is the rate at which chemical reactions in the body happen.

Metabolic rate is affected by inheritance, activity and the ratio of muscle to fat in the body.

People who exercise are usually fitter than those who don't.

Blood cholesterol level is affected by diet and by inherited factors.

Carbohydrates fats proteins vitamins minerals malnutrition deficiency disease metabolism cholesterol

Lesson activities

Starter

1 Comparing diet and exercise habits Survey students about their eating habits and their exercise regime. This could be in the form of a short questionnaire provided at the start of the lesson or through a question and answer session.

2 What makes up a healthy diet Introduce the idea of a healthy diet, brainstorm ideas and get a class consensus on what a healthy diet should comprise. Assess the results of the class discussion and identify and correct any misconceptions.

3 Metabolic rate Introduce the concept of metabolic rate.

Main

1 B1 1.1a Energy value of food Students find the energy value of several different biscuits to allow comparisons to be made. Comparisons can be made between different biscuits of the same type and different types of biscuits. [Prac] (See Teacher and Technician sheet and Student Practical sheet for full details.)

2 Key terms for diet and health – play the matching game. [AT]

3 Effects of exercise Show students a video of a personal trainer explaining his job.

Plenaries

1 Ask students to share feedback from the practical activity.

2 Initiate a class discussion about issues arising from the video.

Homework

1 Use the Food Standards Agency Teens – food myths web page to look at myths surrounding food and the eight tips for eating well. This activity can be extended to help dispel any further myths suggested by the class. Students can also be invited to propose any other tips for eating well (properly).

2 The Food Standards Agency Ages and stages web page includes practical nutrition advice for different ages or stages in life. There is a wealth of information for parents with young babies, requirements of growing children and advice for women who want to become pregnant. The site also includes advice aimed specifically at men, women, teenagers and older people.

3 Worksheet B1 1.1c covers balanced diet, the effect of exercise and glycaemic index.

Points to note

- The nutritional information from the packets of biscuits will need to be photocopied so the students can compare their findings with the values given by the manufacturers.
- The activity could be carried out on other dry food products.
- Body fat callipers could be used to show the relationship between fat and muscle.

Route to A*

Although respiration is an Additional Science topic, the concept of metabolism could be extended to include aerobic respiration.

Answers to Student Book questions

Science skills

- **a** More than two-thirds of children aged 11–15 eat no vegetables each day. One-third of 11-year-olds have at least one sugary drink each day. These children eat sweets and chocolate every day. Their inactive lifestyles mean that they do not use all the energy they obtain from foods. (Excess energy-food is stored as fat.)
- **b** 69%.
- **c** One reason, e.g. girls might think that physical activity is 'unfeminine' or not attractive to boys.
- **d** The mass of the food and the volume of the water.

Answers

1. **(a)** To provide energy. **(b)** For healthy functioning of cells.
2. A disease that occurs when we do not eat enough of a particular mineral or vitamin.
3. Amount of fat in the diet; inheritance.
4. Metabolic rate is the speed at which your body uses energy.
5. Lifestyle, age, ratio of muscle to fat and inheritance all affect metabolic rate.
6. Too much food and a lack of exercise result in an increase in body mass. Regular exercise increases metabolic rate. An increase in metabolic rate increases the rate of energy use and results in a decrease in body mass, because the body uses its fat stores to provide this energy.

B1 1.2 Slimming plans

Link to the specification

B1.1.1b A person loses mass when the energy content of the food taken in is less than the amount of energy expended by the body. Exercise increases the amount of energy expended by the body.

B1.1.1d Inherited factors also affect our health; for example cholesterol level.

How Science Works

SKU: B1.1 bullet point 2: Evaluate information about the effect of lifestyle on development of disease; B1.1 bullet point 3: Analyse and evaluate claims made by slimming programmes, and slimming products.

CA: B4.5.4 Draw conclusions using scientific ideas and evidence, by: (a) writing a conclusion, based on evidence that relates correctly to known facts; (b) using secondary sources.

B1 1.2 Slimming plans

Learning objectives

- evaluate claims made by slimming programmes
- analyse and evaluate claims made for slimming programmes and products.

New Slimcredible contains 100% natural ingredients that amazingly:
- burn fat
- block hunger pangs from reaching your brain
- boost your concentration
- speed up your metabolism.

Slimcredible

Using Slimcredible, you can lose up to one dress size in just two weeks!

Our unique formula contains a blend of guarana, lemongrass, green tea, *Garcinia cambogiam*, L-carnitine and the Acai berry.

Years of scientific studies have shown that this combination of organic ingredients, amino acids and the renowned Brazilian superfood the Acai berry massively boost your weight loss power.

Figure 1 Can you trust all adverts?

Do you believe what you read?

People in the UK spend around £2 billion a year on products that claim to help them lose weight.

Currently, manufacturers are not compelled by law to prove that their products work and can make claims that are unsupported by evidence.

The advert in Figure 1 shows how a fictitious company tries to get people to buy their slimming product as a way of losing mass. The advert tries to convince you that this product works. Many companies use adverts like this. The claims made in the adverts are rarely based on scientific evidence but rather on hearsay. Having an understanding of how evidence is used to provide **reliable** results enables you to question what you read and to make informed decisions.

Medical experts say that there is only one way to lose weight, which is to eat healthy foods and keep energy intake below energy use. Exercise increases the amount of energy used by the body.

Science skills Adverts showing photographs of a person before and after losing weight by using a slimming product used to be common. This type of advertising has now been banned.

a Suggest reasons why the evidence in this kind of advert should be regarded as unreliable.

Examiner feedback

Information aimed at consumers almost always uses the term 'weight', but exam questions refer to the correct term 'mass'.

Slimming drugs warning

Trading standards officials investigated a variety of slimming products offered for sale over the Internet. They found that three-quarters of the products tested made false claims. Most companies could not provide reliable evidence to back up their weight-loss claims. These are some of the claims that companies make about their products:

- tablets that enable the body to burn fat before food is digested
- pills that allow people to lose weight without dieting or exercising
- a product that burns fat while people are asleep.

Health experts warn that if a product or a diet programme sounds too good to be true, it probably isn't good for you and isn't true.

Science skills Diet Trials was a study organised by the BBC and a group of scientists. The study compared four popular commercial weight-loss programmes with a control group. The diets were:

- the Slim-Fast plan: a meal replacement approach
- Weight Watchers' Pure Points programme: an energy-controlled diet with weekly group meetings
- Dr Atkins' New Diet: a self-monitored low-carbohydrate eating plan
- Rosemary Conley's Eat Yourself Slim diet and fitness plan: a low-fat diet and a weekly group exercise class.

300 overweight people matched for age, sex and mass were randomly divided into the five groups for the study.

6

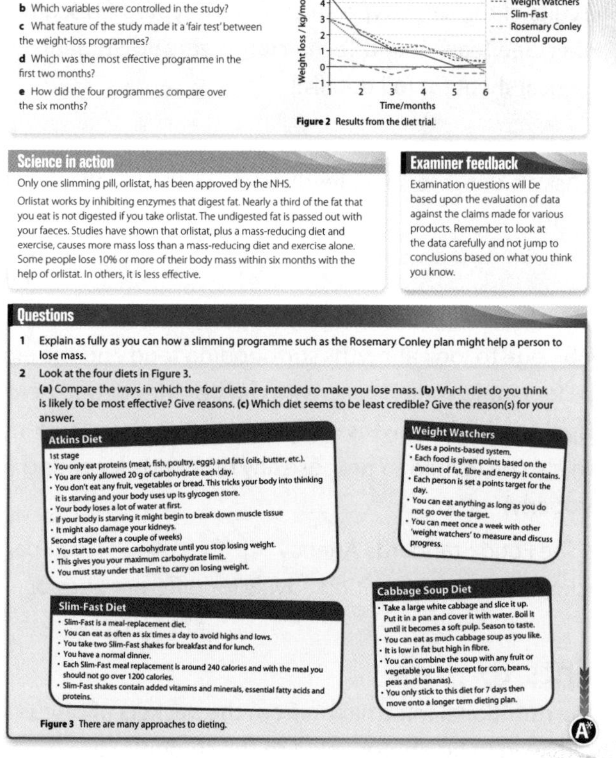

Figure 2 shows some of the data from the study.

b Which variables were controlled in the study?

c What feature of the study made it a 'fair test' between the weight-loss programmes?

d Which was the most effective programme in the first two months?

e How did the four programmes compare over the six months?

Figure 2 Results from the diet trial.

Science in action

Only one slimming pill, orlistat, has been approved by the NHS.

Orlistat works by inhibiting enzymes that digest fat. Nearly a third of the fat that you eat is not digested if you take orlistat. The undigested fat is passed out with your faeces. Studies have shown that orlistat, plus a mass-reducing diet and exercise, causes more mass loss than a mass-reducing diet and exercise alone. Some people lose 10% or more of their body mass within six months with the help of orlistat. In others, it is less effective.

Examiner feedback

Examination questions will be based upon the evaluation of data against the claims made for various products. Remember to look at the data carefully and not jump to conclusions based on what you think you know.

Questions

1 Explain as fully as you can how a slimming programme such as the Rosemary Conley plan might help a person to lose mass.

2 Look at the four diets in Figure 3.
(a) Compare the ways in which the four diets are intended to make you lose mass. **(b)** Which diet do you think is likely to be most effective? Give reasons. **(c)** Which diet seems to be least credible? Give the reason(s) for your answer.

Atkins Diet

1st stage
- You only eat proteins (meat, fish, poultry, eggs) and fats (oils, butter, etc.).
- You are only allowed 20 g of carbohydrate each day.
- You don't eat any fruit, vegetables or bread. This tricks your body into thinking it is starving and your body uses up its glycogen store.
- Your body loses a lot of water at first.
- If your body is starving it might begin to break down muscle tissue
- It might also damage your kidneys.

Second stage (after a couple of weeks)
- You start to eat more carbohydrate until you stop losing weight.
- This gives you your maximum carbohydrate limit.
- You must stay under that limit to carry on losing weight.

Weight Watchers
- Uses a points-based system.
- Each food is given points based on the amount of fat, fibre and energy it contains.
- Each person is set a points target for the day.
- You can eat anything as long as you do not go over the target.
- You can meet once a week with other 'weight watchers' to measure and discuss progress.

Slim-Fast Diet
- Slim-Fast is a meal-replacement diet.
- You can eat as often as six times a day to avoid highs and lows.
- You take two Slim-Fast shakes for breakfast and for lunch.
- You have a normal dinner.
- Each Slim-Fast meal replacement is around 240 calories and with the meal you should not go over 1200 calories.
- Slim-Fast shakes contain added vitamins and minerals, essential fatty acids and proteins.

Cabbage Soup Diet
- Take a large white cabbage and slice it up. Put it in a pan and cover it with water. Boil it until it becomes a soft pulp. Season to taste.
- You can eat as much cabbage soup as you like.
- It is low in fat but high in fibre.
- You can combine the soup with any fruit or vegetable you like (except for corn, beans, peas and bananas).
- You only stick to this diet for 7 days then move onto a longer term dieting plan.

Figure 3 There are many approaches to dieting.

A*

Healthy bodies 7

Learning objectives

Most students should be able to:
- calculate Body Mass Index (BMI)
- evaluate information about the effect of lifestyle on development of disease
- analyse and evaluate claims made by slimming programmes, and slimming products

Some students should also be able to:
- relate cholesterol levels to heart disease (not on spec) [Ext]

Key points

A person loses mass when the energy content of the food taken in is less than the amount of energy expended by the body.

Exercise increases the amount of energy expended by the body.

Data can be used to evaluate claims about slimming products and slimming programmes.

ActiveTeach Resource: Video of a dietician explaining her job – *Video*
Slimming down – *Venn diagram – sorting terms*

Body Mass Index | diet | slimming plan | metabolism

Lesson activities

Starter

1 Effects of extra body weight Ask students whether they find it easier to walk with or without rucksacks on their backs. Ask them to describe the differences, and why it is more difficult to walk with something heavy. Ask them to list the effects that the extra weight had on their body, e.g. more easily out of breath, get hotter more quickly. This leads into the problems associated with being overweight, such as high blood pressure, pressure on joints, etc.

2 Slimming down Show students the ActiveTeach video of a dietician explaining her job, and then do the Venn diagram term sorting as a class activity. [AT]

Main

1 Obesity Emphasise what is meant by being obese as opposed to being overweight. The BMI calculation on **Worksheet B1 1.2a** should clarify this point.

2 Causes of weight gain The reasons for being overweight are important. It is not always a case of eating the 'wrong' foods. Thyroid problems, infirmity and lack of mobility may have an effect. Social and emotional issues may also play a part, so it is important to stress the need for understanding and sensitivity when dealing with weight issues. Stress the idea that weight loss should be fat loss. We can all lose weight if we lose water but this weight is put back on just as quickly.

3 Dieting: worksheet B1 1.2a enables students to study four popular ways of dieting.

Plenaries

1 Ask students to produce a concept map about diet.

2 Ask students to exchange feedback from the Slimming plans activity.

Homework

1 Students could research other popular diets and broaden their evidence before they come up with guidelines for losing weight. Alternatively they might scrutinise other diets by using the guidelines they have come up with.

2 Worksheets B1 1.2b and **1.2c** to evaluate slimming programmes and explore the effects of unhealthy diet on lifestyle. [AfL]

Route to A*

Worksheet B1 1.2d relates cholesterol to heart disease (not in specification).

Answers to Student Book questions

Science skills

- **a** No information is given about the size of the sample of people used, or the range of weight loss in participants. Frequently, air-brushing is use to enhance apparent weight loss.
- **b** Age, sex, and body mass were controlled.
- **c** The use of a control group.
- **d** Atkins diet.
- **e** All the programmes were effective. All showed very similar weight loss over the six-month period.

Answers

1 A low-fat diet would reduce the energy content of the food. If the amount of energy used by the body is greater than the energy intake, the person will convert fat into energy and the body will lose mass. Regular exercise will increase the body's metabolic rate, which will increase the rate at which cells convert sugars into energy. These sugars will not then be stored as fat.

2 **(a)** Atkins diet – the amount of carbohydrate is drastically reduced at first, then adjusted to a daily amount that must not be exceeded. So the diet works mainly by reducing the daily intake of carbohydrate below the amount which is used by the body. WeightWatchers® – works on a points system where each food is given a points value and each person is given a daily points target. The total number of points must not be exceeded. So this diet works by restricting the total energy value from all types of food. Cabbage soup – this diet is for rapid, short-term weight loss. The cabbage soup will contain practically no energy. It is supplemented by fruits and vegetables that do not contain much carbohydrate. So it works by severely restricting the intake of carbohydrate and fat for a short period. Slim-Fast® – works on eating specially prepared meals, each with a restricted energy content. The special meals contain restricted amounts of carbohydrates and fats.

(b) The WeightWatchers® diet is the most likely to be effective because it reduces the calorie intake overall rather than just one food group, so a dieter cannot replace the carbohydrates omitted by eating more fats, for example. It allows the dieter to eat a wide range of foods to obtain the nutrients the body needs and remain motivated.

(c) The cabbage soup diet is the least credible since it consists of eating large amounts of a food with practically no nutritional value, then supplementing it with a restricted range of fruits and vegetables. The diet is dangerous since it contains little or no protein and fat, both of which are needed for a healthy body.

B1 1.3 Pathogens

Link to the specification

B1.1.2a Microorganisms that cause infectious disease are called pathogens.

B1.1.2b Bacteria and viruses may reproduce rapidly inside the body and may produce poisons (toxins) that make us feel ill. Viruses damage cells in which they reproduce.

B1.1.2f Semmelweiss recognised the importance of handwashing in the prevention of spreading some infectious diseases. By insisting that doctors washed their hands before examining patients, he greatly reduced the number of deaths from infectious diseases in his hospital.

How Science Works

SKU: B1.1.2 bullet point 1: Relate the contribution of Semmelweiss in controlling infection to solving modern problems with the spread of infection in hospitals.

CA: B4.3.1 Make observations, by: carrying out practical work and research, and using the data collected to develop hypotheses; B4.5.4 Draw conclusions using scientific ideas and evidence, by: (a) writing a conclusion, based on evidence that relates correctly to known facts; (b) using secondary sources; (c) identifying extra evidence that is required for a conclusion to be made; (d) evaluating methods of data collection.

B1 1.3 Pathogens

Learning objectives

- explain what causes infectious disease and how diseases are spread
- explain how pathogens cause disease
- describe the contribution made by Semmelweiss to controlling infection in hospitals today.

Transmitting infections

Up to 5000 people die each year from infections picked up in hospitals in England. The problem actually affects 100 000 people and costs the NHS a thousand million pounds. It is thought that deadly infections are spread because **hygiene** rules are broken. For example doctors and nurses do not always wash their hands or use hand gel between treating patients.

A senior nursing officer said: 'Levels of cleanliness have deteriorated in recent years. I have seen dust under beds, cotton wool buds on the floor and dirty needles dumped in discarded meal trays. There are guidelines about changing the curtains around beds, cleaning floors and cleaning bathrooms but these are often ignored.'

Potentially fatal infections are carried in dust mites and a study has shown that improving ward cleanliness can reduce infections. Hospitals now employ infection control specialists to reduce the number of infections.

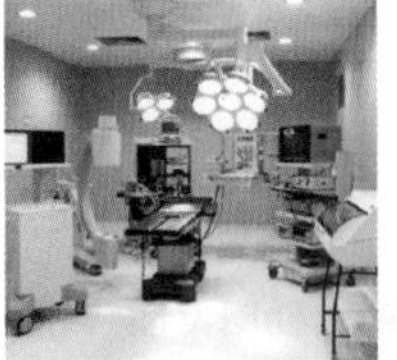

The standard of hygiene in hospitals needs to be high to avoid infections spreading. Think about ways hygiene can be improved in hospitals.

Ignaz Semmelweiss

Microorganisms are the tiny living things that can only be seen using a microscope. They are everywhere, including in the food you eat and inside you. Microorganisms that cause illness or disease are types of **pathogens**.

Ignaz Semmelweiss was a doctor in the mid-1800s. He wondered why so many women died of 'childbed fever' soon after giving birth. He also noticed that student doctors carrying out work on dead bodies did not wash their hands before delivering a baby. When he got them to wash their hands in a **chlorinated** hand wash before delivering babies, fewer women died. He concluded that something was carried by the doctors from the dead bodies to the women.

Science skills

a What was Semmelweiss' observation?

b What was his hypothesis?

The table shows Semmelweiss' original data.

c Why did Semmelweiss calculate the percentage of deaths on each ward rather than relying on the number of deaths?

d What conclusions can be drawn from this data?

Year span	Hospital ward	Number of deaths	Number of patients	Deaths (%)
1833–1838 (same number of doctors and midwives in each ward)	Ward 1	1505	23 509	6.4
	Ward 2	731	13 097	5.81
1839–1847 (medical students and doctors in ward 1; midwives in ward 2)	Ward 1	1989	20 204	9.84
	Ward 2	691	17 791	2.18
1848–1859 (chlorinated hand wash used)	Ward 1	1712	47 938	3.57
	Ward 2	1248	40 770	3.06

Figure 1 Semmelweiss's original data.

Taking it further

Bacterial cells do not have a nucleus like animal and plant cells. Instead, the genes are found in a looped chromosome and in **plasmids**, small seperate rings of genetic material. Plasmids are used by genetic engineers to transfer genes into both animal and plant cells.

8

The discovery of pathogens

Louis Pasteur and Joseph Lister studied 'objects' that became known as 'microorganisms'. Pasteur proved that there were '**germs**' in the air and that they carried infection and disease. Lister developed a special soap called carbolic soap. He insisted that all medical instruments, dressings and even surgeons should be cleaned with it before any operation. More of Lister's patients stayed healthy than those of other surgeons.

Chemicals that are used to clean wounds or get rid of sores, such as nappy rash, are called **antiseptics**. Chemicals that are used to clean work surfaces and other places where pathogens might be found are called **disinfectants**.

Semmelweiss showed that keeping things clean helps to stop the spread of pathogens. We call this hygiene. Hygiene is about keeping things clean to reduce the risk of disease. Washing removes the dirt and grease that pathogens stick to and use as a source of energy to multiply.

Microorganisms

Pathogens are the 'germs' identified by Semmelweiss, Pasteur and Lister. Two of the main types are:

- **bacteria** – cause cholera, boils, MRSA, typhoid, tuberculosis
- **viruses** – cause warts, herpes, polio, flu, mumps, measles, smallpox.

Spreading disease

Bacteria and viruses can pass from one person to another. This is how some diseases spread and affect many people. You can become infected by pathogens in the air you breathe, the food you eat, the liquids you drink, and by touching someone. By making sure that your environment is clean, you lessen the chance that you will become infected.

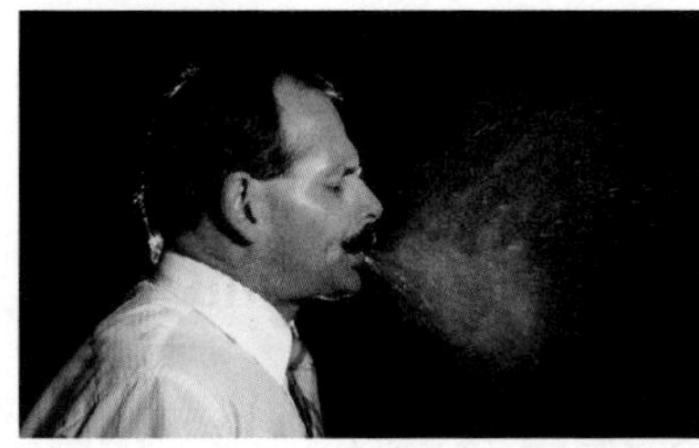

Passing on pathogens.

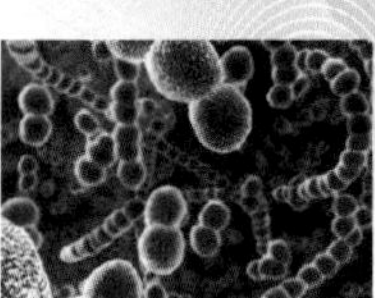

These spherical bacteria are the type that cause sore throats.

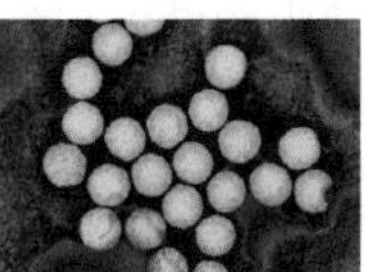

Polioviruses cause the disease polio. They are one thirtieth the diameter of the bacteria above.

Examiner feedback

Do not use the term 'germ' in answers. The general term to use is pathogen. If you use the terms 'bacteria' or 'virus', make sure that they correctly apply to the disease in the question.

Questions

1. What is a pathogen?
2. Name two types of pathogen.
3. Give two ways in which pathogens pass from one person to another.
4. Explain the difference between an antiseptic and a disinfectant.
5. Explain fully why it is important to wash your hands after visiting the toilet.
6. Write a hygiene memo with 10 bullet points for hospital staff. Base your memo on the scientific principles that Semmelweiss applied to his work.

A*

Healthy bodies 9

Learning objectives

Students should be able to:

- explain how bacteria and viruses make us ill
- relate the contribution of Semmelweiss in controlling infection to solving modern problems with the spread of infection in hospitals.

Key points

Infections are caused by microorganisms called pathogens.

Examples of pathogens include bacteria and viruses.

Semmelweiss recognised the importance of hand-washing in preventing the spread of infections.

ActiveTeach Resource: Transmitting diseases – *Sorting activity*

Pathogen microorganisms bacteria virus antiseptic disinfectant Semmelweiss

Lesson activities

Starter

1 Before the students come in to class, sprinkle fluorescent powder in the doorway. Once the class is settled tell them what you have done. Show the students that the powder fluoresces under UV light. Show them that their shoes have powder on, and that the floor is also covered.

2 Ask students to list everything they have touched since going to the toilet this morning. Ask whether they washed their hands or not. Ask them to imagine what might happen if everybody in the class had not washed their hands.

Main

1 Ask volunteers to apply fluorescent lotion to their hands, then shake hands with their friends and touch various surfaces in the room. Get other students to touch the same surfaces. Then check everybody's hands for fluorescent dye – everyone tested should have some amount of 'contamination'. Then use the volunteers to demonstrate how much hand washing is required to remove all of the dye.

2 **Worksheet B1 1.3b** looks at hygiene, particularly in the context of hospital hygiene. Discuss with students how the work of Semmelweiss is relevant to infection control today.

3 **Worksheet B1 1.3c** looks at upper respiratory tract infections (URTIs). Discuss with students other ways in which the body prevents infections.

Plenaries

1 Provide a key word in the bottom box and ask the students to give a definition of each.

2 Ask students to discuss ways of reducing cross-infection in hospitals.

Homework

1 Ask students to research the work of Florence Nightingale and Robert Koch.

2 **Worksheet B1 1.3d** relates the story of Eyam to the transmission of disease. [Ext]

Route to A*

Students' scientific method, i.e. observation, hypothesis, investigation, theory, could be developed via Semmelweiss activity.

Answers to Student Book questions

Science skills

- **a** Student doctors did not wash their hands between working on dead bodies and delivering babies.
- **b** Student doctors were carrying infection from dead bodies to patients.
- **c** There were very large differences in the numbers of patients on the two wards.
- **d** Death rates were highest when babies were delivered both by midwives and doctors. The death rates on the ward where babies were delivered by midwives only was about 25% of that where doctors delivered babies. When doctors and their students washed their hands before delivering babies, the death rate was reduced by about two-thirds.

Answers

1. A pathogen is an organism that causes an infection.
2. Bacteria and viruses are types of pathogen.
3. By touch, in food and drinks, and via the air in the breath.
4. Antiseptics are substances that can be used to kill pathogens on the surface of the human body or on kitchen surfaces without causing irritation or damage to the skin. Disinfectants are much 'stronger' than antiseptics: they kill pathogens but would cause damage to the human body. They are used to clean surfaces in bathrooms and toilets.
5. Bacteria multiply rapidly in the intestines so faeces contain large numbers of them. Some of these bacteria may cause food poisoning if they are transferred to food by unwashed hands.
6. Ten points, for example: before your shift, remove all wrist and preferably hand jewellery; before your shift, cover cuts and abrasions with a waterproof dressing; ensure your fingernails are clean; wash dirty hands with liquid soap and warm water, rubbing with handwash for at least 15 seconds, rinsing thoroughly and drying with paper towels; always decontaminate your hands before any contact with the patient; always decontaminate your hands after any activity that could result in contamination; even if your hands look clean, use an alcohol-based handrub before each contact with a patient, rubbing it in thoroughly to all parts of the hand until the hands are dry; decontaminate shared equipment every time after use; keep the hospital thoroughly clean and free from dust and soiling; make sure you understand your individual responsibility for maintaining cleanliness in the hospital environment.

B1 1.4 Defence against disease

Link to the specification

B1.1.2c The body has different ways of protecting itself against pathogens.

B1.1.2d White blood cells help to defend against pathogens by:

- ingesting pathogens
- producing antibodies, which destroy particular bacteria or viruses
- producing antitoxins, which counteract the toxins released by pathogens.

B1 1.4 Defence against disease

Learning objectives

- **describe how pathogens make us ill**
- **explain how white blood cells protect us against pathogens**
- **explain how we become immune to pathogens.**

Immunity

This boy has a condition known as SCID, also called 'bubble boy' disease. He would not survive outside of his 'bubble' because he has no natural defence against pathogens; he is not **immune** to them.

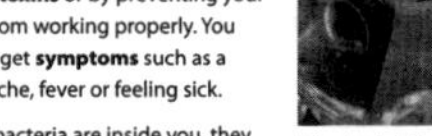

A boy in a bubble.

Bacteria and viruses make you ill by releasing poisonous chemicals called **toxins** or by preventing your cells from working properly. You might get **symptoms** such as a headache, fever or feeling sick.

Once bacteria are inside you, they can multiply rapidly, doubling in number about every 20 minutes. Viruses multiply by entering the cells in your body. They use the chemicals inside the cell to make copies of themselves. The new viruses burst out of the cell ready to invade other body cells. This damages or even destroys the cell.

Examiner feedback

You do not need to know the structure of either a bacterium or a virus, but you must know that antibiotics do not affect viruses.

Cells to fight pathogens

Your body has different ways of protecting itself against pathogens. **White blood cells** are specialised cells that defend your body against pathogens. There are several different types of white blood cell. Some **ingest**, that is, take into the cell, any pathogens that they come across in your body. Once the pathogen is inside the cell, the white blood cell releases **enzymes** to **digest** and destroy it.

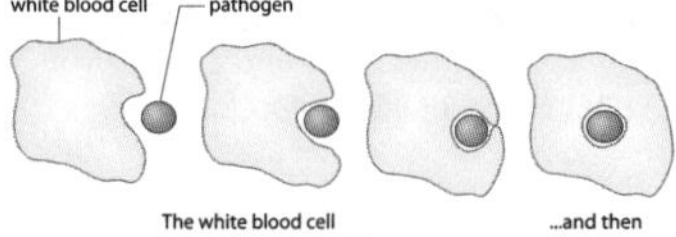

Figure 1 Some white blood cells ingest and destroy pathogens.

Other white blood cells release chemicals called **antibodies**, which destroy pathogens. A particular antibody can only destroy a particular bacterium or virus, so white blood cells learn to make many different types of antibody. For example, when a flu virus enters the body, antibodies are made that destroy the flu virus. After the virus has been destroyed, flu antibodies remain in the blood and act quickly if the same pathogen enters in the future. White blood cells also produce **antitoxins**. These are chemicals that prevent the toxins made by pathogens from poisoning your body.

Taking it further

Your blood group is determined by the molecules present on the surface of your red blood cells. If you have type A blood, you have antibodies against type B molecules. So, if cells with type B molecules get into your body, they will be clumped together by antibodies, causing a blood clot. If your blood cells have neither A nor B molecules on their surfaces, you are blood type O, and if they have both, you are type AB.

For blood transfusions, people with group O blood are said to be universal donors and people with group AB blood are said to be universal recipients. Explain why.

Examiner feedback

Make sure that you are quite clear about the difference between an antibody and an antitoxin. You may come across the term 'antigen' in your studies. This term will not appear in the examination. Do not use the term unless you fully understand what it means.

10

Some measles viruses get into your body.

Your white blood cells make antibodies and memory cells for the measles virus.

antibodies

white blood cell

The antibodies attack the measles viruses, and kill them.

If the measles virus gets into your body again, your memory cells know what kind of antibody to make straight away.

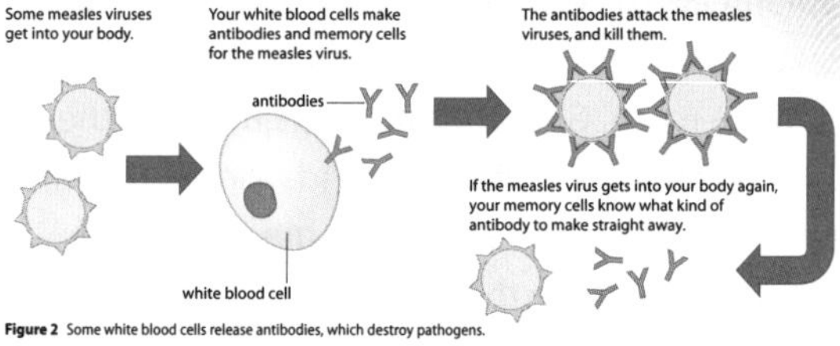

Figure 2 Some white blood cells release antibodies, which destroy pathogens.

Life-long protection

Once your white blood cells have destroyed a type of pathogen, you are unlikely to develop the same disease again. This is because your white blood cells will recognise the pathogen the next time it invades your body and produce the right antibodies very quickly to kill the pathogen before it can affect you. This makes you immune to the disease.

Science skills

Figure 3 shows what happens when someone is infected by a particular pathogen. The graph also shows what happens when the person is infected a second time by the same pathogen.

a How long did it take to start producing antibodies: **i** after the first infection **ii** after the second infection?

b Explain why antibodies were produced more quickly after the second infection.

c Suggest why the person did not become ill after the second infection.

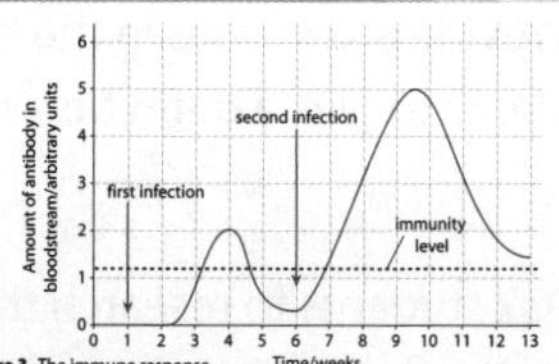

Figure 3 The immune response.

Questions

1. **(a)** Classify the following as B, caused by bacteria, or V, caused by viruses: chicken pox, measles, tuberculosis, mumps, rubella, dysentery, smallpox, cholera, polio, influenza. **(b)** Which of these have you had? **(c)** Which of these have you had only once? **(d)** Which have you had more than once? **(e)** Which are you not immune to?
2. What is meant by immunity?
3. What is meant by a symptom?
4. Explain the difference between antibody and antitoxin.
5. Describe the ways in which pathogens make us feel ill.
6. Describe the ways in which white blood cells protect us against pathogens.
7. Write a paragraph to explain fully why you do not usually suffer from a particular infectious disease more than once.

A*

Science in action

Antibodies are not all useful. Some antibodies produced by a pregnant woman can cause problems for her unborn baby. These antibodies destroy the baby's red blood cells. In severe cases the baby is given a blood transfusion before birth. All pregnant mothers are screened for production of these antibodies so that the problem can be anticipated and dealt with.

Healthy bodies 11

Learning objectives

Students should be able to:

- explain the role of white blood cells in defence
- explain the role of white blood cells in life-long protection [H].

Key points

Microorganisms such as bacteria and viruses that cause infections are called pathogens.

Pathogens produce toxins that make us feel ill.

White blood cells protect the body against pathogens by

- ingesting them
- producing antibodies to destroy the pathogens
- producing antitoxins that counteract the toxins produced by pathogens.

White blood cell   antigen   antibody   toxin   antitoxin   ingestion   immunity   enzyme

Lesson activities

Starter

1 Start with the number 1 and ask students to double it, then double it again, and again. Do this 10 times. Explain to students that bacterial numbers double about every 20 minutes. Now challenge students to work out how many bacteria there will there be in 24 hours from one original cell.

2 Show a video of Iwan Thomas talking about the effect of illness on athletes.

Main

1 The body is a fortress against attack by 'alien' pathogens. The fight against infection is an 'intragalactic' (as opposed to 'inter') war of alien proportions. Ask students to draw cartoons of some of these 'aliens' (antigens and antibodies, etc.). This activity introduces students to an understanding of the role of antibodies in defence.

2 Ask students to recall why attacks by pathogens may make us feel ill. Then ask students to suggest ways in which the body might respond to such attacks.

3 The diagram on **Worksheet B1.1.4a** introduces the role of white cells in defence.

Plenaries

1 Phagocytes destroy pathogens by engulfing them like Pac-Man. Lymphocytes make antibodies that latch on to pathogens so that they can be destroyed. Ask students to use these ideas to draw a quick cartoon strip for each type of white cell, showing how it destroys pathogens.

2 Ask students to consider how future 'alien' attacks could be forestalled.

Homework

1 Questions on **Worksheet B1 1.4b** reinforce work on how pathogens multiply and how white cells seek out and destroy them.

2 Students could research leukaemia – its causes and effects.

Points to note

- Most work with live blood cells is now banned, but a look at prepared slides or bioviewer work would supplement the worksheets well.

Route to A*

Additional homework/research ideas: the whole area of white cells is full of interesting features such as killer T cells, helper cells and suppressor cells. Students could be asked to find out what each of these types of cells are and what their functions are (not on specification).

Answers to Student Book questions

Taking it further

Group O blood cells have neither A nor B molecules, so they will not be clotted by the recipient's antibodies.

Group AB blood has neither anti-A nor anti-B antibodies so transfused blood cells will not be clotted.

Science skills

a (i) About 9 days. **(ii)** Production started almost immediately.

b White cells recognise the pathogen after the previous infection, so can respond immediately.

c Production of antibodies occurs much faster, before the pathogens can have an effect.

Answers

1 **(a)** Bacteria cause tuberculosis, tetanus, dysentery and cholera; the rest are caused by viruses; answers to parts **(b)**, **(c)**, **(d)** and **(e)** will be individual to students (although no-one should have had smallpox), but the answer to **(d)** will normally be 'none' and the answer to **(c)** should correspond to **(b)**; the answer to **(e)** should be diseases not listed in **(b)**, although it is possible to get influenza and chicken pox more than once.

2 Immunity means being protected against infection by having antibodies.

3 A symptom is an outward sign of a disease such as a pain or a headache.

4 Antitoxins neutralise poisons produced by pathogens; antibodies kill pathogens.

5 Bacteria reproduce rapidly and produce toxins; viruses reproduce inside the body's cells, and when these body cells burst toxins are released into the bloodstream.

6 Some white cells engulf pathogens, some produce antibodies to kill pathogens, and some produce antitoxins to neutralise the effects of toxins produced by pathogens.

7 White cells detect pathogens and produce antibodies in response to their presence. Some white cells retain a 'memory' of these pathogens. If the pathogens enter the body again, they are recognised and antibodies are quickly produced.

B1 1.5 Treating and preventing disease

Link to the specification

B1.1.2e The immune system of the body produces specific antibodies to kill a particular pathogen. This leads to immunity from that pathogen. In some cases, dead or inactivated pathogens stimulate antibody production. If a large proportion of the population is immune to a pathogen, the spread of the pathogen is very much reduced.

B1.1.2g Some medicines, including painkillers, help to relieve the symptoms of infectious disease, but do not kill the pathogens.

B1.1.2h Antibiotics, including penicillin, are medicines that help to cure bacterial disease by killing infectious bacteria inside the body. Antibiotics cannot be used to kill viral pathogens, which live and reproduce inside cells. It is important that specific bacteria should be treated by specific antibiotics. The use of antibiotics has greatly reduced deaths from infectious bacterial diseases. Overuse and inappropriate use of antibiotics has increased the rate of development of antibiotic resistant strains of bacteria.

Ideas for practical work

Growing microorganisms in Petri dishes to demonstrate sterile technique and growing pure cultures (*See* **B1 1.8a**).

The use of pre-inoculated agar in Petri dishes to evaluate the effect of disinfectants and antibiotics.

Computer simulations; the growth of bacterial colonies in varying conditions; action of the immune system and the effect of antibiotics and vaccines.

How Science Works

SKU: B1.1 bullet point 2: Explain how the treatment of disease has changed as a result of increased understanding of the action of antibiotics and immunity.

CA: B4.1.1 Develop hypotheses and plan practical ways to test them, by: (a) being able to develop a hypothesis; (b) being able to test hypotheses; B4.2.1 Assess and manage risks when carrying out practical work, by: (a) identifying some possible hazards in practical situations; (b) suggesting ways of managing risks; B4.5.4 Draw conclusions using scientific ideas and evidence, by: (a) writing a conclusion, based on evidence that relates correctly to known facts.

B1 1.5 Treating and preventing disease

Learning objectives

- explain how diseases are treated using medicines and antibiotics
- explain how vaccination make us immune to pathogens
- evaluate data relating to the success of vaccination campaigns.

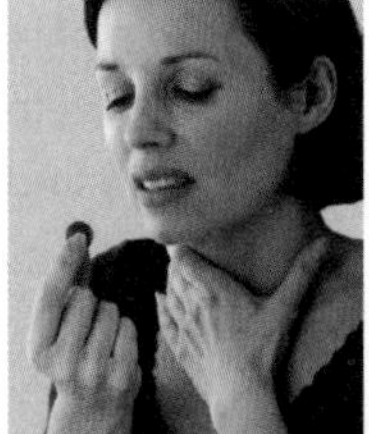

How will this throat lozenge help?

Feeling ill

If you have a sore throat you might take throat lozenges to reduce the pain. The sore throat is a symptom caused by a pathogen that has infected your body. This **medicine** helps to relieve the symptom but it will not kill the pathogen.

Killing bacteria

Antibiotics are medicines that help to cure diseases caused by bacteria. You take antibiotics to kill bacteria that get inside your body. Doctors use many different antibiotics to treat people. **Penicillin** was the first antibiotic to be discovered.

Antibiotics can't kill viruses. Because viruses live and reproduce inside body cells, it is difficult to develop medicines that kill viruses without damaging body cells and tissues.

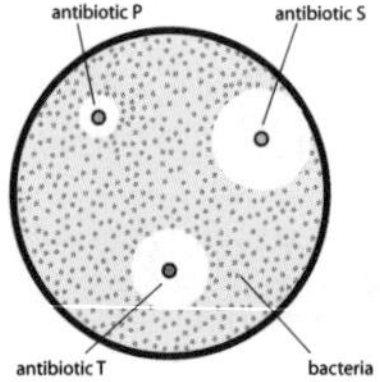

Figure 1 Finding out which antibiotic works best.

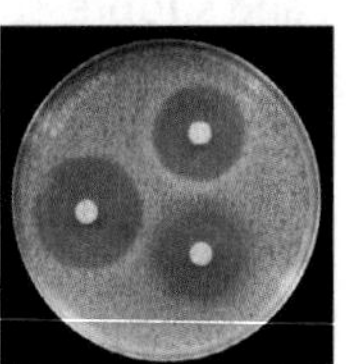

Which antibiotic is most effective?

The effect of different antibiotics on bacteria can be measured in the laboratory. This is done by using small discs of paper containing antibiotics. The discs are placed in a dish containing bacteria growing on a **gel**. The photograph shows the effect of three antibiotics. The clear zone that forms around each disc is where bacteria have been killed. Figure 1 shows the results of testing three other antibiotics. Gel tests are useful, but the body is more complicated than a gel. The results in the body may be different.

A quick jab

Immunity to a disease can be gained without ever having had the disease. A newborn baby receives antibodies from its mother in the first few days that it feeds on her milk. When you were a young child you were probably **immunised** to protect you from very harmful diseases, such as whooping cough, measles and polio. **Immunisation** (**vaccination**) usually involves injecting or swallowing a **vaccine** containing small amounts of a dead or weak form of the pathogen.

12

Because the pathogen is weak or inactive, the vaccine does not make you ill, but your white blood cells still produce antibodies to destroy the pathogen. This makes you immune to future infection by the pathogen. Your white blood cells will recognise the pathogen if it gets into your body and respond by quickly producing antibodies. The pathogen does not get a chance to reproduce enough to make you ill.

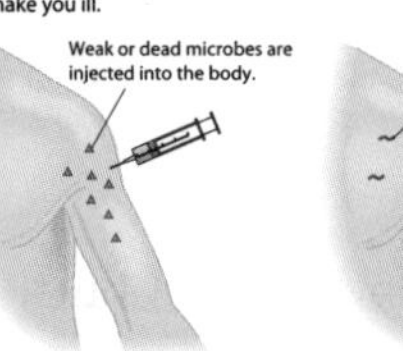

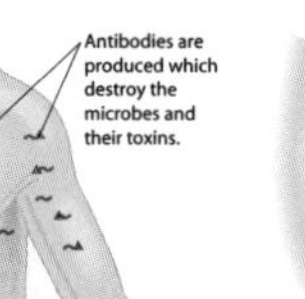

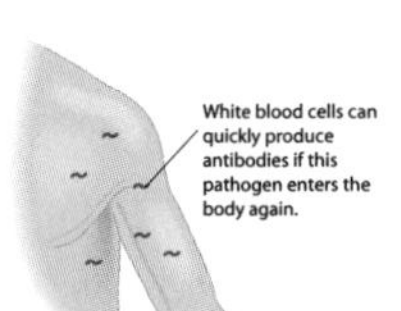

Figure 2 How vaccination works.

Science skills

The level of antibody in the blood after some vaccinations does not get high enough to give protection. In this case, a second, or booster, injection of vaccine a few weeks or months later is needed. The graph shows the level of antibodies in a person's blood following a first and second injection of a vaccine.

a What was the difference in arbitrary units in the level of antibody between the first and second injection?

b Explain why the person became immune after the second injection but not the first.

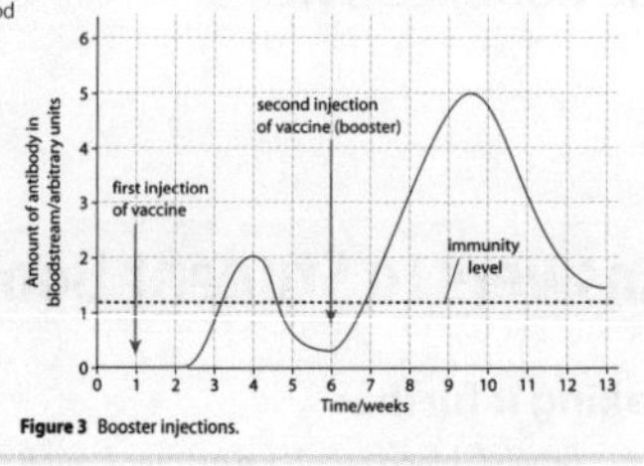

Figure 3 Booster injections.

Questions

1. What symptoms might you have if you catch a cold?
2. What is the most common type of medicine *that is not on these two pages* that is used to treat the symptoms of an infectious disease?
3. Which antibiotic in Figure 1 – P, S or T – works best against this bacterium?
4. Explain why antibiotics can be used to treat bacterial infections but not viral infections.
5. Rubella is a pathogen that can pass across the placenta. Why is it important that girls are vaccinated against rubella?
6. Explain how vaccination protects you against a disease, but does not cause you to develop the disease.

A*

Examiner feedback

It is important that you understand why viruses cannot be killed by antibiotics.

Healthy bodies 13

Learning objectives

Students should be able to:

- explain that some medicines relieve disease symptoms but do not kill pathogens
- explain why antibiotics can be used against bacterial infections, but not viral infections.
- explain how vaccination makes the body immune to a particular disease.

Medicine | antibiotic | penicillin | immunisation | vaccination | vaccine

Key points

Painkillers relieve the symptoms of diseases but do not kill the pathogens.

Antibiotics such as penicillin can cure bacterial diseases by killing the bacteria.

Antibiotics do not work on viruses because they live inside body cells. It is difficult to kill the virus without killing the cells they live in.

People can be immunised using dead or inactive forms of a pathogen in a vaccination to stimulate the white blood cells to produce antibodies and makes the body immune.

White blood cells recognise the pathogen if it gets into your body and respond by quickly producing antibodies.

Lesson activities

Starter

1 Alexander Fleming's famous experiment Explain that when Alexander Fleming left his experiment, growing bacteria on some nutrient broth (agar), on a shelf he forgot to put the lid on one of the dishes. Show students two Petri dishes, one with a lid and one without. Both should be labelled showing nutrient broth (a jelly) and both should be smeared with bacteria which have discoloured the surface of the broth. The one with the lid is covered entirely with bacteria, the one without the lid has little rings of clear jelly where no bacteria have grown. Ask students the following questions:

- Describe everything that Alexander Fleming saw, including how the two dishes are similar and how they are different.
- Which dish has places where bacteria have not grown?
- Why have bacteria not grown in some places? Where did the bacteria come from that landed on the dish?

Main

1 Practical sheet B1 1.5a is geared towards carrying out an aseptic exercise to study either antibiotics, antibacterial agents or antiseptics. The students might compare one type of antibacterial agent with another or use different dilutions of the same antibacterial agent. The area cleared can be calculated by putting graph paper under the dish and counting squares. For extension a procedure for calculating the surface area cleared using (πr^2) can be used.

2 Use **Worksheet B1 1.5b** in conjunction with lesson B1 1.5 in the Student Book to consolidate understanding of antibiotics and vaccination.

Plenaries

1 Ask students to make a list of antibacterial products they might find in the home. Once they have a list of these products, ask them to separate them into two groups – those which are antiseptics and those which are disinfectants.

2 Ask students to discuss variability in the results obtained from the practical activity.

Homework

1 Worksheet B1 1.5c uses Millennium development goals to pull together methods for reducing disease incidence.

2 Students could research development of the PfCP-2.9 malaria vaccine in China.

Route to A*

Students could research the contribution of Ernst Chain to the commercial development of penicillin after Fleming's discovery.

Answers to Student Book questions

Science skills

a Three abitrary units.

b Because a few weeks after the first injection, the concentration of antibodies drops below the immunity level.

Answers

1 Cough, runny nose.

2 The most common medicines used to treat symptoms are painkillers.

3 S works best, because it has the widest clear area around it where it has killed bacteria.

4 Viruses invade body cells; antibiotics cannot enter cells so do not kill viruses.

5 If a girl is not vaccinated and becomes infected while pregnant, the virus will pass across the placenta and infect the baby, causing harm such as deafness and brain damage.

6 The vaccine contains a dead or weakened form of the pathogen. The dead or weakened form of the pathogen still stimulates the white blood cells to produce antibodies. However, the pathogen cannot reproduce or produce toxins.

B1 1.6 Controlling infection

Link to the specification

B1.1.2h Overuse and inappropriate use of antibiotics has increased the rate of development of antibiotic resistant strains of bacteria.

B1.1.2i Many strains of bacteria, including MRSA, have developed resistance to antibiotics as a result of natural selection. To prevent further resistance arising it is important to avoid over-use of antibiotics.

B1.1.2j Mutations of pathogens produce new strains. Antibiotics and vaccinations may no longer be effective against a new resistant strain of the pathogen. The new strain will then spread rapidly because people are not immune to it and there is no effective treatment. Higher Tier candidates should understand that:

- antibiotics kill individual pathogens of the non-resistant strain
- individual resistant pathogens survive and reproduce, so the population of the resistant strain increases
- now, antibiotics are not used to treat non-serious infections, such as mild throat infections, so that the rate of development of resistant strains is slowed down.

How Science Works

SKU: B1.1 bullet 3: Evaluate the consequences of mutations of bacteria and viruses in relation to epidemics and pandemics.

B1 1.6 Controlling infection

Learning objectives

- explain how strains of bacteria can develop resistance to antibiotics
- explain the consequences of the overuse of antibiotics and of mutations of bacteria and viruses
- describe how epidemics and pandemics occur.

Taking it further

Bacteria may develop antibiotic resistance in several ways. These include mutating to:

- deactivate the antibiotic before it reaches the inside of the bacterial cell
- pump antibiotic out of the bacterial cell
- alter the protein on the bacterial cell so that the antibiotic cannot recognise the cell
- produce enzymes to destroy the antibiotic.

Figure 2 A mutation sometimes occurs when bacteria reproduce.

Dr Semmelweiss's recommendations (lesson B1 1.3) two centuries on.

Antibiotic resistance

HOSPITAL SUPERBUG KILLS BABY

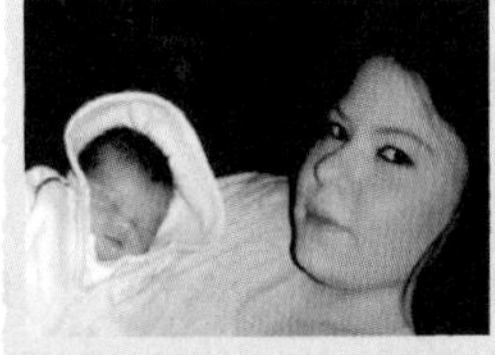

A one-day-old baby boy was killed by the hospital superbug MRSA.

Baby Luke was only 36 hours old when he died.

Luke was born showing no signs of bad health, but within a day he became ill.

Figure 1 Newspaper article about a hospital 'superbug'.

Bacteria grow and divide every 20 minutes. Each new bacterium is exactly the same as the one it came from. Sometimes a bacterium is produced that is slightly different to the others. This is called a **mutation**.

The mutation might result in the bacteria being **resistant** to existing antibiotics, so that the bacteria are no longer killed by antibiotics. When an antibiotic is used, the non-resistant bacteria are killed but a small number of resistant bacteria remain. The resistant bacteria survive and reproduce. Continued use of the antibiotic causes the number of resistant bacteria to increase. This is an example of **natural selection** (see lesson B1 7.2).

You should always complete a course of antibiotics, even if you start to feel better. If you do not complete a course of antibiotics, it is likely that some bacteria will survive. You could become ill again and need a second treatment course. There would be more chance of resistant bacteria developing.

Scientists are continually developing new antibiotics to replace those that are no longer effective.

Superbugs

Methicillin-resistant *Staphylococcus aureus* (**MRSA**) is a variety of *S. aureus* that is resistant to methicillin and most of the other antibiotics that are usually used to treat bacterial infections. MRSA is responsible for hundreds of deaths of hospital patients every year in the UK.

Patients who die with MRSA are usually patients who were already very ill. It is often their existing illness, rather than MRSA, that is given as the cause of death on the death certificate. In these cases, MRSA is only 'mentioned' on the death certificate.

All UK hospitals now have campaigns to prevent the spread of MRSA.

14

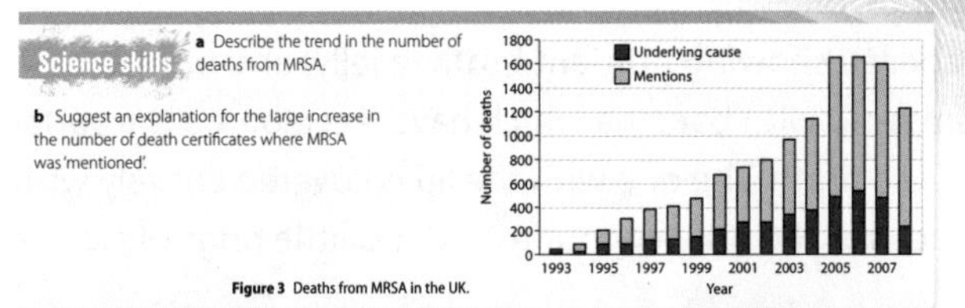

Figure 3 Deaths from MRSA in the UK.

Preventing more superbugs

To prevent more and more types of bacteria becoming resistant, it is important to avoid overusing antibiotics. This is why antibiotics are not used to treat non-serious infections like a sore throat. Doctors should only prescribe an antibiotic to treat a serious disease. By avoiding overusing antibiotics, you increase the likelihood that they will work when you really do need them.

Changing viruses

Flu, or influenza, is a viral disease that affects many people every year. Most people recover within one to two weeks, but flu can cause serious illness and death, especially in very young children and old people. Flu viruses are always mutating, producing new strains. Because the new strain is so different, people will have no immunity to it. This allows the new strain to cause more serious illness and to spread quickly from person to person.

When an outbreak of flu affects thousands of people in a country it is called a flu **epidemic**. Sometimes flu spreads very rapidly around the world, affecting people in many countries. This is called **pandemic** flu. In 2009 a pandemic flu called 'swine flu' developed. The UK government organised vaccination for all vulnerable people and stockpiled millions of doses of Tamiflu, an **antiviral** drug.

Figure 4 An old NHS advert.

Examiner feedback

It is important that you are clear about the difference between an epidemic and a pandemic.

Questions

1 What is MRSA?
2 Name the process that produces antibiotic-resistant strains of pathogens.
3 Explain why patients are advised to always complete a course of antibiotics.
4 Explain why antibiotics are not used to cure viral infections.
5 Suggest why antiviral drugs are only used to treat the most dangerous infections.
6 Explain why the 'swine flu' virus spread rapidly around the world.
7 Explain in terms of natural selection why doctors should not over-prescribe antibiotics.

A*

Science in action

Tamiflu belongs to a family of drugs known as neuraminidase inhibitors. These drugs prevent viruses spreading from cell to cell. When a virus enters a cell it uses the cell's materials to make multiple copies of itself. It also directs the cell to produce an enzyme that will cut through the cell membrane to release the new viruses. Neuraminidase inhibitors block the action of this enzyme. So they do not kill the virus but they do stop it spreading from cell to cell. White blood cells will then eventually develop antibodies to kill the virus.

Healthy bodies 15

Learning objectives

Most students should be able to:

- explain why mutant strains of bacteria may spread rapidly through a population causing epidemics or pandemics

Some students should also be able to:

- explain development of resistant strains in terms of natural selection. [Ext]

Key points

Mutations of pathogens produce new strains.

Antibiotics and vaccinations may not be effective against a new strain of the pathogen. The new strain will then spread rapidly because people are not immune to it and there is no effective treatment.

An epidemic occurs when thousands of people become ill with a disease.

A pandemic occurs when a disease spreads quickly throughout the world.

It is important to prevent the overuse of antibiotics in order to slow down the rate of development of resistant strains.

Mutation | resistant | natural selection | MRSA | epidemic | pandemic

Lesson activities

Starter

1 Show a videoclip such as Could MRSA lurk in your home? – BBC Science. This introduces the idea of the omnipresence of bacteria.

Main

1 Ask students to use the BBC Health article on MRSA to research issues around MRSA and lead to class discussion.

2 Introduce the concept of natural selection in higher organisms, using common examples such as the peppered moth, then apply this to resistant/non-resistant bacterial strains.

3 Ask students to complete **Worksheet B1 1.6a** to consolidate their understanding of MRSA.

Plenary

1 Get the students to share findings from the research activity.

2 Discuss ways of breaking the antibiotic – resistant strain – new antibiotic – new resistant strain cycle.

Homework

1 **Worksheet B1 1.6b** is a homework sheet requiring research into swine flu.

Route to A*

Ask students to research the government's response to the 2009 swine flu epidemic in terms of cost effectiveness.

Answers to Student Book questions

Science skills

a Deaths increased, slowly at first, then more rapidly until 2006. After 2006 there was a decrease in the number of deaths.

b The most likely explanation is increased vigilance for signs of the disease at post-mortem examination.

Answers

1 MRSA is a bacterium that is resistant to a wide range of antibiotics.

2 Mutation.

3 If the course of antibiotics is not completed, some bacteria may survive; these might mutate into resistant strains.

4 Antibiotics don't work on viruses. Viruses live inside body cells, so killing the virus would involve killing the body's cells.

5 Antivirals are very expensive but, more importantly, overuse on trivial diseases could result in viruses becoming resistant to antivirals.

6 The flu virus had mutated, so its antigens were not recognised by white cells. These did not produce antibodies quickly. Existing vaccines were useless because the antibodies produced by vaccination were not effective against the mutated virus.

7 In a population all the bacteria are competing for resources. Resistant strains may out-compete non-resistant strains. If the non-resistant strains are killed off by antibiotics, the resistant bacteria have nothing to keep them in check so they become the dominant strain. The possibility of being infected by a resistant strain then rises considerably.

B1 1.7 Vaccination programmes

Link to the specification

B1.1.2l People can be immunised against a disease by introducing small quantities of dead or inactive forms of the pathogen into the body (vaccination). Vaccines stimulate the white blood cells to produce antibodies that destroy the pathogens. This makes the person immune to future infections by the microorganism. The body can respond by rapidly making the correct antibody, in the same way as if the person had previously had the disease. MMR vaccine is used to protect children against measles, mumps and rubella.

How Science Works

SKU: B1.1 bullet 4: Evaluate the advantages and disadvantages of being vaccinated against a particular disease.

CA: B4.5.4 Draw conclusions using scientific ideas and evidence, by: (a) writing a conclusion, based on evidence that relates correctly to known facts; (b) using secondary sources.

B1 1.7 Vaccination programmes

Learning objectives

- evaluate the advantages and disadvantages of being vaccinated against a particular disease.

Immunisation programmes

Immunisation provides protection against several diseases that used to be very common in children. An example is the **MMR** vaccine, a combined vaccine that makes your body develop immunity to measles, mumps and rubella. Each of these diseases is caused by a virus that is easily spread from someone with the disease to someone who is not immune.

Vaccines such as MMR have saved millions of children from illness and even death. Before a measles vaccine was available, an average of approximately 250 000 children developed measles and 85 children died every year, and many others suffered severe symptoms.

If enough people in a community are immunised against certain diseases, then it is more difficult for that disease to get passed between those who aren't immunised. This is because most people who come into contact with the carrier are immunised, so the disease is less prevalent in the population, and therefore even those who are not immunised are less likely to get it. Medical experts recommend that at least 90% of the population should be vaccinated to prevent epidemics of a disease.

Route to A*

About 85% of UK children have been vaccinated against measles. The World Health Organisation has set a vaccination target of 95%. Explain why it is important to reach the World Health Organisation target.

Science skills

a What was the maximum number of cases of measles in any one year before a vaccine against the disease was introduced?

b What was the maximum number of cases of measles in any one year after the introduction of the measles vaccine?

Number of people with measles/in thousands: 0, 200, 400, 600, 800; Year: 1950, 1960, 1970, 1980, 1990; measles vaccination started; MMR vaccination started

Figure 1 The graph shows the effectiveness of the immunisation programme against measles.

Examiner feedback

Many examinations give data about the number of cases of disease and percentage vaccination.

The data will often have two different *y*-axis scales. Take time before you answer the questions to familiarise yourself with the key to the two sets of data and the different *y*-axis scales.

Remember to give arguments both for and against if you are asked to evaluate such data. Conclude your answer with a reasoned conclusion. It is not sufficient to write 'I think the pros outweigh the cons'.

Concern about vaccines

Children who are not vaccinated are much more likely to develop serious illnesses. Whooping cough is a disease that can cause long bouts of coughing and choking, making it hard to breathe. The disease can be very serious and can kill babies under one year old. More than half the babies under one year old with whooping cough need to be admitted to hospital and many need intensive care.

In the 1970s, parents were concerned about possible **side effects** of the whooping cough vaccine and fewer children were vaccinated against whooping cough. As a result, major outbreaks of whooping cough occurred, with thousands of children being taken into hospital.

16

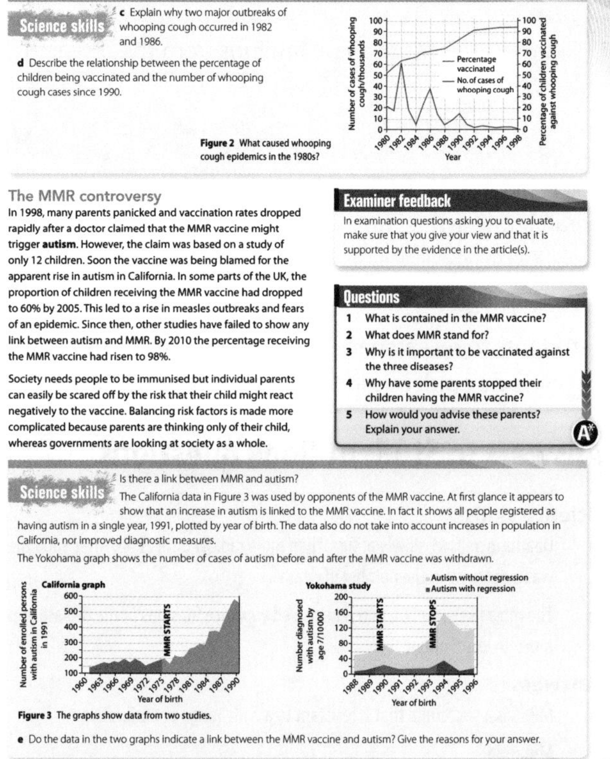

Science skills

c Explain why two major outbreaks of whooping cough occurred in 1982 and 1986.

d Describe the relationship between the percentage of children being vaccinated and the number of whooping cough cases since 1990.

Figure 2 What caused whooping cough epidemics in the 1980s?

The MMR controversy

In 1998, many parents panicked and vaccination rates dropped rapidly after a doctor claimed that the MMR vaccine might trigger **autism**. However, the claim was based on a study of only 12 children. Soon the vaccine was being blamed for the apparent rise in autism in California. In some parts of the UK, the proportion of children receiving the MMR vaccine had dropped to 60% by 2005. This led to a rise in measles outbreaks and fears of an epidemic. Since then, other studies have failed to show any link between autism and MMR. By 2010 the percentage receiving the MMR vaccine had risen to 98%.

Society needs people to be immunised but individual parents can easily be scared off by the risk that their child might react negatively to the vaccine. Balancing risk factors is made more complicated because parents are thinking only of their child, whereas governments are looking at society as a whole.

Examiner feedback

In examination questions asking you to evaluate, make sure that you give your view and that it is supported by the evidence in the article(s).

Questions

1 What is contained in the MMR vaccine?
2 What does MMR stand for?
3 Why is it important to be vaccinated against the three diseases?
4 Why have some parents stopped their children having the MMR vaccine?
5 How would you advise these parents? Explain your answer.

Science skills

Is there a link between MMR and autism?

The California data in Figure 3 was used by opponents of the MMR vaccine. At first glance it appears to show that an increase in autism is linked to the MMR vaccine. In fact it shows all people registered as having autism in a single year, 1991, plotted by year of birth. The data also do not take into account increases in population in California, nor improved diagnostic measures.

The Yokohama graph shows the number of cases of autism before and after the MMR vaccine was withdrawn.

Figure 3 The graphs show data from two studies.

e Do the data in the two graphs indicate a link between the MMR vaccine and autism? Give the reasons for your answer.

Healthy bodies 17

Learning objectives

Most students should be able to:

- explain how immunisation works in terms of white blood cells.

Some students should also be able to:

- evaluate the advantages and disadvantages of being vaccinated against a particular disease. [Ext]

Key points

Some vaccinations may appear to have side effects, and so it is necessary to examine valid data, then weigh up the advantages and disadvantages of being vaccinated against a particular disease.

MMR autism

Lesson activities

Starter

1 'Thought shower' different vaccinations the students have heard of. Look at vaccination schedules to see what vaccinations are in fact available. Compare the timing/frequency of vaccination for different childhood diseases.

A vaccination schedule can be obtained from the Health Protection Agency.

2 Ask students to do the autism quiz.

Main

1 Get the students to watch the BBC News videoclips: MMR scare doctor denies wrongdoing and MMR doctor struck from register. Through this activity introduce the ideas of ethics in reporting research.

2 In groups, students should consider the MMR research time line on the BBC News website and prepare a reasoned report on Dr Wakefield's work and its effects to present to the class.

Plenary

1 Get the students to present their findings to the class.

Homework

1 **Worksheet B1 1.7a** consolidates student's understanding of this topic

2 Ask students to research methods of treating autism.

Route to A*

Ask students to research the effects of the financial contribution made by Bill Gates into researching a vaccine for malaria. Then ask them to discuss the idea of using a wealth tax to finance medical research.

Answers to Student Book questions

Science skills

- **a** Between 760 000 and 780 000
- **b** Between 180 000 and 200 000.
- **c** The percentage of children vaccinated was only around 62% in 1982 and had still reached only around 72% by 1986. This percentage is insufficient to prevent epidemics.
- **d** The percentage of children vaccinated has risen from around 84% in 1990 to 95% in 1998. The number of cases has consequently fallen from 15 000 to 1000 over the same period.
- **e** The data for California are seriously flawed since they do not take into account rises in population in California or improved methods of diagnosis.

  The data for Japan show that the number of autism cases continued to rise, and remained high after MMR vaccination was discontinued, showing that some other factor(s) is involved.

Answers

1. Dead/weakened viruses.
2. Measles, mumps and rubella.
3. All of them can cause serious damage to the body; it is important that over 90% of children are vaccinated to prevent epidemics.
4. Fear of side effects such as autism.
5. Advise parents that the risk of damage from disease is much greater than the risk of damaging side effects, and point out that research has been carried out on large numbers of children in many countries into side effects and that none of the research has shown a link between the vaccine and autism.

B1 1.8 Keeping things sterile

Link to the specification

B1.1.2m Uncontaminated cultures of microorganisms are required for investigating the action of disinfectants and antibiotics. For this:

- Petri dishes and culture media must be sterilised before use to kill unwanted microorganisms
- inoculating loops used to transfer microorganisms to the media must be sterilised by passing them through a flame
- the lid of the Petri dish should be secured with adhesive tape to prevent microorganisms from the air contaminating the culture.

B1.1.2n In school and college laboratories, cultures should be incubated at a maximum temperature of 25 °C, which greatly reduces the likelihood of growth of pathogens that might be harmful to humans. In industrial conditions higher temperatures can produce more rapid growth.

Ideas for practical work

Growing microorganisms in Petri dishes to demonstrate sterile technique and growing pure cultures

How Science Works

CA: B4.2.1 Assess and manage risks when carrying out practical work, by: (a) identifying some possible hazards in practical situations; (b) managing risks.

B1 1.8 Keeping things sterile

Learning objectives

- explain why you need uncontaminated cultures of microorganisms to study the effects of different treatments on them
- describe how apparatus is sterilised and how this achieves pure cultures
- explain how to inoculate a culture medium.

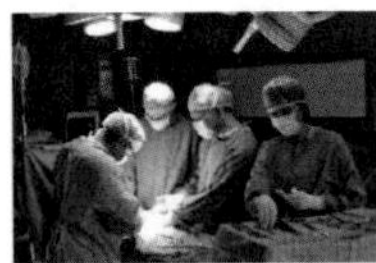

Kitted out to avoid infection.

Examiner feedback

This topic is where your understanding of safety techniques is most likely to be tested. Make sure you can explain the reasons for safety techniques, such as sterilisation, maximum incubation temperature, personal hygiene and disposal of used cultures.

Taking it further

Like animals, most bacteria possess no chlorophyll, so they cannot produce their own food. They cannot eat solid food and have to absorb nutrients through their cell membranes. Like all other living organisms, bacteria use carbohydrates, such as sugars, as an energy source and to produce new cells. Some bacteria need only sugar and mineral ions, such as nitrate, potassium and phosphate, which they use to produce proteins. Other bacteria, particularly pathogenic bacteria, have to obtain proteins and vitamins from external sources.

Growing bacteria

Like all living organisms, bacteria and fungi need nutrients to grow and reproduce. In the laboratory, nutrients are often supplied to the microorganisms, also known as microbes, in a gel called **agar**. Agar is called a growth medium or **culture medium.** It melts at 98 °C and, as a liquid, it can be poured into plastic or glass **Petri dishes.** It solidifies at about 44 °C. Microbes cannot digest agar, so it is not used up as they grow.

Besides nutrients, many microbes need a temperature between 25 °C and 45 °C to grow. In school laboratories, the Petri dishes are put into a cabinet, or an **incubator,** set at a maximum temperature of 25 °C. Pathogens could accidentally be present in the culture dishes, so keeping the temperature at a maximum of 25 °C minimises health risks from them, as they will grow much less well at lower temperatures.

Why do we need to keep things sterile?

The air, the surfaces around you, your skin and clothes all have microorganisms on them. If you culture microorganisms in the laboratory, it involves growing very large numbers of bacterial cells. If safety procedures are not followed, you may accidentally introduce a harmful microbe into a harmless **strain** that you are growing. This would multiply rapidly, just as the harmless microbes do, and would be a greater health risk than if it were a single cell. Sterile or aseptic techniques must therefore be used to prepare uncontaminated cultures.

Glassware and culture media are **sterilised** in an **autoclave** using pressurised steam at a temperature of 121 °C for 15 minutes.

The type of autoclave used in most schools.

The high temperature needed to kill microbes melts plastic, so Petri dishes and disposable instruments are sterilised by **ultraviolet** or **ionising radiation.** This is done commercially. Petri dishes remain sterile inside until the lid is opened.

Safety first

You must wash your hands before and after working with microorganisms. A clean, cleared working surface is also essential. Hair should be tied back, broken skin covered with a plaster and hand-to-face contact avoided while culturing microbes. Work is carried out near the upward draught from a lighted Bunsen burner. The upward movement of air around the burner minimises the risk of airborne microbes falling onto **culture plates.**

Inoculation

Inoculation is the process of transferring microbes to the culture medium. For solid agar, a wire **inoculating loop** is used. It is first sterilised by holding it in a Bunsen burner flame. After cooling the loop for ten seconds, near the Bunsen burner, the microbes can be picked up from the **pure culture** and transferred to the sterile agar by gently sweeping the loop back and forth over the surface.

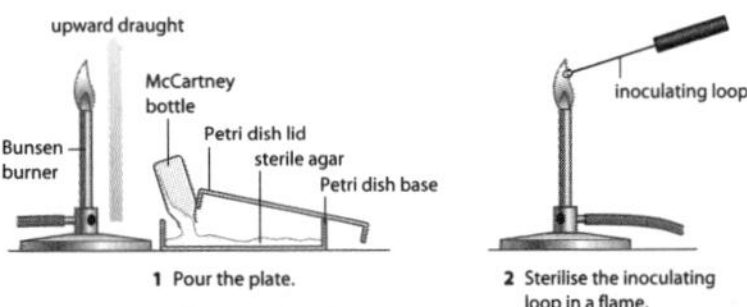

1 Pour the plate.

2 Sterilise the inoculating loop in a flame.

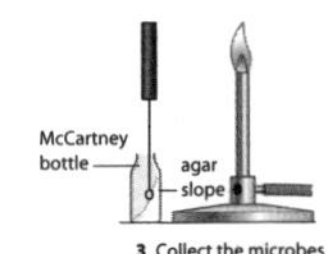

3 Collect the microbes from the pure culture.

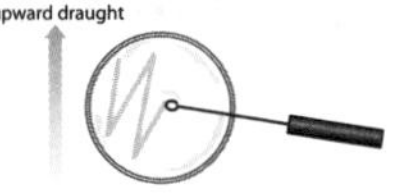

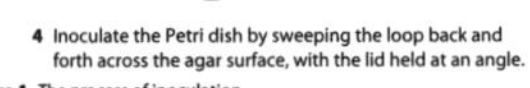

4 Inoculate the Petri dish by sweeping the loop back and forth across the agar surface, with the lid held at an angle.

5 Write the details on the base of the sealed Petri dish.

Figure 1 The process of inoculation.

Before **incubation** the Petri dishes are sealed with adhesive tape to prevent contamination from airborne bacteria. After 24–72 hours, when the results have been noted, the cultures are autoclaved by a technician before disposal.

Questions

1. Give three ways in which microbiological equipment and media can be sterilised.
2. What is meant by 'aseptic'?
3. Give three personal safety precautions that should be taken when experimenting with microorganisms.
4. Describe what would happen if a single cell of a pathogen entered a culture dish.
5. Explain why the wire loop needs to be cooled before picking up the microbes.
6. Suggest why the lid of the Petri dish is not removed completely when introducing the microorganisms.
7. Describe what you should do with your successful culture after an experiment.
8. Explain why agar is suitable as a culture medium for growing bacteria.

18 Healthy bodies 19

Learning objectives

Students should be able to:

- carry out basic sterile techniques
- evaluate their results.

Key points

To investigate the action of antiseptics and antibiotics on microorganisms, uncontaminated cultures of microorganisms are needed.

For this:

- apparatus and culture media should be sterilised in an autoclave to kill unwanted microorganisms
- inoculating loops should be sterilised by passing through a Bunsen flame
- the lid of the culture dish should be sealed to prevent contamination by microorganisms from the air
- in school and college laboratories, cultures should be incubated at a maximum temperature of 25°C; this greatly reduces the likelihood of pathogens growing that might be harmful to humans.

Agar | culture medium | inoculating loop | sterile | incubator | autoclave | culture plate

Lesson activities

Starter

1 Ask students to suggest ways of ensuring that equipment and media used for transferring and growing bacteria are sterile.

Main

1 Growing bacteria B1 1.8a this activity consists of two practicals:

- **a Demonstrating presence of bacteria** In this practical, students transfer bacteria onto agar plates using direct contact with a finger or coin. The plates are left for 48 hours before the results can be analysed.
- **b Testing for contamination** A similar practical, but inoculating the plates using inoculating loops or swabs to take samples from various parts of the laboratory.

Plenary

1 Ask the students to discuss the reasons underlying the use of sterile techniques.

Homework

1 Worksheet B1 1.8b shows students how quickly bacteria multiply.

2 Ask students to research ways in which viruses are cultured and to suggest reasons for the differences in the methods used to culture viruses and bacteria.

Route to A*

Ask students to research cleaning methods in the school and to comment on their findings in light of the results of their practical work.

Answers to Student Book questions

1. Autoclave, ultraviolet, ionising radiation.
2. Free of microorganisms.
3. Any three from: hair tied back, cuts covered with plaster, avoid hand to face contact, wash hands before and after working.
4. Growth and cell division would continue until a colony containing millions of cells would be visible.
5. High temperatures kill microbes; the loop would kill the microbes being transferred.
6. To reduce the risk of microbes from the air contaminating the culture.
7. The culture should be disposed of safely, either using disinfectant or an autoclave.
8. Agar can be sterilised without affecting it chemically; it can be melted for pouring and then it sets. It contains no nutrients, and it is inert, meaning microbial enzymes cannot digest it so it remains solid.

B1 2.1 The nervous system

Link to the specification

B1.2.1a The nervous system enables humans to react to their surroundings and coordinate their behaviour.

B1.2.1b Cells called receptors detect stimuli (changes in the environment).

B1.2.1c Light receptor cells, like most animal cells, have a nucleus, cytoplasm and cell membrane.

B1.2.1d Information from receptors passes along cells (neurones) in nerves to the brain. The brain coordinates the response. Reflex actions are automatic and rapid. They often involve sensory, relay and motor neurones.

B1.2.1e Candidates should understand the role of receptors, sensory neurones, motor neurones, relay neurones, synapses and effectors in simple reflex actions.

Ideas for practical work

- Investigation into candidates' reaction times – measuring reaction times using metre rules, stop clocks or ICT.
- Using forehead thermometers before and after exercise.
- Demonstrating the speed of transmission along nerves by candidates standing in a semicircle and holding hands and squeezing with eyes closed.
- Design an investigation to measure the sensitivity of the skin.
- Demonstrating the knee jerk reaction.

How Science Works

CA: B4.4.1 Show an understanding of the value of means, by: (a) appreciating when it is appropriate to calculate a mean; (b) calculating the mean of a set of at least three results; B4.5.2 Review methodology to assess fitness for purpose, by: (a) identifying causes of variation in data; (b) recognising and identifying the cause of random errors. When a data set contains random errors, repeating the readings and calculating a new mean can reduce their effect: (c) recognising and identifying the cause of anomalous results; (d) recognising and identifying the cause of systematic errors.

B1 2.1 The nervous system

Learning objectives

- describe the receptors that detect different stimuli
- explain how your nervous system enables you to react to your surroundings and coordinates your behaviour
- describe a reflex action
- analyse a response in terms of stimulus, receptor, effector and response.

Waiting for the starting signal.

The nervous system

The difference between winning and losing a race might be down to how quickly you start. It is all about reaction time. This is the time between hearing the gun and reacting to it.

The **nervous system** is made up of three main parts: the **brain**, the **spinal cord** and **neurones**, or nerve cells.

It has **receptors** in the:

- eyes that are sensitive to light
- ears that are sensitive to sound and to changes in position, thus enabling us to keep our balance
- tongue and in the nose that are sensitive to chemicals and enable us to taste and smell
- skin that are sensitive to touch, pressure, pain and to temperature changes.

The nervous system.

Receptors are cells that detect stimuli or changes in the environment. Each receptor cell, e.g. light receptor cells in the eye, like all animal cells, contains a **nucleus** and **cytoplasm** surrounded by a **cell membrane**.

Information from receptors, e.g. in your nose if you smell something burning, passes along neurones to the brain. The information passes along the neurones as signals called **impulses.** The brain then coordinates the response by sending information to the appropriate organs.

There are three types of neurone:

- **sensory neurones** carry impulses from the receptor to the spinal cord
- **relay neurones** carry impulses through the spinal cord and up to the brain and from the brain back along the spinal cord
- **motor neurones** take impulses from the spinal cord to an **effector**.

An effector can be a muscle that is made to **contract,** or a **gland** that secretes a chemical, for example a hormone.

Route to A*

Some drugs are used in medicine because they affect reflex pathways.

- The drug curare prevents muscles from contracting, thereby making surgery easier. At what place in a reflex action does curare probably act?
- Dentists inject the drug procaine into gums so that they can drill into teeth without causing pain. What is the most probable reason for procaine preventing pain?

20

Neurones are not joined to each other. There is a small gap between them called a **synapse**. When an impulse reaches the end of a neurone, a chemical is released. This travels across the gap, and starts an impulse in the next neurone. This means the message can only travel in one direction (see Figure 1).

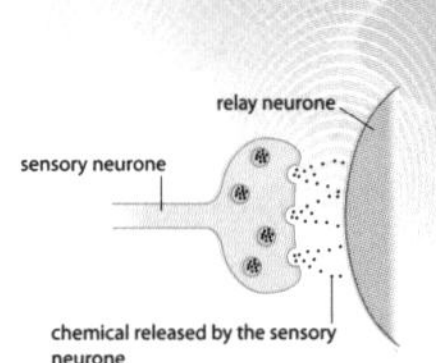

Figure 1 Chemicals released by a sensory neurone travel across the synapse to the relay neurone.

Reflex actions

When pain is detected by a sensory receptor in your finger, it sends an impulse along a sensory neurone to a relay neurone in your spinal cord. The relay neurone sends an impulse in an arc via a motor neurone to an effector, a muscle, which contracts, pulling your hand away. This is called a **reflex action**. It is automatic and very quick (see Figure 2). There are other types of reflex actions such as coughing and blinking. These are needed to protect us from being hurt or from damage to our tissues, e.g. foreign bodies in airways or eyes.

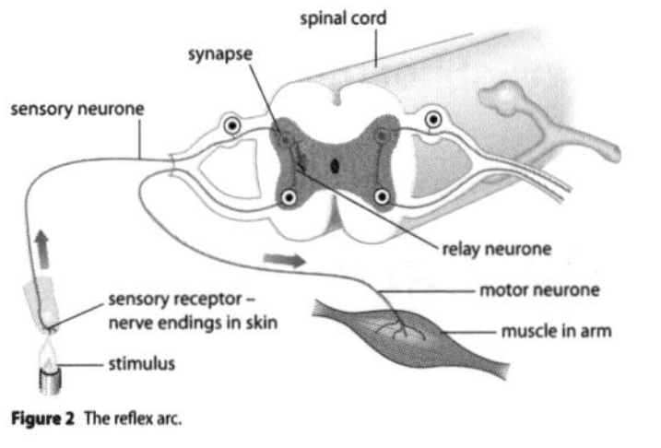

Figure 2 The reflex arc.

Examiner feedback

You should practise looking at different diagrams of the reflex arc and working out what is happening in each part.

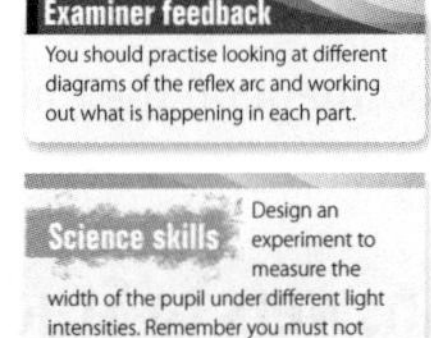

Science skills

Design an experiment to measure the width of the pupil under different light intensities. Remember you must not touch the surface of the eye.

a What are the independent, the dependent and the control variables?

b Explain what you will do to make sure your experiment produces reliable results.

Questions

1. Identify six stimuli that you respond to and state where in the body the receptors for these are located.
2. Some people suffer from a disease called motor neurone disease. **(a)** Suggest which part of the nervous system it affects. **(b)** What will people with this disease have difficulty doing?
3. Coughing, sneezing and blinking are examples of reflex actions. **(a)** Identify what part of the body each reflex action protects. **(b)** Identify the receptor in each reflex action. **(c)** Identify the effector in each reflex action.
4. People taking part in motor sports wear head, neck and back protection. Why is it important to protect each of these areas?
5. Suggest how a sprinter might improve his reaction time.
6. The diagram shows the knee-jerk reflex. When the leg is tapped with a hammer just below the knee, the leg straightens. Describe fully the sequence of events in this reflex arc.

receptors that are very sensitive to the muscle being stretched suddenly
quadriceps – effector muscle
knee cap
sensory neurone
tendon
hamstrings
synapse
motor neurone
spinal cord

Figure 3 The knee-jerk reflex.

Coordination and control 21

Learning objectives

Students should be able to:

- identify and explain the role of the key parts of the nervous system including senses, neurones, brain, spinal cord and effectors
- understand that the nervous system enables humans to react to their surroundings and co-ordinate their behaviour
- explain the pathway of information from stimulus to response
- understand what is meant by a reflex action.

ActiveTeach Resource: Stimulus and response – *Video*
Multiple stimuli – *Video*

Key points

The body has receptors sensitive to light, sound, changes in position, chemicals, touch, pressure, pain and temperature changes.

Reflex actions are rapid and automatic. They involve sensory, relay and motor neurones.

Effectors bring about responses. Effectors may be muscles or glands.

Effector	impulse	motor neurone	neurones	receptor	reflex arc
relay neurone	sensory neurone	spinal reflex	stimuli	synapse	

Lesson activities

Starter

1 Comparing reaction times Put students in pairs and get them to play a less 'violent' alternative to slaps where they must grab a screwed up piece of paper from each other's hand. Ask the students: Who is best? Why are they the best? What are the stimuli prior to reacting? Introduce the idea of reaction time difference.

2 Ask students to think about what other kinds of receptors they have that might be used in reflex actions.

Main

1 Stimulus and response Show the video of the athlete in the starting block from the ActiveTeach. What the stimulus is for the athlete and what is the response to the stimulus? [AT]

2 Multiple stimuli and responses Show the video from the ActiveTeach where the athlete describes what it is like to run in front of a crowd at a competition. Ask students to list all the stimuli that the athlete mentions.[AT]

3 The response process Discuss the sequence of events that links the stimulus to the response (this does not have to be definitive, rather an AfL exercise to identify prior knowledge, misconceptions, etc.).

4 There are three different practical exercises but students only really need to do the first practical (ruler drop). The other two are supplementary, depending on the time available and ability of the group. They do however involve different receptors and effectors.

- **a Reaction time** Students compare their reaction times in catching a falling ruler under various circumstances.
- **b Knee jerk reflex** Students test the knee jerk reflex on each other and attempt to prevent it.
- **c Blink reflex** Students test the blink reflex and attempt to prevent it.

Plenaries

1 Ask students to list as many reflex actions as possible, then to discuss the possible effects on the body if each reflex did not work.

Homework

1 Worksheet B1.2.1b The homework sheets reinforce work covered in the Student Book on parts of the nervous system and the pathway from detecting a stimulus to responding. It looks at how reflex actions work. [AfL]

2 Ask students to research conditioned reflexes.

Route to A*

- At the junction between a motor neurone and the muscle.
- It prevents impulses passing along sensory neurones.

Answers to Student Book questions

Science skills

a The independent variable is the light intensity. The dependent variable is the width of the pupil.

Control variables include intensity of background illumination, the distance of the light sources from the eye, age and gender of student.

b To obtain reliable results at least three measurements of pupil width should be taken at each light intensity for each student, and the mean width calculated. The experiment should then be repeated on other students.

Answers

1 Six from: light – eyes; sound – ears; chemicals – nose and tongue; temperature changes – skin; touch – skin; pain – skin; changes in position – ears.

2 **(a)** Motor nerves. **(b)** Controlling their muscles.

3 **(a)** Coughing – lungs; sneezing – nostrils; blinking – eyes. **(b)** Coughing – touch receptors; sneezing – chemical receptors; blinking – light receptors. **(c)** Coughing – breathing muscles, sneezing – facial muscles, blinking – eyelid muscles.

4 Head – to protect the brain from damage; neck and back – to prevent damage to the spinal cord.

5 A sprinter could improve reaction time by getting a colleague to video practice starts, measuring reaction time from the videos, then adjusting starting position accordingly.

6 Tapping moves the knee cap and slightly stretches the attached muscles. Receptors in the muscle detect the stretch stimulus. Impulses pass along a sensory neurone to the central nervous system. In the nervous system the impulse is transmitted by chemicals across a synapse, first to a relay neurone, then to a motor neurone. The motor neurone carries the impulse to an effector that is a muscle. The muscle contracts to straighten the leg.

B1 2.2

Controlling our internal environment

Link to the specification

B1.2.2a Internal conditions that are controlled include:

- the water content of the body – water leaves the body via the lungs when we breathe out and via the skin when we sweat to cool us down, and excess water is lost via the kidneys in the urine
- the ion content of the body – ions are lost via the skin when we sweat and excess ions are lost via the kidneys in the urine
- temperature – to maintain the temperature at which enzymes work best
- blood sugar levels – to provide the cells with a constant supply of energy.

How Science Works

CA: B4.1.1 Develop hypotheses and plan practical ways to test them, by: (a) being able to develop a hypothesis; (b) being able to test hypotheses; (c) using appropriate technology.

B1 2.2

Controlling our internal environment

Learning objectives

- describe how water leaves the body via the lungs, skin and kidneys
- describe how ions are lost through the skin as sweat, and the kidneys as urine
- explain why it is important that blood sugar concentration and blood ion concentration are regulated
- explain why body temperature is kept at 37 °C.

Refuelling during a marathon.

When we exercise

During a marathon, runners top up with sports drinks several times. Why do they need to do this?

Figure 1 compares the rate of heat production and the body temperature of a marathon runner during a race with those of the same athlete at rest.

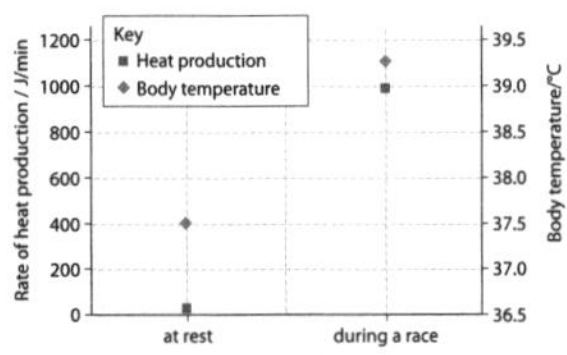

Figure 1 Body changes during a marathon.

Why is our body temperature kept at 37 °C?

Your body tries to stay at a steady internal temperature, around 37 °C. This is the temperature at which enzymes in your body work best. Enzymes speed up chemical reactions in the body. Without enzymes your body would not be able to work properly. The process of keeping things constant and balanced in your body is called **homeostasis**.

Salt (sodium chloride) contains sodium and chloride ions. These are needed to help our body work properly. Too much salt can be dangerous, but so is too little. Sodium and chloride levels in the blood are controlled by the kidneys. These ions are also lost when we sweat.

If the balance of ions and water changes in our bodies, cells do not work so well. Sports drinks help to replace both the water and the ions.

Sports drinks also contain **glucose**. This helps to top up the athlete's blood sugar levels during the marathon. To work properly, body cells need a constant supply of glucose for their energy needs. This glucose is supplied by the blood.

Figure 2 shows the effect of temperature on the rate of an enzyme-controlled reaction. If our bodies were cooler than 37 °C, the chemical reactions in our cells would be much slower. Above 37 °C these reactions rapidly slow down. If we heat enzymes above 45 °C, their structure changes and they stop working.

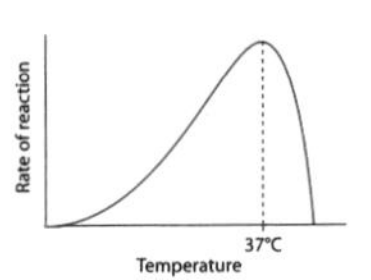

Figure 2 How temperature affects the rate of a reaction involving an enzyme.

Heat exhaustion and heatstroke

Heat exhaustion and heatstroke are two heat-related health conditions. Both can be very serious.

Heat exhaustion is when the core temperature rises to 40 °C. At that temperature, the levels of water and salt in the body begin to drop. This causes symptoms such as nausea, feeling faint and heavy sweating. If left untreated, heat exhaustion can sometimes lead to heatstroke.

Heatstroke happens when a person's core temperature rises above 40 °C. Cells inside the body begin to break down and important parts of the body stop working. Symptoms of heatstroke can include confusion, rapid shallow breathing and loss of consciousness. If left untreated, heatstroke can cause multiple organ failure, brain damage and death.

If a person with heat exhaustion is taken quickly to a cool place and given plenty of water to drink, they should begin to feel better within half an hour and experience no long-term effects. Heatstroke is very serious and should be treated immediately. Treatment involves quickly cooling down the body to lower the core temperature by using ice packs or a cold bath/shower.

Balancing the water budget

To stay healthy, the body needs to balance the gain and loss of both water and ions. Besides losing water when we urinate, pass faeces and sweat, we lose water in the air we breathe out. This is why a mirror becomes misty if we breathe on it.

The **kidneys** control the balance of water and ions in the body. They do this by producing a fluid called **urine**. Urine contains the excess salts and water that the body does not need. It also contains other waste materials.

Science in action

If the amount of water in the blood is too low, a hormone called anti-diuretic hormone (ADH) is released from the pituitary gland in the brain. ADH activates the kidney to reduce the amount of water lost in the urine. The retained water passes back into the bloodstream to stop you from losing too much water (dehydrating).

Sports scientists have developed a urine colour chart to help athletes gauge how much water to drink during training. If the urine is too dark in colour, the urine is too concentrated. This tells the athlete that they are not drinking enough water to replace the water lost via sweating.

Science skills The amount of water entering the body should balance the amount of water leaving the body.

a How much water would this person have to drink to compensate for the amount of water lost?

b What proportion of water loss was via the skin?

c Construct pie charts to show the water budget.

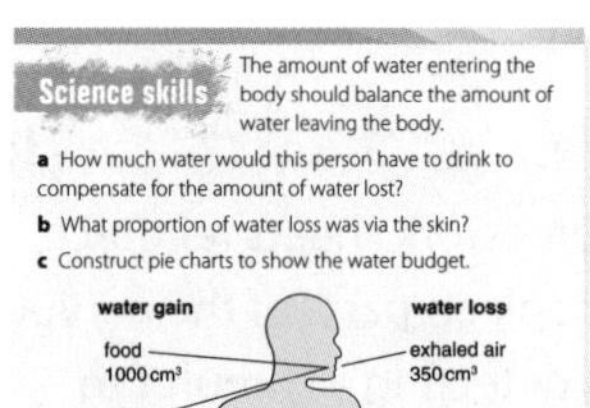
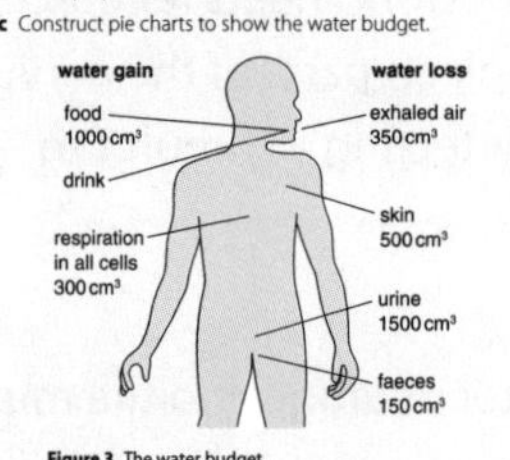

Figure 3 The water budget.

Questions

1. Looking at Figure 1:
   (a) By how much does body temperature rise during a marathon?
   (b) Calculate the percentage increase in heat production by a marathon runner during a race.
2. (a) If you sweat a lot, what will happen to your: (i) salt levels (ii) water levels? (b) Why might this be dangerous?
3. Why does an athlete's blood sugar level fall during a race?
4. A person suffering from severe dehydration continues to produce urine, making the body even more dehydrated. Suggest why the body continues to produce urine under these conditions.
5. Many drinks cause the body to lose more water in the urine. These drinks are called diuretics. Alcohol, caffeine and fizzy drinks are all diuretics. Why is it not a good idea to drink these when you feel thirsty?
6. Describe in detail how conditions in the body are kept constant. A*

22 Coordination and control 23

Learning objectives

Students should be able to:

- know that body temperature has to be maintained at a level at which enzymes work best
- know that blood sugar provides cells with energy
- know that water leaves the body via the lungs, skin and kidneys
- know that salt is lost through the skin when we sweat and via the kidneys in urine
- understand that all of the above are controlled by homeostasis.

Key points

Conditions which should be kept constant in the body include:

- the water content of the body – excess water is lost via the kidneys in the urine
- the ion content of the body – excess ions are lost via the kidneys in the urine
- temperature – to maintain the temperature at which enzymes work best
- blood sugar levels – to provide the cells with a constant supply of energy.

ActiveTeach Resource: How to avoid sports injuries – *Video*
Causes of cramp – *Video*
Importance of drinking fluids during exercise – *Video*

Dehydration enzymes ions homeostasis glucose kidneys urine lungs skin

Lesson activities

Starter

1 Demonstration of homeostatic control during exercise Start with some exercise. Ask students to run on the spot, do star jumps and press ups. Some students may be unable to do these and gentler exercise might be more appropriate. Keep them exercising until they are visibly sweating and tiring (about 5 minutes). Once finished, get them to look at each other and describe and explain what they see (e.g. hot, flushed, breathing heavily). This is an AfL-type exercise designed to find out what they already know about homeostasis and the level of details their explanations involve.

2 How to avoid sports injuries ActiveTeach video explaining how injuries can be avoided by athletes including the role that diet and warming up plays. [AT]

Main

1 B1 2.2a Temperature and exercise In this activity, students measure the effect of exercise on skin temperature.

2 Causes of cramp ActiveTeach video. Discuss how 'failure' of homeostasis results in cramp. [AT]

3 Importance of drinking fluids during exercise ActiveTeach video showing Iwan Thomas talking about sports drinks and the importance of drinking water during training and competitions. [AT]

Plenary

1 Start with the idea that the sea is salty. Ask students what effect swallowing sea water would have on blood concentration. Once this is established, students should be able to complete the sequence and describe how it is regulated back to normal.

Homework

1 Students could research homeostasis associated with breathing. Ask them to consider what is added/removed and why.

2 Worksheet B1 2.2b consolidates understanding of homeostasis.

Points to note

- Homeostasis is developed as a topic in Unit BY3 and you should therefore leave detailed discussions of homeostatic mechanisms until that unit is taught.

Route to A*

- Ask students to research methods of temperature control in reptiles and to suggest explanations for the different methods used by mammals and reptiles to control body temperature.

Answers to Student Book questions

Science skills

a $2500 - 1300 = 1200\ cm^3$

b $500 \div 2500 = 0.2$

c Two pie charts of the same size for water gain and water loss, or one with the balanced water budget.

Answers

1 **(a)** $39.3 - 37.5 = 1.8$ °C **(b)** $1000 - 40 = 960$; $960 \div 40 \times 100$; increase = 2400%.

2 **(a) (i)** Increase. **(ii)** Decrease. **(b)** Body cells will not function correctly.

3 Sugar is respired to release the energy needed to run.

4 Urine removes waste products from the body; if urine production stopped these waste products would build up to dangerous levels.

5 Drinks containing diuretics will speed up the rate at which the body loses water in urine; they will cause even more dehydration.

6 Temperature – heat is produced by respiration in cells. Shivering helps the body to generate heat. Sweating helps the body to release excess heat. We take in water both in food and drink. Water is also produced during respiration. We lose water via sweat and breathing. The kidney gets rid of excess water in urine. We take in mineral ions in food and in some drinks. The kidneys get rid of excess ions in the urine. Hormones control blood sugar level.

B1 2.3 Controlling pregnancy

Link to the specification

B1.2.2b Many processes within the body are coordinated by chemical substances called hormones. Hormones are secreted by glands and are usually transported to their target organs by the bloodstream.

B1.2.2c Hormones regulate the functions of many organs and cells. For example, the monthly release of an egg from a woman's ovaries and the changes in the thickness of the lining of her womb are controlled by hormones secreted by the pituitary gland and by the ovaries.

B1.2.2d Several hormones are involved in the menstrual cycle of a woman. Hormones are involved in promoting the release of an egg.

- follicle stimulating hormone (FSH) is secreted by the pituitary gland and causes eggs to mature in the ovaries. It also stimulates the ovaries to produce hormones including oestrogen
- luteinising hormone (LH) stimulates the release of eggs from the ovary
- oestrogen is secreted by the ovaries and inhibits the further production of FSH.

B1 2.2e The uses of hormones in controlling fertility include:

- giving oral contraceptives that contain hormones to inhibit FSH production so that no eggs mature
- oral contraceptives may contain oestrogen and progesterone to inhibit egg maturation
- the first birth-control pills contained large amounts of oestrogen. These resulted in women suffering significant side effects
- progesterone-only pills lead to fewer side effects
- birth-control pills now contain a much lower dose of oestrogen, or are progesterone only
- giving FSH and LH in a 'fertility drug' to a woman whose own level of FSH is too low to stimulate eggs to mature, for example in *in vitro* fertilisation (IVF) treatment.
- IVF involves giving a mother FSH and LH to stimulate the maturation of several eggs. The eggs are collected from the mother and fertilised by sperm from the father. The fertilised eggs develop into embryos. At the stage when they are tiny balls of cells, one or two embryos are inserted into the mother's uterus (womb).

B1 2.3 Controlling pregnancy

Learning objectives

- explain the role of the hormones FSH, LH and oestrogen in the menstrual cycle
- explain the role of FSH as a fertility drug
- explain the role of hormones in oral contraceptives.

Hormones

Many of our body processes are controlled by chemicals called **hormones.** These are produced by organs called glands. The hormones pass from glands into the bloodstream, which transports them around the body. Each hormone affects one or more organs, known as the target organs.

The menstrual cycle

Every month, an egg (**ovum**) develops inside a female ovary. At the same time, **oestrogen** causes the lining of the womb (**uterus**) to become thicker, ready to receive a growing embryo. If the egg is not fertilised, the womb lining breaks down, causing bleeding from the vagina. The monthly cycle of changes that take place in the ovaries and womb is called the **menstrual cycle**. The menstrual cycle is controlled by several hormones. The action of the hormones involved is summarised in Figures 1 and 2.

Examiner feedback

You are only required to learn the roles of FSH, LH and oestrogen in the menstrual cycle. FSH starts with the letter F. Use this to remember that FSH is the first hormone to be secreted in the menstrual cycle. Remember that FSH stimulates eggs to mature; it does not cause egg release. Oestrogen does not cause egg release. LH starts with the letter L. Use this to remember that LH is the last of the three hormones to be produced. LH stimulates egg release.

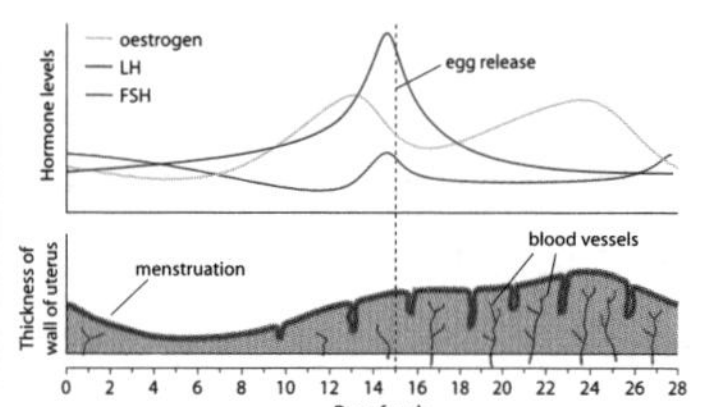

Figure 1 The effects of the menstrual cycle.

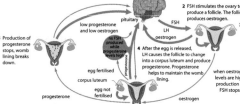

1 Each month the pituitary gland at the base of the brain starts to produce follicle–stimulating hormone (FSH).

2 FSH stimulates the ovary to produce a follicle. The follicle produces oestrogen.

3 Oestrogen prepares the uterus for a fertilised egg; a surge of LH triggers egg release.

4 After the egg is released, LH causes the follicle to change into a corpus luteum and produce progesterone. Progesterone helps to maintain the womb lining.

5 Production of progesterone stops, womb lining breaks down.

pituitary
FSH
LH
oestrogen
low progesterone and low oestrogen
no FSH produced while progesterone levels high
progesterone
egg fertilised
corpus luteum
egg not fertilised
when oestrogen levels are high, production of FSH stops.
progesterone
oestrogen

Figure 2 The menstrual cycle.

24

The contraceptive pill

A woman can take the contraceptive pill to stop her from becoming pregnant. The pill contains hormones that have the same effect on the pituitary gland as oestrogen. These hormones stop the pituitary gland making the hormone **FSH**. This means that no eggs will mature in the ovaries.

Benefits and problems

The first contraceptive pills contained large amounts of oestrogen. These resulted in women suffering significant side effects such as the formation of blood clots, which can block vital arteries.

There are now two types of contraceptive pill available, 'combined' and 'mini pill'. The combined pill contains a much lower dose of oestrogen along with another hormone called progesterone. The mini pill contains progesterone only. The mini pill causes fewer side effects but must be taken punctually in order for it to work and is less reliable than the combined pill.

The combined pill decreases the chance of getting cancer of the womb by 50% and cancer of the ovaries by 40%. There is an increased risk, however, that women taking the pill will develop blood clots.

Fertility drugs

If a woman's own level of FSH is too low, her ovaries will not release eggs and she cannot become pregnant. Infertility can be treated by injecting FSH into the blood. FSH acts as a fertility drug by stimulating the ovaries to produce mature eggs.

Unfortunately, the treatment does not always work, or sometimes it may cause more than one egg to be released. This can result in twins, triplets, quadruplets or even more.

Science skills

a Imagine you are a doctor. Using the data in the table, what would you say to a woman who wanted to go on the pill and was worried about side effects?

Table 1 The risk of blood clots.

Situation	Risk in cases per 100 000 women
women not on the pill	8
women taking combined pill	25
women taking mini pill	15
women who smoke	100
pregnant women	85

Questions

1 (a) How many days are there in a typical menstrual cycle?
(b) On which day does the concentration of FSH peak?

2 What causes menstruation?

3 What is the role of FSH in the menstrual cycle?

4 What is the relationship between oestrogen concentration in the blood and the thickness of the lining of the womb?

5 The most difficult time for a female athlete to race well is the week before menstruation and the week after ovulation. The best time for female athletes to race is thought to be just before ovulation, between days 9 to 12.
(a) Study the changing levels of oestrogen in Figure 1 and explain the connection between the oestrogen level and athletic performance.
(b) Design a training schedule for a female athlete so that she can train and race at peak performance. Think about the menstrual cycle and how it affects performance.
(c) How might taking the contraceptive pill help with race training and performance?

6 Explain why:
(a) FSH can be used as a fertility drug
(b) oestrogen can be used as a contraceptive drug
(c) the mini pill is better in some respects, and worse in others, than the combined pill.

7 There are two forms of 'morning-after' pill (emergency contraceptive pill). Pills containing high doses of oestrogen and progesterone will immediately stop ovulation. The other type of pill prevents a fertilised egg from implanting into the lining of the womb. Evaluate the use of these two types of 'morning-after' pill.

A*

Coordination and control 25

Learning objectives

Most students should be able to:

- understand the role of FSH, LH and oestrogen in the menstrual cycle of a woman
- be able to explain the role of FSH and LH in fertility
- understand the differences between the different types of contraceptive pill.

Some students should also be able to:

- evaluate the benefits of, and the problems that may arise from, the use of hormones to control fertility. [Ext]

Key points

Hormones are chemicals that control many processes in the body such as the menstrual cycle.

In the menstrual cycle:

- FSH stimulates eggs to mature in the ovary
- Oestrogen causes the lining of the womb to increase in thickness.
- LH triggers egg release.
- FSH can be given to women to help them get pregnant.
- Oestrogen and/or progesterone can be given to a woman to prevent pregnancy.

Follicle stimulating hormone (FSH) luteinising hormone (LH) menstrual cycle menstruation oestrogen progesterone uterus hormone gland fertility contraception

Lesson activities

Starter

1 The menstrual cycle Show students a linear diagram of the changes in thickness of the uterus lining over the course of the menstrual cycle and get them to speculate what it is (there should be some interesting comments). Give clues to lead students to the correct conclusion. Questions that you could ask as clues include: Where is the mid-point of the picture? Can you show this point labelled as 14? Can you show the start labelled as 0 and the end as 28? Can you describe what happens from 0 to 28?

Main

1 Hormones in the menstrual cycle. Worksheet B1 2.3a leads the students through a series of tasks that show what happens as the menstrual cycle progresses. In effect they construct a timeline picture showing how hormones influence what takes place over time. Ask students to use a different colour for each line that is drawn.

2 Worksheet B1 2.3b Ethics of contraceptive trials Students use the worksheet as a basis for discussion and prepare a report for the plenary.

Plenaries

1 Recent research has shown that the chances of a woman getting pregnant decrease after about 35 years of age. Ask students: Which hormones affect fertility? What might be happening to hormones as a woman gets older? What can be done to improve fertility after the age of 35?

2 Students report back on the ethics of the contraceptive trial.

Homework

1 Much research has been done around the area of menstruation, exercise and fertility. The cycle is also linked to eating disorders such as anorexia. This is a good area for students to research in terms of understanding menstruation and issues relating to it. However, it is a subject that needs approaching with sensitivity.

2 Worksheet B1 2.3c consolidates understanding of fertility and contraception.

Points to note

- The specification does not require knowledge or understanding of the actions of progesterone, but high ability students may well consider the role of this hormone for a fuller understanding of the menstrual cycle. There are religious issues associated with birth control; teachers should be aware of students' sensitivities in this area.

Route to A*

Students might research alternative methods of delivering hormonal contraceptives such as implants.

Answers to Student Book questions

Science skills

a The risks of a blood clot are very low if you do not smoke as well. The risks are lowest with the mini pill, but still higher than for a woman who is not on the pill.

Answers

1 **(a)** 28. **(b)** 14.

2 The breakdown of the womb lining causes menstruation.

3 FSH stimulates the maturation of an egg and stimulates the production of oestrogen by the ovaries.

4 Increasing oestrogen concentration increases the thickness of the womb lining.

5 **(a)** Athletic performance peaks when oestrogen levels are rising to their peak. **(b)** Light training during menstruation, increasing in intensity for maximum performance on day 14; gradual wind down until start of next menstrual cycle **(c)** Pills that contain oestrogen will increase performance and can push on the day of ovulation giving a longer 'race window'.

6 **(a)** FSH stimulates an egg to mature in the ovary and it stimulates the production of oestrogen; oestrogen stimulates the thickening of the womb lining; both these increase favourable conditions for fertilisation and implantation of an egg. **(b)** Oestrogen inhibits the production of FSH so eggs do not mature in the ovaries. **(c)** The mini pill has fewer side effects, but is not as reliable if not taken exactly as prescribed.

7 Both pills are advantageous in that they prevent unwanted pregnancies. Both types of pill could encourage irresponsible sexual behaviour. The high oestrogen/progesterone pill gives a higher risk of side effects such as blood clotting. The second type of pill has ethical objections because it kills a human embryo.

B1 2.4 Evaluating the benefits of fertility treatment

Link to the specification

B1.2.2e The uses of hormones in controlling fertility include:

- giving oral contraceptives that contain hormones to inhibit FSH production so that no eggs mature: oral contraceptives may contain oestrogen and progesterone to inhibit egg maturation; the first birth-control pills contained large amounts of oestrogen, these resulted in women suffering significant side-effects; birth-control pills now contain a much lower dose of oestrogen, or are progesterone only; progesterone-only pills lead to fewer side-effects;
- giving FSH and LH in a 'fertility drug' to a woman whose own level of FSH is too low to stimulate eggs to mature, for example in In Vitro Fertilisation (IVF) treatment: IVF involves giving a mother FSH and LH to stimulate the maturation of several eggs. The eggs are collected from the mother and fertilised by sperm from the father. The fertilised eggs develop into embryos. At the stage when they are tiny balls of cells, one or two embryos are inserted into the mother's uterus (womb).

How Science Works

SKU: B1.2 bullet point 1: Evaluate the benefits of, and the problems that may arise from, the use of hormones to control fertility, including IVF.

B1 2.4 Evaluating the benefits of fertility treatment

Learning objectives

- explain the principles underlying IVF treatments
- evaluate the benefits of, and the problems that may arise from, the use of hormones to control fertility, including IVF.

Interfering with nature?

Sixty-six-year-old Adriana Iliescu became the world's oldest mother when she gave birth to a daughter following fertility treatment.

Ms Iliescu is a retired professor who lives alone. She said she had delayed having a child so she could concentrate on her academic career. Ms Iliescu became pregnant through IVF, using donated sperm and eggs, and this was her third attempt at having a baby.

Figure 1 Interfering with nature?

In vitro fertilisation

Many women are infertile because of blocked oviducts, or fallopian tubes. This means that eggs cannot travel from the ovaries to the womb. Nor can sperm travel upwards to meet an egg. This type of infertility can be treated by using ***in vitro* fertilisation (IVF).** This literally means fertilisation in a test tube, which led to the term '**test-tube baby**'.

The first stage of IVF is to obtain eggs from the woman. She is given injections of FSH to stimulate the **maturation** of several eggs. Eggs are then collected just before they are released from the ovary.

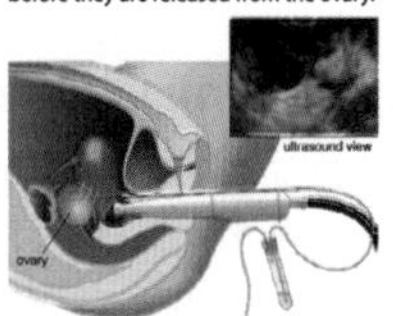

Figure 2 Using ultrasound to view the ovary, the doctor inserts the needle through the wall of the vagina into the ovary and removes the eggs for use in IVF.

The eggs are fertilised with sperm from the father outside the body and the fertilised eggs are allowed to divide to form **embryos**, as shown in Figure 3. At the stage when the embryos are still just balls of cells, some are inserted into the woman's womb.

removal of egg (aspiration)

insemination

incubation

embryo transfer into womb

Figure 3 IVF procedure.

What are the statistics?

The average success rate for IVF treatment using fresh eggs, i.e. eggs that have not been stored frozen, in the UK is shown in Table 1.

The typical cost of a cycle of IVF treatment is approximately £5000–8000. On top of this, the couple will have to pay for the costs of consultation, drugs and tests. The single biggest risk from IVF treatment is multiple births, and particularly triplet births. Many women decide to abort one of these triplets, because multiple births carry potential health risks for both the mother and the unborn children.

26

Science skills Multiple birth babies are more likely to be premature and below normal birth mass. Premature babies have a much higher risk of most of the problems associated with early childhood.

The risk of death before birth or within the first week after birth is more than four times greater for twins and almost seven times greater for triplets than for single births.

The incidence of **cerebral palsy**, a form of brain damage, is approximately five times higher for twins and approximately 18 times higher for triplets than for single births.

Table 1 IVF statistics for 2007 in the UK.

Women aged	Success rate (%)
under 35	32.3
35–37	27.7
38–39	19.2
40–42	11.1
43–44	3.4
44+	3.1

a How is the success of IVF treatment affected by age? Suggest an explanation for this.

b Currently 0.5% of IVF births are triplets, down from almost 4% in the early 1990s. Twenty per cent of IVF births are twins. Suggest an explanation for this.

c Imagine that you are a doctor. What advice would you give to a couple who were considering IVF treatment? Use the information above in your answer.

Science in action

Some couples cannot have children because the man's sperm are too weak to penetrate the egg. These couples may be helped by intracytoplasmic sperm injection (ICSI).

As in IVF, the woman is given fertility drugs to stimulate eggs to mature and to be released. Sperm is collected from the man: a semen sample. A single sperm is then injected directly into the woman's egg with a very delicate needle. The egg will reseal itself after the needle is withdrawn, just as it does in natural fertilisation when the sperm breaks through its outer membrane. The fertilised egg is then allowed to develop for a few days before being transferred back into the woman's uterus in the form of an embryo.

Questions

1. Should Ms Iliescu, Figure 1, have been given fertility treatment? Give arguments for and against.
2. Explain why FSH can be used as a fertility drug.
3. A drug called **clomiphine** is often used instead of FSH. This drug blocks the effect of oestrogen on the pituitary gland. Explain how clomiphine works as a fertility drug.
4. Two embryos are sometimes inserted into the mother, even if she only wants one child. Suggest why.
5. Write a leaflet for couples about to have IVF treatment. Describe and explain the procedures involved. Include diagrams where necessary.
6. During normal IVF, a woman undergoes several weeks of hormone injections. The treatment can lead to a condition called ovarian hyperstimulation syndrome, resulting in a build-up of fluid in the lungs and, very rarely, death. The syndrome occurs in about 1% of standard IVF cycles, but in about 10% for some women. An IVF cycle may cost up to £4300.

   In *in vitro* maturation (IVM), hormone treatment lasts for less than 7 days. Eggs are collected from the ovaries while still immature, then matured in a laboratory for up to 48 hours before being injected with a single sperm. A few days after fertilisation, the embryos are implanted into the womb. The cost of each IVM cycle is £1700.

   In IVM treatment, the risk of abnormalities in the sex chromosomes, and of birth deformities and cancer in the babies, while small, is greater than in IVF.

   Evaluate the use of IVM rather than IVF in treating infertility. A*

Science skills Think about the ethical implications of IVF. Here are some opinions. Some people are concerned that it is not natural; others think that an older mother will be unable to cope when the child is a teenager. Some people are concerned about the rights of a woman to be a mother against those of unused embryos. Other people ask whether enough is known about the long-term effects of these techniques. Many people ask why it is acceptable for older men to become fathers, when for an older woman to become a mother is seen as unacceptable.

Coordination and control 27

Learning objectives

Students should be able to:

- describe the process of IVF
- evaluate the benefits of, and the problems that arise from the use of IVF.

Key points

IVF involves giving a mother FSH to stimulate the maturation of several eggs.

The eggs are collected from the mother and mixed with sperm from the father.

The fertilised eggs develop into embryos.

At the stage when they are tiny balls of cells, one or two are inserted into the mother's womb.

Lesson activities

Starter

1 Ask students to watch the BBC video "Woman, 70, in 'oldest new mum' claim".

2 Ask students to watch the associated videos on the same site to introduce issues surrounding the use of IVF.

Main

1 **Evaluating fertility treatments** Students read the BBC News article about a woman of 62 who had IVF, and use it as a starting point for a discussion in groups, who should consider the questions on **Worksheet B1 2.4a**.

2 **IVF statistics** Students work in groups to prepare graphical representations of data from the HFEA in **Worksheet B1 2.4b**. They prepare suggested explanations of trends to present to the class.

Plenaries

1 Ask the groups to report their conclusions from activity B1 2.4a to the whole class.

2 Ask the groups to report their conclusions from activity B1 2.4b to the whole class.

Homework

1 Ask the students to use the Internet to research ICSI.

2 **Worksheet B1 2.4c** consolidates knowledge and understanding of IVF.

Points to note

- Consider students' religious sensitivities when dealing with the issues surrounding this topic.

Route to A*

Ask students to research the role of progesterone in the menstrual cycle and pregnancy. They should then use a copy of the graph from B1 2.3c and add a curve for progesterone to it. They could then sketch another graph to show the curves for the four hormones if the egg is fertilised.

Answers to Student Book questions

Science skills

a There is approximately a 90% reduction in success rate between under 35 and 44+. A possible reason is the decrease in responsiveness of the ovary and womb cells to hormones.

b Because of the increase in risk to both mothers and babies of multiple births, doctors are now inserting mainly single embryos into women.

c The couple should have the treatment at as young an age as possible because success rate falls rapidly at ages above 35, and they should have a single embryo implanted because of the high risks associated with multiple births.

Answers

1 Arguments for include personal freedom and the right to motherhood. Arguments against would be that the mother might not survive to raise the child to adulthood. There is a large age gap between mother and child. The procedure would be more dangerous to both mother and child for a woman of this age.

2 FSH stimulates eggs to mature in the ovary and it also stimulates the secretion of oestrogen; oestrogen then stimulates the build-up of the womb lining. These conditions favour implantation of a fertilised egg.

3 Oestrogen inhibits the production of FSH; increased FSH production causes eggs to mature in the ovaries; so blocking oestrogen production allows more cells to mature and so increases chances of fertilisation.

4 Two embryos are sometimes implanted to decrease failure rates for a woman who has had previous unsuccessful treatments; each treatment cycle is very expensive and unpleasant for the mother, so every effort is made to ensure success.

5 The following points must be covered in the leaflet with relevant diagrams: the woman is given injections of FSH to stimulate the maturation of several eggs in the ovary. The eggs are then collected just before they are released from the ovary. The eggs are fertilised with sperm from the father in the laboratory. The fertilised eggs are then allowed to divide to form embryos. When the embryos are balls of cells, one or two are inserted into the woman's womb.

6 Advantages of IVM: cheaper; fewer hormone injections used; reduced risk of ovarian hyperstimulation; shorter treatment. Disadvantages of IVM: higher risk of abnormal sex chromosomes/birth defects/baby cancer than with IVF.

Evaluation: IVM better because less risk to mother outweighs small risk to baby

or

IVF better because no risk to baby and a small risk to mother.

Plant responses

Link to the specification

B1.2.3a Plants are sensitive to light, moisture and gravity:

- their shoots grow towards light and against the force of gravity
- their roots grow towards moisture and in the direction of the force of gravity.

B1.2.3b Plants produce hormones to coordinate and control growth. Auxin controls phototropism and gravitropism (geotropism).

B1.2.3c The responses of plant roots and shoots to light, gravity and moisture are the result of unequal distribution of hormones, causing unequal growth rates.

Ideas for practical work

- the effect of light on the growth of seedlings
- the effect of gravity on growth in germinating seedlings
- the effect of water on the growth of seedlings
- using a motion sensor to measure the growth of plants and seedlings.

How Science Works

CA: B4.1.1 Develop hypotheses and plan practical ways to test them.

B1 2.5

Plant responses

Learning objectives

- describe the responses of plant roots and stems to gravity, light and water
- explain these responses to light and gravity in terms of the distribution of hormones.

Phototropism

Plants need light for **photosynthesis**, but they are rooted in soil so they cannot move from place to place to obtain maximum light.

The photograph shows seedlings that have been grown in three different conditions:

- grown in light coming from the left
- grown in darkness
- grown in all-round light.

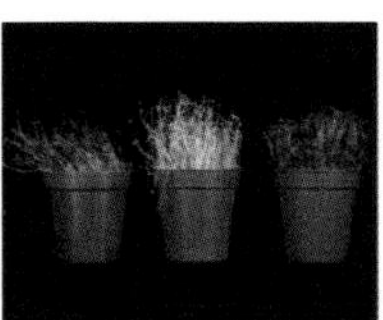

Plant stems grow towards the light.

The stems in the right-hand pot have grown normally.

The stems in the centre pot have grown straight up, and are much longer than the stems in the other two pots because they received no light.

The stems in the left-hand pot have grown towards the light. This response to directional light is called **phototropism**. Plants stems are **positively phototropic**, that is they grow towards the light stimulus.

Which part of the stem detects the stimulus?

Charles Darwin did some of the earliest experiments on phototropism. Figure 1 shows one of them.

This experiment showed that the tip of the stem is the receptor for the light stimulus.

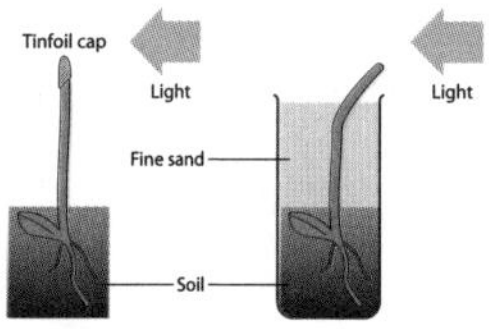

Figure 1 Darwin's experiment.

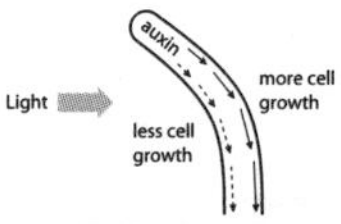

Figure 2 The effector in phototropism.

What is the effector in phototropism?

The response of growing towards the light is brought about by unequal growth. Cells on the shaded side grow longer than cells on the side nearest the light. Growth of cells in the stem is stimulated by hormones called **auxins**. Auxins are produced by the stem tip and are transported downwards. If the stem is placed in **unidirectional** light, more auxin is transported down the shaded side so the cells on this side grow faster, thus bending the stem towards the light.

Gravitropism

Gravitropism.

The pot shown in the photograph on the left was placed in the vertical position until the stem was a few centimetres tall. The pot was then placed on its side. One day later the stem had turned to grow vertically as shown.

Stems are **negatively gravitropic** – they grow away from the direction of the force of gravity. Roots are **positively gravitropic** – they grow in the direction of the force of gravity.

28

Growing away from gravity means that a stem beneath the soil will eventually find light. Growing downwards into the soil means that a root will help to keep the plant anchored in the soil.

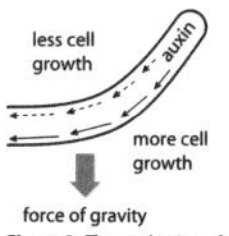

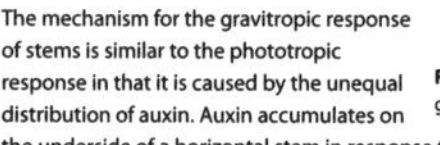

Figure 3 The mechanism of gravitropism in stems.

The mechanism for the gravitropic response of stems is similar to the phototropic response in that it is caused by the unequal distribution of auxin. Auxin accumulates on the underside of a horizontal stem in response to gravity. The cells on the underside grow faster than those on the upper side and the stem grows upwards.

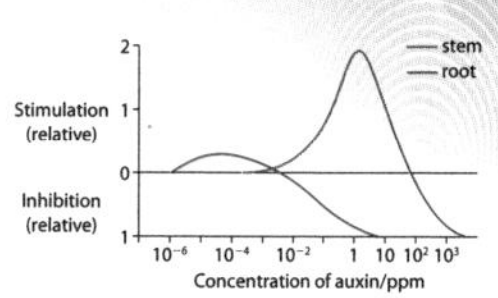

Figure 4 The effect of auxin concentration on root and stem cell growth.

If a root is placed in the horizontal position it will grow downwards. This means that the cells on the upper side grow faster than the ones on the underside. However, auxin accumulates on the underside of the root as it does in the stem. So why does the root go downwards? The reason is that the concentration of auxin that stimulates stem growth inhibits root growth, as shown on the graph in Figure 4.

Taking it further

In stems, a photodetector causes auxin-transporter proteins to move into the side membranes of cells. In roots, it is thought that organelles called amyloplasts settle by gravity to the bottom of cells near the root tip. The amyloplasts cause auxin-transporter proteins to move into the cell membranes. These proteins move auxins downwards out of the cells.

Using agar and mica

Figure 5 shows one of the experiments that scientists did to show that gravity causes unequal distribution of auxin. Agar is **permeable** to auxins but mica is impermeable.

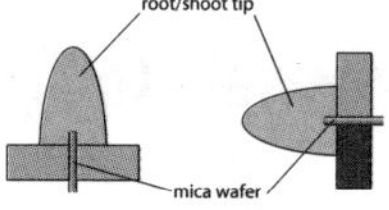

Figure 5 The distribution of auxins in a gravitropic response.

Hydrotropism

Figure 6 shows what happens when a root is stimulated by both the force of gravity and a directional water stimulus. The root grows towards the water. It is **positively hydrotropic**.

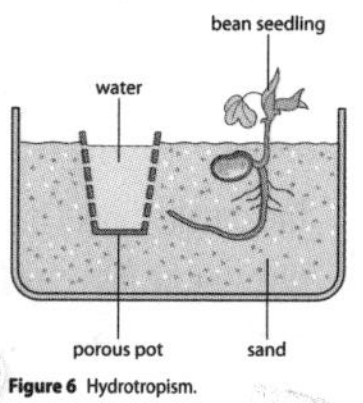

Figure 6 Hydrotropism.

Examiner feedback

Make sure you understand that stem cells and root cells have different responses to the same concentration of auxin and this is why stems grow upwards and roots grow downwards.

Questions

1 Name the type of substance that brings about plant responses.
2 Why is mica used in experiments on plant responses?
3 Suggest an explanation, other than the effect of gravity, for the root in Figure 6 growing towards the water.
4 What is the receptor in a tropic response?
5 What is the effector in a tropic response?
6 Name the response of a plant organ to: **(a)** directional light **(b)** the force of gravity **(c)** water.
7 Explain fully why roots grow in the direction of the force of gravity, but stems grow away from the direction of the force of gravity.
8 Compare and contrast the response of a plant shoot to light with a pain withdrawal.

A*

Coordination and control 29

Learning objectives

Most students should be able to:

- describe the responses of plants to light, gravity and water
- explain the role of auxin in phototropism and in gravitropism.

Some students should also be able to:

- appreciate the mode of action of auxins on cell walls. [Ext]

ActiveTeach Resource: How plants grow in response to a stimulus – *Video*

Key points

Stems are positively phototropic and negatively geotropic.

Roots are positively geotropic and positively hydrotropic.

Auxins are hormones that affect the growth of plant cells.

Auxins are produced by the tips of roots and stems.

Tropisms are caused by the unequal distribution of auxins in stems and roots.

The concentration of auxin that stimulates stem growth inhibits root growth, so roots respond to gravity and light in the opposite way to stems.

Phototropism	phototropic	gravitropism	gravitropic
hydrotropism	hydrotropic	hormone	auxin	unidirectional

Lesson activities

Starter

1 Why plants need tropisms Ask students to think about the problems associated with not being able to move from place to place (plants) compared with being motile (animals).

Main

1 B1 2.5a Phototropism In this activity, students investigate the effect of unidirectional light on plant stems

2 B1 2.5b Gravitropism In this activity, students investigate the effect of gravity on the growth of plant roots.

Plenaries

1 Ask students to report findings to the rest of the class.

2 How plants grow in response to a stimulus Ask students to watch the ActiveTeach video to consolidate understanding of tropisms. [AT]

Homework

1 Worksheet B1 2.5c consolidates understanding of the role of auxins in tropisms. [AfL]

2 Students research the action of gibberellins.

Route to A*

Students research the action of auxins in cell wall (not on specification).

Answers to Student Book questions

1 Auxins/hormone.

2 Mica is used because it is impermeable to hormones/auxins.

3 Water is essential for plant growth so plant roots exhibit hydrotropism (although it is difficult to observe in underground roots).

4 The root tip or shoot tip is the receptor.

5 Unequal growth rates of cells is the effector.

6 **(a)** Phototropism. **(b)** Geotropism. **(c)** Hydrotropism.

7 It is advantageous for roots to grow downwards to anchor the plant and to find water and mineral ions; it is advantageous for plant stems to grow upwards where they are most likely to reach the light they need for photosynthesis.

8 Neurones are involved in the reflex action to pain. Plants do not have neurones; rather, the response involves hormones. Reflex actions have specialised receptor cells: plant do not have specialised receptor cells, but have sensitive regions. The effector in the reflex action is a muscle. The effector in a tropism is the unequal growth rates of cells. A reflex action is rapid, a tropism is much slower. A reflex action is not a permanent effect, but a tropism is usually a permanent effect.

B1 2.6 Using plant hormones

Link to the specification

B1.2.3d Plant growth hormones are used in agriculture and horticulture as weedkillers and as rooting hormones.

Ideas for practical work

The effect of rooting compounds and weedkillers on the growth of plants.

How Science Works

SKU: B1.2 bullet point 2: Evaluate the use of plant hormones in horticulture as weedkillers and to encourage the rooting of plant cuttings.

CA: B4.1.1 Develop hypotheses and plan practical ways to test them, by: (a) being able to develop a hypothesis; (b) being able to test hypotheses; (c) using appropriate technology. B4.3.2 Demonstrate an understanding of the need to acquire high quality data, by: (a) appreciating that, unless certain variables are controlled, the results may not be valid. B4.4.2 Demonstrate an understanding of how data may be displayed, by: (a) drawing tables; (b) drawing charts and graphs; (c) choosing the most appropriate form of presentation. B4.4.1 Show an understanding of the value of means, by: (a) appreciating when it is appropriate to calculate a mean; (b) calculating the mean of a set of at least three results. B4.5.4 Draw conclusions using scientific ideas and evidence, by: (a) writing a conclusion, based on evidence that relates correctly to known facts; (b) using secondary sources.

B1 2.6 Using plant hormones

Learning objectives

- describe the principles underlying the use of plant hormones as weedkillers and rooting powders
- evaluate the use of plant hormones in horticulture.

Selective weedkillers

Most gardens in the UK have a lawn. The biggest problem with lawns is keeping them free of **weeds**. There are two common ways of doing this: pull each weed up by hand or spray the lawn with a **selective weedkiller**.

A selective weedkiller in action on the left.

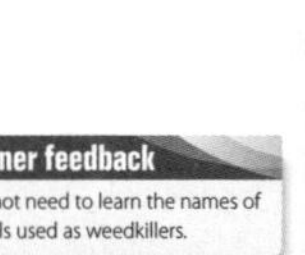

Examiner feedback

You do not need to learn the names of chemicals used as weedkillers.

The effect of weedkiller.

The most common selective weedkiller is **2,4-D**, short for 2,4-dichlorophenoxyacetic acid.

2,4-D has a chemical structure similar to that of auxins, but it has a much greater effect. 2,4-D is rapidly absorbed by broad-leaved plants. It accumulates in the stem and root tips and causes uncontrolled growth as shown in the photograph.

The growth is so abnormal that the plant dies. 2,4-D is not absorbed by narrow-leaved plants such as grasses, so when it is sprayed on a lawn, the weeds are killed but the grass is unaffected. 2,4-D is a selective weedkiller.

Agent Orange

During the Vietnam war in the 1960s, American aircraft sprayed wide areas of Vietnam with 2,4-D. The codename for this spray was Agent Orange. Agent Orange was an equal mixture of 2,4-D and another hormone, 245T. The concentration of 2,4-D in the spray caused the leaves of the jungle trees to fall off. The purpose of this was to deny hiding places to the North Vietnamese soldiers. Unfortunately the spray came into contact with both Vietnamese and Americans. There was a significant increase in the proportion of children born with birth defects during and after the war. According to the Vietnamese Ministry of Foreign Affairs, 4.8 million Vietnamese people were exposed to Agent Orange, resulting in 400 000 deaths and disabilities and 500 000 children born with birth defects.

Follow-up studies on American soldiers show a higher incidence of several diseases than in the general population.

30

Rooting powders

Horticulturists use cuttings to produce large numbers of identical plants. Part of a plant shoot is cut off and the end of the stem is dipped in **rooting powder**. The end of the stem is then pressed into damp **compost**. After a few days, roots develop from the cut stem. Rooting powders contain auxins that stimulate the stem cells to develop into roots.

Using rooting powder.

Ripening fruit

The gas **ethene (ethylene)** is a plant hormone. It is produced by fruits as they ripen. One effect of ethylene is to stimulate the reactions that convert starch into sugar. A ripe fruit tastes much sweeter than an unripe one.

Science in action

Bananas grown in the tropics are picked while they are green, which means they are unripe.

They are transported in this state in well-ventilated containers. On arrival at their destination country, the bananas are placed in 'banana rooms'. Ethylene is then pumped into the 'banana room' to ripen them.

Science skills

A student investigated the effectiveness of a rooting powder on three different plant **species**: begonia, geranium and rose. Begonia and geranium are herbaceous (non woody) plants. Rose is a woody bush. The student dipped equal sized pieces of shoots of the three species into rooting powder, then pushed the ends of the stems into damp compost. The student also pushed untreated pieces of shoot from each species into the compost. After two weeks the student measured the total length of roots produced by each species. The results are shown in the table.

a Give two ways in which the student could have improved the investigation.

b Give the two main conclusions that can be drawn from the student's results.

Species	Total length of roots produced/cm	
	Hormone treated shoots	Untreated shoots
Begonia	1.50	0.80
Geranium	0.75	0.40
Rose	0.00	0.00

Practical

Design a controlled investigation to find out if apples ripen faster if stored with bananas.

For 'storage' you could place an unripe apple and a banana into a plastic bag, then seal it.

To compare ripeness of apples, you could cut them in half, then stain with iodine/potassium iodide solution. The more blue/black colour, the more starch.

Questions

1. Name the type of substance used as weedkillers and rooting powders.
2. What is the main difference between the effect of weedkillers on plant stems and that of rooting powders?
3. Suggest why the containers for transporting bananas are well ventilated.
4. Suggest the advantages of transporting bananas in their unripe form, then placing them in 'banana rooms'.
5. Why do selective weedkillers kill only broad-leaved plants?
6. What is the advantage to horticulturists of using rooting powders?
7. Explain the advantages to distributors of using fruit-ripening hormones.
8. How should new weedkillers be trialled before being marketed?

A*

Coordination and control 31

Learning objectives

Most students should be able to:

- interpret the results of their own weedkiller investigation
- evaluate the use of a weedkiller investigation.

Key points

Selective weedkillers contain hormones similar to auxins.

Selective weedkillers work by over-stimulating the growth of broad-leaved plants.

Rooting powders contain hormones that stimulate stem cells to grow into roots.

Hormones are used to control ripening in fruits.

Selective weedkiller | 2,4-D | glyphosate

Lesson activities

Starter

1 Show students a picture of an East Anglian wheat crop. Ask them to imagine the same area two hundred years ago with hosts of farm workers weeding the crop. Ask them to suggest what social changes have been brought about by modern agricultural methods

2 Introduce the Agent Orange story from the Student Book.

Main

1 B1 2.6a Investigating a weedkiller In this activity, students investigate the effect of different dilutions of a selective weedkiller on 'bedding' plants.

2 Ask students to carry out the HSW task from lesson B1 2.6 of the Student Book in groups.

3 Ask students to consider the effect on wildlife of the increasing use of weedkillers in gardens.

Plenary

1 Students bring together the results for the different dilutions of the weedkiller.

Homework

1 Worksheet B2.6b presents data for evaluation on the use of weedkillers to control weeds in a rice crop.

2 Students report back their plans for the HSW investigation from the Student Book.

Points to note

- Teachers may wish to give information about the mechanisms involved in rooting and in weedkilling but should note that such detail is not required by the specification.

Route to A*

Ask students to research the possible link between the most recently developed pesticides and the reduction in bee populations. Ask them to consider how far research supports a link between the two.

Answers to Student Book questions

Science skills

a Use several pieces of shoot for each species. Control the amount of rooting powder applied to each shoot.

b The rooting powder is effective for herbaceous shoots, but not woody shoots. The treated shoots grew approximately double the length of roots as the untreated plants.

Answers

1 Hormone/auxin.

2 Weedkillers cause uncontrolled growth; rooting powders cause cells to differentiate to form tissues.

3 The containers are well ventilated to prevent the build-up of ethylene, which would cause the bananas to ripen too soon.

4 The bananas can be made to ripen just before they go on sale, lengthening their shelf life.

5 Selective weedkillers kill only broad-leaved plants because they are not absorbed by narrow-leaved plants such as grasses.

6 Plants reared from cuttings can go on sale much sooner because they develop root systems much more quickly.

7 The fruit all ripen within a short time; growers can organise labour in advance to pick the fruit, and transport it to market.

8 Wide-scale trials should be organised to test its effectiveness compared with existing weedkillers. These tests should include persistence (i.e. to make sure it does not persist in the environment). The cost of manufacture should be compared with that of existing products to ensure it can be sold at a competitive price. There should be tests on animal cells to see if it is toxic to animals. There should be tests on pregnant animals to ensure that it does not cause birth deformities.

B1 3.1 Developing new drugs

Link to the specification

B1 3.1a Scientists are continually developing new drugs.

B1 3.1b When new medical drugs are devised, they have to be extensively tested and trialled before being used.

Drugs are tested in a series of stages to find out if they are safe and effective.

New drugs are extensively tested for toxicity, efficacy and dose: in the laboratory, using cells, tissues and live animals; in clinical trials involving healthy volunteers and patients.

Very low doses of the drug are given at the start of the clinical trial. If the drug is found to be safe, further clinical trials are carried out to find the optimum dose for the drug. In some double blind trials, some patients are given a placebo, which does not contain the drug. Neither the doctors nor the patients know who has received a placebo and who has received the drug until the trial is complete.

B1 3.1c Candidates should be aware of the use of statins in lowering the risk of heart and circulatory diseases.

B1 3.1d Thalidomide is a drug that was developed as a sleeping pill. It was also found to be effective in relieving morning sickness in pregnant women. Thalidomide had not been tested for use in pregnant women. Unfortunately, many babies born to mothers who took the drug were born with severe limb abnormalities. The drug was then banned. As a result, drug testing has become much more rigorous. More recently, thalidomide has been used successfully in the treatment of leprosy and other diseases.

How Science Works

SKU: B1 3 bullet point 1: Evaluate the effect of statins in cardiovascular disease.

CA: B4 4.1 Show an understanding of the value of means by: (a) appreciating when it is appropriate to calculate a mean; (b) calculating the mean of a set of at least three results. B4 4.2 Demonstrate an understanding of how data may be displayed by: (a) drawing tables, (b) drawing charts and graphs, (c) choosing the most appropriate form of presentation. B4 5.3 Identify patterns in data by: (a) describing the relationship between two variables and deciding whether the relationship is causal or by association.

B1 3.1 Developing new drugs

Learning objectives

- explain the stages in developing and testing a new drug
- describe the failures in the testing of thalidomide
- evaluate the effect of statins on cardiovascular disease.

Developing new drugs

Drugs used to treat disease need to be safe, effective, chemically **stable**, and successfully taken in and removed from the body. The treatment of disease is always being improved by the development of new drugs. However, before a new drug can be used, it is put through several tests and has to pass each stage. As the newspaper extract in Figure 1 shows, this is not always without risk.

All **clinical trials** are **double-blind trials** in which some patients are given a dummy medicine, called a **placebo,** which does not contain the drug, as a control group. Neither the doctors nor the patients know who has received a placebo and who has received the drug being tested, until the trial is complete.

SIX TAKEN ILL AFTER DRUGS TRIAL

Six men remain in intensive care after being taken ill during a clinical drugs trial in north-west London

The healthy volunteers were testing an anti-inflammatory drug at a research unit based at Northwick Park Hospital when they suffered a reaction.

Relatives are with the patients, who suffered multiple organ failure. Two men are said to be critically ill.

An investigation has begun at the unit, run by Parexel, which said it followed recommended guidelines in its trial.

The men were being paid to take part in the early stages of a trial for the drug to treat conditions such as rheumatoid arthritis and leukaemia until they were taken ill on Monday within hours of taking it.

Eight volunteers were involved, but two were given a placebo at the unit, which is on Northwick Park Hospital's grounds, but is run independently.

Figure 1 Drugs tests sometimes go wrong.

Science in action

Animal testing in the cosmetic industry is especially undertaken for make-up and soaps. Rabbits are the main animals used in these tests. Guinea pigs are used to test sunscreen products. The tests are done to find whether the products will produce reactions and allergies .

Many people are uneasy about the use of animals to test make-up and soaps. Scientists have developed 'non-animal' alternatives including the following.

- Human skin model tests are now in use, including EpiDerm™ (cultured human skin) test, which has been accepted almost universally as a total replacement for skin testing in rabbits
- Human skin left over from operations or from people who have donated their bodies to science is used to measure the rate at which chemicals are able to penetrate the skin.

Table 1 The main stages in the testing of a new drug.

Stage	Purpose
laboratory	animals or tissues used in a laboratory to find out the level of **toxicity** and to find out if the drug works
phase 1 clinical	low doses are tested on a small group of healthy people to evaluate its safety, and identify side effects
phase 2 clinical	tested on a larger group of people to see if it is effective, to further evaluate its safety and to determine the optimum dose
phase 3 clinical	tested on large groups of people to confirm its effectiveness and monitor side effects

34

When drug testing fails

Starting in 1957, **thalidomide** was given to women in the first few months of pregnancy to help them sleep and to overcome the effects of morning sickness. Many women who took the drug gave birth to babies with limbs that weren't properly formed. The drug was banned worldwide in 1961 after it was confirmed that it caused tragic birth defects. The testing of thalidomide was incomplete, because it had not been tested on pregnant animals. The total number of babies damaged by thalidomide throughout the world was about 10 000.

Recently, thalidomide has been used very effectively to treat a serious disease called **leprosy**. However, some pregnant women with leprosy have obtained the drug without doctor's advice, and once again children are being born with deformed limbs.

The result of not testing thalidomide.

Testing statins

Drugs called **statins** have been developed to lower blood cholesterol levels.

Science skills

A study into statins was carried out in a leading UK hospital. The study involved 20 536 patients aged between 40 and 80 with heart disease. The health of these patients was monitored closely over a five-year period.

A total of 10 269 of the patients took a **simvastatin** tablet daily, whilst 10 267 received a placebo every day. Patients were randomly placed into the 'statin' group or the 'placebo' or control group.

The main conclusion of the study was that simvastatin is safe and reduces the risk of people having a heart attack or a stroke.

a This type of study is called a **randomised controlled trial**.

i What feature of the study was randomised?

ii How was a control used in the study?

b It is important that studies to assess drugs are highly reliable. What features of this study show that the findings are reliable?

Examiner feedback

Make your own mnemonic to remember the sequence of events in drug testing.

T – tissues for toxicity

H – healthy people for side effects

P – patients for effectiveness

D – patients for dose

Questions

1 **(a)** What conditions was thalidomide designed to treat? **(b)** What test was omitted during the development of thalidomide?

2 What is a double-blind trial?

3 What is a placebo?

4 Suggest why only a few people are used in phase 1 of a clinical trial.

5 Suggest why phase 2 is carried out after phase 1 and not at the same time.

6 Once a drug is on sale, why does it still have to be monitored?

7 Some doctors have used the results of the above statin trial to suggest that all children should be given statins daily. Do you agree with these doctors? Explain the reasons for your answer.

A*

Drugs: use and abuse 35

Learning objectives

Students should be able to:

- describe the stages in the testing of a new drug
- explain why the testing of thalidomide was not complete and describe the consequences of this
- evaluate the use of statins in treating cardiovascular disease.

Key points

New drugs are tested to see if they are toxic and then tested in clinical trials on people to check whether they are effective and whether they have any side effects.

Thalidomide is an example of a new drug that was not tested sufficiently. It was given to pregnant women, resulting in terrible birth defects and the banning of the drug.

Statins are drugs that lower the cholesterol level in the blood and so treat and prevent heart disease.

Clinical trial double blind leprosy placebo statin thalidomide

Lesson activities

Starter

1 The thalidomide tragedy Look at and discuss photographs of people born with abnormalities caused by thalidomide.

2 A drug trial gone wrong Discuss news reports surrounding the drug trial in a London hospital (March/April 2006) in which several volunteers were made critically ill; e.g. BBC News – Drug trial.

Main

1 Worksheet B1 3.1a Drug development introduces the idea that chemicals can interfere with chemical reactions in body tissues.

2 Introduce section on thalidomide in Student Book lesson B1 3.1. Discuss ethics of trialling thalidomide on thalidomide patients.

3 Students individually complete the HSW task on a statin trial in Student Book lesson B1 3.1.

Plenaries

1 Class discussion of the results of student experiment B1 3.1a.

2 Ask students what would be the following stages after successfully testing the effect of the drug 'salt' on body tissues.

Homework

1 Worksheet B1 3.1b brings together the required understanding of drug testing.

2 Research the benefits and side-effects of statins.

Route to A*

Ask students to research the idea of modelling to replace the testing of drugs on animals.

Answers to Student Book questions

Science skills

a **(i)** Whether a patient receives the statin or the placebo was randomised.
(ii) The control was the group who received the placebo – the tablet that did not contain the drug.

b The large number of participants, the use of a control, and the double-blind method all make the trial reliable.

Answers

1 **(a)** Thalidomide was designed as a sleeping pill and to control morning sickness.
(b) Tests on pregnant animals were omitted.

2 A double-blind trial is a trial in which neither doctor nor patient knows who gets the drug and who gets the placebo.

3 A placebo is a dummy medicine that looks like the drug but does not contain the drug.

4 If the drug is toxic, then only a few people will be affected and need treatment.

5 Side effects might be masked by toxic effects.

6 So far it has only been tested on a sample of the population; rare side effects might not have shown up.

7 An argument for is that it would reduce the risk of heart disease and early death. An argument against would be that statins have not been used long enough to discover any long-term side effects. Also, the tests were not carried out on children so there could be other side-effects that we don't know about. Parents should always be given the choice as to what medication a child takes.

B1 3.2 Recreational drugs

Link to the specification

B1 3.1e Candidates should be aware of the effects of misuse of the legal recreational drugs, alcohol and nicotine. Candidates should understand that the misuse of the illegal recreational drugs ecstasy, cannabis and heroin may have adverse effects on the heart and circulatory system

B1 3.1g The overall impact of legal drugs (prescribed and non-prescribed) on health is much greater than the impact of illegal drugs because many more people use them.

B1 3.1h Drugs change the chemical processes in people's bodies so that they may become dependent or addicted to the drug and suffer withdrawal symptoms without them. Heroin and cocaine, are very addictive.

How Science Works

SKU: B1.3 bullet point 2: Evaluate different types of drugs and why some people use illegal drugs for recreation. B1.3 bullet point 3: Evaluate claims made about the effect of prescribed and non-prescribed drugs on health.

CA: B4.5.1 Distinguish between a fact and an opinion, by: (a) recognising that an opinion might be influenced by factors other than scientific fact. (b) identifying scientific evidence that supports an opinion.

B1 3.2 Recreational drugs

Learning objectives

- explain why some people use drugs for recreation
- describe how drugs change the chemical processes in the body and explain how this can lead to addiction.

What is a drug?

Many drugs are extracted from natural substances. They have been used by people from different cultures for medicines and recreation for thousands of years. **Alcohol** has been fermented from fruit and grain since at least ancient Chinese times, about 9000 years ago.

MAY DAY CELEBRATIONS END IN TRAGEDY

Hundreds of students followed a centuries-old tradition and jumped off Magdalen Bridge at dawn on May Day into the River Cherwell at Oxford.

However, most of them were drunk after all-night parties and they ignored police warnings that the river was too low this year. The result was at least ten students with serious injuries to spines, legs and ankles.

Would students do this if they were sober?

A **drug** is any chemical that alters how our body works. Drugs that affect our **central nervous system (CNS)** control the movement of chemicals across the synapses. The natural chemicals in our nervous system have shapes that fit receptors in our bodies like a key in a lock. Drugs have similar shapes to these chemicals and mimic, or copy, what they do.

receptor

drug

Figure 1 Some drugs mimic chemicals released across the synapses.

People take drugs for recreational or medical reasons. Most drugs were originally used to deal with injury or sickness. Drug abuse occurs when people take too much of a drug or use it for the wrong reasons. Spanish explorers learned from indigenous South Americans to chew on coca plant leaves to keep awake. Today it is used to make cocaine.

If some drugs are used a lot, your body builds up a tolerance to them. This means you must use more of the drug to get the same effect. As a drug is used more often and in greater amounts, your body becomes more dependent on it. This means you will find it difficult to manage without the drug and will need to take it regularly. This leads to addiction. You are addicted when you cannot manage without taking the drug.

When you try to stop taking a drug you are addicted to, you suffer from withdrawal symptoms. These can include feeling sick, headaches and flu-like symptoms. More severe withdrawal symptoms include tremors and fits.

Why do people use drugs?

Drugs are not just taken for medical reasons; some drugs are also taken for pleasure. These drugs are called **recreational drugs**. Some recreational drugs are legal, for example alcohol, **caffeine** and **nicotine** in tobacco, but other recreational drugs are illegal, for example, **cannabis**, **cocaine**, **heroin** and **ecstasy**. Ecstasy, cannabis, cocaine and heroin may have adverse effects on the heart and circulatory system.

Many people smoke cannabis as a recreational drug because it alters their mood. Some of these people think that cannabis is harmless because it is similar to smoking tobacco or drinking alcohol. Many scientists think that the evidence shows that cannabis can cause psychological problems. However, other scientists are uncertain whether cannabis actually causes these problems.

However, it isn't only illegal drugs that can be dangerous. Research has shown that tobacco and alcohol cause thousands of deaths in Britain every year. The NHS has to spend far more money on treating the effects of legal drugs than illegal drugs, because far more people use them. Many people would argue that these drugs should be made illegal. Others argue for the decriminalisation of all drugs, in order to make their use safer, cut down crime associated with the cost of illegal drugs, and to stop criminal gangs from making huge profits from the drugs trade.

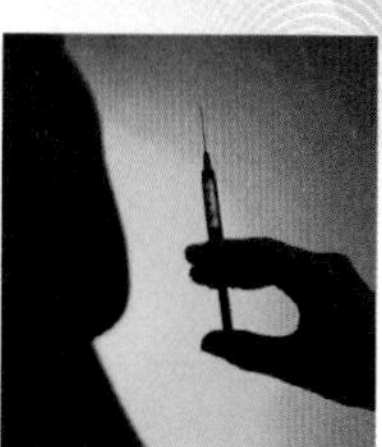

Heroin addicts have to inject themselves frequently or they suffer severe withdrawal symptoms.

Taking it further

There is a 'reward centre' in the brain that affects our behaviour. One cause of a feeling of pleasure is the accumulation of a substance called dopamine in synapses in this centre. Normally, another substance, dopamine re-uptake transporter, causes the dopamine to be reabsorbed. Cocaine blocks the action of the dopamine re-uptake transporter, so dopamine remains in the synapses and the feeling of pleasure persists.

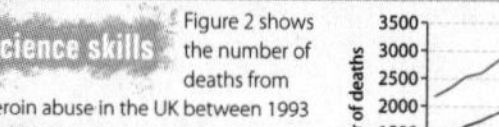

Science skills Figure 2 shows the number of deaths from heroin abuse in the UK between 1993 and 2008.

a Compare and contrast the number of deaths from heroin abuse between men and women from 1993 to 2008.

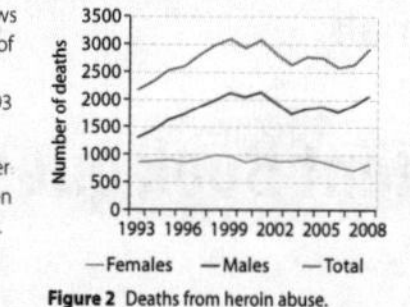

Figure 2 Deaths from heroin abuse.

Questions

1. Explain what is meant by a recreational drug.
2. **(a)** Give two examples of legal recreational drugs. **(b)** Give two examples of illegal recreational drugs.
3. Explain why drugs can alter the way we behave.
4. 'Tonics' sold to people in America in the 1800s contained heroin. **(a)** What would a person feel having taken this 'tonic'? **(b)** What long-term problems might they have suffered?
5. Why might taking heroin lead to you getting HIV, AIDS or other infections?
6. What is meant by 'withdrawal symptom'?
7. Why do more people die from using nicotine and alcohol than heroin and cocaine?
8. Explain fully how a person becomes addicted to a drug.

A*

Learning objectives

Most students should be able to:

- explain how a person becomes addicted to a drug
- explain why the overall impact of legal drugs (prescribed and non-prescribed) on health is much greater than the impact of illegal drugs because many more people use them.

Some students should also be able to:

- evaluate different types of drugs and why some people use illegal drugs for recreation [Ext]
- evaluate claims made about the effect of prescribed and non-prescribed drugs on health. [Ext]

Key points

Drugs change the chemical processes in the body, so people may become addicted to them and suffer withdrawal symptoms.

People use legal and illegal drugs recreationally.

The impact of legal drugs on health is much greater than that of illegal drugs as more people use them.

Addiction alcohol caffeine cannabis central nervous system cocaine ecstasy recreational drug

Lesson activities

Starter

1 Ask students to list as many drugs as they can, legal and/or illegal.

2 Ask students to put the drugs into groups that have similar effects on the body. There is no need to get involved with details. [AfL]

Main

Two tasks are available. They could be done in successive lessons, or the class could be split into two halves, one for each activity.

1 B1 3.2a Substance use and abuse Research task: students work in groups to collect information. Have information cards available on each type of drug being researched. Alternatively, students could use the Internet for their research.

2 B1 3.2b Drug addiction A research exercise in which students investigate the ways that various addictive drugs interact with the human nervous system. Internet access will be needed in order for students to read the BBC News articles: BBC News – Addiction and BBC News – Hospital drugs raid.

Plenary

1 Groups report their findings to the rest of the class.

Homework

1 Worksheet B1 3.2c brings together knowledge and understanding of the topic.

Points to note

- Although it may be interesting to bring in knowledge about the effects of specific drugs, these are not required by the specification.

Route to A*

Ask students to research the differences between the government's classification of drugs as Class A, B, C and scientists' opinions on the harm caused by drugs; then to suggest reasons for the differences.

Answers to Student Book questions

Science skills

a Deaths of women always less than deaths of men. Deaths of women almost constant, deaths of males fluctuate. Both show peak in 1999, both show rise in 2008.

Answers

1 A recreational drug is a drug taken for pleasure.

2 **(a)** Alcohol and tobacco, for example. **(b)** Heroin and cocaine, for example.

3 Drugs alter chemical processes in our bodies and can affect our brains.

4 **(a)** Euphoric. **(b)** Addiction to the 'tonic'.

5 Infection from shared hypodermic needles.

6 When a person becomes addicted to a drug, their body chemistry changes, resulting in a craving for the drug if the person stops using it.

7 There are more deaths because many more people use alcohol and tobacco.

8 All drugs change the chemical processes in our bodies. When your body gets used to the change, it may become dependent on the drug. People become addicted to drugs when their whole body chemistry changes. They suffer withdrawal symptoms if they stop taking the drug.

B1 3.3 Establishing links

Link to the specification

B1 3.1f Cannabis is an illegal drug. Cannabis smoke contains chemicals which may cause mental illness in some people.

How Science Works

SKU: B1.3 bullet point 4: Consider the possible progression from recreational drugs to hard drugs.

CA: B4 4.2 Demonstrate an understanding of how data may be displayed by drawing charts and graph. B4 5.1 Distinguish between a fact and an opinion, by: (a) recognising that an opinion might be influenced by factors other than scientific fact, (b) identifying scientific evidence that supports an opinion. B4 5.4 Draw conclusions using scientific ideas and evidence, by: (a) writing a conclusion based on evidence that relates correctly to known facts, (b) using secondary sources, (c) identifying extra evidence that is required for a conclusion to be made, (d) evaluating methods of data collection.

B1 3.3 Establishing links

Learning objectives

- evaluate evidence for a link between smoking cannabis and mental illness
- evaluate the evidence indicating the possible progression from non-addictive recreational drugs to addiction to hard drugs.

A harmless joint?

Many people smoke cannabis as a recreational drug; it helps them to 'chill out'. However, there is mounting evidence of a link between smoking cannabis and mental illness. There is also some evidence that smoking cannabis can lead to addiction to hard drugs, in other words, that it is a **'gateway' drug**.

Many people think that smoking a joint is harmless, but is it?

Science skills Figure 1 shows the government classification of drugs and their harm rating compiled by independent experts.

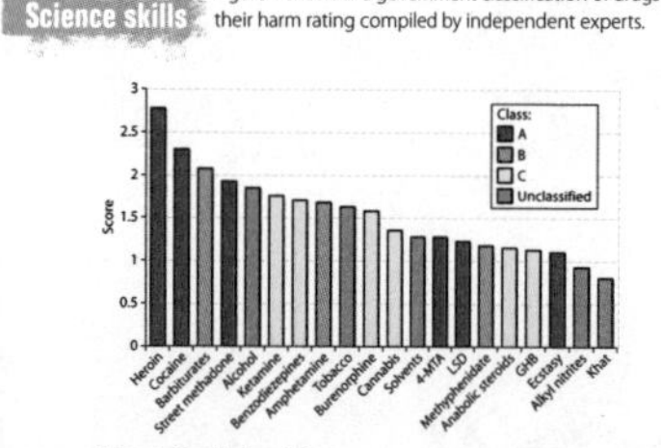

Figure 1 Classification of drugs.

a How does the government classification compare with the harm rating by independent experts?

Is there evidence for a link between cannabis smoking and mental illness?

Patients with mental illness may lose contact with reality or suffer from delusions. Here are some results of research into cannabis and mental illness.

New Zealand scientists followed 1000 people born in 1977 for the next 25 years. They interviewed people about their use of cannabis at the ages of 18, 21 and 25. The questions were about their mental health. The researchers took into account factors such as family history, current mental disorders, and illegal substance abuse.

The scientists' findings were:

- mental illness was more common among cannabis users
- people with mental illness did not have a greater wish to smoke cannabis
- cannabis probably increased the chances of developing mental illness by causing chemical changes to the brain
- there was an increase in the rate of mental illness symptoms after the start of regular use of cannabis.

Examiner feedback

In examination questions you may be given data and asked to draw conclusions from this data. Always read the data carefully and do not make assumptions on what you may believe to be the answer from your knowledge.

38

Scientists studied 45 000 Swedish male conscripts (men called up for army service). This was 97% of the male population aged 18–20 at that time. They followed these men for the next 15 years. They found the men who smoked cannabis heavily at the age of 18 were six times more likely to develop schizophrenia in later life than those who did not smoke cannabis.

Table 1 Drugs studies.

The Amsterdam Study	The Home Office Study	The view of Drugscope
Four surveys, covering nearly 17 000 people, were carried out in Amsterdam in the 1990s. Amsterdam then had 5000 hard drug users in its population of 700 000 and a much larger proportion of cannabis users. There were 300 'coffee shops' in the city where cannabis was freely available. The surveys showed that cannabis users typically start using the drug between the ages of 18 and 20. Cocaine use usually starts between 20 and 25. However, the study concludes that cannabis is not a stepping stone to using cocaine or heroin. The study also claims that most of the evidence that cannabis is a gateway to the use of hard drugs is circumstantial. It found that there was little difference in the probability of an individual taking up cocaine regardless of whether or not they had used cannabis.	This study used information from the 1998/99 Youth Lifestyles Survey (YLS), which contains information taken from over 3900 interviews with young people on their own experiences of drug use. The study found that the age for use of soft drugs is less than the age for use of most hard drugs. However, there was no significant link between soft drug use and the risk of later involvement with crack and heroin. There was a significant but small link between soft drug use and the use of social drugs ecstasy and cocaine.	A spokesman for the UK charity Drugscope backed the study's findings. He told BBC News Online: 'Sixty per cent of young people aged 20–24 have used cannabis, but only 1% of that age group have used harder drugs.' He said people who used harder drugs were less likely to have 'risk-averse' lifestyles and more likely to have misused other substances, including cannabis, tobacco and alcohol.

Questions

Regarding the Swedish study:

1 What type of scientific research was this?
2 How can the reliability of surveys be improved?
3 What were the control variables in the investigation?
4 What did the investigation show about the link between cannabis and psychosis?

Regarding the Amsterdam Study, the Home Office Study and the view of Drugscope:

5 Do you think that the data from these studies are reliable? Explain the reasons for your answers.
6 Give two conclusions common to all three studies.
7 Give one possible reason for progression from soft drugs to hard drugs.
8 Consider all the evidence on these two pages. Does using soft drugs lead to taking hard drugs? Explain the reasons for your answer. A*

Science in action

People may not judge evidence on its scientific strength, but on other criteria. For example, a famous scientist may be taken more seriously than an unknown one, and politicians may disregard scientific advice that they know will be unpopular with voters. We are more likely to accept evidence that agrees with our own views than evidence that contradicts them. Did you dismiss any evidence on this page that disagrees with your opinions?

Drugs: use and abuse 39

Learning objectives

Students should be able to:

- evaluate evidence for a link between smoking cannabis and mental illness
- evaluate data on the progression from soft drugs to hard drugs.

Key points

Scientists have carried out various studies that showed:

- an increase in the rate of mental illness symptoms in people who started using cannabis regularly
- the probability of an individual taking up cocaine is not greatly affected by whether or not he or she has used cannabis
- a significant but small link between soft drug use and the use of social drugs ecstasy and cocaine
- people who used harder drugs were more likely to have risky lifestyles and to have misused other substances, including cannabis, tobacco and alcohol.

Lesson activities

Starter

1 'Thought shower' on cannabis and its effects and whether students feel it is safe to use.

Main

1 **B1 3.3a Cannabis debate** This research activity will help students identify the arguments for and against the legalisation of cannabis.

2 Students should use their research to debate 'Should cannabis be legalised?'

Plenary

1 Student debate using the information they have researched.

Homework

1 **Worksheet B1 3.3b** considers the links between several recreational drugs and mental illness.

2 Students consider the data and questions in lesson B1 3.3 in the Student Book.

Route to A*

Research the therapeutic uses of cannabis and relate its mode of action to the relief of each condition.

Answers to Student Book questions

Science skills

a The class A drugs heroin and cocaine are rated more harmful than all the other drugs. Some class A drugs have a lower harm rating than recreational drugs such as alcohol and tobacco. Many unclassified drugs have higher harm ratings than classified drugs.

Answers

1 The research was a survey.

2 Reliability can be improved by increasing sample size and by increasing the randomness of the sample.

3 The control variables are gender (all male), age (all 18–20 at the start of the investigation), and occupation (all conscripts).

4 The investigation showed a correlation between smoking cannabis and schizophrenia/psychosis: cannabis smokers were more likely to develop psychosis than non-smokers. However, cannabis smokers do not all develop psychosis so there is no direct causal link.

5 A large number of interviews increased reliability, but people do not always tell the full truth when interviewed.

6 There is no direct link between using soft drugs and hard drugs; users of hard drugs are less likely to have 'risk-averse' lifestyles.

7 Once you start using cannabis you are more likely than before to encounter other drugs being sold illegally and be encouraged to try them.

8 It is difficult to come to a firm decision because much of the research is done via questionnaire and we do not know how reliable the responses are. There is no direct causal link as shown by the fact that less than 1% of soft drug users progress to hard drugs. However, there is a higher incidence of hard drug taking from people who have previously used soft drugs. A more important factor seems to be risk-averse lifestyle.

B1 3.4 Steroids and athletics

Link to the specification

B1.3.1i There are several types of drug that an athlete can use to enhance performance. Some of these drugs are banned by law and some are legally available on prescription, but all are prohibited by sporting regulations. Examples include stimulants that boost bodily functions such as heart rate; and anabolic steroids which stimulate muscle growth.

How Science Works

SKU: B1.3 bullet point 5: Evaluate the use of drugs to enhance performance in sport and consider the ethical implications of their use.

B1 3.4 Steroids and athletics

Learning objectives

- describe how steroids can be used as performance-enhancing drugs in athletics
- evaluate the use of drugs to enhance performance in sport and consider the ethical implications of their use
- describe the effects of using steroids on health.

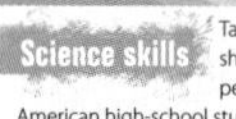

Table 1 shows the percentage of American high-school students who admitted to using steroids to build up muscle in the last year.

Table 1

	Percentage of males	Percentage of females
Social class		
Low	2.2	0.8
Low-middle	1.5	2.3
Middle	2.5	1.2
High-middle	0.6	2.3
High	1.6	0.1
Race		
Native American	9.7	0.0
Other Asian	1.4	0.0
Hispanic	0.0	2.6
Black	0.6	3.7
White	1.3	0.2

a Describe the patterns present in the data for steroid use.

Using steroids to cheat in athletics

Marion Jones winning gold in the 2000 Olympics…

At the 2000 Olympics, sprinter Marion Jones became the first female athlete to claim five medals in a single Games, three of them gold. Eight years later, Jones was headline news again. She was sentenced to serve six months in prison for lying to investigators after admitting her performances in Sydney had been enhanced by **steroids**.

'I have no-one to blame but myself for what I've done,' she said after her admission. 'Making the wrong choices and bad decisions has been disastrous.'

What are steroids?

In ancient times it was known that **testes** were required for the development of male sexual characteristics. In 1849 a scientist called Berthold removed the testes from cockerels, which then lost their sexual function. Then he removed the testes and transplanted them into the birds' abdomens. This time the sexual function of the birds was unaffected. Berthold showed that 'male hormones' passed from the testes into the blood.

In the 1930s, the male hormone was identified as **testosterone**. Scientists were then able to synthesise testosterone and other hormones that acted in the same way. These hormones are called steroids.

In 1954, the Soviet Union dominated the World Weightlifting Championships. They also easily broke several world records. It was soon discovered that the weightlifters had used steroids during their preparation. The use of steroids in athletics had begun. By the 1970s most athletics authorities had banned the use of steroids.

40

In 1996 scientists investigated the effect of high doses of testosterone on the performance of weightlifters. Forty experienced male weightlifters were randomly assigned to one of four groups: two groups were given a placebo, one group with and one without exercise, and two groups were given testosterone, one group asked to exercise, the other not. The investigation lasted six weeks. The scientists tried to match each group for diet, training and weightlifting experience.

The scientists then measured the strength of each weightlifter and his fat-free body mass, which is the total body mass minus the estimated mass of fat in his body. They found that:

- body mass increased only in the two testosterone-treated groups
- fat-free body mass increased only in the exercise groups
- the greatest change in fat-free mass was in the testosterone plus exercise group
- percentage body fat did not change in any group
- muscle size increased more in the testosterone groups than in either placebo group
- strength increased in both testosterone groups, as well as in the exercise group receiving placebo
- strength increase was greater in the exercise group with testosterone than in the exercise group with placebo.

Other scientific studies have shown that there is a significant **placebo effect** in studies with weightlifters. In most of these studies, strength increased considerably in subjects who received placebo, but who were told they were receiving steroids.

Weightlifters need to develop large muscles.

Is it harmful to take steroids?

The poster shows some of the known side effects of steroids.

Questions

1. What is the effect on a male of removing the testes?
2. What conclusions can be drawn from the results of the 1996 study on testosterone about the effectiveness of using steroids in training?
3. What is the natural function of testosterone?
4. Give two ways in which using steroids enhances athletic performance.
5. Give two ways in which using steroids may affect health in women.
6. Explain what is meant by the 'placebo effect'.
7. Suggest a reason for the ban on the use of steroids.
8. Imagine you are an athletics coach. One of your athletes says that she knows that several of her competitors are taking steroids. She does not want them to out-perform her. What advice would you give her?

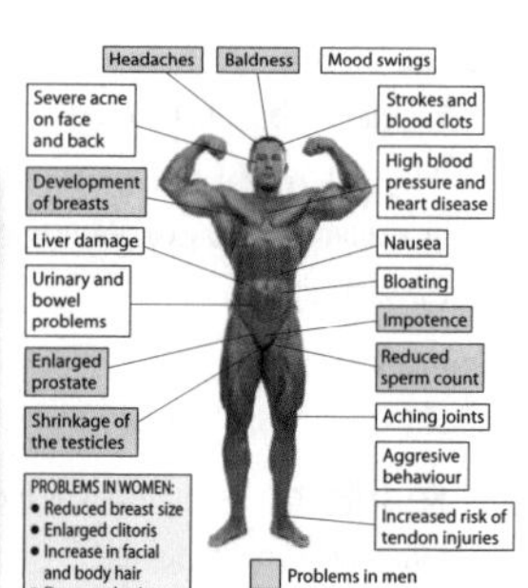

Figute 1 The possible side effects of using steroids.

Drugs: use and abuse 41

Learning objectives

Students should be able to:

- recall that steroids and other performance-enhancing drugs are used by some athletes
- evaluate the use of drugs to enhance performance in sport
- consider the ethical implications of using performance-enhancing drugs.

Key points

Steroids are performance-enhancing drugs that are banned by most athletics authorities.

There are ethical and health issues involved with taking steroids to enhance performance.

Placebo effect steroid testes testosterone

Lesson activities

Starter

1 Watch the BBC Sport video of David Millar talking about how team pressures led to him taking performance-enhancing drugs.

Main

1 Students read the BBC Ethics article on types of performance-enhancing drug (print it out or access it on the web), then answer the questions on **Worksheet B1 3.4a**.

2 Students complete the HSW skills box in lesson B1 3.4 in the Student Book.

Plenary

1 Student debate: 'Is it possible to make sure that athletes have not used performance-enhancing drugs in the run-up to an event?'

Homework

1 **Worksheet B1 3.4b** looks at anabolic steroids.

2 **Worksheet B1 3.1c** considers the use of stimulants in athletics.

Route to A*

Research ways of building up muscles that do not involve the use of drugs. Write a pamphlet explaining why these methods are more advisable than using drugs.

Answers to Student Book questions

Science skills

a Higher overall use in males. Highest 'individual' use in native American males. Highest 'individual' use in black and hispanic females. Highest use in middle social class for males and low-middle and high-middle for females.

Answers

1 Loss of sexual function.

2 Using steroids will increase body mass and muscle strength, but the effect is enhanced by exercise and there is a large placebo effect when only muscle strength is considered.

3 Testosterone initiates the development of male sexual characteristics.

4 Increased muscle mass and increased strength, for example.

5 Reduced breast size, increased body hair, deepened voice and menstrual problems, for example.

6 The placebo effect is increased performance by an athlete who thinks they have been given the drug.

7 A reason for the ban is to give all athletes a fair chance.

8 Extra exercise is much better than taking steroids because it is almost as effective and has none of the side effects of steroids. If you are detected taking steroids you will be banned. Using steroids is against the spirit of fair competition.

B1 3.5 ISA practice: testing hand-washes

In the Student Book, each ISA practice is contained on one double-page spread. However, you can, if you prefer, use the sheets provided in the Teacher and Technician Planning Pack and the Activity Pack to more closely mirror the experience of a real ISA which would then take place over several lessons and/or as homework.

Link to the specification – How Science Works

Scientific investigations often seek to identify links between two or more variables. [4.1.1]

Scientists need to ensure repeatability, reproducibility and validity in evidence. [4.3.3]

There is a link between the type of graph used and the type of variable represented. [4.4.2]

The patterns and relationships observed in data represent the behaviour of the variables in an investigation. However, it is necessary to look at patterns and relationships between variables with the limitations of the data in mind in order to draw conclusions. [4.5.3, 4.5.4]

In evaluating a whole investigation the repeatability, reproducibility and validity of the data obtained must be considered. [4.5.2]

ISA practice: testing hand-washes

Scientists are investigating the best hand-wash to use in a hospital. Your task is to do an investigation to compare the effect of antiseptic-based hand-washes and soap-based hand-washes on the growth of bacterial colonies.

Hypothesis

There is a link between the type of antibacterial substance used and the growth of bacteria.

Section 1

1 In this investigation you will need to control some of the variables.

(a) Name one variable you will need to control in this investigation. *(1 mark)*

(b) Describe briefly how you would carry out a preliminary investigation to find a suitable value to use for this variable. Explain how the results will help you decide on the best value for this variable. *(2 marks)*

2 Describe how you are going to do your investigation. You should include:

- the equipment that you would use
- how you would use the equipment
- the measurements that you would make
- a risk assessment
- how you would make it a fair test.

You may include a labelled diagram to help you to explain your method.

In this question you will be assessed on using good English, organising information clearly and using specialist terms where appropriate. *(9 marks)*

3 Design a table that will contain all the data that you are going to record during your investigation. *(2 marks)*

Total for Section 1: 14 marks

Section 2

A group of students, Study Group 1, investigated how effective two different hand-washes were in killing bacteria. They decided to place a drop of each hand-wash onto an agar plate and measured the radius of the clear zone that appeared. They repeated their results three times. Figure 1 shows the results they obtained.

Soap-based hand-wash	Antiseptic-based hand-wash
Radius of the clear zone in cm	Radius of the clear zone in cm
Plate 1 disc 1 0.8, disc 2 0.4, disc 3 0.6	Plate 1 disc 1 1.6, disc 2 1.6, disc 3 1.2
Plate 2 disc 1 0.8, disc 2 0.8, disc 3 0.8	Plate 2 disc 1 1.4, disc 2 1.8, disc 3 1.8
Plate 3 disc 1 0.6, disc 2 0.6, disc 3 0.8	Plate 3 disc 1 1.2, disc 2 1.4, disc 3 1.4

Figure 1 Results from Study Group 1's investigation.

4 (a) (i) What is the independent variable in this investigation?

(ii) What is the dependent variable in this investigation?

(iii) Name one control variable this investigation. *(3 marks)*

(b) Plot a graph to show the link between the type of hand-wash used and the radius of the clear zone. *(4 marks)*

(c) Do the results support the hypothesis? Explain your answer. *(3 marks)*

Below are the results of two other study groups.

Table 1 shows the results of another two students, Study Group 2.

Table 1 Results from Study Group 2.

	Mean radius of clear zone/cm		
	Plate 1	Plate 2	Plate 3
Soap-based hand-wash	0.4	0.6	0.5
Antiseptic-based hand-wash	1.5	1.7	1.2

Study Group 3 is a group of scientists who also investigated the effectiveness of a range of different hand-washes. The scientists investigated how well the 14 different hand-hygiene methods A–N, shown in Table 2, worked.

For their investigation the scientists recruited 70 volunteers. The volunteers were asked to wash their hands only with non-antimicrobial hand soap for seven days before the investigation. Five volunteers used each of the methods A–N during the investigation.

Each volunteer:

- washed hands with non-antimicrobial soap
- spread a standard suspension of a red-coloured bacterium over the hands for 45 seconds
- air-dried the hands for 60 seconds.
- used one of the hand hygiene methods, A–N, for 10 seconds
- rinsed the hands for 10 seconds.

Table 2 Hand hygiene methods used by Study Group 3.

Method	Active ingredient	5p3.568	Method of application
A	60% ethyl alcohol	gel	waterless hand rub
B	61% ethyl alcohol	lotion	waterless hand rub
C	61% ethyl alcohol and 1% CHG	lotion	waterless hand rub
D	62% ethyl alcohol	foam	waterless hand rub
E	70% ethyl alcohol and 0.005% silver iodide	gel	waterless hand rub
F	0.5% parachlorometaxylenol and 40% SD alcohol	wipe 256 cm²	waterless hand wipe
G	0.4% benzalkonium chloride	wipe, 296 cm²	waterless hand wipe
H	0.75% CHG	liquid	hand wash
I	2% CHG	liquid	hand wash
J	4% CHG	liquid	hand wash
K	1% triclosan	liquid	hand wash
L	0.2% benzethonium chloride	liquid	hand wash
M	non-antimicrobial soap	liquid	hand wash
N	tap water	liquid	hand wash

Each volunteer's hands were then sampled for the red-coloured bacterium by:

- placing each hand into a large latex glove containing 75 cm^3 of a sterile sampling solution
- having the glove massaged for 30 seconds.

5 cm^3 of the sampling solution was then spread over a nutrient agar plate. The agar plates were incubated at 25 °C for 24 hours, after which the number of colonies of the red-coloured bacterium was counted. Each colony had developed from a single bacterium.

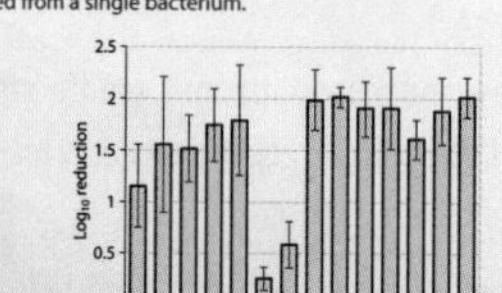

Figure 2 Some of the scientists' results.

A log reduction of 1 means that there are 10 times fewer bacteria in the sample.

A log reduction of 2 means that there are 100 times fewer bacteria in the sample.

A log reduction of 3 means that there are 1000 times fewer bacteria in the sample.

The line associated with each bar on the chart shows the range of results for each hand hygiene method.

The scientists from Study Group 3 carried out a second investigation using similar techniques, but this time using a virus instead of a bacterium.

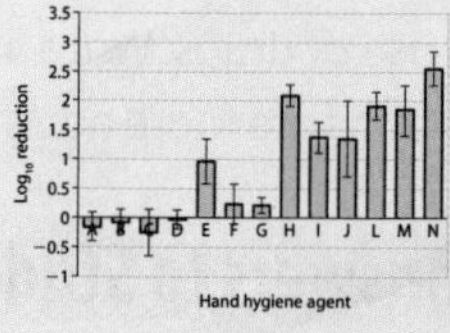

Figure 3 Results from Study Group 3's second investigation.

5 Describe one way in which Study Group 2's results are similar to or different from the results from Study Group 1, and give one reason why the results are similar or different. *(3 marks)*

6 (a) Summarise briefly the results from Study Group 3. *(3 marks)*

(b) Does the data from the study groups support the hypothesis being investigated? To gain full marks you should use all of the relevant data from Study Groups 1, 2 and 3 to explain whether or not the data supports the hypothesis. *(3 marks)*

(c) The data from the other groups only gives a limited amount of information. What other information or data would you need in order to be more certain as to whether or not the hypothesis is correct? Explain the reason for your answer. *(3 marks)*

(d) Use the results from Study Groups 1, 2 and 3 to answer this question. What is the relationship between the type of hand-wash and the effect on bacteria? How well does the data support your answer? *(3 marks)*

7 Look back at Study Group 1's method. If you could repeat the investigation, suggest one change that you would make to the method, and give a reason for the change. *(3 marks)*

8 Suggest how ideas from your investigation and the scientists' investigations could be used to advise hospitals about the type of hand-washes to use. *(3 marks)*

Total for Section 2: 31 marks
Total for the ISA: 45 marks

42 43

Learning objectives

Most students should be able to:

- identify the independent and dependent variables in the hypothesis
- make some notes on two methods to investigate the hypothesis
- identify a method to establish the range of the independent variable, or the value of a control variable that will give a range of values for the dependent variable
- obtain some data to process and produce a graph or bar chart
- identify any trends that may be present in the data
- relate that trend to the hypothesis under investigation.

Some students should also be able to:

- make a risk assessment of their chosen method
- question the evidence to establish its repeatability and /or reproducibility.

anomalous result | calibration | control measure | errors: random | systematic and zero
hazard | mean | range | repeatable | reproducible | uncertainty | validity
variables: control | categoric | continuous | dependent | independent

Key points

Investigations should be designed so that patterns and relationships between variables can be identified.

It is important to ensure repeatability, reproducibility and validity in evidence when designing and evaluating investigations.

The choice of graph used depends upon the type of variable represented.

When drawing conclusions, the limitations of the data must be kept in mind.

Lesson activities

Starter

1 Show either a picture/bottle of hospital hand-wash, or antibacterial hand-wash. Students should answer the questions: What is it? When should it be used? Why is it used? How does it work?

2 Tell students that they will be carrying out an investigation into the hypothesis: 'There is a link between the type of antibacterial substance used and the growth of bacteria.' Suggest a suitable context, e.g. infection control in hospitals.

Main

1 Researching and planning Students need to research at least two different methods of investigating the hypothesis above. Please refer to the **B1 ISA practice 1 Teacher and technician sheet.** They can complete their research/notes for homework. See the **ISA practice Student research notes sheet.**

2 Ask two students to read their notes on one of the points. Get the class to decide whose notes are best, with a reason. Repeat until all the points are covered.

3 Give students the **B1 ISA practice 1 Section 1 paper.**

4 In a following lesson students set up their investigation and record and process their results. Students can work in groups to obtain the data. Please refer to the **B1 ISA practice 1 Student practical sheet.**

5 Students should process the data individually in **controlled** conditions. A bar chart or graph should be plotted and the trend of the graph/bar chart identified and a conclusion made.

6 Students should pool their results so that a class results table can be produced ready for the **B1 ISA practice 1 Section 2 paper.**

7 Give students the **B1 ISA practice 1 Section 2 paper.**

Plenary

1 Students discuss sources of possible errors and ways to overcome them.

Homework

After the practical, ask students to write brief notes about ways in which they could improve their investigation. They should mention how to reduce errors and what further data or information they would need to confirm their conclusion.

Points to note

- With able students simply outline the points they need to cover. You should adjust delivery to match the time that it takes to obtain meaningful results. You should in your discussions remain focussed on the hypothesis.
- Students should describe a complex relationship between the independent variable and the dependent variable.

Route to A*

Students' risk assessment should include sensible risks, with a clear indication of the likelihood of the hazard occurring and how to sensibly control the risk. They should avoid basic laboratory rules.

Ask students to critically evaluate their data and explain that the findings are only valid within the range of the independent variable, whose range may be quite limited.

Answers to Student Book questions

6 **(a)** Liquid hand-washes work better than alcohol-based washes, for both viruses and bacteria. This is most clear in the virus study (1). All the agents are effective against bacteria (1). Method E (alcohol and silver iodide) is the most effective alcohol-based agent (1).

(b) The student states that overall the data strongly supports the original hypothesis and quotes data that supports this (1).
In Study Group 3 increasing concentrations of alcohol are increasingly effective.
CHG reduces the effectiveness of the hand-rub.
CHG is most effective at 2%.
Tap water is as good as CHG at 2% (1).
Study Group 2 and Study Group 1 suggest that soap-based hand-wash is less effective than antiseptic-based hand-wash, with some figures quoted (1).
Figure 3 data is irrelevant to the hypothesis as it deals with viruses not bacteria.

(c) Suggests at least one other piece of information that would be needed to form a firm conclusion (2). The reason for the need for this other information is clearly stated (1).

(d) Liquid hand-washes are better than all other types as samples H–M all show much larger reductions in bacteria. (1) All liquid hand-washes give nearly a 100 times fewer number of bacteria. Only L performs worse than the best hand rub (E). This is also the case for viruses. (1) F and G waterless hand-wipes are the worst. Lotions, gels and foams containing alcohol are effective. (1)

For the full mark scheme, see the Teacher and Technician Planning Pack.

B1 4.1 Plant adaptations

Link to the specification

B1 4.1a To survive and reproduce, organisms require a supply of materials from their surroundings and from the other living organisms there.

B1 4.1d Organisms, including microorganisms, have features (adaptations) that enable them to survive in the conditions in which they normally live.

B1 4.1f Animals and plants may be adapted for survival in the conditions where they normally live, e.g. deserts, the Arctic.

(Animals may be adapted for survival in arctic and dry environments by means of: changes to surface area; thickness of insulating coat; amount of body fat; camouflage.)

Plants may be adapted to survive in dry environments by means of: changes to surface area, particularly of the leaves; water-storage tissues; extensive root systems.

Ideas for practical work

Investigate the effect on plant growth of varying their environmental conditions, e.g. degrees of shade, density of sowing, supply of nutrients.

How Science Works

SKU: B1.4 bullet point 1: Suggest how organisms are adapted to the conditions in which they live. B1.4 bullet point 2: Observe the adaptations, e.g. body shape, of a range of organisms from different habitats. B1.4 bullet point 3: Develop an understanding of the ways in which adaptations enable organisms to survive.

CA: B4 3.2c Recognising the value of further readings to establish repeatability and accuracy. B4 4.1b Calculating the mean of a set of at least three results.

B1 4.1 Plant adaptations

Learning objectives

- describe some features (adaptations) of plants that help them grow well in different conditions
- describe specific adaptations that help plants survive in dry environments
- explain how different adaptations to the environment help plants to survive.

Adapting to the environment

All organisms need food, water and **nutrients** to grow. They get these from the environment where they live. Different environments have different **physical conditions**, such as temperature, and amounts of light, water and nutrients. To grow well and produce offspring, an organism needs particular features that help it get what it needs from its environment. We call these features **adaptations**.

Growing in the cold

Where it is very cold, such as in the Arctic tundra, few plants can grow because ice forming inside cells can damage them. These plants often have a rounded shape that helps to **insulate** the inner parts and keep them warmer.

In coniferous forests of the northern hemisphere, the temperature is a little warmer, but heavy snow is a danger as it can break branches if it piles up.

The leaves and branches of coniferous trees allow snow to slide off quickly without damage.

Growing in rainforests

In a tropical rainforest, the temperature may be good for growth but rainfall can be so heavy that it damages leaves. Many leaves have shiny surfaces and pointed tips to the leaves to help the rain run off quickly, or are divided into many sections so water can pass through easily. At the top of the trees, there is plenty of light for **photosynthesis**, but the forest is usually so dense that plants growing near the forest floor get little light.

Many plants can grow in a tropical rainforest where it is warm all year round but they need adaptations for other conditions.

The red backs of the leaves help ground-level plants capture more light for photosynthesis.

Science skills

a How would you investigate the effect of different amounts of shade, or different levels of nutrients, on the growth of plants?

Examiner feedback

The conservation of water by plants living in dry conditions and the efficient uptake of water when water is available, through adaptations in the root systems, are ideas that are often questioned in exams.

Growing in the dry

Plants, like cacti, that grow in places where it is dry have very wide root systems to collect as much water as possible when it rains, or very deep root systems that can tap into water far underground. They may also have thick leaves or a thick body that contains tissue for storing water that the plant can use when there is a **drought**.

Tiny holes, called **stomata**, in the surfaces of leaves let in carbon dioxide for photosynthesis, but these holes also let water out. Plants in dry areas must reduce water loss through stomata, so they may have no leaves at all. A few stomata in the stem surface are protected by hairs or by being placed deep in ridges. This reduces the speed of air moving across the stomata and so reduces the rate of evaporation. The plant can continue to photosynthesise because the stems are green.

50

The effect of soil

The amount of nutrients in the soil will affect plants. Where the soil contains many nutrients, many different kinds of plants may be able to grow. However, few plants grow well on poor acid soil because it contains so few nutrients. For example, sundew plants get extra nutrients by trapping insects on their leaves and digesting them.

The sundew plant lives in waterlogged and nutrient-poor soil.

The hairy surface of the cactus reduces the speed of air flow across the stomata and so reduces the rate of evaporation of water from the plant.

Examiner feedback

It is important not just to describe the adaptations of an organism to particular conditions in the environment, but also to explain why those adaptations increase the chances of survival.

Questions

1 Describe one adaptation of a plant to extreme cold, and explain how this helps the plant to survive.
2 Describe three adaptations of rainforest plants to their environment and explain how they help plants to survive.
3 A rainforest leaf that is split into sections can be bigger than one that isn't split. Explain why this is an advantage.
4 List as many ways as possible that plants which live in dry conditions can make sure they have enough water during long droughts, and explain the importance of each way.
5 In a tropical rainforest the tallest trees are over 60 m, below which are 'layers' of smaller trees and shrubs. Suggest the different adaptations you would expect to see in the tallest trees and the shrubs.
6 Marram grass grows on sand dunes on sea shores and has very deep roots. The leaves are curled, with the stomata tucked inside. Explain as fully as you can how these adaptations help the marram grass to survive.
7 Sundew plants grow slowly. Explain in detail why sundew plants are only found on poor acid soils.
8 The leaves of coniferous trees are thin, waxy needles that remain on the tree all year round. The stomata are hidden in pits in the needle surface. Explain in as much detail as you can why these and other adaptations of conifer trees help them dominate northern landscapes. A*

Science in action

High concentrations of metals in soil are usually poisonous to plants. However, a few plants are adapted to these conditions. These plants can be grown on the spoil heaps from mines where metals such as copper and lead have been extracted. The plants help to remove the metals from the soil, which makes it less poisonous for other plants.

Taking it further

At A level you will learn how plants change the environment in which they live, such as by creating soil around their roots or drying out wetlands. These changes create conditions that are better suited to other plants, which may change conditions in other ways. The gradual replacement of one group of species with others over time is called succession.

Interdependence and adaptation 51

Learning objectives

Most students should be able to:

- describe different features (adaptations) of plants that help them grow well in different conditions
- describe adaptations that help plants survive in dry environments.

Some students should also be able to:

- explain how different adaptations to the environment help plants to survive. [H]

Key points

Plants need to be adapted to the conditions in their environment for survival. Plants living in dry conditions may have extensive root systems, reduced surface areas, or water-storage tissues to help them survive a lack of water. Plants living in cold areas have shapes that help them to cope with the extreme cold or to shed snow to avoid damage.

Lesson activities

Starter

1 Show students a photograph or video of plants living in extreme conditions, such as an arid region or on polar tundra, and ask them to describe the challenges for plants living there.

2 Some students may be able to describe some of the adaptations that help the plants to survive, but the key idea to get across is that if a plant cannot grow and reproduce in those conditions, the species will die out in that area.

Adaptation | driptip | drought | insulate | physical condition | stomata

Main

1 What is the 'environment'? Students need to understand that the environment of an organism includes not only the physical factors, such as light or warmth, but also other organisms including predators, parasites, prey and anything else that they interact with. Use a photograph of a landscape including plants and animals as a stimulus, and start a discussion on 'what makes up the environment?' Ask students to identify elements in the photograph that are part of that environment.

2 B1 4.1a Plant growth In this practical, students measure and compare the area of leaves from plants that have been growing in full sun or in shade. Another focus of the activity is considering how to increase the reliability of measurements from living organisms. (If the leaves are provided, allow ~30 minutes; allow additional time if students are to collect leaves.)

3 B1 4.1b Surviving with little water In this activity students choose one organism from the worksheet that can survive in arid conditions. They should carry out further research on its adaptations to the environment and prepare a poster or short report on their findings. Although lichens are not strictly plants, they are given as an example because their use as pollution indicators is covered in lesson 4 6.

Plenaries

1 Show students the same image or video as given in the starter and ask them to describe, and possibly explain, the adaptations of the plant to the conditions. If they find this difficult, ask them to suggest what else they would need to research in order to answer the question. [AfL]

2 Give students 5 minutes to sketch a plant that shows physical adaptations to a particular environment, such as very cold, very warm or very wet. They should annotate their sketch to identify the key adaptations. [AfL]

Homework

1 Either use books or the Internet to investigate the adaptations of plants in other extreme conditions, such as the rainforest, or as used to rehabilitate spoil heaps from mineral mining.

2 Worksheet B1 4.1c provides some revision questions on this lesson as well as asking students to apply their knowledge to a new example.

Points to note

- This is a fairly simple topic as it builds on earlier work at KS3 and even KS2 on adaptations. To extend this for higher-ability students, focus the tasks on explanation of how an adaptation improves survival and reproductive success.

Route to A*

Students could research some of the physiological mechanisms that allow plants to live in some of the more extreme environments, such as the presence of oils and waxes that reduce the risk of damage by freezing, or behavioural mechanisms such as losing leaves in times of drought or in cold seasons. Students should use their findings to try to explain how these adaptations evolved.

Answers to Student Book questions

Science skills

a Grow a large number of identical plants in controlled conditions where only one of these factors (amount of shade or amount of nutrients) is changed. Use a range of different amounts of shade (measured using light meter) or nutrients (measured into watering solution) and keep all other factors the same for all plants as far as possible (e.g. grown at same temperature). After a few weeks, measure growth of all plants (e.g. by height of plant, or average leaf area), and take means of all measurements for each value of the controlled variable.

Answers

1 Any suitable adaptation, plus explanation of how this increases survival: e.g. small hummock shape, reduces damage from ice formation in cells because inner parts insulated and so are warmer.

2 Any three suitable adaptations, e.g. shiny top surface to leaf, drip tip, divided leaves, which prevent damage to leaves from heavy rain by helping rain to run off easily or through leaves.

3 A larger leaf can capture more light for photosynthesis.

4 Adaptations include deep or wide root systems, thick leaves or body containing water-storage tissue, reduced leaves, no leaves, and hairs; root systems capture as much water as possible from the soil; water-storage tissues store water inside plant for when conditions are dry; reduction to leaves and surface area, and hairs, reduce rate of loss of water from plant.

5 The tallest trees would have smaller leaves because they are more exposed to wind and rain damage. Shrubs would have larger leaves because they are shaded by trees, so get less sun, and are more likely to have drip tips, split leaves and shiny leaf surfaces to reduce damage from heavy rainfall.

6 The deep root system helps the plant to get water from a large area; the stomata being tucked away reduces the rate of evaporation of water. Both of these adaptations are due to lack of water. In sand, water drains very quickly so drought conditions happen easily. Also, wind speeds on the sea shore can be much higher than inland as there is nothing to slow them down. The adaptations make it possible to live where other plants cannot.

7 On other soils they would quickly be shaded by other plants that grow more quickly. This means they would be unable to get light for photosynthesis, so they would die. Other plants cannot get enough nutrients on poor acid soils to grow well so they don't grow there. This means sundew plants have space to grow and reproduce on acid soils.

8 Northern areas are covered in snow for several months, and water is frozen during this time so not easy for plants/trees to take up. The stomata being in pits is an adaptation that reduces water loss because air movement across stomata is reduced and the rate of evaporation is less. Waxy needles reduce the risk of damage caused by freezing as there is less water in the needles. Being evergreen means they can photosynthesise as soon as light levels increase sufficiently in spring, and later into autumn than (deciduous) trees that lose their leaves over winter. The shape of the trees and needles means that snow is shed more easily so that damage to branches is limited. Deciduous trees have none of these adaptations so coniferous trees dominate in colder areas.

B1 4.2 Animal adaptations

Link to the specification

B1 4.1a To survive and reproduce, organisms require a supply of materials from their surroundings and from the other living organisms there.

B1 4.1d Organisms, including microorganisms, have features (adaptations) which enable them to survive in the conditions in which they normally live.

B1 4.1f Animals and plants may be adapted for survival in the conditions where they normally live, e.g. deserts, the Arctic.

Animals may be adapted for survival in dry and arctic environments by means of: changes to surface area; thickness of insulating coat; amount of body fat; camouflage.

Plants may be adapted to survive in dry environments by means of: changes to surface area, particularly of the leaves; water-storage tissues; extensive root systems.

Ideas for practical work

Investigate the behaviour of woodlice using choice chambers.

Computer simulations to model the effect on organisms of changes to the environment.

How Science Works

SKU: B1.4 bullet point 1: Suggest how organisms are adapted to the conditions in which they live. B1.4 bullet point 2: Observe the adaptations, e.g. body shape, of a range of organisms from different habitats. B1.4 bullet point 3: Develop an understanding of the ways in which adaptations enable organisms to survive.

CA: B4.1.1b Being able to test hypotheses – plan a fair test to investigate their hypothesis. B4.3.2.a Appreciating that, unless certain variables are controlled, the results may not be valid. B4.4.2b Drawing charts and graphs.

B1 4.2 Animal adaptations

Learning objectives

- explain how animals are affected by physical factors such as temperature and availability of water
- understand the ways in which adaptations enable organisms to survive
- describe various adaptations of animals for survival in dry desert environments and cold polar environments
- evaluate data related to the distribution of animals.

Staying warm

Where environmental conditions, such as temperature and water availability, are extreme, animals also need particular adaptations to survive and grow well.

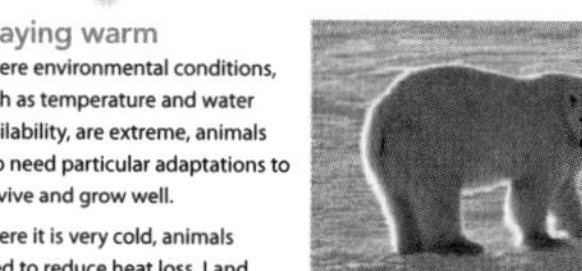

Before winter, the polar bear grows a thicker coat and eats lots of food. When there is no food, it can reduce its rate of energy use to conserve fat reserves.

Where it is very cold, animals need to reduce heat loss. Land mammals, such as polar bears and caribou, have very thick fur that insulates them from the air so that body heat is lost more slowly to the cold environment. Extra fat, in a layer under their skin, increases the insulation and can give the animal energy when food is scarce. During the summer, these animals **moult**, or shed the outer thick layer of fur so that it is easier to lose body heat. Sea mammals, such as seals, need a very thick layer of fat to insulate against heat loss to the water.

Science in action

Studying the hollow hairs of caribou, which live in the frozen north of Canada, showed that the air inside the hairs acts as good insulation from the cold. This led to the development of hollow polyester fibres for use in duvets and insulated clothing to keep us warm.

Keeping cool and avoiding thirst

In deserts, there is very little water for much of the time. It can also be very hot during the day and very cold at night.

Small desert animals, such as the hopping mice of Australia, live mostly in burrows where the temperature is more constant and not as extreme as above ground. They also do not need to drink water, as they get all the water they need from their food. Their kidneys **excrete** urine that contains very little water. Large desert animals, such as camels, can tolerate higher levels of dehydration than non-desert species.

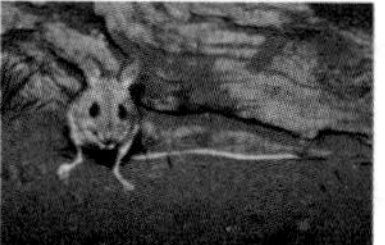

Desert hopping mice can usually only be found on the surface at dawn and dusk.

Science skills

Table 1 The surface area and volume of different sizes of cubes.

Length of one side/cm	Surface area of cube/cm^2	Volume/cm^3
1	6	1
2	24	8
3	54	27
4	96	64

a Calculate the surface area to volume ratio for each cube.

b Heat is generated in an animal's body by the *volume* of tissue. Heat is lost by an animal from the *surface area* of its body. The larger the surface area to volume ratio, the faster the animal will lose body heat. Which size loses heat faster: the smallest or the largest?

Examiner feedback

You will not be asked about Bergmann or Allen in an exam. However, you should be able to explain how the surface area to volume ratio of an animal has a direct effect on where it can live and why. Remember that a large animal has a large surface area, but a small surface area to volume ratio.

Body size and shape rules

The 19th century biologist Carl Bergmann observed that birds and mammals of the same or similar species tend to be larger and heavier when they live in colder climates. 'Bergmann's rule' states that there is a correlation between body mass and average annual temperature. Bergmann's explanation for the correlation was that animals lose heat at the surface of their bodies so, if two animals are shaped identically, the temperature of the larger one will drop less rapidly.

Average body mass/arbitrary units
3.6 3.4 3.2 3.0 2.8 2.6 2.4
−20 −15 −10 −5 0 5 10
Average annual temperature/°C

Figure 1 Body mass of many different animals compared with temperature where they live.

Science skills How would you test the idea that penguins huddling in Antarctic winters is a behavioural adaptation to the cold?

Huddling penguins.

Joel Allen gathered data relating climate to variation in animals. Allen's rule states that the extremities of organisms (limbs, tails and ears) of animals that need to maintain their temperature, such as mammals, are longer in warm climates than in cold climates because they act as heat-radiating organs.

The kit fox lives in the hot dry regions of Mexico.

The Arctic fox lives in northern Canada.

Questions

1 Describe the adaptations of the polar bear to life in the Arctic, and explain how they help it survive.
2 **(a)** Explain how small animals can survive life in the desert. **(b)** Suggest what adaptations large desert animals need to survive, and how these adaptations enable them to survive.
3 Use the information about surface area and volume of cubes to predict what impact body size in animals will have in: **(a)** cold climates **(b)** hot climates.
4 Do the data shown in the graph in Figure 1 support Bergmann's rule? Explain your answer.
5 Do the kit fox and Arctic fox comply with Allen's rule? Explain your answer.
6 Use Bergman's rule to help explain why Emperor penguins huddle during polar winter storms.
7 During the Arctic winter, a mother polar bear stays in a den with her cubs. Explain fully why this is an adaptation to living in polar conditions.
8 Whale blubber is not just a layer of fat, but includes blood vessels that can be adjusted to allow more or less blood near to the skin. Explain in as much detail as you can why a whale needs such a complex system.

A*

52

Interdependence and adaptation 53

Learning objectives

Students should be able to:

- explain how animals are affected by physical factors such as temperature and availability of water
- describe various adaptations of animals for survival in dry desert environments and cold polar environments.
- evaluate data related to the distribution of animals.

Key points

Adaptations to conditions in the environment help animals to survive.

Animals in hot, dry environments are often small. This helps them to lose heat and also means they can hide underground from extremes of temperature.

Insulation with thick body fat and fur, and small extremities help animals in polar conditions to reduce heat loss.

Lesson activities

Starter

1 Ask students what they would need to take on an expedition to polar regions to help them survive. For each suggestion, they should explain why they would need it. Focus on suggestions that protect against the harsh environmental conditions.

2 Ask students to compare their list with any adaptations they can think of that animals have to living in those regions.

Insulate moult

Main

1 B1 4.2a Investigating huddling as an adaptation This is a simple investigation that requires students to understand the importance of calibrating thermometers when using more than one. It generates good data for analysis using line graphs. Use of a spreadsheet or graphing program would be applicable. (~40 minutes) As preparation for the practical, the YouTube video of Penguin behaviour, including huddling, could be used as a stimulus for discussion.

2 B1 4.2b Woodlice choice chambers This practical gives students the opportunity to plan and carry out an experiment that tests the preference of woodlice for variation in one condition: either light/dark or damp/dryness. If different groups investigate each condition, then comparison of results could form the basis of a discussion on which condition is the more important for woodlice, and how reliable the evidence is to support the conclusion. (~40 minutes)

3 Students could carry out their own research into the adaptations of an animal to either life in polar regions or in exceedingly arid conditions. They could present their findings in a poster, slideshow or short report.

Plenaries

1 Ask students to prepare a mind map of all that they have learnt about animal adaptations to cold and to dry regions. This could be done as an individual activity after which students work in pairs and then small groups to compare their maps and identify gaps in their own understanding. [AfL]

2 Ask students to prepare the clues for a crossword using all the key words from this and the previous lesson on plants, and any other relevant words. Their crossword should include at least eight clues. If there is time, they could try their clues out on another student.

Homework

1 Either use books or the Internet to find examples of new materials used for clothing in extreme conditions, and compare the features of these materials with the adaptations of animals that live in those conditions to identify similarities and differences in the way they work.

2 Worksheet B1 4.2c compares the physiological adaptations of camels to living in arid conditions with the way human bodies work.

Points to note

- Students will have covered this topic at a lower level in KS3 and possibly KS2. To extend it fully for higher-ability students, focus the tasks on explanation of how an adaptation improves survival and reproductive success.

Route to A*

Students could research some of the physiological adaptations to extreme conditions, such as presence of 'antifreeze' in animals that live in very cold conditions, or the metabolism of fat in hibernation. Students should try to explain how these adaptations could have evolved.

Answers to Student Book questions

Science skills

a Length 1, surface area/volume 6; length 2, surface area/volume 3; length 3, surface area/volume 2; length 4, surface area/volume 1.5.

b The smallest.

c Measure out two squares of 1 m^2 on the ground outside, ideally on a cold, windy day. See how many students can stand in one square; put one student in the other. After a specific time period, measure the air temperature in the centre of the huddle and the centre of the other square. Ask the students to describe whether they feel warm/cold in different positions in the huddle and alone.

Answers

1 Large body size and small ears help reduce heat loss; thick fur and a fat layer below the skin insulate against heat loss; it can reduce energy use when there is no food to conserve fat. (Also white fur is camouflage – described further in next topic.)

2 **(a)** They may live underground, or hide below ground when it is too hot or too cold. They get water from food. **(b)** Adaptations to reduce water loss, to cope with being dehydrated and with lack of food, and to cope with being very hot or very cold because they cannot hide from the conditions. For example, camels are adapted to survive without water for a week or more; they store fat in their hump(s) to use when food is scarce; their internal body temperature can fluctuate far more than most mammals, which means that they can conserve water by not sweating when the external temperature increases; they have thick fur which can insulate against the hot as well as the cold.

3 **(a)** Cold: better to have a small surface area to volume ratio to reduce the rate of heat loss, i.e. a large bulky body and small extremities. **(b)** Hot: better to have a large surface area to volume ratio, to increase the rate of heat loss, i.e., a small slender body with large extremities such as ears.

4 The trend on the graph is that average body mass decreases as average annual temperature increases, although there is great variation in body mass at any particular temperature. The graph generally supports Bergmann's rule.

5 The kit fox has much larger ears than the Arctic fox, which supports Allen's rule because the Arctic fox lives in colder conditions.

6 By huddling together, the penguins act more like one individual with a much larger volume and, in proportion, reduced surface area exposed to the cold air. This fits with Bergmann's rule that in colder conditions organisms tend to be larger and heavier.

7 The cubs are much smaller than their mother so they have a higher surface area to volume ratio; they are at greater risk of losing body heat to the environment. In the den, the snow insulates the mother and cubs, and so less energy is wasted moving about and the cubs can grow faster before moving out of the den.

8 Blubber is an insulator; it helps to insulate the whale from the cold water in which it swims so that the whale doesn't have to use more energy to keep its body temperature higher than that of the water. When a whale swims fast, it will generate extra heat; it needs to lose this heat to the water. Increasing blood flow through the blubber carries this heat nearer to the skin where it can be lost to the water.

B1 4.3

Surviving the presence of others

Link to the specification

B1 4.1b Plants often compete with each other for light and space, and for water and nutrients from the soil.

B1 4.1c Animals often compete with each other for food, mates and territory.

B1 4.1g Animals and plants may be adapted to cope with specific features of their environment, e.g. thorns, poisons and warning colours to deter predators.

Ideas for practical work

'Hunt the cocktail stick' using red and green cocktail sticks on a green background.

Investigate the distribution of European banded snails.

Investigate the effect on plant growth of varying their environmental conditions, e.g. degrees of shade, density of sowing, supply of nutrients.

Carrying out a survey of European banded snails.

How Science Works

SKU: B1.4 bullet point 1: Suggest how organisms are adapted to the conditions in which they live. B1.4 bullet point 4: Suggest the factors for which organisms are competing in a given habitat.

CA: B4 3.2a Appreciating that, unless certain variables are controlled, the results may not be valid. B4.3.2b Identifying when repeats are needed in order to improve reproducability. B4 5.4a Writing a conclusion, based on evidence that relates correctly to known facts. B4 5.4d Evaluating methods of data collection.

B1 4.3

Surviving the presence of others

Learning objectives

- describe some adaptations that plants and animals have to avoid being eaten
- describe some adaptations that help animals and plants to compete for resources
- suggest the factors for which organisms are competing in a habitat
- explain why animals compete for mates and territories.

Keeping others away

The environment of an organism includes not only the physical conditions but also other plants and animals. If an organism is to grow, mature and produce offspring, it must avoid being eaten by other organisms.

Many organisms have special adaptations to avoid being eaten. Many plants, for example, cacti, have physical deterrents such as thick spines to deter herbivores. Other plants, like ragwort, use chemical deterrents such as poisons that taste unpleasant or can kill.

Many animals also use poison to deter predators. They advertise their poison with bright colours. Other animals hide from predators using **camouflage**. The colours and patterns on their bodies make them much more difficult to see against their usual background.

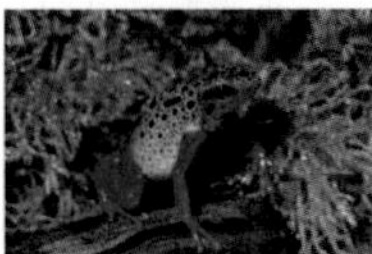

The blue poison dart frog boldly sits in full view of potential predators.

a European banded snails come in a wide variety of shell colours and patterns.
How would you test the idea that the variety is the result of camouflage against predation by birds?

Competing for resources

It is rare that there is so much of a resource that all organisms can get what they need. When resources are limited, organisms have to **compete** with each other. Those organisms that are most successful in getting the resource will grow better and produce more offspring.

Plants compete with each other for water, light and nutrients if they are growing close together. Some ground-living plants in woodland, such as bluebells, are adapted to grow, flower and set seed before the trees have fully grown their leaves and block out the Sun.

Bluebells cannot compete with trees in leaf for the light they need.

Animals of different species may compete with each other for the same food. For example, a leopard may kill an antelope to eat, but there will be many other animals, including lions and hyenas, that could take the antelope from the leopard. Leopards often take their kills up into a tree to keep them from other animals.

Animals of the same species may also compete with each other for resources other than food. In species where males mate with many females, competition to father the next generation can be intense.

Many birds have **territories** when they are breeding. They keep other birds out of it to give them enough space to rear their young. Robins need a territory that is large enough to provide all the food they need for their young. However, birds that feed away from the nest site, such as gannets or penguins, will have small nesting territories, just large enough to be out of pecking distance of other adults.

Science in action

We plant crop plants so close together that they compete heavily with each other. To help them grow better, we add nutrients in fertilisers, and water when it doesn't rain. Even then, competition has an effect.

Mass of seeds produced/kg/m²: 0, 1.0, 2.0, 3.0, 4.0
Number of seeds sown/m²: 0, 200, 400, 600, 800, 1000

Figure 1 Graph of yield versus density at planting.

Questions

1 Using the graph in Figure 1, describe how the seed yield of a crop depends on the density of plants in the crop.

2 Suggest why polar bears are white.

3 The robin is well known for its red breast and for singing loudly in spring. **(a)** What are the disadvantages of these adaptations? **(b)** What are the advantages?

4 **(a)** Copy the table headings from below and complete your table to show all the resources that animals might compete for. **(b)** Give examples of animals for each resource. **(c)** Explain how each animal is adapted to compete for that resource.

Resource	Example	Adaptation

5 Explain why blue poison dart frogs are blue as well as poisonous.

6 **(a)** It takes a lot of energy for a male peacock to grow his tail feathers and display them. Why does he bother? **(b)** Suggest an advantage to the females (in terms of genes) who mate with the male giving the best display.

7 Annual poppies (plants that live only one year) often suddenly appear on land that has recently been cleared of plants, but not in the following year. Explain this observation as fully as you can in terms of competition.

8 Using examples from what you have learnt so far, describe conditions in which plants may compete for light, water and nutrients.

9 Another strategy for avoiding predation is to look like something dangerous: for example, hoverflies look like wasps, but have no sting. Evaluate the advantages and disadvantages to the hoverfly and wasp of this similarity.

A*

Male peacocks display their huge tail feathers and call when there are females around. The male with the best display will mate with most females.

Science in action

We can model the effect of camouflage on the success of predators hunting and catching prey. A simple example would be using different coloured sticks on different coloured backgrounds and seeing which colours are selected by a human 'predator' in a limited time. Conservationists use computer models to investigate the effect of predator numbers on prey numbers, and vice versa, to help predict the effect of changing conditions on populations.

Learning objectives

Students should be able to:

- describe some adaptations that plants and animals have to avoid being eaten
- describe some adaptations that help animals and plants to compete for resources
- explain why animals compete for mates and territories.
- apply evidence from investigation into camouflage to explain real examples.

Key points

Plants compete with each other for light, and for water and nutrients from the soil.

Animals may compete with each other for food, mates and territory.

Animals and plants may deter predators with thorns, spines, poisons and warning colours.

Some animals use camouflage to hide from predators or prey.

ActiveTeach Resource: Adaptations against grazing – *Video*

Camouflage compete territory

Lesson activities

Starter

1 Ask students to compare how busy it is shopping early on a normal day compared with shopping on a sales day. What are the 'resources' that shoppers are looking for? How does the behaviour of the shoppers change in a popular store? Try to elicit the idea of competition between individuals when resources are limited.

2 Show students one or two short video clips, such as a male bird of paradise displaying to a female, and male red deer roaring and fighting in the presence of a female herd. Ask students what the videos have in common, what the males are competing for, and why it is worth the males using so much energy (in display and/or fighting) when it could jeopardise their survival.

Main

1 B1 4.3a Density of sowing This practical gives students an opportunity to plan an experiment to test the effects of density of sowing seeds on the growth of plants and to consider how to apply the evidence from any results to real-life contexts. If time and space allow, the plans could be carried out over a period of one or two weeks. (~30 minutes for plan)

2 B1 4.3b Predators and camouflage In this practical students collect and analyse data on the effect of camouflage on predation. (~40 minutes)

3 B1 4.3c Banded snail survey This activity encourages students to create predictions about the effect of changing conditions on camouflage in banded snails. The activity will benefit from access to the Internet to find the results of snail surveys, which can be used to test their hypotheses.

4 Plant adaptations Show the ActiveTeach video clip about some of the adaptations plants have developed against grazing. [AT]

Plenaries

1 Ask students to create clues for a crossword for the following words: camouflage, competition, adaptation, predation, territory, nutrient, warning colour. They could test their clues on a friend, or create the crossword using a crossword programme from the Internet. [AfL]

2 Give students three minutes to jot down as many examples as they can think of for competition in plants and in animals. They should identify which feature of the environment is being competed for in each case. Take examples from around the class and ask other students if they agree with them. [AfL]

Homework

1 Students could research other examples of camouflage, including that of predators (stripes on tigers, spots on leopards) to help them get closer to their prey without being noticed.

2 Worksheet B1 4.3d gives students the opportunity to apply their knowledge on competition to explain the impact of grey squirrels on red squirrel distribution.

Points to note

- This lesson will give students a chance to challenge some established, but incorrect ideas, such as red squirrel numbers are decreasing because they are attacked by grey squirrels or, in the cocktail stick experiment, that the poorly camouflaged sticks will die out, when in fact they may remain in small numbers because they are more difficult to 'hunt' when spread out.

Route to A*

Students should try to find out how scientists have tried to test and explain the evolution of complex male form and behaviour, and why it is thought to be driven by female mating choice.

Answers to Student Book questions

Answers to B1 4.3 can be found on p.204

B1 4.4 Extreme microorganisms

Link to the specification

B1 4.1d Organisms, including microorganisms, have features (adaptations) that enable them to survive in the conditions in which they normally live.

B1 4.1e Some organisms live in environments that are very extreme. Extremophiles may be tolerant to high levels of salt, high temperatures or high pressures.

How Science Works

SKU: B1.4 bullet point 1: Suggest how organisms are adapted to the conditions in which they live.

CA: B1 5.1b Identifying scientific evidence that supports an opinion. B4 5.4b Using secondary sources. B4 5.4c Identifying extra evidence that is required for a conclusion to be made.

B1 4.4 Extreme microorganisms

Learning objectives

- describe some extreme conditions that microorganisms can live in
- analyse the adaptations that microorganisms need to survive in some extreme conditions
- explain how bacteria that live in extreme conditions are important for other organisms.

Extreme temperatures

Organisms that can survive in the most extreme conditions are called **extremophiles**, and they are mostly microorganisms. In such conditions, there are few other organisms to compete with, but the adaptations needed to survive are extreme too.

The single-celled alga *Chlamydomonas nivalis* contains an extra-red pigment that protects it from the intensely bright light in snowy places that would destroy other cells. The colour also absorbs radiation, helping to keep the cells warmer than the snow around them. After the winter, when the cells have been buried by more snow, they grow **flagella** that help them move back up to the surface.

Examiner feedback

Be careful not to write that all extremophiles are microorganisms. A few animals are extremophiles, such as the Pompeii worm, which lives in extremely hot water close to deep sea vents (below), and tardigrades (microscopic animals often called water bears), which can survive temperatures as high as 151°C and as low as −270°C.

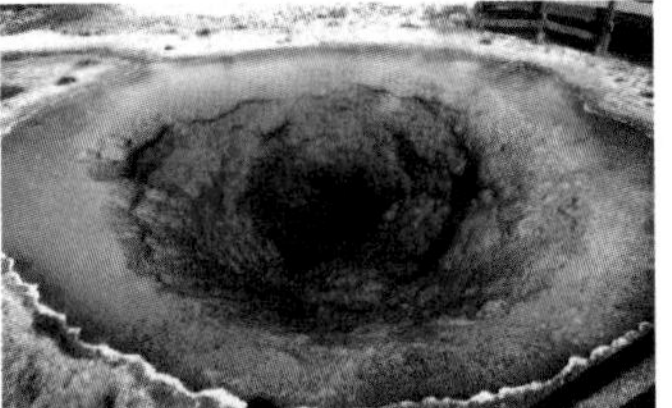
The temperature of the water here is over 60 °C, but there are many kinds of bacteria living in the water and around the edges of the hot spring.

Extreme high temperatures can be found in a few places on Earth, such as around hot springs, or around **hydrothermal vents** deep in the ocean. The heat comes from the rocks below ground. Most organisms die above about 40 °C because the proteins in their cells break down. Bacteria that survive at higher temperatures have proteins that don't break down as easily.

All the organisms living around this hydrothermal vent deep in the ocean depend on chemosynthetic bacteria.

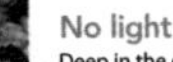

No light

Deep in the ocean, water pressure is great and there is no light. Amazingly, there are large communities of organisms that can live around hydrothermal vents on the ocean floor. They all depend on bacteria that use **chemosynthesis**, which combine chemicals from the water using heat to make sugars for food. These bacteria are the **producers** in these communities, like green plants on the Earth's surface.

Too many nutrients

Organisms need nutrients to make chemicals inside their cells. If the concentration of nutrients outside the cells gets too high, it draws water out of the cells. For most organisms this is fatal. Some microorganisms, however, have high levels of other chemicals, such as **amino acids** or sugars, inside their cells that stop the water moving out.

56

This lake is so salty that the man floats. This concentration of salt in his body would kill him, while the bacteria that make the water pink thrive in it.

Science in action

Soy sauce is made by fermenting soy beans. The fermentation needs microorganisms to break down the proteins in the beans. The strains of microorganisms used for fermentation must also tolerate high salt levels.

Many kinds of bacteria live in conditions of low oxygen inside the cow's gut and help to digest the grass. Without them, the cow could not survive on a diet of grass.

Too little oxygen

Most large organisms depend on oxygen for **aerobic respiration**, but in a few places there is very little or no oxygen, such as deep below ground. Here there are microorganisms that are adapted to get their energy in other ways. Some use chemicals, such as sulfur, instead of oxygen to release energy in **anaerobic respiration**. Another example of anaerobic respiration is the **fermentation** of glucose by yeast.

Questions

1 List the advantages and disadvantages of being an extremophile.

2 List all the extreme conditions described on these pages, and describe adaptations that make survival possible in those conditions.

3 The ability of microorganisms to live in extreme conditions makes life possible for many other organisms. Explain what this statement means.

4 Two competing theories for the origin of life on Earth are that:
- bacteria from other planets came to Earth on meteorites
- bacteria first originated around hydrothermal vents because the surface of the Earth was too extreme.

(a) Explain why both these theories are possible. **(b)** What else would you need to know in order to evaluate which theory was the more likely?

5 Suggest why microorganisms are more able to live in extreme conditions than larger organisms.

6 A student had some onions. She filled two jars with onions and added pickling vinegar. After six months, the onions she hadn't pickled had gone mushy, but the onions in one jar were still crunchy. After two years she opened the second jar and the onions were mushy. Explain these observations.

7 There are an estimated 10 times more bacterial cells in your body than human cells. Most of these bacterial cells live in your gut and play an important role in digestion. Evaluate the advantages and disadvantages of using antibiotics for curing infections. A*

Science in action

In November 1969, astronauts brought a camera back from the Moon that had been there since April 1967. Live bacteria were found growing inside the camera. Having contaminated the camera on Earth, these *Streptococcus mitis* bacteria survived 31 months in the vacuum of the moon's atmosphere.

Taking it further

Without the microorganisms in your gut you would be very ill, and might not even be able to live. They not only help you digest your food, they also produce vitamins that you need to stay healthy, but that aren't found in food. They also help 'train' your immune system to recognise what is foreign and should be attacked, and what is safe and should be left alone.

Interdependence and adaptation 57

Learning objectives

Students should be able to:

- describe some extreme conditions that microorganisms can live in
- analyse the adaptations that microorganisms need to survive in some extreme conditions
- explain how bacteria that live in extreme conditions are important for other organisms.
- evaluate evidence for the possibility of extremophile bacteria living on Mars. [H]

Key points

Microorganisms can be found in a wide range of extreme conditions.

Microorganisms that live in extreme conditions have particular adaptations that make survival possible.

Life on Earth may have started with microorganisms that could tolerate extreme conditions.

Lesson activities

Starter

1 Ask students to suggest the most extreme environments they know of on Earth. They should be able to explain why they have made their suggestion. Discussion should focus on what living organisms need from their environment and why some conditions are more suitable for life than others.

2 Ask students to make a quick list of the factors that plants need from their environment, and a list of the factors that animals need from their environment. Discuss any differences between the two lists. Then ask students to consider the conditions that microorganisms need from their environment and discuss the similarities and differences from their earlier lists. [AfL]

Aerobic respiration anaerobic respiration chemosynthesis extremophile
fermentation hydrothermal vent flagella producer

Main

1 Extremophiles Using the BBC Worldwide - Extremophiles, ask students to make notes about some extreme conditions that microorganisms survive in, and the limitations that their adaptations create for the organisms (i.e. that they cannot live in 'normal' conditions). Ask students why an astrobiologist is looking on Earth for life rather than out in Space. Students could then extend this to research the different kinds of extremes that bacteria, as well as the few multicellular extremophiles, can survive, including temperature, salinity, pH and desiccation. They could prepare a short report showing what they found out, and complete the sentence: 'The most extreme environment that organisms can survive is…', giving reasons for their choice.

2 B1 4.4a Is there life on Mars? Worksheet for class discussion. See Teacher and Technician Planning Pack for full details.

3 The video clip Shooting bugs at high speed looks at an experiment to investigate whether life (in the form of bacteria) could have come to Earth from space rather than have evolved here, an idea known as panspermia. Ask students to consider what conditions the bacteria need to survive in order to move around the Solar System. (You will need to remind students that they will get no marks for using the term 'bug' in its colloquial form to mean microorganism as in the video clip.) They should also consider the validity of the experiment – how well can the results from this experiment support the idea of panspermia?]

Plenaries

1 Ask students to work in pairs to produce three bullet points covering key ideas learnt in this lesson. Take examples from around the class and create discussion to agree on the three most important. [AfL]

2 Ask students to complete sentences related to this topic using at least two different connectives (e.g. because, but, when, and). Suitable sentences include: Organisms are found in the most extreme environments…; Most extremophiles are bacteria…; Extremophile bacteria could have been the first life on Earth….

Homework

1 Tell students that scientists are trying to discover which species of bacteria live in Lake Vostok, which is 4000 m under the Antarctic ice sheet. Ask students to write a list of precautions the scientists need to take to prevent samples from the lake being contaminated with bacteria at the surface, and to explain why those precautions will help.

2 Worksheet B1 4.4b includes questions on the normal gut flora of humans that practise what students have learnt in this and earlier lessons on adaptation and competition.

Points to note

- Students of higher ability should be asked to explain some of the adaptations that bacteria have to survive extreme conditions. Note that will require them to understand a little of the structure of bacteria, particularly the cell wall.

Route to A*

Students could research the physiological mechanisms that make it possible for extremophiles to survive extreme conditions. This may lead on to topics of biochemistry beyond student's understanding, so they should try to summarise the mechanisms rather than explain them in detail.

Answers to Student Book questions

Answers

1 Advantage: don't have to compete with other organisms because nothing else can live there;
disadvantages: need special adaptations to survive, and if conditions change may not be able to survive any longer.

2 Freezing cold: red colour in alga absorbs heat and protects from intense light, has flagella to move up to surface after winter.
Extreme heat: bacteria around hydrothermal vents have proteins that don't break down at high temperatures.
Extreme darkness: bacteria deep in the oceans use chemosynthesis to make food where there is no light.
Extreme salt: microorganisms in water contain high concentrations of other chemicals to stop water from being removed from the cell.
No oxygen: bacteria in a cow's gut can carry out anaerobic respiration without the need for oxygen.

3 Microorganisms that live in extreme conditions can provide nutrients that other organisms need for life: e.g. around hydrothermal vents where there would be no life if the bacteria could not survive, in the gut of cows (and other ruminants) where digestion by microorganisms of plant chemicals that cows can't digest makes it possible for cows to live on a diet of grass.

4 **(a)** We know that there are bacteria now that can survive in both sets of conditions. **(b)** Any suitable suggestions, such as evidence of bacteria on meteorites, evidence of conditions on early Earth, practical experiments that test survival of bacteria in conditions found in space (no air, high light intensity, very cold) or in conditions found around hydrothermal vents (high pressure, high temperature, high levels of nutrients, no light).

5 Unlike larger organisms, microorganisms do not need to evolve complex body systems to cope with extreme conditions.

6 The vinegar prevents the growth of many microorganisms (because it is acidic). Without the vinegar, the decay organisms start to break down the onions straight away. With vinegar, noticeable decay is prevented within six months. However, some bacteria can survive acidic conditions. They produce noticeable decay of the onions after 6 months and within 2 years in vinegar.

7 Antibiotics kill bacteria. The advantage of using them is that they can treat infections that are dangerous to human health, or even fatal. The disadvantage is that they also kill other bacteria. Many bacteria play an important role in the body of keeping us healthy (as in digestion of our food by gut bacteria, the products of which we then absorb). If those bacteria are killed, then we can become unwell.

B1 4.5 The effect of changing environments

Link to the specification

B1 4.2a Changes in the environment affect the distribution of living organisms.

B1 4.2b Animals and plants are subjected to environmental changes. Such changes may be caused by living or non-living factors such as a change in a competitor, or in the average temperature or rainfall.

B1 4.2d Environmental changes can be measured using non-living indicators such as oxygen levels, temperature and rainfall.

Ideas for practical work

The use of maximum-minimum thermometers, rainfall gauges and oxygen meters.

How Science Works

SKU: B1.4 bullet point 5: Evaluate data concerned with the effect of environmental changes on the distribution and behaviour of living organisms.

CA: B4 3.2a Appreciating that, unless certain variables are controlled, the results may not be valid. B4 3.2d Considering the resolution of the measuring device.

B1 4.5 The effect of changing environments

Learning objectives

- describe some ways in which environmental changes can be monitored
- describe examples of how the changes in the environment are affecting the distribution of organisms and explain why these changes are taking place
- evaluate evidence for the impact of environmental change on behaviour and distribution of species.

Changing environments

Organisms have adaptations that help them survive well in particular conditions, so if those conditions change it may make it more difficult for them to live in that place, or it may make it easier for other organisms to come into the area and compete. Either way, this may cause a change in the **distribution** of species.

Practical

Using a maximum–minimum thermometer and rainfall gauge, keep a weather diary for a month, recording a range of environmental conditions such as temperature and rainfall. Describe how the weather changed during that month.

Figure 1 A maximum–minimum thermometer and rainfall gauge.

Science in action

Many environmental groups are carrying out long-term surveys of organisms to help identify the effects of climate change and to predict what will happen to species in the future. Examples include surveys of birds, butterflies and bees. Some groups ask for help from the public to make their surveys as extensive as possible.

Figure 2 The temperature record for central England since 1772. The blue lines are yearly measurements shown as the difference from the average for 1961–90; the red line is a 20-year running mean of annual-average anomalies.

Environmental conditions are always changing. In the UK weather changes with the seasons. We also get different weather depending on which way the wind is blowing. Organisms that live in the UK can cope with this amount of change, so how much change is needed to affect them?

Short-term changes, such as freak storms that cause flooding, or occasional extreme temperatures, can kill organisms. However, the distribution of a whole species is more likely to be affected by long-term changes in climatic conditions.

Temperature records from thermometer measurements for England suggest that recently there has been an increase in average temperature. Similar changes are being seen in other parts of the world, and scientists think that this explains changes in the distribution of some species.

58

The effect on birds

In 1996 little egrets started breeding in southern England, expanding their breeding range from Europe. Other changes are happening too. Some birds, such as blackcaps and chiffchaffs, that used to migrate south for winter are now staying all year round as there is usually more insect food still available for them.

Chiffchaffs are mainly insect eaters. Insects either die or hibernate during cold winters.

Other species seem to be suffering a lack of food. In 2008 there were reports that breeding numbers of sea bird species, such as puffins and kittiwakes, that live in the North Sea decreased rapidly in the previous few years. The average temperature of the sea had increased by about 1 °C and scientists linked this to a loss of sand eels, which the birds feed on.

Examiner feedback

It is important to realise that even if the world is warming up, the effect is not the same for every country. There are circumstances that could result in the average temperatures in the UK becoming colder.

Sand eels are the main food source for puffins and their chicks in the summer.

The effect on bees

Recently there has been a rapid decrease in the numbers of bees, both wild and those kept by bee keepers. Many reasons for this have been suggested, including climate change and loss of wildflowers due to increased building and farming. Cold, wet springs make it difficult for bees to get food when they need to start building new colonies. Also, warmer winters make it easier for a mite parasite to survive. This parasite has destroyed bees in many hives. However, loss of a range of food plants due to farming might also be a cause.

Questions

1 The data for the temperature graph in Figure 2 were manipulated in several ways before graphing. Suggest reasons for each of the following: **(a)** only recent data from sites similar to the historical sites were included, not the recent data collected from all over the UK **(b)** the red line is an average of several years, which smoothes out short-term variations.

2 Describe the trends of temperature shown in the graph in Figure 2.

3 **(a)** Suggest one advantage to the blackcap or chiffchaff of staying in the UK over winter. **(b)** Suggest one disadvantage.

4 **(a)** Explain why we cannot be sure that climate change is causing the decrease in numbers of bees. **(b)** Suggest what research should be carried out on bees to identify what is happening to them.

5 Swallows are insect-eating birds that return to the UK in early April to breed; suggest how changes in the climate may affect breeding populations of swallows.

6 Describe as fully as you can, with examples, the possible effects of climate change on species in the UK.

7 Bees fed a diet of five different pollens produced more glucose oxidase than bees fed with only one kind of pollen. Glucose oxidase preserves honey and food for bee larvae from microorganisms that cause disease. Explain as fully as you can how an increase in farming might lead to a decrease in bee numbers.

8 Design a web page highlighting the urgency for finding a solution to the decline in bee numbers. You should provide no more than 100 words and one illustration.

A*

Science in action

Bees are pollinators of many plants, including many of our crop plants. It is estimated that the UK earns about £200 million each year from crops pollinated by bees. Urgent research is needed to explain how quickly numbers are changing, and what the main causes are, if we are to stop an effect on our harvest **yields**.

Bees are essential for the **pollination** of many plants.

Interdependence and adaptation 59

Learning objectives

Students should be able to:

- describe some ways in which environmental changes can be monitored
- describe examples of how the changes in the environment are affecting the distribution of organisms and explain why these changes are taking place
- evaluate evidence for the impact of environmental change on changing distribution of species
- explain the value and impact of running means on identifying long-term trends in data.

Key points

Changing environmental conditions can affect the distribution of species, because the adaptations they have are no longer useful or because invading species can compete better.

Long-term data collection is needed to measure changing climate.

ActiveTeach Resource: Climate change – *Spreadsheet*

Lesson activities

Starter

1 Ask students to suggest what they would consider are the first signs of spring each year. Encourage discussion about why those signs occur when they do, such as whether they are linked to increase in temperature or to an

Distribution yield

increase in daylight hours. Ask them to suggest how they would measure whether spring was getting earlier, as many people suggest.

2 Give students 3 minutes to jot down examples of how environmental factors, such as light, warmth, water and nutrient availability, change over the short-term of a day or longer, such as a year, decade or century. Take examples from around the class, and ask how the different timescales of changes might affect living organisms.

Main

1 B1 4.5a Recording the weather Refer to sheet in Teacher and Technician Planning Pack.

2 B1 4.5b Where have the bees gone? Refer to sheet in Teacher and Technician Planning Pack.

3 B1 4.5c Climate change and laying date Refer to sheet in Teacher and Technician Planning Pack.

Plenaries

1 Give students the statement: 'Environmental change is harming organisms' and ask students to think of one example that supports the statement and one that is against. Take examples from around the class until all have been considered. Students should briefly discuss the relative merits of each example. [AfL]

2 Tell students that scientists have discovered that the number of 'sprogs' is decreasing rapidly. Ask them to note down how they would go about trying to identify if climate change is the cause, and which other factors they might need to consider. Take examples from around the class for discussion on how to design the experiment to produce reliable results. [AfL]

Homework

1 Worksheet B1 4.5d includes questions on the interpretation of data about the response of organisms to changing environmental conditions. The sheet explains the interpretation of standard error bars on graphs, although you may wish to discuss this further with students in class beforehand.

2 Ask students to write a short article for the school website about the impact of environmental changes on organisms and the concerns that people should consider about the future of species in the UK.

Points to note

- Although this lesson includes measuring environmental conditions, students should be made aware that not all changes to species distribution are the effect of climate change. For example, changes to bee distribution may be linked more to changing environmental use by humans than to climate.
- Measuring the distribution of organisms is covered fully in B2, hence techniques for sampling distribution of organisms are not covered here.

Route to A*

Many media reports now state 'climate change' as the obvious culprit for changes in organisms, but this is not always the case. Ask students to find an example of a media report in which climate change has been invoked as the reason why the distribution of some organisms is changing. They should evaluate the report for its accuracy of content, and reliability of conclusions.

Answers to Student Book questions

Answers

1 **(a)** To make sure the comparison of recent and historical data was valid; recent data from all over might skew the data in a different way. **(b)** It is easier to see long-term change; variability in the short-term can be large, which would swamp long-term gradual change.

2 Up to about 1920, the long-term average was mostly below the 1961–90 value; then it increased above that value for the early part of the 20th century. Since 1990 it has increased rapidly.

3 **(a)** any suitable point, e.g. it does not waste energy flying long distances; males can set up a territory earlier than birds that did migrate. **(b)** If there is an extremely cold winter, then birds that stay are more likely to die as food is killed off.

4 **(a)** There are many other possible factors affecting bee numbers. **(b)** Any suitable suggestion, e.g. compare loss of food plants in different areas with effect on bee numbers, practical work on survival and impact of parasitic mite on bees.

5 Increasing temperature might change the availability of the insects that swallows depend on for food when they are in the UK. If they depend on particular insect species, and the distribution of that species moves (such as further north), then there may be less food for the swallows and their numbers will decrease. However, if swallows feed on many species of insect, and the number of insects in general increases with increasing temperature, then the number of swallows could also increase.

6 Species that live in warm areas may extend their range further north and increase in numbers, such as the little egret. Species that are adapted to cold areas may die out, such as the snow bunting. Species that depend on a particular food at a particular time, such as the puffin and kittiwake, may decrease in number if the food appears at a different time due to climate change.

7 Farming replaces areas of mixed plants, such as woodland, hedgerow and meadow, with large areas of very few kinds of plants, such as wheat or grass for cows. If bees are not able to get a range of pollen then they produce less glucose oxidase, so allowing growth of microorganisms on food for larvae. As a result, the growth of larvae will suffer and so there will be fewer bees.

8 The 100-word article should include the following basic points: Plants need pollination to produce seed. Bees pollinate many kinds of plants. These plants include many of our crops, such as wheat, that we use to make our food. It also includes all the vegetable and fruit plant species that we eat. Without bees, the plants will make less seed/fruit and we will have less to eat.

B1 4.6 Pollution indicators

Link to the specification

B1 4.2a Changes in the environment affect the distribution of living organisms.

B1 4.2c Living organisms can be used as indicators of pollution:

- lichens can be used as air pollution indicators particularly of the concentration of sulphur dioxide in the atmosphere
- invertebrate animals can be used as water pollution indicators and are used as indicators of the concentration of dissolved oxygen in water.

B1 4.2d Environmental changes can be measured using non-living indicators such as oxygen levels, temperature and rainfall.

Ideas for practical work

Investigating the effect of phosphate on oxygen levels in water using jars with algae, water and varying numbers of drops of phosphate, then monitor oxygen using meter.

Investigations of environmental conditions and organisms in a habitat such as a pond.

How Science Works

SKU: B1.4 bullet 5: Evaluate data concerned with the effect of environmental changes on the distribution and behaviour of living organisms.

CA: B4 1.1a Being able to develop a hypothesis; B4 5.2c Recognising and identifying the cause of anomalous results. B4 5.3a Describing the relationship between two variables and deciding whether the relationship is causal or by association.

B1 4.6 Pollution indicators

Learning objectives

- describe some ways in which human activity is changing the distribution of organisms
- explain why lichens can be used to monitor air pollution
- explain how aquatic invertebrates can be used to monitor water pollution.

Pollution changes the environment

Pollution from human activity damages the environment and the organisms that live there. Many industrial processes burn fossil fuels for energy or to release other chemicals for manufacture. Some of the waste gases from this burning are poisonous, or are acidic; when they dissolve in water droplets in cloud, they can form **acid rain**. The acid is damaging to many plants and animals.

We also pollute water by releasing chemicals directly into it, for example when too much fertiliser is put on farmland or when chemicals are released from factories or sewage treatment plants into the water. There are laws against causing air and water pollution, but they can be difficult to monitor and enforce.

Science skills

The lower the pH, the more acidic a solution is.

a Describe the relationship between the number of species of plants and the acidity of the water in a pond.

b Give two explanations for the relationship between number of species of insect larvae and water acidity.

c How could you improve the reliability of your answers?

Table 1 Pond data.

Pond	pH of water	Number of species of insect larvae	Number of species of plants
1	4.4	4	8
2	4.8	5	11
3	5.7	9	16
4	6.6	19	23
5	8.1	14	21

The lichen on the left is a clean-air species. The lichen on the right tolerates some air pollution.

If there is a high level of pollution, organisms may be killed and the distribution of species will change. We can use the presence of organisms that are particularly affected by, or tolerant of, pollution as **pollution indicators**.

Lichens and air pollution

Lichens are often found on trees and walls. There are many different species; some can only grow where there is no air pollution while others are tolerant of different kinds of air pollution.

Surveys of lichens can show quickly and easily how polluted the air has become since the lichens started growing. Recent surveys indicate that sulfur-intolerant species are colonising city areas where they had died out, showing that sulfur dioxide pollution in these areas has decreased.

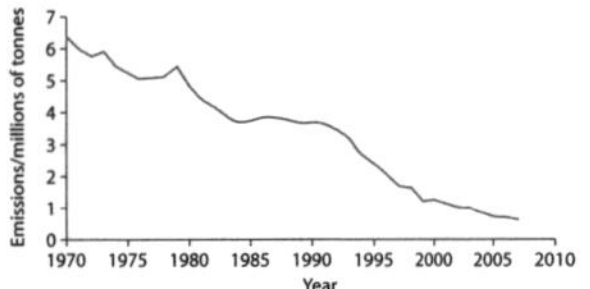

Figure 1 Sulfur dioxide emissions into air in the UK have reduced as we changed to low-sulfur fuels, and because of laws that control emissions from industry.

Practical

Carry out a lichen survey in your area, and use the species you find to decide where there is the most air pollution.

Aquatic invertebrates as pollution indicators

Most **aquatic** organisms get the oxygen they need for respiration directly from the water they live in, not from air. Fertilisers and sewage contain high levels of nitrogen and phosphate. If they drain into water, they can cause plants, algae and bacteria to grow rapidly and use up the oxygen during respiration.

As oxygen concentration drops, some organisms, such as mayfly nymphs, die because they can't get the oxygen they need. Other organisms can survive in water that has a very low oxygen concentration because they have special adaptations. The bloodworm is red because it contains haemoglobin, which combines with oxygen, as it does in our red blood cells. Different aquatic invertebrates can tolerate different oxygen concentrations, so we can use their presence or absence to indicate how polluted the water is.

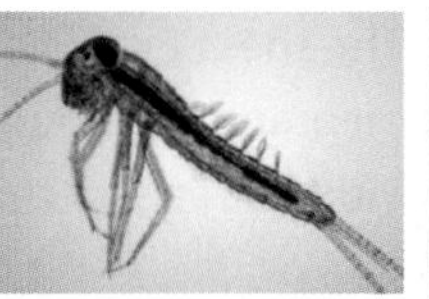

The mayfly nymph (left) can only live in unpolluted water, but the bloodworm (right) can survive in highly polluted water.

Questions

1. Define the word *pollution* and give examples of air and water pollution.
2. Explain why adding nitrogen to water reduces the oxygen concentration of the water.
3. In the 1970s it was shown that forests in Scandinavia, far from any industrial areas, were being damaged by acid rain. Suggest how this could happen.
4. Explain how bloodworms are adapted to low oxygen concentration.
5. Use the graph in Figure 1 to suggest what you would expect to see from lichen surveys: **(a)** from the Scottish Highlands in 1970 and today **(b)** in the centre of Manchester in 1970 and today. Explain your answers.
6. Compare the use of lichen surveys with roadside air pollution monitoring, and suggest the advantages and disadvantages of each.
7. Explain in detail why it may be easy to identify the source of water pollution caused by a poisonous chemical but difficult to find the source for high levels of nitrate in water. A*

Science in action

Gas analysers are fixed beside major roads and in cities so that air pollution can be measured continuously. This helps councils identify areas and times of increased risk of pollution.

We can measure the concentration of dissolved oxygen in water using an oxygen meter.

Science in action

The Biological Monitoring Working Party has a procedure for assessing water quality using aquatic invertebrates. Each type of invertebrate scores a number according to how likely they are to be found in clean (highest value) or polluted water (lower values). An average score is calculated from all the organisms found. This makes it easier to compare the amount of pollution in rivers, streams and lakes in different parts of the country.

Taking it further

Historical evidence from the distribution of dark and light forms of peppered moths shows evolution in action. Pollution (in the form of soot in smoke) resulted in an increase in the proportion of dark forms because they were camouflaged on sooty tree branches. Now air is cleaner, the proportion of light forms has increased because these are less visible against the natural colour of tree bark.

Learning objectives

Students should be able to:

- describe some ways in which human activity is changing the distribution of organisms
- explain why lichens can be used to monitor air pollution
- explain how aquatic invertebrates can be used to monitor water pollution
- evaluate the usefulness of organisms as pollution indicators.

Key points

The distribution of different species of lichens can be used as an indicator of air pollution.

The distribution of different species of aquatic invertebrates can be used as an indicator of water pollution.

ActiveTeach Resource: Water samples – *Spreadsheet*

Lesson activities

Starter

1 Describe a lichen as an organism that grows on walls and trees. Ask students to suggest a link between litmus paper and the lichen. Prompt for a suitable answer by asking them what the litmus paper does, and link the answer of the presence of acidity indicating the presence of air pollution.

2 Ask students to consider how useful an organism that indicates the presence or absence of pollution could be.

Acid rain	aquatic	lichen	pollution	pollution indicator

Main

1 B1 4.6a Phosphate and oxygen in water Refer to sheet in Teacher and Technician Planning Pack.

2 B1 4.6b Investigating freshwater organisms Refer to **Worksheet B1 4.6b**, **Worksheet B1 4.6c** and the ActiveTeach activity *Water samples*. [AT]

3 What's in your backyard? The Environment Agency has a website containing interactive maps that students could use to identify sources of air and water pollution in their local area. The maps contain more information than students need, so they should be directed to focus on sulphur pollution on the air pollution map, and water pollution. They should identify a range of sources of pollution and consider the local effects of that pollution on living organisms.

Plenaries

1 Play 'indicator hangman' by choosing one of the indicator species mentioned in the lesson. Pick three students and ask each in turn to give you a letter. If the letter is in your word, write it in the correct position on the board. Students should suggest the word as soon as they can and gain points for the number of blanks left in the word. Repeat with another suitable word. [AfL]

2 Give students a few minutes to jot down as many advantages and disadvantages they can think of for using living organisms as pollution indicators. Take examples from around the class, and when most have been covered, ask students to decide in which conditions they would use organisms to indicate pollution and in which conditions it would not be useful. [AfL]

Homework

1 Worksheet B1 4.6d includes questions on the use of lichens for indicating the presence of sulphur dioxide in the air.

2 Students could research examples of changing water quality since the mid-1900s, using examples such as salmon and other freshwater fish as indicators of clean water. They should also look at the measures used to try to improve water quality in rivers (such as the Thames) where pollution was once a major problem.

Points to note

- Surveying lichens in the UK for distribution in relation to sulphur dioxide pollution will no longer provide useful data because legislation has reduced atmospheric sulphur dioxide concentration to low levels. However, lichen species distribution is still strongly affected by atmospheric nitrogen oxides as these are more difficult to control.

Route to A*

Direct students to the online Open Air Laboratories (OPAL) lichen survey which is being carried out with support from the Field Studies Council and Natural History Museum. From this, they could analyse the changing distribution of lichens in the UK, and assess the use of other pollution indicators that are being surveyed, such as tarspot on sycamore leaves.

Answers to Student Book questions

Science skills

a As acidity increases (pH gets lower), fewer plant species are found, suggesting that acidity damages plants. Most plant species are found around pH6.6. Fewer are found at pH8.1, but the difference is quite small and each pH measurement comes from a different pond. Therefore it is difficult to tell from this small sample if higher pH also damages plants.

b Increasing acidity between pH6.6 and pH4.4 could be damaging larvae, or there are fewer kinds of plants for larvae to feed on at lower pH levels.

c Need to gather evidence from more ponds to check if the findings from these ponds are similar.

Answers

1 Any definition that means the same as: adding materials to the environment that can damage living organisms. Air pollution examples include sulfur dioxide gas from industry (also nitrogen oxides from traffic exhaust). Water pollution includes high levels of nutrients/nitrogen from fertiliser run-off or from sewage, chemicals from industry leaked into water system.

2 Nitrogen is a nutrient that plants need for healthy growth; extra nitrogen will make it possible for water plants to grow faster, so they respire faster, taking oxygen from the water.

3 Pollutant gases released into the air from industry were carried in the wind to Scandinavia; there they fell in rain, increasing acidity and damaging forests.

4 Haemoglobin combines easily with oxygen, so when oxygen concentration is low it helps the worm absorb any oxygen from the water much more effectively.

5 **(a)** The Scottish Highlands are far from industry and not heavily populated, so in 1970 would expect that there would have been many sulfur-intolerant species then and still will have now – so little change. **(b)** Central Manchester is a big industrial and highly populated area, so in 1970 there would have been a lot of air pollution in the city from houses, industry and traffic and so mostly sulfur-tolerant lichens would have been found. Now we would expect to also find sulfur-intolerant lichens because of reduced sulfur dioxide concentration in air.

6 Lichen surveys show long-term changes because lichens take a long time to grow – if newer species are different to old ones, that can infer a change in air pollution. Easy to do, doesn't require special equipment.
Roadside monitoring shows changes over days, or even hours, and gives numeric, quantitative data about chemicals being measured. Requires special equipment that needs maintaining to work well. Produces a lot of data that can be recorded by computer for analysis.

7 Very few industries produce poisonous chemicals, and different industries produce different chemicals, so it is likely that there will be only one or two possible sources for a leak of a specific poisonous chemical. Nitrogen-containing chemicals can come from farmland, from sewage and other sources. Although sewage is treated at particular places, so that a leak could be easily associated with a source, fertilisers are spread over all farmland, so over-use at a particular place (leading to run-off into the river) would be difficult to identify.

B1 5.1 Energy in biomass

Link to the specification

B1.5.1a Radiation from the Sun is the source of energy for most communities of living organisms. Green plants and algae absorb a small amount of the light that reaches them. The transfer from light energy to chemical energy occurs during photosynthesis. This energy is stored in the substances that make up the cells of the plants.

B1.5.1b The mass of living material (biomass) at each stage in a food chain is less than it was at the previous stage. The biomass at each stage can be drawn to scale and shown as a pyramid of biomass.

B1.5.1c The amounts of material and energy contained in the biomass of organisms is reduced at each successive stage in a food chain because:

- some materials and energy are always lost in the organisms' waste materials
- respiration supplies all the energy needs for living processes, including movement. Much of this energy is eventually transferred to the surroundings.

How Science Works

SKU: B1.5 bullet 1: Interpret pyramids of biomass and construct them from appropriate information.

CA: B4.5.2a Identifying causes of variation in data.

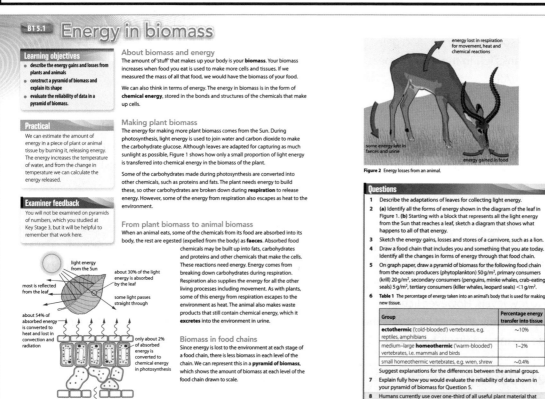

B1 5.1 Energy in biomass

Learning objectives

- **describe the energy gains and losses from plants and animals**
- **construct a pyramid of biomass and explain its shape**
- **evaluate the reliability of data in a pyramid of biomass.**

Practical

We can estimate the amount of energy in a piece of plant or animal tissue by burning it, releasing energy. The energy increases the temperature of water, and from the change in temperature we can calculate the energy released.

Examiner feedback

You will not be examined on pyramids of numbers, which you studied at Key Stage 3, but it will be helpful to remember that work here.

About biomass and energy

The amount of 'stuff' that makes up your body is your **biomass**. Your biomass increases when food you eat is used to make more cells and tissues. If we measured the mass of all that food, we would have the biomass of your food.

We can also think in terms of energy. The energy in biomass is in the form of **chemical energy**, stored in the bonds and structures of the chemicals that make up cells.

Making plant biomass

The energy for making more plant biomass comes from the Sun. During photosynthesis, light energy is used to join water and carbon dioxide to make the carbohydrate glucose. Although leaves are adapted for capturing as much sunlight as possible, Figure 1 shows how only a small proportion of light energy is transferred into chemical energy in the biomass of the plant.

Some of the carbohydrates made during photosynthesis are converted into other chemicals, such as proteins and fats. The plant needs energy to build these, so other carbohydrates are broken down during **respiration** to release energy. However, some of the energy from respiration also escapes as heat to the environment.

From plant biomass to animal biomass

When an animal eats, some of the chemicals from its food are absorbed into its body, the rest are egested (expelled from the body) as **faeces**. Absorbed food chemicals may be built up into fats, carbohydrates and proteins and other chemicals that make the cells. These reactions need energy. Energy comes from breaking down carbohydrates during respiration. Respiration also supplies the energy for all the other living processes including movement. As with plants, some of this energy from respiration escapes to the environment as heat. The animal also makes waste products that still contain chemical energy, which it **excretes** into the environment in urine.

light energy from the Sun
most is reflected from the leaf
about 30% of the light energy is absorbed by the leaf
some light passes straight through
about 54% of absorbed energy is converted to heat and lost in convection and radiation
only about 2% of absorbed energy is converted to chemical energy in photosynthesis
about 44% of absorbed energy is lost in evaporation

Figure 1 What happens to light energy falling on a leaf.

Biomass in food chains

Since energy is lost to the environment at each stage of a food chain, there is less biomass in each level of the chain. We can represent this in a **pyramid of biomass**, which shows the amount of biomass at each level of the food chain drawn to scale.

62

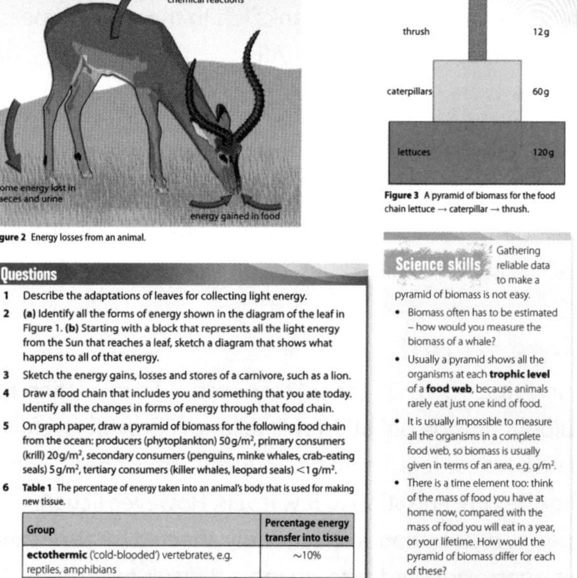

Figure 2 Energy losses from an animal.

Figure 3 A pyramid of biomass for the food chain lettuce → caterpillar → thrush.

Questions

1 Describe the adaptations of leaves for collecting light energy.

2 **(a)** Identify all the forms of energy shown in the diagram of the leaf in Figure 1. **(b)** Starting with a block that represents all the light energy from the Sun that reaches a leaf, sketch a diagram that shows what happens to all of that energy.

3 Sketch the energy gains, losses and stores of a carnivore, such as a lion.

4 Draw a food chain that includes you and something that you ate today. Identify all the changes in forms of energy through that food chain.

5 On graph paper, draw a pyramid of biomass for the following food chain from the ocean: producers (phytoplankton) 50 g/m², primary consumers (krill) 20 g/m², secondary consumers (penguins, minke whales, crab-eating seals) 5 g/m², tertiary consumers (killer whales, leopard seals) <1 g/m².

6 **Table 1** The percentage of energy taken into an animal's body that is used for making new tissue.

Group	Percentage energy transfer into tissue
ectothermic ('cold-blooded') vertebrates, e.g. reptiles, amphibians	~10%
medium–large **homeothermic** ('warm-blooded') vertebrates, i.e. mammals and birds	1–2%
small homeothermic vertebrates, e.g. wren, shrew	~0.4%

Suggest explanations for the differences between the animal groups.

7 Explain fully how you would evaluate the reliability of data shown in your pyramid of biomass for Question 5.

8 Humans currently use over one-third of all useful plant material that grows on Earth every year. Explain fully the impact of an increasing human population on other life in terms of energy flow. A*

Science skills

Gathering reliable data to make a pyramid of biomass is not easy.

- Biomass often has to be estimated – how would you measure the biomass of a whale?
- Usually a pyramid shows all the organisms at each **trophic level** of a **food web**, because animals rarely eat just one kind of food.
- It is usually impossible to measure all the organisms in a complete food web, so biomass is usually given in terms of an area, e.g. g/m².
- There is a time element too: think of the mass of food you have at home now, compared with the mass of food you will eat in a year, or your lifetime. How would the pyramid of biomass differ for each of these?

Each of these issues will affect the data that are collected.

Examiner feedback

Remember what you learned about the digestive system at Key Stage 3. It will help you understand this chapter, although you will not be examined on it at GCSE.

Energy 63

Learning objectives

Students should be able to:

- describe the energy gains and losses from plants and animals
- draw a pyramid of biomass and explain its shape
- evaluate the reliability of data in a pyramid of biomass.
- construct Sankey diagrams to describe energy flow in a community.

ActiveTeach Resource: Pyramids of biomass – *Powerpoint presentation*

Key points

Energy flows from sunlight, through plants and animals in a food chain and is lost to the environment as heat energy.

The biomass of each level in a food chain is usually less than in the previous level.

A pyramid of biomass is a scale representation of the amount of biomass in each level of a food chain.

Lesson activities

Starter

1 Ask students to create a mind map around the term *food web* and use it to assess what they have remembered from work in KS2 and KS3 on food chains and feeding relationships. Return to the mind maps for the plenary.

2 Give students 4 minutes to jot down all the ways that they gained and lost energy yesterday. In each case, ask them to identify which form the energy was in. Take examples from round the class, to make sure that chemical energy in food, body tissues and waste, and heat energy have all been considered. Then ask where the heat energy has come from. This should remind students of the link between respiration and energy.

Biomass chemical energy egest excrete faeces food web photosynthesis pyramid of biomass respiration trophic level

Main

1 Pyramids of biomass The ActiveTeach presentation *Pyramids of biomass* contains a series of slides. On the first slide, ask students to comment on what the sketched pyramid shows. Attempt to elicit responses such as 'the amount of biomass in each trophic level of a food chain', or 'how the amount of biomass in a trophic level gets less higher up a food chain'. Then ask students to describe the key difference between the sketch and Figure 2 in the Student Book lesson B1 5.1: Figure 2 shows numbers in grams while the sketch does not. Introduce the terms *qualitative* and *quantitative* and use the two diagrams to illustrate the differences. The next part of the presentation explains how to construct a pyramid of biomass. At the end of the presentation, students use graph paper to construct their own pyramids using the data on the last slide. [AT]

2 B1 5.1a Measuring biomass in food chains This practical gives students an opportunity to discover some of the limitations in the data described in pyramids of biomass.

3 B1 5.1b Sankey diagrams This activity introduces students to the use of another model, the Sankey diagram, which describes energy transfers in a system. This may be familiar from work in other areas of science and can help to reinforce the concept of energy generally in systems. If not, students may need help in interpreting the first diagram. Skills Sheet 36 could support the activity. Students will need graph paper to complete this activity.

Plenaries

1 Return to the mind maps that students created in *Starter 1*. Ask them to check what they had written, and then to add anything that they have learnt in this lesson, including the use and evaluation of models for describing complex living systems. [AfL]

2 Ask students to quickly sketch and annotate diagrams that show the energy gains and losses for a producer and for a consumer. Take examples of annotations from students and collate them onto sketches on the board. Ask students to explain any differences between the annotations on the two diagrams. [AfL]

Homework

1 **Work sheet B1 5.1c** provides some questions on the construction and evaluation of pyramids of biomass.

2 Ask students to write a short report on the value of using models to describe complex systems, with specific reference to pyramids of biomass, and Sankey diagrams if covered in the lesson.

Points to note

- The specification refers to 'energy loss'– although in other sciences it is considered more appropriate to talk about energy transfer, to avoid conflict with the theory that energy can neither be created nor destroyed, in this area of biology the old term is still used.

Route to A*

Ask students to research pyramids of energy and write a short report (max. one side of A4) on how they are calculated, how they differ from pyramids of biomass, and evaluating their usefulness in comparison with pyramids of biomass.

Answers to Student Book questions

1 Flat surface that is wide and thin to intercept as much light as possible; green chlorophyll to capture light energy.

2 **(a)** Light energy from sunlight, heat energy released to environment, chemical energy in plant material. **(b)** Diagram showing a block representing 100%, showing clearly the following breakdown (a Sankey diagram would be appropriate but is not essential): 30% absorbed, 70% reflected or passes straight through; the 30% is then broken down further, so approx.16% (i.e. 54% of 30%) of original energy converted to heat, approx.13% (44% of 30%) lost in evaporation, approx.0.6% (2% of 30%) used in photosynthesis.

3 Sketch showing carnivore, energy gain from food, energy loss as heat to environment and as chemical energy in faeces and urine, energy stored as chemical energy in animal tissues.

4 Any suitable chain that starts with a producer and ends with human, e.g. grass ⟶ cow (burger) ⟶ human; energy changes should show light energy from sunlight to plant transferred to plant as chemical energy, chemical energy in plant and animals transferred as heat energy to environment or as chemical energy in next organism in chain.

5 Pyramid of four levels, producers at bottom and tertiary consumers at top, each level of same height but width drawn to scale as far as possible to show values indicated.

6 Endotherms use some of the energy from their food to keep their body temperature stable and usually above the temperature of their surroundings, so less of the energy from food can be used for making body tissue.
Small endotherms have a higher surface area to body ratio, so they lose heat to the environment faster than a larger endotherm; so they will use even more energy to maintain their body temperature.
Ectotherms do not need to use energy from food to maintain a constant body temperature, so more of that energy can be used to make new tissues.

7 Compare the data with similar data from other studies, to see if they show a similar range of values; check how the data were collected, and decide if the methods used would provide reliable results; attempt to repeat some of the measurements to check how repeatable they are.

8 Any energy taken from the system as plants by humans means that energy is not available to other animals. The amount of plants on Earth cannot increase. So an increasing human population will take more energy, in the form of plants. This will reduce the amount of energy, and therefore the number of other consumers on Earth. It may not affect the number of decomposers as they feed on all dead and waste organic matter, including humans.

B1 5.2 Natural recycling

Link to the specification

B1.6.1a Living things remove materials from the environment for growth and other processes. These materials are returned to the environment either in waste materials or when living things die and decay.

B1.6.1b Materials decay because they are broken down (digested) by microorganisms. Microorganisms are more active and digest materials faster in warm, moist, aerobic conditions.

B1.6.1c The decay process releases substances that plants need to grow.

B1.6.1d In a stable community, the processes that remove materials are balanced by processes that return materials. The materials are constantly cycled.

Ideas for practical work

Design and carry out an investigation to measure the rate of decay of bread by, for example, exposing cubes of bread to air before placing them in sealed Petri dishes at different temperatures and/or different moisture levels.

Potato decay competition, using fresh potatoes. Candidates decide on the environmental conditions and the rate of decay is measured over a two week period.

How Science Works

CA: B4.3.2a Appreciating that, unless certain variables are controlled, the results may not be valid; B4.4.2c Choosing the most appropriate form of presentation; B4.5.4a Writing a conclusion, based on evidence that relates correctly to known facts.

B1 5.2 Natural recycling

Learning objectives

- explain what happens during decay
- describe and explain the best conditions for microbial decay
- explain the importance of decay for the continual recycling of nutrients in the environment.

Taking it further

Studies can show how energy is transferred in natural ecosystems. Although we think mostly of the large plants and animals we can see, most of the energy in an ecosystem is within the microorganisms that cause decay.

Science in action

Microbial decay plays an important role in helping us treat sewage (waste water from bathrooms and kitchens). Microorganisms in the sewage use nutrients from the breakdown of faeces, urine and other materials for growth. Cleaning the microorganisms out of the water removes the nutrients too, making it safe to return the water to rivers, streams and lakes.

A matter of life and death

The tissues of your body are made of many elements, which you get from your food. We call these elements nutrients because we need them for growth. A lack in any one of these over a long period would affect your growth and health.

Table 1 Important nutrients in a human body.

Nutrients	Percentage of body weight	Role in body
nitrogen	3.2%	forms part of proteins, DNA in all cells
calcium	1.8%	strengthens bones and teeth, needed for nerve and muscle activity
phosphorus	1.0%	part of DNA, also strengthens bones and teeth
sodium	0.2%	needed for nerve and muscle activity
iron	0.007%	haemoglobin in red blood cells carries oxygen

During photosynthesis plants make **carbohydrates**, which contain only carbon, hydrogen and oxygen. To grow well, the plant must have other nutrients, such as nitrogen for proteins and **DNA**, magnesium to make chlorophyll, and calcium to build strong cell walls. Plants absorb these nutrients when they take in water surrounding their roots. This removes the nutrients from the environment and makes it possible for animals to get what they need in their food. However, until the nutrients are returned to the soil, they are no longer available to plants.

Returning the nutrients to the soil only becomes possible when the plants or animals die, or when animals produce waste materials such as faeces and urine. The **decay** of this dead and waste material releases the nutrients back to the environment.

What is decay?

Decay is the digestion, or **rotting**, of complex **organic** substances to simpler ones by microorganisms such as fungi and bacteria. Since microorganisms have no gut, digestion happens outside their cells and the simpler nutrients are absorbed. This gives the microorganisms the nutrients they need for growth. Some of the simpler nutrients are left in the soil which means plants are now able to absorb them through their roots.

Fungus causing decay of an orange. The white part is a mass of fungal threads, and the grey/green parts are fruiting bodies.

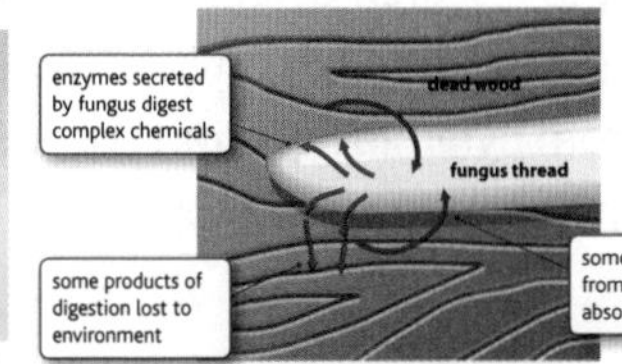

Figure 1 Decay organisms break down complex chemicals into smaller molecules that they can absorb.

The best conditions for decay

Decay microorganisms don't usually have a thick protective coating, so they easily dry out. They often grow below the surface of the material that they are decaying. However, many microorganisms are more active when there is plenty of oxygen for respiration, so they cannot live far beneath the surface. Like other organisms, the rate of the reactions in the cells of microorganisms is affected by temperature. When it is colder, they cannot grow as quickly, so decay is usually faster in warm, moist conditions.

Science skills

a Which conditions would you test to investigate the best conditions for the decay of plant material?

b How would you carry out your investigation?

c How would you control variables?

In 1991, the body of a man was found in the Italian Alps after the deep ice above it had melted. The remains were dated at 3300 BC and still had skin and some hair.

In winter, dead leaves cover the ground, but by midsummer most of the leaves will have decayed.

Essential recycling

Without decay, there would be no recycling of nutrients in the environment, and there would eventually be no life. In **stable** natural communities, where there is little change over time in the plants and animals that live there, there is a balance between the nutrients removed from the soil by plants and the return of nutrients to the soil by decay. The nutrients are constantly cycled.

Questions

1 Describe one similarity and one difference in the way that microorganisms and animals digest their food.

2 Explain why the only parts of a fungal mould that you can usually see are the fruiting bodies.

3 The leaves in the forest photograph fell in November. Explain why they are still there in February but not in June.

4 **(a)** Draw a diagram to show the cycling of nutrients through the environment and living organisms.
(b) Use your diagram to explain the essential role of decay in nutrient cycling.

5 Put the following environments in order of decomposition rate of dead material, starting with the fastest, and justify your order: hot desert, Canadian coniferous forest, polar tundra, tropical rainforest.

6 Many gardeners put their garden waste on a compost heap to decay. Explain why the temperature inside the compost heap gradually increases over the first few weeks.

7 Explain fully why the 5000-year-old remains of the ice-man still had skin and hair.

8 Although rainforests are the most productive areas of plant growth on Earth, their soils are nutrient-poor. Explain as fully as you can the reasons for this apparent discrepancy.

A*

Learning objectives

Students should be able to:

- explain what happens during decay
- describe and explain the best conditions for microbial decay
- explain the importance of decay for the continual recycling of nutrients in the environment.

Key points

Microorganisms digest dead plant and animal material as their source of food. Most microorganisms that cause decay prefer warm moist conditions.
In stable communities, nutrients are constantly cycled between the living organisms that remove them from the environment and microorganisms that return them to the environment.

ActiveTeach Resource: Death and decay – *Interactive activity*

Lesson activities

Starter

1 Set the following scenario: a sheep dies on a mountainside – 1 year later only the skeleton of the sheep remains. Ask students to write bullet point notes to describe and explain what happened. Take examples from around the class and discuss any similarities and differences in useful responses.

2 Revise earlier work on the environmental factors that plants need to grow well. If not mentioned, prompt for nutrients, and ask where the plants get these from and how they got there. Introduce the term *decomposer* and ask students to suggest what it means. Explain that most decomposers are microscopic (such as fungi and bacteria), which is why we often overlook them and also their importance in ecosystems.

Carbohydrate decay organic nutrient rotting stable

Main

1 B1 5.2a Temperature and the rate of decay This is a simple practical investigating the effect of temperature on the rate of decay of bread cubes. It is good preparation for the competition below.

2 B1 5.2b The great potato decay competition In this activity, students will compete as a class to cause the greatest rate of decay in fresh potato. They must first discuss as a class the competition conditions, to make it fair, and then plan their own set-up.

3 Natural nutrient cycling Instead of answering Q4 in lesson B1 5.2 in the Student Book, students could draw a diagram or create a poster to display the various steps in nutrient cycling, such as in a woodland. The cycle should include plants (producers), animals (consumers) and decay organisms and should show the flow of nutrients through the organisms and the environment. Students should define the term 'nutrient' in their diagram and use the diagram to explain how nutrients, in contrast to energy, cycle through ecosystems. The ActiveTeach resource could be used here. [AT]

Plenaries

1 Ask students to write down three questions that can be answered from what has been learnt in this lesson. Take examples from around the class and ask other students to answer the questions. [AfL]

2 Give students 3 minutes to write bullet-point notes for an essay titled 'The importance of microorganisms in recycling nutrients in the environment'. Take examples from around the class to make sure all the key points have been covered. [AfL]

Homework

1 Worksheet B1_5.2c provides questions about the process of mummification that will exercise students' understanding of the conditions that decay microorganisms need for growth.

2 Ask students to use the method of the practical work in **B1 5.2a** to prepare a plan for an investigation into the effect of different moisture levels on the rate of decay of bread cubes.

Points to note

- Fungi are important decomposers, and technically many of them are not microscopic. However, students should appreciate that the parts of fungi that we usually see (such as mushrooms, toadstools and moulds) are mainly fruiting body structures, and that the main part of the 'body' of a fungus is the mycelium, a mat of fine threads which is usually below the surface of the decaying material.

Route to A*

Ask students to find out about the nitrogen cycle and evaluate the role of microorganisms in that cycle, both for returning nitrogen to the atmosphere so that it can continue to cycle through larger organisms and in helping plants get the nitrogen they need for healthy growth.

Answers to Student Book questions

Science skills

a Suitable conditions would include temperature and moisture level.

b Investigation should test one independent variable at a time, for example either temperature or moisture level; should show suitable methods for adjusting the independent variable and measuring accurately; should show suitable method for measuring amount of decay, either by visual assessment to give qualitative measurement or e.g. by weighing to give quantitative value; adequate time must be allowed to give measurable change in dependent variable; adequate health and safety precautions should be considered.

c Other variables that should be controlled include any other potential independent variables, as well as materials used both for decay (e.g. dead plant materials) and to provide the environment in which decay occurs (e.g. soil).

Answers

1 Similarity: they break down complex molecules into simpler ones (with enzymes). Difference: animals digest food in their gut, microorganisms digest food that surrounds them.

2 The fungal threads are below the surface where they are protected from drying out. The fruiting bodies need to be in the air to disperse spores in the wind.

3 Conditions are too cold over winter for growth of decay organisms. During spring air temperature rises, so microorganisms can start to grow and break down the leaves.

4 **(a)** Diagram that shows nutrients in soil water, passing into plants through roots, passing to animals in food, passing through dead plants and animals to decay organisms, returning to soil water from decay organisms. **(b)** If dead material was not decayed, there would be no cycle and eventually nutrients would run out, plants would stop growing, etc.

5 Tropical rainforest, hot desert, coniferous forest, polar tundra: in order of heat and moisture, so although a desert is hotter than a rainforest, there is less moisture, which will reduce the rate of growth of decay microorganisms. (It is possible that desert is even less than coniferous forest, if rainfall fails for several years.)

6 The decay in the compost heap is caused by decay organisms and microorganisms. As they feed on the dead material, they grow and reproduce so their numbers increase. The energy for growth and reproduction comes from respiration, and some of the energy released in respiration is transferred to the surroundings as heat energy. As the numbers of organisms increase, so more respiration occurs and more heat energy is transferred to the heap.

7 Soft tissue is usually decayed rapidly after death by microorganisms. Soon after death he must have been covered with snow/ice, as there was little damage to the soft tissues. The ice made it too cold for the growth of decay microorganisms. Also the ice excluded air, so microorganisms that need oxygen could not grow. The body remained covered with ice for nearly 5000 years, when it was exposed by ice melt. If it hadn't been discovered quickly, decay microorganisms would have started to grow and destroy the soft tissues.

8 Good plant growth needs lots of nutrients, but the soil doesn't have lots. Decay microorganisms usually grow best in warm moist conditions. Conditions for decay are good in rainforests. Any dead organic material is rapidly decayed in a rainforest. The nutrients are rapidly reabsorbed by the plants/trees, so the plants can grow well.

B1 5.3 Recycling issues

Link to the specification

B1.6.1b Materials decay because they are broken down (digested) by microorganisms. Microorganisms are more active and digest materials faster in warm, moist, aerobic conditions.

Ideas for practical work

Investigate the rates of decay using containers (e.g. thermos flasks) full of grass clippings, one with disinfectant, one with dry grass, one with wet grass and one with a composting agent. If the container is sealed, a thermometer or temperature probe can be placed through a cotton wool plug to monitor the temperature.

How Science Works

SKU: B1.6 bullet 1: Evaluate the necessity and effectiveness of schemes for recycling organic kitchen or garden waste.

CA: B4.5.4b Using secondary sources.

B1 5.3 Recycling issues

Learning objectives

- outline the methods by which food and animal wastes can be recycled
- describe the advantages of recycling organic wastes
- identify some of the difficulties with recycling wastes
- evaluate different methods for recycling organic wastes.

A load of rubbish

In 2009 a report on UK household waste estimated that we throw away about 8.3 million tonnes of food and drink each year. This is the equivalent of an average household throwing away £50 every month. Of the total, over 7.6 million tonnes goes in the waste-bin or down the drain.

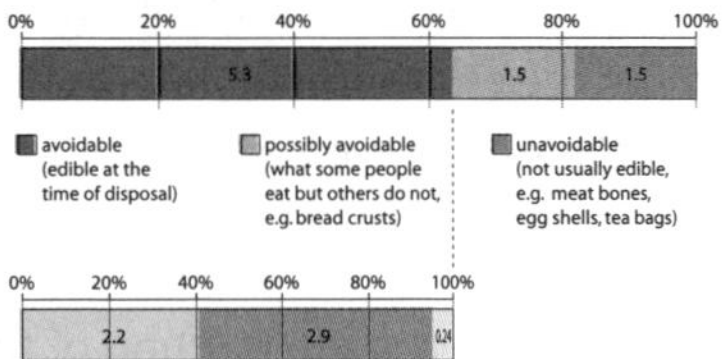

Figure 1 The amount of food and drink waste generated in the UK in 2009 (millions of tonnes per year).

Examiner feedback

You do not need to know what methanogens are, but you should know about the effect of methane in the atmosphere.

The problem with organic waste

Food and drink wastes are organic, which means they originally come from plants and animals. These wastes decay as bacteria and fungi grow on them. Until recently much of the waste in the UK was disposed of in **landfill sites**. Once organic wastes are buried, the usual decay organisms cannot grow because there is not enough oxygen for aerobic respiration. Other decay microorganisms, called **methanogens**, can grow anaerobically. They release a gas called methane, which is not only highly flammable, but also more active in global warming than carbon dioxide.

In 1999, the European Landfill Directive set out plans to reduce the area used for landfill in all European countries for several reasons, including pollution. This has led to more waste recycling in the UK. Most councils now ask us to separate out garden waste, cans, glass and sometimes plastics for collection, but only a few collect food wastes separately. This is because meat waste is very attractive to pests like rats – the waste needs to be protected while it is waiting to be collected.

Landfill tips need to be vented in a controlled way for many years after tipping has ended, otherwise methane that forms as the refuse decays might explode or create fires that burn below the surface for weeks.

Collecting food waste separately means another separate bin for each house as well as special collection trucks.

66

A selection of choices

The traditional way of managing garden and vegetable kitchen waste is the **compost heap** in the garden. The waste is piled up and microbial decay breaks it down into compost that you can add to the garden soil. Many councils now collect this as 'green' waste and make compost on a large scale in a process called **windrow composting**. This needs a lot of space, and the composting material must be turned regularly to keep the oxygen level high, but it doesn't need any special equipment.

Other councils collect all garden and kitchen waste, including meat, together. By law, this needs composting in large containers until the meat waste is broken down, in a process called **in-vessel composting**. Composting is then completed using the windrow process. An advantage is that conditions can be monitored inside the containers, and maintained at the correct temperature and moisture levels for more rapid decay in the early stages. The higher temperatures also kill **pathogens** and the seeds of **weed** plants.

Another process uses **anaerobic digestion** by the methanogenic bacteria that cause problems on landfill sites. Food waste is put into large **digesters** and air is excluded. The methanogens break down the material and release methane and other gases. The methane is collected and burnt to produce heat, which can be used to heat buildings or for making electricity. This process can't use wood waste because these microorganisms cannot break it down.

In all these processes, the solid end materials can be used for soil conditioning, in gardens, parks or in agriculture.

Examiner feedback

You need to be able to compare different methods of dealing with organic waste, but the terms 'windrow composting' and 'in-vessel composting' do not need to be remembered for your exam.

A traditional compost heap in the garden can create the right conditions for vegetable waste to decay in a few months.

Questions

1 **(a)** What proportion of the food and drink that we waste in the UK could potentially be avoided? **(b)** Describe methods that would help us to reduce the amount of food and drink waste that we produce.

2 List the problems with disposing of food waste on landfill sites. Explain your choices.

3 Explain why meat waste must be composted in containers for the first part of in-vessel composting.

4 Explain how the recycling of food waste mimics the natural process of nutrient recycling.

5 Another way of dealing with all household waste is to burn it. Argue the environmental advantages of recycling food waste rather than burning it.

6 Draw up a table to show the different ways in which councils are managing waste food. For each way, list the advantages and disadvantages of each process.

7 Using the data in the graphs, create a poster to inform householders how and why they should increase the amount of waste they recycle to the maximum possible.

8 Some councils are considering fining households that put recyclable material into refuse that is not recycled. Prepare a memo for discussion listing the advantages and problems with this. A*

Science in action

Gardeners need to create the right conditions inside the compost heap to raise the temperature high enough to kill seeds of weed plants, and disease-causing fungi. So the heap must be kept sheltered from rain, and the right balance of fresh and dead material added plus a little soil to bring in the right microorganisms. Turning the heap every few weeks makes sure enough oxygen gets to all parts.

Route to A*

When evaluating a process, make sure you identify the advantages and disadvantages of the various approaches and then compare these to come to a decision about which gives the best result.

Energy 67

Learning objectives

Most students should be able to:

- outline the methods by which food and animal wastes can be recycled
- describe the advantages of recycling organic wastes
- identify some of the difficulties with recycling wastes
- evaluate different methods for recycling organic wastes.

Some students should also be able to:

- evaluate the use of a proxy for a measurement. [Ext]

Key points

In the UK we throw away a lot of food and green waste, which causes problems at landfill sites.

There are several schemes now for recycling green and food waste, which have different advantages and disadvantages.

Lesson activities

Starter

1 Tell students that in July 2009 a fire inside a landfill tip on Guernsey was thought to have finally gone out (BBC News: Guernsey landfill fire). It was estimated to have been burning for 4 years. Ask students to use what they learnt in the last lesson to suggest what made the fire possible and why it took so long to stop burning. Answer: the decay of food materials within the refuse dumped at the tip released flammable gases that caught fire due to the heat produced from respiration of the decay microorganisms.

2 Ask students what they are supposed to do with vegetable and food waste at home. Most councils now collect these separately and some families may compost their own if they are gardeners. Ask students to suggest why garden and food waste is collected separately, and what the council does with it.

Anaerobic digestion	compost heap	digester	in-vessel composting
landfill site	methanogen	organic pathogenic	windrow composting

Main

1 B1 5.3a Composting grass In this activity, students will plan an investigation, and if possible carry out their plan, into the effects of some conditions on the rate of decay of grass clippings.

2 The effectiveness of recycling schemes Students should research one or more recycling schemes for organic kitchen or garden waste. They could look at what some local councils are doing. They should prepare a report or presentation that explains the need for such schemes, and compare and evaluate some different approaches.

3 Worksheet B1 5.3b provides some data from the WRAP final report *Performance analysis of mixed food and garden waste collection schemes* published in 2010. Further data on this and other studies can be found on the WRAP website. Students could work together in groups to produce their own advisory report for a local authority on the best collection schedule to use to capture food waste for recycling.

Plenaries

1 With the students' suggestions, draw a mind map to summarise all that they have learnt in this and the previous lesson. Students should suggest words to add to the map and how they should be added, justifying their suggestions. [AfL]

2 Ask students to complete sentences about recycling using at least two different connectives (e.g. but, because, and, when). Suitable sentences include: Much of our food is wasted …; Organic waste is a problem …; Recycling organic food can be difficult... [AfL]

Homework

1 Work sheet B1 5.3c provides questions about the setting up of a compost heap for recycling food and garden waste that will exercise students' understanding of the conditions that provide the most rapid decay.

2 Ask students to design a poster to encourage people to dispose of food and garden waste properly for recycling rather than in the residual waste bin.

Points to note

- Students do not need to remember the terms *methanogen*, *in-vessel composting* or *windrow composting* for their exams, although they may be presented with information about them during the exam.

Route to A*

Students could research the different approaches to recycling carried out in other European countries and attempt to explain why different countries have different attitudes to recycling. Using some of the examples they find, they could outline ways in which the UK could improve its recycling efforts and suggest ways of encouraging individuals, industry and councils to do this.

Answers to Student Book questions

1 **(a)** (5.3 + 1.5) / 8.3 = 0.82 = 82% **(b)** Any suitable suggestions that relate to the lower bar in the diagram, such as not buying more than we need for a period of time, or not preparing too much for a meal.

2 Any suitable problems, such as: food waste decays resulting in the release of methane; methane can cause fires or explosions, and adds to problems of global warming; food waste attracts vermin such as rats; landfill sites take up lots of space for a long time.

3 To prevent attracting vermin such as rats; after that extra stage, it will not attract them.

4 Breakdown of dead plant and animal material by microorganisms, and return of nutrients to the ground (as fertiliser for food waste recycling).

5 Burning releases all carbon to air as carbon dioxide, which is linked to global warming; fewer nutrients are left in ash for returning to the soil.

6 Table similar to the following:

Method	Advantages	Disadvantages
windrow compositing	cheap	cannot treat meat waste
in-vessel composting	can monitor conditions for fastest decay while in vessel can include meat waste	cost of equipment
anaerobic digestion	treats all but wood waste; produces methane which can generate heat or electricity	cost of equipmnent

7 Poster needs to contain the following:
- how much that is not recycled but that could be
- should identify and give example of the three groups of waste: avoidable, possibly avoidable, unavoidable
- should identify and give examples of the reasons for wasting avoidable waste
- should identify simple ways of avoiding wasting avoidable waste
- should explain the benefits/needs of recycling more waste
- should present information as clearly and attractively as possible.

8 Memo to include the following points: Advantages: makes people more aware of how they are separating their rubbish; makes people more aware of how important it is to recycle as much as possible; helps councils achieve their recycling targets more easily. Problems: added burden for householders; creates extra work (cost) to check bins to make sure people are using the different types correctly; extra work (cost) involved in issuing/collecting fines.

The carbon cycle

Link to the specification

B1.6.2a The constant cycling of carbon is called the carbon cycle. In the carbon cycle:

- carbon dioxide is removed from the environment by green plants and algae for photosynthesis
- the carbon from the carbon dioxide is used to make carbohydrates, fats and proteins, which make up the body of plants and algae
- when green plants and algae respire, some of this carbon becomes carbon dioxide and is released into the atmosphere
- when green plants and algae are eaten by animals and these animals are eaten by other animals, some of the carbon becomes part of the fats and proteins that make up their bodies
- when animals respire some of this carbon becomes carbon dioxide and is released into the atmosphere
- when plants, algae and animals die, some animals and microorganisms feed on their bodies
- carbon is released into the atmosphere as carbon dioxide when these organisms respire
- by the time the microorganisms and detritus feeders have broken down the waste products and dead bodies of organisms in ecosystems and cycled the materials as plant nutrients, all the energy originally absorbed by green plants and algae has been transferred
- combustion of wood and fossil fuels releases carbon dioxide into the atmosphere.

B1 5.4 The carbon cycle

Learning objectives

- describe how plants remove carbon from the atmosphere and use it to make chemicals in their bodies
- explain how carbon passes between living organisms and is returned to the atmosphere
- interpret a diagram of the carbon cycle.

Capturing carbon dioxide

Imagine a carbon atom that is part of a carbon dioxide molecule in the air. If that carbon dioxide molecule gets too close to a plant, it might be taken into a leaf. There, during photosynthesis, it will be changed into an organic carbon compound called glucose, a carbohydrate. This is known as **fixing** carbon because it removes carbon from the physical environment.

If the glucose is used for respiration, it will be converted to carbon dioxide and released back into the air. However, it might instead be changed into complex carbon compounds, such as the carbohydrates, proteins and fats in plant tissue.

Carbon compounds in animals

If a plant is eaten by an animal, the plant's tissues will be broken down during digestion. Some of the carbon compounds in it will be absorbed through the animal's gut and made into more carbohydrates, proteins, fats or other complex compounds. The rest will leave the animal's body as faeces.

Some of the carbon compounds made inside the animal will be converted to glucose for respiration, then transformed back into carbon dioxide, which will be released into the atmosphere. Other carbon compounds may become part of the animal's body tissues, or may be excreted in urine. If the animal is eaten by a predator, these processes will happen in that animal.

If plants and animals are not eaten, and just die, **detritus feeders**, such as worms and fly larvae, will feed on the dead bodies. They also feed on the faeces and urine excreted by animals. They break down the complex carbon compounds and use them to make more carbon compounds in their bodies, releasing some carbon as carbon dioxide to the air from respiration. Decomposer organisms, such as fungi and bacteria, continue the process of decay. They break down carbon compounds even further, using some to make carbon compounds in their bodies and using some for respiration, releasing carbon dioxide.

The full cycle

When large quantities of organisms, such as trees or plankton, are buried over long timescales, heat and pressure will change them into **fossil fuels**, such as coal and oil.

The **combustion** of fuels formed from organisms, including fossil fuels and wood, releases carbon dioxide into the air.

Whenever the carbon is returned to the atmosphere as carbon dioxide, it is possible that it may be captured by a leaf and fixed again in photosynthesis. This starts the process over again. This constant cycling of carbon through carbon compounds in living organisms and carbon dioxide in the air is called the **carbon cycle**.

In terms of chemicals and energy, we can see that although plants are able to take nutrients and carbon dioxide from the environment, and capture energy from sunlight, only the nutrients and carbon dioxide can be continuously cycled between the environment and living organisms. All the energy that is captured by plants will eventually be transferred as heat to the environment. This energy cannot be used by living organisms, so there is no energy cycle.

carbon in carbon dioxide from respiration
carbon in carbon dioxide enters leaf and becomes part of glucose (photosynthesis)
carbon in protein and fats
carbon in starch and carbohydrates

Figure 1 How carbon from the air is changed into carbon compounds in a potato plant.

Examiner feedback

Remember that plants photosynthesise during the day, taking carbon dioxide from the atmosphere, and plants respire all the time, releasing carbon dioxide back into the atmosphere.

68

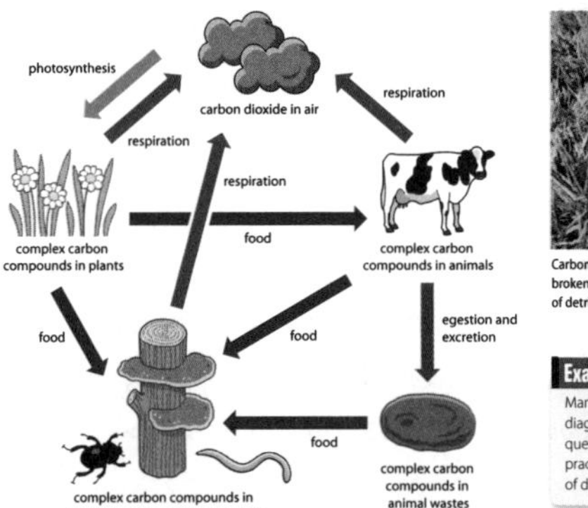

Figure 2 The natural carbon cycle.

Carbon compounds in this cowpat will be broken down and used by many different kinds of detritus feeders and decomposers.

Examiner feedback

Many different styles of carbon cycle diagram can be used in examination questions. Make sure that you have practised interpreting different styles of diagram.

Questions

1 What is photosynthesis, and what is its role in the carbon cycle?

2 What contribution do plants make to the carbon cycle?

3 Draw a diagram to show what happens to the carbon in an animal that is eaten by a predator.

4 It is possible that one of the carbon atoms in your body was once in the body of William Shakespeare. Explain how this could happen.

5 Explain how human activity modifies the carbon cycle shown in Figure 2.

6 In China, silkworms are grown on mulberry bushes that surround fish ponds. The faeces from feeding silkworms, and waste from the processing of silk, are returned to the ponds. Carp fish feed on water plants in the ponds, and are harvested for human consumption. Figure 3 shows the biomass in kilograms per hectare for the parts of this system. Describe what the diagram shows as fully as possible.

silkworm rearing and processing
cocoon 2700
raw silk 206
mulberry 36700
silkworm waste 18400
waste water 37500
pupae 2300
2290
187
1150
pond

Figure 3 Biomasses.

7 The silkworm/carp pond arrangement is an example of a natural recycling system. Identify which parts of the system are not shown in the diagram and suggest as far as you can why they were not included.

8 Explain as fully as possible why the carbon cycling in the silkworm/carp pond arrangement is self-sustaining, and consider conditions in which this might change.

A*

Energy 69

Learning objectives

Students should be able to:

- describe how plants remove carbon from the atmosphere and use it to make chemicals in their bodies
- explain how carbon passes between living organisms and is returned to the atmosphere
- interpret a diagram of the carbon cycle
- identify the form in which the carbon is passed from one process to the next in the carbon cycle.

Key points

The carbon cycle shows how carbon cycles between the air as carbon dioxide and within organisms as complex carbon compounds.

Carbon is removed from the atmosphere by plants during photosynthesis and returned to the atmosphere by respiration by all living organisms.

Lesson activities

Starter

1 Ask students what photosynthesis and respiration have in common, and allow them 3 minutes to jot down as many ideas as they can. Take examples from around the class to revise what students already know about these processes. There is no need to correct answers at this point, though do encourage discussion if conflicting ideas arise.

2 Give students 3 minutes to jot down all examples of carbon compounds that they can remember within organisms and the natural environment. If students find this straightforward, they could be challenged to identify the processes that change one compound into another.

Carbon cycle | detritus feeder | fix

Main

1 B1 5.4a Carbon dioxide processes Refer to sheet in Teacher and Technician Planning pack.

2 B1 5.4b Carbon cycle jigsaw Refer to sheet in Teacher and Technician planning pack.

3 Carbon cycle role play Arrange students into groups, and ask them to write a label on an A4 sheet for each stage of the carbon cycle. The stage should indicate the organisms, not the processes in the cycle. The students should then take one label and arrange themselves in order of the carbon cycle, so they can pass a ball between them to represent carbon as it moves through the cycle. Challenge students to identify the process each time the ball is passed.

Plenaries

1 Ask students to write clues for a crossword that includes as many key words from B1 Chapter 5 as possible. They should test their clues against a friend to see how successful they are.

2 Ask students to write down the three most important facts that they have learnt in the last two lessons. They should share their facts with a neighbour and the pair should choose the three most important from those. Repeat the exercise in fours, then eights, then as a class vote on the three most important overall.

Homework

1 Work sheet B1 **5.4c** provides questions about using the carbon cycle as a model for making predictions.

2 Ask students to investigate the amounts of carbon stored in various sinks within the carbon cycle. It is likely that they will come across alternative models of the carbon cycle during this activity, so you should identify how far they should extend the model they have learnt here.

Points to note

- If students carry out any research on the carbon cycle, they will come across alternative models to the one described in this lesson which focuses only on living organisms and the air. Although discussing alternative models can help to identify their limitations in describing complex systems, make sure students are aware that they will not need to remember more than is given in the lesson for their exams.

Route to A*

Main task 2: Students research other carbon cycles that include other carbon reservoirs, and make adjustments to their own model to take in any differences they consider are reasonable.

Main task 3: Students identify the form in which the carbon exists within each stage of the carbon cycle, within limits, e.g. proteins/ fats/carbohydrates within organisms rather than specific chemicals. Students could also use the chemical formulae for all reaction equations rather than just words.

Answers to Student Book questions

1 Photosynthesis is the formation of food (glucose) by plants when they combine carbon dioxide and water using the energy of sunlight. Photosynthesis removes carbon dioxide from the atmosphere and fixes it as complex carbon compounds in living organisms.

2 Carbon dioxide is used by plants to make complex carbon compounds during photosynthesis; during respiration carbon dioxide is released from complex carbon compounds.

3 Diagram that shows carbon entering the animal, as complex carbon compounds in food, some of this being egested in faeces, the rest taken into the animal's body. The complex carbon compounds in the animal's body then are lost as complex carbon compounds in urine, as carbon dioxide to the atmosphere after respiration, pass to another organism that eats it (a predator) and the remains pass to a decomposer.

4 A carbon atom in a complex carbon compound in a human body over 400 years ago could have cycled between the atmosphere as carbon dioxide and within other organisms as complex carbon compounds many times. If it was fixed from the atmosphere as part of a plant that you ate, it could easily become part of your body.

5 Combustion of fuels, including fossil fuels and wood, is returning additional carbon dioxide to the atmosphere beyond what is returned by the natural process of respiration.

6 36 700 kg/ha of mulberry is eaten by silkworms. The silkworms produce 2700 kg/ha of cocoons, which in turn produce 206 kg/ha of silk. 18 400 kg/ha of waste (in the form of faeces, etc.) from the silkworms falls into the pond. In addition 37 500 kg/ha of waste water from processing silkworms, plus 2300 kg/ha of dead pupae from processing is returned to the ponds. Carp eat the plants in the pond. A total of 3627 kg/ha of carp are harvested for people to eat.

7 There are several parts of the system not identified in the diagram: the water plants that the carp feed on; the waste produced by the carp in the form of faeces and urine; and the decomposer/decay organisms that break down the carbon compounds in all the waste in the ponds. Estimating the amount of water plant growth could be done by harvesting the plants in one pond and measuring their biomass, so it is not clear why this is not included unless it is difficult to separate plants from microorganisms. Estimating the waste produced by carp could be done by keeping carp in laboratory conditions and collecting faeces to measure the mass, but the amount of faeces produced depends on the amount of food eaten, so it would be difficult to translate the lab results into estimates for the real system. Estimating the biomass of decomposers would be very difficult as many of them are microscopic.

8 Carbon enters the system as carbon dioxide taken up by mulberry leaves in photosynthesis. It is converted to complex carbon compounds that then pass to the silkworms. From the silkworms, carbon compounds pass to the ponds in faeces or waste from the process, and some is lost from the system as silk. Carbon compounds in the ponds pass via decomposers to pond plants and carp. At every stage in the food chain, some carbon is lost as carbon dioxide in respiration. Carbon compounds are also removed from the system in the carp, as food for people. As long as the amount of carbon lost to the system in the harvesting of silk and carp does not exceed the input of carbon dioxide from the atmosphere in the photosynthesis of the plants, the system will remain stable. Increased harvesting, climate change (which affects the rates of photosynthesis and respiration), the addition of other organisms, or pollution could all affect this balance.

B1 6.1 Gene basics

Link to the specification

B1.7.1 a The information that results in plants and animals having similar characteristics to their parents is carried by genes, which are passed on in the sex cells (gametes) from which the offspring develop.

B1.7.1 b The nucleus of a cell contains chromosomes. Chromosomes carry genes that control the characteristics of the body.

B1.7.1 c Different genes control the development of different characteristics of an organism.

B1.7.1 d Differences in the characteristics of different individuals of the same kind may be due to differences in:

- the genes they have inherited (genetic causes)
- the conditions in which they have developed (environmental causes)
- or a combination of both.

Ideas for practical work

Look at variation in leaf length or width, pod length, height. Compare plants growing in different conditions – sun/shade.

How Science Works

CA: B4.3.2f Identifying the range of the measured data; B4.4.1b Calculating the mean of a set of at least three results.

B1 6.1 Gene basics

Learning objectives

- describe how genes are small sections of chromosomes in a cell's nucleus
- explain how different genes control the development of different characteristics
- explain how variation in characteristics is caused.

Basic characteristics

All organisms have **characteristics**, for example, coat colour in dogs, and often some characteristics look like those of one parent and others look more like those of the other parent.

Genes control characteristics

We **inherit** some characteristics from our parents. This is because we were formed when a sex cell (a **gamete** called an egg) from our mother fused with a sex cell (a gamete called a sperm) from our father. The nucleus of each gamete contains **chromosomes** that are made up of **genes**. So we receive some genes from each parent.

This puppy has inherited some characteristics from each parent.

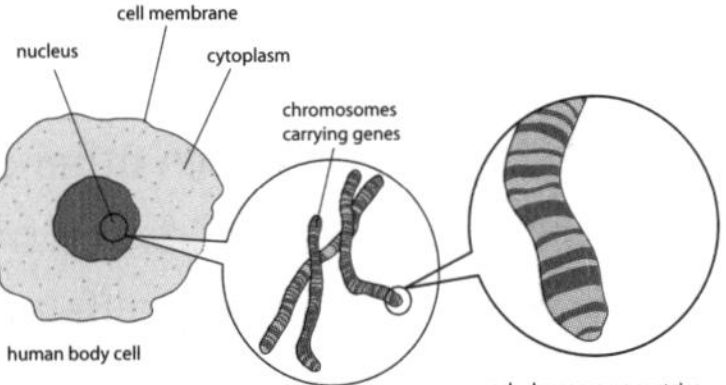

Figure 1 Chromosomes in the nucleus.

Each chromosome carries thousands of genes. There are genes for height, hair colour, blood type, the length and shape of your bones, the size and shape of your hands and so on. Each gene 'codes' for a particular characteristic. Genes are the instructions for making every part of you, and as you grow, so the genes affect the way that you grow. Except for identical twins, we all have slightly different combinations of genes, which is why we all look different.

Examiner feedback

Note that you may see the bands shown here in photographs. They are the effect of staining, not the individual genes. There are many more genes than bands that can be seen.

Examiner feedback

There is often confusion by students in examinations between gametes, chromosomes and genes. Make sure that you know the difference.

The cause of variation

Many of our characteristics are controlled by **genes**. One example is a gene called OCA2, which is found on chromosome 15. This gene carries instructions for making the substance that gives eyes, hair and skin colour. As genes can be passed from parent to offspring in gametes, these characteristics are inherited. However, not all of the differences between the characteristics of individuals come from the genes. Some, such as muscle strength, are mainly due to differences in lifestyle and in our environment. These differences cannot be inherited.

Variation that is strongly affected by the environment, such as height, often shows **continuous variation**, where there is a gradual change from one extreme to the other. However, variation caused by a single gene is usually **categoric**, in separate groups.

Science in action

The Human Genome Project has mapped all of the chromosomes in a human nucleus. Scientists are now trying to identify which part of each chromosome is a particular gene. With this detailed information, scientists hope to speed up the process of looking for cures for human disorders that are caused by faulty genes.

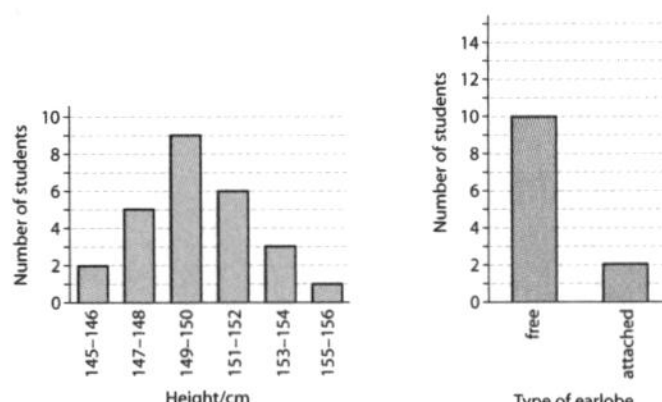

Figure 2 The graph on the left shows continuous variation, and the one on the right shows categoric variation.

Many characteristics are affected by both environment and genes. For example, if you have two tall parents, you are likely to have the genes for tallness, but if you do not grow well as a child (as a result of poor nutrition or illness) you may not grow as tall as your genes would allow. As research continues on human genes, it is becoming clear that many characteristics that we would have previously considered the result of environment, such as obesity, may also be partly the result of inherited genes.

Questions

1 **(a)** Look at the photograph of the dogs. Identify as many characteristics of the puppy as you can that are from each parent. **(b)** Explain why the puppy has these characteristics.

2 Describe the relationship between nucleus, chromosomes and genes.

3 The parents of a child were both champion marathon runners. Will the child also be a champion marathon runner? Explain your answer.

4 Look at the graphs in Figure 2: **(a)** Which characteristic is the result of genetic factors alone? Explain your answer. **(b)** The graph for types of earlobe shows the results for boys. In the same survey, all 14 girls had free earlobes. Is the conclusion that all girls have free earlobes valid? Explain your answer.

5 Group the following characteristics of rose plants into three groups: variation due to genes, variation due to environment, variation due to genes and environment. For each characteristic, justify your choice of group.
flower colour, plant height, size of leaf, time of flowering, shape of leaf, presence or absence of thorns

6 Explain how you would investigate whether variation in a human characteristic was the result of genes or the environment, or a combination of the two.

7 Many people think obesity is caused by environmental effects, but research shows there may be a genetic cause too. Explain in detail the importance of this discovery.

Any differences between these identical twins are the result of the environment.

Science skills

If you carried out a survey of human characteristics to see if they were controlled by genes, the environment or both, how would you set up the survey to help you get reliable results?

Science in action

Some human disorders are caused by genes and some by environment, and some by a mixture of the two. In order to understand why some people have the disorders, scientists compare different aspects of people who have them and people who don't to see if they can find any correlations. For example, comparing people who smoke with those who don't helped to identify the link between smoking and cancer. This kind of study is called epidemiology.

Taking it further

A chromosome is much more than a string of genes that code for characteristics. It includes packaging molecules so genes are only used when needed. The rest of the time the chromosome is neatly folded and protected so that it does not get damaged.

Learning objectives

Most students should be able to:

- describe how genes are small sections of chromosomes in a cell's nucleus
- explain how different genes control the development of different characteristics
- explain how variation in characteristics is caused.

Some students should also be able to:

- calculate and explain the value of standard error of a mean to identify significant differences between samples. [Ext]

ActiveTeach Resource: Genetics and variation – *Interactive activity*

Key points

Parents pass their characteristics to their offspring in the genes on the chromosomes of their sex cells (gametes).

The nucleus of a cell contains the chromosomes.

Different genes code for different characteristics.

Some characteristics are controlled by genes, some by the environment and some by a combination of both.

Lesson activities

Starter

1 Carry out a 'Consider All Possibilities' exercise using the statement 'A plant is not very tall'. Possible answers: it is still growing; it has not received enough light/nutrients, etc.; it has had a disease; its parents were not very tall. Students' responses will allow you to draw out what they remember about inherited and environmental causes of variation from earlier work.

Categoric variation characteristic chromosome continuous variation gamete gene inherit

2 Ask students to jot down any characteristics that they feel they have inherited from their parents, and any that they think are not. Take examples, and arrange them on the board into the two groups. Ask students to suggest how the characteristics within a group are similar to each other, and how those in the separate groups are different. It doesn't matter at this stage if students find it difficult to agree which group a characteristic should go in as this will be covered later in the lesson.

Main

1 **B1 6.1a Measuring variation** Refer to sheet in Teacher and Technician Planning Pack.

2 **B1 6.1b Human characteristics survey** Refer to sheet in Teacher and Technician Planning Pack.

3 The ActiveTeach resource *Genetics and variation?* shows the relationship between genes, chromosomes and cells. This relationship can be difficult for students to understand, but the animation should help them visualise it. [AT]

Plenaries

1 Ask students to look at the photo of dogs in the Student Book and describe which characteristics the young animal has inherited from each of its parents. Ask them to give reasons for their choices. Ask them then to suggest any of the characteristics that could change with time as a result of the environment. [AfL]

2 Give students 1 minute to jot down as many different ways in which the individuals in the classroom vary. Then ask them to identify whether each type of variation is the result of genes, environment or both. Take examples from around the class and ask if other students agree with the cause. Discuss any differences in opinion and ask students how they would set about finding the main cause. [AfL]

Homework

1 Provide students with the following word list and ask them to create a crossword with clues that includes all the words, and any other related words from this lesson: cell, characteristic, chromosome, environment, gene, gamete, nucleus, inherit, parent, variation.

2 **Worksheet B1 6.1c** provides students with a sample answer to a data interpretation question on characteristics. Students are asked to improve the supplied answer. They will need graph paper to complete their answer.

Points to note

- Although we say things like 'he has his father's eyes' there are few, if any, human characteristics that are controlled by a single gene. Although tongue rolling, attached/free ear lobes and eye colour are often quoted as such, as more research is done on them results suggest they are controlled by several or many genes. However, characteristics in other organisms are controlled by single genes, such as coat colour in mice and flower colour in some plants. These will be studied in more detail in Additional Science and at AS or A level.

Route to A*

Ask students to research examples of characteristics mentioned recently in the media that vary in humans. These are most likely to be in relation to health/disease, such as cancer, diabetes or Alzheimer's. They should research the evidence for genetic causes and environmental causes, and use their findings to explain any differences in the way the research is being carried further or treatment developed.

Answers to Student Book questions

Science skills

For reliable results, you need comparable groups for characteristics that vary with age and gender, such as separating male and female height or weight data, separating age groups into adults and smaller age groups for younger people. You also need to take measurements from as large a number of people as possible in order to take averages to even out variation between individuals within a group.

Answers

1 **(a)** from the parent on the left: grey/black and white markings, shorter hair, shape of head; from the parent on the right: floppy ears. **(b)** It inherited the genes for the characteristics from its parents.

2 The nucleus contains the chromosomes; the chromosomes are made up of genes.

3 Possibly – the child may inherit genes for muscle type and body shape that make it more likely, but unless the child trains (and avoids accident) properly then it is unlikely to be a champion.

4 **(a)** Ear lobe type, because it is discontinuous. **(b)** No, because it is a small sample size. Without a much larger sample size, it is not valid to suggest that girls cannot have attached ear lobes.

5 Flower colour: genetic because it is not usually affected by environment. Plant height: mostly environmental due to effect of water, nutrients and warmth on growth, but may include genetic component (i.e. a limit to how tall or short the plant can be). Size of leaf: mostly environmental, as for plant height. Time of flowering: mostly genetic but some environmental, as temperature and/or amount of light can adjust the timing a little. Shape of leaf: genetic as usually the same for all plants of that species. Presence or absence of thorns: genetic as usually the same for all plants of that species.

6 Any suitable answer with appropriate explanation, such as: compare the characteristic in identical twins because it will be the same in both if it is genetic; look at the distribution of measurements of that characteristic in a large number of people, if it is continuous then is more likely to have an environmental component than if it is categoric.

7 An environmental cause would be linked simply to taking in more energy from food than is lost through body processes and exercise. This would explain obesity as a result of eating too much and/or exercising too little. If there is a genetic link, then people with the gene that promotes obesity might find it more difficult to lose weight while eating the same amount as someone without the gene. If the doctor knew whether or not you had the gene, they could provide better advice on how to keep weight down and avoid obesity.

B1 6.2 Different types of reproduction

Link to the specification

B1.7.2a There are two forms of reproduction:

- sexual reproduction – the joining (fusion) of male and female gametes. The mixture of the genetic information from two parents leads to variety in the offspring
- asexual reproduction – no fusion of gametes and only one individual is needed as the parent. There is no mixing of genetic information and so no genetic variation in the offspring. These genetically identical individuals are known as clones.

B1.7.2b New plants can be produced quickly and cheaply by taking cuttings from older plants. These new plants are genetically identical to the parent plant.

Ideas for practical work

Investigate the optimum conditions for the growth of cuttings, of, e.g. Mexican hat plants, spider plants, African violets.

B1 6.2 Different types of reproduction

Learning objectives

- describe the key features of sexual and asexual reproduction
- explain how sexual reproduction leads to variety in the offspring and why asexual reproduction produces identical offspring
- explain the advantages and disadvantages of the different forms of reproduction.

Sexual reproduction

The variation described in lesson B1 6.1 is the result of **sexual reproduction**. This kind of reproduction occurs when the nucleus of a sperm cell (male gamete) fuses with the nucleus of an egg cell (female gamete) to produce a fertilised cell. When the gametes are formed, they only receive half of the chromosomes that are in a body cell. So the fertilised cell gets half its chromosomes from the mother and half from the father. The process of producing gametes ensures that it is highly unlikely that any two gametes will contain the same variations of genes.

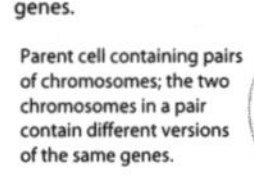
Parent cell containing pairs of chromosomes; the two chromosomes in a pair contain different versions of the same genes.
(Note: this diagram is highly simplified.)

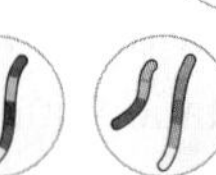

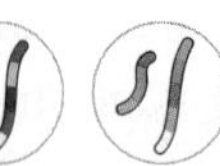

Four possible different sex cells.

Figure 1 Each sex cell gets one chromosome from each pair in the parent cell.

The variation in the genes in each gamete, and the mixing of genes from the father and mother, make it very unlikely that two offspring from the same parents will be alike, unless they are identical twins formed from the same fertilised cell.

Many species of plants and animals, like these damselflies, use sexual reproduction to produce offspring.

Asexual reproduction

Another way to produce offspring is by **asexual reproduction**. Here the offspring are produced from the division of cells in the parent without the need for **fertilisation** by a sperm cell. So the cells of the offspring contain exactly the same chromosomes as the parent. All the offspring are genetically identical and are called **clones**.

Asexual reproduction can happen much more quickly than sexual reproduction. For example, in one summer, there may be up to 40 generations of cabbage aphid. This is a great advantage for a pest such as aphids that need to reproduce rapidly in the short time when food is available.

Some plants also reproduce asexually. For example, couch grass produces new plants from underground stems, called **runners**, which help it spread quickly in an area to outcompete other plants. Plants that live in places where it is either too hot or too cold for growth during part of the year, may form underground **storage organs**, like potatoes, each of which can form a new plant in the next growing season.

Female aphids can give birth to live young without fertilisation by a male aphid.

74

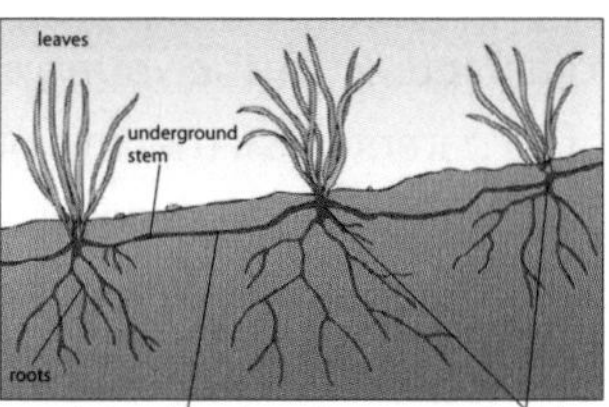
leaves
underground stem
roots
new plants grow from underground stems by asexual reproduction
new plants will have identical genes

Figure 2 When the new couch grass plant has enough roots to grow on its own, the runner may die off.

A tray of leaf cuttings from an African violet plant. The dark leaves were taken from the parent plant. Some of these have formed roots and are starting to grow into new plants with brighter green leaves.

Applications of asexual reproduction

We can make clones of plants artificially by copying the natural asexual process, such as taking potatoes from an old plant and planting them separately. For some plants we can also take **cuttings**. These are parts cut off a plant, usually from a stem or leaf. The cuttings grow roots and develop into new plants. This can produce lots of new plants more quickly than by sexual reproduction, and more cheaply because it is quicker.

Questions

1. Explain why the offspring from sexual reproduction are not identical to: **(a)** their parents **(b)** other offspring from the same parents.
2. Explain why the offspring from asexual reproduction are clones.
3. Draw up a table to show the advantages and disadvantages of sexual and asexual reproduction.
4. A student grows African violet plants. Which technique should he use to: **(a)** try to produce a plant that has a new flower colour? **(b)** produce many plants with this same new colour? Explain your answers.
5. Aphids reproduce asexually all summer, but late in the season winged males and females are produced. These mate and the females lay eggs that overwinter and hatch in spring. **(a)** Are females that hatch from overwintering eggs identical or not? Explain your answer. **(b)** What is the advantage of producing aphids that are able to fly in autumn? **(c)** Explain the advantages of both kinds of reproduction in the aphid life cycle.
6. Use your table from question 3 to suggest the best form of reproduction in the following situations. Justify your answers. **(a)** A weed plant starts growing in cleared soil. **(b)** An aquatic animal produces offspring that will drift downriver to live in other areas.
7. A student has been given a *Bryophyllum* plant to set up an experiment to show as clearly as possible the variation in leaf size caused by temperature. Write a plan for how she should set up the experiment, explaining each step.

A*

Practical

Leaf cuttings can easily be taken from an African violet plant and used to test the best conditions for forming new plants. They can also show how much variation is the result of environment, as the new plants are genetically identical.

Examiner feedback

It is important that you understand why asexual reproduction is so important in economic terms.

Taking it further

Bacteria reproduce mainly asexually, so populations can grow rapidly. Occasionally, they reproduce sexually, producing variation in the offspring. However, they also contain small rings of genetic material called plasmids that they can pass to other bacteria, without reproduction (as no new individuals are formed). Plasmids can carry genes for antibiotic resistance, so resistance can be passed quickly between different types of bacteria.

Variation 75

Learning objectives

Students should be able to:

- describe the key features of sexual and asexual reproduction
- explain how sexual reproduction leads to variety in the offspring and why asexual reproduction produces identical offspring
- explain the advantages and disadvantages of the different forms of reproduction.

Key points

In sexual reproduction, male and female gametes fuse, carrying genes from each parent.

The mixture of genetic information from two parents leads to variation in the offspring.

There is only one parent in asexual reproduction, and all offspring are identical clones of that parent.

Identical plants can be produced quickly and cheaply from cuttings taken from a parent plant.

Asexual reproduction | clone | cutting | fertilise | gamete | runner | sexual reproduction | storage organ

Lesson activities

Starter

1 Show students an example of vegetative reproduction in plants. This could be a spider plant that is producing runners with new plants, a sprouting potato tuber or the top of a carrot plant that has been left for a few days on damp paper towel to start sprouting. Ask students to describe what is happening. Elicit the fact that new plants are being made without the need for fertilisation, i.e. there is only one parent. Ask students to suggest other examples.

2 Write the word *reproduction* in the middle of the board and ask students to suggested related words and how they should be linked to create a mind map on the topic. This will help you assess what students remember from work in KS3 on this.

Main

1 B1 6.2a Taking cuttings This practical gives students the opportunity to learn how to grow new plants from cuttings of a mature plant.

2 Reproduction research Ask students to research examples of asexual reproduction in animals, such as how *Hydra* reproduce by budding, or how malaria parasites multiply inside the host. For each kind of animal, students should explain what advantage this form of reproduction gives them.

Plenaries

1 Prepare a list of 10 words or phrases relating to sexual and asexual reproduction, such as fusion of sex cells, one parent, clones are produced, many offspring produced quickly, etc. These could be written on the board or provided on cards. Ask students to link each word correctly to the headings 'Asexual reproduction' and 'Sexual reproduction'. [AfL]

2 Ask students to write questions for which the key words for this lesson are the answers. They could try their questions out on a friend to see if the questions are good and sufficiently challenging. [AfL]

Homework

1 Worksheet B1 6.2b provides some standard questions on asexual and sexual reproduction.

2 Worksheet B1 6.2c provides some more challenging questions on asexual and sexual reproduction.

Route to A*

Ask students to research the question 'Why did sexual reproduction evolve?' They should produce a short report (less than one side of A4) that shows how scientists explain the evolution of something so complex and at risk of failure compared with producing clones of oneself.

Answers to Student Book questions

1 **(a)** Half of their genes come from each parent, so they will have some characteristics of each parent. **(b)** Each gamete carries different genes, so all the offspring will be different as they were formed from different gametes.

2 They all receive the same genes from their parent.

3 Table similar to the following:

	Sexual reproduction	Asexual reproduction
advantages	produces variation in offspring good when environment changes	unless conditions change, all offspring will be well suited to environment faster than sexual reproduction
disadvantages	takes longer than asexual reproduction wastes energy as only some offspring will be suited to environment and others will die	if environment changes, all offspring will suffer same fate as no variation

4 **(a)** Sexual reproduction, using pollen from one plant on the flower of another, because he wants variation that is different to what there was before. **(b)** Asexual reproduction, such as leaf cuttings from the one plant, because he wants many clones of the plant (new plants that all have the same genes and so the same characteristics).

5 **(a)** Not identical, because they were the product of sexual reproduction. **(b)** They can move around to find a mate. **(c)** Sexual reproduction produces variation that will hopefully mean that some offspring will be well suited to any change in conditions the following year; asexual reproduction of females that have grown well means they can have many more offspring in the same time which should also grow well in the same place.

6 **(a)** Asexual reproduction, because it is fast so can outcompete other plants that use sexual reproduction; also conditions are not likely to be different in the same area so if parent grows well then offspring should too. **(b)** Sexual reproduction, because conditions will probably be different downriver, so variation in offspring will hopefully mean some are well suited to the different conditions.

7 First the student should take cuttings from the plant to produce as large a number of clones as possible. This will eliminate the effect of genetic variation as all the plants will be clones. A large number will allow the use of repeats to remove any random effects in the experiment. She should choose a suitable range of temperatures over which plants grow (e.g. 5–35 °C) and set up several plants in each temperature, controlling all other variables (such as light, water and nutrients) as far as possible. The plants should be allowed to grow for several weeks, then a number of leaves that have formed since the experiment started should be selected for measurement. Measurements of leaves for each temperature should be averaged, and the averages compared.

B1 6.3

Cloning plants and animals

Link to the specification

B1.7.2c Modern cloning techniques include:

- tissue culture – using small groups of cells from part of a plant
- embryo transplants – splitting apart cells from a developing animal embryo before they become specialised, then transplanting the identical embryos into host mothers
- adult cell cloning – the nucleus is removed from an unfertilised egg cell. The nucleus from an adult body cell, e.g. a skin cell, is then inserted into the egg cell. An electric shock then causes the egg cell to begin to divide to form embryo cells. These embryo cells contain the same genetic information as the adult skin cell. When the embryo has developed into a ball of cells, it is inserted into the womb of an adult female to continue its development.

Ideas for practical work

Investigate the best technique for growing new plants from tissue cultures (e.g. cauliflower).

How Science Works

SKU: B1.7 bullet 1: Interpret information about cloning techniques and genetic engineering techniques. B1.7 bullet 2: Make informed judgements about the economic, social and ethical issues concerning cloning and genetic engineering, including GM crops.

CA: B4.2.1b Suggesting ways of managing risks; B4.3.1 Making observations by carrying out practical work and research, and using the data collected to develop hypotheses.

B1 6.3 Cloning plants and animals

Learning objectives

- explain how plants are grown using tissue culture
- describe what embryo transplants are
- describe how clones are made by adult cell cloning
- interpret information about cloning and explain the advantages and disadvantages of different methods.

Tissue culture

Plant growers have grown new plants from cuttings for many centuries. Now they can also grow new plants using just a few cells from the parent plant. This is known as **tissue culture** and is another form of cloning.

Cells are taken from the tip of a shoot and placed on a jelly that contains nutrients and a chemical that helps the cells to divide. They make a small ball of cells called a **callus**. The callus can be split to make new calluses. Each callus is then put on a jelly that contains different chemicals to encourage roots and shoots to form. When the new plants are large enough, they are planted into compost. Tissue culture makes it easier to grow thousands of new plants from one original one.

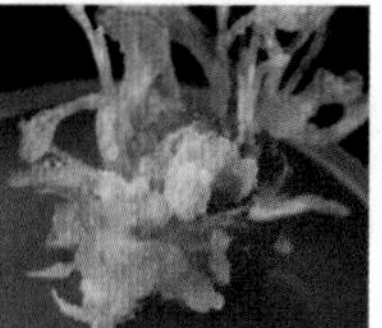

Forming new plants in tissue culture.

Science in action

One of the great advantages of tissue culture is that the cells from the shoot tip are usually free of disease-causing pathogens that are in the rest of the plant. This is particularly important in producing new banana plants, because bananas usually reproduce asexually by runners, so infection can easily pass from the parent plant to the offspring. This is helping farmers in Africa to produce enough food where banana diseases usually devastate crops.

Embryo transplants

When animals reproduce, most of the cells in the embryo **specialise** before the animal is born. Specialised animal cells, such as muscle cells, cannot change into other kinds of cell. This means that cloning animals is much more difficult than cloning plants, but it can be done.

One way is called **embryo transplanting**. An egg is fertilised with sperm in a laboratory. When it has divided to make four or eight cells, before they start to specialise, the cells are separated to start making new embryos. These are transplanted into the womb of **host mothers** where they grow until they are ready to be born.

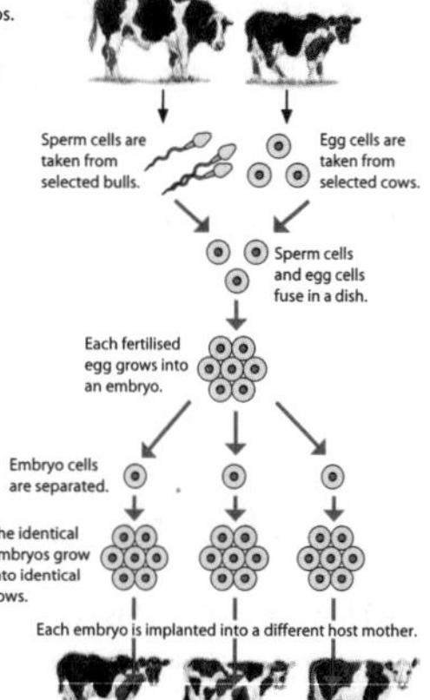

Sperm cells are taken from selected bulls.
Egg cells are taken from selected cows.
Sperm cells and egg cells fuse in a dish.
Each fertilised egg grows into an embryo.
Embryo cells are separated.
The identical embryos grow into identical cows.
Each embryo is implanted into a different host mother.

Figure 1 Embryo transplanting means farmers can get many more offspring from their best animals.

Adult cell cloning

Another animal cloning technique is **adult cell cloning**, where the nucleus of an unfertilised egg cell is removed and replaced with the nucleus of a body cell, e.g. skin cell, from an adult animal. The egg cell can then be given an electric shock so that it starts to divide like a normal embryo. The embryo will contain the same genetic information as the adult body cell. Although this was first done successfully with sheep, it has been repeated for many animal species. People are concerned that it could be used to make human clones, but scientists are using the technique to make replacement cells for problems such as spinal cord damage.

sheep X

sheep Y

Cell taken from the udder of an adult sheep.

Unfertilised egg cell taken, and the nucleus removed.

Nucleus extracted and used.

Nucleus from udder cell inserted into unfertilised egg cell. An electric shock causes the cell to start dividing to form a ball of cells (an embryo).

sheep Z

The embryo is placed into the womb of another sheep to develop. The first lamb born by this process, in 1996, was called Dolly.

Figure 2 Adult cell cloning.

Science skills

It took 277 attempts using adult cell cloning to create a cell that successfully grew into a healthy sheep. Most attempts fail because the cells do not develop normally. As an adult, Dolly was mated and produced healthy lambs, but she developed arthritis (usually occurs in much older sheep) and was put down at the age of six because of lung cancer. The scientists who bred her said her early death was not the result of being a clone, but other scientists think that using an 'old' nucleus could cause the animal to age faster than normally. What are the pros and cons of continuing adult cell cloning research?

Science in action

Since Dolly the sheep was created, the same technique has been used in many other species, including cats and dogs. For about US$50 000 you could have your pet dog or cat cloned. However, although the clone would look like your pet, it probably wouldn't behave exactly the same way.

Questions

1 **(a)** How is tissue culture different from taking cuttings? **(b)** How is tissue culture the same as taking cuttings?

2 Are all animals produced by embryo transplanting clones? Explain your answer.

3 Why would it make sense for a farmer to use an expensive technique such as embryo transplanting rather than allowing bulls and cows to mate as usual?

4 Look at the diagram in Figure 2, which shows how Dolly the sheep was produced. The three adult sheep were all different species. Which sheep was Dolly a clone of? Explain your answer.

5 Draw a flow chart to show all the steps in tissue culture.

6 Describe how adult cell cloning could be used to create a human clone.

7 Tissue culture is being used increasingly to save rare and endangered plant species. Explain as fully as you can the advantages and disadvantages of using tissue culture for this, rather than collecting seed as scientists used to do.

8 Evaluate the disadvantages of producing a human clone using adult cell cloning.

A*

Learning objectives

Most students should be able to:

- explain how plants are grown using tissue culture
- describe what embryo transplants are
- describe how clones are made by adult cell cloning
- interpret information about cloning and explain the advantages and disadvantages of different methods.

Some students should also be able to:

- explain fully the social and economic impact of tissue culture methods on the lives of small farmers. [Ext]

Key points

Tissue culture uses small groups of plant cells to produce many clones of a parent plant.

Embryo transplants can be used to split cells from an animal embryo and then to transplant them into host mothers to produce cloned animals.

Adult cell cloning transfers a nucleus from a body cell into an unfertilised egg from which the nucleus has been removed to produce a cloned animal.

The cloned animal has the same genetic characteristics as the body cell from which the nucleus was taken.

Lesson activities

Starter

1 As students come into class, give each one a sticky note. Ask them to write down three things they learned from the last two lessons on asexual and sexual reproduction. Ask them to give a confidence rating to each of their statements

Adult cell cloning | callus | embryo transplant | host mother | specialise | tissue culture (red, amber or green) and post them on the board. Pick five statements from the board that have low confidence ratings and throw a related question to the whole class. These points can be picked up on in this lesson. [AfL]

2 Write the word *clone* in the middle of the board and ask students to suggest related words and how they should b e linked to create a mind map on the topic. This should revise what was learnt in the last lesson as well as knowledge students bring from other learning. [AfL]

Main

1 B1 6.3a Tissue culture This practical gives students the opportunity to clone African violet plants using tissue culture techniques. It will take about 6 weeks to complete.

2 B1 6.3b The human cloning debate The worksheet for this activity could be completed as a simple comprehension activity. Alternatively it could be used as the basis for a class debate on whether human cloning should be allowed or not. Students could take the role of each of the people quoted on the worksheet. Further research could be used to prepare each argument for presentation to the 'jury'.

3 Watch the video clips (BBC Archive – Jimmy's Global Harvest) showing the use of tissue culture bananas in Kenya. The first shows how the tissue culture is done, and the second describes the economic impact on farmers. Students need to know that new banana plants are generally created by taking cuttings from old plants. Any cuttings will have viral and other diseases of the parent plant. Using tissue culture reduces the risk of the young plants being infected.

Plenaries

1 Ask students to quickly jot down one advantage and one disadvantage for each of the following techniques: tissue culture, embryo transplants, adult cell cloning. Take examples from around the class and ask students to identify whether the answers relate to social, economic or ethical issues, or a mix of these. Continue until you feel that all the main issues have been covered. [AfL]

2 Ask students to write glossary definitions for the key words for this lesson. Take examples from around the class and discuss any differences in the definitions in order to come up with a class definition for each. [AfL]

Homework

1 Students could use the Internet to research recent examples of cloning in the news, to discover how the technique is progressing and the ethical, social and economic issues that it is raising.

2 Worksheet B1 6.3c contains some questions on the various techniques covered in this lesson.

Route to A*

Ask students to research the history of cloning animal cells, which goes back to the 1950s and beyond. They should explain how the research has developed over time, what difficulties were overcome at each stage, and suggest where the research may be heading in the future.

Answers to Student Book questions

Science skills

Advantages: might help to provide treatments for disorders caused by damaged cells, such as paralysis caused by spinal cord damage; research helps develop techniques that will improve success rate.

Disadvantages: practical problems with high failure rate, economic costs of failing much of the time (ethical problems of creating an embryo that won't be allowed to grow into an individual).

Answers

1 **(a)** It uses much smaller pieces of plant tissue. **(b)** It produces many clones of the same plant using pieces of plant tissue.

2 Yes, because they came from cells separated from an embryo so would all have the same chromosomes/genes.

3 If he has a prize cow and bull that produce quality calves from mating, he will get more calves from this pair using embryo transplanting than by usual mating (it will also save the prize cow going through pregnancy, which has risks).

4 Dolly was a clone of sheep X, because that was where the nucleus with all the genes for Dolly came from.

5 Removing and preparing small pieces of tissue from shoot tip ⟶ placing in/on jelly containing chemicals (hormones) to stimulate cell division ⟶ separating cells of callus into other jelly with hormones to produce more calluses ⟶ placing callus on jelly with different chemicals (hormones) to stimulate root and shoot growth ⟶ planting small plants into compost when large enough to handle.

6 Take an unfertilised human egg cell and remove the nucleus. Take the nucleus from a body cell of the person that is to be cloned, and put it in the egg cell. Stimulate the cell to divide and develop into an early embryo. Place the embryo into the womb of a woman.

7 Advantages: can get thousands of plants from one; means not removing thousands of seeds where they naturally grow so more seeds can be left to germinate where they are endangered/rare; growing more plants by tissue culture more likely to be successful because not all seeds germinate, so an expedition to collect seed that failed to germinate would be a waste of time and money; can take parts of existing plants so can leave the rest where they are endangered and cause minimal damage to environment.

Disadvantages: all plants grown from tissue culture will have identical genes, so no variation unless parts of many live plants are brought back to the lab; problems of storage of lots of bits of live plant tissue while transporting to the lab.

8 Risk of failure is very high using current techniques; so may take time and a lot of money. Even if an embryo is successfully created there is no guarantee it will produce a healthy individual. The clone may be more at risk of age-related or other diseases as a result of using the cytoplasm of the body cell. Human cloning is only likely to happen if a person is prepared to pay a lot of money (and go against the law) to make a clone of themselves. There is no guarantee that the clone will be completely identical to the original person, because environmental factors affect many characteristics as well as genes.

B1 6.4 Modifying the genetic code

Link to the specification

B1.7.2d In genetic engineering, genes from the chromosomes of humans and other organisms can be 'cut out' using enzymes and transferred to cells of other organisms.

B1.7.2e Genes can also be transferred to the cells of animals, plants or microorganisms at an early stage in their development so that they develop with desired characteristics.

- New genes can be transferred to crop plants.
- Crops that have had their genes modified in this way are called genetically modified crops (GM crops).
- Examples of genetically modified crops include ones that are resistant to insect attack or to herbicides.
- Genetically modified crops generally show increased yields.

How Science Works

SKU: B1.7 bullet 1: Interpret information about cloning techniques and genetic engineering techniques. B1.7 bullet 2: Make informed judgements about the economic, social and ethical issues concerning cloning and genetic engineering including GM crops.

B1 6.4 Modifying the genetic code

Learning objectives

- describe how genes can be cut out and transferred into other cells
- explain why we cut out genes and transfer them into other cells
- explain the result of transferring genes into organisms in the early stages of development
- interpret information about genetic engineering.

Genetic engineering

The genetic information in all organisms works in the same way, whether it comes from a plant, an animal or a bacterium. Therefore, we can take a gene for a particular characteristic from a chromosome of an individual of one species and insert it into an individual of a different species and it will produce the same characteristic. This is called **genetic engineering**. The organism that contains the new gene has been **genetically modified** (GM), and is called a **transgenic organism**.

Genetic engineering has many practical applications. For example, we can transfer the gene for making the hormone insulin from a human cell into a bacterium. Insulin is a hormone that is needed by some diabetic people to prevent them becoming very ill. It is possible to grow many genetically modified bacteria on a large scale in bacterial fermenters. This means we can make a lot of human insulin more cheaply and safely than before. We now use GM bacteria to make human growth hormone and a vaccine to protect against infection by the disease hepatitis B.

This mouse contains a gene from a fluorescent jellyfish that glows under blue light.

Insulin gene cut out of chromosome using enzymes.
insulin gene
bacterial DNA
Human insulin gene inserted into bacterial DNA.
Bacterial DNA inserted back into bacterium.
Bacterium reproduces asexually making many identical bacteria with the human insulin gene.
Insulin gene makes insulin.
Insulin extracted and purified for use.

Figure 1 How genetically modified human insulin is produced.

Examiner feedback

Although you may come across the term *transgenic* in your research, you do not need to remember it for your exam.

Science in action

The demand for insulin for treating diabetes is very great, so scientists are looking for new, faster and cheaper processes for producing it. One current possibility is to use genetically modified plants, such as safflower.

Before we could make GM bacteria to produce human insulin, the insulin was extracted from dead animals, such as pigs. This not only meant there was less insulin available, but the insulin produced was not identical to human insulin and could cause health problems.

It is also possible to insert a gene into some of the body cells rather than an early embryo. This means that only those body cells make what the gene codes for, and the gene cannot be passed on to offspring. Scientists are developing ways of treating human diseases caused by faulty genes, such as cystic fibrosis, in this way.

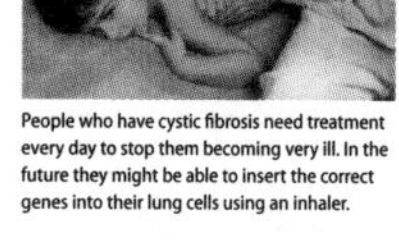

People who have cystic fibrosis need treatment every day to stop them becoming very ill. In the future they might be able to insert the correct genes into their lung cells using an inhaler.

Transferring genes at an early stage

Genes can also be transferred into a plant or animal embryo at an early stage in their development. As the organism grows, all the cells in its body will have a copy of the inserted gene, so all cells can develop the desired characteristics. This technique is most commonly used to make GM food plants. However, it is also very important in research for causes and treatments of human diseases. Mice have been genetically modified so that they can be used to study human cancers, or to investigate the effect of changes to particular genes that cause human diseases. Using mice like this has rapidly increased our knowledge and means treatments will be developed sooner.

Science skills

Inserting genes into human embryos is illegal. Although it could help cure genetic diseases, there are many arguments against it:

- treatment would be expensive, so would only wealthy people get it?
- the parents choose the treatment not the child who gets it – is this right?
- what if parents could choose other genes for insertion, such as for height or intelligence?

This mouse is genetically modified so that it can be used to find out more about human cancers, how they are caused and how they can be treated.

Questions

1. Define the term *genetic engineering* in your own words.
2. Explain why we can transfer a characteristic from one species into a different species.
3. Suggest why the insertion of genes into a human embryo is illegal in most countries.
4. Draw a flow chart to describe how human growth hormone could be produced by genetically modifying bacteria.
5. List as many advantages as you can for producing human insulin from genetically engineered bacteria.
6. Should a parent have the right to choose to have a gene inserted into their embryo so that their child does not have a genetic disease? Justify your answer.
7. Compare as fully as you can the effect of inserting genes into body cells with the effect of inserting genes into embryo cells.
8. Evaluate the ethical and social issues of using GM mice to research the causes and treatment of human diseases such as cancer.

Examiner feedback

It is important that you appreciate the ethical concerns some people have about gene therapy and why it continues to be the focus of much debate.

Taking it further

Plasmids from bacteria are one of the main methods scientists use for transferring genes into bacteria to make genetically modified bacteria. This process copies the natural process that many types of bacteria use for exchanging genetic material.

78 Variation 79

Learning objectives

Most students should be able to:

- describe how genes can be cut out and transferred into other cells
- explain why we cut out genes and transfer them into other cells
- explain the result of transferring genes into organisms in the early stages of development
- interpret information about genetic engineering.

Some students should also be able to:

- evaluate different methods of genetic engineering for different purposes.

Key points

Genes can be cut out of a chromosome of one organism and inserted into of another organism.

Genes can be inserted into cells, so that just these cells produce the characteristic from those genes.

Genes inserted into an early-stage embryo will be copied in every body cell so the whole organism will produce the characteristics controlled by those genes.

ActiveTeach Resource: Genetic modification – *Video/animation*
The effects of inserting genes – *Powerpoint slideshow*

Lesson activities

Starter

1 Write the following words on the board: gene, characteristic, chromosome, nucleus. Give students a few minutes to write questions for which these words are the answers. Take examples from the class. You may wish to revisit these at the end of the lesson and ask students to rewrite the questions in relation to genetic engineering.

 Genetic engineering | genetic modification | transgenic organism

2 Ask students to consider any characteristics that they know of in one kind of organism which could be useful in another organism, e.g. a lion that made chlorophyll in its skin wouldn't have to spend as much time hunting. They should choose three that they think are the most useful, then apply what they know about genetic and environmental control of characteristics to identify those that could be created by transferring the appropriate gene from one organism to the other.

Main

1 B1 6.4a The process of genetic engineering This activity provides reinforcement on the stages of genetic engineering using bacteria. The extension activity asks students to research other vectors for the transmission of DNA between cells and to identify the advantages of each method for particular purposes.

2 The ActiveTeach video *Genetic modification* explains at a very simple level how genetic modification can be used to produce animals and plants with new characteristics. For each example ask students to suggest an advantage and, if possible, a disadvantage with producing the transgenic organism. [AT]

3 The ActiveTeach presentation *The effects of inserting genes* is a slideshow that compares the techniques of the insertion of genes into early embryos (genetic engineering) and into adult cells (gene therapy) from the perspective of their long-term impact, and it provides a few examples of each. [AT]

Plenaries

1 Give students the following sets of words and ask them to write one sentence for each set:

a gene, transfer, vector
b DNA, enzyme, nucleus
c genetic engineering, characteristic, embryo.

Take examples from around the class and encourage discussion on how to improve them.

2 Ask students to quickly jot down the stages in the production of a transgenic plant that contains a gene for insect resistance which has been taken from a bacterium. Take examples of each stage from around the class to compile a class list of stages. This will help students identify any stages that they have missed or misunderstood. [AfL]

Homework

1 Worksheet B1 6.4b provides examples of how genetic engineering is being used in areas other than crop development. Students should use these examples as a focus for their own research into the advantages and disadvantages of genetic modification.

Points to note

- Students will come across the terms *vector* (the method of transferring genes into another organism) and *plasmid* (the bacterial DNA that is separate from the main DNA of a bacterium, used commonly for genetic transfer) in their research on methods of genetic modification. Although it will be helpful for their understanding to know the meaning of these terms, they will not need to remember them for their exams.
- Note that GM crops are covered in greater detail in the next lesson.

Route to A*

Ask students to research how the media present stories about genetic engineering. Some are more factual, others more sensationalist. Students should choose one of each style and criticise them both for scientific accuracy, accessibility for the intended audience, and then summarise what each story is trying to achieve in its audience.

Answers to Student Book questions

1 Anything similar to: inserting a gene from one organism into another so that it produces a characteristic.
2 Genes work the same way in all organisms, so a gene from one organism will create the same characteristic (such as make a protein) in another species.
3 Most people are unhappy with the idea that it would change the cells of the new individual completely.
4 Cut human growth hormone gene from human chromosome using enzymes → insert gene into bacterial chromosome → put bacteria into conditions where they grow and multiply rapidly → bacteria will produce growth hormone → extract and purify hormone.
5 Cheaper than extracting insulin from animals; can be produced in much larger quantities and faster; less likely to cause problems with health.
6 Either yes or no with suitable justification, such as: yes, because it will prevent the child suffering from the disease; no, because we do not have the right to make decisions for others.
7 Inserting into body cells causes only those cells to make the characteristic, the gene cannot be passed on to offspring; inserting into embryo cells means all cells get the gene, including gametes, so all cells have the potential to make the characteristic, and the gene can be passed on to offspring.
8 Ethical issues include the creation of genetically modified mice that are only being used for research. Also, is it right to create genetically modified mice that we know will suffer from human diseases such as cancer? However, most people think that it is better to research on mice than on humans.

Social issues include the fact that this kind of research speeds up the development of knowledge of the causes and possible treatment of human cancers. This means that fewer people may end up suffering or dying from cancer.

B1 6.5

Making choices about GM crops

Link to the specification

B1.7.2e Genes can also be transferred to the cells of animals, plants or microorganisms at an early stage in their development so that they develop with desired characteristics.

- New genes can be transferred to crop plants.
- Crops that have had their genes modified in this way are called genetically modified crops (GM crops).
- Examples of genetically modified crops include ones that are resistant to insect attack or to herbicides.
- Genetically modified crops generally show increased yields.

B1.7.2f Concerns about GM crops include the effect on populations of wild flowers and insects, and uncertainty about the effects of eating GM crops on human health.

How Science Works

SKU: B1.7 bullet 2: Make informed judgements about the economic, social and ethical issues concerning cloning and genetic engineering, including GM crops.

B1 6.5

Making choices about GM crops

Learning objectives

- describe how GM crops are produced
- explain some of the issues surrounding the use of GM crops
- evaluate claims related to the production of GM crops.

Science in action

Evidence from trials carried out by GM seed companies show that herbicide-resistant crops produce greater yields than non-resistant crops. Trials by other scientists working with farmers often show a decreased yield in GM crops. One study in the USA showed that GM soybean produced about 4700 kg/ha compared with over 5170 kg/ha from the nearest similar non-GM variety. These scientists suggest that inserting the gene has damaged other parts of the plant development, which affects yield.

Making GM crops

Plants can be genetically modified by inserting the required gene into the cells of an early embryo. Often a bacterium, called *Agrobacterium*, is used to get the new gene inside the nucleus of the cells where it can join with the cell's DNA.

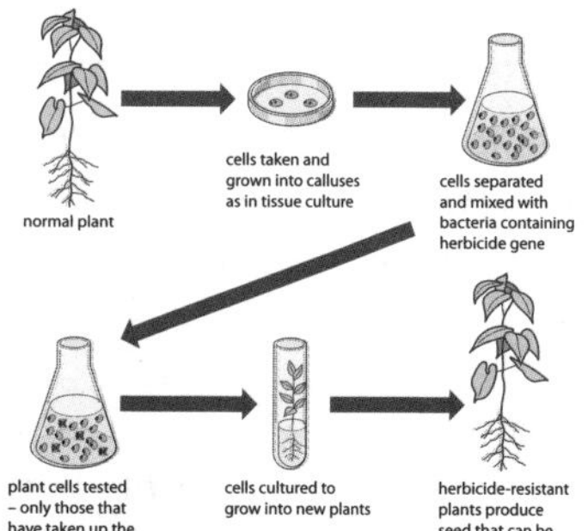

normal plant
cells taken and grown into calluses as in tissue culture
cells separated and mixed with bacteria containing herbicide gene
plant cells tested – only those that have taken up the new gene are kept
cells cultured to grow into new plants
herbicide-resistant plants produce seed that can be planted in fields

Figure 1 Producing GM plants.

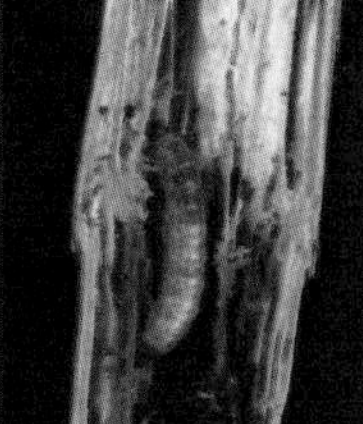

In Africa, the maize stalk borer damages plants and reduces crop yields by 20–40% on average.

Different modifications

Many GM crops have a gene for **herbicide** resistance. While a crop is growing, other plants compete for water and nutrients in the soil. These weed plants can reduce the amount of food harvested from the crop (the **yield**). Farmers use herbicides to kill plants, but these chemicals can damage the crop plants as well. Using crops that are resistant to a particular herbicide means that the crop can be sprayed with that herbicide to kill weeds without damaging the crop.

Some crop plants are modified with a gene for a poison that kills insects that try to eat the plant. Pest damage reduces crop yield, so GM crops should produce a greater yield.

The pros and cons of GM crops

One concern with GM crops is that the seed costs more than normal seed, and the companies that produce seed for herbicide-resistant crops also produce the herbicide that the crop is resistant to. This is good for those companies but not necessarily good for farmers.

80

Another concern is gene transfer through **pollination**. Pollination can happen occasionally between plants that are closely related. As crop varieties were bred originally from wild varieties, if those wild types are weeds growing nearby, then the inserted gene could be transferred to them. Research in Canada has shown that the gene for herbicide resistance has been transferred to weed species within six years of growing GM crops.

Using GM varieties changes the way farmers look after their crops, which can also affect the environment. Growing insect-resistant crops can benefit other species of insects because chemical insecticides, which kill other insect species as well as the pest, are not used. However, where herbicide-resistant varieties have been grown on a large scale, there is no evidence of reduced use of chemicals that kill a wide range of plant species and this means that the variety of wildflowers is reduced, which will affect insect and bird species that feed on them.

People are also concerned about the safety of the foods produced from the crops. Although the foods are tested on animals to make sure they don't cause health problems, we have no idea yet if there are any problems caused by eating GM foods over a long time.

Much more research is needed if GM crops are to help feed the increasing human population.

Questions

1. Explain why plant embryos are used for genetic modification.
2. Sketch a diagram to show how weeds can reduce crop yield.
3. Suggest any disadvantages of using crops that are modified to resist insect attack.
4. Explain how using an insect-resistant crop variety could help the environment.
5. No GM crops are grown for sale in the UK at the moment, but there are licensed scientific trials. Should this be allowed? Justify your answer.
6. A small-scale farmer in Kenya is considering growing GM maize that is resistant to stalk borer. How would you evaluate the advantages and disadvantages of this so that you could advise on the best choice?
7. Genetic engineering and tissue culture are two possible solutions to the problem of creating disease-free bananas. Explain fully why using tissue culture is more likely to be the better approach for poor farmers in Africa.
8. Explain as fully as you can why results for yield in trials on GM crops by the companies that make the seed might be more positive about increased yields than the results from other scientists.

A*

Spraying a field with herbicide will get rid of not just the weeds, but also the animals that feed on the weeds, and animals that feed on those animals.

POTATOES
NOT
MUTATOES!
GOOD

Opinion on the value of GM crops is divided because people are not sure about long-term effects.

Examiner feedback

You will be expected to understand and present both sides of the ethical debate on GM crops, and not just give your own point of view.

You will be expected to apply the knowledge and understanding you have gained on your course to new examples.

Variation 81

Learning objectives

Most students should be able to:

- describe how GM crops are produced
- explain some of the issues surrounding the use of GM crops
- evaluate claims related to the production of GM crops.

Some students should also be able to:

- evaluate the potential for GM and other technologies to improve crop production in poor areas. [Ext]

Key points

Crop plants have been genetically modified for herbicide resistance or insect resistance.

People are concerned that GM crops may harm the environment or human health.

We need good evidence on which to base judgements about GM crops.

Lesson activities

Starter

1 Write the words *genetic modification* on the board and ask students to suggest words that can be used, and how they should be linked, to create a mind map on the topic. This will help to revise what was learnt in the last lesson, and could be revisited as suggested in *Plenary 2*.

Herbicide pollination weed yield

2 Ask students to suggest the problems that farmers have with damage caused to crops. (If necessary, remind them about competition between plants, and the problems of pest/herbivores covered in Chapter 4.) Ask them to suggest characteristics that could be useful in these plants to reduce the problems, and therefore which genetically controlled characteristics scientists could be looking for.

Main

1 B1 6.5a GM crops in the UK This activity focuses on a study carried out by the Government over 3 years on the effects of GM crops on the environment. This is a useful opportunity to raise the issue of biodiversity. Killing off weeds means we get more yield from the crop, but also means there are no food plants for many species of insects and birds. Is this a good thing or a bad thing?

2 B1 6.5b The GM food debate In this activity, students prepare for a debate on whether or not GM foods should be allowed for sale in the UK. The worksheet presents some facts and opinions that can be used to organise the different perspectives of the debate. Students should carry out further research to prepare their arguments.

3 Ask students to research websites that discuss the merits and disadvantages of GM crops. Useful sites include: Monsanto, Gene Watch, Friends of the Earth, The Food Standards Agency, and Greenpeace. Students should try to work out whether the website is for or against the growing of GM crops, or presents a balanced argument (note that some sites are very subtle about their attitude, suggesting balance but generally providing a pro or negative stance). They should identify quotes from each site to use as evidence for the site's general attitude to the debate.

Plenaries

1 Ask students to work in small groups to think of two questions that they would like to ask a researcher working on genetic modification of crop plants. After a few minutes, take selections from the class to write on the board. Try to get a list of the five most important questions from the students' point of view. [AfL]

2 Revisit the mind map created in *Starter 1* and ask students to suggest any additions or amendments that could be made as a result of what they have learnt in the lesson. They should justify any changes that they suggest and, if other students do not agree, encourage discussion to produce a consensus view.

Homework

1 Ask students to prepare a poster, slideshow or report on the arguments for and against the growing of GM crops in the UK.

2 Worksheet B1 6.5c is a comprehension activity about some of the advantages and disadvantages of growing GM crops. The extension question will need further research on the effect of factors other than technology in the development of crops to help poor farmers.

Route to A*

Ask students to research and then write a short report (one side of A4) on the following question 'Can GM crops solve the world's food shortages?' The report should refer to the claims made, who makes them and why, and should present arguments for or against – either approach is acceptable as long as the arguments are suitably supported by scientific evidence.

Answers to Student Book questions

1. So that all the cells of the plant contain the inserted gene.
2. Diagram should include: weeds and crops growing close together; roots of weeds and crops competing to get water and nutrients from soil; as crop plants get less water and nutrients when weeds are close, they cannot grow as well, so they cannot produce as much yield.
3. The seed will probably be more expensive than normal seed.
4. Using an insect-resistant crop means you don't have to spray with chemical insecticides that kill not just the pest, but also other insects; this leaves more food for insect-eating birds, and therefore for the predators that feed on the birds.
5. Either yes or no with suitable justification, such as: yes, because otherwise there is no way of getting the evidence on which to base decisions; no, because if it causes damage there will be no way to put things right again.
6. Any suitable suggestions, such as: comparing cost of seed of normal and GM varieties with expected yields, to see which gives best profit; checking to see if there are other ways of controlling pest effectively without using GM seed; considering cost of any chemicals used with normal variety, plus their impact on other insect species; checking for any change to farming practice between the varieties (e.g. does the GM variety need more fertiliser?) and what impact this has on farmer and environment.
7. Tissue culture is a simpler method than genetic modification. That means the plants produced will be cheaper. This is important to poor farmers who have little money. It also means they aren't tied to buying from one particular company, who control prices. Both methods should produce disease-free plants, but tissue culture should guarantee better quality because it produces clones – so using good-quality starting plants will more likely give good-quality offspring.
8. Bias because the company wants to convince people to buy their seed. The company may only carry out limited trials that don't give the full range of conditions that plants growing in normal farming conditions, in large fields, may experience. Company may only compare the GM yield with varieties that make the GM crop look good, while scientists should be comparing results of GM crop with the nearest equivalent so that they can draw valid conclusions.

B1 7.1 Evolution of life

Link to the specification

B1.8.1a Darwin's theory of evolution by natural selection states that all species of living things have evolved from simple life forms that first developed more than three billion years ago.

B1.8.1d Studying the similarities and differences between organisms allows us to classify living organisms into animals, plants and microorganisms, and helps us to understand evolutionary and ecological relationships. Models allow us to suggest relationships between organisms.

How Science Works

SKU: B1.8 bullet 1: Interpret evidence relating to evolutionary theory.

B1 7.1 Evolution of life

Learning objectives

- **describe how life on Earth has changed as a result of evolution**
- **interpret an evolutionary tree**
- **explain how the similarities and differences between organisms helps us to understand evolutionary and ecological relationships.**

Science skills

Scientists have different ideas about how life began on Earth. For example, bacteria-like cells may have arrived from other parts of our solar system, or they might have formed from chemical reactions that happened on Earth. How would you evaluate the claims of these suggestions?

Examiner feedback

You will find different ways of grouping organisms, but all you need to learn for your exam are three groups: microorganisms, plants and animals.

Life on Earth

The first evidence of life on Earth is found in rocks that are just over 3500 million years old. These rocks contain shapes that look like **fossils** of bacteria.

Scientists estimate that there are over 30 million species of organisms on the Earth today.

Relationships between living organisms

Most organisms can be quite easily classified into three main groups:

- microorganisms – single-celled organisms, such as bacteria
- plants – organisms that photosynthesise, mostly multi-celled
- animals – mostly multi-celled organisms that get their energy from eating other organisms.

Grouping organisms is known as **classification**. Studying the features of organisms carefully can help us decide how to classify them. When we group according to features, we have to be careful about how we interpret the results. Some features are strongly adapted to the environment, so organisms may be a similar shape because they have a similar lifestyle, that is, they show an **ecological relationship**.

Table 1 The main characteristics of mammals and fish.

Mammal	Fish
eggs fertilised inside the body usually give birth to live young mothers make milk for young usually have hair or fur get oxygen from air using lungs	eggs usually fertilised outside the body get oxygen from water using gills body covered in scales

Some features, such as the structure of the bones and their arrangement in the skeleton, can help us group organisms in a way that makes better predictions. For example, humans and dolphins share more characteristics than dolphins and sharks, so they are grouped as mammals. If we found an animal that shared characteristics with a human and a dolphin, we could predict that it also had other mammalian characteristics..

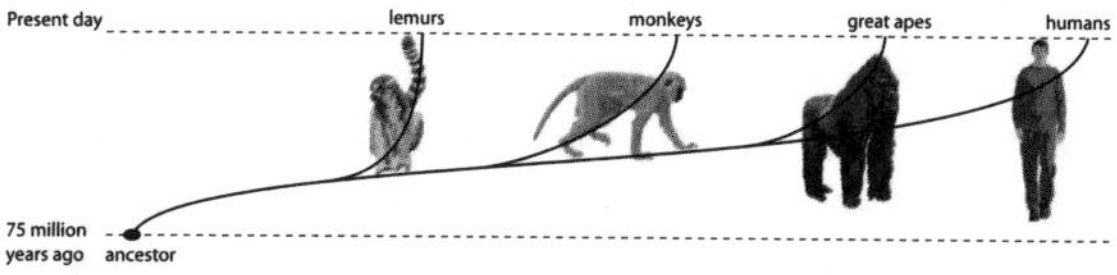

Figure 1 This diagram shows how closely humans are related to some other animals.

If we group animals according to how many similar characteristics they have, we get a diagram like this. This shows that humans are more like apes than monkeys, and more like monkeys than lemurs. This kind of diagram can be interpreted as an **evolutionary relationship**, where the different groups evolved from a **common ancestor**. It doesn't show that the modern great apes became humans, because both apes and humans have evolved since that last common ancestor.

Fossil evidence

Fossils are evidence of organisms that lived in the past. When a new fossil is discovered, scientists use characteristics in the fossil to help classify it with other fossils and with the same groups of organisms that we have today. If fossils are also grouped according to age, we can see that characteristics change over time. For example in fossils of ancient horse-like animals, we can see how the tooth structure and leg bone structure have changed.

The change in species over time is called **evolution**. So arranging similar fossil species to show how they changed over time is called an evolutionary relationship.

From all the fossil species that have been discovered, scientists believe that all the species that are living now evolved by changing gradually from the very simple cells that lived on Earth more than three billion years ago.

Questions

1 An organism contains chlorophyll. How should it be classified, and why?
2 You discover a new fossil skeleton. Explain what would be done so that it could be classified.
3 Explain why dolphins and sharks look similar.
4 In an early classification, snakes were grouped with earthworms. Suggest why this happened.
5 Snakes are now classified as vertebrates (a bony skeleton), and earthworms are invertebrates (no bones). What does this imply about their evolution?
6 Describe the evolutionary tree of humans and other animals in as much detail as you can.
7 Explain in detail what Figure 2 shows.
8 'Life began on Earth 3500 million years ago.' How accurate do you think this statement is? Explain your answer.

A*

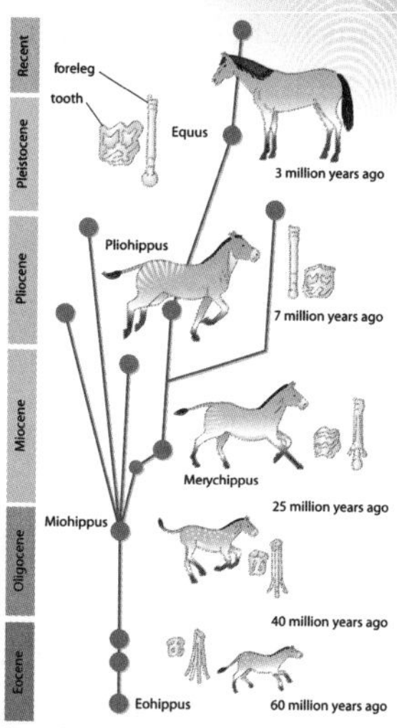

Figure 2 Evolution of the horse, based on teeth and bones from fossils. The tree-like shape is a suggested evolutionary relationship between the species.

Examiner feedback

You will be expected to explain how evolutionary trees are models that can be used to describe the relationship between organisms through time.

Learning objectives

Most students should be able to:

- describe how life on Earth has changed as a result of evolution
- interpret an evolutionary tree
- explain how the similarities and differences between organisms help us to understand evolutionary and ecological relationships.

Some students should also be able to:

- explain how the use of models, such as evolutionary trees and time lines, can help us to explain how life evolved on Earth from the simplest organisms. [Ext]

Key points

It is thought that all life on Earth evolved from simple life-forms that existed over three billion years ago.

We can use the characteristics of organisms to identify ecological and evolutionary relationships, and to classify them into the main groups.

Extinction may be caused by changes in the physical conditions of the environment, or by changes in other organisms, such as a new predators, diseases or competitors.

Lesson activities

Starter

1 Show students a group of at least six random objects (e.g. pencil, piece of paper, paperclip, ruler, exercise book and biro) and give them 5 minutes to classify them into related groups. Take examples of classifications from around the class, and draw out the key point of selecting characteristics and how the choice impacts on the final grouping.

2 Give students 2 minutes to jot down three key facts that they know about evolution. Take examples from round the class until you feel you have covered most of the points that could be expected from KS3 learning. [AfL]

 Classification common ancestor ecological relationship evolutionary relationship evolution fossil species

Main

1 B1 7.1a Time line for life on Earth This activity asks students to create a time line for life on Earth to indicate key moments in the evolution of life. Students could do this individually on an A4 sheet, or a class display could be prepared as a group activity in which students share out the questions on the worksheet to research. Students may need help in calculating and marking the main baseline. For a class display, students could find images of the organisms to include if there is sufficient space.

2 B1 7.1b The origin of life on Earth In this activity students sort various statements according to how well they act as evidence for the two main competing theories of the origin of life on Earth. Students could carry out further research to find more evidence for the two theories and could debate the strength of current evidence in order to decide which they think is the more convincing.

Plenaries

1 Give students a set of answers to which they have to write questions. As there may be more than one possible question that would give each answer, this activity is best done individually or in small groups. When students have had enough time to write their questions, you can compile a list on the board with contributions from each group. Suitable answers include: ecological relationship; over 4500 million years ago; common ancestor; origin of life.

2 Give students three minutes to write dictionary definitions for all the key words in this lesson. Take examples from around the class and discuss any differences between definitions for each word. [AfL]

Homework

1 Worksheet B1 7.1c uses the example of classification of mammals from bones and from DNA to show the need for corroborating evidence (in this case, from geology).

2 Worksheet B1 7.1d provides a further opportunity to interpret an evolutionary tree. The example given is the evolutionary relationship between the great apes and humans.

Route to A*

Students could research in greater detail the appearance of the main plant and animal phyla to add to the time line of life on Earth. They should use their findings to describe the main trends in evolution (e.g. the increasing complexity of body structure, evolution of characteristics that made life on land possible) in both plants and animals.

Answers to Student Book questions

Science skills

To test the idea that life came from beyond Earth you need to show that:

- life can survive in space (a vacuum with high levels of solar radiation, etc.)
- there is some way that life could get from space to Earth easily (e.g. meteors)
- there are examples of life in space/on other planets of the kinds first seen on Earth
- life beyond Earth existed at the time that the first signs of life appear on Earth.

To test the idea that life arose on Earth, you would need to show that:

- it is possible for organic chemicals to be formed from smaller inorganic chemicals by natural processes that do not include those that only occur inside living cells
- those chemicals and the processes needed to make organic chemicals existed somewhere on Earth at the time that the first signs of life appear on Earth.

Answers

1 Chlorophyll is used for photosynthesis, so the organism should be classified as a plant.

2 The structure of the bones, and their relationship within the skeleton, must be studied in detail, then compared with living organisms to get the closest match on as many characteristics as possible in order to get the best classification.

3 They both swim fast to catch food, so their shape and smooth surface help this. They also both catch food while moving at speed, so sharp teeth are an adaptive feature for this.

4 They have similar body shapes, i.e. long and thin without any limbs, and move across the ground by changing the shape of their body.

5 This suggests the two groups have very different evolutionary histories.

6 Humans, great apes, monkeys and lemurs are closely related and all evolved from a common ancestor. Lemurs were the first group to evolve on a separate line from the common ancestor of monkeys, great apes and humans. Then the monkeys began to evolve on a separate line from the ancestors of great apes and humans. Finally the great apes and human groups started to evolve separately. The tree shows that of all the groups, humans are most closely related to great apes.

7 The diagram shows the relationship between fossil and modern horse species over 60 million years based on similarities in their teeth and forelegs. *Eohippus* was a small species that lived 60 million years ago and had a small tooth and a short foreleg with four toes. *Miohippus* was a descendant of *Eohippus* that lived about 40 million years ago and was slightly larger, with a larger tooth and only three toes on its foreleg. *Merychippus* was one of the descendants of *Miohippus* that lived around 25 million years ago. It was larger again, with a larger more complex tooth and although it still had three toes, the two side toes were reduced in size compared with the central one. *Pliohippus* was one of the descendants of *Merychippus* and lived around seven million years ago. Its tooth was larger and more complex in structure and it had only one toe on its foreleg. *Equus*, the modern horse alive now, is a direct descendant of *Pliohippus*, and is much larger. Its tooth is also larger and more complex in structure, and the hoof on the foreleg is much larger than that of its ancestor.

8 It is difficult to be accurate at this distance in time. It depends on the accuracy of mechanisms for dating the rocks. It also depends on there being rocks at the surface of the Earth that are of this age, because most have been destroyed by geological processes. It would be more secure if there was other supporting evidence, such as from several different sites on the Earth's surface, or from other parts of the solar system.

B1 7.2 Evolution by natural selection

Link to the specification

B1.8.1e Evolution occurs via natural selection:

- individual organisms within a particular species may show a wide range of variation because of differences in their genes
- individuals with characteristics most suited to the environment are more likely to survive to breed successfully
- the genes that have enabled these individuals to survive are then passed on to the next generation.

B1.8.1f Where new forms of a gene result from mutation there may be relatively rapid change in a species if the environment changes.

How Science Works

SKU: B1.8 bullet 1: Interpret evidence relating to evolutionary theory.

B1 7.2 Evolution by natural selection

Learning objectives

- describe the impact of natural selection on variation in individuals
- explain how species evolve as a result of natural selection
- explain why the rate of change in a species may vary.

Evidence for evolution

Fossils show us that there have been other species on Earth than the ones we see today, and that they have changed over time. We can also see from breeding species, such as dogs, that the characteristics we select can be changed over time. These are two lines of evidence for the **theory of evolution**, but they don't help us understand how the change happens.

These dogs belong to the same species, but different characteristics were selected by humans in each breed.

Individuals of the same species may have different characteristics, such as slightly longer legs.

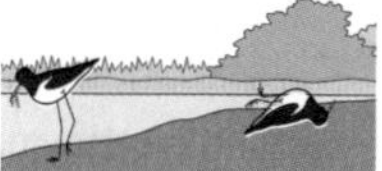

Individuals struggle to survive. Some die because of lack of food or may be eaten by predators.

Individuals with useful characteristics are more likely to survive, and pass on their characteristics to the next generation. The long-legged bird can get food but the short-legged one cannot.

Figure 1 Natural selection results in changes in characteristics.

Natural selection

Charles Darwin (1809–1882) spent years carefully observing organisms, asking questions and investigating the answers. What he saw was:

- organisms produce many more offspring than survive to adulthood
- there is variation between the individuals of a species and in the offspring they produce
- characteristics are passed from one generation to the next
- the individuals that are best adapted to the environment are the ones that survive and produce more offspring in the next generation.

Darwin deduced from his observations that the characteristics that were best adapted to the environment were the ones that would increase in the population in the next generation. He called this process **natural selection** because he was suggesting that nature – the environment – was selecting which characteristics were most successful.

How evolution occurs

Darwin suggested that evolution occurred because the environment changed. When the environment changes, different characteristics may be better suited to the new conditions. The individuals with those characteristics will be more likely to survive and breed. Darwin used the evidence of human selection of characteristics in breeding animals such as dogs and pigeons to support this idea.

Darwin thought that after enough time had passed, the characteristics in a population would have changed so much that we would consider those organisms to be a new **species**.

84

Genes and mutation in evolution

The idea of genes did not become widely known until 50 years after Darwin published his ideas on evolution. So he could not explain how characteristics were passed from parent to offspring. He also did not know that the variation in inherited characteristics between individuals is caused by their having different forms of genes, and these different forms are caused by random changes, or **mutations**, in the genes.

Many of these mutations have no effect on survival, but some are disadvantageous or fatal, often resulting in a miscarriage during pregnancy, and some can increase survival. For example, DNA evidence suggests that humans (*Homo sapiens*) first evolved in Africa and then spread out across the world. All African populations have dark skins that protect them from the damaging effects of sunlight, but all human societies in northern areas have pale skins. This is the result of random genetic mutation, which improves the health of people in these areas. So it would have been a good adaptation and selected for by the environment in northern areas.

It has been estimated that a baby has about 100 mutations that are different from its parents' genes.

The rate of change in a species is not constant. It depends on how quickly the environment changes and how difficult it is to survive in the new conditions. In difficult conditions, only the few variations that make survival possible will get passed on to the next generation and all other variations will die out. If conditions change so much that no variations can survive then all individuals will die and the species will become extinct.

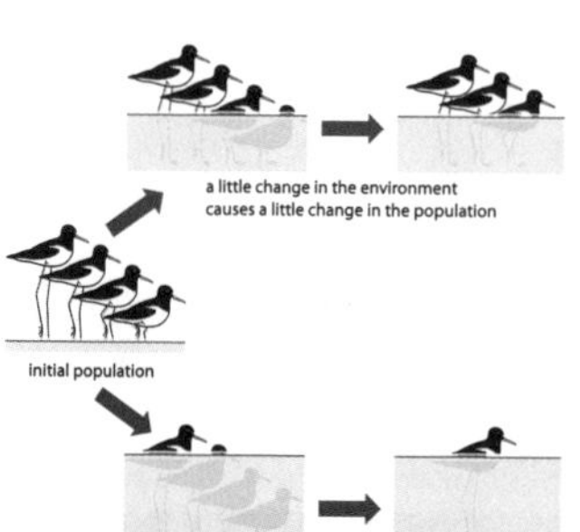
a little change in the environment causes a little change in the population
initial population
a large change in the environment causes a rapid change in the population

Figure 2 Rate of change in a species.

Questions

1. Define the terms *natural selection* and *evolution*.
2. Explain how the evidence from changing characteristics in animal breeding can be used to support the theory of evolution.
3. Mutation can occur anywhere in genes as a cell divides. Explain why only mutations that occur in gametes are important for evolution.
4. Explain how natural selection can change the characteristics of a species.
5. Explain why Darwin deduced from his observations that the best adapted characteristics should increase in a population.
6. Without mutation, there could be no evolution. Explain this statement.
7. Antibiotics are used to kill bacteria. Mutations for antibiotic resistance are rare. Use what you know about natural selection to: **(a)** explain why the increase in bacteria resistant to antibiotics has been so rapid **(b)** suggest ways to limit the increase in antibiotic-resistant bacteria.
8. After heavy fishing using large-mesh nets for many years in the North Sea, scientists have found that the size at which some fish species start breeding has decreased. Use evolutionary theory to explain why.

A*

Evolution 85

Learning objectives

Students should be able to:

- describe the impact of natural selection on variation in individuals
- explain how species evolve as a result of natural selection
- explain why the rate of change in a species may vary.

Key points

Natural selection is the process by which individuals with characteristics that are best adapted to the environment are more likely to survive and produce most offspring.

Evolution is the change in species over time, and occurs as a result of natural selection and changes in the environment.

Mutation of genes produces the variation that natural selection works on.

Lesson activities

Starter

1 Ask students to work in pairs to write linked sentences that contain the words adaptation, survival and competition. Take examples from around the class to identify any areas of learning that need reinforcing before attempting to discuss natural selection.

2 Show students a selection of images of different varieties of dog (such as at a Crufts dog show) and remind students that these all belong to the same species. Give students 3 minutes to work with a partner to suggest how the different varieties came to be. Take examples from around the class – accept any sensible suggestion at this stage.

Main

1 B1 7.2a Surviving environmental change This card game helps students to understand how changing conditions can change the predominant characteristics of a species. It will also show that no characteristic is wholly dependent on the environment. Students should work through lesson B1 7.2 in the Student Book before attempting the card game. (~15 mins)

Mutation natural selection species theory of evolution

2 Ask students to research examples of natural selection on the Internet or in books. Suitable examples include the effect of climate change on the size of birds in North America in terms of Bergman's rule (see Student Book lesson B1 4.2 and also BBC – Earth News), melanic (black) forms of moths such as *Biston betularia*, Darwin's mockingbirds and finches, and sickle cell trait in humans. They should try to explain the change in the examples they have found in terms of differential survival of individuals with different variations of a characteristic.

3 Ask students to draw a cartoon strip or prepare a slideshow to explain how natural selection causes change in a population. They could extend their work to explain how the rate of change in a species can be varied by the 'strength' of the selection factor, i.e. the proportion of individuals that can survive it.

Plenaries

1 Ask each student to write down three things that they think the person sitting next to them should have learnt and when they would have learnt it. Then ask students to ask each other in pairs whether they agree on the things they should have learnt. Ask them to agree a final list of the three most important points. [AfL]

2 Following on from *Starter 1*, ask students to work in pairs to explain how different varieties of dogs were developed, and why pedigrees (dogs with the perfect characteristics for the variety) are so important for maintaining each variety. Gives students 3 minutes to do this, then take examples from the class. Encourage discussion if there are differences in explanations. [AfL]

Homework

1 Worksheet B1 7.2b gives students the challenge of applying the theory of evolution by natural selection to the increasing problem of antibiotic resistance in bacteria.

2 Worksheet B1.7.2c is more challenging and anticipates one of the criticisms of Darwin's theory of evolution, that of how the theory can explain periods of rapid evolution. Darwin's theory will be covered in greater detail in lesson 7.3.

Points to note

- Point B1.8.1f in the specification is confusing. All variation in the forms of a gene is the result of mutation. Change in a species depends on there being sufficient variation from mutation in a population for natural selection to act on, but the rate of change in a species is dependent on the 'evolutionary pressure', i.e. how advantageous or deleterious a characteristic is in comparison to other characteristics in the population in terms of survival in the environment. The greater the evolutionary pressure, the greater the rate of change.

Route to A*

Ask students to research the 'founder effect', where the limited range of genetic variation in a small population reaching an island, for example, has a significant effect on the evolution of that species through natural selection. They should use their findings to describe and explain an example of the founder effect, such as Galapagos tortoises.

Answers to Student Book questions

1 Definitions that are similar to the following:
   - natural selection – the process by which individuals with variants of characteristics (caused by mutations to genes to create different forms of the genes) that are best adapted to the environment, are more likely to survive and successfully reproduce, becoming more common in a population over successive generations
   - evolution – the change in characteristics of the organisms of a species over time

2 Breeding of dogs shows that characteristics in a group of individuals can be changed over time by selecting which individuals breed and produce offspring (pass on their characteristics).

3 Only genes in gamete cells are passed to offspring during sexual reproduction, so only changes to the genes (mutations) in gametes can possibly result in changes to characteristics in the offspring.

4 If there is variation in characteristics (e.g. leg length/speed of running) within a group of organisms of the same species (population):
   - a new selection factor (such as change in water level, faster predator) affects the survival of individuals, such that those with particular variants of a characteristic survive better than those with other variants
   - individuals with adaptive variants (e.g. long legs/faster runners) of the characteristic survive and reproduce while those who don't are killed and don't produce offspring
   - the next generation shows more individuals with the adaptive variant

5 Darwin realised that if individuals with characteristics that were best adapted to the environment were the ones that were more likely to survive to reproduce, and they produced more offspring, because characteristics are passed from parent to offspring then there would be a higher proportion of individuals with the best-adapted characteristics in the next generation.

6 Mutation produces variation; if there is no variation then any changes in the environment will increase or decrease the chance of survival for all individuals by the same amount, so there will be no change – no evolution.

7 **(a)** Most bacteria are killed by an antibiotic, so only the rare mutants that are resistant will survive; as there will be no competition for them with other bacteria, they can reproduce rapidly to produce a resistant population. **(b)** Reduce use of antibiotics so selection for resistance is reduced; use several different antibiotics at the same time, as the chances of any bacteria being resistant to them all is less, although if there was a mutant bacterium that survived, it would be able to increase rapidly after other bacteria are removed, so this is a risky strategy.

8 Fishing is a selection factor – individuals that are caught can no longer breed. Only large fish are caught by nets of large mesh size. Small fish escape capture. Any fish that escapes capture and is able to breed will contribute more offspring to the next generation than fish that are caught. So breeding at small size is an advantage when there is heavy fishing. There will be more, smaller breeding fish as fishing continues.

B1 7.3 The development of a theory

Link to the specification

B1.8.1b The theory of evolution by natural selection was only gradually accepted because:

- the theory challenged the idea that God made all the animals and plants that live on Earth
- there was insufficient evidence at the time the theory was published to convince many scientists
- the mechanism of inheritance and variation was not known until 50 years after the theory was published.

B1.8.1c Other theories, including that of Lamarck, are based mainly on the idea that changes that occur in an organism during its lifetime can be inherited. We now know that in the vast majority of cases this type of inheritance cannot occur.

How Science Works

SKU: B1.8 bullet 1: Interpret evidence relating to evolutionary theory. B1.8 bullet 2: Suggest reasons why Darwin's theory of natural selection was only gradually accepted. B1.8 bullet 3: Identify the differences between Darwin's theory of evolution and conflicting theories, such as that of Lamarck. B1.8 bullet 4: Suggest reasons for the different theories.

B1 7.3 The development of a theory

Learning objectives

- explain why Darwin's theory was only gradually accepted
- interpret evidence relating to evolutionary theory
- evaluate different theories of evolution
- explain why Darwin's theory is the most commonly accepted theory of evolution.

Other theories of evolution

Two centuries ago, some scientists, other than Darwin, had developed other ways of explaining the diversity of species on Earth. Most people at the time thought that God had created everything. Richard Owen (1804–1892) was a biologist who tried to explain the similarities between species by suggesting that God created basic plans that were developed in different ways. The problem with Owen's theory is that it could not be tested scientifically using experiments.

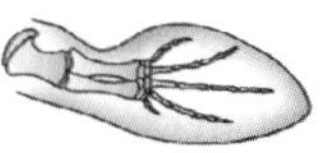
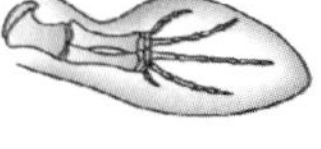
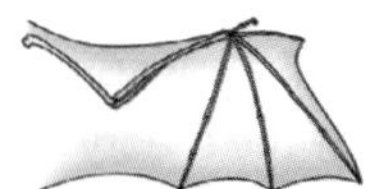

Figure 1 Owen used the examples of a bat's wing and a whale's flipper as evidence for his theory.

To reach food in deeper water, wading birds stretch their legs. This makes their legs slightly longer.

Having slightly longer legs is passed on to the next generation. Birds in this generation also stretch their legs.

Over many generations, the wading birds' legs become much longer.

Figure 2 How Lamarck's theory explains the evolution of long-legged birds.

An important theory in Darwin's time had been suggested by Jean-Baptiste Lamarck (1744–1829). Lamarck challenged the ideas of his time by suggesting that species can change; most scientists then believed that they were always the same. He developed his idea to say that the environment caused changes in species, and that these changes were passed on to the offspring.

The problems with Darwin's theory

When Darwin published his theory in 1859, he knew many people would reject it because it didn't consider God as the creator of species. However, many scientists had difficulty accepting Darwin's theory for other reasons. For them, the problem was that there was little evidence for natural selection causing change and creating new species. This is because it usually takes a long time for a new species to evolve. In addition, Darwin could not explain how characteristics were passed from parent to offspring. This would only be understood after Gregor Mendel's work on inheritance was widely published around 1900, and the concept of genes was developed.

This cartoon of 1871 ridiculed Darwin's idea that apes and humans are related.

Taking it further

Modern studies of inheritance show that Lamarck's theory is not entirely wrong in some cases, because of the way that genes are controlled. If a gene that had been active in a parent is 'switched off', it may remain switched off in any children they may have later. The study of changes in characteristics without a change in genes is called epigenetics.

The acceptance of Darwin's theory

Darwin's theory has now been used to make predictions that can be tested scientifically. One example was the work of Peter and Rosemary Grant in the 1970s, who used the theory to predict the effect of drought on the beaks of finches in the Galapagos Islands. The Grants saw that drought produced harder seeds. They predicted that the birds that got the most food and produced the most offspring would be those with the larger, stronger beaks so, in years following drought, beak size should increase.

86

Science skills The graphs show the sizes of finch beaks in a year after no drought (1976) and a year after drought (1978). The blue arrows show the mean beak depth.

a Describe the results and compare them with the Grants' prediction. Explain how this evidence supports Darwin's theory.

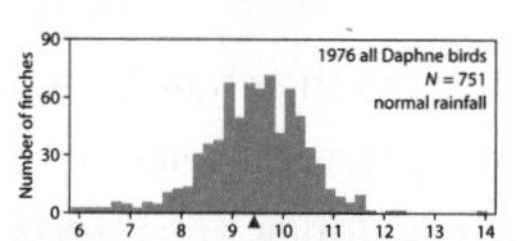

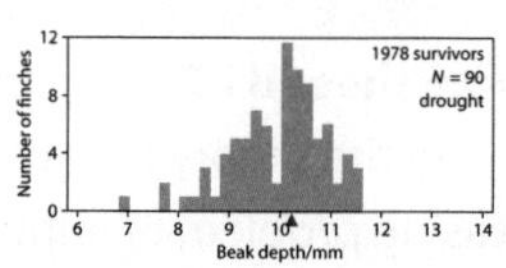

Figure 3 Changes to beak size in finches following drought.

The theory also satisfactorily explains many observations such as why new species evolve rapidly when a new environment occurs. For example, Lake Victoria in Africa is less than 15 000 years old, but contains over 500 species of one kind of fish that are found nowhere else in the world. All these species are most closely related to one species of river fish that lives in the area, and each species is adapted in slightly different ways – some are fast-swimming predators, some graze on weed in shallow water, and others have strong jaws to crush shellfish.

Darwin's theory is now generally accepted as the best explanation for how evolution occurs.

Taking it further

The studies of other scientists have modified Darwin's theory since his death. The theory that is generally held now is called modern Darwinism. Aspects of this theory continue to be debated by scientists as new information is discovered about genes and evolution.

Questions

1 Owen's ideas were not a scientific theory. Explain why.

2 (a) Suggest how Owen used the examples of the bat's wing and whale's flipper as evidence for his idea. (b) How would Darwin have explained the similarities and differences between the bat's wing and whale's flipper?

3 Compare Lamarck's explanation of the evolution of long legs in birds with Darwin's explanation in lesson B1 7.2. Identify the similarities and differences in the explanations.

4 (a) Why do you think the cartoon of Darwin was drawn? (b) What assumption does the cartoon make about humans and apes, and how does this differ from Darwin's ideas?

5 Explain why Darwin's theory was only gradually accepted.

6 Look at the graphs of finch beaks in Figure 3. Explain how this evidence supports Darwin's theory.

7 Suggest why Owen, Lamarck and Darwin are all considered to be scientists, but had different theories of evolution.

8 Suggest how the variety of fish species in Lake Victoria may have evolved. Explain your answer.

Evolution 87

Learning objectives

Most students should be able to:

- explain why Darwin's theory was only gradually accepted
- evaluate different theories of evolution
- explain why Darwin's theory is the most commonly accepted theory of evolution.

Key points

There have been many theories to explain the variety of species, some scientific and some not.

Scientific theories make predictions that can be tested, and explain many different observations.

Lesson activities

Starter

1 Explore what students already understand by the term *theory* by asking them to write definitions for the words *hypothesis*, *idea* and *theory*. They should discuss their definitions in small groups, to create a group definition. Take examples from around the class, without comment, and ask the class to decide on the best definition for each. Then give students a scientific dictionary definition for each and ask them to identify any differences between the class definition and the dictionary definition, and the implications of the definitions for scientific study.

2 Ask students to work with a partner to write down three key facts that they know about Charles Darwin. Take examples from around the class and compile a master set of facts that can be revisited in *Plenary 2*.

Main

1 B1 7.3a Beliefs and hypotheses Refer to sheet in Teacher & Technician Planning Pack.

2 B1 7.3b Conflicting ideas Refer to sheet in Teacher & Technician Planning Pack.

3 Ask students to carry out their own research on the arguments surrounding Darwin's theory of evolution after the publication of *On the origin of species*. They should identify the key protagonists in the debate and summarise the arguments for and against Darwin's ideas.

Plenaries

1 Carry out a 'Consider All Possibilities' exercise using the statement 'A person does not agree with a new scientific theory'. Possible answers: the theory has not been tested properly; there is no explanation for why the theory works; it goes against religious beliefs; there is some evidence that the theory does not account for.

2 Ask students to jot down the three most important facts about Darwin's theory of evolution by natural selection. Return to the master set of facts about Charles Darwin and compare the lists. As a class agree a final set of the 'three most important facts about Charles Darwin'. [AfL]

Homework

1 Students could research recent examples of evidence that support Darwin's theory of evolution through natural selection.

2 **Worksheet B1 7.3c** presents a series of questions that summarise this lesson.

Points to note

- The religious arguments against the theory of evolution, including creationism and 'intelligent design', are not covered in this specification. However, students need to be aware that many websites discussing evolution are presented from this stance.
- The word 'theory' in common usage often simply means 'an idea'. The purpose of this lesson is to give it the scientific meaning of an idea that can be tested using scientific method. It is essential for students to gain this understanding if they do not already have it.
- The guidance in the specification about Lamarck's theory refers to occasional inheritance of acquired characteristics. This refers to epigenetics, which requires an understanding of the way in which genes are expressed and how that expression can be controlled by other genes or chemical reactions during gene expression. As this is likely to be beyond the knowledge of most students, it has only been included as an extension activity for the most able.

Route to A*

Ask students to research the meaning of the term epigenetics. This is a fairly recent idea in genetics and could be viewed as an example of Lamarckism that is correct. Students should use their research to write a few short paragraphs to answer the question 'Was Lamarck right after all?

Answers to Student Book questions

Science skills

a In 1976, a year after normal rainfall, the average beak depth was around 9.4 mm; in 1978, a year after drought, the average beak depth was around 10.1 mm. This shows an increase in beak depth of about 0.6 mm, which matches the prediction. The evidence supports Darwin's theory because it shows how a change in the environment changes the breeding success of individuals in relation to how well adapted they are to cope with the change.

Answers

1 Although Owen tried to use evidence to support his idea, it is not one that can be tested with experiment and predictions; therefore it is not scientific.

2 **(a)** The bone arrangement in the wing and flipper are similar, although the proportions are different; Owen would have suggested that God had a basic plan for a mammal front limb that was adjusted a little for each. **(b)** Darwin would have said that they both evolved from a common ancestor with the basic limb structure.

3 Lamarck's explanation says that the individual is changed by the environment and passes that change directly on to their offspring; Darwin's explanation says that only those individuals that have inherited from their parents the best adaptations to the environment will survive and pass the characteristics for those adaptations on to their offspring.

4 **(a)** To make people think his idea was silly and that therefore their ideas were better. **(b)** It suggests that Darwin (a human) is an ape, whereas what Darwin's theory really suggested was that modern apes and humans evolved along separate lines from a common ancestor in the past; the cartoon actually gets the science wrong.

5 It took time to produce the range of evidence needed to convince most people that it was a valid theory.

6 The graphs show that beaks get longer after drought. This evidence is explained successfully by the theory, because birds with longer and stronger beaks will get more food during a drought and so be more likely to produce offspring. As a result, the following year there will be more birds with longer and stronger beaks.

7 They were all scientists as they were using observation and evidence to produce their theories. Their theories differed because they made different assumptions: Owen assumed God was involved; Lamarck assumed the changes happened to the individuals in their lifetime; Darwin assumed there was a way of passing on characteristics (as we now know, as genes) that the environment could select for.

8 The single species that lived in the river could have moved into the lake as it started to form because there would have been food there and no competition or predators. As the lake increased in size there would have been many different sets of conditions for the fish to live in, such as gathering food off the bottom of the lake or feeding in the open water at the surface. Different conditions would select for different adaptations, so different varieties of fish would evolve, eventually becoming separate species.

B1 7.4

ISA practice: the growth of mould on bread

In the Student Book, each ISA practice is contained on one double-page spread. However, you can, if you prefer, use the sheets provided in the Teacher and Technician Planning Pack and the Activity Pack to more closely mirror the experience of a real ISA which would then take place over several lessons and/or as homework.

Link to the specification – How Science Works

Scientific investigations often seek to identify links between two or more variables. [4.1.1]

Scientists need to ensure repeatability, reproducibility and validity in evidence. [4.3.3]

There is a link between the type of graph used and the type of variable represented. [4.4.2]

The patterns and relationships observed in data represent the behaviour of the variables in an investigation. However, it is necessary to look at patterns and relationships between variables with the limitations of the data in mind in order to draw conclusions. [4.5.3, 4.5.4]

In evaluating a whole investigation the repeatability, reproducibility and validity of the data obtained must be considered. [4.5.2]

ISA practice: the growth of mould on bread

Scientists are investigating the best advice to give to supermarkets about storing and displaying bread. Your task is to investigate the effect of temperature on the growth of mould on bread.

Hypothesis

It is suggested that there is a link between temperature and the rate at which bread goes mouldy.

Section 1

1 In this investigation you will need to control some of the variables.
 (a) Name one variable you will need to control in this investigation. *(1 mark)*
 (b) Describe briefly how you would carry out a preliminary investigation to find a suitable value to use for this variable. Explain how the results will help you decide on the best value for this variable. *(3 marks)*

2 Describe how you are going to do your investigation. You should include:
- the equipment that you would use
- how you would use the equipment
- the measurements that you would make
- how you would make it a fair test.

You may include a labelled diagram to help you to explain your method.

In this question you will be assessed on using good English, organising information clearly and using specialist terms where appropriate. *(6 marks)*

3 Think about the possible hazards in your investigation.
 (a) Describe one hazard that you think may be present in your investigation. *(1 mark)*
 (b) Identify the risk associated with the hazard you have described, and say what control measures you could use to reduce the risk. *(2 marks)*

4 Design a table that will contain all the data that you are going to record during your investigation. *(2 marks)*

Total for Section 1: 14 marks

Section 2

A group of students, Study Group 1, investigated the effect of temperature on the growth of mould on bread.

- Their teacher gave them two slices of bread, each of which had a colony of mould growing on it.
- They measured the width of the colonies then placed each of the slices of bread inside separate plastic bags. They placed one plastic bag a shelf in the laboratory. They placed the other plastic bag in a refrigerator.
- On each of the next four days, they removed the slices of bread from the bags, measured the width of the mould colonies then replaced the bread in the bags. The bags were returned to the shelf in the laboratory and the refrigerator respectively.

Figure 1 shows their results.

bread kept in laboratory		bread kept in refrigerator
4 cm	Day 1	4 cm
6 cm	Day 2	5 cm
10 cm	Day 3	6 cm
15 cm	Day 4	7 cm
20 cm	Day 5	8 cm

Figure 1 Group 1's investigation.

5 (a) (i) What is the independent variable in this investigation?
 (ii) What is the dependent variable in this investigation?
 (iii) Name one control variable this investigation. *(3 marks)*
 (b) Plot a graph to show the link between temperature, time and the diameter of the mould colony. *(4 marks)*
 (c) Do the results support the hypothesis? Explain your answer. *(3 marks)*

Below are the results of three other study groups.

Table 1 shows the results of another group of students, Study Group 2.

Table 1 Results from Study Group 2.

Temperature at which bread was stored/°C	Number of days the bread stayed mould-free
0	10.0
10	5.0
20	3.5
30	2.4
40	1.6
50	1.0

A third group of students, Study Group 3, also investigated the hypothesis. Figure 2 is a graph of their results.

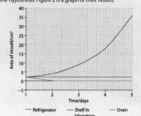

Figure 2 Study Group 3's results.

Study Group 4 was a group of scientists investigating the best conditions for storing bread in supermarkets. They investigated the effect of temperature on the rate at which the bread went stale. Figures 3 and 4 show their results.

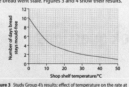

Figure 3 Study Group 4's results: effect of temperature on the rate at which bread goes mouldy.

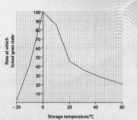

Figure 4 Study Group 4's results: effect of storage temperature on rate at which bread goes stale.

6 Describe one way in which the results of Study Group 2 are similar to or different from the results of Study Group 1, and give one reason why the results are similar or different. *(3 marks)*

7 (a) Draw a sketch graph of the results from Study Group 2. *(3 marks)*
 (b) Does the data support the hypothesis being investigated? To gain full marks you should use all of the relevant data from the first set of results and Study Groups 2 and 3 to explain whether or not the data supports the hypothesis. *(3 marks)*
 (c) The data from the other groups only gives a limited amount of information. What other information or data would you need in order to be more certain as to whether or not the hypothesis is correct? Explain the reason for your answer. *(3 marks)*
 (d) Use the results from Study Groups 2, 3 and 4 to answer this question. What is the relationship between the temperature and the growth of mould on bread?
 How well does the data support your answer? *(3 marks)*

8 Look back at the investigation method of Study Group 1. If you could repeat the investigation, suggest one change that you would make to the method, and give a reason for the change. *(3 marks)*

9 Suggest how ideas from your investigation and the scientists' investigations could be used to advise supermarkets about the best ways of storing and displaying bread. *(3 marks)*

Total for Section 2: 31 marks

Total for the ISA: 45 marks

88 89

Learning objectives

Most students should be able to:
- identify the independent and dependent variables in the hypothesis
- make some notes on two methods to investigate the hypothesis
- identify a method to establish the range of the independent variable, or the value of a control variable that will give a range of values for the dependent variable
- obtain some data to process and produce a graph or bar chart
- identify any trends that may be present in the data
- relate that trend to the hypothesis under investigation.

Some students should also be able to:
- make a risk assessment of their chosen method
- question the evidence to establish its repeatability and /or reproducibility.

anomalous result calibration control measure errors: random systematic and zero hazard mean range repeatable reproducible uncertainty validity variables: control categoric continuous dependent independent

Key points

Investigations should be designed so that patterns and relationships between variables can be identified.

It is important to ensure repeatability, reproducibility and validity in evidence when designing and evaluating investigations.

The choice of graph used depends upon the type of variable represented.

When drawing conclusions, the limitations of the data must be kept in mind.

Lesson activities

Starter

1 Show students a slice of mouldy bread (in a sealed bag). Ask the students to explain what it is, why it has happened, and would they eat it.

2 Tell students that they will be carrying out an investigation into the hypothesis: 'It is suggested that there is a link between temperature and the rate at which bread goes mouldy.' Suggest a suitable context, e.g. storing bread at home.

Main

1 Researching and planning Students need to research at least two different methods of investigating the hypothesis above. Please refer to the **B1 ISA practice 2 Teacher and technician sheet.** They can complete their research/notes for homework. See the **ISA practice Student research notes sheet.**

2 Ask two students to read their notes on one of the points. Get the class to decide whose notes are best, with a reason. Repeat until all the points are covered.

3 Give students the **B1 ISA practice 2 Section 1 paper.**

4 In a following lesson students set up their investigation and record and process their results. Students can work in groups to obtain the data. Please refer to the **B1 ISA practice 2 Student practical sheet**.

5 Students should process the data individually in **controlled** conditions. A bar chart or graph should be plotted and the trend of the graph/bar chart identified and a conclusion made.

6 Students should then pool their results so that a class results table can be produced ready for the **B1 ISA practice 2 Section 2 paper.**

7 Give students **the B1 ISA practice 2 Section 2 paper**.

Plenary

1 Students discuss sources of possible errors and ways to overcome them.

Homework

After the practical ask students to write brief notes about ways in which they could improve their investigation. They should mention how to reduce errors and what further data or information they would need to confirm their conclusion.

Points to note

- With able students simply outline the points they need to cover. You should adjust delivery to match the time that it takes to obtain meaningful results. You should in your discussions remain focussed on the hypothesis.
- Most supermarket bread needs a long time to go mouldy as it has lots of preservatives added.
- Students should consult a range of sources, starting with old text books, their notebooks, and the Student Book for ideas. They can also use the Internet if available.
- Students should describe a complex relationship between the independent variable and the dependent variable.

Route to A*

Students' risk assessments should include sensible risks, with a clear indication of the likelihood of the hazard occurring and how to sensibly control the risk. They should avoid basic laboratory rules.

Ask students to critically evaluate their data and explain that the findings are only valid within the range of the independent variable, whose range may be quite limited.

Answers to Student Book questions

7 **(a)** Both axes labelled (1), a suitable curve drawn (1), an indication given (arrow or numbers) of the direction of increase in value of axes (1).

(b) The student states that overall the data strongly supports the original hypothesis and quotes some data from the tables that supports this (1).
There is an appreciation that there is some conflicting evidence.
Critical appraisal of data to include: Study Group 1 shows that cooler has slower growth rate of mould; Study Group 2 suggests that above 15 °C temperature is not so important; Study Group 3 has the oven, which is not relevant as the mould will be killed at this temperature (which is not given) (1); Study Group 3 mould grows in size at the laboratory temperature, but not in the refrigerator (1).

(c) Suggests at least one other piece of information that would be needed to form a firm conclusion (2). The reason for the need for this other information is clearly stated (1).

(d) States that the rate of mould growth and temperature are linked as increasing temperature reduces days the bread is mould free (1), and uses data from Study Groups 2 or 4 to back this up (1). Realisation that this may be limited from Study Group 2 data (1).
For the full mark scheme, see the Teacher & Technician Planning Pack.

B2 1.1 Animal building blocks

Link to the specification

B2.1.1a Most human and animal cells have the following parts:

- a nucleus, which controls the activities of the cell
- cytoplasm, in which most of the chemical reactions take place
- a cell membrane, which controls the passage of substances into and out of the cell
- mitochondria, which is where most energy is released in respiration
- ribosomes, which is where protein synthesis occurs.

B2.1.1e Cells may be specialised to carry out a particular function.

Ideas for practical work

Observation of cells under a microscope, e.g. sprouting mung beans to show root hair cells.

Computer simulations to model the relative size of different cells, organelles and molecules.

How Science Works

SKU: B2.1 bullet point 1: Relate the structure of different types of cells to their function.

B2 1.1 Animal building blocks

Learning objectives

- describe the structure and function of the parts of animal cells
- explain what controls chemical reactions in cells
- explain how animal cells may be specialised to carry out a particular function.

Animal cells

Animals, including humans, are made up of millions of tiny cells. You can see some of the structure of these cells through a light microscope that can magnify up to 400 times.

Each cell is surrounded by a very thin **cell membrane** that holds the cell together. The cell membrane also controls what goes into and out of the cell.

Cells contain smaller parts called **organelles**. These include the **nucleus**, **mitochondria** and **ribosomes**. The organelles have particular jobs in the cell. The single **nucleus** controls the cell's activities and it is surrounded by watery **cytoplasm**. Without the nucleus the cell will die. It contains **DNA**, the **genetic** material that provides the instructions for synthesising the chemicals the cell needs, like **enzymes**. Inside the cytoplasm hundreds of chemical reactions take place and these reactions are controlled by the enzymes.

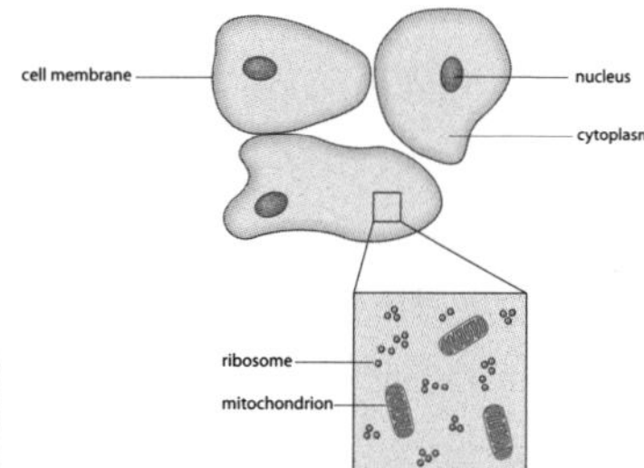

Figure 1 The organelles found in animal cells.

Electron microscopes** magnify up to 500 000 times and show us details of smaller organelles, such as mitochondria. These use **glucose** in respiration to release energy for the cell. Ribosomes are the smallest organelles. They build up, or synthesise, **proteins** from smaller, simpler compounds called **amino acids**. Proteins are molecules that are used to make other parts of the cell and other chemicals, such as enzymes. The cells of most animals, including humans, have the same organelles.

Route to A*

When describing cells, the term 'ultrastructure' refers to organelles that are only visible with the electron microscope. Use 'ultrastructure' in your answer to the following question:

Describe the relationship between amino acids, proteins and ribosomes.

Taking it further

Ribosomes measure about 20 nm in diameter. Besides being present singly in the cytoplasm, as in Figure 1, they may be present in a chain or attached to an organelle called the rough endoplasmic reticulum (rough ER). You will be expected to know about rough endoplasmic reticulum for AS and A-level Biology.

Specialised animal cells

The cells in Figure 1 line the inside of your mouth. They are called simple **epithelial cells** and line cavities and tubes, like blood vessels in your body. Many different types of cell are found in your body. They have different shapes and many have special features that are related to what they do. These cells are called **specialised cells**. Some examples are shown in Figure 2.

100

a Spindle-shaped muscle cells have fibrils and can shorten in length.

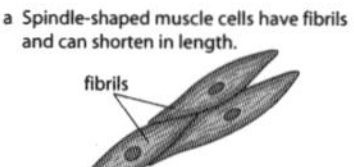

b Sperm cells have a tail to help them move to find the egg. They also have a high number of mitochondria to release energy for movement.

tail

c Nerve cells have long fibres that carry electrical impulses. Branches of cytoplasm at each end of the cell facilitate communication with other nerve cells.

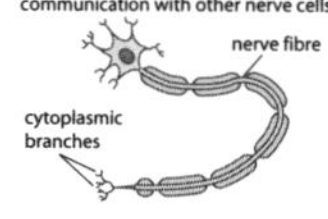

d These specialised epithelial cells have tiny hair-like structures, called cilia, on their free surface. They are known as ciliated epithelial cells. The cilia sway constantly back and forth to move particles along.

cilia

Figure 2 Examples of specialised cells (a muscle cell; b sperm cell; c nerve cell; d epithelial cell).

Science in action

Scientists study human cells using the light microscope. Cells are collected from **organs** and fluids throughout the body. Pre-cancerous changes, cancer and some infections can be detected and diagnosed. Cancerous cells are usually smaller than the cells surrounding them and they also have enlarged nuclei.

Science skills

Table 1 Numbers of mitochondria.

Type of human cell	Average number of mitochondria per cell (to the nearest 100)
liver	1900
kidney	1500
skin	200
small intestine	1600
muscle	1700

a What is the range in the number of mitochondria in human cells?

b Explain which method you would use to display this data.

Examiner feedback

The independent variable is the one that is being changed by the investigator. It goes on the *x*-axis of a graph.

The dependent variable is the result that is seen when the independent variable changes. It goes on the *y*-axis of a graph.

A line graph is drawn only when both variables can have any numerical values.

Questions

1 Explain how it is possible to see the parts of human cells, such as the nucleus.
2 Explain how substances that enter and leave cells are controlled.
3 Why are mitochondria found in large numbers in muscle cells?
4 Ribosomes synthesise proteins. Explain what this means.
5 Explain why the nucleus of the cell is important.
6 Look at Figure 2. **(a)** Give two differences between a muscle cell and a ciliated epithelial cell. **(b)** Most cells don't move. How does each of the following help a sperm cell to move: **(i)** tail **(ii)** mitochondria **(iii)** its shape? **(c)** The epithelial cells shown help to sweep mucus containing dust out of the lungs. Describe how they are adapted for this job.
7 Compare and contrast a nerve cell and a sperm cell, both structurally and functionally.
8 Select three examples of specialised animal cells and explain how the special features of each one adapts the cell for its function. A*

Cells and cell structure 101

Learning objectives

Most students should be able to:

- describe the structure and function of the parts of animal cells
- explain what controls chemical reactions in cells
- explain how animal cells may be specialised to carry out a particular function.

Some students should also be able to:

- explain how the three types of mammalian muscle are each specialised to carry out a specific type of muscle contraction. [Ext]

ActiveTeach Resource: Animal cells – *Interactive labelling activity*

Key points

Animals, including humans, are made up of millions of tiny cells.

All animal cells are surrounded by a cell membrane that contains cytoplasm.

Cytoplasm contains organelles that include the nucleus, mitochondria and ribosomes.

Each organelle has a particular job to do:

- the nucleus controls the cell's activities
- mitochondria release energy for the cell through respiration
- ribosomes synthesise proteins.

Animal cells are specialised to carry out particular functions, e.g.

- muscle cells contract causing movement
- sperm cells can move to find the egg cell.

Cell membrane	cytoplasm	DNA	enzymes	genetic	mitochondria	nucleus
organelles	organs	proteins	respiration	ribosomes	specialised cells	

Lesson activities

Starter

1 Give students the term 'animal cell'. Ask them to list as many words as they can that they associate with the term. Once they have done this, ask them to group the words into sensible categories and give each group a name. This should give you a clear understanding of their prior understanding from Key Stage 3.

2 Complete a spider diagram that introduces cells.

Main

1 B2 1.1a Animal cells In this practical activity, students make a slide of liver cells and draw three cells under high power. A prepared slide of involuntary muscle provides the opportunity for pupils to compare the structure of two different animal cells. (~25 mins)

2 B2 1.1b Specialised animal cells In this activity, students use a section of the mammalian gut to examine and compare several types of specialised animal cells. Students can then estimate the width of typical cells from each region and find a mean value for them. (~30 mins)

3 B2 1.1c Animal cell specialisation Worksheet B2 1.1c provides an opportunity to test students' understanding of cell structure and function.

4 ActiveTeach has an animation showing the different parts of animal cells and their function. [AT]

Plenaries

1 Provide a drawing of the shape of an unspecialised animal cell with the nucleus labelled. Ask the students to name other parts of the cell and describe their appearance and their function. Together build up an annotated diagram.

2 You could extend this to assess their recall of cell specialisation by giving the names of two cell types shown in Figure 2 of the Student Book and asking the students how each cell's structure is an adaptation for its function.

Homework

1 Students use the Internet to research:
- single celled animals
- chemicals found in the cytoplasm
- cell membranes.

2 They then produce a PowerPoint presentation to report back to the class.

3 Worksheet B2 1.1d provides opportunities to test students' understanding of cell structure and function.

Points to note

- Cells shown in the Student Book are not drawn to scale. Smooth (involuntary) muscle is shown as the structure of striped (voluntary) muscle is atypical of cells.
- Students should not make slides using their own cells.
- Enzymes are covered in more detail in lessons B2 4.2–4.5.
- If students have not used microscopes before, a demonstration and safety talk will be needed. If students have used microscopes before, a reminder on how to focus may be needed to ensure the slides are not damaged. If you do not have enough microscopes to go around, the students can work in groups or the slides can be projected so that the whole class can see the cells. It is recommended that a demonstration of making slides is undertaken.

Route to A*

Higher achievers can be given a wider variety of animal cells to examine and report on their specialisations. Challenge the students to find out what is the minimum number of cells that can be measured to provide a consistent mean value.

Answers to Student Book questions

Route to A*

The ultrastructure of cells reveals ribosomes in the cytoplasm. Ribosomes synthesise proteins from amino acids.

Science skills

a 200–1900.

b A bar chart, as the independent variable is not continuous.

Answers

1. By using a light microscope or an electron microscope.
2. The cell membrane controls which substances enter and leave the cell.
3. Mitochondria use glucose to release energy (respiration). Movement needs a large amount of energy so muscle cells can contract. Muscle cells therefore need large numbers of mitochondria to provide that energy.
4. Ribosomes build up proteins from smaller, simpler components (amino acids).
5. The nucleus contains DNA, which gives instructions for the synthesis of chemicals in the cytoplasm. This controls all activities of the cell. Without it the cell will die.
6. **(a)** A muscle cell is spindle-shaped and contains filaments that can shorten. A ciliated epithelial cell is cuboid and has many hairs, or cilia, on its free surface. **(b) (i)** Moves back and forth to propel the sperm along. **(ii)** Release energy for movement. **(iii)** Streamlined to aid swimming. **(c)** They have cilia that move constantly back and forth on their free surface, propelling mucus across the surface
7. Both types of cell have a nucleus, ribosomes, mitochondria, cytoplasm and a cell membrane. They are both elongated in shape (but nerve cells are much longer). The sperm cell can move from place to place but the nerve cell cannot move. Both ends of the nerve cell have branches, but the sperm cell does not. The sperm cell needs many mitochondria to provide energy for movement but the nerve cell does not.
8. Examples answers include: a muscle cell brings about movement; cytoplasm contains fibrils that can shorten in length. A sperm cell moves to find the egg; it has a tail to propel it along and many mitochondria to release energy. A nerve cell communicates with other cells; it has a long fibre that carries electrical impulses.

B2 1.2 Plant and alga building blocks

Link to the specification

B2.1.1b Plant and algal cells also have a cell wall made of cellulose, which strengthens the cell. Plant cells often have:

- chloroplasts, which absorb light energy to make food
- a permanent vacuole filled with cell sap.

B2.1.1e Cells may be specialised to carry out a particular function.

Ideas for practical work

Observation of cells under a microscope, e.g. sprouting mung beans to show root hair cells.

How Science Works

SKU: B2.1 bullet point 1: Relate the structure of different types of cells to their function.

B2 1.2 Plant and alga building blocks

Learning objectives

- **describe the structure and function of the parts of plant cells**
- **explain how plant cells may be specialised to carry out a particular function**
- **compare and contrast animal and plant cells.**

Route to A*

Leaves contain two different types of mesophyll cells that you can distinguish between. Figure 1 shows palisade mesophyll cells, which are adapted, by the presence of many chloroplasts, to trap light energy for photosynthesis.

Find out the name of the other type of mesophyll cells in a leaf and learn what their function is.

Plant cells

Like animal cells, plant cells usually have a cell membrane, nucleus, mitochondria, ribosomes and cytoplasm. Unlike animal cells, plant cells also have a **cell wall**, made of a carbohydrate called **cellulose**. The cellulose in the cell wall is in the form of tiny fibres. Together, these fibres are very strong so the cell wall supports the cell and strengthens it. Algae are also made of cells that have a cell wall made of cellulose. Examples of algae include seaweed and microscopic, single-celled algae that grow on tree trunks or in fish tanks, giving the water a green colour. Some plant cells also have organelles called **chloroplasts** in their cytoplasm. Inside the chloroplasts is a green pigment called **chlorophyll**. Chlorophyll is a chemical that plants use in **photosynthesis** to absorb the Sun's light energy. In photosynthesis, light energy is converted to chemical energy in the form of glucose, as food for the plant.

In the centre of many plant cells there is a large, permanent, liquid-filled space called a **vacuole**. The liquid in the vacuole is called **cell sap** and it contains sugars, salts and water. When it is full the vacuole supports the cell, making it firm. If the vacuole is less full, the cell is not so firm.

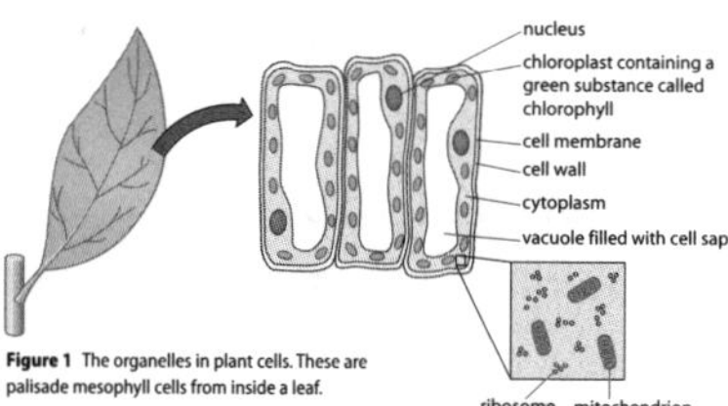

Figure 1 The organelles in plant cells. These are palisade mesophyll cells from inside a leaf.

Root hairs on a germinating seed.

Specialised plant cells

Many plant cells are specialised to carry out particular jobs.

- **Palisade mesophyll cells** are found in the leaf and are packed with chloroplasts. They are the main photosynthetic cells.
- **Root hair cells** have extensions into the soil to absorb water and dissolved mineral ions. These extensions are the actual root hairs. They are long and narrow so they can fit between soil particles. A thin film of water surrounds each soil particle and it contains the dissolved mineral ions.

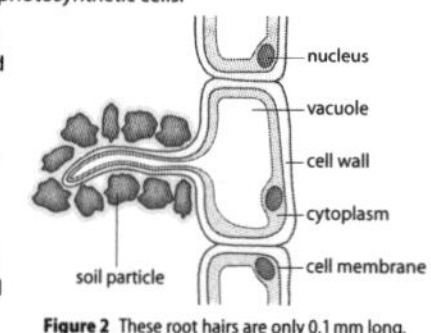

Figure 2 These root hairs are only 0.1 mm long. Each root end has thousands of these cells.

102

- **Xylem vessels** are made up of empty dead cells, arranged as long tubes of cell wall only, with no end walls between them. The cell wall has various chemicals added to it in xylem, so it does not rot away. Xylem vessels transport water from the roots, up through the stem to the leaves.

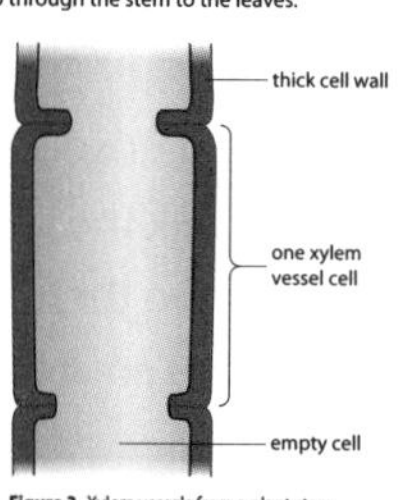

Figure 3 Xylem vessels from a plant stem.

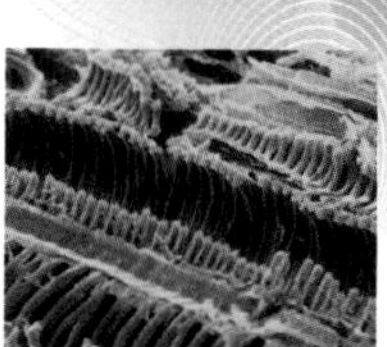

Scanning electron microscope photo of a section through a rhubarb stem, showing a xylem vessel cut open. Magnification ×290.

Two students were measuring cells with a microscope. They used a clear plastic ruler, calibrated in mm, clipped to the microscope. The magnification of the microscope was ×10.

a Suggest how many cells they should measure to give a reliable result. Explain your answer.

b The students reported that one type of cell was 0.3 mm in diameter. Comment on the accuracy of the result bearing in mind the resolution of the ruler.

Practical

Figure 4 You can make slides of plant cells and look at them through a light microscope.

Questions

1. Why is the cell wall important in an algal cell and what is the cell wall made from?
2. Explain why plants need: **(a)** a nucleus **(b)** mitochondria **(c)** a cell membrane **(d)** ribosomes.
3. List three facts about chloroplasts.
4. What fills the large, permanent space in a plant cell? What chemicals does it contain and what is its function in the cell?
5. Explain fully the advantage of palisade cells having lots of chloroplasts.
6. Suggest which parts of a plant might not contain chloroplasts. Explain your answer.
7. Compare and contrast the structures of animal and plant cells.
8. Look at Figures 2 and 3. Explain how root hair cells and xylem vessels are adapted for their function in the plant.

Examiner feedback

Distinguish carefully between the cell wall and cell membrane. A cellulose cell wall is present in plant, but not animal, cells and it allows all substances in solution to pass through it. A cell membrane is present in every cell and allows some substances to pass through, but not others. Cellulose is only found in plant and algal cells.

Cells and cell structure 103

Learning objectives

Most students should be able to:

- describe the structure and function of the parts of plant and algal cells
- explain how plant cells may be specialised to carry out a particular function
- compare and contrast animal and plant cells.

Some students should also be able to:

- list a range of habitats where algae can be found [Ext]
- explain why root hairs are only found just behind the root tip and what cell process takes place at the root tip. [Ext]

ActiveTeach Resource: Plant cell structures – *Interactive matching activity*

Key points

Plant cells usually have a cell membrane, nucleus, ribosomes and cytoplasm, like animal cells.

Unlike animal cells, plant and algal cells also have a cell wall made of cellulose.

Some plant cells have organelles called chloroplasts that contain chlorophyll that is used in photosynthesis.

A vacuole is a large permanent space filled with liquid and is present in the centre of many plant cells.

Specialised plant cells carry out particular functions e.g.

- Root hair cells absorb water and dissolved mineral ions from the soil.
- Palisade cells are packed with chloroplasts and found in leaves.

Lesson activities

Starter

1 Draw a plant cell on the board and ask students to list as many structures as they can that a plant cell has. This should allow you to assess their prior understanding from Key Stage 3.

2 Thought shower to identify different types of plant cells in a stem or root.

Cell sap | cell wall | chlorophyll | chloroplasts | photosynthesis | vacuole

Main

1 B2 1.2a Plant and algal cells Students make slides of onion cell epidermis and algae. Examination of the slides under a microscope and drawing cells of each will enable the students to compare the structure of plant and algal cells. (~30 mins)

2 B2 1.2b Specialised plant cells Observation of root hair cells of germinating mung beans under the microscope is followed by use of a prepared slide of a vertical section through a leaf. The latter provides students with the opportunity to examine and compare several types of specialised plant cells and to relate structure to function. (~30 mins)

3 B2 1.2c Making plants strong This is a planning activity for an investigation into modelling the strength of plant stems. It provides the opportunity to incorporate criteria into the investigation that should provide valid evidence. (planning ~25 mins)

4 ActiveTeach has a matching activity showing the different parts of plant cells and their functions. [AT]

Plenaries

1 Show the students a flower and a fruit/vegetable and ask the students to list the organelles found in the cells of the flower and fruit/vegetable. Let them suggest any specialisations related to the functions the cells might have.

2 List the organelles that have been observed in plant cells. With help from the students, produce a table to compare plant and animal cells.

Homework

1 Worksheet B2 1.2d provides opportunities to test students' understanding of plant and algal cell structure and plant cell specialisation.

2 Students use the Internet to research the types of cells found in wood. They should note whether the cells are living or dead, their shape and their length. Students should tabulate their findings in a Word document.

Points to note

- Most of the wood of trees is made up of two types of xylem. 'Old' wood does not conduct water and forms the majority of a tree trunk. Only the outermost, thin layer of xylem carries water.
- The actual diameter of an unspecialised plant cell is approximately 20 μm. The diameter of a xylem vessel is approximately 75 μm.
- Diatoms are one of the most common types of phytoplankton and have a cell wall made of silica. In oceans it is estimated that they are responsible for up to 45% of the primary production.
- If students carry out the practical after the planning exercise in Worksheet B2 1.2c, care is needed with use of weights. The plan requires the student to do a risk assessment, but this must be approved by the teacher.

Route to A*

Higher achievers can be given the opportunity to:

- investigate the range of types of algae and habitats where they can be found
- explain about the different regions of a root and why root hairs are only found in one specific area.

Answers to Student Book questions

Route to A*

Spongy mesophyll cells have a large, free surface area. They absorb carbon dioxide for photosynthesis and release oxygen.

Science skills

a At least 10 cells because repeated readings improve the reliability of the data.

b The students should be able to estimate the size to the nearest 0.5 mm, as this will be half a division on the ruler scale and it will be seen clearly under the microcope at x10 magnification. The size of any cell measured should be rounded up or down to the nearest 0.5 mm. The size of the cell the students measured to be 0.3 mm should therefore be given to be 0.5 mm.

Answers

1 The cell wall is made of cellulose and gives the algal cell strength and support.

2 Plants need: **(a)** a nucleus to control the cell's activities, **(b)** mitochondria to use glucose in respiration to release energy for the cell, **(c)** a cell membrane to control what goes into and out of the cell and **(d)** ribosomes to synthesise proteins.

3 Three facts, e.g. chloroplasts are found in the cytoplasm; they contain chlorophyll; they absorb light energy.

4 Cell sap is found in the vacuole. It contains sugars, salts and water. It keeps the cell firm and supports it.

5 There are lots of chloroplasts in palisade cells because they are the main photosynthetic tissue and provide sugar for the plant.

6 Roots, because they are not exposed to light so can't photosynthesise, so have no need for chloroplasts.

7 Both plant and animal cells have a nucleus, cytoplasm, cell membrane, mitochondria and ribosomes. In addition, plant cells have a cell wall and a vacuole containing cell sap, but animal cells do not.

8 Root hairs of cells are long and narrow so they can fit between soil particles to absorb water and mineral salts from the film of water around the soil particles. Their shape gives a large surface area to volume ratio, which aids absorption. Xylem vessels are made up of empty dead cells, arranged as long tubes of cell wall only, with no end walls between them. The cell walls of xylem vessels have various added chemicals so they do not rot away.

B2 1.3 Bacteria and yeast cells

Link to the specification

B2.1.1c A bacterial cell consists of cytoplasm and a membrane surrounded by a cell wall; the genes are not in a distinct nucleus.

B2.1.1d Yeast is a single-celled organism. Yeast cells have a nucleus, cytoplasm and a membrane surrounded by a cell wall.

Ideas for practical work

Making model cells.

How Science Works

SKU: B2.1 bullet point 1: Relate the structure of different types of cells to their function.

B2 1.3 Bacteria and yeast cells

- describe the structure of a bacterial cell
- describe the structure of a yeast cell
- compare and contrast the structure of a bacterial cell and yeast cell.

The most abundant cells on Earth

Tens of billions of bacteria may be present in a handful of soil. You have more bacteria in your intestines and on your skin than cells in your body. Bacteria are **unicellular organisms**. Each single cell can live on its own and carry out all the seven characteristics of living organisms. A microscope is needed to see bacteria, so they are known as **microbes** or **microorganisms**. They are found in and on plants and animals, and worldwide in habitats as diverse as deserts, deep oceans, snow and boiling mud.

Examiner feedback

The mnemonic 'Mrs Gren' will help you to remember the seven characteristics of living things. They are: movement, reproduction, sensitivity, growth, respiration, excretion and nutrition.

The structure of a bacterial cell

Under the electron microscope we can see the internal structure of a bacterial cell. A bacterium consists of cytoplasm surrounded by a membrane and an outer cell wall. The cell wall is semi-rigid and not made from cellulose. There is no nucleus, and no other organelles, except ribosomes. The cytoplasm contains a loop of DNA that contains most of the cell's **genes**.

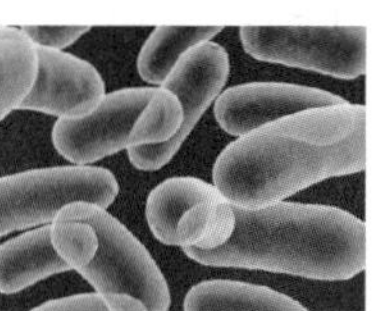

Bacteria under the electron microscope.

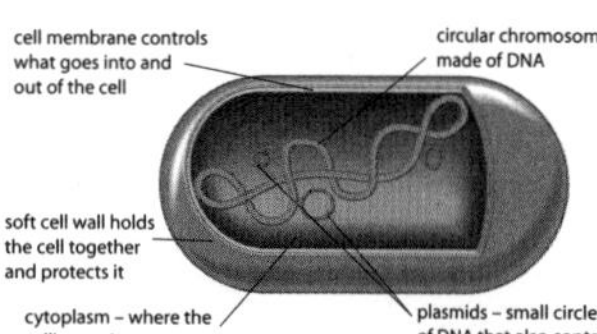

Figure 1 Internal structure of a bacterial cell.

Taking it further

Bacterial cells have no nucleus and no other organelles surrounded by a membrane. They are known as prokaryotic cells.

Yeast cells have a membrane-bound nucleus and other organelles. They are known as eukaryotic cells. Animal and plant cells are also eukaryotic.

Science skills

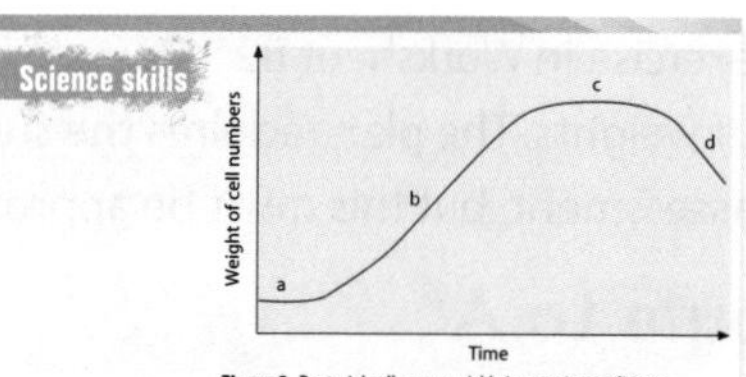

Figure 2 Bacterial cells grow quickly in certain conditions.

a Suggest which region of the graph corresponds to ideal growth conditions.

b Give a reason for your answer to part **a**.

c Suggest what is happening to the bacteria in region 'd' of the graph.

104

Yeast is a single-celled microscopic fungus

Some fruits – like grapes, plums and apples – often have a pale grey 'bloom' on their surface. This is partly due to naturally occurring yeast. If you have ever polished a plum or apple by rubbing it on your clothes you have removed the natural yeast. Yeast occurs on plant leaves, flowers and in the soil. Yeasts are also found in dust, water, milk and even on some of the inside surfaces of our body, such as the linings of the body cavities and various tubes.

Yeast growing on fruit skins.

Structure of a yeast cell

You can buy a block of fresh yeast for baking bread. Each square centimetre of it contains millions of individual yeast cells.

Each yeast cell is oval or spherical and has a nucleus, cytoplasm, mitochondria, a vacuole and a cell membrane surrounded by a cell wall. Yeast cells are about 10 times bigger than bacterial cells.

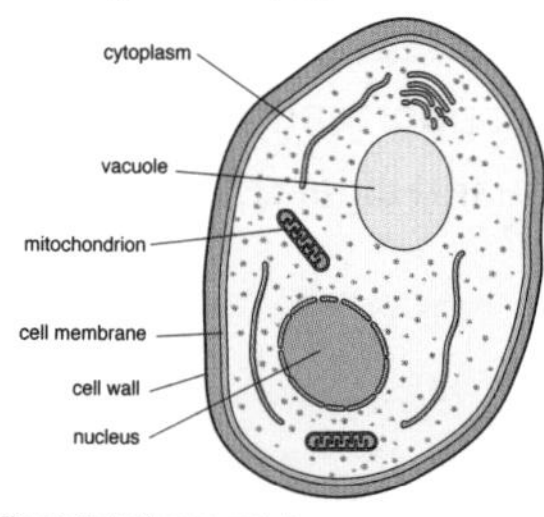

Figure 3 Section through a yeast cell.

Compressed yeast. Each 1-cm^3 block contains millions of yeast cells.

Questions

1 Why do we refer to bacteria as microorganisms?
2 Name and describe the only organelle found in bacterial cells.
3 Where is the genetic material found in bacterial cells and what is it made of?
4 What type of organism is a yeast cell?
5 Name and describe the organelle that contains genes in a yeast cell.
6 (a) Give three similarities in structure between bacterial and yeast cells.
(b) Give two differences in structure between bacterial and yeast cells.
(c) How much bigger are yeast cells than bacterial cells?
7 Give two ways that yeast can be used in the home and describe two forms that yeast could be in when it is bought.
8 Explain, as fully as you can, where bacteria and yeast are found naturally and why they are usually found in such large numbers.

Science in action

Breweries use vast amounts of yeast. It is sent to them in granulated form from suppliers called maltsters. Yeast cells survive even when they are dehydrated. Yeast produces the alcohol in beer.

Route to A*

A question that asks you to compare two organisms, such as bacteria and yeast, requires you to give similarities *and* differences between the two. Use the mark allowance to help you to supply a suitable number of marking points in your answer.

Cells and cell structure 105

Learning objectives

Most students should be able to:

- describe the structure of a bacterial cell
- describe the structure of a yeast cell
- compare and contrast the structure of a bacterial and yeast cell
- explain what a bacterial plasmid is
- list a range of locations where yeast can be found naturally
- describe how yeast can be preserved for baking or brewing.

Key points

Bacteria are unicellular and microscopic.

Bacterial cells have an outer membrane, cytoplasm and a cell wall not made of cellulose.

There is no distinct nucleus in bacterial cells. The genes are in a loop of DNA in the cytoplasm.

Yeast is a single-celled fungus.

Yeast cells have a nucleus, cytoplasm and a membrane surrounded by a cell wall.

 DNA electron microscope genes microbes microorganisms plasmid unicellular organisms

Lesson activities

Starter

1 Show students some empty yogurt pots and note what it says on them about the bacterial content of the food and any claims of health benefits from eating it.

2 Show the students a drum/sachet of baking or brewing yeast. Pass the yeast round so that the pupils can smell it and ask them to say what the smell brings to mind. Stress that dehydrated yeast granules are *not* individual yeast cells.

Main

1 B2 1.3a Bacterial and yeast cells Students make slides of diluted yogurt to allow them to see *Lactobacillus* bacteria. Slides of a yeast culture are also made. The relative size of the two types of microorganisms can be appreciated (~20 mins)

2 B2 1.3b Model bacterial and yeast cells Playdough, plastic film, foil, etc. are used to make 3-dimensional models of a bacterial and/or yeast cell. Differences in structure between the two types of cell can be clearly seen and spatial relations of the 3-dimensional organelles can be appreciated. (~30 mins)

3 B2 1.3c Importance of yeast This worksheet requires production of a spider diagram. This is followed by Internet research on one of four aspects of yeast. Information gathered is used to make an A5 'Fact Flyer'. (~30 mins)

Plenaries

1 Draw up a table to compare the similarities and differences between bacterial and yeast cell structure. Enlist the students' help in completing this.

2 Brainstorm types of food and drink that involve microbial content/involvement. Encourage suggestions from the cuisine of different countries and stress the preservative benefits of microbial action on milk (by creating a low pH in which most bacteria cannot survive).

Homework

1 Worksheet B2 1.3d provides practice using HSW skills of data presentation, prediction and experimental design.

2 Ask students to research information provided by the Natural History Museum about: The search for life: Astrobiology and the limits within which life can survive.

Points to note

- Bacteria are difficult to see, even with ×40 objective lens. Refer to the Student Book lesson B2 1.3 to see rod-shaped bacteria.
- Sterilised milk (UHT) does not need refrigerating until its packaging is opened.
- Sterilisation kills all bacteria.
- There are many different types of yeast. Specific varieties only live in precise locations and soil types and this is one reason for the differences in regional wines from a specific country.

Route to A*

Students could find out which European research departments collaborated in sequencing the yeast genome.

Alternatively, the most able students might like to find out more about genome sequencing in other microorganisms.

Answers to Student Book questions

Science skills

a Region b.

b The weight of cell numbers increases continually, showing cell numbers are growing.

c The cells are dying.

Answers

1 A microscope is needed to see them because they are very small.

2 Ribosomes are the only organelles found in bacterial cells. They are tiny, solid, spherical structures when seen with an electron microscope.

3 The genetic material is found in a loop of DNA in the cytoplasm.

4 Yeast is a single-celled, microscopic fungus.

5 The nucleus contains the genes in a yeast cell. It is the largest organelle present in the cell and is usually spherical.

6 **(a)** Both bacterial and yeast cells have cytoplasm, a membrane and a cell wall. **(b)** Yeast cells have a nucleus, mitochondria and a vacuole (choose two) and bacterial cells do not. **(c)** Yeast cells are about 10 times bigger than bacterial cells.

7 Yeast can be used in brewing wine or beer and making bread. It can be bought as either dehydrated granules or as fresh yeast compressed into a block.

8 Bacteria can be found in and on plants and animals and worldwide in habitats as diverse as deserts, deep oceans, snow and boiling mud. Yeast occurs on plant leaves, flowers and fruit and in the soil. Yeasts are also found in dust, soil, water, milk and even on some of the inside surfaces of our body, such as the linings of the body cavities and various tubes. Both are found in very large numbers because they are very tiny and have a rapid rate of reproduction.

B2 1.4 Getting in and out of cells

Link to the specification

B2.1.2a Dissolved substances can move into and out of cells by diffusion.

B2.1.2b Diffusion is the spreading of the particles of a gas, or of any substance in solution, resulting in a net movement from a region where they are of a higher concentration to a region with a lower concentration. The greater the difference in concentration, the faster the rate of diffusion.

B2.1.2c Oxygen required for respiration passes through cell membranes by diffusion.

Ideas for practical work

Computer simulations to model the process of diffusion.

Diffusion of ammonium hydroxide in a glass tube using litmus as the indicator.

Investigate how temperature affects the rate of diffusion of glucose through Visking tubing.

B2 1.4 Getting in and out of cells

Learning objectives

- describe the process of diffusion
- explain diffusion through cell membranes
- describe how the difference in concentration can affect the rate of diffusion
- explain what a partially permeable membrane is.

Diffusion of gases

You can smell the perfume released by a flower because smelly particles spread through the air. The smell can spread many metres. The movement of the perfume particles through the particles of air is called **diffusion**.

As you get closer to the flower the smell gets stronger. This is because there are more smelly particles of gas near the flower. We say that the **concentration** of perfume particles is higher nearer the flower. The sense of smell detects chemicals in the form of a gas. Gas molecules diffuse rapidly through the air.

Science in action

In England in July 2007, smoking was banned in all enclosed public places and workplaces to prevent inhalation of smoke by non-smokers. This is called passive smoking and occurs due to diffusion of the particles in cigarette smoke through the gases in the air.

high concentration — net movement — low concentration

Figure 1 Particles move from areas of high concentration to areas of low concentration.

Route to A*

When defining diffusion, include the term 'net movement' and finish by saying that diffusion carries on until the particles in an area are equally distributed.

Diffusion of liquids

When a **soluble** substance is placed in water, the particles that make up the substance will start to diffuse. The particles move in random directions, and bump into each other and into the water particles. They start all clumped in one place, but this movement spreads them out slowly. When the particles are clumped together, they have a high concentration. When they are more spread out, they have a lower concentration. As they spread more, the concentration of the particles throughout the water eventually becomes equal.

A difference in concentrations of a substance between two areas is called a **concentration gradient**. If you start with a much greater concentration in one place than the other, diffusion will be faster than if the concentrations in the two places are nearly the same.

Practical

(a)

(b)

(c)

A slice of boiled beetroot is put in water at 12 noon (a). Diffusion is shown at 6 am (b) and 6 pm (c).

106

Diffusion through cell membranes

All plant and animal cells have a cell membrane. The cell membrane has tiny holes through which small particles can pass by diffusion. We say that cell membranes are **partially permeable membranes** because large particles cannot get through.

If the concentration of small particles on each side of a membrane is different, then more particles will diffuse through the membrane from the concentrated solution to the dilute solution. The overall or **net movement** of particles is from a higher concentration to a lower concentration. Diffusion results in an even distribution of particles on both sides of a membrane.

partially permeable membrane; start; after a few hours; high concentration; low concentration; equal concentrations; net movement

Figure 2 When the concentrations are different, the net movement of particles is from the higher concentration to the lower concentration.

Examiner feedback

It is important to remember that even when there is a big difference in concentration, diffusion occurs in both directions. There is a *net* movement from high to low concentration.

Route to A*

Remember that plant and algal cells require oxygen for respiration too, but because their rate of respiration is low, compared with animals, the rate of diffusion of oxygen into their cells is lower too.

All living organisms need oxygen for respiration. Oxygen molecules are small molecules that can pass through cell membranes by diffusion. There are five cell membranes for oxygen to pass through from an air sac, or **alveolus**, in the lungs, to a red blood cell that carries the oxygen round the body. The rapid rate of diffusion keeps the cells alive. It enables oxygen to get into the blood fast enough to be transported to body cells.

Questions

1 Name one sense that a butterfly uses to find a flower that is far away.
2 Explain how the perfume of the flower reaches the butterfly.
3 Where is the concentration of perfume particles highest: near the flower or far from it? Explain your answer.
4 Explain what we mean by 'partially permeable membrane'.
5 Explain how cell membranes control which particles pass through them by diffusion.
6 Explain what we mean by 'net movement'.
7 If milk is poured into a mug of hot, black coffee and not stirred, explain, using the word 'diffusion', why the coffee changes colour from black to medium brown.
8 Cells need oxygen for respiration. Explain how oxygen can get into cells.

Taking it further

A short diffusion distance increases the rate of diffusion.

From the inside of an alveolus to the inside of a red blood cell the distance is 5 × the width of a cell membrane. Find out what this distance is.

Cells and cell structure 107

Learning objectives

Most students should be able to:

- describe the process of diffusion
- explain diffusion through cell membranes
- describe how the difference in concentration can affect the rate of diffusion
- explain what a partially permeable membrane is.

Some students should also be able to:

- describe how temperature can affect the rate of diffusion [Ext]
- explain how agricultural practices make use of insect pheromone diffusion to protect crops. [Ext]

ActiveTeach Resource: Diffusion experiment – *Mark sample answers activity*

Key points

Gases and any substance in solution can diffuse.

During diffusion there is a net movement of particles from a region where they are at a higher concentration to a region of lower concentration.

The greater the difference in concentration, the faster the rate of diffusion.

Dissolved substances can move into and out of cells by diffusion e.g. oxygen for respiration.

Alveolus	concentration	concentration gradient	diffusion
membranes	net movement	partially permeable membrane	soluble

Lesson activities

Starter

1 Cut an onion at the front of the class or squeeze some garlic. Ask students to raise their hand when they can smell it. Ask how the smell got to them and why it took longer for students at the back and sides of the room to smell it than those near the front.

2 Use the practical display in lesson B2 1.4 of the Student Book that shows colour diffusion from a slice of boiled beetroot.

Main

1 B2 1.4a Diffusion of ammonia in air During a demonstration, students time when squares of red litmus turn blue as ammonia diffuses along a glass tube. Results are tabulated, graphed and evaluated. (~35 mins)

2 B2 1.4b Diffusion through a partially permeable membrane This practical gives students the opportunity to study the effect of diffusion across a partially permeable membrane (Visking tubing). Students will need to understand the colour reaction of starch with iodine before they begin, so they can interpret their findings correctly. Details of the practical are given in **Student practical sheet B2 1.4b** which suggests that students set it up with the iodine solution inside the Visking tubing. With some groups, you may also wish to ask them to set up the opposite (i.e. with the starch inside the Visking tubing) so they can see diffusion happening in both directions through the membrane. (~30 mins)

3 Worksheet B2 1.4c provides an opportunity to assess the students' understanding of diffusion. For high achievers you can extend the last question by asking what effect exercise will have on the concentration of carbon dioxide in the cell and on the rate of diffusion into the blood. (~20 mins)

Plenaries

1 ActiveTeach includes an interactive activity relating to diffusion of large and small molecules on either side of a partially permeable membrane. This is a 'mark a sample answer' activity. Use it to assess the students' understanding of diffusion rate and concentration gradient. [AT]

2 Add 1 grain of potassium manganate(VII) into a test tube using a glass tube; remove the tube slowly to prevent disturbing the water. Some diffusion will be seen immediately. Then produce a similar tube that was set up between 24 hours and 1 hour before the lesson. Invite the class to explain what has happened.

Safety: Potassium manganate(VII) is oxidising and harmful and will stain skin.

Homework

1 Students research the special features of the membranes that make up the blood/brain barrier in humans.

Route to A*

1 Ask more able students to research ichneumon wasps that feed on the larvae of cabbage white butterflies, to find out how the wasps locate the larvae.

2 When a smoke alarm is triggered smoke/fumes diffuse from the site of the fire to the alarm. Ask students to find out what type of particles trigger fire alarms and at what concentrations.

Answers to Student Book questions

Taking it further

$5 \times 7\,\text{nm} = 35\,\text{nm}$.

Answers

1 The sense of smell.

2 It diffuses through the air.

3 It is highest nearest the flowers. When the perfume particles are released they diffuse away from the flower in many different directions.

4 Partially permeable membranes allow small particles to pass through, but not large ones.

5 The cell membrane has gaps that only certain molecules can fit into and pass through.

6 Net movement is the overall direction and amount of movement.

7 The milk and coffee particles diffuse through the volume of liquid and both become spread out, blending together the dark brown and white particles to produce a medium brown colour.

8 Oxygen molecules are small enough to diffuse through the gaps in the partially permeable membrane. Oxygen will pass down the concentration gradient by diffusion from high concentration outside the cell to low concentration inside the cell.

B2 1.5 Specialised organ systems

Link to the specification

B2.2.1a Large multicellular organisms develop systems for exchanging materials. During the development of a multicellular organism, cells differentiate so that they can perform different functions.

B2.2.1b A tissue is a group of cells with similar structure and function.

B2.2.1c Organs are made of tissues. One organ may contain several tissues.

B2.2.1d Organ systems are groups of organs that perform a particular function. The digestive system is one example of a system in which humans and other mammals exchange substances with the environment.

B2.2.2a Plant organs include stems, roots and leaves.

B2.2.2b Examples of plant tissues include: epidermal tissues, mesophyll, xylem and phloem.

How Science Works

SKU: B2.1 bullet point 1: Relate the structure of different types of cells to their function.

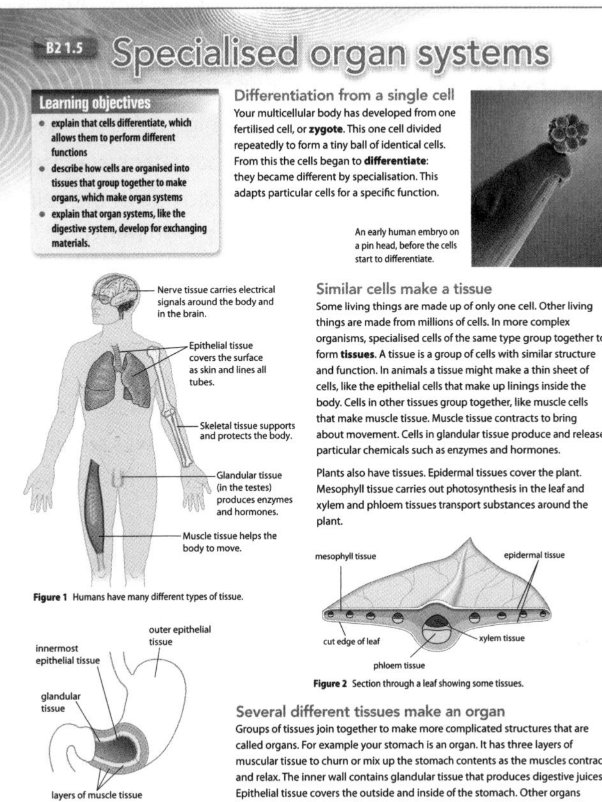

B2 1.5 Specialised organ systems

Learning objectives

- explain that cells differentiate, which allows them to perform different functions
- describe how cells are organised into tissues that group together to make organs, which make organ systems
- explain that organ systems, like the digestive system, develop for exchanging materials.

Differentiation from a single cell

Your multicellular body has developed from one fertilised cell, or **zygote**. This one cell divided repeatedly to form a tiny ball of identical cells. From this the cells began to **differentiate**: they became different by specialisation. This adapts particular cells for a specific function.

An early human embryo on a pin head, before the cells start to differentiate.

Figure 1 Humans have many different types of tissue.

Similar cells make a tissue

Some living things are made up of only one cell. Other living things are made from millions of cells. In more complex organisms, specialised cells of the same type group together to form **tissues**. A tissue is a group of cells with similar structure and function. In animals a tissue might make a thin sheet of cells, like the epithelial cells that make up linings inside the body. Cells in other tissues group together, like muscle cells that make muscle tissue. Muscle tissue contracts to bring about movement. Cells in glandular tissue produce and release particular chemicals such as enzymes and hormones.

Plants also have tissues. Epidermal tissues cover the plant. Mesophyll tissue carries out photosynthesis in the leaf and xylem and phloem tissues transport substances around the plant.

Figure 2 Section through a leaf showing some tissues.

Figure 3 A section through the stomach's tissues.

Several different tissues make an organ

Groups of tissues join together to make more complicated structures that are called organs. For example your stomach is an organ. It has three layers of muscular tissue to churn or mix up the stomach contents as the muscles contract and relax. The inner wall contains glandular tissue that produces digestive juices. Epithelial tissue covers the outside and inside of the stomach. Other organs in your body include your heart, brain, liver and lungs. Organs have a specific function. The function of the stomach is the storage and digestion of food.

108

Several different organs make a specialised organ system

Systems are groups of organs that perform a particular function. The digestive system in humans and other mammals is one example of a system where substances are exchanged with the environment. Food enters the body, is broken down and absorbed into the blood. Undigested food with some added waste chemicals is returned to the environment.

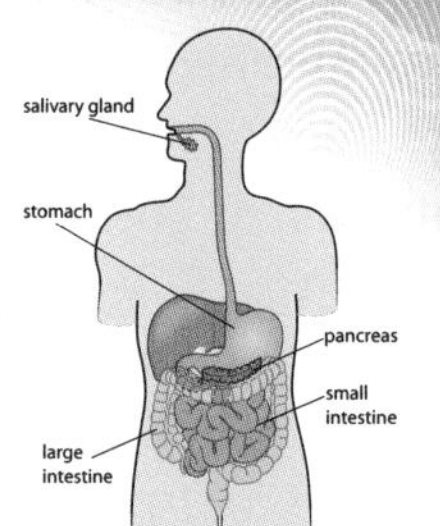

Figure 4 Some organs in the digestive system.

Science skills Read the information below about the digestive system and then construct a table to show it.

The digestive system includes glands such as the pancreas and salivary glands that produce digestive juices. Digestion occurs mostly in the stomach and small intestine. Absorption of soluble food occurs in the small intestine. In the large intestine, two processes occur: water is absorbed into the blood from the undigested food and faeces are produced.

Plant organs

You have just been studying the hierarchy of cell organisation in animals. You may have realised, when looking at Figure 2, that a leaf is a plant organ, as it contains several different types of tissue and has the specific function of photosynthesis in the light. Two other plant organs are roots and stems. Roots absorb water and minerals. The stem holds the leaves in a good position to catch as much light as possible. Leaves are where photosynthesis occurs in plants when they are in the light.

Questions

1 What is the function of: **(a)** epithelial tissue **(b)** glandular tissue?
2 Define an organ and write down six organs in your body.
3 Arteries are blood vessels carrying blood away from the heart. Suggest what the functions of the following tissues are in an artery: **(a)** epithelial tissue **(b)** muscular tissue.
4 Draw a table listing four plant organs and their functions. Suggest why plants need organs.
5 Outline how you could see plant cells for yourself, in a leaf you were given in the laboratory.
6 Using the stomach as an example of an organ, describe three types of tissue it contains and the function of each tissue's cells.
7 Name a system in humans where substances are exchanged with the environment. Explain how three organs are involved in the example you have given.
8 Explain the terms 'differentiate' and 'specialise', by referring to human cells and tissues.

A*

Taking it further

Xylem, the main supporting tissue in plants, is distributed differently in stems and roots. In stems it is found as distinct oval patches arranged in a circle, while in roots it is found as a central cylinder.

Suggest what forces a plant stem and root are subject to as they grow and survive in the air and soil respectively.

How will the arrangement of xylem in the root and shoot equip them for their survival?

Route to A*

Suggest one other organ system in humans and mammals, in addition to the digestive system, where substances are exchanged with the environment.

Cells and cell structure 109

Learning objectives

Most students should be able to:

- explain that cells differentiate, which allows them to perform different functions
- describe how cells are organised into tissues that group together to make organs, which make organ systems
- explain that organ systems, like the digestive system, develop for exchanging materials.

Some students should also be able to:

- describe the arrangement of vascular tissue in plant organs [Ext]
- list the organs of the digestive system and give their functions. [Ext]

Key points

After differentiation the cells of multicellular organisms become adapted for specific functions.

Tissues are groups of cells with a similar structure and function e.g. muscle tissue.

Organs may contain several types of tissue and carry out a particular function e.g. the heart.

Organ systems are groups of organs that perform a particular function e.g. the digestive system.

Lesson activities

Starter

1 Ask the students to put a hand over their biceps muscle and flex it. Elicit the fact that the biceps is made of many muscle cells and tell them it is called muscle tissue. Ask them to suggest the reason for grouping many muscle cells together. This could lead on to brainstorming other types of tissue.

2 Refer to the striking photograph in lesson B2 1.5 of the Student Book. Discuss with the students in outline how a human baby develops from the ball of cells. Use the terms 'differentiate' and 'specialise'.

Differentiate | epithelial | organs | tissues | zygote

Main

1 B2 1.5a Cells and tissues in a celery stem Refer to sheet in Teacher and Technician Planning Pack.

2 B2 1.5b Organs and organisms Refer to sheet in Teacher and Technician Planning Pack.

3 Worksheet B2 1.5c Cells make tissues make food Refer to sheet in Teacher and Technician Planning Pack.

Plenaries

1 Write the words 'cell', 'tissue' and 'organ' on the board and give students 5 minutes to link them in a concept map. As a class activity add other useful words, including examples.

2 Write the following types of tissues on separate slips of paper: nerve tissue, epithelial tissue, skeletal tissue, glandular tissue, muscle tissue, mesophyll tissue, epidermal tissue, phloem tissue, xylem tissue. Put the slips into an opaque plastic bag. Divide the students into two groups. Offer the bag to one team to draw out a slip. The function of the tissue must be given. The bag is passed over to the other team and the process repeated until all the slips have been used.

Homework

1 Worksheet B2 1.5d is a crossword that will give students an opportunity to revise keywords for this chapter.

2 Ask the students to create a spreadsheet in Excel to show the types of tissue in the heart, kidney and lungs. Suggest they enter 'histology' in their search engine to start.

Route to A*

Ask high achievers to choose three organ systems in humans and to draw a diagram of each, showing the organs involved in relation to one another.

Students use the Internet to research four types of human epithelial tissue. For each type, students should list the structural features and how these equip the cell for a particular function.

Answers to Student Book questions

Science skills

System	Organs	Tissues	Function
digestive	pancreas salivary gland	glandular	produce digestive juices
digestive	stomach small intestine	glandular	produce digestive juices
digestive	small intestine	epithelial	absorption of food
digestive	large intestine	epithelial muscle	water absorption faeces formation

Taking it further

Stems are subject to buffeting forces of wind. An interrupted ring of xylem tissues allows the stem to flex without snapping. Roots need to force their way through the soil and a central mass of xylem strengthens the root to exert pressure on the soil.

Route to A*

The respiratory system exchanges the gases of oxygen and carbon dioxide with the environment.

Answers

1 **(a)** Epithelial tissue is a lining and a covering tissue. **(b)** Glandular tissue produces and releases chemicals such as enzymes and hormones.

2 An organ is a group of tissues that performs a specific function. Examples include: arteries, heart, brain, liver, stomach and lungs.

3 **(a)** Epithelial tissue forms a lining and a covering of an artery. **(b)** Muscular tissue contracts to help push blood along.

4 Four from:

Plant organ	Function
stem	holds the leaves in a good position to intercept light
root	absorbs water and minerals
leaf	photosynthesis
flower	reproduction
seed	protect plant embryo and serve as a food source
fruit	protect seeds and aids in seed dispersal

5 Take a thin transverse section through a leaf, mount on a slip and view using a light miscroscope.

6

Tissue in the stomach	Function
epithelium	forms a lining and a covering layer
muscle	mixes the stomach contents – food and digestive juices
glandular	produces chemicals to help digestion

7 Example: digestive system. The pancreas and salivary glands produce digestive juices. Digestion occurs in the stomach and small intestine. Absorption of soluble food occurs in the small intestine. In the large intestine two processes occur: water is absorbed into the blood from the undigested food and faeces is produced.

8 Cells become different, or differentiate, as they specialise, or develop, adaptations to do particular jobs. Two examples of specialised cells and what they do: e.g. muscle – contract; epithelial – provide coverings/linings; glandular – produce chemicals. A tissue is a group of similar cells; suitable example of a tissue.

B2 2.1 Photosynthesis

Link to the specification

B2.3.1a Photosynthesis is summarised by the equation:

carbon dioxide + water (+ light energy) $\longrightarrow$ glucose + oxygen

B2.3.1b During photosynthesis:

- light energy is absorbed by a green substance called chlorophyll, which is found in chloroplasts in some plant cells and algae
- this energy is used by converting carbon dioxide (from the air) and water (from the soil) into sugar (glucose)
- oxygen is released as a by-product.

Ideas for practical work

Investigate the effects of light, temperature and carbon dioxide levels, (using Cabomba, algal balls or leaf discs from brassicas) on the rate of photosynthesis.

Investigating the need for chlorophyll for photosynthesis with variegated leaves.

The use of sensors to investigate the effect of carbon dioxide and light levels on the rate of photosynthesis and the release of oxygen.

How Science Works

SKU: B2.3 bullet point 1: Interpret data showing how factors affect the rate of photosynthesis.

B2 2.1 Photosynthesis

Learning objectives

- describe photosynthesis in an equation
- describe the role of chloroplasts and chlorophyll in photosynthesis
- explain energy conversion in photosynthesis
- explain that oxygen is a by-product of photosynthesis.

A life-giving chemical reaction

The word 'synthesis' means to combine or to join together to create something new. 'Photo' means light. Photosynthesis uses light energy and two simple molecules: carbon dioxide from the air and water from the soil, to make a more complex molecule called glucose. Oxygen is also released as a **by-product**. Photosynthesis happens in a series of reactions that can be summarised by the equation:

$$\text{carbon dioxide} + \text{water} \xrightarrow{\text{light energy}} \text{glucose} + \text{oxygen}$$

Glucose is a larger molecule than carbon dioxide and water, and contains more energy in its bonds. This energy can be used for growth. Plants make glucose by photosynthesis.

light energy from the Sun
glucose produced
water from the roots
carbon dioxide from the air
oxygen out into the air

Figure 1 Photosynthesis produces sugar.

Photosynthesis takes place in chloroplasts

Chlorophyll is a green pigment that is found in chloroplasts. Chloroplasts are found mainly in palisade cells in the upper layer of leaves. The chlorophyll absorbs light energy, which is used to convert carbon dioxide and water into glucose.

A variegated plant.

Some plants have green and white leaves. These leaves are called **variegated** leaves and many cultivated plants have them. Only the green parts contain chlorophyll. Photosynthesis can only take place in the green parts of the leaves.

Some algae can photosynthesise

Green algae are organisms that have some different characteristics to plants. They do, however, have chloroplasts and can photosynthesise. You may have seen green algae in ponds and streams in summer. Also, seaweeds are algae. **Plankton** contains the most numerous types of algae. They are single celled and microscopic and are found in the surface layers of lakes, rivers and oceans.

These algae can photosynthesise.

Investigating photosynthesis

One of the easiest ways to see if a plant is photosynthesising is to test it for **starch**. Any excess sugar produced during photosynthesis is stored as the insoluble product starch and this will stain blue-black with the iodine test. In the photograph of the two leaves, the brown leaf is showing the brown iodine stain because no starch is present in it. It has not photosynthesised. The other leaf is stained blue-black because it contains starch. This tells us that the leaf has photosynthesised. Before iodine is added to the leaves they are plunged into boiling water and decolourised by heating in ethanol.

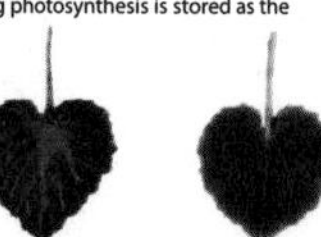

The iodine test for starch. If starch is present the leaf turns blue-black.

110

You can also check that oxygen is produced in photosynthesis by collecting and testing it with a glowing splint. The easiest way to do this is by using pondweed, a plant that lives under water.

Practical

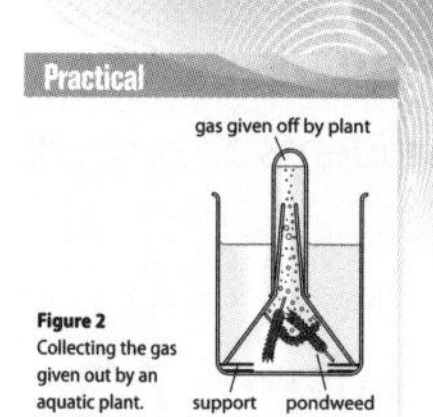

Figure 2 Collecting the gas given out by an aquatic plant.

Science skills

The easiest way to measure the rate of photosynthesis is to measure the rate at which oxygen is produced. The two sets of apparatus shown in Figure 3 do this in different ways.

a What two measurements do you need to make in order to calculate the rate at which oxygen is produced?

b Which set of apparatus in the diagram would give the more reliable data: A or B? Explain the reason for your answer.

c Table 1 shows results obtained from this experiment. Suggest the most suitable method of displaying the results.

Table 1 Results from experiment.

Light intensity/ arbitrary units	Rate of movement of meniscus/mm in 5 min
0	0
2	3
4	6
6	9
8	12
10	12

d How many times should the experiment be repeated to make the results reliable?

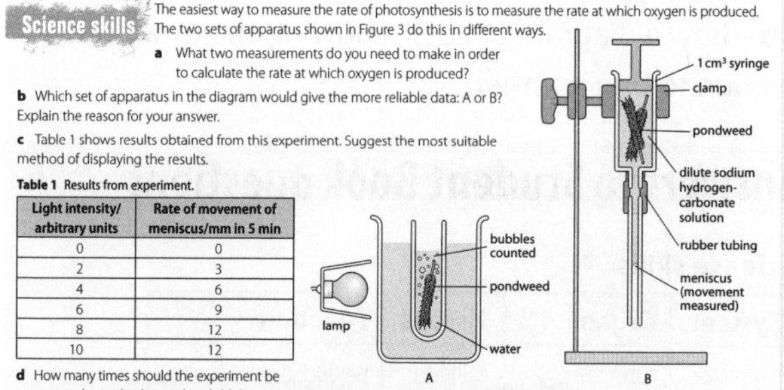

Figure 3 Measuring the rate of photosynthesis.

Questions

1 **(a)** What are the reactants in photosynthesis? **(b)** Where do they come from? **(c)** Why is light needed for photosynthesis?
2 What are the products of photosynthesis and how are they useful to the plant?
3 Explain the role of chlorophyll in photosynthesis.
4 A farmer forgets to water the crops when the weather is dry. What effect will this have on photosynthesis?
5 Describe the appearance of variegated leaves. If you had two leaves of the same type and size, that had been kept in the same conditions but one was variegated and the other was not, suggest with reasons which would have the higher rate of photosynthesis.
6 How could you test a leaf from a plant that has been kept in a dark cupboard for 3 days to see if it had been photosynthesising? What result would you expect from the test?
7 Some tiny green algae grow on the surface of ponds. If a pond gets completely covered by these, the larger plants underneath them die. Suggest why.
8 Pondweed is a plant that lives under water. Explain how it obtains glucose.

A*

Plants: obtaining food and growth 111

Learning objectives

Most students should be able to:

- describe photosynthesis in an equation
- describe the role of chloroplasts and chlorophyll in photosynthesis
- explain energy conversion in photosynthesis
- explain that oxygen is a by-product of photosynthesis.

Some students should also be able to:

- name two types of phytoplankton that live on the surface of the oceans [Ext]
- explain that light is needed to develop chlorophyll in plants. [Ext]

Key points

Photosynthesis is the means by which plants produce their own food using the Sun's energy.

The process also requires carbon dioxide, water and chlorophyll.

Oxygen is produced as a waste product of the reaction and glucose as an energy source.

Lesson activities

Starter

1 Give the students the word equation and the symbol equation for photosynthesis. Ask them to identify: i) what factors are needed to make glucose, and ii) what products are produced by photosynthesis.

2 Take some samples of starch-based foods, e.g. breakfast cereal, bread, potato crisps, popcorn, and drop some iodine solution on each one. Use questions and answers to see whether students can recall what iodine solution tests for. Ask students how starch came to be in these foods. Relate this to the process of photosynthesis.

Main

1 B2 2.1a Is light necessary for photosynthesis? Students test leaves that have been partially covered in aluminium foil, to see if they contain starch. The leaf to be tested is drawn to show the area covered by the foil and drawn again after the iodine test to show its distribution in the leaf. (~30 mins)

2 B2 2.1b Using leaf discs to investigate the need for chlorophyll in photosynthesis Green and white discs about 5 mm in diameter are cut with a cork borer from a destarched variegated leaf. After at least 24 hours in bright light the discs are tested for starch. (Set-up 10 mins + 15 mins test for starch; ~ 25 mins total)

3 B2 2.1c Predicting the outcomes of three photosynthesis investigations This worksheet describes investigations relating to carbon dioxide, light and temperature and asks the students to apply their knowledge of the photosynthesis equation to predict the effect of a factor on the outcome of photosynthesis. You may wish to use this worksheet in the next lesson instead.

Plenaries

1 The 20-second starch test and photosynthesis equation. Tell the class that you are looking for verbal contributions to summarise what the starch test and photosynthesis equation are. Appoint a time keeper and a recorder for the whiteboard to put items into the equation and make a list of steps in the starch test. Each person can only speak for 20 seconds.

2 Have a variegated plant, a flower, a vegetable and a fruit to show the students and ask them to write a list of plant parts that can photosynthesise and those that cannot. Use the lists to elicit a discussion of the key role of chlorophyll in photosynthesis.

Homework

1 Worksheet B2 2.1d provides an opportunity for students to test their understanding of photosynthesis.

2 Ask students to research what other pigments besides chlorophyll are present in leaves and if they have a special function. Ask them to find the predominant pigment in leaves of copper beech trees.

Points to note

- Explain at the start that although glucose is made in photosynthesis it is stored as starch.
- Emphasise that starch is stored in plants so it can be used as an energy source in respiration.
- Tell the students that starch is insoluble and so does not affect entry of water into cells by osmosis.
- Plants need to be destarched by being kept in the dark for 48 hours before these experiments are started. This gives time for the starch to be changed into sugar and moved out of the plant before the experimental conditions are applied.

Route to A*

Higher achievers can be given the opportunity to find out the wavelengths of light which are most absorbed by chlorophyll and most used in photosynthesis. They can also research the effect of water depth on photosynthesis and effectively the greatest depth at which photosynthesis is possible.

Answers to Student Book questions

Science skills

a The volume of oxygen given off in a standard time, e.g. 5 minutes.

b Apparatus B because the 1 cm^3 pipette is accurately calibrated and the volume of oxygen released can be measured to provide a continuous variable.

c As a line graph.

d As many times as possible in the time available; preferably five but at least three times.

Answers

1 **(a)** Water and carbon dioxide. **(b)** Water comes from the soil, carbon dioxide comes from the air. **(c)** Light is needed to supply energy.

2 Glucose and oxygen are the products of photosynthesis. Glucose is used for growth and respiration, oxygen is also used for respiration.

3 Chlorophyll absorbs light energy.

4 It will reduce the rate of photosynthesis as water is one of the reactants in photosynthesis.

5 Variegated leaves have some white patches in them. The one that was not variegated would have the higher rate of photosynthesis as all parts of the leaf have chlorophyll and will be able to photosynthesise. The parts of the variegated leaf that are white or yellow will not photosynthesise.

6 Plunge a leaf in boiling water and then heat it in ethanol until all the green colour has come out of it. Add iodine solution to the leaf and if it has been photosynthesising it will turn blue/black, proving that starch is present. The leaf that was in the cupboard will not turn black because it could not photosynthesise without light.

7 The algae block light from entering the water so the large plants below cannot photosynthesise. They die when their food reserves have been used up.

8 Glucose is obtained through photosynthesis: carbon dioxide + water (+ light energy) $\longrightarrow$ glucose + oxygen. Carbon dioxide is dissolved in pond water and oxygen is released into the pond water. Light penetrates the surface layers of water and surrounds the plant, and is therefore readily available for photosynthesis.

B2 2.2 Limiting factors

Link to the specification

B2.3.1c The rate of photosynthesis may be limited by shortage of light, low temperature or shortage of carbon dioxide.

B2.3.1d Light, temperature and the availability of carbon dioxide interact and in practice any one of them may be the factor that limits photosynthesis.

Ideas for practical work

Investigate the effects of light, temperature and carbon dioxide levels, (using Cabomba, algal balls or leaf discs from brassicas) on the rate of photosynthesis.

The use of sensors to investigate the effect of carbon dioxide and light levels on the rate of photosynthesis and the release of oxygen.

How Science Works

SKU: B2.3 bullet point 1: Interpret data showing how factors affect the rate of photosynthesis.

B2 2.2 Limiting factors

Learning objectives

- explain what is meant by a limiting factor
- describe the factors that may limit photosynthesis
- describe how factors that limit the rate of photosynthesis can interact with one another
- interpret a graph showing the interaction of limiting factors.

What limits the rate at which crops grow?

Growing tomatoes is big business. Tomato plants produce our food through photosynthesis. Growers need to know the conditions in which photosynthesis works fastest if they are to harvest the largest possible crop.

Rate of photosynthesis

The rate of photosynthesis is the speed at which photosynthesis takes place. It is affected by the environment. The factors that affect it most are temperature, **light intensity**, availability of carbon dioxide and availability of water. The rate of photosynthesis is limited by low temperature, shortage of carbon dioxide and shortage of light.

If the level of one or more of these is low, the rate of photosynthesis will be slowed down, or limited. The factor that is reducing the rate of photosynthesis is called the **limiting factor**. A limiting factor is something that slows down or stops a reaction even when other factors are in plentiful supply.

Crop plants photosynthesising.

How do variations in the amount of light, carbon dioxide and temperature affect the rate of photosynthesis?

If we are to advise growers we need to investigate how variations in these three factors affect the rate of photosynthesis. When we investigate each factor separately we find that increasing the amount of the limiting factor will increase the rate of photosynthesis, but only up to a certain value. After this rate of photosynthesis has been reached there is no further increase. Some other factor has become a limiting factor. This can be seen in Figure 1 where each graph levels off at 'X'. For the left-hand graph low temperature or low light intensity might be the limiting factor. For the right-hand graph low temperature or shortage of carbon dioxide might be the limiting factor.

Increasing temperature beyond the optimum value for a plant causes the enzymes that control the reactions of photosynthesis to break down or **denature**. This stops photosynthesis.

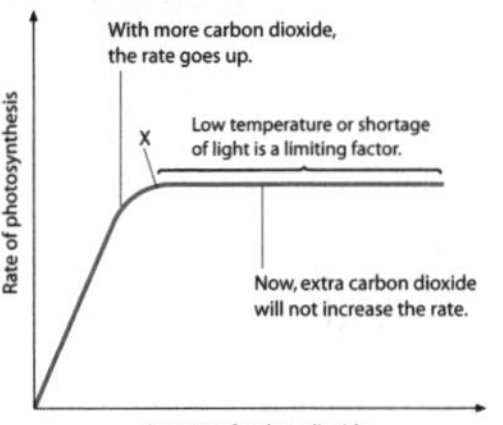

With more light, the rate goes up.
X
Low temperature or shortage of carbon dioxide is a limiting factor.
Now, extra light will not increase the rate.
Rate of photosynthesis
Light intensity

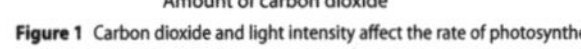

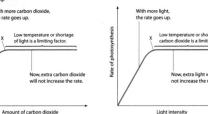

Figure 1 Carbon dioxide and light intensity affect the rate of photosynthesis.

Interaction of limiting factors

In practice, light intensity, temperature and the level of carbon dioxide interact to affect the rate of photosynthesis. Any one of them might be the limiting factor at a specific time of day. For instance at dawn and in the evening the temperature may be low, or in rainy weather thick cloud may reduce the light intensity. The Earth's atmosphere has a very low concentration of carbon dioxide of about 0.04% and carbon dioxide can be a limiting factor when plants grow densely together as crops or in tropical rainforests.

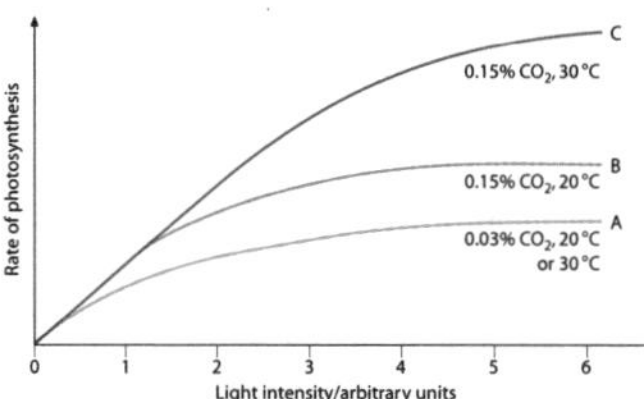

Figure 2 Interaction of limiting factors affects the rate of photosynthesis.

Questions

1. What is meant by the rate of photosynthesis?
2. List three factors that affect the rate of photosynthesis.
3. Explain what a limiting factor is.
4. **(a)** Using the three limiting factors discussed on this page, construct a table and suggest, using ticks, which of them you think may be limiting in the following locations: the Arctic, a hot desert, a tropical rainforest. **(b)** Which other substance in short supply will limit or prevent photosynthesis?
5. Explain the financial implications for a grower of ignoring the concept of limiting factors.
6. Look at the graphs in Figure 1. **(a)** Suggest why increasing the amount of carbon dioxide increases the rate of photosynthesis. **(b)** Suggest why increasing the amount of light can increase the rate of photosynthesis. **(c)** Explain why both graphs level off as the factor continues to increase. **(d)** The percentage of carbon dioxide in the air is about 0.04%. On a warm, sunny day, suggest which factor is limiting the rate of photosynthesis in the middle of a crop. Give a reason for your answer.
7. Look at Figure 2. **(a)** Which curve shows the highest rate of photosynthesis at 6 units of light intensity? **(b)** Which curve shows the lowest concentration of carbon dioxide? **(c)** Explain why curve C is much higher than curve B. **(d)** Suggest why you get curve A even if the temperature is increased from 20°C to 30°C.
8. You have been asked to experiment and find out the rate of photosynthesis of a specimen of pondweed provided by your teacher. Outline what you would do, giving reasons for your proposed method.

A*

Route to A*

Curves with a similar shape to those in Figure 1 are very common in biology. You need to be able to explain why the curves go up to start with and why they then level out.

Taking it further

Plants are **autotrophic** in their nutrition – this means they feed themselves. Plants build up organic molecules from simple inorganic molecules, using light as a source of energy.

The biochemical pathway involved has two main stages: the light-dependent reaction and the light-independent reaction. Suggest which of these stages is mostly limited by temperature.

Learning objectives

Most students should be able to:

- explain what is meant by a limiting factor
- describe the factors that may limit photosynthesis
- describe how factors that limit the rate of photosynthesis can interact with one another
- interpret a graph showing the interaction of limiting factors.

Some students should also be able to:

- plan an investigation to investigate the effect of carbon dioxide, light or temperature levels on photosynthesis [Ext]
- evaluate the benefits of artificially manipulating the environment in which plants are grown. [Ext]

Key points

Certain factors will stop photosynthesis from occurring even when other needed substances are in plentiful supply.

These are called limiting factors

Limiting factors include shortage of light, shortage of carbon dioxide and low temperature.

Lesson activities

Starter

1 Show the class two photographs, preferably of the same scene, of plants in winter and summer. Ask the students to tell you at which time of year most photosynthesis will be going on. During discussions elicit the information that low levels of temperature and light may limit or reduce the level of photosynthesis.

2 Building a self-assembly chair. Explain that to make the chair in 20 minutes, components A, B and C have to be constructed in 5, 10 and 5 minutes respectively. Then ask what the effect on the overall construction time will be if component A takes 7 minutes to make.

3 Establish that one component at a slow rate in a system will slow the whole process down and relate that to photosynthesis.

Light intensity limiting factor

Main

1 B2 2.2a Investigating the effect of carbon dioxide concentration on photosynthesis Refer to sheet in Teacher and Technician Planning Pack.

2 B2 2.2b Planning – How does light intensity affect the rate of photosynthesis of an aquatic plant? Refer to sheet in Teacher and Technician Planning Pack.

3 Worksheet B2 2.2c Managing banana growth in Iceland explores modification of environmental conditions to obtain maximum yield. (~20 mins)

Plenaries

1 Write 'limiting factors of photosynthesis' on the board and ask the students what the three factors are. Go on to ask them how a tomato grower might be able to increase photosynthetic rate. Elicit the facts that this will increase growth rate (bigger tomatoes faster) and hence the amount of crop produced (yield).

2 Give students a list of answers e.g. limiting factor, oxygen, light intensity, glucose, temperature. Ask them to work in small groups to write the questions.

Homework

1 Worksheet B2 2.2d provides an opportunity for students to see how the limiting factor is different in different situations.

2 Ask students to research information about shade and partial shade varieties of plants that can be grown in the UK. They can put their data in an Excel spreadsheet and include the following information: height of plant, time of flowering, annual or perennial, grown from seed or not, evergreen or deciduous. Students can use gardening adverts, catalogues or the Internet as resources.

Points to note

- Interpretation of graphical data is used frequently in this topic.
- *Cabomba* is sold in aquarist shops and departments at garden centres. It is used to aerate tropical fish tanks. You may find it bubbles more vigorously than *Elodea*, but its rather thin fronds are easily broken off.
- *Elodea* can be kept in a tank of tap water all year, but it photosynthesises better in summer.
- In experiments involving bench lamps near to the experimental set-up, a heat shield must be used to prevent the plants overheating and introducing temperature as a variable. A flat-sided vase or tank of water, between the lamp and the plant, is suitable.
- There are alternative practicals available on the SAPS website. Some of these involve the use of algal balls.
- Light intensity is proportional to $\frac{1}{d^2}$ where d is the distance from the light source.

Route to A*

Students research the light conditions required to grow roses for Valentines Day or poinsettias for Christmas. They can also research the temperature range tolerated by some important food crops such as rice, wheat, maize, potatoes and yams.

Answers to Student Book questions

Taking it further

The light-independent reaction.

Answers

1 The speed at which photosynthesis takes place.

2 Light intensity, carbon dioxide concentration, temperature.

3 A limiting factor is something that slows down or stops a reaction even when other factors are in plentiful supply.

4 **(a)**

	Light intensity	Amount of carbon dioxide	Temperature 20 °C
Arctic	✓		✓
Hot desert			
Tropical rain forest		✓	

(b) Water.

5 If photosynthesis is limited by one or more factors the crop will not grow to its full potential. The crop yield will be reduced, and so the grower will have less produce to sell and will make a smaller profit. At the same time, the grower may have spent money enhancing one limiting factor, which would not cause an increase in the rate of photosynthesis if another factor was limiting.

6 **(a)** There is more reactant available. **(b)** There is more energy available for the reaction. **(c)** The graphs level off because some factor other than the given variable, such as temperature, may be limiting. **(d)** Carbon dioxide would be the limiting factor if the plant was adequately watered, as there is enough light and heat energy from the sun.

7 **(a)** Curve C. **(b)** Curve A. **(c)** C has a higher temperature – the lower temperature limits photosynthesis at a lower rate in B. **(d)** Carbon dioxide is the limiting factor.

8 Put the pondweed in a glass tube, to allow light to reach it. Attach a 1 cm^3 pipette to the glass tube; this measures the oxygen given off during photosynthesis. Surround the pondweed with dilute sodium carbonate solution to provide dissolved carbon dioxide. Measure the volume of oxygen given off per minute.

B2 2.3 Uses of glucose produced in photosynthesis

Link to the specification

B2.3.1e The glucose produced in photosynthesis may be converted into insoluble starch for storage. Plant cells use some of the glucose produced during photosynthesis for respiration.

B2.3.1f Some glucose in plants and algae is used:

- to produce fat or oil for storage
- to produce cellulose, which strengthens the cell wall
- to produce proteins.

B2.3.1g To produce proteins, plants also use nitrate ions that are absorbed from the soil.

Ideas for practical work

Taking thin slices of potato and apple and adding iodine to observe under the microscope.

B2 2.3 Uses of glucose produced in photosynthesis

Learning objectives

- **describe how glucose may be converted to insoluble starch, fat or oil and stored in cells**
- **explain that cells use some glucose for respiration**
- **explain that glucose is also used to synthesise cellulose and proteins.**

Energy foods

Many of our energy foods come from parts of plants that are stores of carbohydrate. Potatoes and cereals are part of our **staple** diet. Both store plenty of carbohydrate. These stores are not for the benefit of humans. Stored carbohydrate helps the plants to survive over the winter and to support the growth of new plants the following spring.

Glucose releases energy during respiration

During photosynthesis plants make glucose:

$$\text{carbon dioxide} + \text{water} \xrightarrow{\text{light energy}} \text{glucose} + \text{oxygen}$$

The glucose a plant makes does not stay as glucose for long. Some of it is used for respiration:

$$\text{glucose} + \text{oxygen} \longrightarrow \text{carbon dioxide} + \text{water (+ energy)}$$

The energy released in respiration in plant and animal cells is used in many processes. It is used to build new cells for growth, or for repair of damaged cells. Some energy is used in chemical reactions to change some materials into others. More energy is used to move materials around inside the organism.

Examiner feedback

Remember to use the word 'release' when you are writing about the energy from glucose that is available after respiration. This is because energy cannot be created or destroyed.

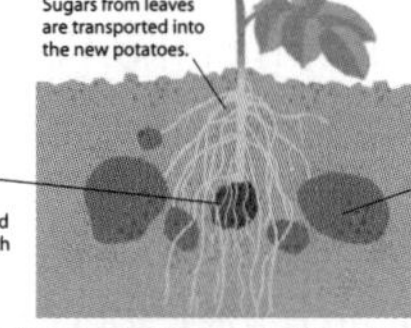

Sugars from leaves are transported into the new potatoes.
Remains of potato formed last year. Starch from this potato was used to provide materials and energy for the growth of this year's potato plant.
New potato forming. Here sugars from the leaves are converted into starch for storage over winter.

Figure 1 Potato plants use some glucose in respiration for growth and some to make potatoes.

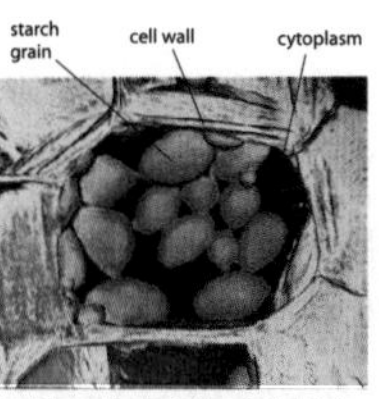

starch grain
cell wall
cytoplasm

Starch is stored in plant cells as starch grains in the cytoplasm. Magnification ×309.

Conversion of glucose to starch

A plant won't use all the glucose it makes straight away. Some glucose needs to be converted to starch and stored for times when the plant can't make enough glucose, for instance when it is too cold.

Starch is useful for storage because it is **insoluble** and doesn't react easily with other chemicals in the cytoplasm. The starch is an **energy store**, because the plant can change it back to glucose when it needs more energy from respiration.

114

Most plant cells contain some starch, but some cells are specially adapted to store a lot of it. For example, potatoes are stem tubers full of starch that grow underground. In the spring, the potatoes provide the energy stores needed to make new potato plants. These grow from buds on the old potatoes. Seeds, such as those of wheat and rice plants, also store a lot of starch. These stores are used to provide the energy needed to make new leaves when the seed germinates.

Conversion of glucose to fat or oil

Some plant seeds, plants, and algae store energy as fat or oil droplets in the cytoplasm. Fats and oils belong to a group called **lipids**. One gram of lipid has a higher energy content than 1 gram of carbohydrate. Lipids provide more glucose for respiration than carbohydrates, such as starch, when cells need it for respiration.

High-energy lipids are formed in some plant and algal cells after photosynthesis.

Synthesis of cellulose and proteins from glucose

When large molecules of cellulose are synthesised, many molecules of glucose are linked together to form strong fibres. This makes cellulose a useful structural material in plant and algal cell walls. It strengthens the cell wall and prevents the cell from bursting when it absorbs water.

All living cells need proteins to form enzymes and cell membranes. Plant and algal cells can synthesise proteins from glucose and other raw materials, such as **nitrates**. Soluble nitrates can be absorbed through cell membranes from soil, or water if the plant is aquatic.

cells containing chloroplasts photosynthesise
cell membranes absorb nitrates

Seaweed uses glucose and nitrates to build its cells.

Questions

1. Look at the equations for photosynthesis and respiration. **(a)** What are the similarities in the two equations? **(b)** What are the differences in the two equations? **(c)** Animals also respire. Where do they get their glucose from for respiration?
2. Give three processes for which a plant needs the energy from the respiration of glucose.
3. Explain what we mean by energy store.
4. Name: **(a)** one plant where starch is stored in stem tubers **(b)** two plants where starch is stored in the seeds **(c)** two fruits that store lipid **(d)** two seeds that store lipid.
5. Explain why potato plants and plants growing from seed need food stores.
6. A wheat grain contains a lot of starch. **(a)** Explain where the starch comes from. **(b)** Explain why the starch is stored in the grain. **(c)** Write down what the starch will be used for by the plant.
7. Why is the formation of cellulose dependent on photosynthesis?
8. Describe the uses of glucose produced in photosynthesis that is not used for respiration or stored as starch.

A*

Taking it further

Cereal crops, which are grown for their seeds, require large amounts of nitrate fertilisers.

Explain the links between seed formation, photosynthesis and nitrates in wheat crops.

Plants: obtaining food and growth 115

Learning objectives

Most students should be able to:

- describe how glucose may be converted to insoluble starch, fat or oil and stored in cells
- explain that cells use some glucose for respiration
- explain that glucose is also used to synthesise cellulose and proteins.

Some students should also be able to:

- explain how starch grains are built up in the cytoplasm of plant cells [Ext]
- relate structure to nutrient content in a wheat seed and the derivation of the component molecules. [Ext]

ActiveTeach Resource: Sugar use in plants – *Interactive labelling activity*

Key points

The carbohydrates made by plants during photosynthesis may be stored as starch or respired.

Fats and oils are produced from some glucose for storage in plants and algae.

The cell wall in plants and algae can be strengthened by the addition of cellulose, fats and proteins formed from glucose.

Nitrates from soil or water are needed to synthesise proteins.

Energy store | insoluble | lipid | nitrate | staple

Lesson activities

Starter

1 Present simple molecular diagrams of glucose and starch and discuss with the students the relative sizes of the molecules. In addition, add 10 g of glucose and 10 g of starch to two separate test tubes of water and stir each with a glass rod. This will allow the students to appreciate the difference in solubility of the two.

2 Show the students photographs of foods such as nuts, cereal grains, olives, rhubarb. Ask the students what the main nutrients are in these foods. Then go on to elicit information about how the plants have produced the nutrients.

Main

1 B2 2.3a Testing plant foods for reducing sugar and starch This student practical allows the testing of plant foods for reducing sugar and starch. Benedict's solution and iodine/KI solution are the reagents used. The reducing sugar test requires a water bath at 98 °C. (~35 mins)

2 B2 2.3b Looking for starch grains in cells This microscope practical requires thin sections of foods such as apple and potato. Sections are stained with iodine/KI solution. (~25 mins)

3 B2 2.3c Staple foods This worksheet explores staple foods around the world and also the nutrients in a wheat grain that have been synthesised by the plant after photosynthesis.

Plenaries

1 Draw a diagram on the board to show a young oak tree in a large plant pot. Ask the students to suggest how the tree will have changed after 5 years if it is just watered, and to explain their answers.

2 Write the following list on the whiteboard: sugar, starch, cellulose, oil/fat, protein. Give the class 3 minutes to write down as many plant foods as they can, that they have eaten in the last 24 hours, containing each item on the list.

3 Use the ActiveTeach labelling activity on 'Sugar use in plants'. [AT]

Homework

1 Worksheet B2 2.3d looks at the different types of complex molecules that are built up from glucose and their uses by the plant.

2 Students can research either 10 types of plants used to produce food oils, or the development of rape seed oil as a suitable food for humans.

Points to note

- The Benedict's test identifies *all* reducing sugars, one of which is glucose. Sucrose, which is used to sweeten tea, coffee, etc., is *not* a reducing sugar.
- Stress to the pupils that starch is *never* found in animal tissues.

Route to A*

Higher achievers can be given the opportunity to research the variety of sugars found in plants. They can also research the differences in molecular structure between starch and cellulose.

Answers to Student Book questions

Taking it further

Absorption of nitrates from the soil and glucose produced in photosynthesis are needed for protein formation. Seeds of cereal crops contain protein.

Answers

1 **(a)** Both equations have carbon dioxide, water, glucose, oxygen and energy in them. **(b)** The products of photosynthesis are the reactants of respiration. **(c)** From the food they eat.

2 For growth, repair of damaged cells, for chemical reactions and to move materials around the plant.

3 A food store that can be changed to glucose and used to release energy during respiration.

4 **(a)** E.g. carrot, parsnip, turnip, swede, potatoes, radish. **(b)** E.g. pea, bean, wheat grain, sweetcorn. **(c)** E.g. olives, avocados. **(d)** E.g. sunflower, corn, sesame, oil seed rape.

5 To provide energy for growth of new plants.

6 **(a)** From the glucose produced during photosynthesis in the leaves. **(b)** So that it can provide energy needed for the wheat seeds to germinate when conditions are suitable next year and produce more wheat plants. **(c)** Starch will be converted back into glucose when needed for the production of cellulose and proteins in the growing plant, and long-term storage as oil or fat/lipid.

7 It is made from glucose, a product of photosynthesis.

8 Glucose is used to produce fat or oil, and for energy storage. One gram of lipid has a higher energy content than one gram of carbohydrate. Glucose is also combined with nitrates (which are also needed for protein formation and come from external sources) to produce proteins. Glucose is also used to form cellulose, which strengthens the cell wall.

B2 2.4

Enhancing photosynthesis in greenhouses and polytunnels

Link to the specification

B2.3.1c The rate of photosynthesis may be limited by:

- shortage of light
- low temperature
- shortage of carbon dioxide.

B2.3.1d Light, temperature and the availability of carbon dioxide interact and in practice any one of them may be the factor that limits photosynthesis.

How Science Works

SKU: B2.3 bullet point 1: Interpret data showing how factors affect the rate of photosynthesis.

B2 2.4

Enhancing photosynthesis in greenhouses and polytunnels

Learning objectives

- explain how greenhouses and polytunnels enable crops to be grown throughout the year
- explain how enhancing limiting factors for photosynthesis can increase crop yield
- evaluate the financial benefits of changing environments to improve growth rates.

All-year salad

In the nineteenth century, most people in this country could only buy lettuces in summer. Now you can eat lettuce grown in the UK at any time of year. Artificially controlling the environment around a crop makes it possible to grow it at times of year when it wouldn't grow as well outside, or in places where it wouldn't grow well, such as very dry places. The conditions outside in fields cannot be easily controlled. Growing crops in **greenhouses** or **polytunnels** makes it possible to control the environment around the plants, including the soil.

Maximising the conditions for photosynthesis.

Healthy eating at any time of the year.

Crops grow when the plants are photosynthesising. The faster the rate of photosynthesis, the better the growth of the plants; the better the growth of plants, the higher the **yield**. Yield is the amount of crop a plant produces. Growers can now get plants to photosynthesise all year round. They can do this by enhancing light, carbon dioxide concentration and temperature.

Taking it further

There are several aspects of light quality that are relevant to photosynthesis and plant growth. In addition to light intensity and duration of the light period, the wavelength of the light is important for photosynthesis.

Find out which wavelengths of light are most useful to photosynthesising green plants.

Enhancing light

Light is rarely a limiting factor in summer, but some growers supplement natural light with artificial light in winter. In industrial greenhouses the problem with enhancing light is making sure that all the plants receive the extra light. Tall plants shade each other if they are not adequately spaced. Supplementary light is usually only economic when the plants are small and then they can be grown more densely.

Enhancing carbon dioxide

The very low concentration of carbon dioxide in the atmosphere (about 0.04%) can limit the rate of photosynthesis when plants are grown closely together. Carbon dioxide levels in a greenhouse can be increased by burning a fuel such as propane or adding the gas through PVC tubing. Growers find that there is a limit to increasing the rate of photosynthesis by increasing the concentration of carbon dioxide. Another factor, such as temperature or light, may then become limiting.

Controlling temperature

Keeping a greenhouse at a temperature of between 25 °C and 30 °C in winter requires heating. Most greenhouses are heated in winter by a boiler and radiators. In summer the temperature in the greenhouse will sometimes exceed 30 °C. This is because heat waves from the Sun are trapped in the greenhouse by being continually reflected. This causes the rate of photosynthesis to decrease. Vents can be opened in the greenhouse roof and blinds can be used to lower the temperature.

Science skills

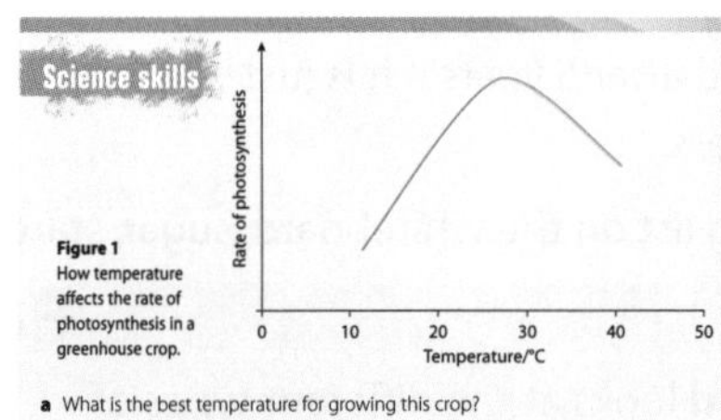

Figure 1 How temperature affects the rate of photosynthesis in a greenhouse crop.

a What is the best temperature for growing this crop?

b At what temperature would you open the roof vents? Explain your answer.

c Describe the change in rate of photosynthesis between 30 °C and 40 °C.

Science in action

When propane is burned, carbon dioxide is produced and heat is released. Liquid carbon dioxide is pure carbon dioxide and is stored in special cylinders. After vaporisation the carbon dioxide is delivered to the plants by PVC tubing with a hole punched in the tubing near each plant.

Scottish strawberries growing in a polytunnel.

Science in action

Pollination is essential to fruit formation. When strawberries are grown in greenhouses or polytunnels, growers import live bees to pollinate the flowers. These imported bees must not be released outside as they may affect the health of British bees.

Questions

1. Give three factors that can be controlled in polytunnels and greenhouses to increase the rate of photosynthesis.
2. **(a)** For each of the factors in your answer to question **1**, explain how a grower can increase that factor in a greenhouse. **(b)** Why would a grower want to increase these factors?
3. Give two advantages of growing crops in controlled environments.
4. Give two disadvantages of growing crops in controlled environments.
5. Suggest why a grower might choose to grow crops in a controlled environment.
6. UK-grown lettuces are available at Christmastime. Explain how this is possible and any disadvantages for growers and consumers.

A*

Examiner feedback

When extracting data from a graph, it is sensible to draw a construction line from the curve of the graph to the relevant axis. This will enable you to read off a value and give an accurate answer.

116

Plants: obtaining food and growth 117

Learning objectives

Most students should be able to:

- explain how greenhouses and polytunnels enable crops to be grown throughout the year
- explain how enhancing limiting factors for photosynthesis can increase crop yield
- evaluate the financial benefits of changing environments to improve growth rates.

Some students should also be able to:

- design a protected environment for growing specified plants on a specified site [Ext]
- express a preference for using polytunnels as opposed to greenhouses for certain crops in some parts of the UK. [Ext]

Key points

Greenhouses enable the growth of year-round crops.

Enhancing limiting factors for photosynthesis can increase yield.

ActiveTeach Resource: Enhancing photosynthesis – *Interactive true or false activity*

Growing crops in greenhouses – *Video*

Soaking up CO_2 – *Video*

Greenhouses polytunnels yield

Lesson activities

Starter

1 Show students some tomatoes and discuss with them where they were grown. Explore the students' existing knowledge of greenhouses and polytunnels.

2 If the school/college has a greenhouse, use it as an example of how a protected environment can be beneficial for growing certain plants. If the school/college does not have a greenhouse, show the students a photograph of a massive greenhouse such as the Palm House at Kew. Discuss with the students how it would feel in there with regard to temperature, humidity and wind.

Main

1 B2 2.4a Design a greenhouse This is a planning and design task for a greenhouse to grow salad crops all year round on a given plot. Students work in groups of two or three. Internet research is required and you may prefer to split the practical into two sessions – one for research and siting the greenhouse, and the second for completing the design and presentation of it to peers.
(~25 mins + 40 mins = 65 mins total)

2 B2 2.4b Managing photosynthesis – a debate This worksheet provides the basis for a debate on the pros and cons of growing food under controlled conditions in greenhouses, to maximise photosynthesis.

3 Worksheet B2 2.4c Be an agricultural expert provides an opportunity for students to apply their knowledge of limiting factors when replying to three fictitious problems from gardeners. This can be used with groups of two or three, or individually.

Plenaries

1 Use the ActiveTeach resources to reinforce students' learning. [AT]

2 Return to the fresh tomatoes used in *Starter 1*. On the whiteboard, with the students' help, build up a source diagram for tomatoes in winter and summer. Most tomatoes are imported during the winter and the students should be able to give the reasons. There may be less carbon emissions from transport costs than from providing heating and lighting to UK greenhouses.

Homework

1 Worksheet B2 2.4d gives students the opportunity to evaluate data.

2 Ask the students to plan how they could organise a tasting session to judge consumer preference for organic versus intensively produced types of fruit or vegetable. Emphasise that it must be a fair test and suggest (if necessary) that the tasters rate the food on a five-point scale.

Points to note

- Some students may be unaware of the enormous size of commercial greenhouses.
- Polytunnels may be alien to some students.
- The mechanisation involved in greenhouses for watering, crop collection, etc. may need explaining.
- Use of fertilisers, or fungicides and insecticides in greenhouse monocultures is usual. You may like to discuss this as a disadvantage of commercial greenhouses.

Route to A*

Ask students to research the automatic sprinkler and ventilation mechanisms used in the hot houses at the Eden Project or Kew Gardens.

Students can also research pineapple growing in the UK in Victorian times. The Lost Gardens of Heligan website is a good place to start.

Answers to Student Book questions

Taking it further

Blue light with a wavelength of 450 nm and red light with a wavelength of 650 nm are most effective in photosynthesis.

Science skills

a 26–28 °C.

b 25 °C as there is still a high rate of photosynthesis yet the plants have not become too hot, as this would cause their rate of photosynthesis to decrease rapidly. Plants often die if they are overheated so the growers need to avoid this.

c There is a continual decrease in the rate of photosynthesis.

Answers

1 Light intensity, temperature and level of carbon dioxide can be controlled in greenhouses to increase the rate of photosynthesis.

2 **(a)** Light – artificial light; temperature – heaters; carbon dioxide – from propane heaters or as a gas. **(b)** To make the plants grow better so that he obtains a higher yield from the crop.

3 Advantages: The crops produce a higher yield; the crops can be grown when the weather and land outside are unsuitable.

4 Disadvantages: the costs for energy and for equipment are high.

5 A bigger yield, or crops grown out of season, will increase the grower's profit.

6 Lettuces can be grown in greenhouses; high light intensity, warm temperature, optimum levels of carbon dioxide and water provide good growing conditions. Conditions outside are cold at Christmas time, with only a few hours of daylight, so the cost of energy for heating and lighting is high. This means the cost of the lettuce will be relatively high, and there will be increased carbon emissions involved in growing the lettuces, which is a disadvantage to both growers and consumers.

B2 2.5

Manipulating the environment of crop plants

Link to the specification

B2.3.1a Photosynthesis is summarised by the equation:

carbon dioxide + water (+ light energy) ⟶ glucose + oxygen

B2.3.1c The rate of photosynthesis may be limited by:

- shortage of light
- low temperature
- shortage of carbon dioxide.

B2.3.1d Light, temperature and the availability of carbon dioxide interact and in practice any one of them may be the factor that limits photosynthesis.

B2.3.1g To produce proteins, plants also use nitrate ions that are absorbed from the soil.

How Science Works

SKU: B2.3 bullet point 2: Evaluate the benefits of artificially manipulating the environment in which plants are grown.

B2 2.5

Manipulating the environment of crop plants

Learning objectives

- explain the advantages and disadvantages of manipulating environmental conditions in which plants grow
- evaluate the practice of manipulation in greenhouses
- interpret data showing how environmental factors affect the rate of photosynthesis.

Economics of enhancing photosynthesis

High energy costs for supplementary heating, lighting and carbon dioxide concentration prohibit some potential growers from using greenhouses and polytunnels. In addition there are one-off costs for building and equipment to set up this type of agriculture. However, it results in a bigger yield, and crops grown out of season usually sell for more money.

Getting carbon dioxide to greenhouse crops

Three ways of supplying carbon dioxide to greenhouse crops are described below. The information in each section is for 4 hectares of greenhouse maintaining a carbon dioxide concentration of 1300 parts per million (ppm).

Propane burner for carbon dioxide enrichment, installed in a greenhouse.

Propane burners

When propane is burned, carbon dioxide is produced and heat is released. Propane is derived from fossil fuel and these fuels tend to contain sulfur as an impurity. If there is sulfur in the fuel, sulfur dioxide will also be released. About 1.4 kg of water is released for each cubic metre of propane burned. The one-off cost of installing the burners is £32 600 and the daily cost of propane is £217.

Carbon dioxide from flue gases

Natural gas is burned in a microturbine, which is used to generate electricity. The heat released during combustion is used to heat water. This can be circulated immediately throughout the greenhouse by pipes, or stored in large tanks for use at night. The carbon dioxide in the flue gas is distributed to the crops through a pipework system. The one-off cost of the equipment is approximately £118 000 and the natural gas fuel for the microturbine costs £84 per day.

Science in action

All of the carbon dioxide released in commercial greenhouses, as described in this chapter, has been produced by burning fossil fuels. The carbon dioxide-enriched atmosphere boosts crop growth. However, carbon dioxide released into the atmosphere by the same combustion process is regarded as one of the main contributors to global warming. Globally, this may reduce crop growth in future decades.

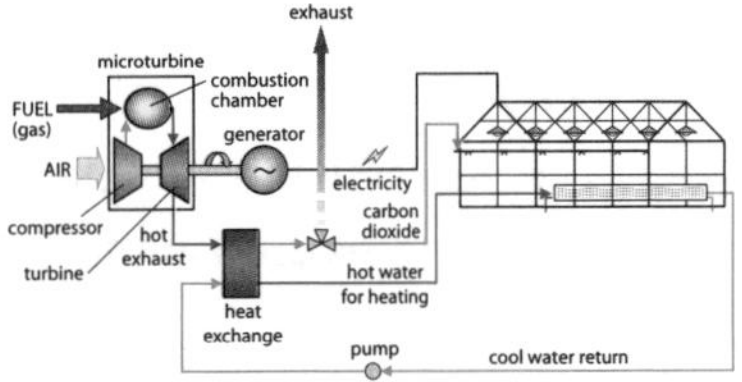

CO_2-enrichment from a combined heat and power (CHP) unit.

Liquid carbon dioxide

Liquid carbon dioxide is pure carbon dioxide. It is delivered in bulk by tankers and stored in special cylinders. The liquid carbon dioxide is vaporised then delivered to the plants by PVC tubing with a hole punched near each plant. The equipment for storing and vaporising the carbon dioxide is rented for £6900 per year and the daily cost of the carbon dioxide is £234. This method of providing carbon dioxide is used more on mainland Europe than in the UK. Once installed, equipment can be expected to last for at least 10 years.

Bulk storage of liquid carbon dioxide.

Science skills

During the day, plants both photosynthesise and respire. The relationship between gross photosynthesis, net photosynthesis and respiration is given in the equation:

gross photosynthesis = net photosynthesis + respiration

Table 1 The rates of gross photosynthesis and net photosynthesis for a cereal crop at different temperatures.

Temperature/°C	Rate of gross photosynthesis/ arbitrary units	Rate of net photosynthesis/ arbitrary units
12	12	10
19	26	24
26	40	37
34	34	27
41	26	11

a Plot a graph of the data in Table 1. Choose suitable scales for the axes. Label each of the curves.

b Describe the effect of temperature on the rate of gross photosynthesis.

c Which factor is limiting the rate of gross photosynthesis between 19 °C and 26 °C? Explain the reasons for your answer.

d The rate of gross photosynthesis is the same at 19 °C as it is at 41 °C. The cereal crop grows more slowly at 41 °C than at 19 °C. Suggest an explanation for this.

Cucumbers are now grown mainly in greenhouses.

Table 2 The yield of cucumbers grown in a well-lit greenhouse under different conditions.

Temperature/°C	Yield of cucumbers/kg per 10 plants	
	0.13% carbon dioxide	0.04% carbon dioxide
12	12	10
19	26	24
26	40	37
34	34	27
41	26	11

e In which conditions did the cucumbers give the greatest yield?

f Would the grower make most profit by using these conditions? Explain the reasons for your answer.

Questions

1 In a table, summarise the advantages and disadvantages of each of the methods of supplying carbon dioxide described above.

2 Imagine you are a grower. Which method would you use? Explain the reasons for your answer. A*

Learning objectives

Most students should be able to:

- explain the advantages and disadvantages of manipulating environmental conditions in which plants grow
- evaluate the practice of manipulation in greenhouses
- interpret data showing how environmental factors affect the rate of photosynthesis.

Some students should also be able to:

- calculate weekly costs for carbon dioxide supply by three different methods [Ext]
- assess the benefits of using hydroponic cultivation in greenhouses. [Ext]

Key points

Enhancing carbon dioxide in greenhouses is expensive; growers need to balance the cost of enhancement against the increase in yield.

Increasing temperature increases the rate of respiration as well as the rate of photosynthesis; therefore raising the temperature too high may result in a decrease in yield.

Increasing one factor may have no effect if another factor is limiting.

Lesson activities

Starter

1 Use the photographs in the Student Book to explain the scale of operations in large commercial greenhouses.

2 List the factors that can limit photosynthesis and invite explanations of how each factor contributes to the process.

Main

1 **Worksheet B2 2.5a Evaluating the economics of enhancing growing conditions in greenhouses** requires students to analyse the information in the Student Book about the economics of supplying CO_2 to greenhouses by three different methods.

2 **Worksheet B2 2.5b Using hydroponics and sensors in commercial greenhouses** explores hydroponics in commercial greenhouse cultivation.

3 **Worksheet B2 2.5c Biological pest control in greenhouses** gives students experience in referencing information obtained from the Internet. (Biological pest control is beyond the remit of the specification, but the task will help the students develop useful skills.)

Plenaries

1 Write 'carbon dioxide enrichment' in the middle of the whiteboard and ask the students to suggest three methods of doing this. Write these below 'carbon dioxide enrichment' and attach them by leader lines. Add to this cascade diagram with the class suggesting advantages, costs, etc. When the diagram is finished it should be a summary of the process.

2 Give the students 3 minutes to write down as many examples as possible of plants grown in commercial greenhouses. Then ask them to name two they would least like to live without during the winter.

Homework

1 **Worksheet B2 2.5d** provides an opportunity for students to engage with examination question mark schemes.

2 Ask students to go to the Eden Project website and find out how environmental conditions are controlled in the rainforest biome.

Points to note

- Students need to be aware of what an area of 4 hectares looks like.
- Calculations are required for Worksheet B2 2.5a and groups of 2–3 students could work together.
- Some time needs to be spent with students explaining the flow diagram in the Student Book.
- It may be worthwhile showing the students photographs of sensors for light and CO_2 in greenhouses.
- Students may not be familiar with greenfly, slugs, nematode worms and marigolds that are mentioned in Worksheet B2 2.5c. Have some images available to show them on the whiteboard.

Answers to Student Book questions

Science skills

a *x*-axis: temperature; *y*-axis: rate of photosynthesis; two line graphs – one for gross photosynthesis, one for net photosynthesis. Both curves labelled.

b An increase in temperature up to 26 °C increases the rate of photosynthesis. At higher temperatures the rate of photosynthesis decreases.

c Carbon dioxide is the limiting factor because in a cereal crop the plants are so dense that there is a very high demand for carbon dioxide when temperatures increase to 25 °C, and the rate of photosynthesis is high.

d At 41 °C some of the cell components like enzymes have been damaged by the high temperature and this prevents cell division and growth.

e At a temperature of 26 °C when there was 0.13% carbon dioxide.

f The grower would have to pay for carbon dioxide enrichment but at a temperature of 26 °C he would only gain an extra 3 kg/10 plants yield of cucumbers, because of the extra carbon dioxide supplied. Heating the greenhouse to 26 °C would cost more than heating to 19 °C but he would gain more money from the extra 14 kg/10 plants yield of cucumbers. He would have to decide if carbon dioxide enrichment was cost efficient.

Answers

1

	Propane burners	Flue gases	Liquid carbon dioxide
Advantages	Release both heat and CO2. Cheaper to install than boilers for flue gases.	Heat released and hot water can be stored. Cheapest to run.	Smaller equipment costs per year.
Disadvantages	Sulfur dioxide may be released.	May contain carbon monoxide.	Space needed externally for storage and equipment. No heating supplied to greenhouse.
Costs	Installation £32 600. Not as cheap to run as flue gas at £217/day.	High cost of installation at £118 000. Low running costs of £84/day.	Most expensive to run at £234/day plus on-going annual rental costs for equipment £6900/year.

2 Choice of method – propane burners, flue gases or liquid carbon dioxide. Two advantages, relevant to chosen method, from table above; two comparisons with other methods in table above; justification for choice.

B2 3.1

Communities of organisms and their environment

Link to the specification

B2.4.1a Physical factors that may affect organisms are:

- temperature
- availability of nutrients
- amount of light
- availability of water
- availability of oxygen and carbon dioxide.

How Science Works

SKU: B2.4 bullet point 1: Suggest reasons for the distribution of living organisms in a particular habitat.

CA: B4.3.1a Carrying out practical work and research, and using the data collected to develop hypotheses.; B4.4.1a Appreciating when it is appropriate to calculate a mean; B4.4.1b Calculating the mean of a set of at least three results; B4.5.3a Describing the relationship between two variables and deciding whether the relationship is causal or by association; B4.5.4b Using secondary sources; B4.5.4d Evaluating methods of data collection.

B2 3.1

Communities of organisms and their environment

Learning objectives

- identify the physical factors that affect the distribution of organisms
- explain how each particular factor affects the distribution of organisms
- calculate the mean, median and mode for environmental data.

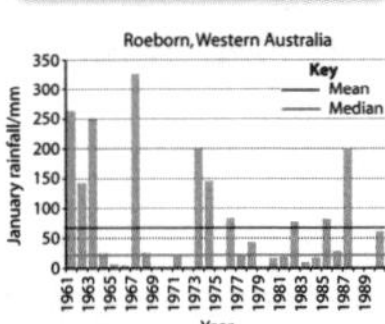

Figure 1 January rainfall for a city in Western Australia.

Examiner feedback

The high rainfall figures in some years are *not* anomalous results – so they cannot be disregarded when calculating the mean. Data can only be disregarded if the measuring technique or equipment is faulty.

Examiner feedback

It is easy to confuse mean, median and mode. Remember:

- mean by writing it as meAn – A = average
- median by writing it as meDian – D = the miDDle letter
- mode by writing it as MOde – MO = MOst common.

Physical factors

Organisms are affected by their environments.

Table 1 Some environmental factors alongside their effects on living organisms, and the methods we use to measure them.

Physical factor	Measurement	Effect on living organisms
temperature	thermometer or probe	In low temperatures metabolism slows right down. This reduces the activities of animals that cannot regulate their body temperatures.
nutrients	chemical analysis	Plants and microorganisms need ions to produce chemicals essential for living processes, so plants do not grow well in nutrient-poor soils.
amount of light	light meter or light sensor	Plants need light for photosynthesis, so only specialised plants can grow well in shade conditions.
availability of water		Most living organisms contain a very high proportion of water, which is essential for all living processes.
availability of oxygen in water or soil	oxygen electrode	Oxygen is essential for aerobic respiration, so only specialised animals can live in water with a low concentration of dissolved oxygen.
availability of carbon dioxide	gas analysis	Carbon dioxide is essential for photosynthesis and may be a limiting factor in some circumstances.

Analysing data

Environmental factors may vary throughout the year or even minute by minute, so before an experiment we must plan data collection and analysis so that the results reflect actual conditions as faithfully as possible.

A student investigating the activity of insects measured the temperature on the school playing field at noon each day for 1 week in summer.

The temperatures, in °C, on the 7 days were

19 21 18 22 18 17 25

To find the **mean** noon temperature for the week, add all seven numbers and divide by seven.

$19 + 21 + 18 + 22 + 18 + 17 + 25 = 140$

$140 \div 7 = 20$

So the mean temperature for the week was 20 °C.

To find the **median** temperature for the week, rearrange the daily temperatures in ascending order and select the one in the middle. If two numbers are left in the middle, add them together and divide by two.

17 18 18 19 21 22 25

So the median temperature for the 7 days is 19 °C.

122

To find the **mode**, group the data and find out how many there are in each group.

17 (1), 18 (2), 19 (1), 21 (1), 22 (1), 25 (1)

There were 2 days when the temperature was 18 °C and only 1 day for each of the other temperatures, so the mode temperature was 18 °C.

If the values you are working with are fairly close together, then calculating the mean gives useful information. However, if the values for a factor are very variable, the median may be more useful.

Figure 1 shows wide variation in January rainfall. The mean is influenced by the very high rainfall in some years. The median gives a far more typical measure of the rainfall.

Science skills

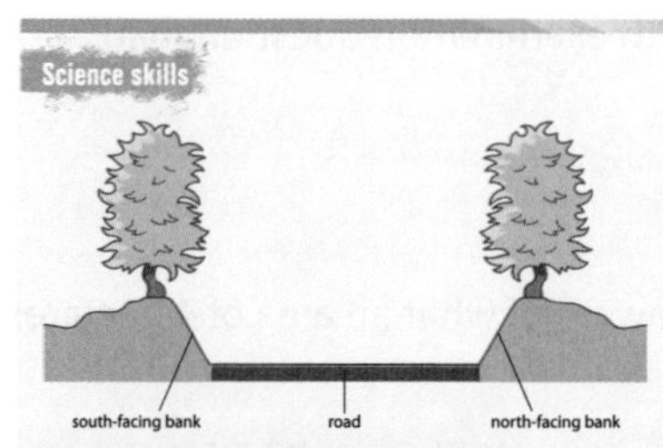

Plant species	Number of plants growing in a 10 m length of bank	
	South-facing bank	North-facing bank
Cow parsley	7	10
Dandelion	8	4
Groundsel	15	10
Lesser celandine	18	8
Thistle	5	1
White deadnettle	23	0

Figure 2 Which factors affect the growth of plants on the banks by a road?

a Describe the pattern shown by the data for most of the plants growing on the banks.

b Which plant does not fit into the general pattern?

c **i** Suggest the two factors that are most likely to affect the general pattern.

ii Name two processes in plants that could be affected by the factors you have named in **i**.

d Suggest one other factor that might affect the general pattern.

Questions

1 Give one way in which an increase in temperature affects organisms.

2 Which factors are essential for the healthy growth of plants in a habitat?

3 When is it best to calculate: **(a)** the mean value for an environmental factor? **(b)** the median value for an environmental factor?

4 The minimum temperature (°C) on each of 7 successive days in a habitat was:

9 9 11 5
14 2 6

Calculate the mean, the mode and the median for this set of data.

5 The graph in Figure 3 shows changes in the populations of two species of plants in an area of deforestation.

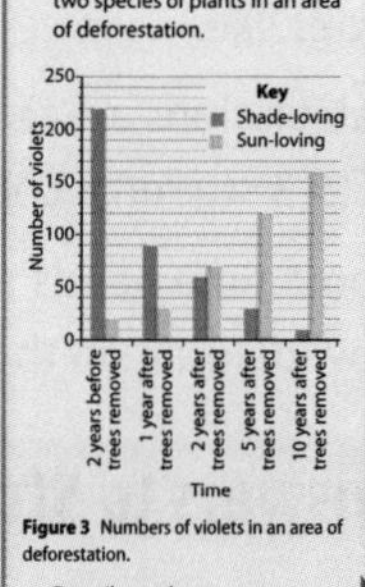

Figure 3 Numbers of violets in an area of deforestation.

Describe and suggest an explanation for the changes in the populations of the two species.

A*

Communities of organisms and their environment 123

Learning objectives

Most students should be able to:

- use the Internet to gather climate information for a particular area
- calculate mean and median using climate data.

Some students should also be able to:

- plan an investigation to find the effect of a physical factor on the distribution of organisms in an area. [Ext]

ActiveTeach Resource: Changing environments – *Matching activity*

Key points

Factors that affect the distribution of organisms include temperature, light, nutrients, water, oxygen and carbon dioxide.

If the values for an environmental factor are fairly close together, the results can be summarised by calculating the mean.

If the values for an environmental factor vary widely, it might be more appropriate to calculate the median (middle value).

The mode is the most common value in a set of data.

Physical factor mean median mode

Lesson activities

Starter

1 Start a concept map on the board with the word 'environment'. Depending on the ability of the students, you could add link words such as 'organism' and 'feeding relationship'. Ask students for other words to link into the map. Aim to revise what they covered in Unit 1 on environment and adaptation.

Main

1 B2 3.1a Investigating physical factors in the environment Students measure the environmental conditions in three different areas on the school playing field and survey the plants found in those areas. (~90 mins) It is not necessary for students to actually carry out the investigation – the lesson could just concentrate on the planning skills required for ISAs.

Plenaries

1 Students share their ideas about the problems involved in measuring environmental factors.

2 In the ActiveTeach 'Changing environments' activity, students match sentences relating to changes in factors and the effect this may have on organisms there, e.g. a large tree shading a large area of lawn – match to an increase in shade-loving plants. [AT]

Homework

1 Worksheet B2 3.1b covers analysing climate data in terms of calculating mean, median and mode.

2 Students should complete the Science Skills exercise in lesson B2 3.1 of the Student Book.

Points to note

- Students need to understand that the 'environment' of an organism includes the physical factors, such as light, warmth, water and soil, as well as biotic factors such as feeding relationships and competition.
- Students may need the opportunity to do some preliminary work to see how much plant distribution varies over the fields and to think about why this happens. This should lead them to thinking of a suitable question to investigate.

Route to A*

Research the statistical methods that ecologists use to test for significant differences in ecological data.

Answers to Student Book questions

Science skills

- **a** Most plants have larger populations on the south-facing bank.
- **b** Cow parsley.
- **c** **(i)** Temperature and light intensity.
  (ii) Photosynthesis and respiration.
- **d** Nutrients.

Answers

1. Increases enzyme activity/metabolism.
2. Suitable light intensity, suitable temperature, supply of nutrients and water.
3. **(a)** When values are reasonably close together. **(b)** When there is a large range of values.
4. Mean 8 °C, median 9 °C, mode 9 °C.
5. Shade-loving species declined rapidly in the first year after trees were removed, then more slowly. The total fell from 220 before trees were removed to 10, 10 years after the trees were removed. Sun-loving species rose steadily after the trees were removed, from an initial 40 to 160 after 10 years. The shade-loving species probably could not compete well for light with faster-growing or taller species of plants. The sun-loving plants need a high light intensity for optimal growth.

B2 3.2 Collecting ecological data

Link to the specification

B2.4.1b Quantitative data on the distribution of organisms can be obtained by:

- random sampling with quadrats
- sampling along a transect.

Ideas for practical work

Investigative fieldwork involving sampling techniques and the use of quadrats and transects; which might include, on a local scale, the:

- patterns of grass growth under trees
- distribution of daisy and dandelion plants in a field
- distribution of lichens or moss on trees, walls and other surfaces
- distribution of the alga *Pleurococcus* on trees, walls and other surfaces
- leaf size in plants growing on or climbing against walls, including height and effect of aspect.

How Science Works

SKU: B2.4 bullet point 2: Evaluate methods used to collect environmental data, and consider the validity of the method and the reproducibility of the data as evidence for environmental change.

B2 3.2 Collecting ecological data

Learning objectives

- explain how quadrats are used to collect information about the distribution of organisms
- explain random and systematic sampling
- analyse information obtained using quadrats.

Monitoring biodiversity

The Government is planning to build a high-speed rail link between London and Birmingham. The outline route passes through countryside that has a large biodiversity. Scientists will survey the wildlife in these areas in order to report on the effects of the proposals on threatened species. Some of the techniques the scientists will use are described below.

How many woodlice live in a wood?

Imagine you want to make a count of the number of woodlice in an area of woodland. Woodlice are tiny, there are very many of them and they are not distributed evenly across their habitat. Because of this it is not easy to find out how many woodlice there are in the wood. Instead of trying to count all the woodlice, we can use **sampling**. We count the numbers in a small area and use this number to estimate the total.

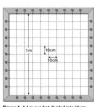

Large numbers of woodlice live in damp woodland soil.

1 m
10 cm
10 cm

Figure 1 A 1 m quadrat divided into 10 cm squares.

Quadrats

The most common method of sampling organisms is to use a **quadrat**. This is a square frame, usually measuring 10 cm, 50 cm or 1 m along each side. Quadrats are usually subdivided into smaller squares.

Science skills A group of four students each placed a 10 cm quadrat on the floor of a wood. Figure 2 shows their quadrats.

a Count the number of woodlice in quadrat A. Use this result to estimate the number of woodlice in 1 m² of woodland.

b Now count the total number of woodlice in quadrats A, B, C and D. Divide the total to find the mean number of woodlice in a 10 cm quadrat. Use the mean number to estimate the number of woodlice in 1 m² of woodland. What does your second estimate tell you about using quadrats?

A
B
leaf litter
woodlouse
C
D

Figure 2 The students' quadrats.

124

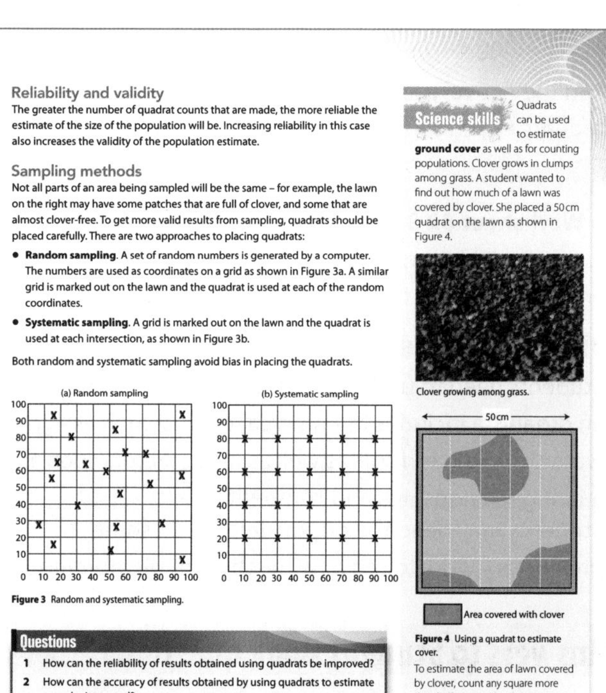

Reliability and validity

The greater the number of quadrat counts that are made, the more reliable the estimate of the size of the population will be. Increasing reliability in this case also increases the validity of the population estimate.

Sampling methods

Not all parts of an area being sampled will be the same – for example, the lawn on the right may have some patches that are full of clover, and some that are almost clover-free. To get more valid results from sampling, quadrats should be placed carefully. There are two approaches to placing quadrats:

- **Random sampling**. A set of random numbers is generated by a computer. The numbers are used as coordinates on a grid as shown in Figure 3a. A similar grid is marked out on the lawn and the quadrat is used at each of the random coordinates.
- **Systematic sampling**. A grid is marked out on the lawn and the quadrat is used at each intersection, as shown in Figure 3b.

Both random and systematic sampling avoid bias in placing the quadrats.

Figure 3 Random and systematic sampling.

Science skills Quadrats can be used to estimate **ground cover** as well as for counting populations. Clover grows in clumps among grass. A student wanted to find out how much of a lawn was covered by clover. She placed a 50 cm quadrat on the lawn as shown in Figure 4.

Clover growing among grass.

50 cm

Area covered with clover

Figure 4 Using a quadrat to estimate cover.

To estimate the area of lawn covered by clover, count any square more than half-covered by clover as a 'clover square'.

c Use the number of 'clover squares' to calculate the percentage of squares covered by clover.

d How could the quadrat be modified to give a more accurate measurement of cover? Give a reason for your answer.

Questions

1. How can the reliability of results obtained using quadrats be improved?
2. How can the accuracy of results obtained by using quadrats to estimate cover be improved?
3. Explain how quadrats could be placed randomly to sample organisms in a habitat.
4. Explain how quadrats could be placed systematically to sample organisms in a habitat.
5. Look again at the quadrats labelled A, B, C and D in Figure 2. **(a)** Where are most of the woodlice found? **(b)** Suggest a hypothesis to explain this distribution. **(c)** Design an investigation to test this hypothesis.

Communities of organisms and their environment 125

Learning objectives

Most students should be able to:

- use a quadrat to estimate cover of a species.

Some students should also be able to:

- evaluate the data obtained from an investigation involving a quadrat. [Ext]

Key points

Quadrats are used to sample the distribution of organisms in a habitat.

The larger the number of quadrats the more reliable the results.

Cover is calculated by counting the number of sub-squares of a quadrat more than half covered by the organism.

To avoid bias, quadrats should be placed in random or systematic positions.

Quadrat random sampling systematic sampling

Lesson activities

Starter

1 At the end of the previous lesson, ask students to look for evidence of a green, powdery growth (*Pleurococcus*) on tree trunks in the vicinity of their homes. Ask them to see if there is any apparent pattern to the areas of the trees on which the *Pleurococcus* grows.

2 Students should spend some time practising with the quadrats as indicated in 'Points to note' below.

Main

1 B2 3.2a Investigating the distribution of *Pleurococcus*
In this activity students estimate the percentage cover of *Pleurococcus* around a tree trunk. (~90 mins)

2 Students carry out the task in lesson B2 3.2 of the Student Book – Estimating woodlice populations.

3 Students carry out the task in lesson B2 3.2 of the Student Book – Estimating clover cover

Plenaries

1 Ask students to suggest environmental factors that might be affecting the distribution of *Pleurococcus*.

2 Ask students to comment on the validity of their results from Main task 1.

Homework

1 Worksheet B2 3.2b covers random sampling of plants in a school.

2 Worksheet B2 3.2c covers using quadrats to estimate population size.

Points to note

- Students should spend some time practising with the 10 cm × 10 cm quadrat to estimate percentage cover before working on the trees. Try making estimates of percentage cover in the lab using grids with a known number of squares shaded. In ecological studies of this type an accuracy of +/− 5–10% will give useful results.

Route to A*

Use a statistical method you researched in lesson B2 3.1 to analyse the data in worksheet B2 3.2c.

Answers to Student Book questions

Science skills

a Number of woodlice = 16, number in 1 m^2 = 16 × 100 = 1600.

b Total number of woodlice = 80, mean = 20, number in 1 m^2 = 20 × 100 = 2000. The greater the number of quadrats, the more accurate the population estimate.

c Number of squares = 6; percentage of squares = (6 × 100) ÷ 25 = 24%.

d Divide into smaller squares. It is equivalent to using more quadrats.

Answers

1 Using more quadrats.

2 Dividing the quadrat into smaller squares.

3 Use random numbers generated by a computer to give coordinates for sampling points on a grid.

4 Place quadrats at all the intersections on a grid.

5 **(a)** Under leaf litter. **(b)** Woodlice prefer dark conditions. **(c)** Construct a choice chamber giving woodlice a choice of light or dark conditions. Place large, equal numbers of woodlice in each half. Leave for standard time. Count the woodlice in each half. Repeat the experiment another two times. Calculate the mean number of woodlice that chose light and dark areas.

B2 3.3 Analysing ecological data

Link to the specification

B2.4.1b Quantitative data on the distribution of organisms can be obtained by:

- random sampling with quadrats
- sampling along a transect.

How Science Works

SKU: B2.4 bullet point 1: Suggest reasons for the distribution of living organisms in a particular habitat; B2.4 bullet point 2: Evaluate methods used to collect environmental data, and consider the validity of the method and the reproducibility of the data as evidence for environmental change.

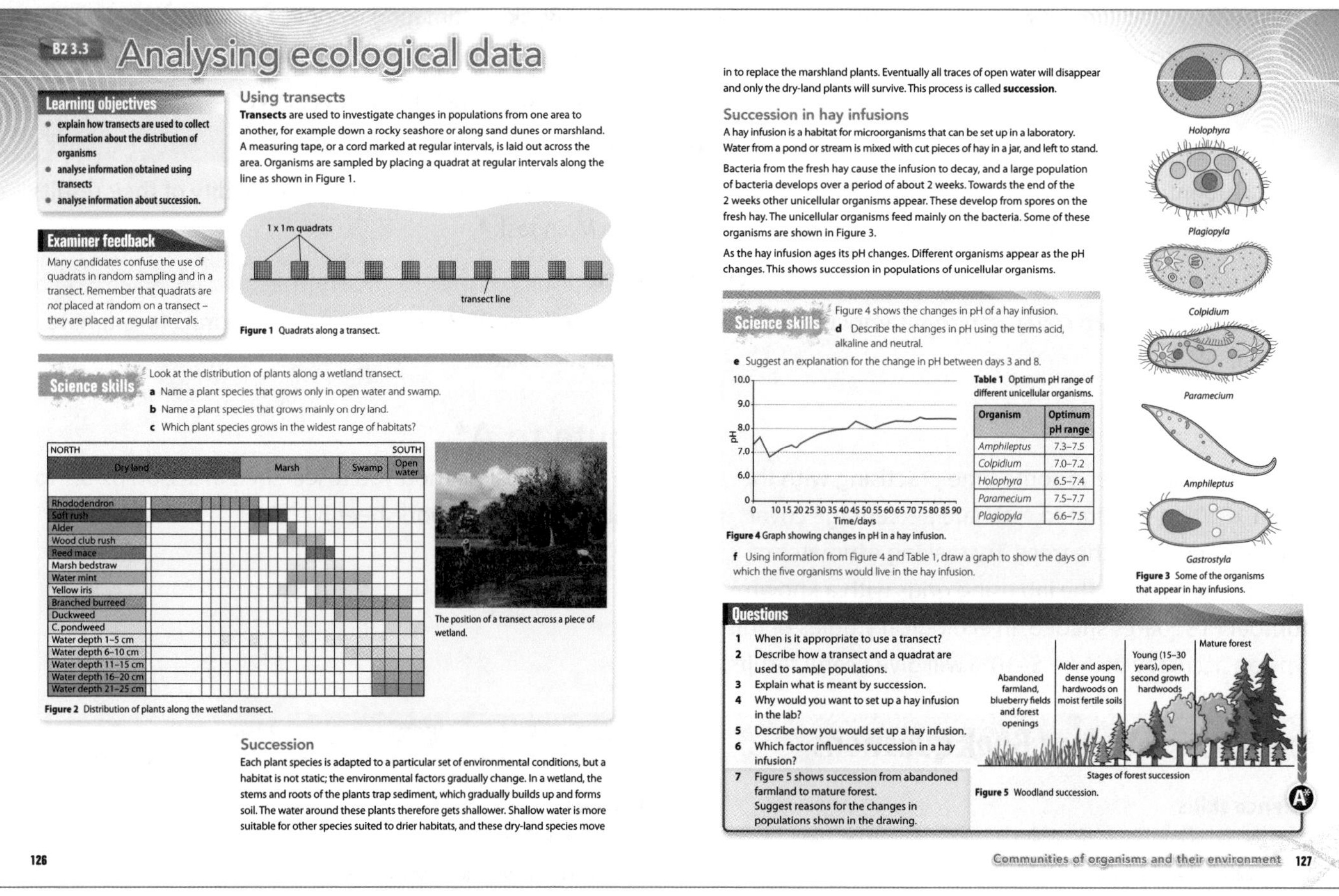

Learning objectives

Most students should be able to:

- understand the use of quadrats and transects to collect ecological data
- suggest reasons for the distribution of living organisms in a particular habitat
- evaluate methods used to collect environmental data.

Some students should also be able to:

- consider the validity and reliability as evidence for environmental change. [Ext]

Key points

Transects are used to measure changes in populations from one place to another.

Quadrats are placed at regular intervals along the transect to sample the populations.

Organisms may change conditions in the habitat so that the conditions become more suitable for other organisms. The change in the populations of organisms is called succession.

Succession in populations of unicellular organisms can be demonstrated in hay infusions.

Quadrat transect succession

Lesson activities

Starter

1 Hold a question and answer session: Ask one student 'What is your favourite TV programme?', and then ask how many others agree with their answer. Is this answer the same as everyone else's?

2 Steer students towards the idea of sampling – which is that you can't ask everyone. Then discuss how many to sample – too few is unrepresentative, too many is time-consuming. Finally, discuss how to sample – this could be random (e.g. pull names out of a hat) or systematic (e.g. every tenth name on the register).

Main

1 Worksheet B2 3.3a Using a transect Students work in groups to carry out a short belt transect following the instructions on the worksheet. They can display their data collected in the form of graphs. (~90 mins)

2 Students carry out the exercise in lesson B2 3.3 of the Student Book – Distribution of plants across a wetland transect.

3 Students carry out the activity in lesson B2 3.3 of the Student Book – Succession in a hay culture.

Plenaries

1 Students can present their finished graphs from *Main task 1* to the rest of the group.

2 When looking at the results it may be an opportunity to discuss why students doing similar transects, e.g. across the same path, get slightly different results, although the trend may be the same.

Homework

1 Worksheet B2 3.3b introduces further examples of the effect of physical factors on the distribution of plants.

2 Worksheet B2 3.3c introduces the mark–release–recapture method of estimating animal populations. NB method is not required knowledge. [Ext]

Points to note

- Most students find the idea of random sampling difficult. The idea of 'throwing a quadrat backwards over one's shoulder' is very common and should be discouraged. Students should understand that using random numbers to select squares on a grid of a habitat is the best way of obtaining a random sample.

Answers to Student Book questions

Science skills

a Canadian pondweed.

b Rhododendron/soft rush.

c Branched burreed.

d From being slightly alkaline, the pH becomes slightly more alkaline for three days then drops to just below neutral by the eighth day. The pH then gradually becomes more alkaline until the 90th day.

e Respiration of the increasing number of bacteria, which releases carbon dioxide, an acidic gas.

f Graph showing appropriate horizontal line for the number of days each species exists, related to its optimum pH and the pH graph.

Answers

1 When conditions change across a habitat.

2 A line is laid across the habitat and a quadrat placed e.g. every metre along the line.

3 The modification of a habitat by organisms, making the habitat more suitable for other organisms.

4 To study the effects of pH on unicellular organisms. This might be useful to scientists measuring the effects of water pollution.

5 Boil some hay in water, leave to cool, decant the infusion then add pieces of fresh hay.

6 pH.

7 Because the abandoned farmland is not harvested, dead plants decay in the soil making the soil more fertile. Alder and aspen can grow in this more fertile soil. These trees grow taller than the original vegetation and out-compete it for light. Meanwhile, some slower-growing hardwood trees have appeared. These out-compete the alder and aspen for light. Very little light now reaches the forest floor so very few ground plants grow.

ISA practice: earthworm distribution

In the Student Book, each ISA practice is contained on one double-page spread. However, you can, if you prefer, use the sheets provided in the Teacher and Technician Planning Pack and the Activity Pack to more closely mirror the experience of a real ISA which would then take place over several lessons and/or as homework.

Link to the specification

3.2 How Science Works

Observing phenomena can lead to the start of an investigation, experiment or survey. Careful observation is necessary before deciding which variables are the most important.

3.6 Controlled assessment

Scientific investigations often seek to identify links between two or more variables. [B4.1.1, B4.3.1.]

Scientists need to ensure repeatability, reproducibility and validity in evidence. [B4.3.3]

There is a link between the type of graph used and the type of variable represented. [B4.4.2]

In evaluating a whole investigation the repeatability, reproducibility and validity of the data obtained must be considered. [B4.5.2]

The patterns and relationships observed in data represent the behaviour of the variables in an investigation. However, it is necessary to look at patterns and relationships between variables with the limitations of the data in mind in order to draw conclusions. [B4.5.3, B4.5.4]

ISA practice: earthworm distribution

A farmer has asked students to investigate how the outside air temperature each month affects the distribution of earthworms in the soil. Earthworms are important in agriculture in the recycling of nutrients in the soil. Earthworms live in burrows in soil. The depth at which they live depends mainly on physical factors in the soil.

Section 1

1 Write a hypothesis about how air temperature affects the distribution of earthworms. Use information from your knowledge of earthworm behaviour to explain why you made this hypothesis. *(3 marks)*

2 Describe how you could carry out an investigation into this factor.

You should include:

- the equipment that you could use
- how you would use the equipment
- the measurements that you would make
- how you would make it a fair test.

You may include a labelled diagram to help you to explain the method.

In this question you will be assessed on using good English, organising information clearly and using specialist terms where appropriate. *(6 marks)*

3 Think about the possible hazards in the investigation.

(a) Describe one hazard that you think may be present in the investigation. *(1 mark)*

(b) Identify the risk associated with this hazard that you have described, and say what control measures you could use to reduce the risk. *(2 marks)*

4 Design a table that you could use to record all the data you would obtain during the planned investigation. *(2 marks)*

Total for Section 1: 14 marks

Section 2

Two students, Study Group 1, investigated how outside air temperature affects the distribution of earthworms in the soil. They measured the air temperature and counted the number of worms in 1 m^2 of soil. Their results are shown in Figure 1.

January	May	September
3°C 22 worms	8°C 92 worms	12°C 30 worms
February	June	October
1°C 8 worms	15°C 12 worms	9°C 52 worms
March	July	November
2°C 12 worms	20°C 5 worms	8°C 78 worms
April	August	December
5°C 38 worms	16°C 18 worms	6°C 52 worms

Figure 1 Study Group 1's results.

5 (a) Plot a graph of these results. *(4 marks)*

(b) What conclusion can you draw from the investigation about a link between outside air temperature and the distribution of earthworms? You should use any pattern that you can see in the results to support your conclusion. *(3 marks)*

(c) Look at your hypothesis, the answer to question 1. Do the results support your hypothesis? Explain your answer. You should quote some figures from the data in your explanation. *(3 marks)*

Below are the results of three more studies.

Figure 2 shows the results from another two students, Study Group 2.

Study Group 2

January	May	September
3°C 22 worms	8°C 68 worms	12°C 40 worms
February	June	October
1°C 2 worms	15°C 13 worms	9°C 48 worms
March	July	November
2°C 6 worms	20°C 12 worms	8°C 65 worms
April	August	December
5°C 30 worms	16°C 17 worms	6°C 59 worms

Figure 2 Study Group 2's results.

128

A third group of students, Study Group 3, decided that another factor might also be affecting the number of earthworms. They decided to find out the rainfall for the area. Their results are shown in Figure 3.

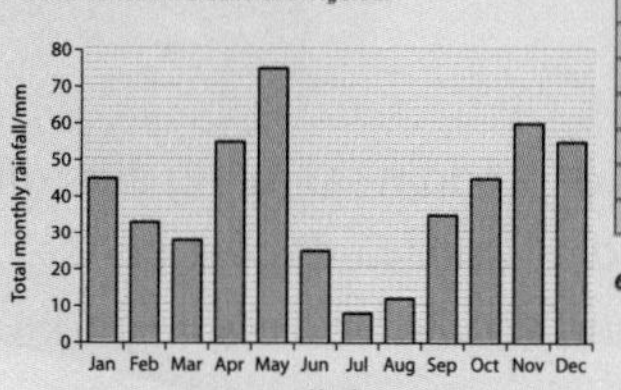

Figure 3 Monthly rainfall data from Study Group 3.

Study Group 4 was a group of scientists in India. They compared earthworm populations in two different national parks, X and Y.

- In each park they sampled eight sites by digging out a piece of soil 25 cm × 25 cm × 20 cm.
- They counted the number of earthworms in each sample.
- They measured the biomass of the worms using an electronic balance.
- They also measured the pH, nitrogen, organic matter, phosphorus, calcium, temperature and moisture content of each sample.

Table 1 shows the mean number and mean mass of earthworms from the two national parks.

Table 1 Mean number and mean mass of earthworms.

Park	Mean number of earthworms/m^3	Mean mass of earthworms / m^3/g
X	82	11.20
Y	17	2.87

Table 2 Average soil characteristics of national parks X and Y.

	Park X	Park Y
pH	6.40	6.02
Total nitrogen as a percentage	0.75	0.58
Organic matter as a percentage	5.13	4.09
Phosphorus as a percentage	0.34	0.23
Potassium as a percentage	0.90	0.63
Nitrate as a percentage	0.23	0.19
Temperature/°C	29.02	29.40
Water as a percentage	26.60	13.66

6 (a) Draw a sketch graph of the results from Study Group 2. *(3 marks)*

(b) Look at the results from Study Groups 2 and 3. Does the data support the conclusion you drew about the investigation in answer to question 5(a)? Give reasons for your answer. *(3 marks)*

(c) The data contain only a limited amount of information. What other information or data would you need in order to be more certain whether the hypothesis is correct or not? Explain the reason for your answer. *(3 marks)*

(d) Look at the results from Study Group 4. Compare the data from Study Group 1 with Study Group 4's data. Explain how far the data shown supports or does not support your answer to question 5(b). You should use examples from Study Group 4 and Study Group 1. *(3 marks)*

7 (a) Compare the results of Study Group 1 with Study Group 2. Do you think that the results for Study Group 1 are *reproducible*? Explain the reason for your answer. *(3 marks)*

(b) Explain how Study Group 1 could use results from other groups in the class to obtain a more *accurate* answer. *(3 marks)*

8 Applying the results of the investigation to a context. Suggest how ideas from the original investigation and the other studies could be used by the farmer in encouraging growth in the numbers of earthworms in his fields. *(3 marks)*

Total for Section 2: 31 marks

Total for the ISA: 45 marks

129

Learning objectives

Most students should be able to:

- make observations and develop into a hypothesis
- identify the independent and dependent variables in the hypothesis
- obtain some data to process
- produce a graph or bar chart from the data obtained
- identify any trends that may be present in the data
- relate that trend to their hypothesis.

Some students should also be able to:

- make a risk assessment of their chosen method, with suitable control measures
- examine the evidence obtained to establish its repeatability and /or reproducibility.

anomalous result calibration control measure hazard hypothesis mean observation prediction range repeatable reproducible research theory uncertainties (errors): random systematic zero validity variables: control categoric continuous dependent independent

Key points

Investigations should be designed so that patterns and relationships between variables can be identified.

It is important to ensure repeatability, reproducibility and validity in evidence when designing and evaluating investigations.

The choice of graph used depends upon the type of variable represented.

When drawing conclusions, the limitations of the data must be kept in mind.

Lesson activities

Starter

1 Show students a choice chamber of maggots. Subject the maggots to cold, heat, light and dark. Ask students to make a hypothesis about the behaviour of maggots from their observations.

Main

1 **Researching and planning** Students need to research, using at least two different sources, a way of investigating earthworm distribution and develop a hypothesis. Suggest a suitable context, e.g. farmers needing to encourage the growth in the number of earthworms in their fields. Please refer to the **B2 ISA practice 1 Teacher and technician sheet.**

2 Students can complete their research/notes for homework. They need to be aware of the likely risks and how to control them. See the **B2 ISA practice 1 Student research notes sheet.**

3 Ask two students to read their notes on one of the points. Get the class to decide whose notes are best, with a reason. Repeat until all the points are covered.

4 Give students the B2 **ISA practice 1 Section 1 paper.**

5 In a following lesson students set up their investigation and record and process their results. Students can work in groups to obtain the data. If several groups have used the same method they may wish to pool results and obtain a mean. Please refer to the **B2 ISA practice 1 Student practical sheet**.

6 Students should process the data individually in controlled conditions. A bar chart or graph should be plotted and the trend of the graph/bar chart identified and a conclusion made.

7 The conclusion should be compared with their hypothesis to identity if their hypothesis has been confirmed or denied.

Plenaries

1 Students discuss sources of possible errors and ways to overcome them.

2 Give students the B2 **ISA practice 1 Section 2 paper.**

Homework

After the practical, ask students to write brief notes about ways in which they could improve their investigation. They should mention how to reduce errors and what further data or information they would need to confirm their conclusion.

Points to note

- Students should describe a complex relationship between the independent variable and the dependent variable.

Route to A*

Students' risk assessment should include sensible risks, with a clear indication of the likelihood of the hazard occurring and how to sensibly control the risk.

Depending on how closely you wish to mirror the real ISA experience all three parts can be done in class or some can be done for homework. You should adjust delivery to match the time that it takes to obtain meaningful results.

Ask students to critically evaluate their data and explain that the findings are only valid within the range of the independent variable, whose range may be quite limited.

Answers to Student Book questions

6 **(a)** Both axes labelled. (1) A suitable curve/line drawn. (1) Indication (arrow or numbers) of direction of increase in value of axes. (1)

(b) The student states that data in Study 1 strongly supports the original hypothesis and quotes some data from tables that supports this. (1)

The student also states that data in Study 2 shows a similar monthly pattern and quotes some data from tables that supports this. (1)

Critical appraisal of data to include:

Data for Study Groups 2 and 3 show the same pattern, although there are significant differences in some of the months.

Data from Study 2 also shows the same monthly pattern so it is impossible from this data to conclude which of the two factors has the more significant effect. (1)

(c) Suggests at least one other piece of information that would be needed to form a firm conclusion. The reason for the need for this other information is clearly stated. (3)

(d) Comment that this experiment was not comparable with the student's investigation because:

- The scientists did not collect monthly data.
- The temperature in the two parks was similar.
- Several other factors were also measured.
- The number and mass of earthworms were measured.
- Measurements were per m^3 rather than m^2. (3)

For the full mark scheme, see the Teacher and Technician Planning Pack.

B2 4.1 Protein structure, shapes and functions

Link to the specification

B2.5.1a Protein molecules are made up of long chains of amino acids. These long chains are folded to produce a specific shape that enables other molecules to fit into the protein. Proteins act as:

- structural components of tissues such as muscles
- hormones
- antibodies
- catalysts.

B2.5.1b Catalysts increase the rate of chemical reactions. Biological catalysts are called enzymes. Enzymes are proteins.

B2 4.1 Protein structure, shapes and functions

Learning objectives

- describe the structure of protein molecules
- explain some functions of proteins in animals
- describe the role of catalysts in chemical reactions
- explain the functions of enzymes in living organisms.

The most diverse biological molecules

Nearly 20% of the fat-free mass of your body is made up of protein – water makes up about 72%. Your hair, skin and nails are made of protein. Protein molecules, in the form of haemoglobin, carry oxygen in your blood and help if you are injured by clotting blood. Throughout the living world proteins are extremely important molecules. They take part in most chemical reactions within cells and are part of the structure of most organelles.

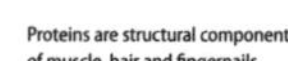

Proteins are structural components of muscle, hair and fingernails.

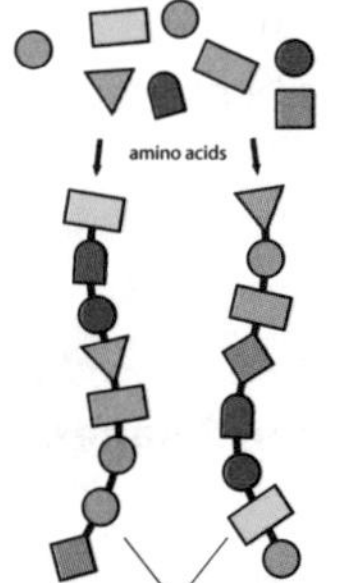

Figure 1 Two different polypeptide chains.

Structure of protein molecules

All proteins contain the same four elements: carbon, hydrogen, oxygen and nitrogen. Proteins are large molecules, known as macromolecules. They are made of a long chain of smaller, soluble molecules called **amino acids**. Twenty different amino acids are found in living organisms. These amino acids are joined together in a long chain, known as a **polypeptide**. Any number of amino acids can be joined together and any of the 20 types of amino acid can be used.

The sequence of the amino acids in the polypeptide chain is specific to every protein. These long chains of amino acids usually bend and fold extensively, forming a precise and specific three-dimensional shape. The shape is held together by chemical bonds. On the surface of the molecule there is often a depression or 'pocket' and this is known as the **binding site**. Other molecules can fit into the protein at the binding site.

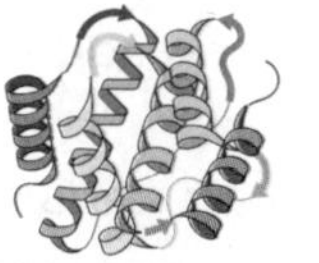

Figure 2 A folded protein contains helical (spiral) sections, and sections where the chain forms a flat zig zag (shown by arrows).

Variety of protein functions

Some proteins form minute fibres. These have very long chains of amino acids and a simple specific shape. These give a framework or structure to some tissues such as muscles. Muscle contraction relies on proteins acting as structural components of muscle tissue.

Hormones are proteins. Insulin is a hormone that your pancreas produces. It controls your blood sugar level within narrow limits no matter what you eat. Antibodies are protein molecules with a precise 3D shape. They are produced by white blood cells to fight off invading pathogens, such as bacteria. This immune reaction helps us to survive attacks from microorganisms.

136

Antibodies fit and lock on to antigens that bacteria carry.

Bacteria with antigens on their surface.

White blood cells with antibodies.

Figure 3 Proteins act as antibodies.

Biological catalysts are made of protein

Thousands of chemical reactions are taking place in the cells of animals and plants all the time. The rate of these chemical reactions is increased by the action of protein enzymes, which are **catalysts**. Catalysts are chemicals that speed up the rate of reactions, but are neither reactants nor products of the reaction. As enzymes speed up reactions in living organisms they are called biological catalysts. They catalyse processes such as respiration, growth, photosynthesis and protein synthesis.

Questions

1. Why are proteins such important molecules throughout the living world?
2. How are amino acids initially arranged in protein molecules?
3. Give three reasons why the amino acid composition of proteins is so varied.
4. Describe how each protein acquires its specific three-dimensional shape.
5. Give four functions of proteins.
6. Look at Figure 1. Using the same colours and shapes to represent amino acids, draw five different polypeptide chains each with eight amino acids.
7. A man cut his chin while shaving. List at least three ways in which proteins in his body are involved in this action and the consequences of it.
8. Explain what is meant by a catalyst. Explain where biological catalysts, or enzymes, act in living organisms, giving examples of two processes in which they are involved. A*

Examiner feedback

Remember 'CHON' to remind you of the four elements that are always present in proteins and amino acids (carbon, hydrogen, oxygen and nitrogen).

Science in action

A cell's proteome is the total amount of proteins present in it at one time. This produces a very large-scale set of data. Scientists use this set of data to construct hypotheses about the ancestry of modern organisms and they illustrate the fundamental importance of proteins in living organisms.

Route to A*

Denaturation of a protein is a change in its characteristic three-dimensional shape, making it no longer functional. It is an irreversible process.

Taking it further

In a polypeptide chain, the amino acids are linked together by chemical bonds called peptide bonds.

Find out what type of chemical reaction takes place between two amino acids when a peptide bond is formed.

Proteins and their functions 137

Learning objectives

Most students should be able to:

- describe the structure of protein molecules
- explain some functions of proteins in animals
- describe the role of catalysts in chemical reactions
- explain the functions of enzymes in living organisms
- describe how polypeptides are folded or coiled to form 3D proteins, held together by chemical bonds.

Some students should also be able to:

- explain that there is a depression or pocket on the surface of some protein molecules, known as a binding site. [Ext]

Key points

Protein molecules are made up of long chains of amino acids that fold very precisely.

Protein molecules have a very specific 3D shape that other molecules can fit into.

Proteins can function as structural molecules, hormones, antibodies and catalysts.

Biological catalysts made of protein are called enzymes. They increase the rate of chemical reactions.

Amino acids | binding site | catalysts | polypeptide

Lesson activities

Starter

1 Refer to the photograph of the baby in lesson B2 4.1 of the Student Book and invite the students to tell you which parts of the baby's physical appearance are made mainly from protein.

2 Write the word 'catalyst' on the whiteboard and have a brain-storming session for 3 minutes about its meaning and associations.

Main

1 Worksheet B2 4.1a Modelling polypeptides and 3D proteins gives instructions for the students to build card models of polypeptides and fold them so they become 3D proteins. (~25 mins)

2 B2 4.1b Modelling protein binding sites In this practical activity, students make plasticine models of proteins with binding sites and complementary reacting molecules. (~20 mins)

3 Worksheet B2 4.1c Keratin: curly or straight hair? is about keratin found in hair, and the effects hair styling products have on keratin. As it requests a PowerPoint presentation to be prepared you may consider revisiting the use of these with students.

Plenaries

1 Return to one of the 3D card protein models made using Worksheet B2 4.1a. Ask the students how it has been formed from separate amino acids. Then go on to ask them what would happen to the 3D molecule if it was subjected to a temperature of 200 °C, as in cooking. Hopefully the students will be able to tell you that the protein will lose its 3D shape.

2 Write the word 'Enzymes?' on the whiteboard. Ask for a verbal definition and use a volunteer as a starter. Everyone in the class must make a valid contribution about enzymes, e.g. name, where found, effect, etc.

Homework

1 Worksheet B2 4.1d provides an opportunity for revision. It explores the variety of proteins and can be used for either classwork or homework.

2 Ask students to research a structural protein called collagen, referring to its function in the body, its involvement in ageing and also beauty products. Findings should be presented in a Word document.

Points to note

- Modelling 3D proteins and protein binding sites is a helpful preparation for the work to come on enzymes.
- You may need to revise the concept of chemical bonding before the practical in Worksheet B2 4.1a that the 3D conformation depends on. This will also provide a reference point for future work on denaturation of enzymes.
- Worksheet B2 4.1c involves downloading images for a PowerPoint presentation.

Route to A*

Students research how insulin's shape is important in its function and the protein content of cell membranes.

Answers to Student Book questions

Taking it further

A condensation reaction.

Answers

1 They take part in most chemical reactions within cells and are part of the structure of most organelles.

2 They are arranged in long chains.

3 Any of the 20 types of amino acid may be present; an amino acid may be present any number of times; the sequence of amino acids in the chain can vary.

4 The long chains are folded very precisely and held together by chemical bonds.

5 Structural components of tissues such as muscles, hair and finger nails; as catalysts (enzymes), hormones and antibodies.

6 Five chains, each with eight amino acids. Each chain needs to be different in sequence of amino acids.

7 Hair contains structural protein. To shave he needs to contract muscles in his arms; muscle contraction is caused by proteins. When the cut starts to bleed proteins in his blood will stop the bleeding.

8 A catalyst speeds up the rate of reactions. Catalysts act in the body cells of all living organisms: respiration, photosynthesis, protein synthesis, etc.

B2 4.2 Characteristics of enzymes

Link to the specification

B2.5.1b Catalysts increase the rate of chemical reactions. Biological catalysts are called enzymes. Enzymes are proteins.

B2.5.2a The shape of an enzyme is vital for the enzyme's function. High temperatures change the shape.

B2.5.2b Different enzymes work best at different pH values.

B2 5.2d The enzyme amylase is produced in the salivary glands, the pancreas and the small intestine. This enzyme catalyses the breakdown of starch into sugars in the mouth and small intestine.

Ideas for practical work

Plan and carry out an investigation into enzyme action using the reaction between starch and amylase at different temperatures, pH and concentrations.

B2 4.2 Characteristics of enzymes

Learning objectives

- explain how enzyme shape is related to function
- describe the effect of temperature on enzyme action
- identify how pH affects enzyme action
- explain how the loss of 3D shape results in denatured enzymes
- interpret graphs to show the optimum conditions for the action of certain enzymes.

Molecules with a vital, special shape

During a chemical reaction the substances that are reacting are chemically rearranged as chemical bonds are broken or formed, to make new substances. We can speed up the rate of some reactions by using an enzyme. The enzyme makes it easier for the reacting substances to come together and be rearranged, so the reaction happens faster.

The starting substance of a reaction is called the **substrate**, and the substance it is converted to is called the **product**. Enzymes work by locking onto substrates. Figure 1 shows how this happens. Because of its precise shape each enzyme will only act on one type of substrate, just like a key that fits into a specific lock. When the substrate has reacted, it no longer fits the space on the enzyme, and so the products leave. This leaves the space free for more reacting substances to fit into the enzyme. The enzyme is not changed by the reaction.

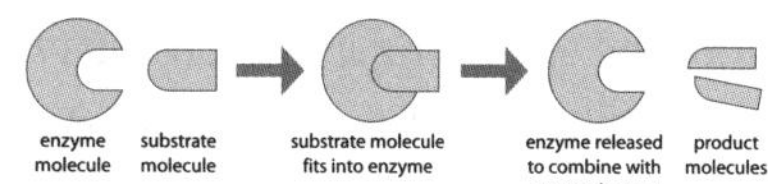

Figure 1 Some enzymes catalyse the breakdown of products.

enzyme molecule

substrate molecule

Figure 2 High temperatures change the shape of the enzyme.

Effect of temperature

Most chemical reactions are speeded up by an increase in temperature. Molecules move around more rapidly as the temperature rises. This causes more collisions to occur between enzymes and substrate molecules, and so increases the rate of reaction.

As the temperature continues to rise above a certain level, 37 °C in humans, the rate of enzyme-controlled reactions falls rapidly. High temperatures change the shape of enzymes: they denature them. A denatured enzyme has a different shape and so cannot lock onto the shape of the substrate. Therefore they no longer speed up the reaction.

Examiner feedback

Enzymes are molecules so they are *not* alive. When they stop working because their shape has changed they are denatured or destroyed, *not* dead and *not* killed.

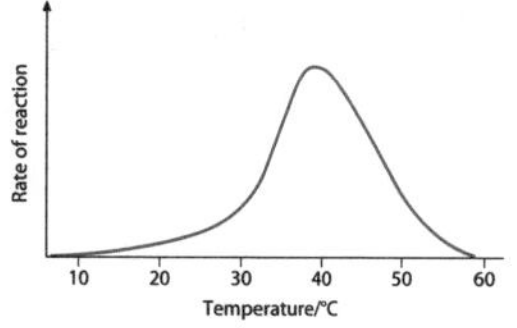

Figure 3 The effect of temperature on an enzyme-controlled reaction.

138

Effect of pH

Different enzymes work best at different pH values. The pH at which an enzyme works best is called the optimum pH. The optimum pH of an enzyme depends on the pH conditions where the enzyme works. For example, intestinal enzymes work best in alkaline conditions and have an optimum pH of 8. Stomach enzymes have an optimum pH of 2 because the stomach is acidic. Intestinal enzymes will not work at all in very acidic conditions.

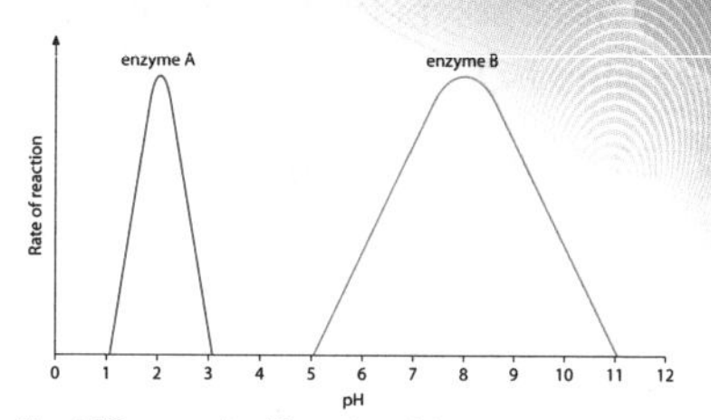

Figure 4 Different enzymes have different optimum pH values.

Science skills

Potato cells contain an enzyme called catalase. This enzyme speeds up the breakdown of hydrogen peroxide. As hydrogen peroxide breaks down, bubbles of oxygen are released forming a froth. A group of students investigated how changing temperature affects the action of catalase. They were provided with potato tissue and hydrogen peroxide and were told that catalase leaves the potato across its cut surfaces. The students decided to measure the rate of reaction by recording the height of froth formed in each test tube.

Table 1 The results of the investigation.

Temperature/°C	Height of froth/cm
15	2.5
25	4.2
35	4.5
45	4.1
55	3.5

a Suggest a suitable control for this investigation.

b What is the independent variable in this investigation?

c One group of students carefully cut the potato into small discs. They used a ruler to make sure the discs were all cut to the same size. Another group of students added the same mass of potato to each test tube.

- **i** Why is it necessary to add the same amount of potato to each tube?
- **ii** Which method is the more accurate – measuring the size or the mass? Give reasons for your answer.

Questions

1. Describe what would happen if we did not have enzymes in our bodies.
2. Explain why the shape of an enzyme affects the way it works in a reaction.
3. High temperatures destroy the shape an amino acid chain makes. **(a)** What effect would high temperatures have on an enzyme-controlled reaction? **(b)** Explain your answer.
4. How does pH affect the rate of enzyme action?
5. **(a)** Make a list of four reactions that you know are catalysed by enzymes. **(b)** Describe two processes in a plant that would be affected if it contained no enzymes.
6. Look at the results in Table 1. Explain the rate of reaction when the temperature increases from: **(a)** 15 to 35 °C **(b)** 35 to 55 °C.
7. Explain why a graph of temperature versus rate of reaction for two human digestive enzymes usually shows a single curve but a graph of pH versus reaction rate of two different digestive enzymes may have two separate curves.
8. Explain as fully as you can why enzymes are sometimes described as a lock that substrates, acting as a key, fit into.

A*

Proteins and their functions 139

Learning objectives

Most students should be able to:

- explain how enzyme shape is related to function
- describe the effects of temperature on enzyme action
- identify how pH affects enzyme action
- explain how the loss of 3D shape results in denatured enzymes
- interpret graphs to show the optimum conditions for the action of certain enzymes.

Some students should also be able to:

- explain the effect of temperature on enzyme action [Ext]
- describe how enzymes achieve their specific 3D shape. [Ext]

Key points

The shape of an enzyme enables substrates to fit into it.

High temperatures change the shape of enzymes and stop them working.

This change in enzyme shape is called denaturation.

Every enzyme has a specific pH at which it works best.

Lesson activities

Starter

1 Show the class two zips – one broken and one that works. Explain that it is possible to make the 'teeth' of the broken zip fit together but that it is a slow and fiddly process. The zipper makes it possible to open and close teeth quickly and easily by placing the teeth in exactly the right position so that they can fit together or be separated. It is likely that students will not have looked at a zip this closely before, so allow time during the lesson for all of them to have a close look at both zips. Use the idea of something that makes an action happen more quickly and introduce the terms 'catalyst' and 'enzyme'.

2 Introduce enzymes and how they control chemical reactions. Put the word equations for photosynthesis and respiration on the board and explain that many different enzymes are involved in each process and that the equations are just summaries.

Denature product substrate

Main

1 B2 4.2a The effect of pH on the enzyme catalase In this practical, students use filter paper discs soaked in solutions of catalase at different pHs. The time taken for the discs to rise to the surface is measured. (~30 mins)

2 B2 4.2b The optimum temperature for amylase This is a planning activity. The practical could be performed in a subsequent lesson; either or both parts of the activity can form the basis of a Controlled Assessment practical. (~25 mins + 35 mins)

3 Worksheet B2 4.2c The shape of enzymes explores and reinforces enzyme shape.

Plenaries

1 Tell students that the way enzymes act with reacting substances is often called the 'lock-and-key' model. If you have a lock and key, it would be useful to model the action of 'making a change', i.e. locking or unlocking the lock with the key. Give students 5 minutes to work in small groups or individually to produce a brief comparison of the lock-and-key analogy with how enzymes work. They should consider how useful the analogy is and, depending on the ability of the students, what its limitations are.

2 Ask students to produce labelled diagrams of enzymes and reactants and how they fit together. Then ask students to modify their diagrams to show why enzymes stop functioning when they are denatured.

Homework

1 Worksheet B2 4.2d revises the properties of enzymes.

2 Students use the Internet to find out what the most abundant enzyme in plants is, then make a PowerPoint presentation of the information they have discovered.

Points to note

- It may be useful to tell students that within processes such as photosynthesis and respiration there are many stages, with many chemicals, the details of which they will learn in AS and A level courses. What they need to understand at this point is that each step within each process is catalysed by a different enzyme, so they may come across many enzyme names in their research.
- It is important for students to realise that when an enzyme is denatured, the enzyme's shape has changed so that the reacting molecule can no longer fit into the active site.
- Human amylase is used in Worksheet B2 4.2b but it is important for students to realise that plants produce amylase too, and to understand why it is produced.

Route to A*

1 Students investigate the effect of the reactant molecule's (substrate's) concentration on the rate of enzyme action.

2 Give students a series of graphs showing the rate of enzyme action, e.g. at different temperatures or pHs, and ask them to explain what is happening in molecular terms at each stage.

Answers to Student Book questions

Science skills

a A tube with hydrogen peroxide and no catalase.

b Height of froth.

c i To standardise the amount of reacting tissue so that results at different temperatures can then be compared.
  ii In this case measuring the size is more accurate because surface area needs to be standardised. This is because the enzyme will leave the potato through its surface where the cells are cut.

Answers

1 Biochemical reactions would happen too slowly to maintain life.

2 The shape of an enzyme is designed to bring reacting substances close together. Without enzymes, the substances of the reaction won't be brought close together, so won't react as well.

3 **(a)** They will slow the reaction down. **(b)** The 3D shape of the enzyme will be altered, as it is denatured by the high temperature. The substances therefore won't fit as well in the enzyme so they won't react with each other as easily.

4 Each enzyme works best at a specific pH. On either side of this pH the rate of enzyme action slows down or stops.

5 **(a)** Any four for one point each, e.g. digestion reactions, e.g. breakdown of starch to sugars (by amylase), breakdown of fats to lipids (by lipases), breakdown of proteins to amino acids (by proteases), respiration reactions (glucose + oxygen → carbon dioxide + water + energy), reactions involved in protein synthesis, photosynthesis reactions (carbon dioxide + water (using light energy) → glucose + oxygen). **(b)** Growth – formation of new cells; photosynthesis – manufacture of energy-rich molecules; reproduction – formation of sex cells (any two).

6 **(a)** The molecules of enzyme and substrate have more kinetic energy as the temperature increases. They collide more frequently and with more force, increasing the rate of reaction. **(b)** 35 °C is the enzyme's optimum temperature and soon after that the enzymes begin to be denatured and can no longer catalyse the reaction so the rate of reaction falls.

7 All enzymes are affected in a similar way by temperature but digestive enzymes tend to operate in a narrow pH range. If the pH range was, for example, pH 3–8, one enzyme might only react in pH 3–4 and another in pH 7–8.

8 Enzymes have a precise shape, like a lock, and only act on one type of substrate, like a key that fits a certain lock. When the substrate has reacted, it no longer fits the space on the enzyme and so the products leave.

B2 4.3 Digestive enzymes

Link to the specification

B2.5.2c Some enzymes work outside the body cells. The digestive enzymes are produced by specialised cells in glands and in the lining of the gut. The enzymes then pass out of the cells into the gut where they come into contact with food molecules. They catalyse the breakdown of large molecules into smaller molecules.

B2.5.2d The enzyme amylase is produced in the salivary glands, the pancreas and the small intestine. This enzyme catalyses the breakdown of starch into sugars in the mouth and small intestine.

B2.5.2e Protease enzymes are produced by the stomach, the pancreas and the small intestine. These enzymes catalyse the breakdown of proteins into amino acids in the stomach and the small intestine

B2.5.2f Lipase enzymes are produced by the pancreas and small intestine. These enzymes catalyse the breakdown of lipids (fats and oils) into fatty acids and glycerol in the small intestine.

B2.5.2g The stomach also produces hydrochloric acid. The enzymes in the stomach work most effectively in these acid conditions.

B2.5.2h The liver produces bile, which is stored in the gall bladder before being released into the small intestine. Bile neutralises the acid that was added to food in the stomach. This provides alkaline conditions in which enzymes in the small intestine work most effectively.

Ideas for practical work

Using small pieces of cooked sausage, use 2% pepsin and 0.01 M HCl in water baths at different temperatures to estimate the rate of digestion. This can also be carried out with 2% trypsin and 0.1 M NaOH. The concentration of both enzymes can be varied.

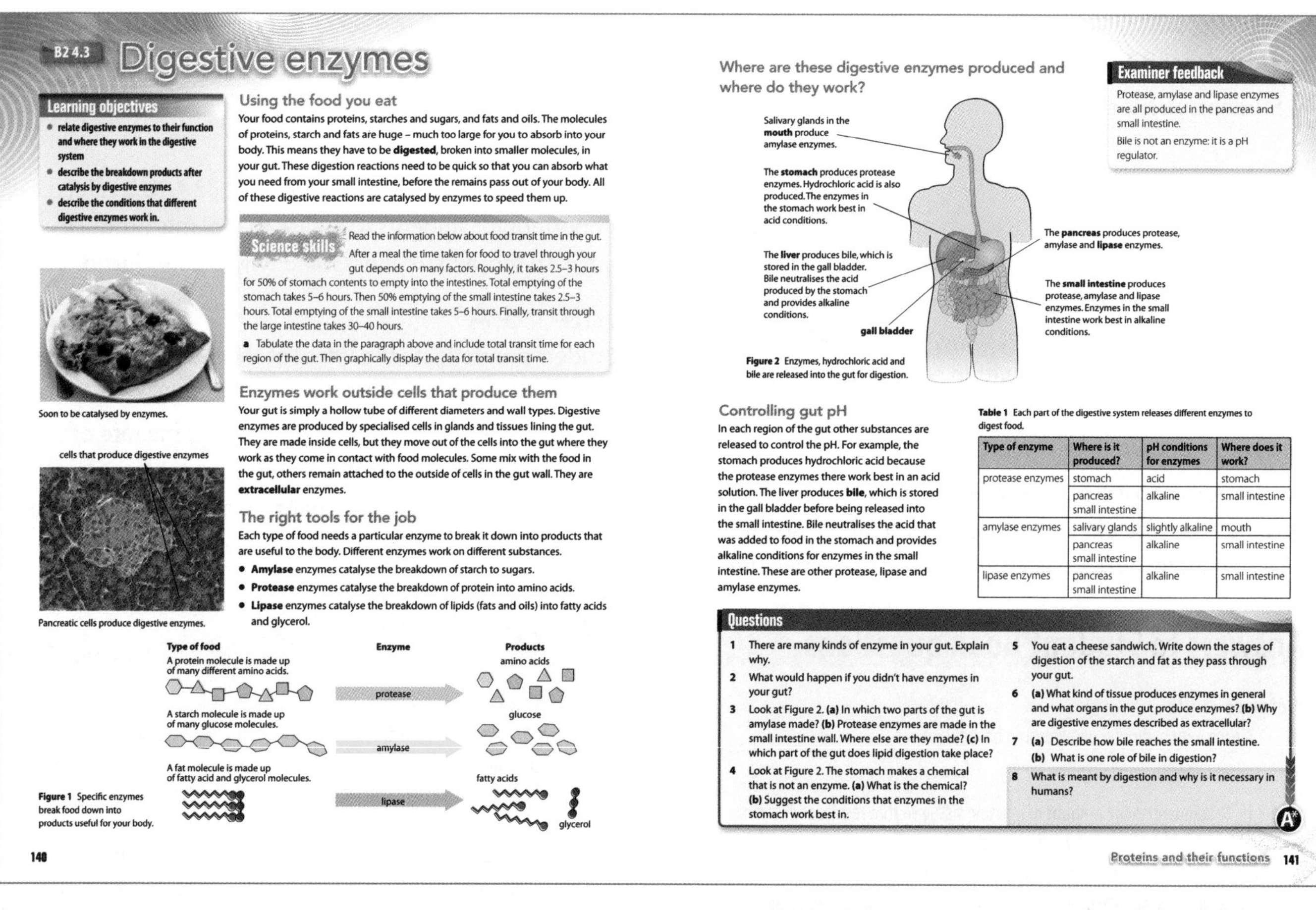

B2 4.3 Digestive enzymes

Learning objectives

- relate digestive enzymes to their function and where they work in the digestive system
- describe the breakdown products after catalysis by digestive enzymes
- describe the conditions that different digestive enzymes work in.

Using the food you eat

Your food contains proteins, starches and sugars, and fats and oils. The molecules of proteins, starch and fats are huge – much too large for you to absorb into your body. This means they have to be **digested**, broken into smaller molecules, in your gut. These digestion reactions need to be quick so that you can absorb what you need from your small intestine, before the remains pass out of your body. All of these digestive reactions are catalysed by enzymes to speed them up.

Science skills Read the information below about food transit time in the gut. After a meal the time taken for food to travel through your gut depends on many factors. Roughly, it takes 2.5–3 hours for 50% of stomach contents to empty into the intestines. Total emptying of the stomach takes 5–6 hours. Then 50% emptying of the small intestine takes 2.5–3 hours. Total emptying of the small intestine takes 5–6 hours. Finally, transit through the large intestine takes 30–40 hours.

a Tabulate the data in the paragraph above and include total transit time for each region of the gut. Then graphically display the data for total transit time.

Soon to be catalysed by enzymes.

cells that produce digestive enzymes

Pancreatic cells produce digestive enzymes.

Enzymes work outside cells that produce them

Your gut is simply a hollow tube of different diameters and wall types. Digestive enzymes are produced by specialised cells in glands and tissues lining the gut. They are made inside cells, but they move out of the cells into the gut where they work as they come in contact with food molecules. Some mix with the food in the gut, others remain attached to the outside of cells in the gut wall. They are **extracellular** enzymes.

The right tools for the job

Each type of food needs a particular enzyme to break it down into products that are useful to the body. Different enzymes work on different substances.

- **Amylase** enzymes catalyse the breakdown of starch to sugars.
- **Protease** enzymes catalyse the breakdown of protein into amino acids.
- **Lipase** enzymes catalyse the breakdown of lipids (fats and oils) into fatty acids and glycerol.

Figure 1 Specific enzymes break food down into products useful for your body.

140

Where are these digestive enzymes produced and where do they work?

Figure 2 Enzymes, hydrochloric acid and bile are released into the gut for digestion.

Examiner feedback

Protease, amylase and lipase enzymes are all produced in the pancreas and small intestine.

Bile is not an enzyme: it is a pH regulator.

Controlling gut pH

In each region of the gut other substances are released to control the pH. For example, the stomach produces hydrochloric acid because the protease enzymes there work best in an acid solution. The liver produces **bile**, which is stored in the gall bladder before being released into the small intestine. Bile neutralises the acid that was added to food in the stomach and provides alkaline conditions for enzymes in the small intestine. These are other protease, lipase and amylase enzymes.

Table 1 Each part of the digestive system releases different enzymes to digest food.

Type of enzyme	Where is it produced?	pH conditions for enzymes	Where does it work?
protease enzymes	stomach	acid	stomach
	pancreas small intestine	alkaline	small intestine
amylase enzymes	salivary glands	slightly alkaline	mouth
	pancreas small intestine	alkaline	small intestine
lipase enzymes	pancreas small intestine	alkaline	small intestine

Questions

1 There are many kinds of enzyme in your gut. Explain why.

2 What would happen if you didn't have enzymes in your gut?

3 Look at Figure 2. **(a)** In which two parts of the gut is amylase made? **(b)** Protease enzymes are made in the small intestine wall. Where else are they made? **(c)** In which part of the gut does lipid digestion take place?

4 Look at Figure 2. The stomach makes a chemical that is not an enzyme. **(a)** What is the chemical? **(b)** Suggest the conditions that enzymes in the stomach work best in.

5 You eat a cheese sandwich. Write down the stages of digestion of the starch and fat as they pass through your gut.

6 **(a)** What kind of tissue produces enzymes in general and what organs in the gut produce enzymes? **(b)** Why are digestive enzymes described as extracellular?

7 **(a)** Describe how bile reaches the small intestine. **(b)** What is one role of bile in digestion?

8 What is meant by digestion and why is it necessary in humans?

A*

Proteins and their functions 141

Learning objectives

Most students should be able to:

- relate digestive enzymes to their function and where they work in the digestive system
- describe the breakdown of products after catalysis by digestive enzymes
- describe the conditions that different digestive enzymes work in
- explain how digestive enzymes work outside body cells
- describe the function of the liver in digestion as a producer of bile, and what the function of bile is.

ActiveTeach Resource: Digestive enzymes – *Matching activity*

Key points

Digestive enzymes pass out of specialised cells into the gut where they catalyse the breakdown of large food molecules.

The three types of digestive enzymes are proteases, amylases and lipases.

The pH in different regions of the gut is controlled so that enzymes work most effectively.

Amylase	bile	digested	extracellular	gall bladder	lipase
liver	mouth	pancreas	protease	small intestine	stomach

Lesson activities

Starter

1 Give each student a small piece of bread or a plain, unsweetened biscuit and ask them to chew on it until it completely breaks down in the mouth. Note that the food must be prepared hygienically as in a food technology lesson. Also, be sensitive to any students with food allergies. Ask students what they notice about the taste as they chew. They should find that the food starts to taste sweeter as the starch (which doesn't taste sweet) in the food is digested to glucose (which does taste sweet). Use this to introduce the idea of digestive enzymes. These are enzymes that are secreted and act outside the cells in which they were made.

2 Issue diagrams of the digestive system and discuss the sites of production of the different enzymes. Students annotate the diagrams as the discussion takes place.

Main

1 B2 4.3a Effect of pepsin concentration on digestion In this practical activity, students weigh cubes of sausage before and after the experiment. (~30 mins)

2 B2 4.3b Digestion of fat A practical investigation into the digestion of olive oil by lipase, in the presence of bile salts. It makes use of an indicator, bromothymol blue. (~35 mins)

3 Worksheet B2 4.3c Investigating digestion looks at the enzymes involved in digesting different types of foods. ActiveTeach has a matching activity relating to the enzymes used in digestion. [AT]

Plenaries

1 Give students 5 minutes to think of a plus, a minus and an interesting response to the statement 'The human body does not need enzymes to digest food.' Take examples of answers from the class, and discuss any misconceptions that may have arisen.

2 Divide the class into four groups. One group names an enzyme, the second group says where it is produced, the third group says what is digested and the fourth group gives the product(s) of digestion.

Homework

1 Worksheet B2 4.3d is an opportunity for students to revise enzyme action in the digestive system.

2 Students use textbooks and the Internet to find out about the cells in the lining of the small intestine that manufacture and release enzymes.

Points to note

- Bile salts are a constituent of bile and cause emulsification.
- The breakdown of starch, protein and fat into smaller molecules are all hydrolysis reactions, involving the addition of a molecule of water.
- Digestive enzymes are continuously removed from the gut as food passes through it.

Route to A*

1. Ask higher achievers to research the structure of the stomach lining and to differentiate between glands that produce hydrochloric acid and those that produce enzymes, in a PowerPoint presentation.
2. Ask students to research precisely where and how gastric bands are fitted, as a surgical aid to weight loss. The risks and benefits of the procedure can be evaluated.

Answers to Student Book questions

Science skills

a

Region of gut	Time to pass through (hours)	
	50%	100%
stomach	2.5–3	5–6
small intestine	2.5–3	5–6
large intestine		30–40

Displayed as a bar chart, with *x*-axis showing region of gut and *y*-axis showing total transit time in hours.

Answers

1 There are different substances in food that need to be digested.

2 You wouldn't digest food and wouldn't be able to absorb it.

3 **(a)** Any two from mouth, pancreas and small intestine. **(b)** Pancreas and stomach. **(c)** Small intestine.

4 **(a)** Hydrochloric acid. **(b)** Acidic conditions.

5 The starch in the bread starts to be broken down by salivary amylase in the mouth. It continues to be broken down to glucose by amylase – produced in the pancreas and small intestine – in the small intestine. Fat is broken down to fatty acids and glycerol by lipase – produced in the pancreas and small intestine – in the small intestine.

6 **(a)** Glandular tissue produces enzymes. The gut, salivary glands, pancreas and small intestine are organs that produce enzymes. **(b)** Digestive enzymes work outside the cells that produce them, either mixed with the food or on the outside of the cells in the gut wall.

7 **(a)** It is made in the liver and passes to the gall bladder where it is stored until needed, when it passes into the small intestine. **(b)** To neutralise the acid from the stomach. The enzymes in the small intestine work better in an alkaline liquid.

8 Our food contains proteins, starches and sugars, and fats and oils. The molecules of proteins, starch and fats are much too large for us to absorb into our body as they are. This means they have to be digested, broken into smaller molecules, in our gut. These digestion reactions need to be quick so that we can absorb what we need from our small intestine, before the remains pass out of the body.

B2 4.4 Enzymes used in industry

Link to the specification

B2.5.2i Some microorganisms produce enzymes that pass out of the cells. These enzymes have many uses in the home and in industry.

In the home:

- biological detergents may contain protein-digesting and fat-digesting enzymes (proteases and lipases)
- biological detergents are more effective at low temperatures than other types of detergents.

In industry:

- proteases are used to 'pre-digest' the protein in some baby foods
- carbohydrases are used to convert starch into sugar syrup
- isomerase is used to convert glucose syrup into fructose syrup, which is much sweeter and therefore can be used in smaller quantities in slimming foods.

B2.5.2j In industry, enzymes are used to bring about reactions at normal temperatures and pressures that would otherwise require expensive, energy-demanding equipment. However, most enzymes are denatured at high temperatures and many are costly to produce.

How Science Works

SKU: B2.5 bullet point 1: Evaluate the advantages and disadvantages of using enzymes in the home and in industry.

B2 4.4 Enzymes used in industry

Learning objectives

- explain why microorganisms are useful in enzyme technology
- describe how three types of enzyme are used in the food and drinks industry
- describe some industrial uses of enzymes
- evaluate the uses of enzymes in industry.

Enzymes from microorganisms

Vast amounts of microorganisms, such as bacteria, are grown in industry to supply us with useful enzymes. Many of the enzymes produced by microorganisms are passed out of the cell, which enables scientists to use the enzyme from the microorganism. Microorganisms can be grown relatively cheaply inside vats, known as fermenters, and no expensive equipment is needed. As they can multiply very rapidly, microorganisms produce large amounts of enzymes quickly. The fermenter is kept at 28 °C so energy costs for enzyme production are low.

Millions of bacteria can be grown quickly in these fermenters. Enzymes extracted from the liquid are used for many purposes.

Enzyme technology

For many years, inorganic catalysts (those not containing carbon) have been used in industrial reactions: for example, iron is used in the production of ammonia in the **Haber process**. Recently there have been many developments in the use of enzymes as industrial catalysts, a process known as **enzyme technology**. Enzymes are highly efficient catalysts: only a small amount of enzyme is needed to produce a large quantity of product. This is why they are more useful in industrial processes than inorganic catalysts.

Enzymes in the food and drinks industry

Enzymes are now used a lot in the catering industry. In some baby foods, proteases are used to help 'pre-digest' the proteins. This makes the food softer, or less fibrous, for babies to eat and easier for babies to digest.

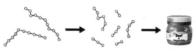

Figure 1 Protease enzymes are used to break down long-chain protein molecules into short chains that are easier for babies to digest.

Enzymes are also used in the production of sugar syrups used as sweeteners in the food and drinks industry. It is cheaper to get starch than sugars from plants to use in our food. Starch can be obtained from potatoes and cereals that are cheaper than sugar sources like sugarcane and sugar beet. Starch can be converted to sugar syrup using **carbohydrases** to catalyse the reaction. This means we can make products like sugary drinks, cakes and sweets more cheaply.

Fructose and glucose are both sugars with the same energy value. Isomerase is an enzyme used to convert glucose syrup into fructose syrup. Fructose is a much sweeter sugar than glucose, so less needs to be added to foods and drinks to make them taste sweeter. This is very useful in the production of slimming foods and low-calorie drinks.

Stage 1: production of glucose syrup

starch from maize grains

Carbohydrase enzymes are added to the starch to digest it into glucose.

↓

glucose syrup

Stage 2: conversion of glucose to fructose

glucose syrup

isomerase enzyme

↓

fructose syrup

Figure 2 Carbohydrase and isomerase enzymes are used in the production of sweeteners.

142

Science skills

The amount of fructose produced is affected by how fast the glucose syrup flows through the reactor containing immobilised enzymes. Figure 3 shows the result of increasing the rate of flow of glucose syrup into the reactor.

a What rate of flow should scientists use in the reactor? Explain your answer.

b How much more fructose is produced when the rate of flow is increased from 3 to 4 dm^3/min?

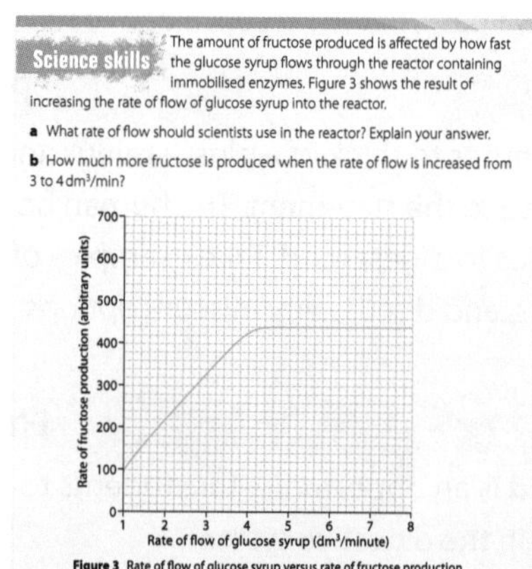

Figure 3 Rate of flow of glucose syrup versus rate of fructose production.

Questions

1. Which organisms produce the enzymes obtained in industry?
2. Where are these organisms grown and how are the enzymes obtained?
3. Give two advantages to industry of using enzymes.
4. What do the following enzymes digest: **(a)** protease **(b)** carbohydrase **(c)** lipase?
5. **(a)** Give three examples of the use of enzymes in the food industry.
   (b) For each example, name the type of food the enzyme works on and the reason for using an enzyme in the food production.
6. Evaluate the use of enzymes in the food industry.
7. Explain fully how protease enzymes in the food industry could be used over and over again to break down large protein molecules into smaller ones.
8. Evaluate the use of immobilised enzymes in the food industry.

A*

Science in action

When a reaction is complete, the enzyme and product are mixed up with each other. It is very expensive for an industry to keep producing enzymes and to keep separating products from enzymes. To avoid this expense scientists have found ways of fixing enzymes to the surface of small beads. This is called immobilising the enzyme. The diagram shows how isomerase enzymes fixed in this way can be used over and over again. It also means that there are no enzyme molecules mixed with the product, as they are all trapped in the beads.

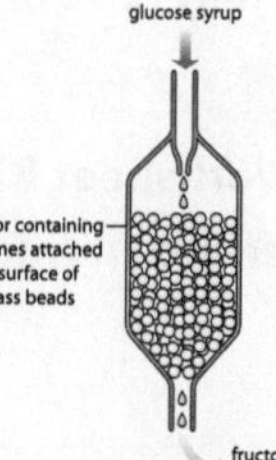

Figure 4 Immobilised enzymes can be used over and over again.

Taking it further

Isomers are molecules that contain the same types and numbers of atoms, but arranged in different ways.

Proteins and their functions 143

Learning objectives

Most students should be able to:

- explain why microorganisms are useful in enzyme technology
- describe how three types of enzyme are used in the food and drink industry
- describe some industrial uses of enzymes
- evaluate the uses of enzymes in industry.

Some students should also be able to:

- describe how enzymes are produced by bacteria in fermentation [Ext]
- explain how enzymes can be immobilised for use in industry and the advantage of immobilisation. [Ext]

Key points

Some microorganisms produce enzymes, which pass out of the cells.

Microorganisms are grown on an industrial scale in fermenters to collect useful enzymes.

The enzymes produced by bacteria include proteases, carbohydrases and isomerases.

Uses of enzymes in the food and drinks industry include production of baby foods, sugar syrups and sweeteners.

ActiveTeach Resource: Fermentation systems – *Video*

Carbohydrases | enzyme technology | Haber process

Lesson activities

Starter

1 Refer to the photograph of an industrial fermenter in lesson B2 4.4 of the Student Book and explain that this is where bacteria that produce enzymes are grown. Ask the students why the technician in the photograph is wearing protective clothing and a face mask. ActiveTeach includes a video of the operation of an industrial fermenter. [AT]

2 Show the students a jar of baby food or a photograph of one and a tin of meat or fish and ask them to suggest why enzymes may have been involved in the production of the baby food but not the meat or fish in the tin. Elicit the fact that babies who are just starting to eat solid food can cope with it better if it is partially digested or of a softer texture. To achieve this texture without enzymes involves a lengthy cooking process.

Main

1 B2 4.4a The effect of a pineapple enzyme on protein Refer to sheet in Teacher and Technician Planning Pack.

2 B2 4.4b Using amylase immobilised by alginate beads Refer to sheet in Teacher and Technician Planning Pack.

3 Worksheet B2 4.4c Producing enzymes for use in industry Refer to sheet in Teacher and Technician Planning Pack.

Plenaries

1 'If I ...' Organise a continuation game where the starter chooses one of the following: baby food, birthday cake, light cola. The game proceeds as follows:

a The starter says, e.g. 'If I were eating birthday cake it may have used sugars produced by ...'

b Next contributor – carbohydrase enzymes which ...

c Next contributor – convert starch to sugar.

The game continues with the other foods – ask for volunteer contributors.

2 Ask the students to indicate whether they think using enzymes in the food industry is an advantage or not. Discuss their reactions with them.

Homework

1 Worksheet B2 4.4d can be used as a revision opportunity for students to apply what they have learned during the lesson.

2 Ask students to prepare a PowerPoint presentation in response to the question 'Do enzymes produced in industry support or undermine a healthy diet?'

Points to note

- Enzymes, being proteins, cause allergic reactions in some individuals. It is recommended that enzyme solutions do not come into contact with the skin.
- Many low-calorie foods use aspartame as a sweetener rather than fructose.
- You may need to outline the process of canning pineapple so that students realise a high temperature is used.

Route to A*

1 Students can use the Internet to research the use of enzymes in the textile industry.

2 Ask students to research the types of microbes used to produce enzymes for use in the chemical industry.

Answers to Student Book questions

Science skills

a 4.4 dm^3/min, as this gives the highest rate of fructose production: any faster and no more fructose is produced.

b 80 arbitrary units.

Answers

1 Bacteria.

2 They are grown in large fermenters and release enzymes into the liquid in the vat.

3 Lowers costs by saving energy; no need for expensive equipment.

4 **(a)** Protein. **(b)** Starch. **(c)** Fat.

5 (a and b) Three examples, e.g. baby foods: the protein is pre-digested, making it easier to digest; diet foods: glucose is changed to fructose, which is sweeter so less is needed; sweets, cakes, etc.: starch can be used as a raw ingredient as it is cheaper to obtain than sugar. Enzymes then change it to sugar. This makes the products cheaper to produce.

6 Enzymes can be used over and over again, saving money. This helps to lower the cost of food. Some cheaper foods produced, like cakes and sweets, have a high energy value, which is not helpful in the fight against obesity. Enzymes can be used to produce fructose sugar used in diet foods. Pre-digested baby foods provide a safe and convenient food for babies without lengthy preparation time.

7 Protease enzymes could be fixed onto the surface of small beads. The protein, with large molecules, is passed through a reactor of immobilised enzymes. At the base of the reactor the protein molecules have been made smaller; the enzyme is still in the reactor and can be used again.

8 Any 2 × 1 marks in favour of using enzymes in the food industry, e.g. convenience of using ready prepared baby foods (protease enzymes); more cheaply produced sugary foods (carbohydrase enzymes); lower calorie foods (isomerise enzymes); using immobilised enzymes ensures there are no enzymes mixed up with the products.

Any 2 × 1 marks against using enzymes in the food industry, e.g. enzymes are used in processed foods that may contain chemical additives for preservation, colour, etc.; enzymes are produced by bacteria; processed food may contain less fibre and less vitamins than fresh food.

1 mark for expressing an opinion about the use of enzymes in the food industry. 1 mark for giving the reason for the opinion.

B2 4.5 Home use of enzymes

Link to the specification

B2.5.2i Some microorganisms produce enzymes that pass out of the cells. These enzymes have many uses in the home and in industry.

In the home:

- biological detergents may contain protein-digesting and fat-digesting enzymes (proteases and lipases)
- biological detergents are more effective at low temperatures than other types of detergents.

In industry:

- proteases are used to 'pre-digest' the protein in some baby foods
- carbohydrases are used to convert starch into sugar syrup
- isomerase is used to convert glucose syrup into fructose syrup, which is much sweeter and therefore can be used in smaller quantities in slimming foods.

Ideas for practical work

Investigating biological and non-biological washing powders at different temperatures to remove different stains from cotton material.

How Science Works

SKU: B2.5 bullet point 1: Evaluate the advantages and disadvantages of using enzymes in the home and in industry.

B2 4.5 Home use of enzymes

Learning objectives

- explain why enzymes are used in biological detergents
- describe the types of enzyme biological detergents contain
- evaluate the use of enzymes in the home and in industry.

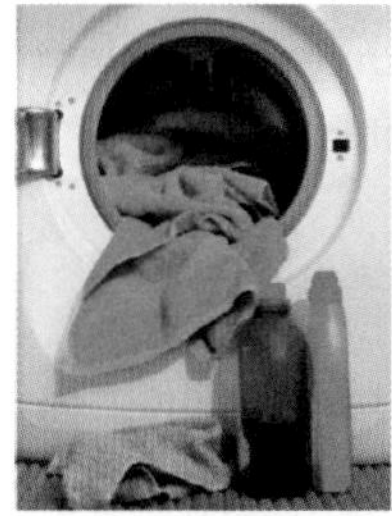

Biological detergents contain enzymes.

Science in action

Recently, manufacturers and retailers have tried to show they care for the environment by recommending that many garments are washed at 30 °C. However, Korean scientists have shown that washing at 30 °C is much worse at removing dust mites and pollen than washing at 60 °C. Allergy sufferers could have a problem with low-temperature washes.

Examiner feedback

An 'evaluate' question requires you to give some advantages and disadvantages and then to make a conclusion. Your conclusion should say whether or not you think enzymes (in this case) are useful, linked to a reason for your judgement.

Enzymes from bacteria

Bacteria help to clean our laundry. This is true if you use biological detergents containing enzymes. The first biological detergents that were produced would only work in warm water. However, proteases and lipases have now been produced that work at much higher temperatures. Most of the enzymes in washing powders are obtained from bacteria living in hot springs, which means the bacteria are adapted to live in water above 45 °C. The enzymes obtained from these bacteria will work at moderately high temperatures. This is useful because the detergents in washing powders, which get rid of greasy stains, work best at higher temperatures.

The enzymes produced by bacteria living in hot springs will work at high temperatures.

Biological detergents

The dirt that we get on our clothes comes from our bodies, our surroundings and from the food we eat. The substances that make up the dirt are mostly proteins, fats and sugars. All washing powders contain detergents to dissolve stains so that they can be washed away. Biological washing powders also contain protease and lipase enzymes. Protease enzymes catalyse the breakdown of proteins present in stains such as blood, grass and egg. Lipase enzymes catalyse the breakdown of lipids in stains such as fat, oil and grease. The protein and fat molecules in stains are broken down into smaller, soluble molecules that dissolve easily in water and can be washed away. In the home, biological detergents are more effective at low temperatures, such as 30 °C, than other types of detergents. For a wash at 60 °C or 90 °C biological detergents are not recommended because most enzymes are denatured at high temperatures and stop working. Some people still use non-biological detergents because they get an **allergic reaction**, such as a skin rash, to the enzymes.

Evaluating enzyme use in home and industry

It helps you to decide if using enzymes is useful or not by looking at their advantages and disadvantages.

Table 1 Advantages and disadvantages of enzymes.

Advantages	Disadvantages
Enzymes bring about reactions at normal temperatures and pressures, saving on energy.	Most enzymes are denatured at high temperatures.
Enzymes save on expensive equipment.	Many enzymes are expensive to produce.
Biological detergents are more effective at low temperatures than other types of detergent.	Allergy sufferers may be allergic to the enzymes and/or require a higher temperature wash to destroy allergens in bedding and clothes.

144

Science skills

A group of students carried out an investigation to find the conditions in which biological washing powders work best. The students used photographic film to demonstrate the action of the washing powders. The film contains black grains stuck on by a layer of gelatin. Gelatin is a protein. When the gelatin is broken down by the enzymes in the washing powder the film becomes clear as the black grains come away.

The students prepared a 1% solution of washing powder by dissolving 1 g of powder in 100 cm^3 of water. Figure 1 shows how the students designed the investigation.

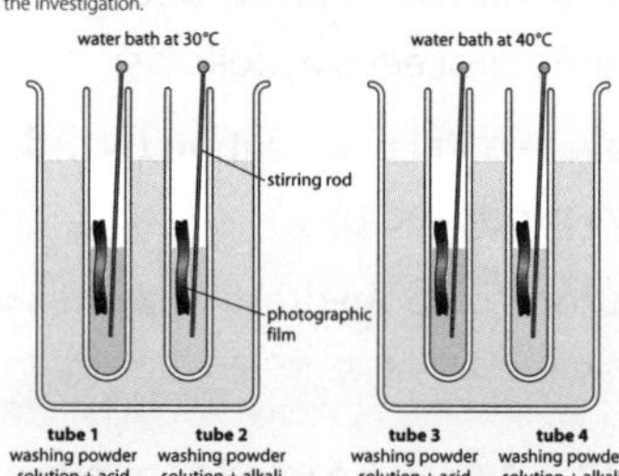

Figure 1 A biological washing powder can dissolve the protein on photographic film.

a Identify the two independent variables.

b What type of variable is the dependent variable?

c **i** Explain why a 1% solution of washing powder was used in all four test tubes.

ii Explain why a stirring rod was used.

d Suggest what the students should do to make their results more reliable.

Table 2 The students' results.

	Tube 1	Tube 2	Tube 3	Tube 4
Temperature/°C	30	30	40	40
pH	4	8	4	8
Time taken for film to go clear/min	not digested	25	40	10

Questions

1 Which organisms produce the enzymes found in biological detergents?

2 Which enzymes digest: **(a)** protein **(b)** fat?

3 Suggest two stains that: **(a)** protease **(b)** lipase would act on.

4 Suggest: **(a)** two advantages of using enzymes to help get clothes clean **(b)** one disadvantage of using enzymes in biological detergents.

5 Explain why it is easier for stains to leave clothes when they have been digested by enzymes.

6 A student washed his clothes using biological detergent on a very hot wash at 90 °C. They still came out with stains on. Explain to him the advantages of using enzymes in detergents and why his clothes would have been washed cleaner if the water temperature had been at 40 °C.

7 Suggest two reasons why hotels do not use biological detergents to wash their cotton sheets.

8 Use Table 1 to evaluate the use of enzymes in home and industry.

A*

Proteins and their functions 145

Learning objectives

Most students should be able to:

- explain why enzymes are used in biological detergents
- describe the types of enzyme biological detergents contain
- evaluate the use of enzymes in the home and industry.

Some students should also be able to:

- list several types of protein-based stains that biological detergents can digest [Ext]
- recognise the importance of different fabrics in holding and releasing their stains or having the potential to be digested by biological detergents. [Ext]

Key points

Biological detergents contain protein-digesting and fat-digesting enzymes (protease and lipase).

The enzymes in biological detergents are produced by bacteria.

There are advantages and disadvantages in using enzymes in detergents.

ActiveTeach Resource: Enzymes in industry – *Interactive matching*
Enzymes in your washing – *True or false quiz*

Lesson activities

Starter

1 Ask students to think about what makes 'dirty' clothes dirty. You could prepare some 'typical' examples to stimulate suggestions, such as food-based stains, mud or grass stains, a grubby collar or cuffs, the 'smelly' sock! Where do the stains come from? What kinds of substances do they contain?

2 Show the students two versions of the same brand of detergent – biological and non-biological. Also show the students detergents in different forms, e.g. powder, gels, tablets, liquid. Discuss with the students which type and form of detergent they would choose or which is used to wash their clothes and why.

Main

1 **B2 4.5a Domestic uses of enzymes** This is a non-quantitative investigation into the action of biological detergents on gelatine, agar and egg yolk. (~30 mins)

2 **B2 4.5b Washing at different temperatures** This practical activity investigates the effect of temperature on the cleaning power of a biological detergent. (~35 mins)

3 **Worksheet B2 4.5c Problems with enzymes** contains two fact files related to allergies for the students to assess.

Plenaries

1 Ask students to work in small groups to sketch out an advert for a biological detergent. The advert should show how the enzyme works and the advantages of using the biological detergent. Select examples to share the key points of the advert with the class.

2 Look at the packaging of three different brands of biological detergent. Ask students what associations they have of using the colour green. Does it relate to living things in some way? Go on to discuss why biological detergents are usually packaged in green. Some students may associate the colour green with eco-friendly and this aspect of using biological detergents should be discussed too.

3 Use the ActiveTeach resources to consolidate learning. [AT]

Homework

1 **Worksheet B2 4.5d** compares doing the laundry 100 years ago with doing the laundry today.

2 Ask students to research allergies and detergents. The National Eczema Society website is a good place to start. Students can put their findings in a Word document.

Points to note

- A range of different washing powders could be compared.
- Many students will have no experience of washing clothes.
- For student practical B2 4.5a, a comparison could be made of the time taken for the detergents to digest the egg and gelatine.
- Any students with known skin allergies should be supplied with plastic gloves.

Route to A*

1 Student practical sheet B2 4.5b could be extended to find the optimum temperature for biological detergent.
2 Invite higher achievers to research the websites of two detergent manufacturers and from them produce a PowerPoint presentation entitled 'Bio versus non-bio detergents'.
3 Ask students to find out why detergent manufacturers have found it necessary to market 'colour' varieties of their detergents.

Answers to Student Book questions

Science skills

a Temperature and pH.

b A continuous variable.

c **i** So that the results in each tube were comparable.
ii To mix the enzyme and substrate.

d Repeat the experiment a few more times and take the average time for each tube.

Answers

1 Bacteria.

2 **(a)** Protease. **(b)** Lipase.

3 Two of each, e.g. **(a)** Blood, beef gravy. **(b)** Ice cream, olive oil.

4 **(a)** Saves energy, less wear on clothes in a shorter wash time. **(b)** Some people may develop an allergic skin rash, or releases enzymes into the water system.

5 Large molecules are broken down into smaller, soluble molecules that dissolve in water and can be washed away from the threads in the fabric that trap large molecules.

6 Biological detergents remove stains at low temperatures, saving energy and saving money. Enzymes are denatured and stop working at high temperatures; therefore stains are not removed at 90 °C.

7 Hotel laundry is washed at a temperature of 60–90 °C for hygiene. Enzymes in biological detergents would be denatured. Some hotel guests may be allergic to enzymes and develop a rash.

8 In industry, advantages are that enzymes bring about reactions at normal temperatures and pressures, saving on energy and saving on expensive equipment. Disadvantages are that most enzymes are denatured at high temperatures, and many enzymes are expensive to produce.
In the home an advantage is that biological detergents are more effective at low temperatures than other types of detergent, and a disadvantage is that allergy sufferers may be allergic to the enzymes and/or require a higher temperature wash to destroy allergens in bedding and clothes.

B2 5.1 Aerobic respiration

Link to the specification

B2.6.1a The chemical reactions inside cells are controlled by enzymes.

B2.6.1b During aerobic respiration (respiration that uses oxygen) chemical reactions occur that:

- use glucose (a sugar) and oxygen
- release energy.

B2.6.1c Aerobic respiration takes place continuously in both plants and animals.

B2.6.1d Most of the reactions in aerobic respiration take place inside mitochondria.

B2.6.1e Aerobic respiration is summarised by the equation:
glucose + oxygen → carbon dioxide + water (+ energy)

B2.6.1f Energy that is released during respiration is used by the organism. The energy may be used:

- to build larger molecules from smaller ones
- in animals, to enable muscles to contract
- in mammals and birds, to maintain a steady body temperature in colder surroundings
- in plants, to build up sugars, nitrates and other nutrients into amino acids which are then built up into proteins.

How Science Works

CA: B4.2.1a Identifying some possible hazards in practical situations.

B4.3.2a Appreciating that, unless certain variables are controlled, the results may not be valid.

B2 5.1 Aerobic respiration

Learning objectives

- **describe how aerobic respiration in mitochondria uses glucose and oxygen to release energy**
- **summarise aerobic respiration with a word equation**
- **explain what cells use the energy released in respiration for.**

Taking it further

The process of releasing energy from substances such as glucose takes place through a complex series of reactions. These reactions occur in different parts of the mitochondrion.

Respiration for energy

Respiration is carried out in plant cells and animal cells all the time to provide the energy that organisms use to stay alive and to do all that they need to do. Without respiration organisms would die.

All these activities need aerobic respiration.

Most animal and plant cells respire aerobically. **Aerobic respiration** literally means respiration using air. More accurately, it uses oxygen from the air. The oxygen is used to chemically break down 'fuel' molecules, usually a simple sugar called glucose. The breakdown of glucose releases energy and produces two waste products – carbon dioxide and water. The overall reaction is:

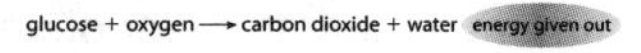

This equation is only a summary. In respiration, glucose is broken down in many separate stages. Like other reactions inside cells, the reactions in respiration are controlled by enzymes.

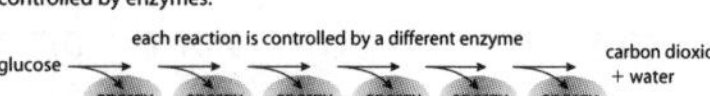

Figure 1 The breakdown of glucose in aerobic respiration involves many stages, each controlled by an enzyme.

Practical

We can use this apparatus to prove that animals produce carbon dioxide during respiration. With adaptation, it can also show that plants produce carbon dioxide during respiration.

to vacuum pump
A B C
limewater
limewater
woodlice
sodium hydroxide solution to remove carbon dioxide
fine metal gauze

Figure 2 Apparatus to demonstrate carbon dioxide production during respiration.

Powerhouses of the cell

Most of the reactions in aerobic respiration occur inside small structures called mitochondria, which are found inside all plant and animal cells. Cells that use a lot of oxygen, such as muscle cells, tend to have many more mitochondria than others. In animals, the glucose comes from the breakdown of food molecules in the gut, or from the breakdown of food stores in the body. In plants, the glucose is a product of photosynthesis.

146

In most animals, oxygen and glucose are carried to all cells in the blood. The waste products of respiration (carbon dioxide and any water the cell doesn't need) are carried away in the blood.

Mitochondria are sometimes called the powerhouses of cells because this is where energy is released in respiration.

Science skills Reactions that are controlled by enzymes are usually affected by temperature. The rate of a reaction usually increases as temperature increases up to around 40 °C, after which it decreases.

a Identify the dependent and independent variables in an experiment to show the effect of temperature on the enzymes that control the reactions of respiration.

Using the energy from respiration

The energy from respiration is used for many processes in a living organism. It can be used to make large, complex molecules from smaller subunits – for example animals build proteins from amino acids or fats from fatty acids. Plants start with even smaller molecules, for example they make amino acids from sugars and nitrogen-containing substances from the soil.

Energy is also needed to break down large molecules into smaller ones, for example during digestion in animals. The smaller molecules can more easily be moved around the body to where they are needed. Animals also need energy to make muscles work and to pump the blood round the body. Mammals and birds also use energy from respiration to keep their body temperature at a constant level above the temperature of their surroundings.

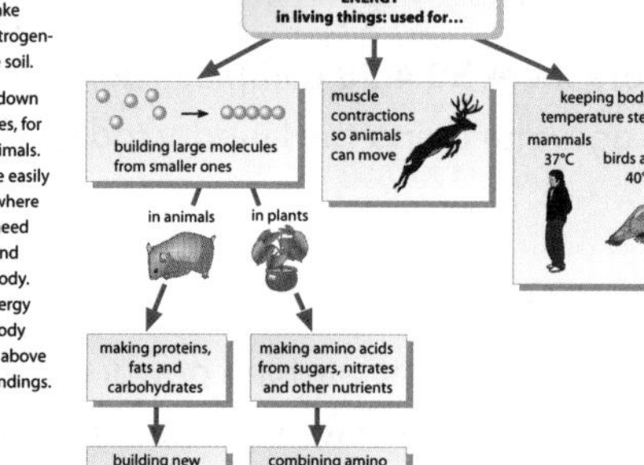

Figure 3 Living things use the energy they get from respiration in many ways.

Questions

1 Make a list of 10 things that you use energy for. Try to include some that allow you to stay alive.

2 **(a)** Where does the glucose for respiration come from in animals? **(b)** Explain how a plant gets the glucose it needs for respiration.

3 A muscle cell has more mitochondria than a brain cell. Suggest a reason for this.

4 Give as many reasons as you can that could explain why one person would be breathing faster than another.

5 The rate of respiration of a mouse, a plant and a lizard are measured as the volume of carbon dioxide used in 1 hour. **(a)** Describe how the plant experiment should be set up to make sure the results are reliable. Explain your answer. **(b)** Explain what must be done to all the results so that they can be compared fairly. **(c)** Put the organisms into order to show how quickly they respired, slowest first. Explain your order.

6 Explain fully the role of the circulatory system in enabling respiration to take place in the cells.

7 Cyanide blocks an enzyme that controls one of the reactions in respiration. Explain fully why cyanide is a very effective poison.

A*

Energy from respiration 147

Learning objectives

Most students should be able to:

- describe how aerobic respiration in mitochondria uses glucose and oxygen to release energy
- summarise aerobic respiration with a word equation
- explain what cells use the energy released in respiration for.

Some students should also be able to:

- compare and contrast experimental investigations of respiration and draw conclusions about which is the most reliable. [Ext]

Key points

Aerobic respiration can be summarised using the word equation:
glucose + oxygen → carbon dioxide + water + energy

Aerobic respiration is a series of reactions, controlled by enzymes, that occur mostly inside mitochondria and release energy from glucose using oxygen from air.

Plants use the energy from respiration for building chemicals such as proteins for growth.

Animals use the energy from respiration for building chemicals to make tissues, for movement, and in mammals and birds for keeping a steady body temperature.

Lesson activities

Starter

1 Breathing concept map: Write the word 'breathing' in the middle of the board. Ask students for related words and how they should be linked to develop a concept map. Aim to cover words related to respiration and to establish their understanding from KS3 learning on this topic. The activity should help you assess what they remember and any misconceptions that students have developed. Keep the concept map to complete in the plenary.

Main

1 **B2 5.1a Measuring respiration** This practical uses a standard set-up to indicate that organisms release carbon dioxide from respiration. It gives students the opportunity to think about how a control could be used to make sure the change to the limewater is the effect of the air breathed out only, and not due to anything else. This will give students an opportunity to revise the importance of using controls in their own work. (Allow ~20 mins to set up, several hours/overnight to run, ~10 mins to collect results.)

2 **B2 5.1b Energy from food** This worksheet supports students in planning an investigation to measure the energy in foods in order to get reliable data. (Planning time + ~ 30 mins practical work.)

3 **Aerobic activity** Ask students to use the Internet or books to research the link between aerobic respiration, fitness and health, and to find out why regular aerobic activity that raises heart rate is recommended by doctors.

Plenary

1 Revisit the concept map begun in the starter activity. Ask students to add any new words or ideas that they have learnt during the lesson.

Homework

1 **Worksheet B2 5.1c** contains questions that revise the lesson and checks that students appreciate that the measurement used in the example (change in pH indicator) is valid for the experiment.

2 **Worksheet B2 5.1d** contains questions on human basal metabolic rate, which links this lesson with the next on changes during exercise. Be sensitive to any students who may have dietary-related problems such as obesity or anorexia. The sheet refers to the recommendations for estimated average requirements for energy for different groups. Q9 emphasises the fact that these data are averages for groups and should not be applied to individual cases, but you may wish to reinforce this. It may help students to remind them of earlier work on metabolic rate in B1 before they use this worksheet.

Route to A*

Students should evaluate as fully as possible the methods used for measuring energy released from food or during activity in order to identify the limitations of the methods. Only investigations in which heat transfer to the surroundings is eliminated will give an accurate measurement, and few investigations achieve this.

Answers to Student Book questions

Science skills

a Independent variable: temperature; dependent variable: rate of reaction.

Answers

1 Any suitable answers; should include movement, growth, repair and breathing.

2 **(a)** From the digestion of food. **(b)** It is made during photosynthesis.

3 Muscle cells need more energy more rapidly (for exercise) than brain cells.

4 One person could be exercising and need the extra oxygen for more energy. Or deliberately choosing to breathe faster, being unwell or that person just naturally breathes at a different rate.

5 **(a)** Must be in the dark so that photosynthesis doesn't occur, as it produces carbon dioxide. **(b)** Divide the rate of respiration by the mass of organism because they will be different sizes, so some have more cells/mitochondria than others. **(c)** Plant, lizard, mouse, because lizard moves more than plant, and mouse moves, but also needs to maintain a body temperature above that of the environment.

6 The blood transports materials around the body to all cells. It carries oxygen from the lungs and glucose from digestion to cells that need these for respiration. It also carries carbon dioxide, the waste product of respiration, from the cells to the lungs for removal from the body, and any excess water to the kidneys for excretion.

7 All cells need to respire to produce energy. If an enzyme cannot carry out its role in a reaction, the reaction will slow down or stop. If respiration stops in any cell for more than a few minutes, the cell dies. So cyanide can kill cells all over the body quickly

B2 5.2 Changes during exercise

Link to the specification

B2.6.1g During exercise a number of changes take place:

- the heart rate increases
- the rate and depth of breathing increases.

B2.6.1h These changes increase the blood flow to the muscles and so increase the supply of sugar and oxygen and increase the rate of removal of carbon dioxide.

B2.6.1i Muscles store glucose as glycogen which can then be converted back to glucose for use during exercise.

Ideas for practical work

Investigating the effect of exercise on pulse rate, either physically or using pulse sensors and data loggers.

Investigating the link between exercise and breathing rate with a breathing sensor.

How Science Works

SKU: B2.6 bullet point 1: Interpret data relating to the effects of exercise on the human body.

CA: B4.1.1c Using appropriate technology; B4.3.2b Identifying when repeats are needed in order to improve reproducibility;

B4.3.2f Identifying the range of the measured data; B4.4.1b Calculating the mean of a set of at least three results; B4.5.2c Recognising and identifying the cause of anomalous results.

B2 5.2 Changes during exercise

Learning objectives

- describe some changes that take place in the body during exercise
- interpret data on the effects of exercise on the human body
- explain that the effect of changes during exercise is to supply sugar and oxygen faster to muscles and remove carbon dioxide more rapidly.

Energy for exercise

Your muscles need energy to contract. This energy comes from respiration. When you exercise you need more energy so that your muscles can contract more frequently and for longer, so the rate of respiration increases the harder you exercise.

When you begin exercising, glucose moves into the mitochondria of muscle cells. As the level of activity increases, more glucose moves out of the blood and into muscle cells. However, if there isn't enough glucose in the blood for the increased level of respiration, then stores of **glycogen** in muscle and liver cells are converted to glucose to supply what is needed.

Breathing rate and heart rate

Respiration needs oxygen and produces carbon dioxide. These gases are also transported around the body in the blood.

To supply all the extra oxygen and sugar that is needed when you exercise, and to remove all the extra carbon dioxide from cells, your blood needs to circulate faster, so your **heart rate** increases.

Oxygen and carbon dioxide in the blood also need to be exchanged faster with the air in the lungs. Your **breathing rate** increases and you breathe more deeply. This increases the volume of air being moved into and out of the lungs.

Figure 1 Concentrations of oxygen and carbon dioxide in the blood change with increasing level of exercise.

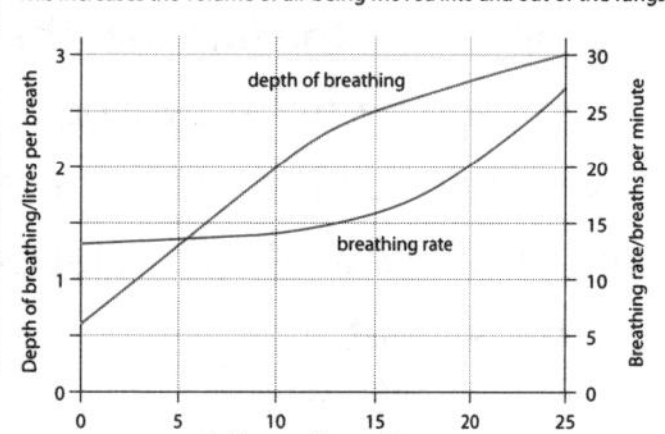

Figure 2 Changes in breathing rate and depth of breathing with exercise.

Examiner feedback

During exercise both breathing rate and heart rate increase, so more oxygen and glucose are transported to the actively respiring cells.

Science skills

Table 1 Data showing the heart rate of someone of average fitness after 1 minute of different levels of exercise.

Exercise level	Heart rate/beats per min
resting	69
gentle	84
moderate	123
vigorous	162

a Explain why heart rate was measured after 1 minute at each level.

b Graph the data and explain the shape of the curve.

c Suggest how the curve might differ for a highly fit athlete and for an unfit person.

If you exercise regularly your body gets fitter and better able to provide the increased blood supply that muscles need during activity. Our bodies are adapted for regular and frequent activity as a result of human evolution. In the UK seven out of 10 adults do not get enough exercise. This is leading to an increase in health problems such as high blood pressure and heart disease.

Heart rate, breathing rate and breathing depth can all be measured while a person exercises.

Science skills

Figure 3 suggests that being unfit is more closely linked to risk of death than being overweight.

d How would you decide if these results are reliable?

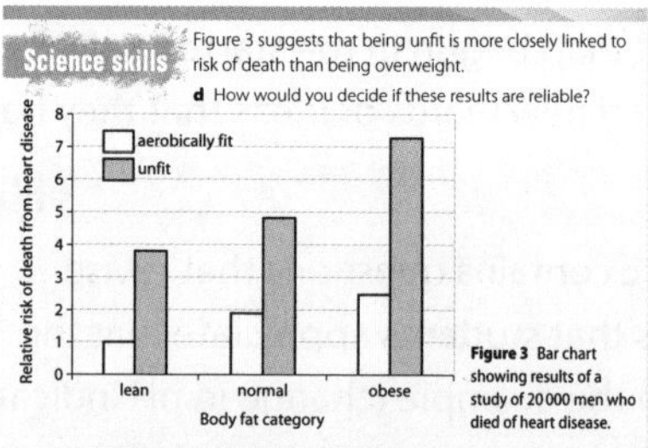

Figure 3 Bar chart showing results of a study of 20 000 men who died of heart disease.

Questions

1 Describe what effect an increasing level of activity has on: **(a)** the oxygen concentration in blood near cells **(b)** the carbon dioxide concentration in blood near cells.

2 The oxygen and carbon dioxide concentrations shown in Figure 1 were measured in venous blood. Explain why these measurements were taken from the veins, not the arteries.

3 Look at Figure 2. **(a)** How many breaths per minute were taken when the person was cycling at 10 km/hour? **(b)** What was the volume of each breath when the person was cycling at 15 km/hour? **(c)** Calculate the total volume of air breathed in and out in 10 minutes when the person was cycling at 20 km/hour. Show your working.

4 **Table 2** Blood supply to different parts of the body. (Skeletal muscles include those of the arms and legs.)

Part of body	Blood flow at rest/cm^3 per min	Blood flow during exercise/cm^3 per min
brain	750	750
heart muscle	300	1200
gut and liver	3000	1500
skeletal muscles	1000	1600

Compare the values at rest and during exercise and explain any changes, or lack of change.

5 Draw a concept map to show how your body responds to increased exercise. Add notes to your map to explain why those changes happen.

6 **(a)** Which has the higher concentration of oxygen, the air in the lungs or the blood coming to the lungs from the tissues? Explain your answer. **(b)** Which has the higher concentration of carbon dioxide, the air in the lungs or the blood coming to the lungs from the tissues? Explain your answer. **(c)** The rate of diffusion of a gas increases if there is a greater difference in concentration. Explain how breathing faster and deeper increase the rate of exchange of oxygen and carbon dioxide between the blood and air in the lungs.

7 For most of human evolution we lived as hunter–gatherers, moving around to find food. Explain in terms of respiration and human evolution why this still affects the way our bodies work, and why this might be the cause of health problems due to being unfit.

A*

Learning objectives

Most students should be able to:

- describe some changes that take place in the body during exercise
- interpret data on the effects of exercise on the human body
- explain that the effect of changes during exercise is to supply sugar and oxygen faster to muscles and remove carbon dioxide more rapidly.

Some students should also be able to:

- explore and explain the impact of exercise on the body. [Ext]

ActiveTeach Resource: Fitness – *Video*

Key points

During exercise, heart rate increases and the rate and depth of breathing also increase.

The changes to heart rate and breathing during exercise increases the supply of oxygen and glucose to muscle cells by the blood, and increases the rate of removal of carbon dioxide.

Muscles store glycogen, which can be broken down to glucose during exercise to supply more energy.

Lesson activities

Starter

1 Choose a relatively fit student who will not be concerned by the attention. Quickly take their pulse and record it on the board. Then ask the student to carry out a simple exercise, such as 20 star jumps, and measure their pulse rate again. It should have increased. Ask students to suggest as many reasons as they can why this change has happened. They could also suggest any other changes they noticed, such as increased breathing rate and depth of breathing.

Main

1 B2 5.2a Changes during exercise This practical gives students the opportunity to plan and then carry out an investigation into the effect of activity on heart rate and breathing rate. (Allow ~15 mins to plan, 20–40 mins to gather data, ~15 mins to analyse.)

2 B2 5.2b Changing heart rate This data analysis sheet gives students the opportunity to investigate results without having to carry out the practical work. Students could use a spreadsheet program to analyse the data. Skills sheets 27 and 28 may help students who need support when working with spreadsheets.

3 Fitness Ask students to research the average heart rate and breathing rate for adults and other age groups, and the effect of increased fitness in athletes on the resting heart rate and breathing rate. Some of this information can be found in the ActiveTeach video clip 'Fitness' and the rest from the Internet or books. Students should consider why heart rate varies so much between individuals, and within the same individual at different times of the day or in particular situations, in order to justify the term 'average heart rate'. [AT]

Plenary

1 On the board, sketch a graph of heart rate and level of exercise like the one from the data in the data box in lesson B2 5.2 of the Student Book. Ask students for suggestions on how to annotate the graph to explain the shape of the curve. Then ask how the curve might differ for someone who is very fit, or for someone who is unfit.

Homework

1 Worksheet B2 5.2c contains some headline statements about health and fitness and presents some questions that will revise what has been learnt in the lesson.

2 If appropriate for your students, ask them to carry out their own 'exercise audit' and to think of simple ways in which they could increase their daily level of activity. If they are already very active, they could consider other members of their family. Explain how important it is to make exercise simple and easy to incorporate as part of normal life, otherwise you are much more likely to give up. They should also explain why exercise has an effect on health and fitness.

Points to note

- During any physical activity, be sensitive to students who find such activity difficult or uncomfortable. If appropriate, pair such students with others who are physically more able and ask them to act as recorders for data collected during the activity.

Answers to Student Book questions

Science skills

a To allow the body to adjust to the new level of activity.

b The curve shows that heart rate increases as level of exercise increases.

c For a highly fit athlete, the curve would most likely start at a lower resting heart rate and show a lower heart rate throughout all levels of exercise, so the curve would sit below the one given in b. For an unfit person, the curve might start at around the same value for resting but increase more steeply with level of exercise.

d Compare the results with those from other studies, to see if they produce similar patterns. If they are similar, then the results are reliable. If not similar, then the way the different studies were set up needs to be compared to see which method was more likely to produce repeatable results.

Answers

1 **(a)** The oxygen concentration decreases. **(b)** The carbon dioxide concentration increases.

2 The venous blood is blood coming from the tissues, including the muscles where most exchange of gases is happening between cells and blood during exercise.

3 **(a)** 14 breaths per minute. **(b)** 2.5 litres per breath.
(c) Total volume in 10 minutes = volume per breath × breaths per minute × 10 = 2.75 × 20 × 10 = 550 litres.

4 Brain – no change because continuing function during exercise is important. Gut and liver – decrease during exercise as not important in activity. Heart muscle – increase so that it can contract harder. Skeletal muscles – increase so that they can work harder.

5 Concept map to include the following:
- heart rate increase – to deliver blood faster to muscles
- breathing rate and depth increase – to exchange gases more quickly between lungs and blood
- muscles – increased need for energy for contraction, so increased rate of respiration, so need increased amounts of glucose and oxygen delivered by blood; also higher production of carbon dioxide, which is changes to blood supply to other parts of the body so that muscles can get more blood.

6 **(a)** Air in the lungs has more oxygen, because blood coming from tissues to the lungs has had the oxygen removed for respiration. **(b)** Blood from the tissues, because carbon dioxide has been added from respiring cells. **(c)** Breathing replaces air in the lungs with air that has more oxygen and less carbon dioxide. This increases the difference in concentration of the gases between the air in the lungs and the blood coming from the tissues, so rate of diffusion increases.

7 Our bodies are adapted through a long evolution to a level of exercise much greater than most people have now. This adaptation means our bodies generally work best at a higher level of exercise than we have now. If we don't get sufficient exercise, the systems of our body may not work as well, leading to ill health.

B2 5.3 Anaerobic respiration

Link to the specification

B2.6.2a During exercise, if insufficient oxygen is reaching the muscles they use anaerobic respiration to obtain energy.

B2.6.2b Anaerobic respiration is the incomplete breakdown of glucose and produces lactic acid.

B2.6.2c As the breakdown of glucose is incomplete, much less energy is released than during aerobic respiration. Anaerobic respiration results in an oxygen debt that has to be repaid in order to oxidise lactic acid to carbon dioxide and water.

B2.6.2d If muscles are subjected to long periods of vigorous activity they become fatigued, i.e. they stop contracting efficiently. One cause of muscle fatigue is the build up of lactic acid in the muscles. Blood flowing through the muscles removes the lactic acid.

Ideas for practical work

Investigating holding masses at arm's length and timing how long it takes the muscles to fatigue.

Investigating the effect of exercise on pulse rate, either physically or using pulse sensors and data loggers.

Designing an investigation using force meters and data loggers to find the relationship between the amount of force exerted by a muscle and muscle fatigue.

How Science Works

SKU: B2.6 bullet point 1: Interpret data relating to the effects of exercise on the human body.

CA: B4.5.4d Evaluating methods of data collection; B4.6.1b Developing scientific ideas as a result of observations and measurements.

B2 5.3 Anaerobic respiration

Learning objectives

- explain how anaerobic respiration supplies energy to muscle cells when insufficient oxygen is available
- describe anaerobic respiration as the incomplete breakdown of glucose
- explain why anaerobic respiration results in an oxygen debt that has to be repaid
- explain why muscles become fatigued after long periods of activity.

Running out of oxygen

If you exercise for a long time, your muscles start to **fatigue**. This means that they don't contract as strongly as they normally do, and cannot do as much work. You feel an increasing weakness and pain or cramps in the muscles.

The cause of fatigue is not well understood because there are many changes happening in muscle during activity. In prolonged activity some chemicals needed for reactions start to run out, and others that are made during activity build up.

This athlete has muscle fatigue after running a marathon.

Taking it further

You will find that advanced texts talk about lactate rather than lactic acid. This is because when lactic acid is in solution in water, it dissociates into negative lactate ions and positive hydrogen ions. However, the two terms mean the same thing in this instance.

Examiner feedback

A different form of anaerobic respiration occurs in many microorganisms, including yeast. It is commonly called fermentation and its end-product is ethanol (ethyl alcohol), not lactic acid as in animal cells. It is important to distinguish between the two processes because of their different end-products.

Another source of energy

Most of the time muscles get the energy to contract from aerobic respiration. However, if you suddenly start exercising vigorously, or if you exercise vigorously for some time, your muscle cells may not be able to get enough oxygen to keep contracting hard.

Fortunately, if oxygen levels in muscle cells are low, the cells can also use **anaerobic respiration**. This process releases energy without the need for oxygen to break down glucose. Anaerobic respiration does not replace aerobic respiration. It provides muscles with extra energy beyond what they can get from aerobic respiration.

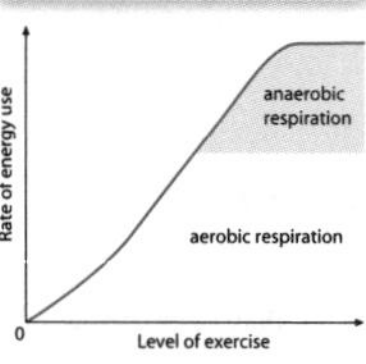

Figure 1 This graph shows the contribution of aerobic and anaerobic respiration to energy production at different levels of activity.

Comparing the two types of respiration

Anaerobic respiration also breaks down glucose, but it does not make the same products as aerobic respiration. The equation for anaerobic respiration is:

glucose → **lactic acid** (energy given out)

Anaerobic respiration produces much less energy per glucose molecule than aerobic respiration. This is because the glucose is only partly broken down and there is still a lot of energy locked in the bonds of the lactic acid molecules. However, the breakdown of glucose to lactic acid is much faster than the breakdown of glucose to carbon dioxide and water, so anaerobic respiration can supply energy quickly.

150

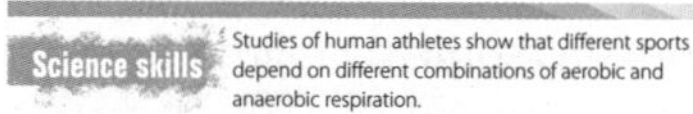

Science skills

Studies of human athletes show that different sports depend on different combinations of aerobic and anaerobic respiration.

Table 1 Types of respiration for different activities.

Activity	Type of respiration
short-distance sprint	mostly anaerobic
middle distance, e.g. 400 m run	anaerobic and aerobic
long distance, e.g. marathon	mostly aerobic

a Explain why different kinds of athletes need to train differently to improve the efficiency of their muscle cells to manage aerobic or anaerobic respiration.

Whales and seals keep lactic acid inside their muscles and out of their blood during diving because they dive for so long and the amount of lactic acid produced could damage other organs.

The oxygen debt

For a while after exercise, we continue to breathe deeply even though our muscles have stopped working as hard. The extra oxygen that our bodies need after exercise is called the **oxygen debt**.

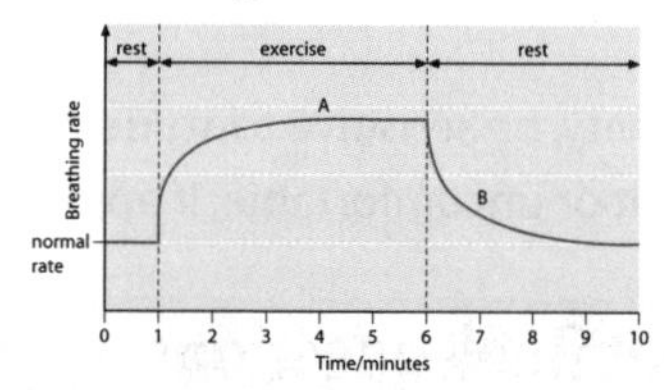

Figure 2 Breathing rate during and after exercise.

Some of the extra oxygen taken in at this time is used to return the body to its resting state. However, if anaerobic respiration has occurred, the lactic acid must also be removed from the muscle cells and recycled. It is transported in the blood to the liver where it is oxidised so that it can be used for aerobic respiration another time, when it is broken down to carbon dioxide and water.

Science in action

It used to be thought that lactic acid caused muscle fatigue, but scientists now realise that it plays an essential part in keeping muscles working when they are being overstimulated during vigorous exercise. Endurance athletes are now trained to develop both their aerobic and anaerobic capacity.

Examiner feedback

Make sure you know what anaerobic respiration is, how it can contribute during exercise and why it results in an 'oxygen debt'.

Questions

1 Explain what we mean by 'muscle fatigue'.
2 State one similarity and one difference between aerobic and anaerobic respiration.
3 Explain why the oxygen concentration in muscle cells may be low during vigorous activity.
4 Give one disadvantage and one advantage of anaerobic respiration compared with aerobic respiration.
5 Look at Figure 2. Explain the breathing rate at points A and B.
6 Why is it an advantage for an endurance athlete to develop both aerobic and anaerobic capacity?
7 Explain fully why whales and seals need a special adaptation to cope with lactic acid.
8 Explain the different proportions of aerobic and anaerobic respiration shown in Table 1.

A*

Energy from respiration 151

Learning objectives

Most students should be able to:

- explain how anaerobic respiration supplies energy to muscle cells when insufficient oxygen is available
- describe anaerobic respiration as the incomplete breakdown of glucose
- explain why anaerobic respiration results in an oxygen debt that has to be repaid
- explain why muscles become fatigued after long periods of activity.

Some students should also be able to:

- evaluate claims that lactic acid causes pain after anaerobic activity. [Ext]

Key points

Muscles become fatigued after long periods of vigorous activity and stop contracting as efficiently.

If insufficient oxygen reaches muscle tissue, it can produce energy through anaerobic respiration.

Anaerobic respiration is the incomplete breakdown of glucose to lactic acid, releasing less energy than aerobic respiration.

After exercise, you continue to breathe deeply to 'repay the oxygen debt' and return the body to normal, including oxidising any lactic acid formed.

Lesson activities

Starter

1 Choose a student who is reasonably fit (but not a muscle builder!) and ask them to stand with one arm outstretched, palm up. Place a copy of the Student Book on their hand and ask them to hold it like that for as long as they can manage. Ask other students to explain what is happening in the student's arm muscles, and how the heart may need to respond, to revise aspects of aerobic respiration from earlier lessons. After 2 or more minutes, ask the student to explain any changes in feeling that are happening in their arm muscles. Ask other students to suggest what changes are occurring in the muscles. Stop the activity after 5 minutes if the student is still managing to hold the book. Ask them to feel their arm muscles and describe any changes that have occurred.

Main

1 B2 5.3a Muscle fatigue and muscle size Refer to sheet in Teacher and Technician Planning Pack.

2 Worksheet B2 5.3b What causes muscle cramps? Refer to sheet in Teacher and Technician Planning Pack.

3 Muscle fatigue Ask students to research the changes that happen in muscle cells during prolonged activity. This will result in many suggestions as to why cells fatigue. Some sources still suggest lactic acid from anaerobic respiration as the cause, although recent medical and scientific research shows that this is unlikely. An interesting debate topic for the class could be 'How could scientists determine what causes muscle fatigue?' This will illustrate the difficulty of identifying one factor from a number of changes that occur simultaneously, and help to explain the confusion about lactic acid for so long.

Plenary

1 Play a 'traffic lights' game to test how well students have learnt the features of anaerobic respiration. Give each student a red, a yellow and a green card. Ask them to hold up the red card if a statement is false, green if it is true and yellow if they are not sure. Offer statements appropriate to the level covered in this topic, such as 'Anaerobic respiration uses oxygen to break down glucose and release energy' (false), 'Muscle cells use anaerobic respiration to release energy when oxygen levels are low' (true).

Homework

1 Worksheet B2 5.3c is a comprehension and graph interpretation sheet related to training to build both aerobic and anaerobic endurance in competition sport.

2 Worksheet B2 5.3d is an alternative comprehension and graph interpretation sheet related to the production of lactic acid in diving animals and humans.

Points to note

- This topic provides some interesting opportunities for comparing results that are apparently based on scientific evidence with those based on true scientific investigation. The role of lactic acid in causing pain and cramps is one example.

Route to A*

Ask students to discuss the role of anaerobic respiration in terms of increasing the chance of survival, and to give a balanced judgement of its advantages and disadvantages.

Answers to Student Book questions

a Different levels of exercise require different amounts of anaerobic respiration, so it would make no sense for a marathon runner to develop anaerobic capacity, but it is essential that a sprint runner develops this as much as possible.

1 Muscle fatigue is when muscles stop contracting as efficiently because of prolonged vigorous exercise.

2 Similarity: both produce energy from the breakdown of glucose. Difference: aerobic respiration breaks down glucose completely to carbon dioxide and water; anaerobic respiration breaks down glucose incompletely to lactic acid.

3 Oxygen has been used up in aerobic respiration and not enough further oxygen is being supplied by the blood.

4 Disadvantage: it doesn't produce as much energy from each molecule of glucose. Advantage: it can continue when oxygen levels are low, so the muscle can continue to contract; or it can produce energy more rapidly than aerobic respiration.

5 A: the raised level of breathing rate is supplying oxygen as fast as possible to the blood. B: breathing rate only gradually reduces after exercise has finished, to repay the oxygen debt.

6 A high aerobic capacity means they can race faster for longer; a high anaerobic capacity means they can increase the amount of energy released beyond what is available from aerobic respiration, so they can go even faster.

7 Diving mammals can only get oxygen at the surface. If they dive for long periods, they will need to generate a lot of the energy in their swimming muscles from anaerobic respiration. This will build up large amounts of lactic acid. Keeping it in their muscles prevents damage to other organs. When they reach the surface, they can get oxygen to oxidise the lactic acid back to glucose.

8 Sprint: requires fast, short burst of energy, faster than aerobic respiration can supply. Middle distance: much of the energy is supplied by aerobic respiration because it needs to be sustained, but on a relatively short distance the athlete can use some anaerobic respiration to supply more energy than aerobic can supply to run faster. Long distance: all aerobic, as energy supply needs to be sustained for a long time, which anaerobic cannot do.

B2 6.1 Cell division

Link to the specification

B2.7.1a In body cells the chromosomes are normally found in pairs. Body cells divide by mitosis.

B2.7.1b The chromosomes contain the genetic information.

B2.7.1c When a body cell divides by mitosis:

- copies of the genetic material are made
- then the cell divides once to form two genetically identical body cells.

B2.7.1d Mitosis occurs during growth or to produce replacement cells.

B2.7.1e Body cells have two sets of chromosomes; sex cells (gametes) have only one set.

B2.7.1f Cells in reproductive organs – testes and ovaries in humans – divide to form gametes.

B2.7.1g The type of cell division in which a cell divides to form gametes is called meiosis.

B2.7.1h When a cell divides to form gametes:

- copies of the genetic information are made
- then the cell divides twice to form four gametes, each with a single set of chromosomes.

B2.7.1i When gametes join at fertilisation, a single body cell with new pairs of chromosomes is formed. A new individual then develops by this cell repeatedly dividing by mitosis.

B2.7.1n The cells of the offspring produced by asexual reproduction are produced by mitosis from the parental cells. They contain the same alleles as the parents.

B2.7.2f Chromosomes are made up of large molecules of DNA (deoxyribonucleic acid) which has a double helix structure.

B2.7.2g A gene is a small section of DNA.

Ideas for practical work

Observation or preparation and observation of root tip squashes to illustrate chromosomes and mitosis.

Using genetic beads to model mitosis and meiosis.

How Science Works

CA: B5.4.2c Demonstrating an understanding of how data may be displayed, by choosing the most appropriate form of presentation.

B2 6.1 Cell division

Learning objectives

- describe how new body cells are produced by mitosis
- explain that new cells are needed for growth or repair, or for asexual reproduction
- describe how gametes (sex cells) are produced by meiosis
- describe the main differences between mitosis and meiosis
- explain how fertilisation produces a new cell with two sets of chromosomes that then divide by mitosis.

Examiner feedback

Chromosomes don't usually stay in pairs or sets, so you won't normally see them like this. However, you need to remember that body cells have two sets of chromosomes, while gametes (sex cells) in many organisms only have one set.

Practical

The cells at the tip of a root or shoot in a plant are dividing rapidly for growth. We can investigate the stages of division in plant cells by making a **root tip squash**.

Taking it further

The division of cells during mitosis and meiosis is considerably more complex than shown here. Each type of division goes through several different phases which are named and described separately. However, it is important to remember that division is one continuous process and these stages run into one another. So, when looking at slides of division, it can be difficult to identify exactly at which stage each cell is.

Chromosome sets

In the body cells of most organisms, there are two sets of genetic information, or **chromosomes**, because one set comes from each parent. For example, humans have 46 chromosomes in almost every body cell, which can be arranged in 23 pairs (two sets of 23).

A human karyotype shows all the chromosomes from one cell arranged in pairs, from biggest to smallest.

Mitosis

During growth, or for replacement of damaged cells, a body needs to make new cells. To do this, existing body cells divide in a type of division that is called **mitosis**.

Before a cell divides, every chromosome is copied. During division, one copy of each chromosome moves to one side of the cell and the other copy moves to the other side. The cell then splits in two, creating two new cells with the same number of chromosomes as the original. Since body cells start with two sets of chromosomes, mitosis will produce more cells with two sets of chromosomes.

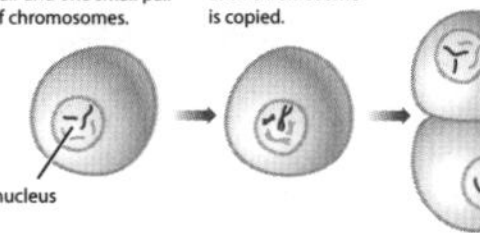
The cell has one large pair and one small pair of chromosomes.
Each chromosome is copied.
When the cell divides in two, each cell gets one new copy of each chromosome.
nucleus

Figure 1 Mitosis of a body cell with four chromosomes (two pairs). The chromosomes are drawn short here, and coloured, so it is easier to see what is happening. They don't really look like this.

154

Mitosis is also the kind of division that occurs during **asexual reproduction**, when new offspring are produced by the division of parent cells. The cells of the offspring receive copies of every chromosome in the parent cell. So the offspring carry the same genes as their one parent, and are called **clones**.

Meiosis

The production of **gametes** (sex cells) in the reproductive organs uses a different kind of cell division, called **meiosis**. In humans, meiosis occurs in the **testes** in men and the **ovaries** in women. During meiosis, each new cell only receives one set of chromosomes, so human gametes only contain 23 chromosomes.

Meiosis begins with a cell that contains two sets of chromosomes. All the chromosomes are copied, as at the start of mitosis. However, in meiosis the original cell divides twice so at the end of the division there are four cells that each contain only one set of chromosomes. In men the four cells then develop into four sperm. In women, one of the four cells becomes an egg.

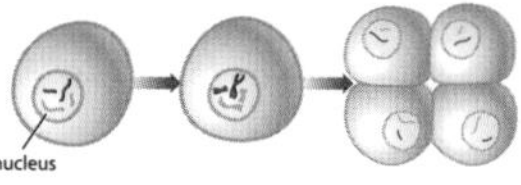
The cell has one large pair and one small pair of chromosomes.
Each chromosome is copied.
The cell divides in two and then in two again. Each new cell gets a copy of one chromosome from each pair.
nucleus
These cells are not identical.

Figure 3 Meiosis of a cell with four chromosomes.

sperm (in testes)

egg (in ovaries)

Figure 2 Gametes are produced in the reproductive organs.

After fertilisation

During **fertilisation**, when an egg cell fuses with a sperm cell, the chromosomes from each gamete come together in the new nucleus. So the fertilised cell contains two sets of chromosomes again. The fertilised cell divides by mitosis, so that every body cell of the new individual will have two sets of chromosomes.

Examiner feedback

Often in science exams if you misspell a word but it looks like the correct word then you will be awarded the mark. You cannot afford to spell either mitosis or meiosis incorrectly as they look too similar to each other.

Questions

1. Which kind of division happens in the cells of a root tip squash? Explain your answer.
2. Explain the purpose of mitosis in most organisms.
3. Draw up a table to compare the similarities and differences between mitosis and meiosis.
4. Explain why an offspring of sexual reproduction will be different from both its parents but an offspring of asexual reproduction will be identical to its parent.
5. Describe the role of mitosis and meiosis in the life cycle of a human.
6. Explain why meiosis is needed before fertilisation can take place.
7. Komodo dragons live on a range of islands in Indonesia, some of which are very small and can only support a few of these large lizards. Scientists assumed they only reproduced sexually, but females in zoos have produced eggs through asexual reproduction. Explain as fully as you can why Komodo dragons may use both forms of reproduction.

A*

Patterns of inheritance 155

Learning objectives

Most students should be able to:

- describe how new body cells are produced by mitosis
- explain that new cells are needed for growth or repair, or for asexual reproduction
- describe how gametes (sex cells) are produced by meiosis
- describe the main differences between mitosis and meiosis
- explain how fertilisation produces a new cell with two sets of chromosomes that then divide by mitosis.

Some students should also be able to:

- compare and contrast models of DNA and mitosis to evaluate the most successful model. [Ext]

Key points

Mitosis is the division of body cells to make identical cells for growth and repair, or in asexual reproduction.

Meiosis is the division of cells in the reproductive organs to produce gametes, which have only one set of chromosomes.

At fertilisation, two gametes fuse to form a cell with two sets of chromosomes, which then divides by mitosis to grow into the new individual.

ActiveTeach Resource: Mitosis and meiosis – *Animation*

Asexual reproduction chromosome clone fertilisation gamete meiosis mitosis ovary root tip squash testis

Lesson activities

Starter

1 Revise work in B1 on 'sexual reproduction' and 'asexual reproduction' by asking students to write a definition for each term. Students then compare their definitions with those of a neighbour and work together to produce improved versions. This can be repeated in fours and eights and then as a class to create class definitions for each term.

Main

1 **B2 6.1a Root tip squash** In this practical activity, students prepare a microscope slide of a root tip squash and practise their microscope skills. (~30 mins)

2 **Mitosis** To help visualise the process as a continuous sequence, there are several videos of mitosis on the Internet which could be helpful, although you may wish to view them without sound as they will introduce detail that students will find confusing at this stage. Videos of meiosis will be too complex for this level. You could first view a complete video without sound, then re-run it and ask students to write their own commentary to explain it. ActiveTeach includes an animation showing mitosis and meiosis. [AT]

3 **Worksheet B2 6.1b Modelling cell division** guides students through modelling the two types of cell division. They will need a selection of different-coloured 'poppit' beads and some short lengths of wire twist or pipe cleaner, plus paper and pencil. Students should manage mitosis without support, but meiosis may need guidance to avoid confusion between the separation of sets of chromosomes and the separation of their copies. The words 'chromatid' and 'homologous chromosomes' have been avoided, but may help more able students distinguish between the two main stages of meiosis.

Plenary

1 Ask students to write the word 'mitosis' and the word 'meiosis' on separate scraps of paper. Read out the following statements one by one and ask students to hold up the name of the correct process: makes gametes; used in asexual reproduction; produces cells with pairs of chromosomes; forms cells with half the usual number of chromosomes; used in growth and repair of cells; forms cells with the full number of chromosomes; produces clones; produces cells with a single set of chromosomes.

Homework

1 Ask students to create a crossword with clues, using all the key words from this lesson and any other suitable words from the lesson.

2 **Worksheet B2 6.1c** provides a set of questions to test understanding of concepts from this lesson.

Points to note

- Students do not need to learn the different stages of mitosis or meiosis for this specification, though they will see different stages of mitosis if they prepare a root tip squash. Viewing a video will help them see the stages as part of a continuous sequence.
- The specification incorrectly suggests that all four cells produced by meiosis always go on to form gametes. In humans, this is only true for males. In females, only one of the four cells will form an egg, the rest are effectively lost.

Route to A*

Students research other models of mitosis and meiosis, using the Internet or books, and develop criteria to evaluate which is the most effective.

Answers to Student Book questions

1 Mitosis, because these are body cells dividing for growth.

2 To produce new cells for growth or to repair damaged tissues.

3

	Mitosis	Meiosis
Similarities	Chromosomes duplicate before division. Produce new cells.	
Differences	Original cell divides once to form two cells. Identical cells formed. Cells formed contain two sets of chromosomes. All body cells divide like this. Needs two parents.	Original cell divides twice to form four cells. Cells formed are not identical. Cells formed contain only one set of chromosomes. Only cells in the reproductive organs divide like this. Occurs in each parent.

4 During sexual reproduction two gametes fuse, each bringing one set of chromosomes from each parent, so the offspring will be a mix of characteristics from both parents. In asexual reproduction, the offspring gets identical copies of the parent cell, so will have the same characteristics as the parent.

5 After fertilisation, all body cells are produced by mitosis. Meiosis then produces the gametes (egg or sperm cells depending on the sex of the person). One male and one female gamete fuse during fertilisation, which completes the cycle.

6 Meiosis produces cells with only one set of chromosomes. In fertilisation, two cells fuse. If both cells had two sets of chromosomes, the result of fusion would be a cell with four sets of chromosomes. Meiosis before fertilisation ensures that the result of fusion is a cell with the usual two sets of chromosomes again.

7 Komodo dragons produce sexually when they can because this increases variability in the offspring, which helps to increase the chance that some will survive if the environment changes. However, females that reach new islands can produce eggs without fertilisation if there is no male present, so the species can spread.

B2 6.2 Differentiated cells

Link to the specification

B2.7.1j Most types of animal cells differentiate at an early stage whereas many plant cells retain the ability to differentiate throughout life. In mature animals, cell division is mainly restricted to repair and replacement.

B2.7.1k Cells from human embryos and adult bone marrow, called stem cells, can be made to differentiate into many different types of cells, e.g. nerve cells.

B2.7.1l Human stem cells have the ability to develop into any kind of human cell.

B2.7.1m Treatment with stem cells may be able to help conditions such as paralysis.

How Science Works

SKU: B2.7 bullet point 5: Make informed judgements about the social and ethical issues concerning the use of stem cells from embryos in medical research and treatments.

B2 6.2 Differentiated cells

Learning objectives

- describe what cell differentiation is and when it happens in animals and plants
- explain what stem cells are and give examples of how they might be used to treat some conditions
- identify and evaluate some of the social and ethical issues surrounding the use of embryonic stem cells.

Taking it further

The process of differentiation (specialisation) involves the switching on and off of genes as the cell develops. This is why all cells have the same genes, but don't all look the same.

Differentiated cells

Your body contains many different kinds of cells, and almost all of them are **differentiated** (specialised) to do different jobs. When an animal egg cell is fertilised it starts dividing to make an **embryo**. The cells in the early stages of an animal embryo can differentiate to form almost any kind of cell. As cell division continues, the cells become increasingly specialised and the range of types of cell they can develop into decreases. By the time you are born, almost all your cells are differentiated.

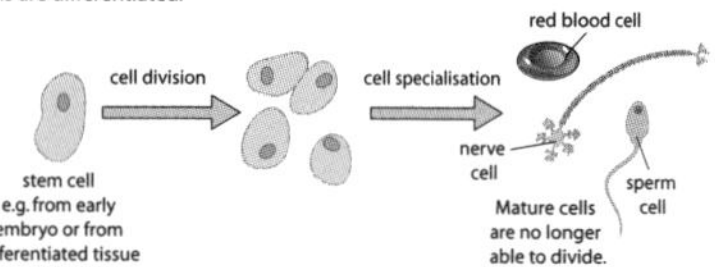

Figure 1 Differentiation of animal cells.

In plants, it is different. Many cells in a fully grown plant keep the ability to differentiate into any kind of cell. We can take cuttings from plant parts or use tissue culture to grow a whole new plant, but we cannot do this in animals.

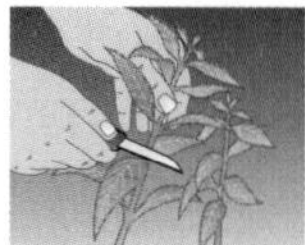

1 Cut shoot from a plant.

2 Dip cut end into hormone rooting powder.

3 Plant in pot of soil as soon as possible after cutting.

Figure 2 In a plant cutting, cells at the cut end divide and differentiate into root cells to form a new root system.

Science in action

Scientists are currently researching how specialised cells can be returned to the stem cell state and then directed to produce new, different specialised cells. The success of this process will change the scientific problems that need tackling to produce effective treatments for people with disorders caused by defective cells, as well as change the ethical issues raised. Society needs to be aware of any changes, and the questions that politicians and the general public will need to consider.

Stem cells

Cells that can differentiate into a range of other cells are called **stem cells**. The cells in an early embryo (**embryonic stem cells**) have the ability to differentiate into any kind of body cell.

In differentiated body tissues there are a few **adult stem cells**, which divide when needed for growth or repair to damaged tissue. However, these cells can normally only differentiate into a limited range of other cells. Stem cells in **bone marrow**, for example, normally only produce different kinds of blood cell.

Using stem cells for treatment

Stem cells are already being used to treat some human disorders, for example bone marrow cells are used to treat leukaemia, a type of cancer in blood cells. New treatments are being developed for many other disorders where cells are damaged, such as to replace damaged nerve cells in people who have been paralysed after their spinal cord was broken in an accident. The advantage of using

156

embryonic stem cells is that they are easier to work with, but a practical disadvantage is that putting cells from one body into another means lots of medication for the rest of the patient's life. Using stem cells created from a patient avoids this problem.

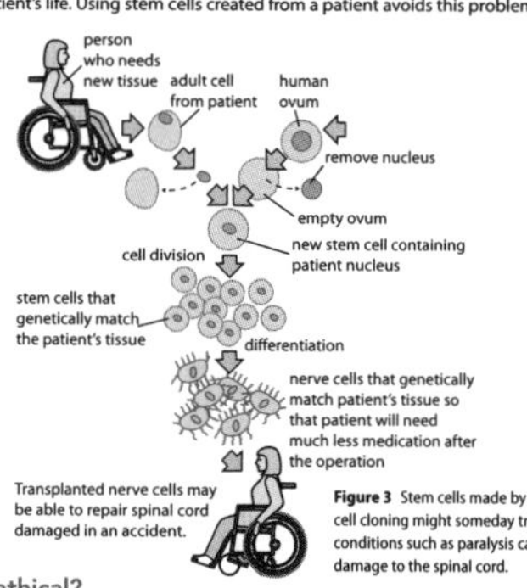

Figure 3 Stem cells made by adult cell cloning might someday treat conditions such as paralysis caused by damage to the spinal cord.

Science in action

Scientists are researching many other ways to encourage adult stem cells to differentiate into a greater range of specialised cells. For example, in March 2010 a boy was given a replacement windpipe with stem cells taken from his own bone marrow. The stem cells were treated to grow into all the kinds of cells needed in the new windpipe. Doctors will monitor the success of this new treatment.

Is it ethical?

Many countries ban the use of embryonic stem cells for treatment. This is partly because research is still trying to solve some of the practical problems they cause, such as the need for lifetime medication. However, there are also **ethical questions**. Some people say that using such embryos is destroying a new life. However, most of the embryos used are those unwanted after fertility treatment and would be destroyed anyway. Research into embryonic stem cells is allowed in many countries because they are easier to extract from tissues than adult stem cells.

Examiner feedback

You will not be expected to remember the details of Figure 3, but it will help you to understand the link between techniques for adult cell cloning and gene therapy. It also shows why people who are against the use of embryos in research and treatment don't like this technique, because an embryo is created and then destroyed.

Questions

1 Explain why we can grow a whole new plant from a leaf but not a complete human from a leg.

2 Define the term 'stem cell' in your own words.

3 List the similarities and differences between embryonic and adult stem cells.

4 Explain how the adult cell cloning technique makes it possible to use the patient's own cells to treat a disorder.

5 Explain why there are ethical problems with using embryonic stem cells.

6 Bone marrow transplant is a form of stem cell therapy that has been used since the 1960s to treat patients with leukaemia. Suggest why this kind of stem cell treatment has been available for so long, while other stem cell treatments are still in the development phase.

7 If a couple have a child that is paralysed due to nerve damage, it is possible to mix their sperm and eggs in the lab to create an embryo from which stem cells could be taken and used to cure the child's paralysis. **(a)** What are the advantages to the child of doing this? **(b)** What are the advantages to the parents? **(c)** Should the law allow this kind of treatment? Explain your answer.

8 Stem cells can be taken from the umbilical cord of a baby just after birth. A parent could decide to do this for a baby and have the cells stored in case they are needed later in life to cure a disorder or paralysis. Storage costs money. Evaluate the advantages and disadvantages of this idea.

A*

Patterns of inheritance 157

Learning objectives

Most students should be able to:

- describe what cell differentiation is and when it happens in animals and plants
- explain what stem cells are and give examples of how they might be used to treat some conditions
- identify and evaluate some of the social and ethical issues surrounding the use of embryonic stem cells.

Some students should also be able to:

- compare and contrast the social and ethical issues of using embryonic stem cells and adult stem cells, and use this to explain the current direction of stem cell research and development. [Ext]

Key points

Most types of animal cells differentiate at an early stage of development, while many plant cells retain the ability to differentiate throughout life.

Animal cells that have started to differentiate can only divide to make similar cells, but stem cells keep the ability to differentiate into many kinds of cell.

Scientists are developing ways of using stem cells to treat conditions such as paralysis.

ActiveTeach Resource: Stem cells – *Video*

Embryonic stem cell use – *Pros and cons debating activity*

Lesson activities

Starter

1 Revise what students learnt in B1 about adult cell cloning by starting to draw the diagram of this from lesson B1 6.3 in the Student Book. Don't tell students what you are drawing but at each stage ask 'Can you see what this is yet?' An alternative would be to provide this as a PowerPoint presentation using the original diagram and building it up as described here. Start with just the cells and arrows of the original diagram. Then label the cell from an udder, the unfertilised egg and the separate nucleus. Then give the hint 'something to do with sheep', and if there is still no response, remind them of Dolly the sheep. Then ask students to recall some of the problems with the technique and with Dolly. Use the answers to elicit discussion about the difference between scientific issues, such as whether or not a technique is successful, and ethical issues, such as whether something is right or wrong.

Adult stem cell | bone marrow | differentiate | embryo | embryonic stem cell | ethical question | stem cell

Main

1 Worksheet B2 6.2a Stem cell questions Refer to sheet in Teacher and Technician Planning Pack and use in conjunction with the ActiveTeach video. [AT]

2 Worksheet B2 6.2b Embryonic stem cell debate Refer to sheet in Teacher and Technician Planning Pack. The ActiveTeach resource 'Embryonic stem cell use' is a pros and cons debating activity. [AT]

3 Stem cells Ask students to research the range of human disorders that stem cells might be used to treat. They should try to identify what it is that these disorders have in common (they are caused by faulty cells) and explain why scientists think that stem cells could be the cure.

Plenary

1 Give each student a card labelled 'true' and a card labelled 'false'. Present a range of statements, some of which are true and some false, related to the content of the lesson, and ask students to show the card which identifies the statement correctly. Suitable examples are: Adult stem cells are only found in adults (F). Ethical questions are about what is right or wrong (T).

Homework

1 Ask students to research recent examples of the use of stem cells in research and treatments. They should find out which kinds of stem cells were used and describe any scientific and/or ethical issues raised by the techniques used.

2 **Worksheet B2 6.2c** presents a series of questions on the use of adult and embryonic stem cells.

Points to note

- This specification focuses on the ethical concerns with using embryonic stem cells, but students should also be aware of some of the problems concerned with using adult stem cells in order to make comparisons.
- If students carry out their own research, they are likely to come across the following words. These definitions may help: Totipotent – a stem cell that can produce any kind of cell (only the very earliest cells of an embryo); Pluripotent – a stem cell that can produce almost any kind of cell (later cells in a young embryo, before the nerve cord forms); Multipotent – a stem cell that can produce many kinds of cell (adult stem cells and older embryo cells).

Route to A*

Ask students to research progress on the development of stem cells and their use in treatments, including iPSCs (induced pluripotent stem cells). Students should identify the scientific and ethical advantages and disadvantages of any new technique for producing stem cells and compare and contrast with the use of embryonic and adult stem cells.

Answers to Student Book questions

1 Plant cells in the leaf retain the ability to differentiate into all the different types of cell in a plant, but animal cells do not so you couldn't get muscle, nerve and bone tissue in a leg to make the other organs in a human body.

2 A cell that retains the ability to differentiate into many kinds of cell.

3 Similarity: both are cells that can differentiate into many kinds of cell. Differences: adult stem cells found in small numbers in tissues, embryonic stem cells are all cells in an early embryo (easier to get at); adult stem cells can differentiate into a more limited range of cell types than embryonic stem cells.

4 The nucleus of the cloned cell cells comes from the patient. This produces stem cells that genetically match the cells in the patient's body, so the patient will not need as much medication for the rest of her life as she would if the stem cells had come from someone else or an embryo.

5 Ethical arguments tackle what people think is right or wrong. Some people think it is wrong to use embryonic stem cells as an embryo must be destroyed to get them. As an embryo is a potential life, they consider this the same as killing someone.

6 Cells in bone marrow are easier to get hold of than stem cells in other tissues where they are scattered through tissue. So they are easier to extract and identify. They also don't need much further preparation before being used for treatment because they naturally produce blood cells to replace blood cells in the patient damaged by cancer/leukaemia. Embryonic stem cells need to be treated to direct them to make blood cells rather than other kinds of cell, as do cells created by adult cell cloning.

7 **(a)** The child will not be paralysed and can live a normal life without lots of treatment. **(b)** The parents won't have to spend so much time and money looking after the child as it grows up. (c) Any suitable answer supported by appropriate explanation, such as: no, because it is not right to destroy the life of an embryo; yes, because it improves the life of the patient, and reduces the strain on their parents and on society in providing support for the patient.

8 Advantages: the cells from the chord are stem cells, so could be used to make any kind of body cell later; the cells are from the baby so they will be genetically identical if used for treatment. Disadvantages: cost of storage may mean that only wealthy people could do this, which is unfair to poorer people; if the baby has a genetic fault (mutation) the cord cells will also have it, so they could only be used for adult cell cloning not to produce new differentiated cells directly.

Genes and alleles

Link to the specification

B2.7.2c Some characteristics are controlled by a single gene. Each gene may have different forms called alleles.

B2.7.2f Chromosomes are made up of large molecules of DNA (deoxyribonucleic acid) which has a double helix structure.

B2.7.2g A gene is a small section of DNA.

B2.7.2h Each gene codes for a particular combination of amino acids which make a specific protein.

B2.7.2i Each person (apart from identical twins) has unique DNA. This can be used to identify individuals in a process known as DNA fingerprinting.

Ideas for practical work

Making models of DNA.

Extracting DNA from kiwi fruit.

How Science Works

CA: B5.2.1a Identifying some possible hazards in practical situations; B5.2.1b Managing risks

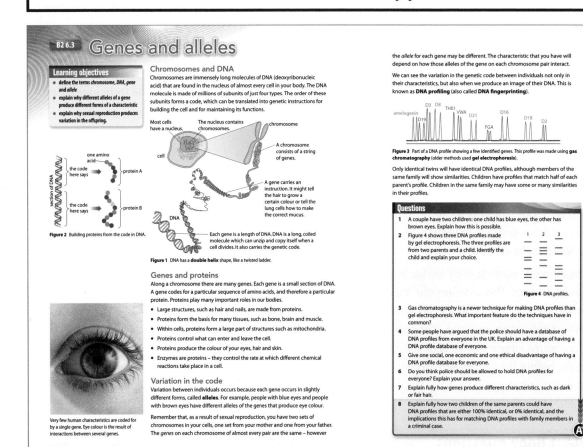

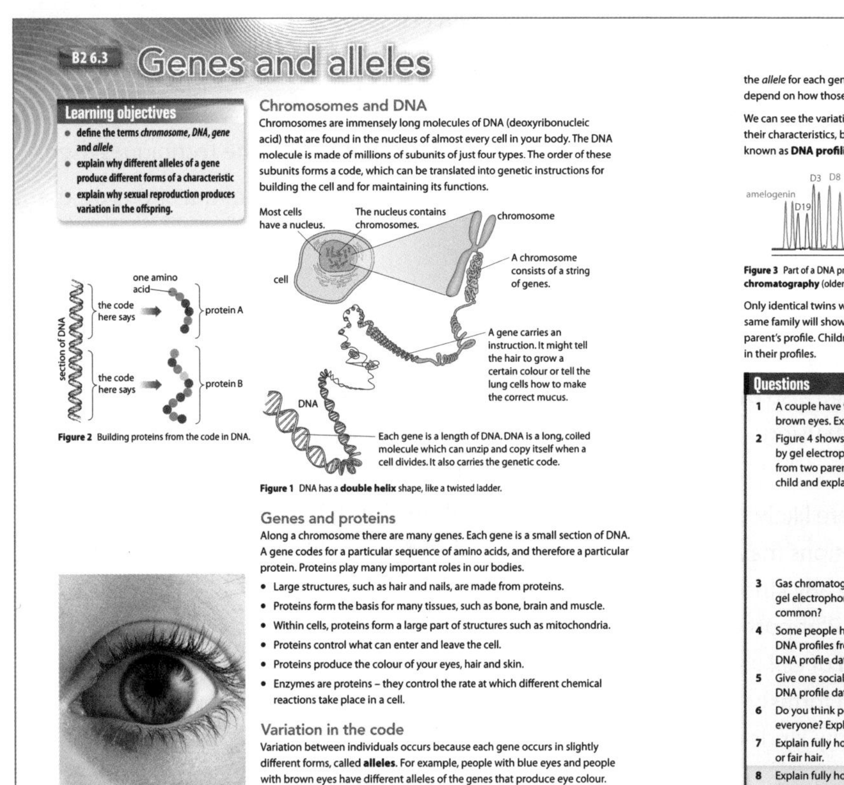

B2 6.3 Genes and alleles

Learning objectives

- define the terms *chromosome, DNA, gene* and *allele*
- explain why different alleles of a gene produce different forms of a characteristic
- explain why sexual reproduction produces variation in the offspring.

Chromosomes and DNA

Chromosomes are immensely long molecules of DNA (deoxyribonucleic acid) that are found in the nucleus of almost every cell in your body. The DNA molecule is made of millions of subunits of just four types. The order of these subunits forms a code, which can be translated into genetic instructions for building the cell and for maintaining its functions.

Figure 1 DNA has a **double helix** shape, like a twisted ladder.

Figure 2 Building proteins from the code in DNA.

Genes and proteins

Along a chromosome there are many genes. Each gene is a small section of DNA. A gene codes for a particular sequence of amino acids, and therefore a particular protein. Proteins play many important roles in our bodies.

- Large structures, such as hair and nails, are made from proteins.
- Proteins form the basis for many tissues, such as bone, brain and muscle.
- Within cells, proteins form a large part of structures such as mitochondria.
- Proteins control what can enter and leave the cell.
- Proteins produce the colour of your eyes, hair and skin.
- Enzymes are proteins – they control the rate at which different chemical reactions take place in a cell.

Very few human characteristics are coded for by a single gene. Eye colour is the result of interactions between several genes.

Variation in the code

Variation between individuals occurs because each gene occurs in slightly different forms, called **alleles**. For example, people with blue eyes and people with brown eyes have different alleles of the genes that produce eye colour.

Remember that, as a result of sexual reproduction, you have two sets of chromosomes in your cells, one set from your mother and one from your father. The *genes* on each chromosome of almost every pair are the same – however the *allele* for each gene may be different. The characteristic that you have will depend on how those alleles of the gene on each chromosome pair interact.

We can see the variation in the genetic code between individuals not only in their characteristics, but also when we produce an image of their DNA. This is known as **DNA profiling** (also called **DNA fingerprinting**).

Figure 3 Part of a DNA profile showing a few identified genes. This profile was made using **gas chromatography** (older methods used **gel electrophoresis**).

Only identical twins will have identical DNA profiles, although members of the same family will show similarities. Children have profiles that match half of each parent's profile. Children in the same family may have some or many similarities in their profiles.

Questions

1 A couple have two children: one child has blue eyes, the other has brown eyes. Explain how this is possible.

2 Figure 4 shows three DNA profiles made by gel electrophoresis. The three profiles are from two parents and a child. Identify the child and explain your choice.

Figure 4 DNA profiles.

3 Gas chromatography is a newer technique for making DNA profiles than gel electrophoresis. What important feature do the techniques have in common?

4 Some people have argued that the police should have a database of DNA profiles from everyone in the UK. Explain an advantage of having a DNA profile database of everyone.

5 Give one social, one economic and one ethical disadvantage of having a DNA profile database for everyone.

6 Do you think police should be allowed to hold DNA profiles for everyone? Explain your answer.

7 Explain fully how genes produce different characteristics, such as dark or fair hair.

8 Explain fully how two children of the same parents could have DNA profiles that are either 100% identical, or 0% identical, and the implications this has for matching DNA profiles with family members in a criminal case.

Science in action

DNA profiling is a key tool in **forensic science**. Tiny samples of tissue such as blood, semen or hair can be used to produce a DNA profile that can help to identify a person who was at the scene of a crime, either by comparing it with a police DNA database or with DNA taken from suspects. However, it cannot specifically identify who carried out the crime.

Practical

DNA can be extracted from any cell with a nucleus, but it is easier to extract from plant cells such as from kiwi fruit.

Science in action

DNA analysis is being used in many areas of science to identify individuals and species, not just in human forensic science. For example, samples taken from whale meat for sale in Japanese markets can show whether or not the meat comes from protected species or from species that are legal to hunt. Comparing the DNA of different species also helps to show evolutionary relationships. For example, evidence from DNA samples taken from fossils of Neanderthal people show that in Europe, where they lived at the same time as *Homo sapiens* (our own species), the two species probably interbred quite frequently.

158 Patterns of inheritance 159

Learning objectives

Most students should be able to:

- define the terms 'chromosome', 'DNA', 'gene' and 'allele'
- explain why different alleles of a gene produce different forms of a characteristic
- explain why sexual reproduction produces variation in the offspring.

Some students should also be able to:

- evaluate the quality of evidence from DNA analysis. [Ext]

ActiveTeach Resource: Genes and protein synthesis – *Key terms quiz*

Key points

Chromosomes are long molecules of DNA, which are made up of many small sections called genes.

A gene codes for a particular sequence of amino acids that forms a specific protein.

Alleles are different forms of a gene and produce different forms of the characteristic.

Every person (except identical twins) has unique DNA and can be identified by their DNA using DNA 'fingerprinting'.

Lesson activities

Starter

1 Give students the following sets of three words and ask them to write a full sentence for each set that contains those words. Take examples from around the class and discuss any variations. This should help to revise work from B1.

- nucleus, chromosome, DNA
- characteristic, gene, chromosome
- variation, gene, environment

Allele chromosome DNA DNA fingerprinting DNA profiling forensic science gas chromatography gel electrophoresis gene

Main

1 B2 6.3a Extracting DNA from fruit This is a standard practical in which DNA is extracted from the nuclei of fruit cells. In their planning of the experiment, students are required to carry out a risk assessment and include appropriate risk management in their method. (~ 30 mins)

2 B2 6.3b Genes make proteins Before giving students this worksheet write the letters EJTQOQUQOG on the board. Tell students that this means something and ask if they can work out what it is. Elicit the idea that it is a code which can be decoded; it is a simple transcription of the word 'chromosome' by using letters that are two further on in the alphabet. When it is decoded we have a sequence of letters that make a word that means something. Similarly, the DNA in our chromosomes is a code which is decoded to form a string of amino acids that make a protein. Consider preparing sheets of squares in 20 different colours, labelled with each of the amino acids, so that students can do this as a cut-and-stick exercise. This can be done simply by creating a table in MS Word of 20 squares and using the colour-fill option. Note insulin is one of the shorter proteins; others can be thousands of amino acids long. Note that students do not need to know the detail given in the worksheet, but this will help them understand how different genes can code for different proteins.

3 If students have difficulty visualising the structure of DNA, give them pieces of scrap paper to cut 'ladder' shapes from. Ask them to twist the ladder vertically, to create a double helix. Explain that each chromosome has many thousands of rungs, and that one gene may contain many rungs. You might like to explain that the ladders are further twisted and coiled many times to form the chromosome shapes that we see during cell division.

Plenaries

1 Ask students to write down three key bullet points that they have learnt from this lesson. Take examples from around the class and ask students to select the three from the list that are most important for the specification.

2 Use the ActiveTeach quiz to consolidate learning. [AT]

Homework

1 Worksheet B2 6.3c contains questions relating to the use of DNA profiling in a criminal case.

2 Worksheet B2 6.3d gives some examples of other uses of DNA profiling and asks questions about the quality of evidence from this technique.

Points to note

- The AQA GCSE Additional Science specification requires that students learn that each gene makes a specific protein. Whilst it may be safe to say that each protein is coded for by one gene, scientists realise that this doesn't mean that one gene = one protein as they used to believe. We have between 20 000 and 25 000 genes in our cells. However, students may find in their research that there are over 90 000 human proteins. There is more to creating proteins than simple decoding of genes, which students will learn more about at A level.

Route to A*

Ask students to carry out research into the complex structure of DNA. They should try to explain why chromosomes are folded many times, and why histones are part of the structure.

Answers to Student Book questions

1. The parents must have different alleles for eye colour, and the children have inherited different alleles.
2. The child is 2, because each of the bars matches either a bar for 1 or 3, i.e. inherited that piece of DNA from that parent.
3. Both techniques identify differences in the DNA.
4. Such a database should make it easier to identify people at the scene of a crime.
5. Social: gives the impression that everyone is a potential criminal. Economic: would need an enormous database to store all the data, which would be costly to set up and run. Ethical: it is a violation of the individual's right to privacy.
6. Any suitable answer supported by an appropriate argument, such as: yes, because it should be easier for the police to catch and punish criminals; no, because already the authorities have too much information about individuals.
7. A gene codes for a sequence of amino acids that make a protein. Proteins play many different roles in our bodies. A gene (or more than one gene) codes for the protein that makes hair colour; different alleles of that gene produce different hair colours.
8. A child inherits one chromosome from each chromosome pair from one parent, and one chromosome from each chromosome pair from the other parent. Although there is a one in two chance that any chromosome of a chromosome pair will become part of the gamete, there is the possibility that each of the two children were formed by the fusion of gametes that could contain exactly the same half of the chromosome pairs from each parent and so be 100% genetically identical. It is also possible that each of the two children were formed by the fusion of gametes that contain the opposite member of each chromosome pair and so be 0% identical. This makes identifying criminals by matching DNA profiles more difficult because two unrelated people may, by chance, have more similar DNA profiles than two brothers or sisters (and even worse with more distant family relations, such as cousins).

Inheriting characteristics

Link to the specification

B2.7.2a Sexual reproduction gives rise to variation because, when gametes fuse, one of each pair of alleles comes from each parent.

B2.7.2b In human body cells, one of the 23 pairs of chromosomes carries the genes that determine sex. In females the sex chromosomes are the same (XX); in males the sex chromosomes are different (XY).

B2.7.2d An allele that controls the development of a characteristic when it is present on only one of the chromosomes is a dominant allele.

B2.7.2e An allele that controls the development of characteristics only if the dominant allele is not present is a recessive allele.

Ideas for practical work

Using genetic beads to model genetic crosses.

How Science Works

SKU: B2.7 bullet point 1: Explain why Mendel proposed the idea of separately inherited factors and why the importance of this discovery was not recognised until after his death; B2.7 bullet point 2: Interpret genetic diagrams, including family trees; B2.7 bullet point 3: Construct genetic diagrams of monohybrid crosses and predict the outcomes of monohybrid crosses and be able to use the terms homozygous, heterozygous, genotype and phenotype; B2.7 bullet point 4: Predict and/or explain the outcome of crosses between individuals for each possible combination of dominant and recessive alleles of the same gene.

CA: B5.6.1a Considering whether or not any prediction made is supported by the evidence.

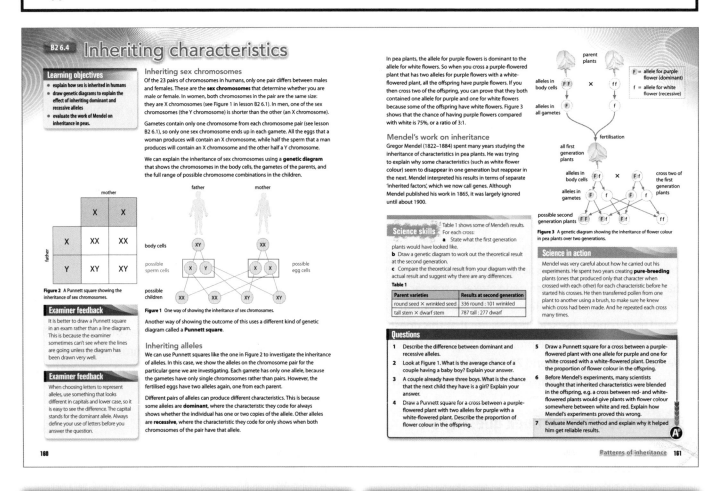

B2 6.4

Inheriting characteristics

Learning objectives

- explain how sex is inherited in humans
- draw genetic diagrams to explain the effect of inheriting dominant and recessive alleles
- evaluate the work of Mendel on inheritance in peas.

Inheriting sex chromosomes

Of the 23 pairs of chromosomes in humans, only one pair differs between males and females. These are the **sex chromosomes** that determine whether you are male or female. In women, both chromosomes in the pair are the same size: they are X chromosomes (see Figure 1 in lesson B2 6.1). In men, one of the sex chromosomes (the Y chromosome) is shorter than the other (an X chromosome).

Gametes contain only one chromosome from each chromosome pair (see lesson B2 6.1), so only one sex chromosome ends up in each gamete. All the eggs that a woman produces will contain an X chromosome, while half the sperm that a man produces will contain an X chromosome and the other half a Y chromosome.

We can explain the inheritance of sex chromosomes using a **genetic diagram** that shows the chromosomes in the body cells, the gametes of the parents, and the full range of possible chromosome combinations in the children.

father \ mother	X	X
X	XX	XX
Y	XY	XY

Figure 2 A Punnett square showing the inheritance of sex chromosomes.

father mother
body cells: XY, XX
possible sperm cells: X, Y
possible egg cells: X, X
possible children: XX, XX, XY, XY

Figure 1 One way of showing the inheritance of sex chromosomes.

Another way of showing the outcome of this uses a different kind of genetic diagram called a **Punnett square**.

Examiner feedback

It is better to draw a Punnett square in an exam rather than a line diagram. This is because the examiner sometimes can't see where the lines are going unless the diagram has been drawn very well.

Examiner feedback

When choosing letters to represent alleles, use something that looks different in capitals and lower case, so it is easy to see the difference. The capital stands for the dominant allele. Always define your use of letters before you answer the question.

Inheriting alleles

We can use Punnett squares like the one in Figure 2 to investigate the inheritance of alleles. In this case, we show the alleles on the chromosome pair for the particular gene we are investigating. Each gamete has only one allele, because the gametes have only single chromosomes rather than pairs. However, the fertilised eggs have two alleles again, one from each parent.

Different pairs of alleles can produce different characteristics. This is because some alleles are **dominant**, where the characteristic they code for always shows whether the individual has one or two copies of the allele. Other alleles are **recessive**, where the characteristic they code for only shows when both chromosomes of the pair have that allele.

160

In pea plants, the allele for purple flowers is dominant to the allele for white flowers. So when you cross a purple-flowered plant that has two alleles for purple flowers with a white-flowered plant, all the offspring have purple flowers. If you then cross two of the offspring, you can prove that they both contained one allele for purple and one for white flowers because some of the offspring have white flowers. Figure 3 shows that the chance of having purple flowers compared with white is 75%, or a ratio of 3:1.

Mendel's work on inheritance

Gregor Mendel (1822–1884) spent many years studying the inheritance of characteristics in pea plants. He was trying to explain why some characteristics (such as white flower colour) seem to disappear in one generation but reappear in the next. Mendel interpreted his results in terms of separate 'inherited factors', which we now call genes. Although Mendel published his work in 1865, it was largely ignored until about 1900.

parent plants
F = allele for purple flower (dominant)
f = allele for white flower (recessive)
alleles in body cells: F F × f f
alleles in all gametes: F, f
fertilisation
all first generation plants
alleles in body cells: F f × F f
cross two of the first generation plants
alleles in gametes: F, f, F, f
possible second generation plants: F F, F f, F f, f f

Figure 3 A genetic diagram showing the inheritance of flower colour in pea plants over two generations.

Science skills

Table 1 shows some of Mendel's results. For each cross:

a State what the first generation plants would have looked like.

b Draw a genetic diagram to work out the theoretical result at the second generation.

c Compare the theoretical result from your diagram with the actual result and suggest why there are any differences.

Table 1

Parent varieties	Results at second generation
round seed × wrinkled seed	336 round : 101 wrinkled
tall stem × dwarf stem	787 tall : 277 dwarf

Science in action

Mendel was very careful about how he carried out his experiments. He spent two years creating **pure-breeding** plants (ones that produced only that character when crossed with each other) for each characteristic before he started his crosses. He then transferred pollen from one plant to another using a brush, to make sure he knew which cross had been made. And he repeated each cross many times.

Questions

1 Describe the difference between dominant and recessive alleles.

2 Look at Figure 1. What is the average chance of a couple having a baby boy? Explain your answer.

3 A couple already have three boys. What is the chance that the next child they have is a girl? Explain your answer.

4 Draw a Punnett square for a cross between a purple-flowered plant with two alleles for purple with a white-flowered plant. Describe the proportion of flower colour in the offspring.

5 Draw a Punnett square for a cross between a purple-flowered plant with one allele for purple and one for white crossed with a white-flowered plant. Describe the proportion of flower colour in the offspring.

6 Before Mendel's experiments, many scientists thought that inherited characteristics were blended in the offspring, e.g. a cross between red- and white-flowered plants would give plants with flower colour somewhere between white and red. Explain how Mendel's experiments proved this wrong.

7 Evaluate Mendel's method and explain why it helped him get reliable results.

A*

Patterns of inheritance 161

Learning objectives

Most students should be able to:

- explain how sex is inherited in humans
- draw genetic diagrams to explain the effect of inheriting dominant and recessive alleles
- evaluate the work of Mendel on inheritance in peas.

Some students should also be able to:

- examine the role of Mendel in the development of the study of genetics. [Ext]

Key points

A dominant allele produces the characteristic when only one copy of the allele is present.

A recessive allele produces the characteristic only when two copies of the allele are present.

Genetic diagrams such as Punnett squares help us to predict the possible offspring between parents with different alleles.

ActiveTeach Resource: Inheritance of sex chromosomes – *Diagram labelling activity*

Inheritance of pea flower colour – *Diagram labelling activity*

Punnett squares – *Spreadsheet*

Dominant genetic diagram Punnett square sex chromosome recessive

Lesson activities

Starter

1 Write the word 'gene' in the middle of the board and ask students to suggest related words and how they should be linked to create a mind map of what they currently know on this topic. This could be revisited at the end of the lesson as an alternative plenary, to add anything new.

Main

1 The ActiveTeach spreadsheet 'Punnett sqaures' can be used whenever suitable in this lesson for explaining genetic crosses. [AT]

2 ActiveTeach also includes two labelling activities. Students could reinterpret the crosses using Punnett diagrams, to provide extra practice. [AT]

3 B2 6.4a Investigating inheritance This practical activity uses counters to model the inheritance of dominant and recessive alleles. ***Expected outcomes*** For the first cross, all 'offspring' should have one counter of each colour. For the second cross, there should be approximately $\frac{1}{4}$ 'offspring' with two dominant alleles, $\frac{1}{2}$ with one dominant and one recessive, and $\frac{1}{4}$ with two recessive alleles. (~30 mins)

4 B2 6.4b Developing ideas This research-based activity helps students link the work of Mendel with the ideas of other scientists of his day and the developing science of genetics in the twentieth century.

Plenary

1 Show students a copy of Figure 3 from lesson B2 6.4 of the Student Book. Play a game of 'traffic lights' to check their understanding. Ask students to indicate whether statements are true or false by showing a red card for false or green card for true, or showing a yellow card if they are unsure. Offer statements such as: 'The allele for white colour is dominant' (F), or 'All the first generation plants had purple flowers' (T).

Homework

1 Students could carry out further research into the work of Mendel. English translations of his papers are available on the Internet and are a good insight into the work of a scientist.

2 Worksheet B2 6.4c provides some questions that will test student's understanding of the inheritance of sex.

Points to note

- Note that only simple monohybrid crosses are required at GCSE level.

Route to A*

Ask students to research the effect of incomplete dominance, where alleles are neither dominant nor recessive, but both act together to produce the phenotype. They should construct genetic diagrams to explain the outcome of crosses between parents with different combinations of alleles that show incomplete dominance.

Answers to Student Book questions

Answers to B2 6.4 can be found on p.205

B2 6.5 Inheriting disorders

Link to the specification

B2.7.3a Some disorders are inherited.

B2.7.3b Polydactyly – having extra fingers or toes – is caused by a dominant allele of a gene and can therefore be passed on by only one parent who has the disorder.

B2.7.3c Cystic fibrosis (a disorder of cell membranes) must be inherited from both parents. The parents may be carriers of the disorder without actually having the disorder themselves. It is caused by a recessive allele of a gene and can therefore be passed on by parents, neither of whom has the disorder.

How Science Works

SKU: B2.7 bullet point 2: Interpret genetic diagrams, including family trees; B2.7 bullet point 4: predict and/or explain the outcome of crosses between individuals for each possible combination of dominant and recessive alleles of the same gene.

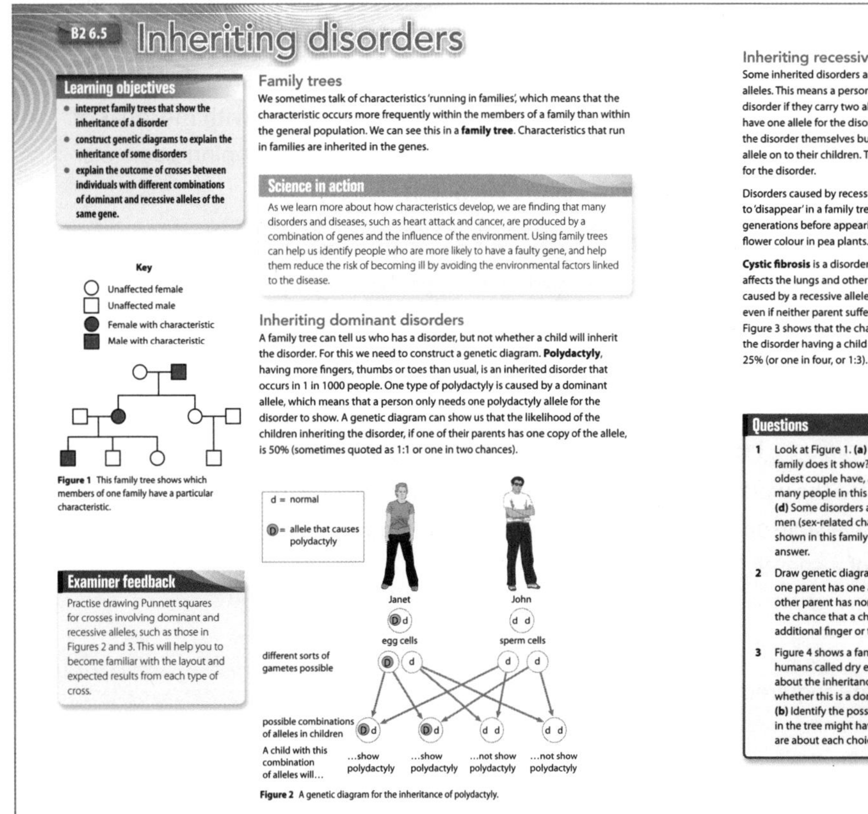

Learning objectives

Most students should be able to:

- interpret family trees that show the inheritance of a disorder
- construct genetic diagrams to explain the inheritance of some disorders
- explain the outcome of crosses between individuals with different combinations of dominant and recessive alleles of the same gene.

Some students should also be able to:

- explain the survival of individuals with inherited disorders in terms of natural selection. [Ext]

Key points

Some disorders are caused by mutations in genes and can be inherited.

Polydactyly is an inherited disorder that can be caused by a dominant allele, and cystic fibrosis is an inherited disorder caused by a recessive allele.

Family trees show the pattern of inheritance of an inherited disorder within a family.

Embryos can be screened for alleles that cause genetic disorders.

Screening embryos raises difficult economic, social and ethical issues.

ActiveTeach Resource: Cystic fibrosis in the family – *PowerPoint*
Punnett squares – *Spreadsheet*

Lesson activities

Starter

1 Ask students for examples of human diseases or disorders and write these on the board. Then ask how people get each of these disorders. If no examples of inherited disorders have been suggested, ask if there are other ways that people may get a disorder. If nothing inherited is suggested, ask what would be the effect if a faulty allele causes a disorder. Try to elicit the fact that this means it could be passed on in the genes from parent to children. Note that there are many inherited disorders, but it is possible that students may not be aware of any at this stage. Also note that some disorders, such as cancer and diabetes, may have a genetic component as well as other causes.

 Cystic fibrosis family tree polydactyly

Main

1 The ActiveTeach spreadsheet 'Punnett squares' can be used whenever suitable in this lesson for explaining genetic crosses. There is an ActiveTeach presentation 'Cystic fibrosis in the family' which explains the inheritance of a recessive disorder. Students could reinterpret crosses for polydactyly and cystic fibrosis with Punnett diagrams to provide extra practice. [AT]

2 Worksheet B2 6.5a Interpreting family trees Refer to sheet in Teacher and Technician Planning Pack.

3 Worksheet B2 6.5b Explaining allele distributions Refer to sheet in Teacher and Technician Planning Pack.

Plenary

1 Ask students to sketch a family tree for an inherited disorder and create some questions about the individuals in the tree that would help someone else work out whether the disorder was caused by a dominant or recessive allele. Take examples from around the class to test the success of the questions.

Homework

1 Students could explore the inheritance of a sex-linked disease such as red–green colour blindness, where the allele for the disorder is carried on the part of the X chromosome that is not matched by the Y chromosome. They should draw genetic diagrams for males and females to explain why the proportion of men and women who have the disorder is different.

2 Worksheet B2 6.5c provides a set of standard questions on the inheritance of recessive and dominant alleles to revise what has been learnt in this lesson.

Points to note

- It is essential that the subject of genetic disorders is covered sensitively, as students may have, or may know friends or relatives with, the disorders mentioned. They may be fully briefed on the outcome of the disorder and be willing to discuss how that affects their point of view of the value of life. Those who are not aware of the consequences could well be distressed to learn of them this way.
- There are several genetic causes of polydactyly, only one of which is a dominant allele. For the purposes of this specification, the other causes are ignored.

Route to A*

Students should be asked to explain all examples of inheritance in terms of natural selection and the survival of individuals best adapted to the environment.

Answers to Student Book questions

1 **(a)** Three. **(b)** Two girls. **(c)** Three. **(d)** No, because in the second generation a woman has the disorder.

2 Using D for polydactyl and d for normal (other suitable letters accepted):

Parents: Dd × Dd

Gametes: D d   D d

Possible offspring: Dd dd Dd dd

2 polydactyl : 2 normal

The chance of having a child with polydactyly is 50%.

3 **(a)** It must be a recessive characteristic because couple 5/6 are not affected, but have a child with the disorder. If a dominant allele caused the disorder, then either 5 or 6 would have dry earwax too.

(b) Individuals 2, 4 and 10 must have two recessive alleles each, so individual 1 must have one recessive allele (that 4 inherits), as have 5 and 6 (since 10 has the disorder). Without further information, it isn't possible to say whether the other people are carriers or have two normal alleles.

4 Someone with a disorder caused by a recessive allele must have two copies of the faulty allele. If their partner doesn't have the disorder, the partner may either be a carrier (have one copy of the faulty allele) or have no faulty alleles.

Using E as the dominant normal allele and e as the recessive faulty allele, we can come up with this punnet square:

		First parent	
		E	E
Second parent	e	Ee	Ee
	e	Ee	Ee

All children will be carriers, but none will have the disorder, so it will appear to skip this generation.

In the next generation, assuming that the first parent is also a carrier, the following cross would be produced:

		First parent	
		E	E
Second parent	E	EE	Ee
	e	Ee	ee

There is a 50% chance that any child will be a carrier, and a 25% chance that they will have the disorder.

5 Family trees. Advantages: they are good for identifying characteristics that are inherited. They show which members of a family have a particular characteristic: that is, where the effects of an allele are visible. Disadvantages: for a recessive allele, this only happens when an individual has two copies of the allele. It can be difficult to tell for certain if an individual is a carrier for that allele.

Genetic diagrams. Advantages: show the probability of inheriting a particular allele and of being affected by it or, for recessive alleles, being a carrier. This can help a couple decide whether or not to have children. Disadvantage: they don't show if a child will definitely get the allele.

B2 6.6 Screening for disorders

Link to the specification

B2.7.3d Embryos can be screened for the alleles that cause these and other genetic disorders.

How Science Works

SKU: B2.7 bullet point 5: Make informed judgements about the economic, social and ethical issues concerning embryo screening.

B2 6.6 Screening for disorders

Learning objectives

- explain that embryos can be screened for genetic disorders
- describe some of the advantages and disadvantages of screening for disorders
- make judgements on some of the issues related to embryo screening.

The problems with genetic disorders

Some genetic disorders can seriously affect the sufferer, making it difficult for them to live a normal life. For example, someone who suffers from cystic fibrosis needs **physiotherapy** every day to remove mucus that is clogging their air passages and lungs. They also need frequent treatment with antibiotics to clear infections caused by microorganisms getting trapped in the mucus.

People with genetic disorders may need extra support and care from their families, and they may need additional medicine and healthcare. Some disorders can even affect how long the person is likely to live.

There are also problems with knowing whether children will inherit a disorder. For example, people with a disorder caused by a faulty dominant allele that doesn't show **symptoms** for many years might pass the allele on to their children before they know they have it. Also, people who are carriers for a recessive disorder may never know they have that allele until their child shows symptoms.

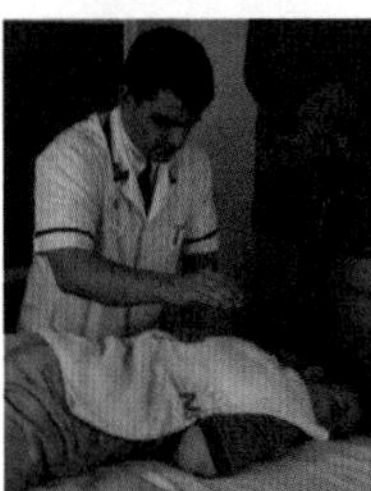

Cystic fibrosis sufferers need firm patting on the back or chest every day to loosen the sticky mucus so they can cough it out.

Making decisions

People who know they have faulty alleles have to make difficult decisions about whether to have children. A couple may have to decide between taking the risk of having an affected child or adopting a child, or even not having children at all.

One way to make these decisions easier is **embryo screening**. Eggs are taken from the woman's ovaries and fertilised by sperm from her partner in a dish in the laboratory. This is called **IVF** (*in vitro* fertilisation). The embryos are tested to see if they carry the alleles for the disorder. Any embryos that do not have the faulty gene can be placed in the womb of the woman to develop into a baby.

Science in action

Embryos conceived naturally can also be tested for genetic disorders, either by removing a sample of fluid from the womb in which the unborn baby is developing, or by taking cells from the unborn baby itself. Both techniques carry a risk of causing the pregnancy to abort, so scientists are looking for another technique that is less invasive, such as testing the mother's blood. All these techniques raise difficult decisions for parents about whether or not to abort a pregnancy if the baby is shown to have a disorder.

Baby Roger Farre's embryo was screened to make sure he didn't have the allele for a disorder caused by a dominant allele.

164

Some people think that embryo screening is a good thing, because it means parents can make decisions about whether or not to raise a child with a genetic disorder and face the problems that might cause. Other people feel that avoiding producing children with a genetic disorder changes how everyone thinks about people with such disorders, and that we should value everyone equally no matter what their genetic make-up.

Many people who are unhappy with the idea of embryo screening are concerned that it could be used to test for all kinds of alleles. Parents might wish to screen embryos for characteristics such as a particular hair colour, or (if scientists can identify them) for characteristics such as intelligence or sporting ability. Deciding when it is and is not acceptable to carry out embryo screening is a decision for society, not scientists. Table 1 shows different kinds of issues we have to think about.

Table 1 Issues around embryo screening.

Type of issue	Explanation
ethical	whether we think something is right or wrong
social	how something affects people, both individuals and all of society
economic	where money is involved

Examiner feedback

You will be given information on unfamiliar examples in the exam and expected to make judgements on them. To get the best marks, remember to consider all the different types of issues, and to suggest how different groups of people may respond differently on those issues. For example, some religious and ethical groups have very strong views on the rights of unborn children; politicians will have views that may be closely linked to popular opinion or to any financial costs such as for medical treatment, as these are supported by money that goes to the government in taxes.

Questions

1 Explain what embryo screening is.

2 Explain how embryo screening could mean that no people in future will be born with genetic disorders that damage health.

3 Explain why it is possible for a parent with an allele for a genetic disorder to pass it on to their children before realising they carry the allele.

4 Give one social and one economic advantage of there being no people with genetic disorders.

5 Is it ethical to avoid producing babies with genetic disorders? Explain the reasons behind your view.

6 Two couples are planning to start families. Jill and Carl have just discovered that Jill's sister has a baby who suffers from cystic fibrosis. Paul and Kim are worried because Paul's father died when he was 42 from a genetic disorder caused by a dominant allele. **(a)** Explain fully the chances that Paul and Kim might have a child with the same disorder that Paul's father had. **(b)** Explain fully the chances that Jill and Carl might have a child with cystic fibrosis. **(c)** Embryo screening is an expensive technique. Should both couples be offered embryo screening to help them have a baby without a genetic disorder? Explain your answer.

7 Some genetic disorders cause a lot of pain and early death, but others, such as some kinds of cancer and blindness, may only cause problems after years of 'normal' health and can be treated by medicine. Should all genetic disorders be treated the same? Present a range of examples to support your argument.

A*

Patterns of inheritance 165

Learning objectives

Most students should be able to:

- explain that embryos can be screened for genetic disorders
- describe some of the advantages and disadvantages of screening for disorders
- make judgements on some of the issues related to embryo screening.

Some students should also be able to:

- evaluate different viewpoints in relation to embryo screening. [Ext]

Key points

Embryos can be screened for alleles that cause genetic disorders.

Screening embryos raises difficult economic, social and ethical issues.

ActiveTeach Resource: Cystic fibrosis: living with the disease – *Video*
Cystic fibrosis: treatment – *Video*

Lesson activities

Starter

1 Tough decisions Ask students for examples of difficult decisions that they have had to make. (Alternatively, tell a story that gives such an example.) What did they do before they made the decision? Did they talk to anyone? Why did they choose that person to talk to? Did that make the decision any easier to make? Was there an obvious right or wrong choice? Explain that there are many decisions we have to make where there is no obvious right choice, and that the decision will be based on what we feel is best based on what we know.

Embryo screening | IVF | physiotherapy | symptoms

Main

1 Many people do not have direct experience of the effect that a genetic disorder can have on life. The ActiveTeach includes two video clips about living with cystic fibrosis and treatments. **Worksheet B2 6.6a Living with cystic fibrosis** contains questions that can be used with the videos to help students understand this perspective before going on to discuss embryo screening. It might be helpful to view the clips first, then rerun them pausing at times to give students the opportunity to complete the answers. Note you may need to explain that nebulised antibiotics are those taken by inhaler. The final clip refers to diagnosis in the womb, and can be omitted if you do not wish to raise this discussion (see Points to note below). [AT]

2 Worksheet B2 6.6b Different points of view gives students an opportunity to consider some of the ethical, social, economic and scientific arguments for and against embryo screening.

3 Debate Ask students to prepare for a debate on the topic of whether embryo screening for genetic disorders should be legal or not. Split the class in two, one half for and the other against, and ask them to research their arguments – Skills sheet 42 may help them plan their arguments. Each side should nominate two or three speakers to present their arguments, after which a class vote should be taken.

Plenary

1 Ask students to write down three key points from the last two lessons on inherited disorders. Take examples from around the class, and then encourage discussion to agree the three most important points. [AfL]

Homework

1 Students could research any recent examples of the application of embryo screening in the news. If these include quotes from different parties, ask students to decide whether the person is discussing an ethical, social or economic aspect of the issue. [AfL]

2 Homework sheet B2 6.6c extends the discussion of whether embryo screening should be made possible in all IVF embryos, since mutations can cause many more disorders than are currently screened for, and looks at the implications of doing so.

Points to note

- The main aim of this topic is to raise discussion on the choices that people have to make, and what might affect the decisions they make. Consideration must be made if there are students in the class who either have, or who know others who have, an inheritable disorder.
- Although the topic is about embryo screening, which can only be done when the eggs are fertilised outside the body, all the issues discussed also apply to techniques such as amniocentesis and chorionic villus sampling which are tests on the fetus in the womb after fertilisation inside the body. These tests can lead to the even greater dilemma of whether to abort a fetus that has an allele for an inherited disease. This is briefly referred to in the final video clip on the ActiveTeach. If you do not wish to discuss this, then do not show this clip.

Route to A*

Students could research examples of other genes that can be screened for in embryos, and should consider the value of doing so and the social and ethical problems that this produces.

Answers to Student Book questions

1 Embryo screening is when an embryo is tested to see if it is likely to suffer from a genetic disorder when it has grown.

2 If everyone with a genetic disorder has their embryos screened before selecting one to develop into a baby, then no babies with the disorder would be born.

3 Some disorders caused by dominant alleles don't show symptoms until beyond the age that the person has children, and carriers of an allele for a recessive disorder won't ever suffer from the disorder, but their children might if the other parent is also a carrier of the allele.

4 Social: life could be better for the children, and for the parents because they wouldn't have to spend as much time caring for an ill child. Economic: it would reduce the cost for parents looking after children with the disorder (such as one parent not being able to work so they can give more care to the child), and the cost to society of providing medical care.

5 Either yes or no, supported by a suitable explanation, such as: yes, because it could reduce the distress of parents looking after a sick child and avoid potential suffering of a child with the disorder; no, because everybody should be treated as of the same value, not thought less of because they aren't the same as everyone else.

6 **(a)** Paul may or may not have the dominant allele, because it doesn't become obvious until later in life (after having children). If Paul has the dominant allele (and Kim doesn't), the chances of passing that allele on to a child are 50% (one in two). If he doesn't (and Kim doesn't either) then they are 0%. **(b)** Jill's sister must have one recessive allele, which the baby has inherited. Jill's sister must have inherited that allele from her parents. So Jill could also have inherited the allele and be a carrier. If Carl is also a carrier, then there is a 25% chance (one in four) that they will have a baby that suffers from cystic fibrosis. If either Carl or Jill is not a carrier, then there is no chance that they will have a baby with cystic fibrosis. **(c)** Any suitable answer with supporting explanation, such as: both couples, because if the baby has the disorder it will seriously affect their life; only Paul and Kim, because the risk of inheriting the dominant allele is twice as great; neither couple, because we should accept everyone as they are and not consider someone with a disorder as being less of a person.

7 Any suitable answer with supporting explanation, but should consider the effect of different kinds of disorder (those that have an effect from birth and those that only become apparent at a later age) on the life of the affected person, their family and society in general. It should also consider how making these kind of checks possible affects the acceptance of society and individuals of genetic disorders and that they may be considered 'abnormal' and unacceptable, when the chances are that many people who were not screened as embryos may carry an allele that causes a disorder. Should also raise the question of how you decide whether one disorder is more acceptable than another.

B2 7.1 Fossil evidence

Link to the specification

B2.8.1a Evidence for early life forms comes from fossils.

B2.8.1b Fossils are the 'remains' of organisms from many years ago, which are found in rocks. Fossils may be formed in various ways:

- from the hard parts of animals that do not decay easily
- from parts of organisms that have not decayed because one or more of the conditions needed for decay are absent
- when parts of the organism are replaced by other materials as they decay
- as preserved traces of organisms, e.g. footprints, burrows and rootlet traces.

B2.8.1c Many early forms of life were soft-bodied, which means that they have left few traces behind. What traces there were have been mainly destroyed by geological activity.

B2.8.1d We can learn from fossils how much or how little different organisms have changed as life developed on Earth.

How Science Works

SKU: B2.8 bullet point 1: Suggest reasons why scientists cannot be certain about how life began on Earth.

B2 7.1 Fossil evidence

Learning objectives

- **describe ways in which fossils form**
- **interpret fossil evidence in relation to evolutionary theory**
- **explain why scientists are not certain about how life began on Earth.**

Examiner feedback

It is important to understand why, in relation to all the organisms that have lived, very few organisms have been found as fossils. You will be expected to explain this in terms of the following:

- Few organisms die in places where good fossilisation can occur.
- Many fossils are in rocks deep below the surface and so have not been discovered.
- Fossils are also destroyed by geological processes.

You will also be expected to understand and explain the impact of this on the challenges of interpreting evolution from fossil evidence.

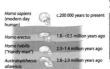

Fossil formation

Fossils are the remains or traces left of organisms that once lived. They can form in several different ways.

The fossil of a skeleton.

Mineral replacement

Minerals in the groundwater replace minerals in the hard parts of the skeleton, such as in bone or shell. Or, if soft tissue doesn't decay, the minerals can fill the spaces in cells and show what soft parts of the body looked like.

A mummified body preserved in a bog.

Mummification

If the growth of decay organisms is prevented by conditions in the ground (e.g. too cold or too acid), the soft tissues are preserved as a **mummy**.

A fossil ammonite.

Moulds and casts

Sometimes a dead organism is pressed into soft sediment. As the organism decays, the shape left in the sediment is filled with other minerals, making a **cast**. The shape in the sediment is a **mould**.

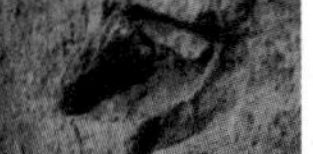

The footprint of a hadrosaur.

Trace fossils

Trace fossils are things made by organisms, such as footprints, burrows or root shapes. These can make casts in the right conditions.

Homo sapiens (modern day human)	c.200 000 years to present
Homo erectus	1.8–<0.5 million years ago
Homo habilis ("Handy man")	2.3–1.4 million years ago
Australopithecus afarensis	3.8–2.9 million years ago

Australopithecus → *Homo habilis*	bigger brain case, smaller teeth and jaws
Homo habilis → *Homo erectus*	flatter jaw, high forehead, intermediate brain case
Homo erectus → *Homo sapiens*	very large brain case, flat face

Figure 1 Evidence from fossil skulls shows how the human head has evolved over time.

A fragmentary record

Only a very small proportion of dead organisms end up in conditions where they can become fossilised; in particular, soft-bodied organisms may decay completely before they can form a fossil. Many fossils that do form are destroyed by geological activity. So fossils tell only a fragment of the story of life on Earth.

We can find out how old fossils are using **radioactive dating** methods. This makes it possible to date the rocks in which the fossils are found, and so date the fossils. Fossils provide key evidence for the **theory of evolution** (see lesson B1 7.1) because we can use them to show how organisms have changed over time.

166

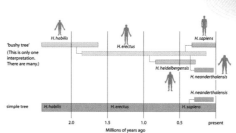

'bushy tree'
(This is only one interpretation. There are many.)
H. habilis
H. erectus
H. sapiens
H. heidelbergensis
H. neanderthalensis
simple tree
H. habilis
H. erectus
H. sapiens
H. neanderthalensis
2.0 1.5 1.0 0.5 present
Millions of years ago

Figure 2 Even when we have many related fossils, as we do for humans, scientists can't always agree how to arrange them in an **evolutionary tree**. Some scientists separate slightly different fossils as individual species, while others group them together into one species.

The earliest life on Earth

We are reasonably certain that the Earth formed about 4600 million years ago, from evidence in the Solar System. Evidence from the earliest rocks suggests that there was life on Earth at least 3500 million years ago. Until around 2000 million years ago the only forms of life on Earth were bacteria. Bacteria are microscopic, so finding fossils of them is difficult. Also, some chemical processes make shapes that look like fossil bacteria. To separate the non-living shapes from real fossil bacteria, scientists analyse the rocks for substances such as proteins and nucleic acids.

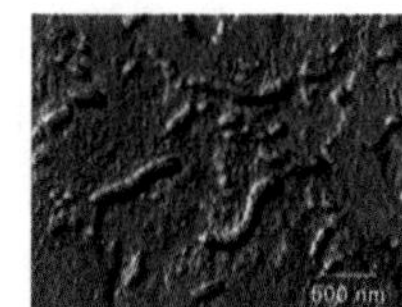

Bacteria-like shapes in this Martian meteorite rock suggest that there may once have been life on Mars. However, many scientists think the shapes are not bacteria.

Questions

1 Look at Figure 1. Describe how skull shape has evolved in humans.
2 What evidence can a mummified fossil give that a mineralised fossil cannot?
3 Give as many reasons as you can why we have so few fossils of all the organisms that once lived.
4 Sometimes geological processes are so great that they fold rocks over and older rocks are found above younger rocks. What evidence could you use to prove this had happened?
5 On a visit to a museum with a 9-year-old child, how would you explain that the 'bones' she sees in a fossil dinosaur are not bone at all?
6 Use evidence from variation in modern humans to explain why there is more than one evolutionary tree proposed for humans.
7 Explain why scientists cannot be certain how life began on Earth.
8 Write an argument to justify how the discovery of feathered dinosaur fossils strengthens support for the theory of evolution.

A*

Science in action

One argument against the theory of evolution in Darwin's time was the problem of explaining something complex, such as a bird's wings. The theory requires that at every stage of evolution any feature must be the best adaptation to the environment so that it is selected for. Recent fossil discoveries have shown that feathers evolved before wings strong enough for flight, suggesting that feathers evolved first for another purpose, such as insulation or display. Flight later became possible as wings got larger.

Organisms changing through time 167

Learning objectives

Most students should be able to:

- describe ways in which fossils form
- interpret fossil evidence in relation to evolutionary theory
- explain why scientists are not certain about how life began on Earth.

Some students should also be able to:

- evaluate evidence relating to evolutionary theory. [Ext]

Key points

Fossils are the evidence of organisms that lived many thousands or millions years ago, and show us how life has changed on Earth.

Fossils provide evidence for evolution.

The evidence we have for life on Earth is not sufficient for scientists to be certain how it began.

Lesson activities

Starter

1 Show students a geological map of Britain that identifies the ages of the major bedrock types. An interactive one is available on the British Geological Survey website. Point out that the age of the rocks gets gradually younger as you go from NW Scotland to SE England. Ask students, since the bedrock is such a mix, what happened to the rest of the rock that was created in each geological era? (The answers are that it is either buried deeper than this map shows or has been destroyed by geological processes including erosion.) Remind students that fossils are found in rocks and ask what has happened to all the fossils that were in the rocks that are now destroyed or deeply buried.

 Cast evolutionary tree fossil mould mummy radioactive dating theory of evolution trace fossil

Main

1 Fossils The BBC set of animations Making fossils helps students explore the conditions in which fossils may or may not be formed, or may be formed then destroyed. Students should take notes from each of the animations and use these to summarise why the fossil record contains so many gaps.

2 Worksheet B2 7.1a The evolution of life contains a set of questions that are best used with the British Geological Survey's interactive timeline of the Earth. This will help students understand the nature of the evidence we currently have for evolution and the problems associated with some of it. The timeline is supported by its own set of teacher notes, some of which might provide additional detail for the most recent events in evolution.

3 Worksheet B2 7.1b Piecing together the evidence provides details about some of the species considered part of human evolution, back to about 4 million years ago. Students can use these to piece together their own possible story of human evolution. They should justify any story that they produce, and more able students should consider more than one possible storyline. If they carry out further research, they will come across a bewildering range of other species names and theories, but this is a good test of understanding just how far limited evidence can be stretched.

Plenary

1 Show students a photo of a fossil (or a real one if you have it), and ask them to note down what evidence could be gained from studying the fossil for its evolutionary relationships, and what limitations there are to that evidence. Take examples from around the class for discussion.

Homework

1 Ask students to research the evolution of a group of living organisms of their own interest. Suitable studies include:

- the evolution of plants from the earliest algae to the dominant flowering plants today
- the evolution of mammals since the extinction of the dinosaurs.

2 Worksheet B2 7.1c provides a set of questions on the relationship between birds and dinosaurs and the impact of the fossil *Archaeopteryx* on deciding evolutionary relationships.

Points to note

- Aspects of this lesson were covered in B1, including the process of mummification in the homework activity for lesson B1 5.2, and the possible origins of life of Earth in a classwork activity for lesson B1 7.1. If not covered then, they would be appropriate for using here also.
- Note that not everyone agrees with the classification of mummies as fossils, in part because they do not form in rock, and also because they are more recent than rock-based fossils. However, they provide huge amounts of detailed evidence for the way some extinct organisms lived and the environments in which they lived.

Route to A*

Students should be expected to explain any examples of evolution in terms of natural selection. This can be difficult when knowledge and understanding of the environment in which the organisms lived is limited. However, students should show an appreciation of the fundamental role of natural selection in any discussion of evolution.

Answers to Student Book questions

1 The brain case has become larger; the face has become flatter; the jaws have become smaller.

2 A mummified fossil still shows signs of soft tissues, such as skin, hair/scales and even internal organs. In a mineralised fossil, the soft tissues usually decay before the hard parts are mineralised.

3 Conditions for good fossilisation only occur rarely. Skeletons can be eaten by scavengers, or broken up by water or wind before being buried. Sediment might be too coarse to take a good impression for mould/cast fossils. We only find fossils when rocks are pushed back to the surface and eroded. Fossils that are made can be destroyed by forces/heat in rock.

4 Use radioactive dating of the rocks, and fossils found in the rocks (compared with fossils in places where there isn't any folding) to date the rocks.

5 Answer should include: bones being buried in sediment, chemicals in bones replaced by minerals in ground water to turn them into rock.

6 Modern humans vary greatly in height, build, skull size, etc. If we simply compared skeletons from two parts of the world, we might decide they are so different that they come from different species. But we know that in reality they are the same species. Scientists can't agree on how much difference in a skeleton/fossil identifies a different species in the fossil record. So their interpretations of evolution will be different.

7 Answer should include: lack of fossil evidence because bacteria are microscopic, what looks like fossil bacteria might just be the result of a chemical process, lack of fossil evidence because most of the rocks of that age have been destroyed by geological processes, and different possible sources such as from space or on Earth from chemical processes.

8 Feathered dinosaur fossils show that feathers appeared before wings, possibly for insulation as a body covering. This adaptation would be an advantage in an environment that was cold, all the time or for just part of the time (e.g. as at night in deserts today), so it would be selected for in those conditions. Small dinosaurs might climb trees to find food that other dinosaurs couldn't reach or to avoid predators, either (or both) of which could improve survival so would be selected for. Gliding from one tree to another would avoid coming back to the ground, saving time wasted in walking or avoiding the risk of predators further. Feathers make a more efficient wing, so the wings with feathers would be selected for. So we can explain the evolution of feathered wings in stages where each new adaptation is a simple development of previous characteristics that are selected for.

B2 7.2 The causes of extinction

Link to the specification

B2.8.1e Extinction may be caused by:

- changes to the environment over geological time
- new predators
- new diseases
- new, more successful, competitors
- a single catastrophic event, e.g. massive volcanic eruptions or collisions with asteroids
- through the cyclical nature of speciation.

B2 7.2 The causes of extinction

Learning objectives

- describe how changes to the physical environment can cause extinction
- describe how other organisms may cause the extinction of species
- evaluate evidence for the causes of mass extinctions.

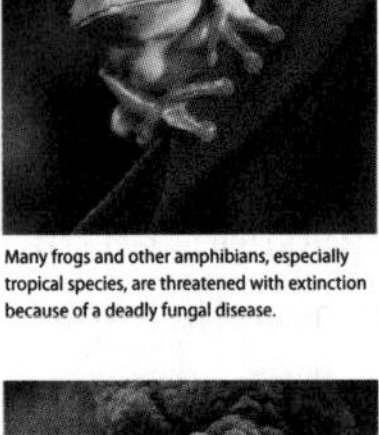

Many frogs and other amphibians, especially tropical species, are threatened with extinction because of a deadly fungal disease.

A series of major volcanic eruptions could produce huge clouds of ash and dust that would block the sunlight and cause a 'global winter'.

Extinction of species

A species evolves as its characteristics change over time. This is driven by **natural selection**, as a result of changes in the physical environment or in the other organisms that live in the same place. If the individuals cannot evolve to survive these changes, the species will become **extinct** (see lesson B1 7.2).

The fossil record shows us that species become extinct, but it cannot tell us why. We need to look for evidence of changes that we think might have caused the extinction. For example, evidence from rocks shows that sea level and temperature have varied greatly over Earth's history. Large or rapid changes in either temperature or sea level could lead to the extinction of species.

Animals that moved from south to north included ground sloths, terror birds and glyptodonts.

Animals that moved from north to south included camels, cats, wolves, deer, rodents and bears.

Figure 1 The green animals were South American species that spread north, and the blue animals were North American species that spread south when the two continents joined.

The different species in an area affect each other, for example through **predation** or **competition**. About 3 million years ago, North and South America joined together for the first time. Before then the two continents had been separate and many species of plants and animals that lived on them were very different. When they joined, some species moved from one continent to the other.

After this exchange, many species quickly became extinct. Some died out because other species moved into their area and competed successfully for resources of food and space. In other cases new predator species came into an area and killed off whole populations of prey species. New diseases that came with the invaders could also have caused some extinction of local species.

Mass extinctions

Sometimes conditions change so rapidly that many species die out at the same time. Such events are known as **mass extinctions**. The worst was about 251 million years ago, when it is thought that over 90% of life on land and in the oceans died out. Another mass extinction about 65 million years ago killed off the last of the dinosaurs.

Most mass extinctions can be linked to rapid changes in sea level or temperature. Some, like the ones 251 million and 65 million years ago, are also linked to volcanic eruptions that lasted over a million years. These would have changed the Earth's climate, affecting both plants and animals. There is some evidence that the extinction 65 million years ago was due to a large asteroid impact.

168

Science skills

a The five worst mass extinctions were 65 million, 205 million, 251 million, c.370 million and c.445 million years ago. Look at the graphs of temperature and sea level change in Figure 2 and suggest what part these factors may have played in these extinctions.

Relative temperature: hot, 0, cold; glacial periods; 542 500 450 400 350 300 250 200 150 100 50 0; Millions of years ago

Sea level change/m: 400, 300, 200, 100, 0, -100, 0; 542 500 450 400 350 300 250 200 150 100; Millions of years ago

Figure 2 Variation in world temperature and sea level over the past 540 million years.

A changed species

Sometimes the fossil record shows one species disappearing and a similar one taking its place. However, this doesn't necessarily mean that an older species died out and the newer species came from somewhere else. It could be that the original species has evolved so much that it is classified as a new species. Sometimes it is not clear which interpretation is true. This is the case for human evolution (see lesson B2 7.1).

Questions

1. Describe the factors that can cause the extinction of a species.
2. It has been estimated that the volcanic eruptions that occurred about 251 and 65 million years ago both lasted between 1 and 2 million years. Explain how they could cause a mass extinction.
3. In the mass extinction 65 million years ago, about 75% of life on Earth became extinct. Suggest what survived.
4. Woolly mammoths became extinct about 8000 years ago. What evidence would you look for to decide whether the extinction of mammoths was the result of climate change or hunting by humans?
5. When scientists looked at a sample of *Australopithecus* fossil bones, some thought there were two species, one larger than the other, while other scientists thought there was just one species. Suggest why.
6. Before South America was connected to North America, many of the large animals were marsupials. Today, only a few marsupials are found there, while many marsupial species live in Australia. Suggest an explanation for this difference.
7. Much of our understanding about how organisms become extinct has come from looking at the impact of humans on the environment today. Using your answer to question 1, explain how this evidence is limited when we try to apply it to examples of extinction in the fossil record.
8. Explain how a large asteroid impact could cause the extinction of life.

A*

Organisms changing through time 169

Learning objectives

Most students should be able to:

- describe how changes to the physical environment can cause extinction
- describe how other organisms may cause the extinction of species
- evaluate evidence for the causes of mass extinctions.

Some students should also be able to:

- evaluate the reliability of conclusions drawn from evidence in the fossil record. [Ext]

Key points

Extinction of species may be caused by many factors, including changes to the environment, new predators or diseases, or new competitors.

Large catastrophic events, such as massive volcanic eruptions or asteroid impacts, may cause mass extinctions.

Species may appear to become extinct in the fossil record because they have changed so much that they look like a different species.

Lesson activities

Starter

1 Write the word 'extinction' on the board and ask students to suggest related words and how they should be linked to create a mind map on the topic. This map could be retained for use as an alternative plenary to revise what has been learnt in the lesson.

Main

1 Worksheet B2 7.2a Why are dinosaurs extinct? Prepares students for a class debate on the cause(s) of the extinction of the dinosaurs. Students should choose one of the suggested explanations and research the evidence for it. You may need to allocate the explanations so that a range of views are presented in the debate. Students are asked to explain not just the extinction of the dinosaurs, but also related details that are often ignored in the general discussion about their extinction. An extension task asks students to question the reliability of conclusions made from the presence or absence of species in the fossil record. Skills sheet 42 may help students prepare their arguments for the debate.

 Competition extinct mass extinction natural selection predation

2 Worksheet B2 7.2b Nearly the end of life? Looks at some of the proposed causes of the greatest mass extinction ever. Although this is a straightforward comprehension sheet of text and questions, it covers such a wide range of knowledge (including global warming and photosynthesis) that it may be better used as a class activity, with students working in small groups to attempt some of the answers.

3 Climate change Ask students to research the evidence for competing theories of climate change and the appearance of modern humans on the extinction of large herbivores in northern Europe, North and South America, and/or Australia. They should present their findings as a poster or slideshow presentation, and try to indicate the level of confidence that exists in the two theories.

Plenary

1 Carry out a 'consider all possibilities' exercise on the statement 'Species X has become extinct'. Possible answers: the environment changed so much that no individuals were well enough adapted to survive and breed; a new competitor arrived in the area that was better adapted to the environment and took over key resources of food or space; a new organism brought a disease that was fatal to species X.

Homework

1 Ask students to research the Great Biotic Interchange that happened when the North American continent joined the South American continent around 3 million years ago. They should identify examples of species that migrated north and those that migrated south, compare these with species that live in these continents now, and try to account for any changes in the last 3 million years.

2 Worksheet B2 7.2c asks students to consider some of the evidence that scientists use to explain the extinction of Neanderthals and to evaluate the interpretation of that evidence in order to judge which provides the most reasonable explanation.

Points to note

- Although the specification for this point has a focus on extinction in evolution, the majority of examples for this today are the result of human activity. If students carry out research on modern examples, they should be encouraged to look at such examples for the deeper reason, as in how the environment has been changed by human activity and how that has led to extinction.

Route to A*

Students should be expected to explain all examples of extinction in terms of natural selection and a failure of the species to adapt to changing environmental conditions, in order to show the fundamental role of natural selection in evolution.

Answers to Student Book questions

Science skills

a The graphs do not show one particular indicator as the cause of extinction. However, there were rapid sea level decreases before the extinctions at 251 and 65 million years ago. There appear to have been large temperature decreases before the extinctions at 445 and 65 millions years ago, a change to rapid cooling at about 370 million years, and a change from rapid warming to cooling at 251 million years. It is difficult to say from these graphs if there was a correlation.

Answers

1 Factors that can cause extinction include changes in the physical environment, such as temperature or availability of water; arrival of a new competitor, predator or disease; massive catastrophes, such as huge volcanic events or asteroid impacts; and gradual change in the characteristics of a species.

2 Ash and dust thrown up into the atmosphere would block out a lot of sunlight. This would reduce the light available for photosynthesis. So many plants would die. This would mean there was little food for animals, so many of them would starve.

3 The ancestors of all living organisms, including flowering plants, mammals and birds.

4 Evidence that the climate had changed significantly, such as temperature and/or availability of water; evidence that humans came into the area where mammoths lived a short while before they became extinct; evidence that humans hunted/killed mammoths from an association of mammoth bones and human artefacts.

5 One species with male being larger than female, as in many modern apes. It would be difficult to tell this from there being two species just by looking at the bones.

6 Australia has remained separated from other landmasses, so (until humans brought many other species in) the marsupials have not had other competitors. When South America connected to North America, many of the marsupial species were out-competed by other (placental) mammals from North America.

7 Evidence for extinction of organisms caused by human activity includes the introduction of new predators, new and more successful competitors, and the introduction of new diseases. We can see the effect these are having as species die out and we investigate the causes. We can also carry out experiments to test our ideas, either in the lab or by comparing different areas where extinction is and isn't occurring. In the fossil record we have very limited information and we also have only the result of what happened. So it is very difficult to say explicitly what caused an extinction when it may have been the effect of several changes, or different changes in different places.

8 Large-scale fires and earthquakes caused by large asteroid impact would have had an immediate impact on plants and animals, killing them directly. Global cooling could be caused by the dust produced. This would have made it difficult for plants to grow. Without plants, the herbivores would have little food and many would have died of starvation. Therefore carnivores would have starved too. The whole food web would be affected if plants were destroyed.

B2 7.3 The development of new species

Link to the specification

B2.8.1f New species arise as a result of:

- isolation – two populations of a species become separated, e.g. geographically
- genetic variation – each population has a wide range of alleles that control their characteristics
- natural selection – in each population, the alleles that control the characteristics which help the organism to survive are selected
- speciation – the populations become so different that successful interbreeding is no longer possible.

B2 7.3 The development of new species

Learning objectives

- describe how new species can arise when populations evolve separately
- explain the role of natural selection in creating new species
- apply the idea of speciation as a result of separation to explain examples of rapid speciation.

Separating populations

One species may evolve over time into a new species as conditions change. However, this gradual change is too slow to explain the rapid increase in numbers of species that is seen sometimes in the fossil record. This fact was once used as an argument against Darwin's theory of evolution, but we know now that natural selection can be the cause of rapid **speciation**.

Imagine a population of birds of one species, as in Figure 1 (a). The individuals will show variation in characteristics because they carry different alleles of many of their genes. If they continue to live in the same area, they will be affected by the same selection processes. The species may change slowly over time if conditions change.

Imagine that one day a storm blows some of the birds hundreds of miles from their home. Some reach an island that is covered in lush green vegetation. Others land on an island covered in rough brown grass. On both islands, the birds begin to adapt to their new environment.

Both islands have predators that eat birds, so camouflage is an important adaptation. Over time, the birds on the green island will be selected for green colour and those on the grass island for brown colour. There may also be other changes in each island population.

Eventually the two populations could become so different that, even if they came back together, they would not be able to breed with each other. They have become different species, as in Figure 1(c).

(a)

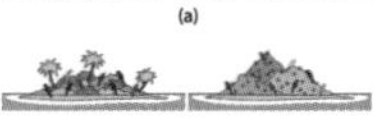

(b)

(c)

Figure 1 Rapid speciation. A population of birds (a) is blown by a storm to two different islands (b). The two groups adapt differently to their new environments (c).

An example of rapid speciation

Lake Malawi in Africa has dried up many times. The lake we know is only about 14 000 years old. There are several hundred species of one type of fish living in the lake. Some of these species are predators, some are herbivores, and some sift food from the mud on the lake floor. They come in many different colours and sizes. However, classification has shown that they all evolved from a few, possibly just one, species of river fish.

Scientists suggest that when the lake started to form, different parts of the lake provided slightly different environments for the river fish, such as open water, shallow muddy bays and deep areas of weed. Adaptations that were better suited to each of these places were selected, so that different forms of the fish evolved in different parts of the lake. Female fish chose to mate with males that came from the same area, so many new species evolved at the same time.

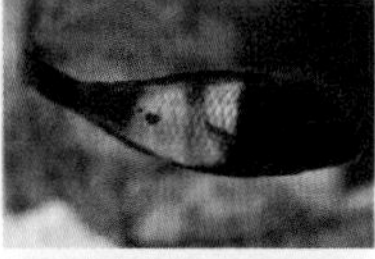

These closely related fish are adapted to very different environments in Lake Malawi.

170

Science in action

In the past, species were classified by looking at their structure. However, DNA evidence is now being used to help identify relationships between species. Some of the results have been surprising. For example, mole species live on most continents: bone evidence suggests they are related, but DNA evidence shows that each species evolved from a completely different animal.

The European mole and the golden mole from South Africa look similar, but they are not closely related. They both spend much of their time underground.

Taking it further

There are different ways in which speciation could be caused. For GCSE, you only need to know how it can result from geographical separation, but you will find other mechanisms suggested. These include genetic mutation, which is common in plants, behavioural separation, particularly where females choose males to mate with based on visible characteristics, and temporal separation, where different groups within the same population breed at different times. All mechanisms of speciation depend on restricting mating (and so exchange of genes) between the individuals of the original population, so that natural selection can act differently on each group.

Questions

1. Draw a flowchart to show how speciation can occur when populations of a species are separated.
2. Explain why separation of populations can lead to a rapid increase in the number of species.
3. **(a)** Suggest why moles from different continents were once classified as one group. **(b)** Suggest how mole species could have evolved to look similar even though they have different ancestors.
4. Suggest why rapid speciation was once an argument *against* the theory of evolution.
5. Explain how female choice of males for breeding supports the process of speciation.
6. Explain the importance of using DNA evidence to identify relationships in speciation.
7. Different species of *Anolis* lizards that live in different environments on one Caribbean island are more closely related to each other than to *Anolis* lizards on other islands. Suggest why.
8. Pollution and a new predator in Lake Victoria have reduced the number of fish species. However, a new species has been discovered that has much larger gills. This enables the new species to live in polluted muddy water where other species, and the predator, cannot live. Outline how this new species could have evolved.

Route to A*

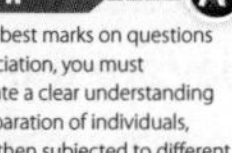

To get the best marks on questions about speciation, you must demonstrate a clear understanding of how separation of individuals, which are then subjected to different selection pressures, can lead to the evolution of individuals that are sufficiently different that they are no longer capable of interbreeding.

Organisms changing through time 171

Learning objectives

Most students should be able to:

- describe how new species can arise when populations evolve separately
- explain the role of natural selection in creating new species
- apply the idea of speciation as a result of separation to explain examples of rapid speciation.

Some students should also be able to:

- evaluate evidence for speciation as a result of geographical separation. [Ext]

Key points

New species can evolve when two populations of a species are separated.

Natural selection, acting on genetic variation, could change the characteristics of the organisms in different ways in each population.

If the two populations become so different that they can no longer interbreed even when they are together, then they are separate species.

Lesson activities

Starter

1 Ask each student to write down a definition of the word 'species'. They should compare their definition with that of their neighbour and try to produce an improved definition in their pair. Repeat this in fours and then eights, then bring all these definitions together for discussion in order to create a class definition. Compare this with the scientific definition of a population of organisms that can all interbreed, and discuss any differences.

Main

1 B2 7.3a Evolution of new species Refer to sheet in Teacher and Technician Pack.

2 Worksheet B2 7.3b Caribbean *Anole* lizards Refer to sheet in Teacher and Technician Pack.

3 Endemic species Ask students to research the endemic species of other 'islands' such as Madagascar, Indonesia and Australia. As well as finding examples of endemic species, they should use evidence about the origin and history of the islands to explain why endemic species evolved on them.

Plenary

1 Ask each student to write down the three most important facts that they have learnt during the last three lessons. Then ask students to share their facts in groups and to compile a master list of facts, including the most common fact learnt and the least common fact. Select a spokesperson for one group at random to share their ideas with the class. Then ask whether other groups had the same 'most common fact'.

Homework

1 Ask students to research the story of Darwin's finches, and to use their findings to explain how the various species of finch on the Galapagos Islands evolved.

2 Worksheet B2 7.3c uses the ideas of evolution in an island situation to explain the evidence for the origins of *Homo floresiensis*.

Points to note

- This lesson only covers the kind of speciation that occurs when two populations of the same species are separated: allopatric speciation. In their research, students may also come across discussion of sympatric speciation, where new species are formed in the same area as a result of different selection pressures (an example being the patterns on some butterfly wings). Crucially, both forms of speciation depend on producing populations that can no longer interbreed and it is easier to explain this in terms of physical separation than in behavioural choice. Students should focus only on allopatric speciation for their exams.
- **Worksheet B1 7.1c Investigating relationships** in B1 looks at how DNA evidence from mammal species matches evidence from the geological record about the break-up of the one supercontinent Pangaea into the continents we have now. This is speciation by physical separation on a major scale, and the worksheet could be revisited from that perspective.

Route to A*

Students should consider the effect of speciation by geographical separation in terms of the 'gene pool' of each population, and be able to explain how differences in evolutionary pressure by the environment on each gene pool results in increasing differences between them.

Answers to Student Book questions

1 Flow chart to include: Separated populations show variation in characteristics in individuals. Physical environment/competitors/predators/diseases in the two areas are different, so natural selection selects for different variations in characteristics. The populations become increasingly different. If they come back together again they are no longer able to breed, so are two species.

2 If there are many different environments, such as many islands or many different conditions in different parts of a lake, then the different conditions can cause the evolution of many new species at the same time.

3 **(a)** Because they have a similar shape and live in a similar way, eating similar food. **(b)** In each continent, a different species started to live underground, and adaptations that made living underground more successful were selected for.

4 Because people couldn't understand how one species could evolve into many different species, and they overestimated how long it would take.

5 If the populations in different areas slowly change due to natural selection, and females choose only to mate with males in the same area, then mixing of characteristics between areas will be reduced and new species can evolve more rapidly.

6 Bone evidence shows the effects of environment as well as genes on characteristics. Differences in DNA are not affected by the environment, so it is easier to tell the difference between two species by their DNA than by appearance, particularly when characteristics are strongly adapted to the environment (such as in moles).

7 It is possible that one species of lizard reached an island and then evolved into several different species, adapted to the different environments on that island. Then one of those species reached another island. Here, new species evolved adapted to the environments on that island. This process was repeated from island to island.

8 Individuals with slightly larger gills cope better in the muddy waters because they can get more oxygen from the polluted water. This would give them an advantage because the predator would not chase them there, so they would be more likely to produce more offspring. Natural selection would continue to select individuals that had even larger gills, which could survive better and leave more offspring. If the females with large gills only mated with males with large gills, this could make a new species.

B2 7.4

ISA practice: carbohydrase enzymes

In the Student Book, each ISA practice is contained on one double-page spread. However, you can, if you prefer, use the sheets provided in the Teacher and Technician Planning Pack and the Activity Pack to more closely mirror the experience of a real ISA which would then take place over several lessons and/or as homework.

Link to the specification

3.2 How Science Works

Observing phenomena can lead to the start of an investigation, experiment or survey. Careful observation is necessary before deciding which variables are the most important.

3.6 Controlled assessment

Scientific investigations often seek to identify links between two or more variables. [B4.1.1, B4.3.1.]

Scientists need to ensure repeatability, reproducibility and validity in evidence. [B4.3.3]

There is a link between the type of graph used and the type of variable represented. [B4.4.2]

In evaluating a whole investigation the repeatability, reproducibility and validity of the data obtained must be considered. [B4.5.2]

The patterns and relationships observed in data represent the behaviour of the variables in an investigation. However, it is necessary to look at patterns and relationships between variables with the limitations of the data in mind in order to draw conclusions. [B4.5.3, B4.5.4]

ISA practice: carbohydrase enzymes

Carbohydrase enzymes are used in industry to break down starch into sugar syrup. A manufacturer of sugar syrup has asked some students to investigate the effect of temperature on the time it takes for carbohydrase to break down starch into syrup.

Section 1

1 Write a hypothesis about how you think temperature affects the rate of enzyme action. Use information from your knowledge of rates of reaction to explain why you made this hypothesis. *(3 marks)*

2 Describe how you could carry out an investigation into this factor.
You should include:
- the equipment that you would use
- how you would use the equipment
- the measurements that you would make
- a risk assessment
- how you would make it a fair test.

You may include a labelled diagram to help you to explain the method.
In this question you will be assessed on using good English, organising information clearly and using specialist terms where appropriate. *(9 marks)*

3 Design a table that you could use to record all the data you would obtain during the planned investigation. *(2 marks)*

Total for Section 1: 14 marks

Section 2

Two groups of students, Study Groups 1 and 2, investigated the effect of temperature on the breakdown of starch by amylase. Figures 1 and 2 show their results.

Temperature 10°C
Starch present after 0, 2, 4, 6, 8, 10, 12, 14, 16 minutes. No starch after 18 and 20 minutes.

Temperature 20°C
Starch present after 0, 2, 4, 6, 8, 10 and 12 minutes.
No starch 14, 16, 18 and 20 minutes.

Temperature 40°C
Starch present after 0, 2, 4 and 6 minutes.
No starch 8, 10, 12, 14, 16, 18 and 20 minutes.

Temperature 60°C
Starch present after 0, 2, 4, 6, 8, 10 and 14 minutes.
No starch 12, 16, 18 and 20 minutes.

Temperature 80°C
Starch present after 0, 2, 4, 6, 8, 10, 12, 14, 16, 18 and 20 minutes.

Figure 1 Study Group 1's results.

4 (a) Plot a graph of these results. *(4 marks)*

(b) What conclusion can you draw from the investigation about a link between the temperature and the rate of enzyme action? You should use any pattern that you can see in the results to support your conclusion. *(3 marks)*

(c) Look at your hypothesis, the answer to question 1. Do the results support your hypothesis? Explain your answer. You should quote some figures from the data in your explanation. *(3 marks)*

Here are the results of three more studies.

Figure 2 shows the results from another two students, Study Group 2.

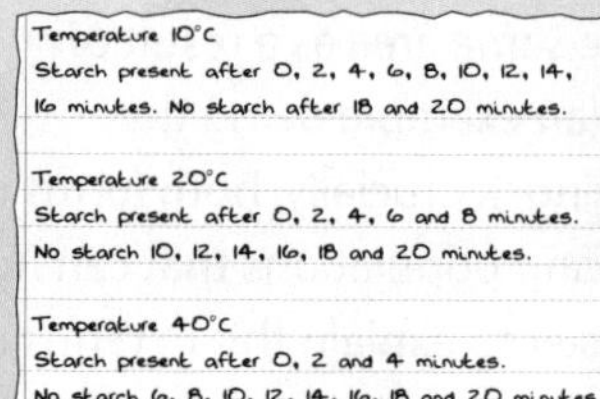

Temperature 10°C
Starch present after 0, 2, 4, 6, 8, 10, 12, 14, 16 minutes. No starch after 18 and 20 minutes.

Temperature 20°C
Starch present after 0, 2, 4, 6 and 8 minutes.
No starch 10, 12, 14, 16, 18 and 20 minutes.

Temperature 40°C
Starch present after 0, 2 and 4 minutes.
No starch 6, 8, 10, 12, 14, 16, 18 and 20 minutes.

Temperature 60°C
Starch present after 0, 2, 4, 6 and 8 minutes.
No starch 10, 12, 14, 16, 18 and 20 minutes.

Temperature 80°C
Starch present after 0, 2, 4, 6, 8, 10, 12, 14, 16 and 18. No starch 20 minutes.

Figure 2 Study Group 2's results.

Figure 3 is a graph drawn from the results of Study Group 3, who carried out another investigation into the effect of a factor on the rate of enzyme action.

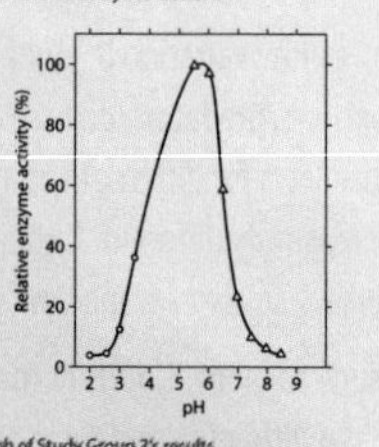

Figure 3 Graph of Study Group 3's results.

Study Group 4 was a group of researchers, who looked on the internet and found Figure 4: a graph showing the effect of temperature on the rate of reaction of a carbohydrase obtained from bacteria.

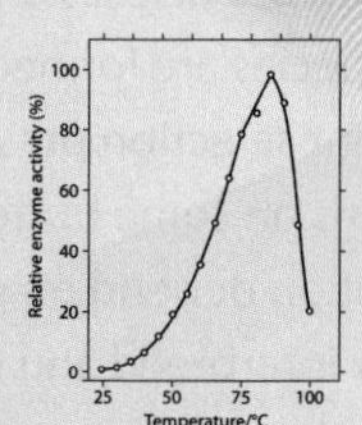

Figure 4 Graph of enzyme activity for a bacterial enzyme.

5 (a) Draw a sketch graph of the results from Study Group 2. *(3 marks)*

(b) Look at the results from Study Groups 2 and 3. Does the data support the conclusion you drew about the investigation in answer to question 5(a)? Give reasons for your answer. *(3 marks)*

(c) The data contain only a limited amount of information. What other information or data would you need in order to be more certain whether the hypothesis is correct or not?
Explain the reason for your answer. *(3 marks)*

(d) Look at the results from Study Group 4. Compare them with the results from Study Group 1. Explain how far the data shown supports or does not support your answer to question 5(b). You should use examples from Study Group 4 and Study Group 1. *(3 marks)*

6 (a) Compare the results of Study Group 1 with Study Group 2. Do you think that the results for Study Group 1 are *reproducible*?
Explain the reason for your answer. *(3 marks)*

(b) Explain how Study Group 1 could use results from other groups in the class to obtain a more *accurate* answer. *(3 marks)*

7 Applying the results of the investigation to a context.
Suggest how ideas from the original investigation and the other studies could be used by the manufacturers to decide on the best temperature at which to use the carbohydrase enzyme to break down starch, and the best source for this enzyme. *(3 marks)*

Total for Section 2: 31 marks

Total for the ISA: 45 marks

172 173

Learning objectives

Most students should be able to:
- make observations and develop into a hypothesis to investigate
- identify the independent and dependent variables
- obtain some data to process
- produce a graph or bar chart from the data obtained
- identify any trends that may be present in the data
- relate that trend to their hypothesis.

Some students should also be able to:
- make a risk assessment of their chosen method, with suitable control measures
- examine the evidence obtained to establish its repeatability and /or reproducibility.

anomalous result calibration control measure hazard hypothesis mean observation prediction range repeatable reproducible research theory uncertainties (errors): random systematic zero validity variables: control categoric continuous dependent independent

Key points

Investigations should be designed so that patterns and relationships between variables can be identified.
It is important to ensure repeatability, reproducibility and validity in evidence when designing and evaluating investigations.
The choice of graph used depends upon the type of variable represented.
When drawing conclusions, the limitations of the data must be kept in mind.

Lesson activities

Starter

1 Show students some starch, e.g. corn flour, and some sugar syrup, e.g. golden syrup. Ask them how the powder can be changed into the syrup. Focus answers on starch being hydrolysed by enzymes to sugars. Explain that this process is used to make sugar syrup industrially in the food industry.

Main

1 Researching and planning Students need to research, using at least two different sources, a way of investigating how enzymes break down starch and develop a hypothesis. Please refer to the **B2 ISA practice 2 Teacher and technician sheet.**

2 Students can complete their research/notes for homework. They need to be aware of the likely risks and how to control them. Suggest a suitable context, e.g. a manufacturer of sugar syrup needing to decide on the best temperature at which to use carbohydrase enzyme to break down starch. See the **B2 ISA practice 2 Student research notes sheet.**

3 Ask two students to read their notes on one of the points. Get the class to decide whose notes are best, with a reason. Repeat until all the points are covered.

4 Give students the **B2 ISA practice 2 Section 1 paper**.

5 In a following lesson students set up their investigation and record and process their results. Students can work in groups to obtain the data. If several groups have used the same method they may wish to pool results and obtain a mean. Please refer to the **B2 ISA practice 2 Student practical sheet**.

6 Students should process the data individually in controlled conditions. A bar chart or graph should be plotted and the trend of the graph/bar chart identified and a conclusion made.

7 The conclusion should be compared with their hypothesis to identity if their hypothesis has been confirmed or denied.

Plenaries

1 Students discuss sources of possible errors and ways to overcome them.

2 Give students the B2 **ISA practice 2 Section 2 paper.**

Homework

After the practical, ask students to write brief notes about ways in which they could improve their investigation. They should mention how to reduce errors and what further data or information they would need to confirm their conclusion.

Points to note

- Students should describe a complex relationship between the independent variable and the dependent variable.
- Depending on how closely you wish to mirror the real ISA experience all three parts can be done in class or some can be done for homework. You should adjust delivery to match the time that it takes to obtain meaningful results.

Route to A*

Students' risk assessment should include sensible risks, with a clear indication of the likelihood of the hazard occurring and how to sensibly control the risk.

Ask students to critically evaluate their data and explain that the findings are only valid within the range of the independent variable, whose range may be quite limited.

Answers to Student Book questions

5 **(a)** Both axes labelled. (1) A suitable curve/line drawn. (1) Indication (arrow or numbers) of direction of increase in value of axes. (1)

(b) The student states that data in Study 1 strongly supports the original hypothesis and quotes some data from tables that supports this. (1)

Critical appraisal of data to include data for Study Groups 2 and 3 show the same pattern, although there are significant differences in some of the times. (1)

A statement is made that indicates that the candidate realises that Case Study 2 is inappropriate because the investigation does not involve a change of temperature.

N.B. If Study 2 has been used inappropriately at any point during the student's answer then one mark should be deducted as the data is irrelevant in this context. (1)

(c) Suggests at least one other piece of information that would be needed to form a firm conclusion. The reason for the need for this other information is clearly stated. (3)

(d) Comment that the investigation plotted relative activity, rather than time taken. Comment that the graph shows a similar pattern, but that the bacterial enzyme has a higher optimum temperature. (3)

For the full mark scheme, see the Teacher and Technician Planning Pack.

B3 1.1 Diffusion and osmosis

Link to the Specification

B3.1.1b Water often moves across boundaries by osmosis. Osmosis is the diffusion of water from a dilute to a more concentrated solution through a partially permeable membrane that allows the passage of water molecules.

B3.1.1c Differences in the concentrations of the solutions inside and outside a cell cause water to move into or out of the cell by osmosis.

How Science Works

CA: B4.1.1 Develop hypotheses and plan practical ways to test them, by: a) being able to make predictions based on a hypothesis; b) being able to test hypotheses; c) using appropriate technology; B4.4.2 Demonstrate an understanding of how data may be displayed, by: a) drawing tables; b) drawing charts and graphs; c) choosing the most appropriate form of presentation. B4.5.4 Draw conclusions using scientific ideas and evidence, by: a) writing a conclusion, based on evidence that relates correctly to known facts; b) using secondary sources; c) identifying extra evidence that is required for a conclusion to be made; d) evaluating methods of data collection.

B3 1.1 Diffusion and osmosis

Learning objectives

- explain that osmosis is the movement of water across a partially permeable membrane from a dilute solution to a more concentrated solution
- interpret information about the effect of solutions of different concentrations on plant and animal cells.

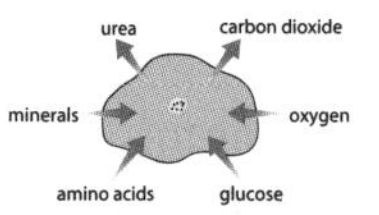

Figure 1 Substances entering and leaving a cell.

Examiner feedback

Be clear when writing about concentration gradients. 'Along' a concentration gradient could mean movement in either direction. 'Down' a concentration can only mean towards the lower concentration.

Taking it further

Cell membranes have specialised molecules called carrier proteins and channel proteins to enable certain molecules and ions to diffuse through. Diffusion via these proteins is called 'facilitated diffusion'.

Movement in and out of cells

Many different types of substance move in and out of the cells of living organisms. Figure 1 shows some of the substances that regularly pass in and out of cells. All cells are surrounded by a cell membrane. It forms a barrier that any substance entering or leaving a cell must pass through. There are three main ways in which substances move in and out of cells: **diffusion**, **osmosis** and **active transport**.

Molecules of gases, such as oxygen and carbon dioxide, are moving about all the time. The molecules of a solution, such as glucose dissolved in water, are also moving in all directions. When molecules move, they spread themselves out evenly. This causes them to move from a higher concentration to a lower concentration until the concentrations become the same. This process is called diffusion. As they move from a higher to a lower concentration, molecules diffuse down a **concentration gradient**. Most substances move into and out of cells by diffusion.

Osmosis

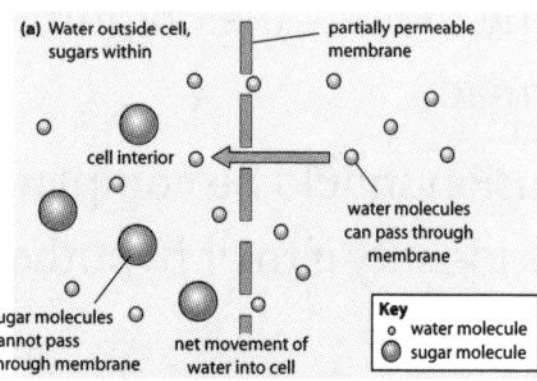

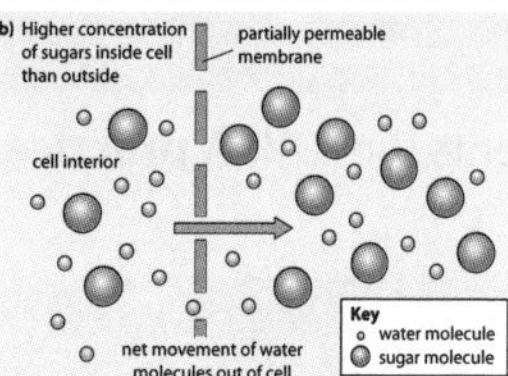

Figure 2 Osmosis.

Water molecules can diffuse through partially permeable membranes, but sugar molecules and most ions generally cannot. A cell membrane has specialised molecules to enable some ions and molecules to move into the cell.

A dilute solution contains more water molecules than a concentrated solution. If a partially permeable membrane separates two solutions of different concentrations, there will be net movement of water molecules from the dilute solution to the concentrated solution. Diffusion of water molecules across a partially permeable membrane is called osmosis.

Osmosis explains the movement of water molecules across plant and animal cell membranes. In a plant, water moves from the soil into root-hair cells, because soil water is a more dilute solution than the solution in the cytoplasm of the cell.

Osmosis also happens between animal cells. However, animal cells have no strong cell wall to protect them, so if too much water enters them they burst. If animal or plant cells lose too much water, the cytoplasm shrinks and the cells cannot function properly.

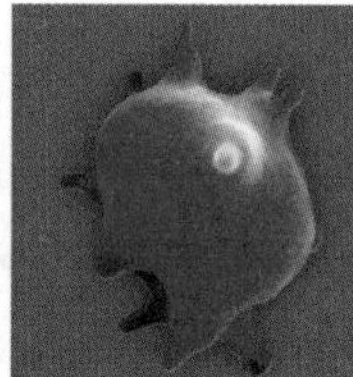

The blood cell in the left-hand photo was in a dilute solution. The right-hand photo shows a blood cell that has changed because it was in a concentrated solution.

Questions

1. What is meant by a 'partially permeable membrane'?
2. What is meant by 'concentration gradient'?
3. Explain how cell membranes control the particles that pass through them.
4. A person drinks a large volume of water very quickly. What effect will this have on the red cells in the blood? Explain why.
5. If we place animal cells in pure water they burst. But plant cells do not burst. Explain why.
6. If a person loses a lot of blood they are given a transfusion of a solution containing ions. What concentration should this solution of ions be? Give the reason for your answer.
7. To prepare fruit salad, a cook cuts up different types of fruit and sprinkles sugar over the pieces. After two hours the fruit is surrounded by syrup (concentrated sugar solution). Explain why.
8. Water moves from the soil into a root hair cell and then through other cells towards the centre of a root. Explain this in terms of osmosis.

Examiner feedback

Remember that the cell wall is permeable to water, ions and sugars. It therefore takes no part in osmosis.

Taking it further

As water continues to enter plant cells by osmosis, the cell contents begin to exert a pressure on the cell wall. This is known as **turgor** pressure. In young plants turgor pressure is the main means of support. When plant cells are placed in a concentrated solution, water leaves the cytoplasm and vacuole by osmosis. Eventually the cytoplasm begins to shrink away from the cell wall. This is known as **plasmolysis**.

Science in action

The main problem facing people on lifeboats in the open ocean is dehydration, even though they are surrounded by water. This is because the concentration of **ions** in seawater is about four times greater than that in our body fluids. Drinking one litre of seawater causes the concentration of ions in our body fluids to rise by about 10 per cent. The effect of the rise is to cause water to move out of the body cells by osmosis, making the cells shrink.

Many lifeboats are now equipped with a reverse osmosis machine to provide drinking water from salt water. Figure 3 shows how it works.

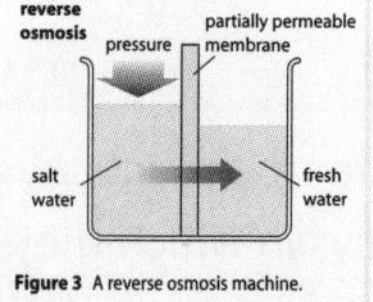

Figure 3 A reverse osmosis machine.

184 Exchanges 185

Learning objectives

Most students should be able to:

- explain that osmosis is the movement of water across a partially permeable membrane from a dilute solution to a more concentrated solution
- describe how water moves between cells by osmosis.

Some students should also be able to:

- explain plasmolysis and turgor. [Ext]

ActiveTeach Resource: Osmosis in plant cells – *Interactive quiz*

Key points

Diffusion is the movement of molecules or ions down a concentration gradient.

Osmosis is the movement of water molecules through a partially permeable membrane from a dilute solution to a more concentrated solution.

Differences in the concentrations of the solutions inside and outside a cell cause water to move into or out of the cell by osmosis.

Diffusion osmosis partially permeable membrane

Lesson activities

Starter

1 Produce a spider diagram to show exchanges in living organisms. Build up the diagram on a flipchart or whiteboard. An example is shown on **Teacher sheet B3 1.1a**.

2 Show the students some dry seeds and some soaked seeds, such as peas. Ask them to explain how the dry seeds have been converted to the other (soaked) seeds and about how the molecules of water moved.

Main

1 Students use **worksheet B3 1.1b Osmosis planning sheet** to help them plan an investigation to study the relationship between the rate of osmosis and concentration of sucrose.

2 B3 1.1c Osmosis In this practical activity, students use Visking tubing to demonstrate osmosis. By giving each group a different concentration of sucrose solution, data for the relationship between sucrose concentration and osmosis can be obtained. (~60 mins)

3 Worksheet B3 1.1d Explaining osmosis consolidates understanding of partially permeable membranes.

Plenaries

1 Collect data from students' experiments and use to prepare class results table and graph.

2 Class quiz: 'Osmosis in plant cells' from ActiveTeach. [AT]

Homework

1 Worksheet B3 1.1e consolidates understanding of osmosis and introduces osmoregulation.

2 Students could research other methods of osmoregulation in animals.

Points to note

- The lesson should build on ideas of diffusion which students covered in B2.
- The idea of net movement through a partially permeable membrane should be consolidated.

Route to A*

The ideas of turgor and plasmolysis outlined in the Student Book could be introduced to the more able students.

Answers to Student Book questions

1 A membrane that lets some substances through, but not others.

2 A region where the concentration of a substance varies from higher to lower.

3 They have specialised molecules to allow certain substances through.

4 The red blood cells swell up. The water the person drinks enters the blood, making it more dilute than the inside of the red blood cells. Water therefore enters the cells by osmosis, and they swell.

5 Plant cells have a cellulose wall outside the cell membrane that stops them from bursting. Animal cells do not have a cell wall.

6 The solution should have the same concentration of ions as the blood to ensure that blood cells and body cells do not shrink or burst.

7 The sugar dissolves in moisture on the cut surfaces of the fruit, forming a very concentrated solution. This solution is more concentrated than the solution in the fruit cells so water leaves the cells via osmosis, producing the syrup.

8 The concentration of the solution inside a root hair cell is greater than that of the solution in the soil. Water enters the root hair cell by osmosis. This movement of water makes the solution inside the root hair cell less concentrated than that in the adjacent root cell, so water moves from the root hair cell into the adjacent cell by osmosis. The same sequence of processes takes place between the next two cells. A concentration gradient is set up across the cells in the root and the water moves down this concentration gradient towards the centre of the root.

B3 1.2

Sports drinks and active transport

Link to the Specification

B3.1.1a Dissolved substances move by diffusion and by active transport.

B3.1.1c Differences in the concentrations of the solutions inside and outside a cell cause water to move into or out of the cell by osmosis.

B3.1.1d Most soft drinks contain water, sugar and ions.

B3.1.1e Sports drinks contain sugars to replace the sugar used in energy release during the activity. They also contain water and ions to replace the water and ions lost during sweating.

B3.1.1f If water and ions are not replaced, the ion/water balance of the body is disturbed and the cells do not work as efficiently.

B3.1.1g Substances are sometimes absorbed against a concentration gradient. This requires the use of energy from respiration. The process is called active transport. Active transport enables cells to absorb ions from very dilute solutions.

How Science Works

SKU: B3.1 bullet point 2: Evaluate the claims of manufacturers about sports drinks.

CA: B4.1.1 Candidates should be able to appreciate that technology such as data logging may provide a better means of obtaining data. They should be able to suggest appropriate technology for collecting data and explain why a particular technological method is the most appropriate.

B4.4.2 demonstrate an understanding of how data may be displayed, by:

- drawing tables
- drawing charts and graphs
- choosing the most appropriate form of presentation.

B4.5.3 identify patterns in data, by:

- Describing the relationship between two variables and deciding whether the relationship is causal or by association.

B3 1.2

Sports drinks and active transport

Learning objectives

- explain why some sports drinks improve performance
- evaluate the claims of manufacturers about sports drinks
- explain the process of active transport.

Rehydration

When we sweat we lose a lot of water, but not quite as many ions. The concentration of ions in sweat is about 1–2 g per litre, which is less than in blood. This leaves us with more ions in our blood than normal. If the balance of ions and water changes in our bodies, cells do not work as efficiently.

Any type of drink will help you to **rehydrate** (replace the water you have lost).

Most soft drinks consist mainly of water, with sugar and flavourings added. Some also contain ions, but the concentration of sugars and ions varies enormously between soft drinks. The sugar content can vary between zero and over 100 g per can, and sodium ions between zero and 150 mg per can. It is important that drinks contain sodium ions since sodium ions are essential for the healthy functioning of most of the body's cells.

Athletes in endurance events such as the marathon need to replace the water and ions they lose as they exercise. Sports drinks help athletes to replace both water and ions as quickly as possible. Athletes also need to replace the glucose that is taken from the blood by the muscles during exercise. The glucose is used to release energy via respiration. Most athletes will drink sports drinks during an event. All sports drinks contain water and ions. Most sports drinks also contain sugar (usually glucose).

Research has shown that the most effective sports drinks contain between 6% and 8% sugar and 120 mg/l sodium ions. Drinks containing these concentrations of sugar and sodium ions are absorbed more quickly than other drinks.

Science in action

Water intoxication (hyponatremia), is caused by drinking excessive amounts of plain water, which causes a low concentration of sodium in the blood. Research has found that, in long-duration endurance events such as ultra-marathons, many competitors finish with low blood sodium concentrations. Those at most risk are those who are on the course the longest, because they tend to drink the most water during the event. Runners who drink extra fluids in the days before the race or those who stop at water stops during the race are also at increased risk of hyponatremia. Investigations have also shown that about 15% of marathon finishers develop hyponatremia from drinking too much water.

Athletes in long-distance endurance events are advised to:

- use sports drinks containing sodium during the event
- increase their daily salt intake several days prior to the event
- try not to drink more than they sweat: about 1 cup of fluid every 20 minutes.

Science skills

Sports scientists investigated the effect of different drinks on the performance of cyclists. The cyclists were given one of four different types of drink and asked to cycle 8 km as fast as possible. The graph shows the results of the investigation.

a Suggest the composition of the placebo.

b **(i)** Which was the most effective drink?

(ii) Suggest why this was the most effective drink.

Time taken to cycle 8 km/min: 12, 11.5, 11, 10.5, 10, 9.5, 9

Drink

high fluid, low sugar
low fluid, high sugar
high fluid, high sugar
placebo drink

Figure 1 Results of sports drink investigation.

186

Active transport

Sometimes the body cells need to move substances from an area of lower concentration to an area of higher concentration. This means moving them against a concentration gradient. This requires energy, which is supplied by respiration. The energy is used to move substances through special channels in the cell membrane. Moving molecules using energy from respiration is called **active transport**. Respiration is carried out in the mitochondria, so cells that use energy for active transport have lots of mitochondria.

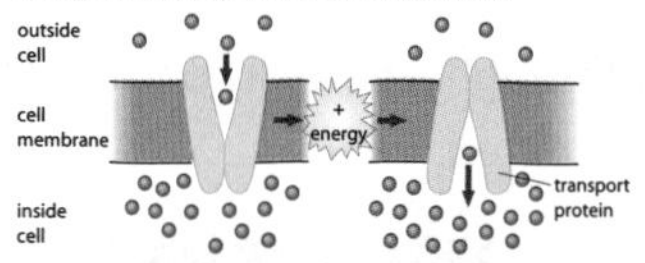

Figure 2 Special proteins create channels for active transport in the cell membrane.

Plants need nitrate ions to make proteins for growth. There is a very low concentration of nitrate ions in soil water surrounding the root. Plants use energy to actively transport nitrate ions across the cell membrane into root cells, against a concentration gradient.

Why do you lose a lot of sweat during a good workout?

Science in action

Posters for a sports drink say that it is the 'water designed for exercise'. The eye-catching television advert for this drink shows an athlete made of water, running, doing cartwheels and back flips, diving into a large pool and swimming away. A voice says: 'Imagine water redesigned for exercise and for better hydration than water alone.' The drink contains 2 g carbohydrate and 35 mg sodium per 100 ml, and provides 10 calories. The ingredients are: water, glucose syrup, citric acid, acidity regulators, flavouring, sweeteners and vitamins.

c Are the makers of this sports drink justified in calling it 'water redesigned for exercise'? Explain the reasons for your answer.

Examiner feedback

Questions on active transport often test your understanding of mitochondria and respiration. If a cell has greater than normal numbers of mitochondria, it has a greater rate of respiration and releases greater amounts of energy. So, cells whose main function is actively transporting substances will have greater numbers of mitochondria.

Sometimes you will be given data involving the use of respiratory poisons. Remember that if respiration stops, active transport will also stop.

Questions

1. What are the main constituents of soft drinks?
2. What are the main differences between a soft drink and a sports drink?
3. Explain why losing a lot of sweat can affect an athlete's performance.
4. Explain why drinking a sports drink can improve an athlete's performance.
5. Give two differences between osmosis and active transport.
6. **(a)** Explain what is meant by 'against their concentration gradient'. **(b)** Why can't this movement be accomplished by diffusion?
7. **(a)** Which organelles in a cell carry out the reactions of respiration? **(b)** Suggest how you would identify a cell that carries out a lot of active transport.
8. Some manufacturers produce drinks containing 'super-oxygenated water'. The manufacturers claim that the extra oxygen in these drinks improves performance by up to 35%. Scientists investigated what happened when runners thought they were getting a performance boost in the form of super-oxygenated water. The athletes completed three separately run 5 km time trials, with half the group drinking a large glass of plain bottled water and the others taking what they thought was super-oxygenated water (but was, in fact, tap water) before they started. Results showed that runners covered the distance an average of 83 seconds faster when they thought they were drinking super-oxygenated water.

   Evaluate the report of the above investigation.

A*

Exchanges 187

Learning objectives

Most students should be able to:

- explain the movement of substances across cell membranes
- explain what is meant by active transport and explain its importance to living organisms
- describe the functions of sports drinks.

Some students should also be able to:

- evaluate manufacturers' claims about sports drinks. [Ext]

ActiveTeach Resource: Do sports drinks boost performance? – *Interactive debating activity*

Key points

Sports drinks contain sugars to replace the sugar used in energy release during the activity. They also contain water and ions to replace the water and ions lost during sweating.

If water and ions are not replaced, the ion/water balance of the body is disturbed and the cells do not work as efficiently.

Substances are sometimes absorbed against a concentration gradient. This requires the use of energy from respiration. The process is called active transport.

Active transport rehydration

Lesson activities

Starter

1 Start with some exercise e.g. running on the spot, star jumps or press ups. Be aware of health problems and advise these students to do gentler exercise. Keep students exercising until they are sweating, about 5 minutes. Discuss effects that losing sweat will have on body functioning.

Main

1 B3 1.2a Movement of ions In this activity students measure the rate of movement of ions through a membrane. (~60 mins)

2 B3 1.2b Movement across membranes This worksheet introduces the concept of active transport.

Plenaries

1 Collect ideas on the similarities and differences between diffusion, osmosis and active transport.

2 Use the ActiveTeach debating activity: Do pupils agree that sports drinks boost performance? [AT]

Homework

1 Worksheet B3 1.2c helps students to understand the use of sports drinks and to evaluate manufacturers' claims about sports drinks.

2 More able students might research the science underlying oral rehydration fluids in the treatment of cholera.

Points to note

- The main point to establish with pupils is that osmosis and diffusion involve net movement down a concentration gradient without the need for energy from respiration, whereas active transport is movement against a concentration gradient with the aid of energy from respiration.

Route to A*

Students could research the role of active transport in kidney functioning.

Answers to Student Book questions

Science skills

a Water and a synthetic sweetener.

b **i** High fluid, high sugar.

ii High sugar replaces the glucose used for energy; high fluid is best for rehydration.

c No, for the following reasons: the drink is a solution, not just water; it contains some sugar and sodium ions so it would be of some help, but the sugar concentration (2%) is below the optimum for rehydration (6–8%).

Answers

1 Water, sugar and ions.

2 The concentrations of sugar and ions in sports drinks are carefully chosen for maximum rehydration and replacement of sugar and ions. Most soft drinks contain too high a concentration of sugars to be effective.

3 The concentration of ions in the blood rises, causing water to leave the cells by osmosis. The shrunken cells work less efficiently.

4 Sports drinks replace the glucose used in releasing energy. They contain water and ions to replace those lost in sweat.

5 Osmosis is movement of water down a concentration gradient. Active transport is the movement of a substance against a concentration gradient. Active transport requires energy from respiration; osmosis does not.

6 **(a)** Movement from a region of low concentration to a region of high concentration. **(b)** Movement against a concentration gradient requires energy from respiration.

7 **(a)** Mitochondria. **(b)** It would have large number of mitochondria.

8 There is no mention of controls – were the runners matched for factors such as age, gender, fitness? There is no mention of the number of athletes – was the number high enough for reliable results? Although a placebo was used, it is best practice that neither scientists nor runners know which drink is the placebo (a double-blind trial). No runners were actually given 'super-oxygenated water'. The trial was repeated three times – this reduces the chance of anomalous results. The results show a placebo effect – runners were faster when they thought the drink was super-oxygenated.

B3 1.3 Exchanges in humans

Link to the Specification

B3.1.1h Many organ systems are specialised for exchanging materials. The effectiveness of an exchange surface is increased by:

- having a large surface area
- being thin, to provide a short diffusion path
- (in animals) having an efficient blood supply
- (in animals, for gaseous exchange) being ventilated.

B3.1.1i Gas and solute exchange surfaces in humans and other organisms are adapted to maximise effectiveness.

B3.1.1j The size and complexity of an organism increases the difficulty of exchanging materials.

B3.1.1k In humans:

- the surface area of the lungs is increased by the alveoli
- the surface area of the small intestine is increased by villi.

B3.1.1l The villi provide a large surface area with an extensive network of capillaries to absorb the products of digestion by diffusion and active transport.

How Science Works

CA: B4.3.1 Make observations, by: carrying out practical work and research, and using the data collected to develop hypotheses.

B3 1.3 Exchanges in humans

Learning objectives

- explain why the size and complexity of an organism increases the difficulty of exchanging materials
- explain how gas and solute exchange surfaces in humans and other organisms are adapted to maximise effectiveness
- explain how the human lung and small intestine are adapted for exchanging materials.

Size and exchanges

Living organisms must exchange substances with the environment. Diffusion is only efficient over short distances, so larger organisms have evolved other mechanisms for exchanging substances.

Small multicellular organisms have adapted by increasing their surface area and decreasing the distance substances have to diffuse. For example, tapeworms live in the intestines of animals. Their bodies are composed of hundreds of flat segments. Being long and flat gives the tapeworm a very large surface area. This allows them to absorb soluble food directly from their surroundings. Being flat means that the distance food has to diffuse to reach the centre of each segment is very short. At no point in a tapeworm's body does food have to diffuse further than 0.1 mm.

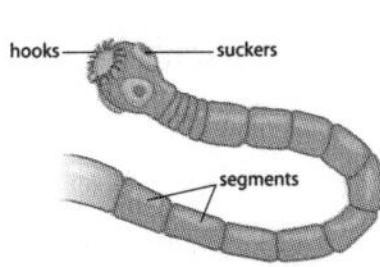

Figure 1 Tapeworms live in intestines and absorb the soluble foods that surround them.

In larger organisms diffusion cannot supply the cells at the centre of the body with food and oxygen. Humans and other mammals have overcome this problem by evolving specialised organs with internal surfaces, such as **alveoli** in the lungs and **villi** in the intestines. Animals with internal exchange surfaces usually have a blood system to transport materials between the exchange surfaces and the tissues.

Alveoli

As you breathe you take in the oxygen you need for respiration, and you also get rid of waste carbon dioxide. In your lungs you exchange the oxygen you need for the carbon dioxide you don't need. This is called gas exchange.

Oxygen and carbon dioxide diffuse rapidly between the air in your lungs and your blood. This is because your lungs are highly specialised for exchanging gases. To carry out gas exchange efficiently, the surface of your lungs needs to have the following features.

- Thin walls so that gases diffuse across only a short distance.
- A good blood supply to transport oxygen and carbon dioxide to and from body tissues.
- A large surface area for diffusion.

Examiner feedback

Do not confuse surface area with surface area to volume ratio (see lesson B1 4.2). Remember that a *large* organism has a large surface area, but a *small* surface area to volume ratio.

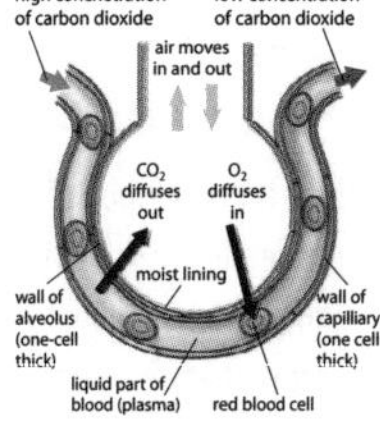

Figure 2 Airway, alveoli and blood supply.

Figure 3 Gas exchange in a single alveolus.

Figure 2 shows the relationship between aveoli and the blood system. Your breathing system takes air in and out of your body. This provides a regular supply of air containing oxygen, and removes air containing carbon dioxide.

The airways of the breathing system end in very small air sacs called alveoli. The walls of the alveoli are where gas exchange happens, and they provide an extremely large surface area for gas exchange. The total surface area of all the alveoli is about 80 m^2. You can see from Figure 3 that the alveolar walls are only one cell thick and each alveolus is surrounded by blood capillaries. The air in each alveolus is very close to the blood flowing in capillaries. This means that oxygen has to diffuse only a short distance to move from the alveolus into the bloodstream, and carbon dioxide has to diffuse only a short distance in the opposite direction.

Villi

The wall of your small intestine is very efficient at absorbing food. It is a specialised tissue for absorption. The small intestine can absorb food efficiently for the following reasons.

- Its inner surface contains many tiny folds called villi. The large number of villi produces a very large surface area for absorption.
- Each villus contains many blood capillaries to transport absorbed food from the small intestine to the rest of the body.
- Each villus is very thin, so that food molecules diffuse over only a short distance to reach the bloodstream. Figure 4 shows how these features allow absorption to take place efficiently.

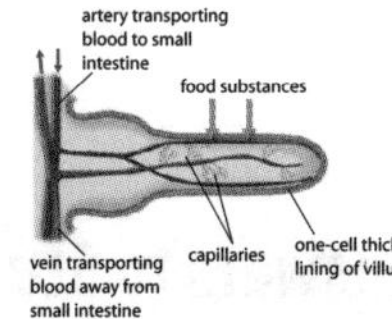

Figure 4 How a villus absorbs food. Each cell of the villus wall has microvilli that further increase the surface area for absorption.

Soluble foods molecules are absorbed into the outer cells of the villi by both diffusion and active transport (see lesson B3 1.2). The soluble food molecules are then moved to the blood capillaries. The blood system distributes the soluble food molecules to the rest of the body.

Questions

1. Explain the effect of having millions of alveoli in the lungs.
2. What features of the alveoli provide a short diffusion pathway?
3. Food molecules diffuse over a short distance to reach the blood. What features of the small intestine provide the short diffusion distance?
4. **(a)** Suggest how steep concentration gradients for oxygen and carbon dioxide are maintained in the lungs. **(b)** Explain why this is important for effective gas exchange in the lungs.
5. What features of the small intestine maintain a concentration gradient of food molecules?
6. Describe one feature of the villus cell that indicates that some food molecules are absorbed by active transport.
7. Explain the advantage of having lining cells with a highly folded cell membrane.
8. Explain fully how large animals have evolved to cope with the problem of exchanging materials with the environment.
   Include information on:
   - how the surface area available for absorption is increased transport mechanisms
   - removal of waste substances from tissues.

A*

188

Exchanges 189

Learning objectives

Students should be able to:

- explain how alveoli are adapted for effective gaseous exchange
- explain how villi are adapted for effective absorption of food.

ActiveTeach Resource: Gas exchange by diffusion – *Interactive labelling activity*

Key points

Large organisms have developed exchange surfaces and transport systems for efficient exchange of materials with the environment.

The effectiveness of an exchange surface is increased by:

- having a large surface area
- being thin, to provide a short diffusion path
- (in animals) having an efficient blood supply
- (in animals) being ventilated.

Alveoli villi capillaries

Lesson activities

Starter

1 B3 1.3a part 1: Teacher demonstration of dissection of fresh lungs of an animal such as a lamb. Show the students the spongy nature of the lungs, the trachea, branching network of bronchi and bronchioles.

Main

1 B3 1.3a part 2: Surface area and rate of diffusion Demonstration using different diameters of Visking tubing and a food dye solution to show that the greater the surface area the greater the rate of diffusion.

2 The ActiveTeach activity shows students how diffusion of gases takes place in the lungs, allowing carbon dioxide to be eliminated and oxygen to be absorbed. [AT]

3 If you have a 5-metre rope or flexible pipe, use it to demonstrate the length of the average human small intestine. Alternatively, get three students to lie down in a long line to give an idea of the length that you are describing. With the rope or pipe, students can attempt to 'pack' it so that it fits within the space of the abdomen. More able students could attempt to estimate the surface area of the inside of the small intestine if there was no folding. This will help give an idea of just how much the villi and microvilli increase the surface area.

4 Show slides of sections through lungs to see alveoli and sections of small intestine to see villi.

5 Worksheet B3 1.3b requires students to mark adaptations of villi on a diagram, then describe how the adaptations enhance the function of the villi.

Plenaries

1 Ask students to list the exchange features of alveoli and villi then compare the way in which each surface is adapted as an exchange surface.

Homework

1 Not all the food substances that are absorbed in the gut are absorbed in the small intestine. Students could research the few substances that are absorbed in the stomach, such as alcohol and aspirin, and try to find out why this is possible.

2 Alternatively, students could research the effect of diet on the intestine length, particularly in animals that vary their diet through the year, such as voles.

3 Worksheet B3 1.3c covers Fick's law and emphysema (this goes beyond the specification).

Points to note

- Most students have difficulty with surface area to volume ratio. They should appreciate that the larger an organism, the larger its surface area. But whereas surface increases by the square of the dimension, volume increases by the cube, so the ratio of surface area to volume decreases as organisms increase in size.

Route to A*

Worksheet B3 1.3d considers adaptations for exchange in fish gills.

Answers to Student Book questions

1 They provide a large surface area for gas exchange.

2 The walls are one cell thick. They are very close to blood capillaries.

3 The intestinal lining is one cell thick. The lining is very close to blood capillaries.

4 **(a)** The air is continually replaced by breathing in and out. Oxygen that diffuses into the blood is moved away as the blood circulates. **(b)** The steeper the diffusion gradient the faster the rate of diffusion.

5 As food diffuses into the blood it is moved away as the blood circulates.

6 It has large numbers of mitochondria.

7 The surface area of the intestinal wall is increased, increasing the rate of diffusion.

8 Diffusion is only effective over short distances. As larger animals evolved they developed internal exchange surfaces, such as alveoli and villi for gas exchange and absorption of food, respectively. Substances absorbed by these surfaces are transported to other parts of the body by a blood system. Similarly, waste substances, such as carbon dioxide, are transported from the tissues to the exchange surface to be excreted.

B3 1.4 Gaseous exchange in humans

Link to the Specification

B3.1.2a The lungs are in the upper part of the body (thorax), protected by the ribcage and separated from the lower part of the body (abdomen) by the diaphragm.

B3.1.2b The breathing system takes air into and out of the body so that oxygen from the air can diffuse into the bloodstream and carbon dioxide can diffuse out of the bloodstream into the air.

B3.1.2c To make air move into the lungs the ribcage moves out and up and the diaphragm becomes flatter. These changes are reversed to make air move out of the lungs. The movement of air into and out of the lungs is known as ventilation.

How Science Works

SKU: B3.1 bullet point 1: Evaluate the development and use of artificial aids to breathing, including the use of artificial ventilators.

CA: B4.1.1: Develop hypotheses and plan practical ways to test them, by: a) being able to make predictions based on a hypothesis; b) being able to test hypotheses; c) using appropriate technology.

B4.2.1: Assess and manage risks when carrying out practical work, by: a) identifying some possible hazards in practical situations; b) managing risks.

B4.3.2: Demonstrate an understanding of the need to acquire high quality data, by: a) appreciating that, unless certain variables are controlled, the results may not be valid; b) identifying when repeats are needed in order to improve reliability; c) recognising the value of repeated readings to establish accuracy; d) considering the resolution of the measuring device.

B4.4.2: Demonstrate an understanding of how data may be displayed, by: a) drawing tables; b) drawing charts and graphs; c) choosing the most appropriate form of presentation.

B3 1.4 Gaseous exchange in humans

Learning objectives

- describe the structure of the human breathing organs
- explain how the action of muscles causes air to enter and leave the lungs
- evaluate the development and use of artificial aids to breathing, including the use of artificial ventilators.

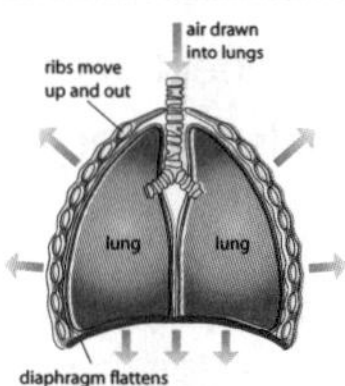

air forced out of lungs

ribs move down and in

lung

lung

diaphragm curves back up

Figure 1 Breathing in (top) and out (bottom).

Breathing

Your lungs are in the upper part of your body, your **thorax**, protected by the **ribcage**. Below the lungs is a sheet of fibre and muscle called the **diaphragm** that separates the thorax from the **abdomen** below. Movements of the ribcage and diaphragm cause you to breathe in and out. The movement of air in and out of the lungs is known as **ventilation**.

To breathe in, two sets of muscles contract at the same time.

- The **intercostal muscles** (muscles between the ribs) contract, pulling the ribs upwards and outwards.
- The diaphragm muscles contract, pulling the central part of the diaphragm downwards.

These changes in the position of the ribs and diaphragm increase the volume of the thorax and expand the lungs. Increasing the volume of a gas decreases its pressure, so the air inside the lungs is now at a lower pressure than the air outside the body. The difference in pressure causes air to move from the outside into the lungs. The process of breathing in is known as **inspiration**.

To breathe out, both the diaphragm and the intercostal muscles relax. Elastic recoil of the lungs and the thorax wall return the lungs to their original size. This decreases the volume of air in the lungs. The pressure of the air inside the lungs is now greater than that of the air outside, so air moves out of the lungs. This process is known as **expiration**.

Some of the air in your lungs is replaced each time you breathe. This keeps a relatively high concentration of oxygen and a relatively low concentration of carbon dioxide in the lungs. At the same time the blood in the capillaries is continually circulating, bringing blood to the lungs with a high concentration of carbon dioxide and a low concentration of oxygen.

Artificial aids to breathing.

A healthy person breathes automatically twenty-four hours each day. However, spontaneous breathing may stop due to disease or injury. If this happens, the patient can be helped to breathe using a mechanical device. There are two main types of device: a machine called a ventilator and a bag that can be compressed manually.

There are two types of ventilator: **negative-pressure ventilators** which cause air to be 'sucked' into the lungs and **positive-pressure ventilators** which force air into the lungs.

Examiner feedback

Do not confuse respiration and breathing. Breathing is the movement of air into and out of the lungs. Respiration is the series of reactions that occur inside cells to release energy from sugars.

Negative-pressure ventilators

The first type of negative-pressure ventilator was the **iron lung**. This type of ventilator was first produced during the 1920s. It was developed for widespread use during epidemics of **poliomyelitis** in the 1940s. In some cases of poliomyelitis, the nerves supplying the breathing muscles ceased to function

190

and the patient stopped breathing. Iron lungs kept many of these patients alive, often for long periods, until the patients recovered.

An iron lung is essentially a large tank enclosing the whole of a patient's body except for the head and the neck. A rubber seal around the patient's neck keeps the tank airtight. A pump removes air from the tank, creating a vacuum. This causes the patient's thorax to expand. Pressure in the lungs decreases, and air from outside moves into the lungs. The vacuum is then released and elastic recoil of the lungs and thorax forces air out of the lungs.

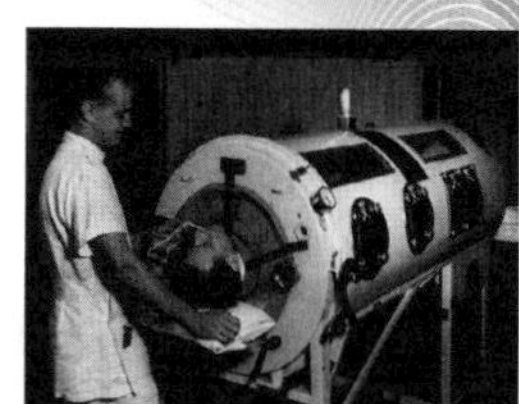

An iron lung in use in the 1920s.

Positive-pressure ventilators

Positive-pressure ventilators were first developed during the 1950s. These machines force air into a patient's lungs through a metal tube inserted through the mouth into the windpipe. The ventilator is most commonly used in operations, during which a patient's muscles are deliberately made to relax to make surgery easier. It is also used to sustain breathing of patients in intensive care units. For long-term use the tube is inserted surgically through the neck into the trachea.

A modern ventilator.

Hand-controlled ventilators

The most common type of hand-controlled ventilator is the bag-mouth-mask ventilator. These ventilators are most often used by paramedics as **resuscitators** to help patients who have stopped breathing after accidents or drug overdoses. Air is supplied via a bag, which can be squeezed manually or operated by a pump.

Questions

1. What is meant by ventilation?
2. Name the muscles that bring about ventilation.
3. Explain the mechanism of inspiration in terms of pressure and volume changes.
4. Explain why air moves out of the lungs during expiration.
5. Explain why some patients who get poliomyelitis need artificial ventilation.
6. Explain how paramedics resuscitate a person who has stopped breathing.
7. Describe how the treatment of breathing failure has changed over the years.
8. Explain how an iron lung keeps a patient alive.
9. Compare and contrast the iron lung and the positive-pressure ventilator machine for long-term care of patients.

A*

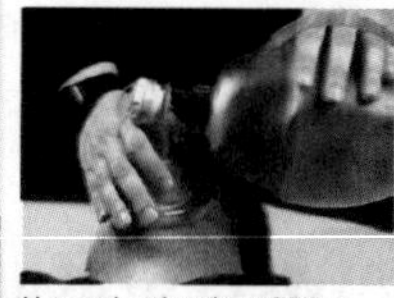

A bag-mouth-mask ventilator or BVM is a normal part of the rescuscitatioj kit for an ambulance crew.

Exchanges 191

Learning objectives

Most students should be able to:

- describe how the breathing system takes air into and out of the body.
- evaluate the development and use of artificial ventilators.

Some students should also be able to:

- explain breathing movements in terms of pressure and volume changes. [Ext]

ActiveTeach Resource: Breathe out… and in again

– Interactive ordering activity

Key points

Inspiration: contraction of the diaphragm and intercostal muscles causes the ribcage to rise and the diaphragm to flatten. These changes cause an increase in the volume of the lungs and a decrease in pressure.

Expiration: the diaphragm and intercostals muscles relax. Elastic recoil forces air out of the lungs.

In an iron lung a pump draws air out of the space around the patient's body, creating a drop in pressure, which results in air being drawn into the patient's lungs.

Positive pressure ventilators force air into a patient's lungs.

Thorax abdomen diaphragm intercostal muscles negative pressure ventilator positive pressure ventilator

Lesson activities

Starter

1 Ask students to put their hands on their chest and take a deep breath in and then out. Ask them to describe the movements of the rib cage during their breathing. Then ask them to place one hand on their chest and one on their abdomen and see whether they can breathe in and out without moving the rib cage. What other part of the body moves with the breath during this kind of breathing?

2 A demonstration using the apparatus shown opposite will help to reinforce the importance of the diaphragm in breathing and the fact that breathing in and out is the result of movements of the diaphragm and rib cage rather than the other way around.

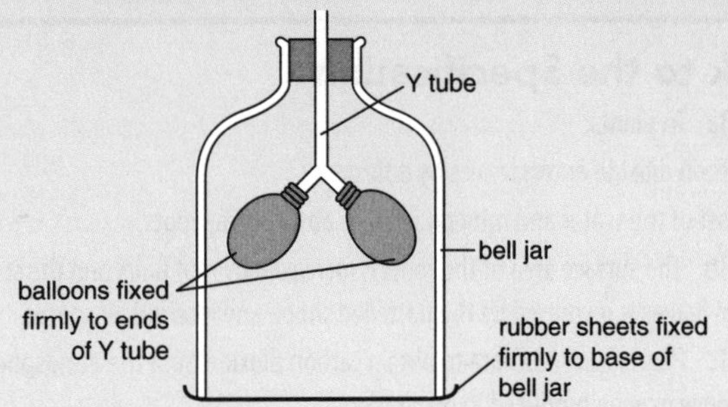

3 The ActiveTeach ordering activity demonstrates the stages of ventilation. [AT]

Main

1 **B3 1.4a Measuring vital capacity** In this activity students design an investigation to compare vital capacity amongst members of the class.

2 **B1.4b Vital capacity** In this activity students carry out the investigation they planned. (~40 mins)

Plenaries

1 Groups report back on the reliability of their data and their conclusions.

Homework

1 **Worksheet B3 1.4c Breathing** Students consider breathing movements in relation to pressure/volume changes. Students then research and evaluate a negative pressure and also a positive pressure ventilator.

Points to note

- At present, students are not taught pressure–volume relationships in physics. Many will find difficulty with this idea both in relation to natural breathing and in considering artificial ventilation. It is worthwhile spending some time examining this inverse relationship.
- The Physics department will probably have a 'Boyle's law apparatus' to help with the explanation.

Answers to Student Book questions

1 The movement of air into and out of the lungs.

2 Intercostal muscles and diaphragm muscles.

3 When the ribs are raised and the diaphragm flattens the volume of the thorax is increased. This results in a decrease in pressure inside the lungs. The higher pressure of the air outside the body draws air into the lungs.

4 The lungs are stretched during inspiration. When the diaphragm and intercostal muscles relax, elastic recoil of the lungs and thorax forces air out.

5 Poliomyelitis affects the nerves that carry impulses to the muscles which bring about breathing. Without impulses these muscles do not contract to bring about breathing movements.

6 The paramedic inserts the mouthpiece of a bag-mouth-mask resuscitator into the patient's mouth. Squeezing the bag forces air into the patient's lungs.

7 The first artificial ventilator was the iron lung. This was developed mainly to help people with poliomyelitis. This worked by sucking air into the patient's lungs. Positive pressure ventilators were developed to sustain the breathing of patients during operations and in intensive care. The most recent development is of bag-mouth-mask resuscitators, which are used to help patients who have stopped breathing due to an accident or a drug overdose.

8 The patient's body is enclosed in a large, sealed tank. Air is pumped out of the tank creating a vacuum. The lower pressure around the patient's body causes the lungs and thorax to expand. The air pressure in the patient's lungs is reduced, which draws higher pressure from the surroundings into the lungs. When the vacuum is released the lungs deflate due to elastic recoil.

9 Both machines help patients who cannot breathe naturally. In the iron lung the whole of the patient's body is enclosed in the machine, meaning that the patient cannot use their limbs. Being enclosed makes nursing and hygiene very difficult. The positive pressure ventilator gives the patient much more freedom, but the metal tube is very uncomfortable. For long-term use, surgery is needed to insert a tube through the neck into the trachea, and this carries a risk of infection.

B3 1.5 Exchange systems in plants

Link to the Specification

B3.1.3a In plants:

- carbon dioxide enters leaves by diffusion
- most of the water and mineral ions are absorbed by roots.

B3.1.3b The surface area of the roots is increased by root hairs and the surface area of leaves is increased by the flattened shape and internal air spaces.

B3.1.3c Plants have stomata to obtain carbon dioxide from the atmosphere and to remove oxygen produced in respiration.

B3.1.3d Plants mainly lose water vapour from their leaves. Most of the loss of water vapour takes place through the stomata.

- Evaporation is more rapid in hot, dry and windy conditions.
- If plants lose water faster than it is replaced by the roots, the stomata can close to prevent wilting.

B3.1.3e The size of stomata is controlled by guard cells, which surround them.

How Science Works

SKU: B3.1 bullet point 3: Analyse and evaluate the conditions that affect water loss in plants.

CA: B4.4.2: Demonstrate an understanding of how data may be displayed, by: a) drawing tables; b) drawing charts and graphs; c) choosing the most appropriate form of presentation.

B4.5.3: Identify patterns in data, by: a) describing the relationship between two variables and deciding whether the relationship is causal or by association.

B4.5.4: Draw conclusions using scientific ideas and evidence, by: a) writing a conclusion, based on evidence that relates correctly to known facts.

B4.6.1: Review hypotheses in the light of outcomes, by: a) considering whether or not any hypothesis made is supported by the evidence.

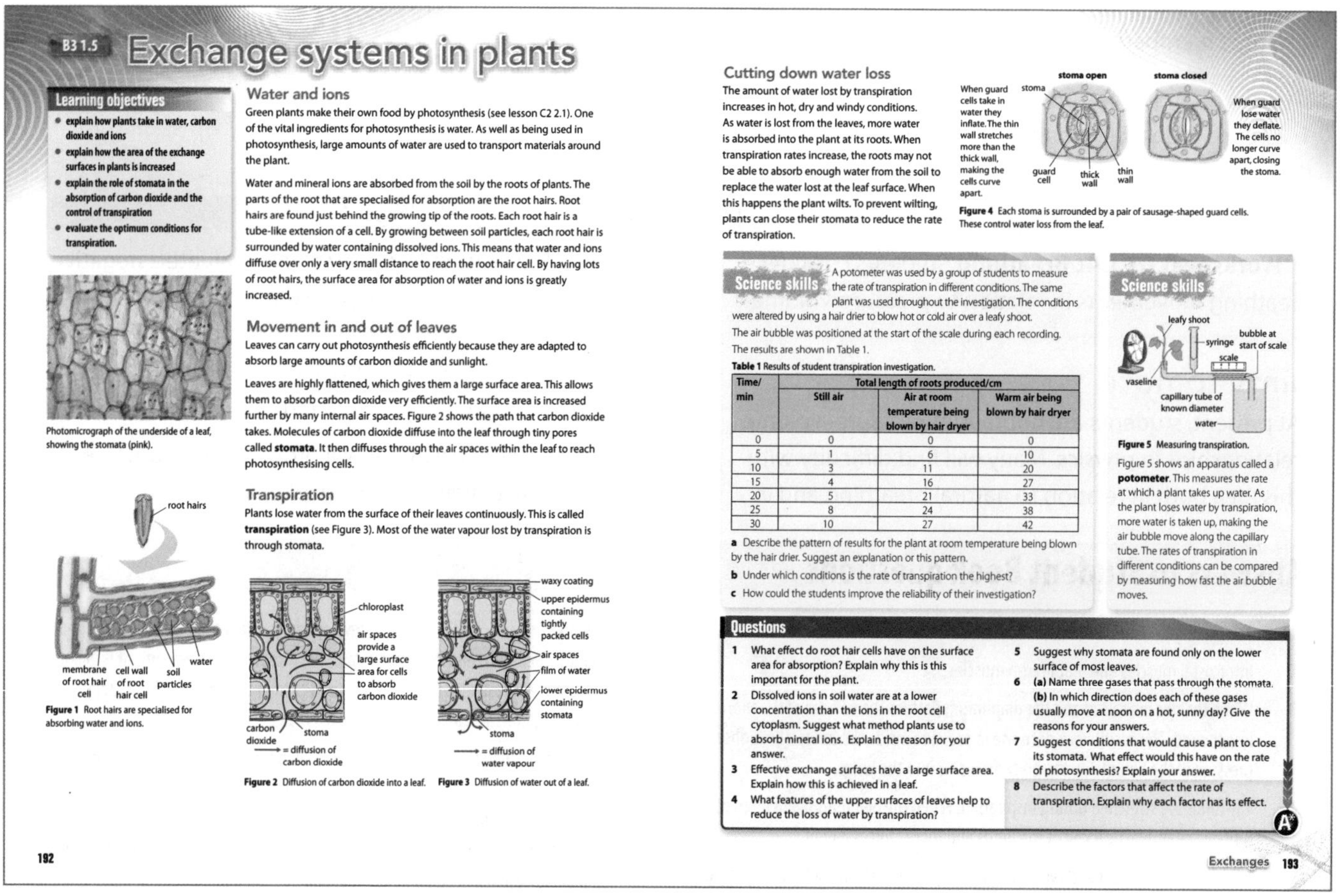

B3 1.5 Exchange systems in plants

Learning objectives

- explain how plants take in water, carbon dioxide and ions
- explain how the area of the exchange surfaces in plants is increased
- explain the role of stomata in the absorption of carbon dioxide and the control of transpiration
- evaluate the optimum conditions for transpiration.

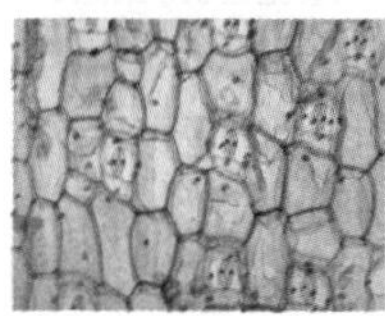

Photomicrograph of the underside of a leaf, showing the stomata (pink).

Water and ions

Green plants make their own food by photosynthesis (see lesson C2 2.1). One of the vital ingredients for photosynthesis is water. As well as being used in photosynthesis, large amounts of water are used to transport materials around the plant.

Water and mineral ions are absorbed from the soil by the roots of plants. The parts of the root that are specialised for absorption are the root hairs. Root hairs are found just behind the growing tip of the roots. Each root hair is a tube-like extension of a cell. By growing between soil particles, each root hair is surrounded by water containing dissolved ions. This means that water and ions diffuse over only a very small distance to reach the root hair cell. By having lots of root hairs, the surface area for absorption of water and ions is greatly increased.

Movement in and out of leaves

Leaves can carry out photosynthesis efficiently because they are adapted to absorb large amounts of carbon dioxide and sunlight.

Leaves are highly flattened, which gives them a large surface area. This allows them to absorb carbon dioxide very efficiently. The surface area is increased further by many internal air spaces. Figure 2 shows the path that carbon dioxide takes. Molecules of carbon dioxide diffuse into the leaf through tiny pores called **stomata**. It then diffuses through the air spaces within the leaf to reach photosynthesising cells.

Transpiration

Plants lose water from the surface of their leaves continuously. This is called **transpiration** (see Figure 3). Most of the water vapour lost by transpiration is through stomata.

root hairs

membrane of root hair cell

cell wall of root hair cell

soil particles

water

Figure 1 Root hairs are specialised for absorbing water and ions.

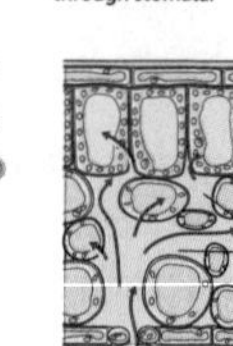

Figure 2 Diffusion of carbon dioxide into a leaf.

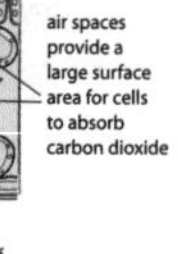

Figure 3 Diffusion of water out of a leaf.

192

Cutting down water loss

The amount of water lost by transpiration increases in hot, dry and windy conditions. As water is lost from the leaves, more water is absorbed into the plant at its roots. When transpiration rates increase, the roots may not be able to absorb enough water from the soil to replace the water lost at the leaf surface. When this happens the plant wilts. To prevent wilting, plants can close their stomata to reduce the rate of transpiration.

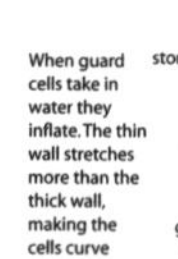

Figure 4 Each stoma is surrounded by a pair of sausage-shaped guard cells. These control water loss from the leaf.

Science skills

A potometer was used by a group of students to measure the rate of transpiration in different conditions. The same plant was used throughout the investigation. The conditions were altered by using a hair drier to blow hot or cold air over a leafy shoot.

The air bubble was positioned at the start of the scale during each recording.

The results are shown in Table 1.

Table 1 Results of student transpiration investigation.

Time/min	Total length of roots produced/cm		
	Still air	Air at room temperature being blown by hair dryer	Warm air being blown by hair dryer
0	0	0	0
5	1	6	10
10	3	11	20
15	4	16	27
20	5	21	33
25	8	24	38
30	10	27	42

a Describe the pattern of results for the plant at room temperature being blown by the hair drier. Suggest an explanation or this pattern.

b Under which conditions is the rate of transpiration the highest?

c How could the students improve the reliability of their investigation?

Science skills

leafy shoot

syringe

bubble at start of scale

scale

vaseline

capillary tube of known diameter

water

Figure 5 Measuring transpiration.

Figure 5 shows an apparatus called a **potometer**. This measures the rate at which a plant takes up water. As the plant loses water by transpiration, more water is taken up, making the air bubble move along the capillary tube. The rates of transpiration in different conditions can be compared by measuring how fast the air bubble moves.

Questions

1 What effect do root hair cells have on the surface area for absorption? Explain why this is this important for the plant.

2 Dissolved ions in soil water are at a lower concentration than the ions in the root cell cytoplasm. Suggest what method plants use to absorb mineral ions. Explain the reason for your answer.

3 Effective exchange surfaces have a large surface area. Explain how this is achieved in a leaf.

4 What features of the upper surfaces of leaves help to reduce the loss of water by transpiration?

5 Suggest why stomata are found only on the lower surface of most leaves.

6 **(a)** Name three gases that pass through the stomata. **(b)** In which direction does each of these gases usually move at noon on a hot, sunny day? Give the reasons for your answers.

7 Suggest conditions that would cause a plant to close its stomata. What effect would this have on the rate of photosynthesis? Explain your answer.

8 Describe the factors that affect the rate of transpiration. Explain why each factor has its effect.

A*

Exchanges 193

Learning objectives

Most students should be able to:

- explain how plant roots and leaves are adapted for exchanging materials
- analyse and evaluate data relating to plant exchanges.

Some students should also be able to:

- evaluate the role of the stomata in the functioning of the plant. [Ext]

Key points

Roots absorb water and ions from the soil. Root hair cells increase the surface area of roots to increase the rate of absorption.

Water is absorbed by diffusion; ions are absorbed by diffusion and by active transport.

Carbon dioxide enters leaves via stomata by diffusion.

The surface area of leaves is increased by their flattened shape and their internal air spaces.

Plants lose water vapour, mainly through stomata in a process called transpiration.

Root hair stomata transpiration

Lesson activities

Starter

1 Briefly revise photosynthesis by giving students 5 minutes to jot down answers to the following questions: what is the equation for photosynthesis, where do the reactants for photosynthesis come from, which conditions affect the rate of photosynthesis, where does photosynthesis happen in a plant and why does it only happen here? Take answers from the class and tackle any weaknesses or misconceptions.

Main

1 Show students cress seedlings that have germinated as far as the root hair stage. Students may notice that the roots developed on their seedlings before the shoot. It is worth explaining that this happens because the seed has a store of starch and doesn't need to photosynthesise immediately. Compare root hairs with villi as absorptive structures.

2 B3 1.5a Investigating stomata In this activity, students use nail varnish peels to observe stomata.

3 B3 1.5b Investigating transpiration This practical allows students to familiarise themselves with the use of a potometer to investigate transpiration. (~60 mins)

Plenaries

1 Students report back on the results of their investigation, considering in particular the reliability of the data and ways in which the procedure could be improved.

Homework

1 Worksheets B3 1.5c and B3 1.5d consolidate knowledge and understanding of exchanges in roots and leaves.

Points to note

- The physical factors that affect transpiration rate should be compared to the way the same factors influence the rate of evaporation from a water surface. It might be useful to compare the rate of transpiration with the rate of drying of washing on an outside line.
- Students should realise that most measures of transpiration are in fact measures of water uptake which may, or may not, be equal to the rate of transpiration.
- For more able pupils a discussion of 'stomata as a necessary evil' might be appropriate.

Route to A*

Students might consider data relating to the shape, behaviour and distribution of stomata in relation to xerophytic conditions.

Answers to Student Book questions

Science skills

a The bubble moved rapidly at first, but then slowed down towards the end of the experiment. As the plant lost more water vapour the stomata began to close, reducing the rate of transpiration.

b Warm, dry and windy.

c Repeating the experiment at each set of conditions would improve reliability.

Answers

1 Root hairs increase the surface area of the root. This increases the rate at which water and ions can be absorbed.

2 Active transport, since the ions are moved against a concentration gradient.

3 The leaf has a flattened shape and large internal air spaces, with stomata connecting the interior to the air.

4 The upper surface of the leaf has a waterproof coating and few or no stomata.

5 It is cooler and this reduces the rate of transpiration.

6 **(a)** Carbon dioxide, oxygen and water vapour.

(b) Carbon dioxide would move into the leaf because the rate of photosynthesis would be greater than the rate of respiration. Oxygen would move out of the leaf for the same reason. Water vapour would move out of the leaf because the stomata would be open to allow carbon dioxide to enter for photosynthesis.

7 The stomata would close in hot, dry or windy conditions. The rate of photosynthesis would fall because less carbon dioxide would be able to diffuse into the leaf.

8 Temperature, humidity and air movement affect the rate of transpiration. Increasing the temperature increases the energy of the water vapour molecules. The molecules move faster and the rate of diffusion increases. Increasing humidity decreases the rate of transpiration. The greater the concentration of water vapour molecules outside the leaf, the less steep the concentration gradient from inside the leaf to outside, and the slower the rate of diffusion of water vapour molecules. Increased air movement moves water vapour molecules away from the leaf. This increases the steepness of the diffusion gradient and water vapour molecules move out of the leaf faster.

B3 2.1 The heart and circulation

Link to the Specification

B3.2.1a The circulatory system transports substances around the body.

B3.2.1b The heart is an organ and pumps blood around the body. Much of the wall of the heart is made from muscle tissue.

B3.2.1c There are four main chambers (left and right atria and ventricles) of the heart.

B3.2.1d Blood enters the atria of the heart. The atria contract and force blood into the ventricles. The ventricles contract and force blood out of the heart.

Valves in the heart ensure that blood flows in the correct direction. Blood flows from the heart to the organs through arteries and returns through veins. There are two separate circulation systems, one for the lungs and one for all other organs of the body.

Ideas for practical work

Dissection of the heart.

B3 2.1 The heart and circulation

Learning objectives

- explain how the heart circulates blood around the body
- explain the advantages of a double circulatory system
- interpret data relating to blood pressure in different types of blood vessel.

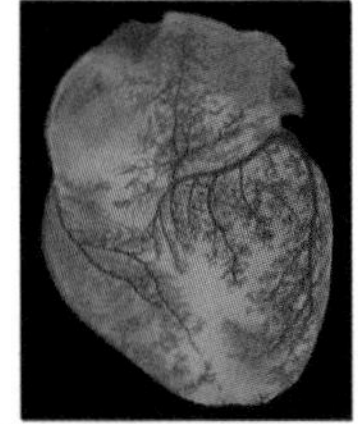

This view of the heart shows the blood vessels carrying blood to the cardiac muscles.

Examiner feedback

The heart is always drawn as though the person was facing you, so the left side of the heart will be on the right side of the drawing.

Science in action

Give a tennis ball a good, hard squeeze. You're using about the same amount of force your heart uses to pump blood out to the body.

Your heart beats about 100 000 times in one day and about 35 million times in a year. During an average lifetime, the human heart will beat more than 2.5 billion times, and pump about 1 million barrels of blood – that's enough to fill more than three supertankers.

In one day, the blood travels a total of 19 000 km.

Pumping blood

Blood flows around your body through a series of blood vessels. These make up your **circulatory system**. Blood is kept flowing around the system by the pumping action of your heart. Your heart beats because the muscles in its walls contract and then relax. When the muscular walls contract, blood is forced out of the heart under high pressure. When the muscular walls relax, the heart fills up with more blood, ready to be pumped out again. Beating at between 60 and 80 beats per minute at rest, your heart is working all the time without pause.

The heart pumps blood out through wide blood vessels called **arteries**. The arteries branch again and again to give narrower vessels that spread throughout the body. Within the organs, the smallest blood vessels are only the width of a red blood cell. These vessels are called **capillaries**.

As they leave the organs, the capillaries join together again and again to form wider vessels called **veins**. By the time they reach the heart all the veins have joined up to form only two large blood vessels.

The heart

The heart is divided into two sides, right and left. Each side consists of two chambers: an upper **atrium** and a lower **ventricle**. Each side has a **valve** that allows blood to flow from the atrium into the ventricle, but prevents backflow. Blood is returned to the heart by two **veins**: the **vena cava** and the **pulmonary vein**. Blood is pumped out of the heart through two **arteries**: the **aorta** and the **pulmonary artery**. Valves at the base of the pulmonary artery and the aorta prevent the backflow of blood into the heart.

Figure 1 shows how the heart works as a pump.

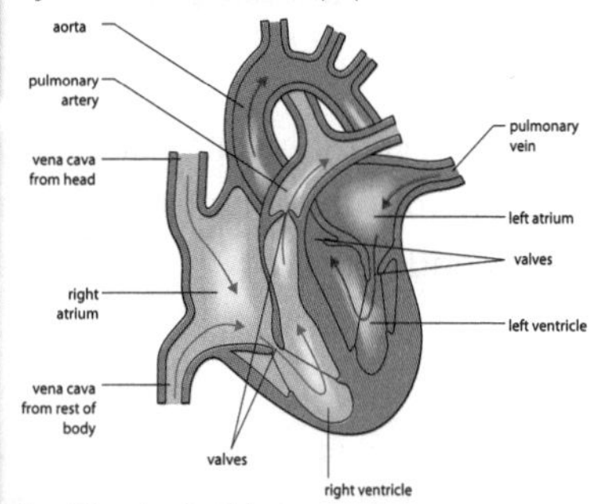

Figure 1 The pumping action of the heart.

Double circulation

The numbers on Figure 2 show the path of blood as it flows through the heart and around the body.

1. Blood from the right ventricle of the heart is pumped out through the pulmonary artery to the lungs.
2. In the lung tissue, oxygen diffuses into the blood and carbon dioxide diffuses out. The blood has become oxygenated.
3. Oxygenated blood from the lungs then returns via the pulmonary vein to the left atrium.
4. Oxygenated blood is pumped through the aorta and arteries to the rest of the body.
5. In respiring tissues, oxygen diffuses from the blood into body cells, and carbon dioxide diffuses from body cells into the blood. The blood has become deoxygenated.
6. Deoxygenated blood is returned by the vena cava to the right atrium.

This is called a double circulatory system because blood travels through the heart twice as it flows around the body. By having a double circulation, oxygenated blood is separated from deoxygenated blood.

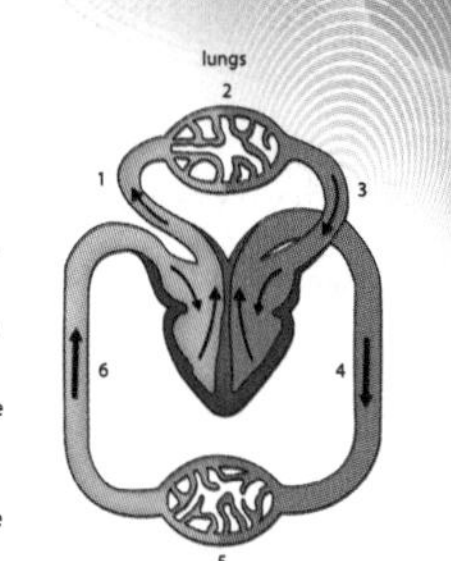

Figure 2 The double circulatory system.

Examiner feedback

Remember that the pulmonary artery is the only artery to carry deoxygenated blood, and the pulmonary vein is the only vein to carry oxygenated blood.

Science skills

Figure 3 shows changes in the pressure of the blood as it passes around the body.

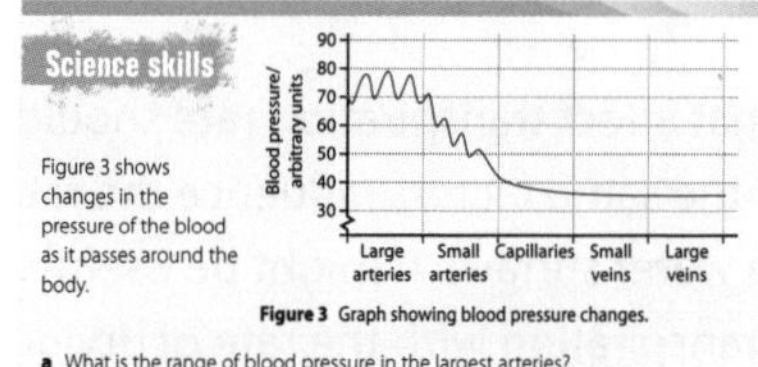

Figure 3 Graph showing blood pressure changes.

a What is the range of blood pressure in the largest arteries?

b In which type of blood vessels does the blood pressure fall the most?

c What is the pressure of blood as it flows back into the heart?

Questions

1. What type of tissue makes up most of the heart?
2. Name the two types of chamber in the heart.
3. Define the following. (a) Artery. (b) Vein. (c) Capillary.
4. Explain why the heart contains valves.
5. Describe the changes in the composition of the blood as it flows through the lungs.
6. Explain what is meant by a double circulatory system.
7. Explain how the structure of the heart is adapted to its function.

194

Transporting material 195

Learning objectives

Students should be able to:

- identify the chambers of the heart and the blood vessels connected to the heart
- describe the passage of blood through the heart
- explain the advantages of a double circulatory system.

ActiveTeach Resource: Structure of the heart – *Labelling activity*
Structure and function of the heart – *Matching activity*

Key points

In the heart cycle:

- blood enters the atria of the heart;
- the atria contract and force blood into the ventricles;
- the ventricles contract and force blood out of the heart;
- valves in the heart ensure that blood flows in the correct direction;
- blood flows from the heart to the organs through arteries and returns through veins.

There are two separate circulation systems, one to the lungs and one to all other organs of the body.

Heart atrium ventricle valve aorta vena cava pulmonary artery pulmonary vein double circulation artery vein capillary

Lesson activities

Starter

1 Write the word 'heart' on the board and, either as a whole-class activity or pair work, ask students to suggest words that can be added to compile a concept map linked to this. After a few minutes, if they have not already been mentioned, introduce the words 'circulation' and 'respiration' and ask how they should be linked to the concept map. It is important at this stage to help students make the link to lungs and small intestine covered earlier. Keep the concept map to return to in the plenary.

Main

1 B3 2.1a Heart dissection In this activity students dissect a heart and relate its structure to function. (~60 mins)

2 B3 2.1b Double structure of the heart consolidates students' understanding of the heart.

3 You may wish to use the ActiveTeach labelling and matching activities. These would be appropriate for either this or the next topic. [AT]

Plenaries

1 Return to the concept map developed in the starter activity and ask students to identify any errors and explain how to resolve them. They should then suggest further words and ideas from the topic to add to the concept map and explain how they should be linked.

Homework

1 Work sheet B3 2.1c introduces the concept of double circulation.

2 Ask students to research on the Internet to find the heart and circulation structure of other groups of animals, such as fish, amphibians and reptiles. If possible, they should compare the effectiveness of the different kinds of circulatory systems.

Points to note

- Students should appreciate that the principal reason for the double circulation is to re-pressurise blood after it has been oxygenated in the lungs. These leads to an understanding of the separation of the heart into two sides dealing with deoxygenated blood and oxygenated blood respectively.
- Students should also appreciate that valves are 'operated' by pressure differences on the two sides of the valve.

Route to A*

Students could research the evolution of the 4-chamber heart, starting with the 2-chamber fish heart and progressing through amphibians, reptiles and birds.

Answers to Student Book questions

Science skills

a Approx. 68–80 units.

b Small arteries.

c Approx. 36 units.

Answers

1 Muscle.

2 Atria and ventricles.

3 **(a)** A blood vessel that carries blood away from the heart. **(b)** A blood vessel that carries blood back to the heart. **(c)** Microscopic blood vessels that carry blood from arteries to veins.

4 Valves prevent backflow of blood from ventricles to atria and from the arteries back into the heart.

5 The concentration of oxygen in the blood rises, while the concentration of carbon dioxide falls.

6 A double circulatory system has a circulation from the heart to the lungs to oxygenate the blood and a second circulation to distribute oxygenated blood from the heart to the rest of the body organs.

7 The heart is composed of muscular tissue that enables it to pump blood around the body. The heart is divided into two sides, left and right, to keep oxygenated blood and deoxygenated blood separate. Each side of the heart is divided into two chambers, one to receive blood (the atrium) and the other to pump blood out of the heart (the ventricle). There are valves between the atria and ventricles to prevent backflow of blood into the ventricles. There are valves at the base of the pulmonary artery and the aorta to prevent the backflow of blood into the heart.

B3 2.2 Blood vessels

Link to the Specification

B3.2.1e Arteries have thick walls containing muscle and elastic fibres. Veins have thinner walls and often have valves to prevent back-flow of blood.

B3.2.1g In the organs, blood flows through very narrow, thin-walled blood vessels called capillaries. Substances needed by the cells in body tissues pass out of the blood, and substances produced by the cells pass into the blood, through the walls of the capillaries.

How Science Works

CA: B4.3.2 Demonstrate an understanding of the need to acquire high quality data, by: d) considering the resolution of the measuring device; e) considering the precision of the measured data where precision is indicated by the degree of scatter from the mean; f) identifying the range of the measured data.

B4.5.4 Draw conclusions using scientific ideas and evidence, by: b) using secondary sources.

B3 2.2 Blood vessels

Learning objectives

- relate the structure of arteries, veins and capillaries to their functions
- explain how substances are exchanged between the blood and the tissues
- interpret data relating to structural features of blood vessels

The circulatory system

Blood is pumped around your body through a system of blood vessels. There are three types of blood vessel: arteries, veins and capillaries.

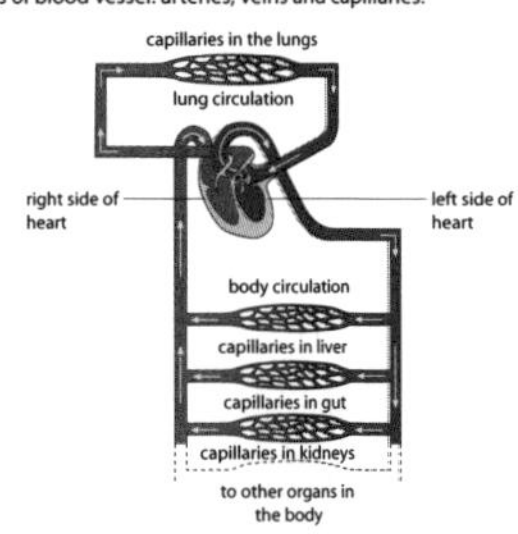

Figure 1 Plan of the blood circulation in humans.

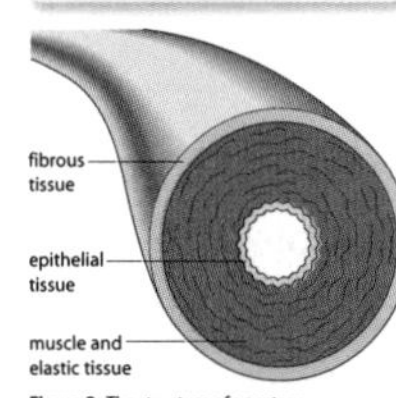

Figure 2 The structure of an artery.

Blood flows out of the heart through arteries. Because it has been pumped from the heart, the blood in arteries is at high pressure. When arteries get to an organ in your body, they branch many times to form capillaries. The capillaries are where substances pass in and out of the blood.

Once they have passed through an organ or tissue, the capillaries join up again to form veins, which return blood back to the heart. The blood flowing through veins is at a much lower pressure.

Arteries

Arteries have thick walls composed largely of muscle and elastic tissue. When the muscle tissue contracts it constricts the flow of blood through the artery. This is how blood flow to the different organs is controlled. The elastic tissue allows the artery to expand when blood is forced into it from the ventricles. When the ventricles relax, recoil of the elastic tissue keeps the pressure of the blood high.

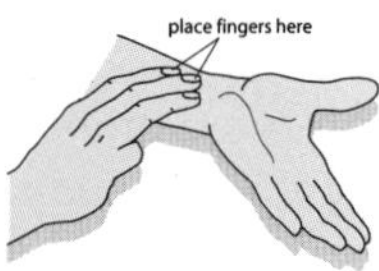

Figure 3 You can feel an artery stretching and recoiling as blood flows along an artery. This is your pulse.

Taking your pulse

Blood does not flow smoothly through arteries. Every time the heart muscles contract, a surge of blood passes along the arteries, causing the artery walls to bulge slightly. When this happens the walls of arteries become stretched. The walls then spring back (recoil) as the heart muscles relax. You can feel arteries stretch and recoil when you feel the pulse in your wrist.

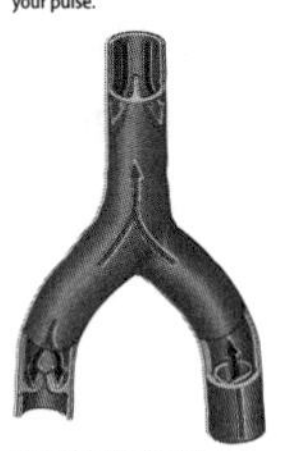

Figure 4 Valves in veins.

Veins

Veins have much thinner walls than arteries. The blood flowing through them is at a much lower pressure than that flowing through arteries. To prevent backflow in long veins such as those in the legs, they have valves.

196

Capillaries

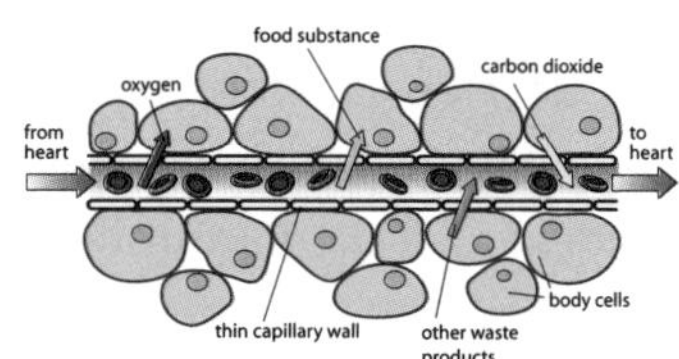

Figure 5 Capillaries exchange substances with tissues.

The smallest blood vessels are called capillaries. This is where substances pass in and out of the blood. Capillaries are so narrow that only one red blood cell at a time can be squeezed through. They also have very thin walls, just one cell thick, that allow substances to pass in and out easily. Substances needed by body tissues, such as soluble foods and oxygen, pass out of the blood, through the capillary wall and into cells. Substances produced by cells, such as carbon dioxide and other waste substances (see lesson B3 3.2), pass into the blood through the walls of the capillaries.

Science in action

If the valves in the veins stop working, blood accumulates, making the veins swell and become unsightly. Such veins are called 'varicose veins'. A common treatment is for the doctor to inject a solution into the vein that causes the vein walls to swell, stick together, and seal shut. This stops the flow of blood and the vein turns into scar tissue. In a few weeks, the vein fades. The blood returns to the heart along alternative vessels.

Science skills

Table 1 gives data about the blood vessels in a small mammal.

Table 1 The blood vessels of a small mammal.

Blood vessels	Mean diameter/cm	Mean length/cm	Total cross-sectional area/cm²	Total volume/cm³
main arteries	0.1	10.0	5	50
small arteries	0.002	0.2	125	25
capillaries	0.0008	0.1	600	60
main veins	0.24	10.0	27	270
other blood vessels				525

a How many times wider than a capillary is a main artery?

b What percentage of the blood is in the capillaries at any one time?

c The main arteries and the main veins have the same mean length. Use data from the table to explain why the volume of blood in the main veins is much higher than that in the main arteries.

d Use information from the table to explain why the pressure of blood in the capillaries is much less than that in the main arteries.

Questions

1. Give the function of each of the following in the wall of an artery. **(a)** Muscle tissue. **(b)** Elastic tissue.
2. Give two differences between the structure of an artery and that of a vein.
3. Describe the structure of a capillary.
4. List the exchanges that occur between the blood in a capillary and the tissues.
5. Explain why cells exchange substances with capillaries rather than with arteries or veins.
6. Explain why veins in the legs have valves.
7. Describe how a molecule of oxygen gets from the air to a muscle cell.

A*

Transporting material 197

Learning objectives

Most students should be able to:

- describe the structure of arteries, veins and capillaries
- relate the structure of arteries, veins and capillaries to their functions
- explain how materials are exchanged between blood in capillaries and the tissues system.

Some students should also be able to:

- relate data concerning blood vessels to their functions. [Ext]

Key points

Arteries have thick walls containing muscle and elastic fibres.

Veins have thinner walls and often have valves to prevent back-flow of blood.

In the organs, blood flows through very narrow, thin-walled blood vessels called capillaries.

Substances needed by the cells in body tissues pass out of the blood and substances produced by the cells pass into the blood through the walls of the capillaries.

Artery | vein | capillary | valve | elastic fibre | muscle

Lesson activities

Starter

1 Ask students what evidence there is for the existence of blood vessels in their own bodies. Answers will probably relate to pulse, superficial vessels in elderly people and perhaps blood loss after an accident.

Main

1 B3 2.2a Looking at arteries and veins. In this practical activity, students observe the structure of arteries and veins from prepared slides. (~40 mins)

2 B3 2.2b Blood vessel data Students carry out exercises using secondary data about blood vessels.

Plenaries

1 Students report back on their results from the practical (Main task 1).

2 Write the key words and other related words from the topic on the board. Give students 5 minutes to write questions to which each word is an answer. Take examples of questions from the class to discuss.

Homework

1 Worksheet B3 2.2c Harvey and Malpighi Students research the contributions of Harvey and Malpighi to our understanding of the circulation of blood.

2 Worksheet B3 2.2d Blood vessels consolidates understanding of the structure and function of blood vessels.

Points to note

- Students should be able to relate data to the structure of blood vessels in relation to their functions. They should appreciate the functions of muscular tissue and elastic tissues in arteries; the differences in the width of arteries and veins; the features of capillaries that enable exchanges to take place between them and the tissues.

Route to A*

Students could research the circulatory systems of arthropods and annelids.

Answers to Student Book questions

Science skills

a 125

b 6.45%

c The veins have a much wider diameter and cross-sectional area. Since their walls are much thinner than artery walls there is a much greater capacity for blood, so the pressure falls.

d The total cross-sectional area of the capillaries is 120 times greater than that of the main arteries. The blood from the arteries has a much greater volume to flow into.

Answers

1 **(a)** Controlling blood flow. **(b)** Maintaining blood pressure.

2 Any two of: arteries have thicker walls; arteries have more muscular tissue; arteries have more elastic tissue; veins are wider than arteries; veins have valves.

3 A microscopic tube with walls one cell thick.

4 Oxygen and soluble foods pass from the capillaries to the tissues; carbon dioxide and other waste substances pass from the tissues into the capillaries.

5 Materials can diffuse easily through capillary walls because they are thin and permeable. The walls of arteries and veins contain many layers of cells.

6 Blood in the veins is at low pressure so it is difficult to move the blood all the way up to the heart. The valves prevent blood flowing backwards between heartbeats.

7 Oxygen diffuses through the walls of the alveoli into lung capillaries. The lung capillaries join up to form the pulmonary vein, which carries oxygenated blood to the left atrium of the heart. Blood passes into the left ventricle of the heart where it is pumped into the aorta. The aorta divides into smaller and smaller arteries and eventually into capillaries in the muscle. Oxygen diffuses out of the capillaries into the muscle cells.

B3 2.3 The blood

Link to the Specification

B3.2.2a Blood is a tissue and consists of a fluid called plasma in which red blood cells, white blood cells, and platelets are suspended.

B3.2.2b Blood plasma transports:

- carbon dioxide from the organs to the lungs
- soluble products of digestion from the small intestine to other organs
- urea from the liver to the kidneys.

B3.2.2c Red blood cells transport oxygen from the lungs to the organs. Red blood cells have no nucleus. They are packed with a red pigment called haemoglobin. In the lungs haemoglobin combines with oxygen to form oxyhaemoglobin. In other organs oxyhaemoglobin splits up into haemoglobin and oxygen.

B3.2.2d White blood cells have a nucleus. They form part of the body's defence system against microorganisms.

B3.2.2e Platelets are small fragments of cells. They have no nucleus. Platelets help blood to clot at the site of a wound.

Ideas for practical work

Observation of blood smears.

How Science Works

SKU: B3.2 bullet point 1: Evaluate data on the production and use of artificial blood products.

B3 2.3 The blood

Learning objectives

- explain the transport functions of blood plasma
- explain how red blood cells transport oxygen
- explain the functions of white blood cells and blood platelets
- evaluate data on the production and use of artificial blood products.

Blood in a bag: what might this be used for?

Your blood

Your blood provides all the cells of your body with the materials they need, as well as removing waste materials. Your cells would soon stop working without a good supply of blood. This is why blood has to be replaced quickly if someone loses a lot of blood in an accident.

Your blood looks like a red liquid, but the liquid part is not red – it is a straw-coloured liquid called plasma. The red colour comes from the billions of red blood cells that are suspended in the plasma. Both the plasma and red blood cells play an important role in transporting substances around the body.

The plasma also carries other cells. **White blood cells** form part of the body's defence system against pathogens. They act in three main ways: producing antibodies, producing antitoxins and engulfing pathogens. **Platelets** are small fragments of cells. They have no nucleus. Platelets help to reduce blood loss by producing a clot at the site of a wound.

Transporting food and waste materials

Plasma is the liquid part of blood. Plasma contains mainly water with a number of dissolved substances, including the following.

- Soluble sugars, amino acids, fatty acids and glycerol are products of digestion in the small intestine. These soluble products are absorbed from the small intestine and transported in plasma to other body organs.
- Carbon dioxide is produced as a waste product of respiration. Carbon dioxide is transported in plasma from respiring cells to the alveoli in the lungs. As blood flows around the alveoli, carbon dioxide is removed from the blood by diffusion and breathed out.
- Urea is a waste product formed from excess amino acids. Urea is made in the liver and transported in blood plasma to the kidneys, where it is removed from the body in urine.

red blood cells
platelets
plasma
white blood cells

Figure 1 The cells in the blood.

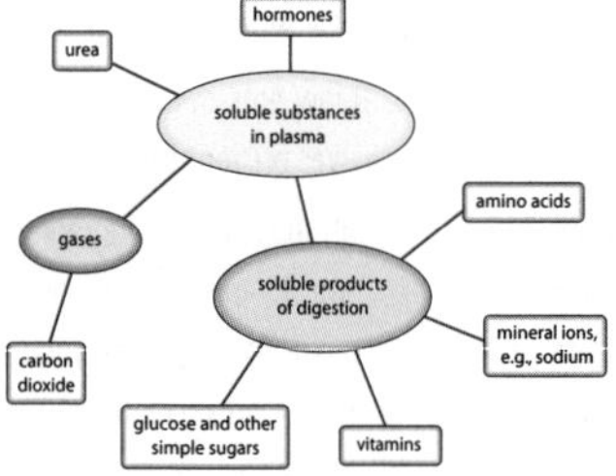

Figure 2 Some of the substances that dissolve in blood plasma.

198

Transporting oxygen

Your blood contains an enormous number of red blood cells. These are very specialised cells that transport oxygen to all the cells of your body. Red blood cells are shaped like a biconvex disc. They are so specialised that they have no nucleus. Each cell is packed with a protein called **haemoglobin**. It is this protein that gives red cells their colour.

As blood flows through the alveoli in the lungs, haemoglobin combines with oxygen to form **oxyhaemoglobin**. When blood flows through respiring tissues, oxyhaemoglobin splits up into haemoglobin and oxygen. The oxygen that is released is used by cells for respiration.

red cells containing oxyhaemoglobin
in the lungs
oxygen
oxygen
oxygen
in respiring tissues
oxygen
oxygen
oxygen
red cells containing haemoglobin (without oxygen)

Figure 3 How red blood cells transport oxygen.

Artificial blood

Scientists have been developing different types of artificial blood since the 1990s. This is to overcome the shortage of blood available for transfusions. Artificial blood could also overcome some of the problems associated with transfusing natural blood. Artificial blood could be sterilised to prevent infections being transmitted. It would avoid problems with mismatching of blood groups and it could be stored for long periods.

Most types of artificial blood are known as **HBOCs** (haemoglobin-based oxygen carriers). Some HBOCs are already in use, e.g., in South Africa where there is a chronic shortage of natural blood for transfusions because of the AIDS epidemic. HBOCs are made from haemoglobin, but doctors cannot transfuse haemoglobin itself into patients because it quickly disintegrates once transfused. There are several ways of preventing this disintegration. The most common is to bind the haemoglobin to a synthetic polymer. HBOCs do not usually remain in the blood for more than a day, compared with the 100-day life of a red blood cell.

A second type of artificial blood contains **PFCs** (polyfluorocarbons). PFCs are entirely synthetic. They are efficient oxygen carriers; they can carry 20–30 per cent more oxygen than plasma. However, they can only be used if the patient is supplied with extra oxygen. PFCs are much smaller than red blood cells. They can be used to supply oxygen to places that cannot be accessed by red blood cells, for example through swollen brain tissue. HBOCs and PFCs still produce some side effects.

Route to A*

Practice evaluation questions like the one below. You will be assessed on using good English, organising information clearly and using specialist terms where appropriate.

Use the information given here on artificial blood to evaluate the use of artificial blood for blood transfusions.

Questions

1. Explain why blood looks red.
2. Which type of cell is most common in the blood?
3. **(a)** Give two differences between a red blood cell and a white blood cell. **(b)** Give two differences between a white blood cell and a platelet.
4. List the substances transported by plasma.
5. Explain what is meant when we say 'haemoglobin combines reversibly with oxygen'.
6. Only one red blood cell at a time can pass along a capillary. Explain how this increases the efficiency of diffusion of oxygen into body cells.
7. EPO is a drug that increases the number of red blood cells in the bloodstream. It is used to treat patients with severe anaemia. Athletes are banned from using this drug because it increases their level of performance. Why does taking EPO enhance athletic performance?
8. Explain how the structure of red blood cells is adapted for their function.

Transporting material 199

Learning objectives

Most students should be able to:

- explain the transport functions of blood plasma
- explain how red blood cells transport oxygen
- explain the functions of white blood cells and blood platelets.

Some students should also be able to:

- evaluate data on the production and use of artificial blood products. [Ext]

Key points

Blood contains red cells, white cells and platelets suspended in a liquid called plasma.

Red blood cells contain haemoglobin to transport oxygen. Haemoglobin combines with oxygen in the lungs to form oxyhaemoglobin. In the tissues oxyhaemoglobin splits up to release oxygen for respiration.

Plasma transports carbon dioxide, urea and the products of digestion.

White blood cells protect us against pathogens by producing antibodies, by producing antigens and by engulfing the pathogens.

Platelets reduce bleeding by forming a clot at the site of a wound.

Artificial blood can be made from haemoglobin or from synthetic compounds that bind with oxygen.

Red blood cell | white blood cell | platelet | haemoglobin | oxyhaemoglobin

Lesson activities

Starter

1 Before looking at the Student Book, ask students to jot down as many substances as they can remember that are transported in the blood. If possible, they should identify where in the body they enter the blood, and where they leave. Take answers from the class until you think they have covered everything – this should include oxygen, carbon dioxide, products of digestion and urea. If any of these have been missed, remind students of the name to prompt for details about where they enter and leave.

Main

1 B3 2.3a Preparing a blood smear The Teacher and technician sheet gives instructions for preparing blood smears, using *CLEAPSS Laboratory Handbook*, Section 14.4. Students then identify the different types of blood cell under a microscope, and draw a red blood cell.

2 Red blood cells The fact that red blood cells have no nucleus means that they have a much shorter life-span than other cells in the body. Ask students to find out how long they survive in the body, what happens to them when they are beginning to break down, where new red blood cells are made and which substances are needed to make them.

3 Student worksheets B3 2.3b and 2.3c provide examples of situations in which the red blood cell count is changed (increased at altitude, decreased in anaemia) to give students further understanding of the importance of red blood cells in carrying oxygen around the body. Students could carry out their own research on either of these to learn more about the changes they cause within the body. The section on 'Artificial blood' in lesson B3 2.3 in the Student Book should be used to develop evaluation skills.

Plenaries

1 Write the key words and other related words from the topic on the board. Give students 5 minutes to write questions to which each word is an answer. Take examples of questions from the class to discuss.

Homework

1 Worksheet B3 2.3d Transporting materials consolidates students' understanding of the functions of blood.

Route to A*

Students could be asked to research tests that can be done on blood, and what normal values are. For example: red cell count, packed cell volume (haematocrit), and haemoglobin levels. More able students may be asked to explain why the normal haematocrit range for adult males is 40–50 per cent, and 36–46 per cent for adult females.

Answers to Student Book questions

Route to A*

Artificial blood can be used to keep patients alive when there is a shortage of natural blood for transfusions. Artificial blood has some advantages over natural blood: it can be sterilised, it does not have to be matched for blood group and it has a long shelf-life. Some types of artificial blood can reach places that red blood cells cannot reach. However, some types of artificial blood do not last for very long, so transfusions have to be repeated frequently. Other types are not as efficient as haemoglobin, so the patient has to be given oxygen as well.

Answers

1 It contains large numbers of red blood cells.

2 The red blood cell.

3 **(a)** Red blood cells have no nucleus, whereas white cells do. Red cells contain haemoglobin; white cells do not. **(b)** White cells are complete cells, whereas platelets are cell fragments. White cells have a nucleus; platelets do not.

4 Carbon dioxide, urea, other waste products, and soluble food materials are transported by plasma.

5 Haemoglobin combines with oxygen in the lungs to form oxyhaemoglobin. In the tissues the oxyhaemoglobin splits up, releasing haemoglobin, plus oxygen for respiration.

6 The red cell travels only slowly along the capillary, giving time for all its oxygen to diffuse out. Much of the surface of the red cell is in contact with the capillary wall, reducing the length of the diffusion path for oxygen.

7 With more red blood cells, an athlete's blood can carry more oxygen, allowing more aerobic respiration and greater energy availability. Anaerobic respiration is less likely, leading to less chance of muscle cramp.

8 Red blood cells contain haemoglobin, which combines reversibly with oxygen, forming oxyhaemoglobin. This allows the blood to absorb large volumes of oxygen in the lungs and transport it to the tissues. Oxygen binds only weakly to haemoglobin, which means that in the tissues it can be released for respiration. The red cell has no nucleus; this allows it to carry more haemoglobin. Its flat shape means that the diffusion path for oxygen to the centre is short. The biconvex disc shape gives the red cell a larger surface area for oxygen to diffuse in and out.

B3 2.4

Stents, artificial heart valves, artificial hearts

Link to the Specification

B3.2.1f If arteries begin to narrow and restrict blood flow stents are used to keep them open.

How Science Works

SKU:

B3.2 bullet point 2: Evaluate the use of artificial hearts and heart valves;

B3.2 bullet point 3: Evaluate the use of stents.

B3 2.4

Stents, artificial heart valves, artificial hearts

Learning objectives

- evaluate the use of stents
- evaluate the use of artificial heart valves
- evaluate the use of artificial hearts.

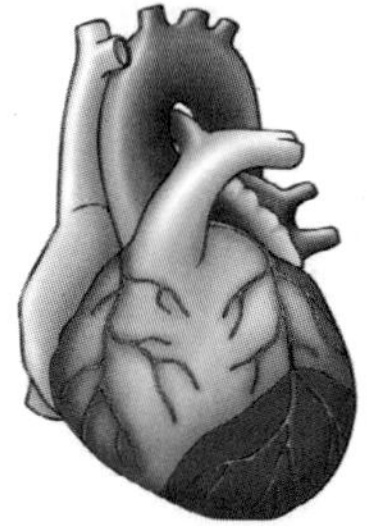

Figure 1 The coronary blood vessels run over the surface of the heart, carrying blood to and from the heart muscles.

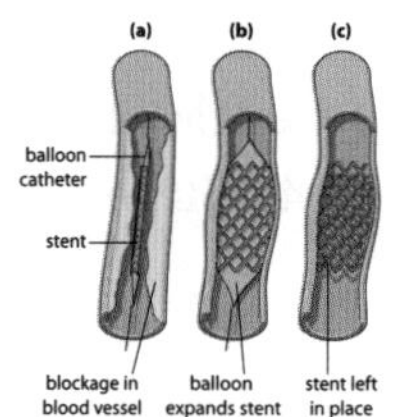

Figure 3 Inserting a stent.

Surgery and stents

Heart muscle needs oxygen to contract efficiently. Oxygenated blood is carried to the heart muscle by the coronary arteries, which branch off the aorta.

In coronary heart disease, layers of fatty material build up inside the coronary arteries and cause them to narrow. This reduces the flow of blood through the coronary arteries. As a result, the heart muscles get less oxygen. In severe cases, the flow of blood to part of the heart muscle ceases and the affected muscle tissue dies; this is what is known as a heart attack.

direction of blood flow

artery wall

fat builds up inside the wall, reducing the diameter of the artery

Figure 2 Fat deposits in the wall of a coronary artery.

There are two methods of treating coronary artery disease: bypass surgery and the use of stents.

In bypass surgery the surgeon uses a piece of a vein from the leg, chest or arm to create a bypass around the blocked portion of coronary artery. The operation requires a general anaesthetic and up to seven days in hospital. It takes up to three months to fully recover.

A stent is a wire metal mesh tube used to prop open an artery. The stent is collapsed to a small diameter and put over a balloon attached to a narrow tube called a 'catheter'. The catheter is inserted into a blood vessel in the leg and manipulated into the area of the blockage in the coronary artery. Then the balloon is inflated, the stent expands, locks in place and forms a scaffold. This holds the artery open. The catheter is then removed. The stent stays in the artery permanently, holds it open and improves blood flow to the heart muscle. However, fatty substances may build up in stents over the years.

Inserting a stent takes 1–2 hours and is carried out under a local anaesthetic. Most patients stay overnight in the hospital for observation, and can resume normal activities within one week. However, fatty substances are not as likely to build up in a bypass as they are in stents.

Replacing heart valves

In most people heart valves operate faultlessly throughout life, but in a few the heart valves can become faulty. There are two main faults:

- the heart valve tissue might stiffen, preventing the valve opening fully
- the heart valve might develop a leak.

Faulty heart valves can be replaced using biological valves taken from humans or other mammals, or by mechanical valves. Figure 4 shows the two types.

Modern mechanical valves consist of two semicircular carbon leaflets that pivot on hinges. The leaflets swing open completely, parallel to the direction of the blood flow.

Mechanical valves are very strong and can last a lifetime, which is why they are often used in young patients. However, mechanical valves damage red blood cells and increase the risk of blood clotting. To minimise this risk, patients have to take drugs that prevent blood clotting for the rest of their lives.

The most common operation using biological valves is to replace the valve in the aorta with the patient's own pulmonary valve, then to replace the pulmonary valve with a valve from a human donor or from a pig's heart. Biological valves do not damage red blood cells, but they have a tendency to become hardened with calcium deposits. This means that after a while they may not open fully.

biological valve (from human or other mammal)

mechanical valve

Figure 4 Artificial heart valves.

Artificial hearts

Some patients with heart disease cannot be treated by using stents or artificial heart valves. For many of these patients there are only two options: a heart transplant or an artificial heart. Artificial hearts are still at the experimental stage and have not been very successful so far.

Figure 5 shows one type of total heart replacement. This artificial heart requires both external and internal power supplies.

Science skills A study was made of 81 patients at high risk of death due to irreversible heart failure. The patients were given an artificial heart as an interim treatment while waiting for a heart transplant. The rate of survival to transplant operation was 79 per cent, compared with 46 per cent in a group of control patients who did not receive an artificial heart. The one-year survival rate among patients who received the artificial heart was 70 per cent, compared with 31 per cent among the controls. The one- and five-year survival rates among patients who received transplants were 86 per cent and 64 per cent, respectively.

a Use information from the diagram and the text to evaluate the use of artificial hearts to treat heart failure.

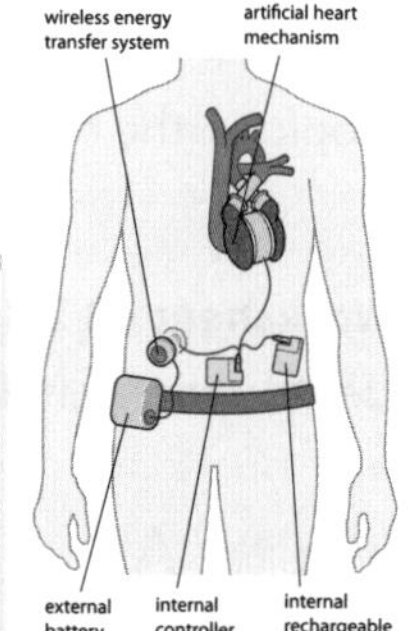

Figure 5 An artificial heart.

Questions

1. Evaluate bypass surgery and stent use as methods of treating blocked coronary arteries.
2. Evaluate the use of mechanical and biological valves as methods of treating heart failure.

200

Transporting material 201

Learning objectives

Students should be able to:

- evaluate the use of artificial hearts, heart valves and stents.

ActiveTeach Resource: Evaluating heart surgery – *Evidence rating activity*

Key points

Coronary heart disease involves narrowing of the arteries supplying the heart muscle with blood, so it is deprived of oxygen.

Bypass surgery uses a piece of a vein from the leg, chest or arm to create a new route around the blocked portion of coronary artery, but it can take the patient months to recover.

Stents may be inserted to prop open the arteries and improve blood flow, but they may clog up over the years.

Heart valves that develop a fault can be replaced, either by biological or artificial valves.

Biological heart valves may harden over time, whereas longer-lasting artificial heart valves increase the risk of blood clots.

Artificial hearts, though still at the experimental stage, can increase the chance of survival for patients awaiting a heart transplant.

Lesson activities

Starter

1 Show a short video of open-heart surgery to illustrate the difficulty of operating on a beating heart.

Main

1 Worksheet B3 2.4a invites students to work in groups to evaluate the methods of treating heart disease in Student Book lesson B3 2.4 and to prepare a report for the plenary session.

2 Evaluating heart surgery Use the ActiveTeach evidence rating activity. [AT]

Plenaries

1 Groups report back on the three evaluation questions from Worksheet B3 2.4a.

Homework

1 Worksheet B3 2.4b invites students to research other models of artificial hearts.

Answers to Student Book questions

Science skills

a The artificial heart requires major surgery to remove the diseased heart and to attach the four great blood vessels so that they do not leak. The patient also needs to have a control unit and a battery fitted inside the thorax. However, the power supply is external and power is transmitted to the devices inside the thorax by a wireless connection.

The heart is only used to keep a person alive while waiting for a transplant; it is not a permanent solution to heart failure. The study shows that the device almost doubles the chance of surviving until a transplant becomes available. The study also shows that the chance of surviving for one year with the artificial heat is more than double that of a control group. However, only 81 patients were studied, so the results might be unreliable.

Answers

1 Both bypasses and stents improve the blood supply to cardiac muscle. The procedure is much shorter for the stent, does not require general anaesthetic, requires less time in hospital and has a shorter recovery time. However, fatty substances are more likely to build up around a stent than in a replacement blood vessel.

2 Mechanical valves are very strong and are likely to last much longer than biological valves. Biological valves have a tendency to become hard and therefore to leak. However, mechanical valves damage red blood cells and lead to a greater risk of blood clotting. Recipients need to take anti-clotting drugs for the rest of their lives. Biological valves do not increase the risk of clotting and the recipients do not need to take anti-clotting drugs.

B3 2.5 Transport systems in plants

Link to the Specification

B3.2.3a Flowering plants have separate transport systems:

- xylem tissue transports water and mineral ions from the roots to the stem and leaves
- the movement of water from the roots through the xylem and out of the leaves is called the transpiration stream
- phloem tissue carries dissolved sugars from the leaves to the rest of the plant, including the growing regions and the storage organs.

How Science Works

CA: B4.1.1 Develop hypotheses and plan practical ways to test them, by: a) being able to make predictions based on a hypothesis; b) being able to test hypotheses. B4.5.4 Draw conclusions using scientific ideas and evidence, by: b) using secondary sources.

B3 2.5 Transport systems in plants

Learning objectives

- explain the role of xylem in transporting water around a plant
- explain the role of phloem in transporting sugars around a plant.

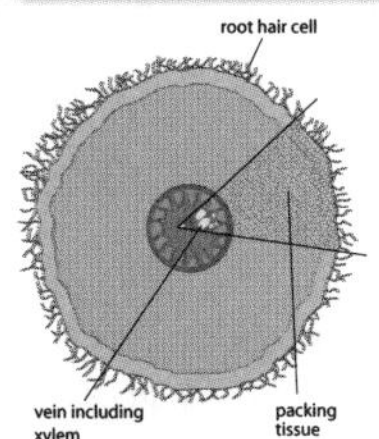

Figure 1 A cross-section across a root.

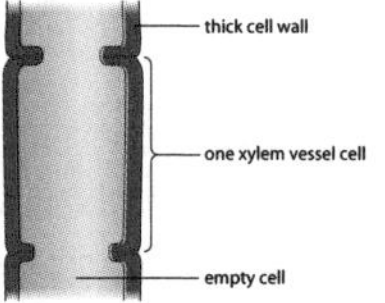

Figure 2 Xylem vessels carry water throughout a plant.

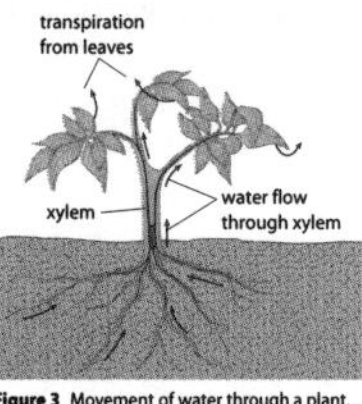

Figure 3 Movement of water through a plant.

Movement of water through a plant

The concentration of **solutes** in water around a plant's root system is lower than the concentration of solutes in the cytoplasm of root hair cells, so water moves into these cells by osmosis (see lesson B3 1.1). This makes their cytoplasm more dilute than the cytoplasm of the cells further inside the root, so water moves from the root hair cells into these cells by osmosis. In this way water travels across the root until it reaches xylem tissue in the centre.

In the leaves, water evaporates from the cells that line the air spaces. The water vapour then diffuses out of the leaf through the stomata and into the air. As the water evaporates, this increases the concentration of the cytoplasm in the cells lining the air spaces, so water moves by osmosis into these cells from the cells that are next to them. This happens from cell to cell across the leaf until the xylem in the leaf vein is reached. There, water moves by osmosis from the vein into the cells that surround it.

Most of the water travels through xylem vessels. These are formed by the breakdown of the end walls of dead xylem cells, forming long tubes. Xylem vessels function like the water pipes in your home. They have thick, rigid walls that stop them from collapsing.

As water moves out of xylem cells in a leaf, the water columns in the xylem vessels are pulled upwards because water molecules stick together. Water is literally pulled all the way from the roots to the top of the plant. This is called the transpiration stream. An enormous amount of energy is needed to do this in tall trees such as redwoods. This energy comes directly from the Sun, which causes water to evaporate from the leaves.

Vascular bundles

Another plant tissue called 'phloem' transports sugars in plants. Phloem tissue is always found next to xylem tissue in **vascular bundles**. Figure 4 shows the position of xylem and phloem in different parts of a plant.

Most of the sugar transported by phloem is carried through sieve tubes. These are similar to xylem vessels, but the end walls of the phloem cells do not break down completely. Instead, they form structures called 'sieve plates'. Mature sieve tubes are not empty, but they have no nucleus. They are always associated with living cells called 'companion cells'. The activity of these companion cells is essential for the activity of phloem.

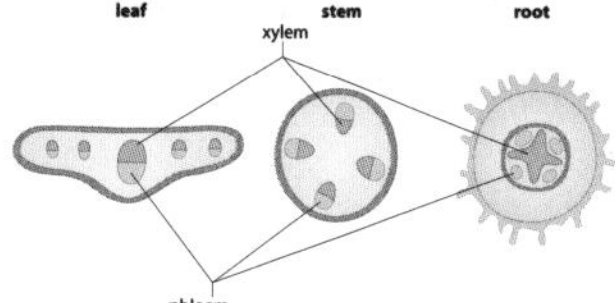

Figure 4 Xylem and phloem in leaves, stems and roots.

Sugars are produced in leaves by photosynthesis. This sugar is then transported to all parts of the plant. All plant cells need sugar for respiration. Plants produce new cells at the tips of roots and stems. These new cells need sugars to grow as well as to respire. Both root tips and shoot tips are supplied with sugars by phloem.

Most plants store large amounts of carbohydrates in underground stems or roots. For example, potatoes store starch and sugar beet stores sugar.

An Italian scientist called Marcello Malphighi first showed that phloem transported sugars, over 300 years ago. He removed a ring of bark from a tree. The bark of a tree contains the phloem. After a few weeks a swelling appeared above the ring. The swollen tissue was rich in sugars. This suggested to Malpighi that sugars were being transported down the tree from the leaves to the roots. He repeated the experiment in winter. This time no swelling appeared. Malpighi correctly concluded that this was because in winter there were no leaves to produce sugars, so no sugars were transported down to the roots.

Giant redwoods can move water up to a height of 100 m.

Scientists have found that the movement of sugars through phloem is much faster than can be explained by diffusion. They have also found that if they poison companion cells, movement of sugar in the phloem stops. Their conclusion is that companion cells assist in the movement of sugars through active transport.

sieve plate
sieve tube
companion cell

Figure 5 Sieve tubes.

Examiner feedback

Remember the different energy sources that are used for transporting substances through the plant.

Movement through the xylem depends on thermal energy from the Sun evaporating water from the leaves. Movement through phloem depends on energy from respiration. So transport through xylem does not require living cells, whereas movement through phloem requires energy released by respiration in mitochondria.

Questions

1. Name the plant tissue that transports the following. **(a)** Mainly water. **(b)** Sugars.
2. In which direction do these occur? **(a)** Water moving through a plant. **(b)** Sugar moving through a plant.
3. **(a)** Describe the structure of a xylem vessel. **(b)** Describe the structure of a sieve tube.
4. Explain how water passes from xylem across a leaf.
5. Explain what causes water to move to the top of a tall tree.
6. Describe the location of vascular bundles in the following parts of plants. **(a)** Roots. **(b)** Stems. **(c)** Leaves.
7. Explain how xylem vessels are adapted to carry out their function.
8. Compare and contrast the mechanisms by which water and sugars are moved through plants.

A*

Science in action

Scientists now use radioactive tracers to follow the movement of sugars around a plant. They label carbon dioxide with a **radioactive isotope** of carbon. The plant takes up this radioactive carbon dioxide and uses it to make sugars. These radioactive sugars can be tracked around the plant using radiation detectors such as Geiger counters or photographic film.

Learning objectives

Most students should be able to:

- describe the movement of water and mineral ions through a plant;
- describe the movement of sugars through a plant.

Some students should also be able to:

- analyse data relating to movement through xylem and phloem. [Ext]

ActiveTeach Resource: How does water move in plants? – *Key terms quiz*

Key points

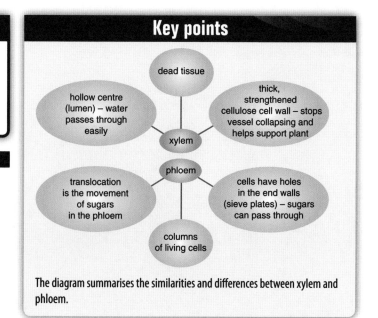

dead tissue
hollow centre (lumen) – water passes through easily
thick, strengthened cellulose cell wall – stops vessel collapsing and helps support plant
xylem
phloem
translocation is the movement of sugars in the phloem
cells have holes in the end walls (sieve plates) – sugars can pass through
columns of living cells

The diagram summarises the similarities and differences between xylem and phloem.

Xylem phloem transpiration stream

Lesson activities

Starter

1 Thought shower on which substances need to be transported by plants, their sources and their 'sinks'.

Main

1 B3 2.5a Xylem and phloem In this activity, students examine celery stalks, which have been standing with their lower ends in a solution of food dye for 24 hours, to detect the position of xylem. Students also examine prepared slides of roots and stems to find the positions of xylem and phloem. (~40 mins)

2 Students imagine that they are David Attenborough, shrunken down to the size of a molecule of water. They plan the voice-over for a TV documentary as a water molecule enters the plant in the root and passes up through the plant and out of the leaves.

3 Students produce a hypothesis about the effect of air movement on movement of water through xylem, then design an investigation to test their hypothesis.

Plenaries

1 Ask students in groups to compare the mechanisms involved in the movement of water through a plant with the mechanism of circulation in humans.

2 The ActiveTeach quiz looks at water transport in plants. [AT]

Homework

1 Worksheet B3 2.5b requires students to consider Malpighi's ring experiment, and consolidates understanding of the transpiration stream.

2 Worksheet B3 2.5c involves data analysis on movement through xylem and phloem.

Route to A*

Students research current theories into the mechanism of transport of sugars through phloem.

Answers to Student Book questions

1 **(a)** Xylem. **(b)** Phloem.

2 **(a)** Upwards from roots to leaves. (b) Upwards to the growing points of stems, and downwards to the growing points and storage tissue in the roots.

3 **(a)** A vertical series of dead, empty cells whose end walls have broken down. **(b)** A vertical series of living cells, without nuclei, whose end walls have formed sieve plates. They have associated companion cells that are essential for the functioning of phloem.

4 By osmosis. As the cells lining the leaf air spaces lose water through transpiration, water passes by osmosis from surrounding cells with more dilute cytoplasm to the cell with the lower concentration of water. Eventually water moves out of the xylem into the last cell in the osmotic series.

5 The Sun provides the energy for water to evaporate from leaves. This sets up a diffusion gradient for water from the xylem to the outside of the leaf. Loss of water from the leaves draws water up the xylem from the roots, because water molecules stick together.

6 **(a)** The vascular tissue is found in the centre of a root. **(b)** The vascular bundles are found in a ring around the stem, xylem to the inside, phloem to the outside. **(c)** In the veins in leaves, with xylem on top and phloem underneath.

7 The end walls of adjacent vertical xylem cells break down to form tubes. Also the cells have no living contents. These two features mean that there is no obstruction to the passage of water up a xylem vessel. It also has thick walls to prevent collapse.

8 The energy for the movement of water comes from the Sun, which evaporates water from the leaves. The energy for the movement of sugars comes from respiration by the companion cells. Movement of water is via dead empty cells in xylem. Movement in phloem is via living cells. Water is pulled up xylem vessels because water molecules stick together. Sugars are moved by active transport in phloem. Because of these factors, water moves in only one direction in xylem, but may move in either direction in phloem.

B3 3.1 Staying in balance

Link to the Specification

B3.3.1a Waste products which have to be removed from the body include:

- carbon dioxide produced by respiration and removed via the lungs when we breathe out
- urea, produced in the liver by the breakdown of amino acids and removed by the kidneys in the urine, which is temporarily stored in the bladder.

B3.3.1b If the water or ion content of the body is wrong, too much water may move into or out of the cells and damage them. Water and ions enter the body when we eat and drink.

How Science Works

CA: B4.1.1 Develop hypotheses and plan practical ways to test them, by: a) being able to make predictions based on a hypothesis; b) being able to test hypotheses (if investigation in activity 1 is completed).

B3 3.1 Staying in balance

Learning objectives

- describe some internal conditions in the body that are homeostatically controlled
- describe processes in which waste products are excreted from the body
- explain why temperature, blood sugar levels, water and ion content are controlled in the body.

In and out

We are constantly taking substances into our bodies, through our lungs and in what we drink and eat. We also make many substances in our bodies during chemical reactions. Some of these substances are waste products that could damage cells or interfere with other reactions if too much collects in the body.

These waste products must be **excreted**, that is, removed from the body. For example, carbon dioxide produced during **respiration** is excreted, mostly through the lungs when we breathe out. Another waste product is **urea**, made from excess **amino acids**, which is excreted through kidneys (see lesson B3 3.2).

We are also continually losing other substances from our bodies when we sweat and breathe, and in **faeces** and **urine**. This continual exchange with the environment means that conditions inside our bodies could change quite rapidly. However, it is essential that this doesn't happen.

There are many substances in our food and drink, including water, many ions and complex chemicals.

The need for balance

There are many processes in the body that keep the key substances and the body temperature within quite narrow limits. These processes are known as **homeostasis**.

Food and drink don't just contain the sugars, proteins and fats that get broken down and absorbed into your body. They also provide water and **mineral ions**, such as the sodium ions and chloride ions that make up salt. These are all small molecules and easily pass across cell membranes. Most cells, including muscle and nerve cells, will only function properly if there is the right balance of ions, such as sodium and potassium ions, on either side of the cell membrane.

Too much water in your cells can cause them to swell and even burst. Too little water can cause cells to shrink and function less efficiently. Lack of water also makes it difficult for other substances to move around. The movement of water in and out of cells is linked to the ion content in the cells. If the ions are not at the right concentration, then the water may move into or out of the cells by **osmosis** (see lesson B3 1.1). Simple sugar molecules, such as **glucose**, can also affect the movement of water by osmosis. Glucose is carried around the body in the blood, so blood glucose concentration must also be kept within limits.

Science in action

People with cholera or dysentery suffer severe diarrhoea and lose water and ions rapidly. Rehydration salts, dissolved in clean water, provide the right balance of ions and water to replace these losses. This cheap but very effective medicine has saved millions of lives.

Marathon runners must drink during a race, or they will become **dehydrated**. Drinking a lot of pure water can cause the body to absorb too much water into cells, causing overhydration, which is also dangerous.

206

You have seen earlier that **enzymes** only work properly within quite a limited range of temperature and pH. Enzymes control so many of the chemical reactions in our cells that we quickly become unwell if these conditions change too much. Carbon dioxide dissolves easily and makes the solution more acidic, which would affect cell reactions if the carbon dioxide was not removed.

Science skills

a Describe the effect of temperature on the rate of reaction.

b In view of the information on enzyme activity in the graph, explain why it is important that body temperature in humans is kept constant at about 37 °C.

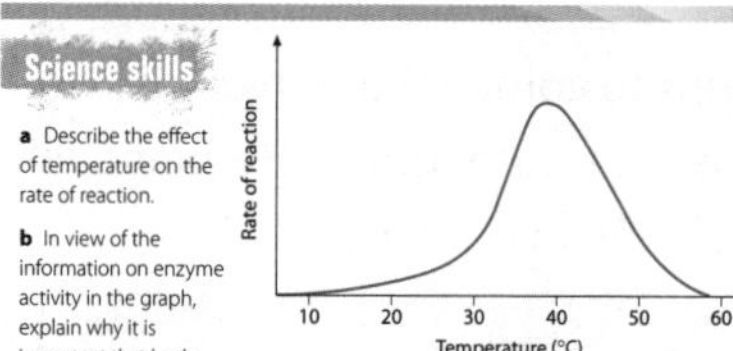

Figure 2 The rate of enzyme-catalysed reactions is affected by temperature.

Two red blood cells: the one on the left is normal, the one on the right has been in a solution that contained a lot of mineral ions.

Questions

1 Write a definition of the term *homeostasis*.

2 Describe and explain the difference between the two red blood cells in the photographs.

3 Suggest what would happen if the red blood cell on the left was put into pure water. Explain your answer.

4 For each of the following, say if the person is likely to become dehydrated or overhydrated. Give a reason for each answer. **(a)** Jenny doesn't have a drink all day. **(b)** Denny drinks two litres of water in one go. **(c)** Benny eats a large pack of salted crisps. **(d)** Penny sits outside for two hours on a hot summer day.

5 Cholera is a disease that causes lots of watery diarrhoea and vomiting and can cause death in a matter of hours. Explain why the death rate from cholera is high and why treatment with rehydration salts dissolved in clean water greatly reduces the death rate.

6 Breathing rate in the body is controlled by homeostatic mechanisms that are more sensitive to carbon dioxide concentration in the blood than to oxygen concentration. (Note that when carbon dioxide dissolves in blood it forms an acidic solution.) Explain as fully as you can why it is important that control of breathing rate involves carbon dioxide receptors. It may help to think about what would happen if carbon dioxide builds up in the cells. A*

Route to A*

When discussing homeostasis, and the effect of changes on the body, remember the effects of temperature and pH on the active site of enzymes. Be prepared to discuss any changes in the body in terms of the importance of enzymes in the control of many body processes, and therefore the key role of homeostasis in keeping the body functioning normally.

Taking it further

Ions play a far more important role in cells than just maintaining osmotic balance. The transfer of sodium ions across cell membranes facilitates the movement of glucose into cells. Cells are also continually exchanging sodium for potassium, to keep cell volume under control. This is particularly important in nerve cells, where the ion exchange across membranes produces nerve impulses. The sodium–potassium pumps in cell membranes account for about one-third of all the cell's energy use.

Homeostasis 207

Learning objectives

Most students should be able to:

- describe some internal conditions in the body that are homeostatically controlled
- describe processes in which waste products are excreted from the body
- explain why temperature, blood sugar levels, water and ion content are controlled in the body.

Some students should also be able to:

- explain fully why waste products must be removed from the body, using knowledge about body processes. [Ext]

Key points

Waste products, such as carbon dioxide and urea, must be excreted from the body so that they do not build up.

The body needs to control temperature and blood sugar levels in order to stay healthy.

Excess water and ions taken into the body in food and drink need to be excreted so that the balance of water and ion content inside and outside cells prevents damage from too much water moving into or out of cells.

ActiveTeach Resource: Keeping in balance – *True or false quiz*

Amino acid	enzyme	excrete	faeces	glucose	homeostasis
mineral ion	osmosis	respiration	urea	urine	dehydrated

Lesson activities

Starter

1 Remind students of earlier work by writing the word *osmosis* in the centre of the board and asking students to suggest related words and how they should be added to create a mind map. Link the effects of water gain and loss on cells with how students as organisms gain and lose water and mineral ions.

2 Ask students for the word equation that summarises aerobic respiration, and write this on the board. Ask them to describe where each of the reactants comes from and what happens to each of the products.

Main

1 Worksheet B3 3.1a Measuring the water in food is a planning exercise. If there is time, then allow students to carry out their investigation and test their hypothesis. (~40–60 min not including heating or drying time)

2 Worksheet B3 3.1b Problems with waste products If students are given the answer to Q1, then it is possible to use this sheet for homework. However, it brings together a wide range of areas of previous learning, including respiration from B1, the effect of pH on enzymes from B2, and the blood system from chapter 2 of B3. Students may need reminding of some of this earlier work to help them complete the answers. You may wish to demonstrate that bubbling oxygen through hydrogen-carbonate indicator does not change the pH of the solution before students complete Q10.

3 The ActiveTeach quiz reinforces work on homeostasis. [AT]

Plenaries

1 Ask students to write a definition of the word *homeostasis*. They should then compare their definition with a neighbour's and work together to produce a better definition. Repeat this in fours, and then eights, then come together as a class to produce the best definition.

2 Ask students whether the removal of water and ions from the body could be considered 'excretion'. If they are unsure, compare the removal of urea with the removal of water and ions – both through the kidneys. They should be prepared to extend the definition of excretion to include not only toxic waste products but also substances in excess in the body.

Homework

1 B3 3.1c Too much and too little This worksheet provides a series of questions on the importance of water and ions in the body in the context of overhydration and dehydration.

2 Ask students to research the range of symptoms caused by dehydration or low ion content in the body.

Points to note

- The specification point about urea production is mainly covered in the next lesson.

Route to A*

Introduce students to the concept of a thermostat, a mechanism that monitors the temperature of a room, and controls temperature in a room by switching the heater on or off at set points. Ask students to use this model to describe the way the body controls water and ion content, and temperature. This should only be done in an outline manner here, so that the detail of the body's control can be added in later lessons.

Answers to Student Book questions

Science skills

a The rate of the enzymatically controlled reactions increases gradually to a peak at around 40 °C, after which it drops rapidly to zero by about 58 °C.

b The best rates of reaction occur across a small range of temperature (between about 35 and 45 °C), so maintaining body temperature within this range will help the body processes to work at their best.

Answers

1 The maintaining of the body's internal balance of materials or temperature within narrow limits.

2 The cell on the left is in its normal state of hydration because it is in balance with the concentration of the solution that it is in. The one on the right has lost water through osmosis because water has been drawn out of it by the ions in the solution.

3 Water would be drawn into the cell by osmosis because the concentration of ions is greater inside than outside. So the cell would swell and eventually burst.

4 **(a)** Jenny would become dehydrated because she would lose water in sweat and in urine, but not gain any. **(b)** Denny would become overhydrated because the water he drinks would be absorbed by his body faster than it was being excreted in urine or sweat. **(c)** Benny would become dehydrated because the salt that his body absorbs from the crisps would draw water out of his cells by osmosis. **(d)** Penny would probably become dehydrated because she will lose a lot of water in sweat, unless she also drinks plenty of water at the same time.

5 Loss of large quantities of water and ions from the body will quickly cause problems with the way cells work. If the damage is too great, then the patient will die. Rehydration salts rapidly replace water and ions in the right balance for cells to continue working properly, so death is much less likely.

6 Carbon dioxide is produced in the reactions of respiration and dissolves in the body fluids, including blood. If the carbon dioxide was not removed, the pH of the fluids would decrease (become more acidic). This would affect chemical reactions in cells that are controlled by enzymes, which work best at normal pH. Oxygen also dissolves in body fluids, but does not affect pH, so its concentration in fluids is not so critical.

[*Note for teachers:* Oxygen concentration is also monitored because cells need oxygen for respiration, but the range of concentration tolerated by the body is much wider than that for carbon dioxide concentration.]

B3 3.2 The role of the kidneys

Link to the Specification

B3.3.1c A healthy kidney produces urine by:

- first filtering the blood
- reabsorbing all the sugar
- reabsorbing the dissolved ions needed by the body
- reabsorbing as much water as the body needs
- releasing urea, excess ions and water as urine.

Ideas for practical work

Test urine from diabetic and non-diabetic people using Clinistix.

How Science Works

CA: B4.5.4 Draw conclusions using scientific ideas and evidence, by: a) writing a conclusion, based on evidence that relates correctly to known facts.

B3 3.2 The role of the kidneys

Learning objectives

- describe how urea is produced from the breakdown of excess amino acids
- explain how healthy kidneys produce urine by reabsorbing glucose, dissolved ions and water needed by the body, and releasing urea and excess water and ions
- outline the role of the kidneys in homeostasis
- explain the value of urine tests for diagnosis in forensics and medicine.

Examiner feedback

Remember that it is the liver that makes urea and the kidneys that excrete urea.

The production of urea

During the digestion of your food, proteins are broken down to amino acids. These are small molecules that pass easily through the gut wall and into the blood. The blood carries the amino acids to cells where they are used for building new proteins.

The body cannot store excess amino acids, so these have to be excreted. They are removed from blood by the liver, which breaks the amino acids down to make a substance called urea. Urea is also a small molecule, so it diffuses easily into the blood. It must be excreted from the body because it is **toxic** in high concentrations and could harm cells and tissues. It is cleared from the blood in the **kidneys**.

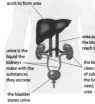

the liver breaks down excess amino acids to form urea

urea passes into the blood to reach the kidneys

urine is the liquid the kidneys make with the substances they excrete

the kidneys clean the blood of substances the body doesn't need, including urea

the bladder stores urine

Figure 1 How excess amino acids are changed to urea, which is then excreted from the body.

Examiner feedback

You will not be expected to know the structure of tubules for your exam, but you will need to understand the role of the processes of filtration and reabsorption in producing urine.

Making urine

You have two kidneys about halfway down your back and inside your abdomen. Each kidney is made up of over one million tubules. The role of the **tubules** is to filter your blood and remove some of the substances your body doesn't need, including urea.

At the start of each tubule is a small capillary network. The cells that line these capillaries have very leaky membranes. This allows a lot of **plasma** (the liquid part of the blood), and the small molecules dissolved in it, to be filtered from the blood, leaving the cells and large molecules behind in the blood vessel.

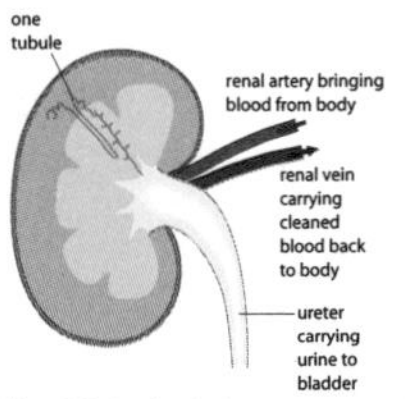

Figure 2 Section through a kidney showing its blood supply.

Each tubule is closely associated with capillaries. As the fluid passes along the tubule, many of the substances in it are absorbed back into the capillary; all the sugar (glucose) is reabsorbed, for example. This is important because the body uses glucose for respiration. Also, any dissolved ions and water that the body needs are reabsorbed. This makes sure that the right balance of water and ions is maintained in the body so that cells and all the processes in them can work properly.

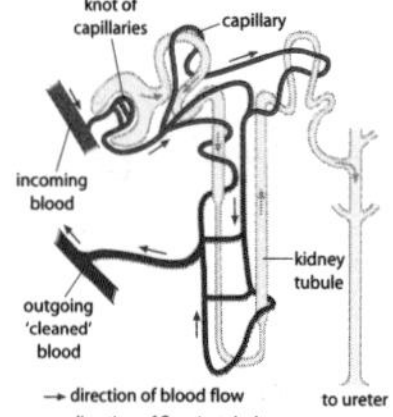

Figure 3 One tubule and its capillary.

208

The fluid that remains in the tubule is called **urine**. It passes to the bladder where it is stored until it is excreted.

The water that is reabsorbed moves back into the blood by osmosis. Some substances are reabsorbed passively from the tubule into the blood by diffusion. Others are actively reabsorbed by active transport, which uses energy.

Science skills

Table 1 shows the concentrations of different substances in the blood, in the liquid filtered off into the kidneys, and in urine.

Table 1 Concentrations of different substances in the blood, kidney filtrate and urine.

Substance	Concentration / grams/100 cm^3		
	blood plasma	kidney filtrate	urine
glucose	0.10	0.10	0.0
mineral ions	0.43	0.43	0.18
protein	6.5	0.0	0.0
urea	0.02	0.02	2.0
water	91.0	91.0	96.0

a Explain the similarities and differences in concentration between the blood plasma and the filtrate.

b Which substance is reabsorbed in the tubule?

c Suggest what would happen to the concentrations in urine of these substances on a hot day.

d Suggest why protein is not part of the filtrate.

Questions

1. Suggest some of the substances dissolved in plasma that could pass into the tubule.
2. Which structures in blood cannot pass into the tubule? Explain your answer.
3. Draw a flow chart to show how excess amino acids are removed from your body.
4. If you drink the same amount of liquid, you will produce less urine on a hot day than on a cold day. Explain why.
5. A doctor may test a patient's urine for glucose. Explain what glucose in the urine might indicate.
6. The reabsorption of glucose and ions in the kidneys uses a combination of diffusion and active transport. Explain fully why both processes are involved.
7. Ethanol (alcohol) is a small molecule that diffuses easily into the blood from the gut and is not actively reabsorbed in the kidneys. Explain why a urine test is an accurate way of measuring blood alcohol concentration and why urine samples must be taken from drivers at the scene of a car accident.
8. Explain fully the role of the kidney in homeostasis.

A*

Science in action

Urine tests are a quick and simple way of identifying what is going on chemically in the body. Doctors use them for diagnosing diabetes and a wide range of other conditions. The police use urine tests to estimate how much alcohol drivers have been drinking. Urine tests can also be used to find out if someone is pregnant.

Practical

When alcohol is added to potassium dichromate, the colour changes from yellow to green. This simple test can identify alcohol concentration in urine.

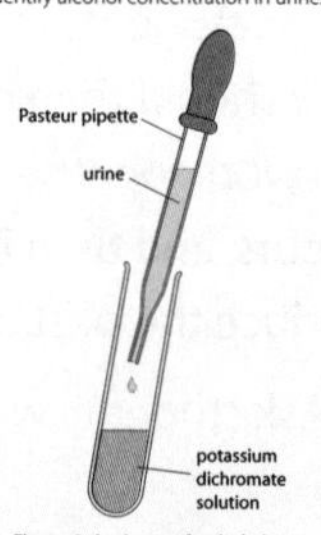

Figure 4 A urine test for alcohol.

Homeostasis 209

Learning objectives

Most students should be able to:

- describe how urea is produced from the breakdown of excess amino acids
- explain how healthy kidneys produce urine by reabsorbing glucose, dissolved ions and water needed by the body and releasing urea, excess water and ions
- outline the role of kidneys in homeostasis.

Some students should also be able to:

- explain how the body homeostatically controls water balance. [Ext]

Key points

Excess amino acids are converted to urea in the liver, which is excreted by the kidneys in urine.

The kidneys filter the blood to form a filtrate in the tubules.

A healthy kidney reabsorbs all the glucose from the filtrate, balances the ions and water needs of the body and excretes urea to make urine.

ActiveTeach Resource: How do your kidneys work? – *Matching activity*

Lesson activities

Starter

1 Start the lesson with a large flask of yellow-coloured water (appropriately coloured for a normal urine sample). Tell students that it is a sample of urine and that they will be analysing it to see what it contains. Give them 5 minutes to jot down a list of substances that they would expect to find, and reasons why they would expect to find them in the urine. This should revise all earlier work on the removal of waste products such as urea, and the control of water in the body.

2 Ask students if they have ever noticed differences in the colour of their urine at different times of day or in different states of hydration. (If they haven't, explain that it is usually darker first thing in the morning when they are less well hydrated and paler when they are well hydrated.) Ask them to suggest why these changes occur and what is causing them.

Main

1 B3 3.2a Testing urine Refer to sheet in Teacher and Technician Planning Pack.

2 The ActiveTeach matching activity will help students understand kidney function and structure. [AT]

3 B3 3.2b Kidney dissection Refer to sheet in Teacher and Technician Planning Pack.

4 Ask students to research the effect of the hormone ADH (anti-diuretic hormone) on the output of urine by the body and how the amount of this hormone that is produced is controlled. They could also investigate the effects of diuretics, such as alcohol and tea, and suggest why doctors may prescribe diuretics for patients who have absorbed poison into their blood.

Plenaries

1 Give students lists of three words and ask them to identify the odd one out, giving reasons for their answers. Suitable lists include: glucose, ions, urea; red blood cell, plasma, oxygen; red blood cell, plasma, carbon dioxide.

2 Ask students to write clues for a crossword on water balance for which the following are the answers: kidney, tubule, urine, glucose, urea, homeostasis, bladder, water. Give students 4 minutes to complete these and then ask them to swap their clues with a neighbour to test them out.

Homework

1 Worksheet B3 3.2c asks questions relating to the use of urine tests.

2 Animals that live in desert conditions need to extract more water from the kidney tubule than those that live in wetter places. Ask students to research the differences in their kidneys which allow this to happen.

Points to note

- During research, students may discover the fact that up to 50% of the urea that is initially filtered from the blood into the kidney tubule is reabsorbed from the tubule. Since we talk about urea being a waste product that is removed by the kidneys, this can be confusing. The reason is that urea is a small molecule and moves back by diffusion along its concentration gradient. However, in the last stage of urine formation water is selectively reabsorbed from the tubule, meaning that the concentration of urea in urine increases even if the actual amount does not. The removal of urea from the blood is a gradual process. Students do not need to understand this for the specification.

Route to A*

Ask students to complete Worksheet B3 3.2d which describes excretory products of other animals and links them to the environments in which they live.

Answers to Student Book questions

Science skills

a All the small molecules (glucose, mineral ions, urea and water) have the same concentration in the blood plasma and filtrate because they filter easily through the capillaries. Larger molecules and blood cells do not pass through the walls of the capillaries, and so they do not appear in the filtrate.

b Glucose.

c The concentrations of mineral ions and urea would increase because more water would be reabsorbed in the tubule to replace water lost in sweat.

d Proteins are too large to pass through the wall of the capillaries.

Answers

1 Glucose, water, urea, mineral ions.

2 Blood cells and anything else that is too large (e.g. protein molecules) to filter through the capillaries into the tubule.

3 Flow chart should show: amino acids from digestion in the blood, excess amino acids removed from blood in liver, amino acids broken down to urea, urea passes back into blood, urea circulates in blood to kidneys, urea filtered out of blood by kidneys, urea as part of urine passes to bladder for storage until excreted.

4 More water will be lost from the body through sweating, so more water will be reabsorbed from the kidney tubules into the blood to maintain homeostasis.

5 Glucose is normally all reabsorbed from the urine because it is an essential molecule for use in respiration by the body. Glucose in the urine shows that something has gone wrong in the body: either that there is too much in the blood and not all can be reabsorbed, or that there is damage to the kidneys.

6 Glucose and ions are small molecules that can pass across cell membranes by diffusion. However, diffusion can only occur while there is a concentration gradient, and diffusion will only occur from the solution where the concentration of the substance is highest to the solution where the concentration is lowest. The body needs to reabsorb all glucose and sometimes extra ions beyond those that are reabsorbed by diffusion. This will be movement against the concentration gradient, so active transport is needed for this.

7 Ethanol will easily be filtered from the blood into the tubule through the capillaries. As the filtrate passes along the tubule, some ethanol will pass back into the blood by diffusion until the concentration of ethanol in the blood and filtrate is balanced. Any ethanol in the urine will give a good indication of the concentration of ethanol in the blood. The urine must be taken as soon after the accident as possible to produce a reliable estimate of blood alcohol concentration at the time of the accident, because the ethanol will be rapidly filtered out of the blood and so its concentration will decrease over time. You can only be charged with being under the influence of alcohol at the time of an accident if there is evidence that your blood alcohol concentration was above the legal limit.

8 The kidney plays a key part in the homeostasis of water, ions, urea and glucose within the body. All these substances need to be controlled within a certain range of concentration in the blood for healthy working of the body. Controlling the concentration in the blood controls their concentration in body cells, because these substances diffuse easily from one to the other. The kidney filters out all these small molecules from the blood at the capillaries. Control of reabsorption by diffusion and by active transport helps maintain these substances within the range of concentrations that the body needs to remain healthy.

B3 3.3 Treatment with dialysis

Link to the Specification

B3.3.1d People who suffer from kidney failure may be treated either by using a kidney dialysis machine or by having a healthy kidney transplanted.

B3.3.1e Treatment by dialysis restores the concentrations of dissolved substances in the blood to normal levels and has to be carried out at regular intervals.

B3.3.1f In a dialysis machine a person's blood flows between partially permeable membranes. The dialysis fluid contains the same concentration of useful substances as the blood. This ensures that glucose and useful mineral ions are not lost. Urea passes out from the blood into the dialysis fluid.

Ideas for practical work

Design a model kidney dialysis machine using Visking tubing as the filter.

How Science Works

SKU: B3.3 bullet point 1: Evaluate the advantages and disadvantages of treating kidney failure by dialysis or kidney transplant.

CA: B4.6.1 Review hypotheses in the light of outcomes, by: b) developing scientific ideas as a result of observations and measurements.

B3 3.3 Treatment with dialysis

Learning objectives

- describe how a person with kidney failure may be treated with dialysis and explain why it has to be carried out at regular intervals
- explain how substances are exchanged between dialysis fluid and the patient's blood across partially permeable membranes to restore normal levels in the blood
- evaluate the advantages and disadvantages of treating kidney failure by dialysis.

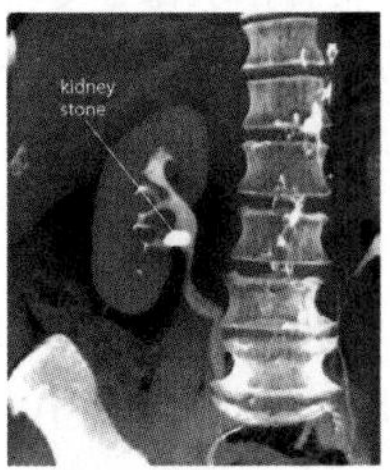

Kidney stones form when salts in the urine crystallise out to make large lumps that block the kidney tubes.

Examiner feedback

Remember that substances in solution diffuse from regions of high concentration to regions of lower concentration.

Route to A*

There is no active transport in a dialyser, so exchange of substances across the membrane is passive only. This is important to remember when contrasting dialysis with the way kidneys work, as it explains the concentrations of substances in the dialysis solution.

Kidney failure

The kidneys play an important role in homeostasis of the body. If they fail to work properly, it can soon cause problems. The concentration of urea in the body increases, and water and ions get out of balance. Kidneys can fail to work properly if they have been damaged in an accident or by disease.

Many things can cause kidney disease, such as infection, diabetes, long-term high blood pressure, or simply blockage of the tubes by hard lumps called kidney stones. Many people have kidney disease, sometimes without even knowing it, because a little damage has little effect on kidney function.

Only a small proportion of people with kidney disease will eventually develop **kidney failure**. This is defined as occurring when the kidneys function at less than 30 per cent of their normal level. At this stage the body can be affected badly by the lack of kidney function. The treatment offered by a doctor will depend on the cause of the disease. For example, kidney stones can be broken up by ultrasound, but other kinds of damage cannot be mended so easily.

Without treatment, a patient with kidney failure will eventually fall into a coma and die from the toxins in the blood, or from a heart attack.

Dialysis treatment

One way of treating kidney failure is **haemodialysis**. This is when a machine takes over the function of the kidneys. Needles are inserted into blood vessels, often in the patient's arm. Blood flows from the patient through a tube to the machine and is returned through another tube. Inside the machine the blood flows through a filter called a **dialyser**.

Inside the dialyser, a partially permeable membrane separates the blood from the dialysing fluid. This fluid contains glucose and useful minerals. It has similar glucose and ion concentrations to those in normal plasma.

If the blood is low in glucose or minerals, these will diffuse into the blood from the dialysing fluid. If their concentration is too high in the blood, then the excess will diffuse out into the dialysing fluid. Waste products, such as urea, diffuse out of the blood, because there are none of these substances in the dialysing fluid.

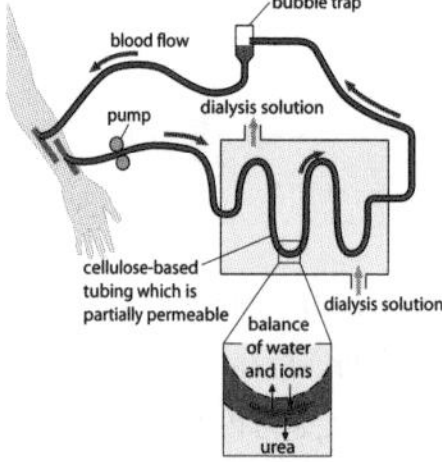

Figure 1 Diffusion into and out of the blood happens in a dialyser just like in the kidney.

210

Practical

We can model the way dialysis works using visking tubing to help understand the process.

a How would you set up the experiment using the apparatus in Figure 2? What would you put in the boiling tube? What would you put in the visking tubing?

b The visking tubing model has limitations when used to explain the mechanism of dialysis. What are these limitations?

sawn-off end of syringe plunger

visking tubing

boiling tube

Figure 2 Modelling dialysis with visking tubing.

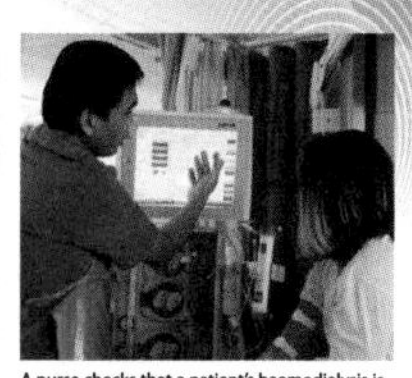

A nurse checks that a patient's haemodialysis is going well.

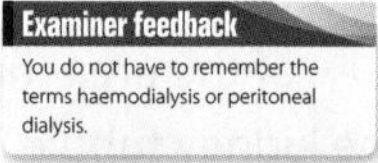

Examiner feedback

You do not have to remember the terms haemodialysis or peritoneal dialysis.

How good is dialysis?

Dialysis only partly copies the action of the kidneys, so people with kidney failure also need to control their diet to prevent a build-up of particular substances, and to avoid taking in too much fluid. Haemodialysis is usually carried out three times a week, for about four hours each time, and often in hospital with medical supervision. Peritoneal dialysis is a similar treatment that is performed continually at home so the patient can move around at the same time. However, patients and their families have the responsibility of making sure the dialysis is carried out properly.

Questions

1. Suggest why people can have kidney disease without knowing it.
2. Explain why a stone blocking urine from leaving the kidney could affect how a kidney works.
3. How is dialysis useful in treating kidney failure?
4. What are the drawbacks of using dialysis for treating kidney failure?
5. Explain how the dialysis machine mimics the normal function of the kidney, and the ways in which it does not mimic the normal function of the kidney.
6. Explain in detail what will happen to the concentration of substances in the blood such as urea and digestion products if the kidneys are failing. What effect will this have on the cells in the body?
7. Explain as fully as possible why people who are on dialysis must control what they eat.
8. Compare the advantages and disadvantages of haemodialysis and peritoneal dialysis, and suggest different groups of people for whom each method would be more suitable. A*

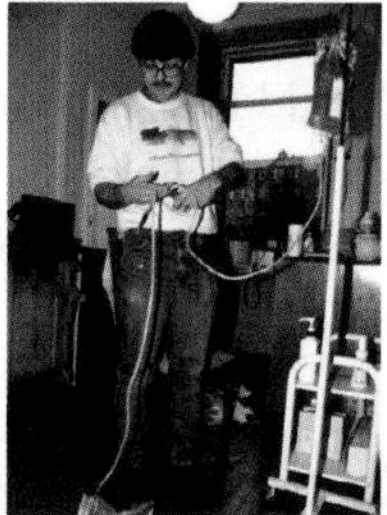

Peritoneal dialysis uses a natural membrane in the abdomen as the dialysis membrane.

Homeostasis 211

Learning objectives

Most students should be able to:

- describe how a person with kidney failure may be treated with dialysis and explain why it has to be carried out at regular intervals
- explain how substances are exchanged between dialysis fluid and the patient's blood across partially permeable membranes to restore normal levels in the blood
- evaluate the advantages and disadvantages of treating kidney failure by dialysis.

Some students should also be able to:

- apply knowledge of diffusion, osmosis and of the way the kidney works to evaluate different methods of dialysis. [Ext]

Key points

Kidney dialysis can be used to treat people suffering from kidney failure.

In the dialyser, substances are exchanged between the dialysing fluid and the blood across a partially permeable membrane to restore the normal balance of those substances in the blood.

Dialysis for treating kidney failure has advantages and disadvantages.

ActiveTeach Resource: How does a dialysis machine work? – *Ordering activity*

Lesson activities

Starter

1 Write the words *osmosis*, *diffusion* and *kidney* on the board and ask students to write three different sentences that include all three words. Ask for examples from around the class and discuss any anomalies or misunderstandings.

2 Ask students to work in pairs for 5 minutes to jot down what effect there would be if the kidneys suddenly stopped working. (Be sensitive to the possibility that a student, or someone they know, may have suffered kidney failure.) Take answers from the class to make sure that they have a clear understanding of the role of the kidneys from the last topic.

Main

1 **B3 3.3a Modelling dialysis** Refer to sheet in Teacher and Technician Planning Pack.

2 The ActiveTeach ordering activity will help students understand the stages in dialysis. If needed, revisit the last lesson to remind students about how the kidneys work. [AT]

3 Ask students to write a letter to a friend who has just been diagnosed with kidney failure and is scared of the idea of dialysis. See the Kidney Dialysis Information Centre and Dialysis – NHS Choices websites for more information.

Plenaries

1 Write the word *dialysis* in the middle of the board and ask students to suggest related words and how they should be linked to create a mind map on the topic. If not suggested, encourage students to include ideas related to advantages and disadvantages.

2 Give students 5 minutes to write down the key problems with dialysis. Take examples from around the class, then ask students to judge whether dialysis is worth the effort. Again, take answers for both 'yes' and 'no' (if there are any), to evaluate this treatment for kidney failure.

Homework

1 **Worksheet B3.3b** Refer to sheet in the Activity Pack.

2 **Worksheet B3.3c** presents a series of questions that tests students' learning in this lesson.

Points to note

- Specification point B3.3.1d and the Skills, Knowledge and Understanding point that refers to transplants are covered in the next lesson.

Route to A*

Expect students to apply their knowledge of diffusion, osmosis and the normal working of the kidney to all work in this lesson.

In addition, this would be a useful opportunity to extend understanding of the role of the kidneys beyond what is needed by the specification. For example, the kidneys play an important part in the formation of red blood cells (by producing erythropoietin) and in the production of vitamin D. Patients suffering from kidney failure and treated with dialysis need regular medication to protect against anaemia and calcium shortage.

Answers to Student Book questions

Practical

a The boiling tube should contain water with concentrations of glucose and ions that are a little lower than normal blood concentrations, but it should contain no urea. The visking tubing should contain a solution of a higher concentration of glucose and ions than in the boiling tube, urea and water. These will model the situation of the patient's blood and haemodialysis solution before dialysis begins.

b This is a static model, whereas in haemodialysis, fresh solution is continually flowing through the machine. This means that, in the model, concentrations of solutes will stabilise at a higher level than would happen in haemodialysis, where solutes that have diffused into the solution are removed and replaced with fresh solution.

Answers

1 Kidney disease sometimes does not produce any symptoms.

2 If the stone blocks the ureter, the urine cannot flow away, so urea and excess water and ions cannot be removed from the blood by that kidney.

3 It keeps the concentration of substances, such as urea, water and dissolved ions at levels that allow normal working of body cells.

4 Frequent regular dialysis means having to be near a hospital or have lots of equipment at home. Patients must also control their diet to stop some substances building up too rapidly. Dialysis takes a lot of time and care to do properly.

5 The dialysis machine exchanges substances by diffusion with the blood until they are in balance either side of the partially permeable membrane. It does not filter the blood as happens in the kidney, and there is no active transport across the membrane to mimic the reabsorption of some substances into the blood as happens in the kidney.

6 Substances that are produced by the body, such as urea, will increase in concentration in the blood. Products of digestion entering the body will not be kept in balance, so concentrations will either increase or decrease much more than normal, depending on how much is taken in. This will change the concentration of the substances in the body cells, and possibly affect the way the cells work.

7 Food and drink contain many substances that are absorbed into the body after digestion. Different foods contain different proportions of different substances, such as ions and proteins. Proteins are broken down to amino acids in digestion, and excess amino acids are converted to urea by the liver. If the balance of ions and water is upset or the concentration of urea in the body increases because the kidneys aren't working properly, then the body could be damaged. Dialysis is only carried out every two or three days, during which time the patient has absorbed many substances from their food and drink. If they take in a high proportion of protein, for example, the body could be damaged between dialysis treatments.

8 Haemodialysis is carried out under medical supervision so there will be someone around who is trained in setting up the dialysis and making sure nothing goes wrong. The disadvantages of haemodialysis are that you have to go to the hospital or clinic every few days to receive that treatment. Substances can get out of balance in the body between treatments, which can damage the body. Peritoneal dialysis can be done at home and can be continuous. This should reduce the risk of damage from toxic urea or an imbalance of ions and water, but depends on the patient and their family being able to use the equipment correctly. Haemodialysis would be better for anyone living on their own as there is nobody at home to help them with the dialysis. It would also be better for anyone living close to a clinic. Peritoneal dialysis would be better for people living far from a treatment centre.

Kidney transplants

Link to the Specification

B3.3.1d People who suffer from kidney failure may be treated either by using a kidney dialysis machine or by having a healthy kidney transplanted.

B3.3.1g In kidney transplants a diseased kidney is replaced with a healthy one from a donor. However, the donor kidney may be rejected by the immune system unless precautions are taken.

B3.3.1h Antigens are proteins on the surface of cells. The recipient's antibodies may attack the antigens on the donor organ as they do not recognise them as part of the recipient's body.

B3.3.1i To prevent rejection of the transplanted kidney:

- a donor kidney with a 'tissue-type' similar to that of the recipient is used
- the recipient is treated with drugs that suppress the immune system.

How Science Works

SKU: B3.3 bullet point 1: Evaluate the advantages and disadvantages of treating kidney failure by dialysis or kidney transplant.

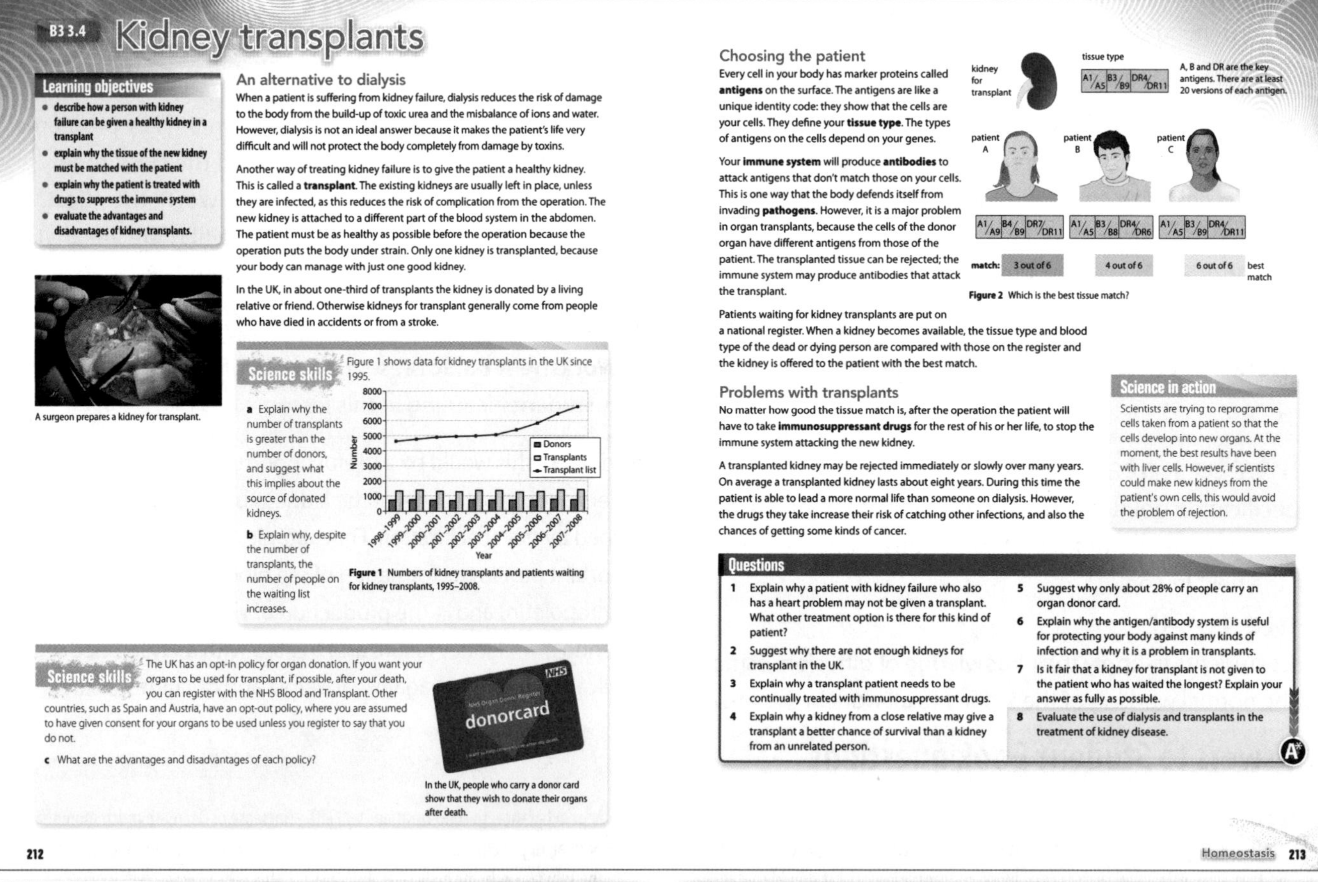

B3 3.4 Kidney transplants

Learning objectives

- describe how a person with kidney failure can be given a healthy kidney in a transplant
- explain why the tissue of the new kidney must be matched with the patient
- explain why the patient is treated with drugs to suppress the immune system
- evaluate the advantages and disadvantages of kidney transplants.

A surgeon prepares a kidney for transplant.

An alternative to dialysis

When a patient is suffering from kidney failure, dialysis reduces the risk of damage to the body from the build-up of toxic urea and the misbalance of ions and water. However, dialysis is not an ideal answer because it makes the patient's life very difficult and will not protect the body completely from damage by toxins.

Another way of treating kidney failure is to give the patient a healthy kidney. This is called a **transplant**. The existing kidneys are usually left in place, unless they are infected, as this reduces the risk of complication from the operation. The new kidney is attached to a different part of the blood system in the abdomen. The patient must be as healthy as possible before the operation because the operation puts the body under strain. Only one kidney is transplanted, because your body can manage with just one good kidney.

In the UK, in about one-third of transplants the kidney is donated by a living relative or friend. Otherwise kidneys for transplant generally come from people who have died in accidents or from a stroke.

Science skills Figure 1 shows data for kidney transplants in the UK since 1995.

a Explain why the number of transplants is greater than the number of donors, and suggest what this implies about the source of donated kidneys.

b Explain why, despite the number of transplants, the number of people on the waiting list increases.

Figure 1 Numbers of kidney transplants and patients waiting for kidney transplants, 1995–2008.

Science skills The UK has an opt-in policy for organ donation. If you want your organs to be used for transplant, if possible, after your death, you can register with the NHS Blood and Transplant. Other countries, such as Spain and Austria, have an opt-out policy, where you are assumed to have given consent for your organs to be used unless you register to say that you do not.

c What are the advantages and disadvantages of each policy?

In the UK, people who carry a donor card show that they wish to donate their organs after death.

212

Choosing the patient

Every cell in your body has marker proteins called **antigens** on the surface. The antigens are like a unique identity code: they show that the cells are your cells. They define your **tissue type**. The types of antigens on the cells depend on your genes.

Your **immune system** will produce **antibodies** to attack antigens that don't match those on your cells. This is one way that the body defends itself from invading **pathogens**. However, it is a major problem in organ transplants, because the cells of the donor organ have different antigens from those of the patient. The transplanted tissue can be rejected; the immune system may produce antibodies that attack the transplant.

Figure 2 Which is the best tissue match?

Patients waiting for kidney transplants are put on a national register. When a kidney becomes available, the tissue type and blood type of the dead or dying person are compared with those on the register and the kidney is offered to the patient with the best match.

Problems with transplants

No matter how good the tissue match is, after the operation the patient will have to take **immunosuppressant drugs** for the rest of his or her life, to stop the immune system attacking the new kidney.

A transplanted kidney may be rejected immediately or slowly over many years. On average a transplanted kidney lasts about eight years. During this time the patient is able to lead a more normal life than someone on dialysis. However, the drugs they take increase their risk of catching other infections, and also the chances of getting some kinds of cancer.

Science in action

Scientists are trying to reprogramme cells taken from a patient so that the cells develop into new organs. At the moment, the best results have been with liver cells. However, if scientists could make new kidneys from the patient's own cells, this would avoid the problem of rejection.

Questions

1 Explain why a patient with kidney failure who also has a heart problem may not be given a transplant. What other treatment option is there for this kind of patient?
2 Suggest why there are not enough kidneys for transplant in the UK.
3 Explain why a transplant patient needs to be continually treated with immunosuppressant drugs.
4 Explain why a kidney from a close relative may give a transplant a better chance of survival than a kidney from an unrelated person.
5 Suggest why only about 28% of people carry an organ donor card.
6 Explain why the antigen/antibody system is useful for protecting your body against many kinds of infection and why it is a problem in transplants.
7 Is it fair that a kidney for transplant is not given to the patient who has waited the longest? Explain your answer as fully as possible.
8 Evaluate the use of dialysis and transplants in the treatment of kidney disease.

A*

Homeostasis 213

Learning objectives

Most students should be able to:

- explain that a person with kidney failure can be given a healthy kidney in a transplant
- explain why the tissue of the new kidney must be matched with the patient
- explain why the patient is treated with drugs to suppress the immune system
- evaluate the advantages and disadvantages of kidney transplants.

Some students should also be able to:

- discuss the scientific and ethical issues surrounding the production of saviour siblings for children who need transplants. [Ext]

Key points

Kidney disease can be treated with a transplanted kidney.

The antigens on the cells in the kidney for transplant must be matched as closely as possible with the cells in the patient's body to reduce the risk of rejection.

A kidney transplant patient will have to take immunosuppressant drugs for the rest of their life to prevent their body making antibodies to the antigens on the cells in the transplanted kidney.

Lesson activities

Starter

1 Revise the last topic by asking students to suggest quickly what the problems are when treating kidney failure with dialysis. Then ask them if they know of other ways to treat organ failure. It is highly likely that some students will suggest organ transplant. Ask students to suggest the advantages of replacing a diseased kidney rather than treating it with dialysis. This can be revisited in the plenary to make sure that students have learnt the correct answers.

Antibody antigen immunosuppressant drug rejection tissue type transplant

2 Choose a word from the keyword lists for the last three topics, and pick three students. Ask each in turn to pick a vowel or a consonant, and write one of the vowels or consonants on the board. If the word has run out of either then nothing is written up. Keep going until one of the three students puts his/her hand up to say what the word is. Then challenge the student to say what the word means and ask the other two students whether they agree or disagree. Then read out the definition from the glossary.

Main

1 Worksheet B3.4a Kidneys for transplant Refer to sheet in Activity Pack.

2 Transplant criteria Ask students to research the criteria on which patients are selected for kidney transplant. They should use their findings to answer the following questions.

- How does the selection process try to be fair to all patients?
- Are people in some areas (such as cities) more likely to be selected than from other areas? Explain your answer.
- Are different age groups treated differently in the selection process? Explain your answer.
- What is a 'multiple pairing donor' scheme?

Plenaries

1 Ask students to imagine that a friend's sister is on dialysis for kidney failure. The friend is thinking about offering to donate one of their kidneys to their sister. Give students 5 minutes to think of two reasons why they should donate, and two why they should not. Take answers from around the class, until you think all sensible examples have been covered.

2 Ask each student to write down a question about something from lessons B3 3.2–3.4. They should write the question on the left of a strip of paper and the answer on the right and then tear the strip in half. Collect the questions and answers separately, then hand them out so that each student gets one question and one answer. Ask one student to read out their question. The student with the right answer then stands and reads out the answer. You may need to restart this task if the original answers to questions are wrong. Do not identify individuals who have made these mistakes; they will learn from any discussion as to what the answer should be.

Homework

1 Worksheet B3.4b Refer to sheet in Activity Pack.

2 Ask students to storyboard an animation that explains why transplanted tissues may be rejected, and what can be done both before and after a transplant operation to minimise the risk of rejection of the transplanted organ.

Points to note

- The parts of specification that refer to dialysis were covered in the last lesson.

Route to A*

Students could research the development in embryo selection for matching tissue types, to produce 'saviour' siblings for young children who need a transplant (more commonly bone marrow, but could be organs such as kidneys). They should consider not only the scientific reasons behind doing this, but also the ethical issues that it raises.

Answers to Student Book questions

Science skills

a People have two kidneys, so a dead person can donate one kidney to each of two patients. As the number of transplants is nearly double that of the number of donors, this implies that most kidneys come from dead donors.

b The number of people needing kidney transplants increases more than the number of organs available for transplant.

c Opt-in: advantage – feeling good about choosing to do it; disadvantage – not enough organs available for donation.
Opt-out: advantage – more organs likely to be available for donation; disadvantage – negative feelings about deciding not to do it. [Ethical question about reducing people's freedom to choose what is done to their bodies.]

Answers

1 A heart problem is a condition that could make a transplant operation very risky so the patient would have to be treated by dialysis.

2 Not enough people are willing to donate their organs, or think about it while they are still alive and able to give permission for their organs to be used after death.

3 The antibodies in the body will continually try to attack the cells of the organ because they are 'foreign'/'not self' and so the production of antibodies has to be suppressed.

4 Since you inherit your antigens from your parents, it is possible that a close relative will have antigens similar to those of the patient. The tissue match will therefore be good and the risk of rejection will be low. Each person can survive on one kidney, so transplant from a living donor is possible.

5 Many people like the idea of their death helping others to live, but it takes effort to get a card, so often people don't bother. They may also dislike thinking about their own deaths or believe that a body should be buried intact, or they may think that surviving relatives will be upset knowing that organs have been removed.

6 Infections are caused by invading cells, so detecting cells as 'not self' helps the body to tackle infection effectively. However, a transplant organ also contains cells that have 'non-self' antigens so the immune system will produce antibodies to destroy the cells in the organ, even though we want the organ to continue working.

7 The answer should be 'yes', because the tissue in the kidney for transplant must match the tissue of the patient as closely as possible to reduce the risk of rejection. This not only avoids wasting the kidney by giving it to someone who has waited longer, but is not a good match, but also avoids the risks of putting them through an operation that is more likely to fail.

8 Dialysis is suitable for all patients suffering from kidney disease. Without it they would soon die from the build-up of urea and excess ions in their body fluids, as these would prevent some normal life processes from happening properly. However, dialysis is inconvenient as it needs to be done several times a week with the patient staying still. Diet needs to be carefully controlled too, to make sure urea and ion concentrations don't increase too quickly from the digestion of food. Normal control of blood concentrations of urea and ions can be achieved by kidney transplant, so the patient can lead a more normal life. However, this requires a good tissue match between the donor and recipient: otherwise the kidney will be quickly rejected. Also, the patient will need to take drugs for the rest of their life to prevent the body rejecting the kidney. These drugs will leave them more susceptible to other infections. Even then, rejection may eventually happen.

B3 3.5 Controlling body temperature

Link to the Specification

B3.3.2a Sweating helps to cool the body. More water is lost when it is hot, and more water has to be taken as drink or in food to balance this loss.

B3.3.2b Body temperature is monitored and controlled by the thermoregulatory centre in the brain. This centre has receptors sensitive to the temperature of the blood flowing through the brain.

B3.3.2c Also temperature receptors in the skin send impulses to the thermoregulatory centre, giving information about skin temperature.

B3.3.2d If the core body temperature is too high:

- blood vessels supplying the skin capillaries dilate so that more blood flows through the capillaries and more heat is lost
- sweat glands release more sweat which cools the body as it evaporates.

B3.3.2e If the core body temperature is too low:

- blood vessels supplying the skin capillaries constrict to reduce the flow of blood through the capillaries
- muscles may 'shiver' – their contraction needs respiration, which releases some energy to warm the body.

Ideas for practical work

Use surface temperature sensors to monitor skin temperature in different conditions.

Plan an investigation to measure the cooling effect of sweating.

How Science Works

CA: B4.2.1 Assess and manage risks when carrying out practical work, by: a) identifying some possible hazards in practical situations; b) suggesting ways of managing risks. B4.5.2 Review methodology to assess fitness for purpose, by: b) recognising and identifying the cause of random errors. When a data set contains random errors, repeating the readings and calculating a new mean can reduce their effect. B4.5.3 Identify patterns in data, by: a) describing the relationship between two variables and deciding whether the relationship is causal by association. B4.5.4 Draw conclusions using scientific ideas and evidence, by: d) evaluating methods of data collection.

B3 3.5 Controlling body temperature

Learning objectives

- describe where, how and why temperature is monitored in the body
- draw a diagram to explain how body temperature is controlled
- explain the role of sweating in maintaining body temperature and how this affects water balance in the body
- apply knowledge of the control of core body temperature to explain changes to the body during exercise.

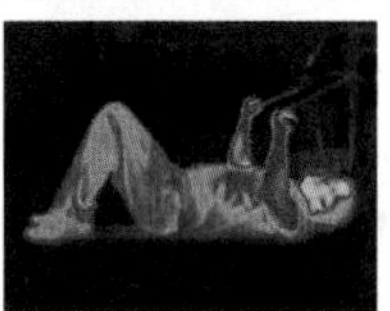

This photograph shows the temperature of a man's body during exercise. The hottest areas are white, cooling through red, yellow and green to blue.

Feedback control

Different parts of our bodies can be at different temperatures but the central **core body temperature**, around the heart, liver, lungs and kidneys, is usually kept steady at about 37 °C.

To keep something steady, you have to **monitor** any changes. There must also be mechanisms for responding to any changes and getting back to the normal position. For example, a thermostat in a room monitors the air temperature. If the temperature falls too low, the thermostat will cause a radiator to switch on and heat the room. When the temperature gets too high, the thermostat will make the radiator switch off, and so the room cools. This kind of control is called **feedback control**.

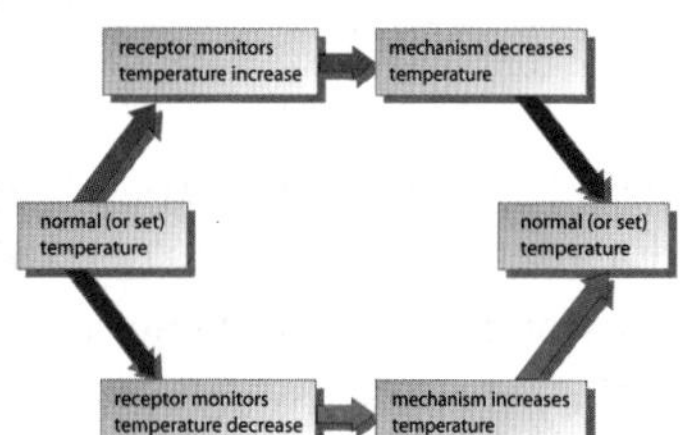

Figure 1 How a feedback control loop works to keep temperature constant.

mechanism to prevent overheating

sweating cools the skin

a lot of heat lost

skin surface

(a) Blood vessels supplying skin capilliaries dilate. More blood flows through capilliaries in the skin.

mechanism to prevent over-cooling

little heat lost

sweating stops

skin surface

(b) Blood vessels supplying skin capilliaries constrict. Less blood flows through capilliaries in the skin.

Figure 2 Control of heat loss through the skin.

Feedback control for body temperature

The **thermoregulatory centre** in your brain contains receptors that monitor internal temperature by detecting changes in the temperature of blood flowing through the brain. Receptors in your skin detect changes in skin temperature. Information from all the receptors goes to the thermoregulatory centre.

If the core body temperature is too high, the thermoregulatory centre sends nerve impulses to the blood vessels supplying **capillaries** near the surface of the skin. This causes them to **dilate** (open wider), so that more blood flows near the skin's surface. The blood warms the body surface, which loses heat by radiation. In addition, you may start to sweat, see Figure 2(a).

If the core body temperature falls too low, the thermoregulatory centre sends nerve impulses to the blood vessels supplying the surface, causing them to **constrict** (get narrower). This reduces blood flow near the surface and reduces heat loss from the blood, see Figure 2(b). In addition, muscles may start to produce rapid small contractions, known as shivering. Respiration provides the energy for these contractions, but some of the energy is transferred as heat energy to the tissues, warming the body.

Sweating

The production of sweat from sweat glands in the skin is also under the control of the thermoregulatory centre. As body temperature increases, watery sweat from these glands is released onto the surface of the skin. In warm conditions, the sweat evaporates to become water vapour. Evaporation requires energy, so as the sweat evaporates it takes energy from the skin, which cools it down. As body temperature falls, sweat production slows down, so there is less evaporation on the skin surface and less cooling. The problem with sweating is that the body loses water and some ions. These have to be replaced from food or drink.

Science skills

a Explain the changes in heat production during and after exercise.

b Describe the mechanisms in the body for increasing heat loss.

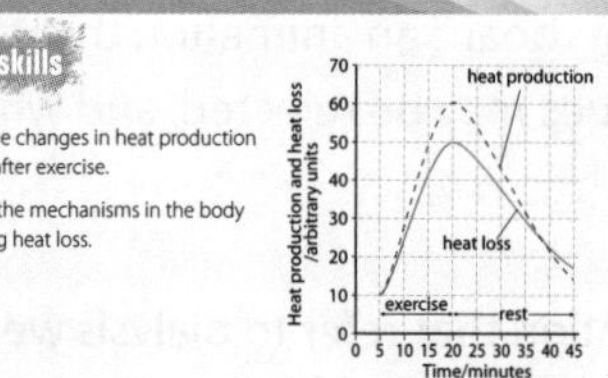

Figure 3 Heat production and loss from a cyclist during exercise and then at rest.

Practical

Thermistors can be attached to the skin in an experiment to monitor how skin temperature responds to changes in external temperature in order to maintain homeostasis inside the body.

c How would you set up such an experiment? What would be your controlled variable?

Questions

1 The temperature of the background in the photo of the man is blue. What does that tell you about the body temperature of the man?
2 Which areas of the man's body are hottest, and which are coolest?
3 Many reactions take place in the cells of the major organs of the body. Using your knowledge of the control of cell reactions, explain why the major organs need to be kept at a steady temperature.
4 Using Figure 1 as a guide, show how your core body temperature stays constant at about 37 °C.
5 Explain fully why you look pink when you are hot.
6 Draw up a table to show how the body detects a change in temperature, and how the body responds to an increase or a decrease in temperature.
7 Describe in detail an investigation that you could use to test reliably the response of skin temperature to changes in activity.
8 Explain as fully as possible the role of the thermoregulatory centre in the brain in maintaining a steady core body temperature.

A*

Taking it further

When considering extreme conditions of heat gain or loss, you need to be aware of all the body's responses in order to explain what is happening. For example, people with severe hypothermia may start to remove clothing. This makes no sense biologically, but decreased activity in the brain as a result of being cold causes disorientation and unpredictable behaviour. Patients who have hyperthermia (body temperature too high) may also become confused and angry because of the effect of temperature on the brain.

Learning objectives

Most students should be able to:

- describe where, how and why temperature is monitored in the body
- draw a diagram to explain how body temperature is controlled
- explain the role of sweating in maintaining body temperature and implications of this on water balance in the body.

Some students should also be able to:

- evaluate the role of physiological and behavioural mechanisms in maintaining core body temperature. [Ext]

Key points

Core body temperature is monitored and controlled by the thermoregulatory centre in the brain, receiving information about temperature from receptors in the brain and skin.

When core body temperature is too high, heat loss from the body is increased by increasing blood flow near to the skin and producing more sweat to evaporate from the skin surface.

When core body temperature is too low, heat loss from the body is reduced by keeping blood flow deeper in the skin, and heat production is increased by shivering of muscles.

Capillary constrict core body temperature dilate monitor shivering thermoregulatory centre

Lesson activities

Starter

1 Explain to students that you are preparing for an expedition into the Sahara Desert, and you will have to carry all your supplies. Ask them to help you prepare a list of what to take. For each (reasonable) suggestion, ask why you will need it. Previous work in the last topic and from KS3 should help students to suggest items that will help to limit heat gain and maintain water and ion content at normal concentrations in the body. Note that many of the suggestions that students are likely to make at this point are behavioural mechanisms (ones we choose to do), such as staying in the shade or wearing clothes to reduce radiation on the skin. The mechanisms that they will learn more about in this topic are physiological mechanisms within the body.

2 Ask students how you could tell by looking at someone whether they were feeling very cold or very warm. They should be able to identify the obvious signs of flushed skin and sweating when hot and lack of flushing/paler skin and raised 'goosebumps' when very cold. Ask if they can suggest why these responses occur.

Main

1 Worksheet B3.5a The cooling effect of sweat will help students plan their own investigation to answer the question 'Does sweat really work?' The planning part of the investigation could be set as a homework task first. (~20 min planning, ~50 min practical work)

2 Skin temperature Demonstrate to students how to use a thermistor to measure skin temperature. Then ask them to plan and carry out an investigation to answer the question 'How does skin temperature vary in different conditions?' They should write a short report to describe and explain their findings.

3 Feedback control This can be a difficult concept for students to understand. Go through the example in the Student Book (a room thermostat controlling a radiator) with students to make sure that they follow the process. If needed, create the diagram that is the answer to question 4 on the board as a whole-class activity.

Plenaries

1 Attach a thermistor to one hand of a student and ask them to place their other hand into a bowl of cold water to which a few ice cubes have been added. Ask other students first to predict what will happen to the temperature of the dry hand, and then to describe and explain what happens. The skin temperature should drop, because the thermoregulatory centre detects a fall in blood temperature from the cold hand and causes all skin capillaries to constrict, keeping warmth deeper in the body.

2 Ask students to sketch and label a graph of changing core body temperature over a period of several hours. They should label their graph to explain what is the 'normal' body temperature and to show what changes may cause the increases and decreases in temperature. They should add values to the y axis to indicate the normal range of body temperature.

Homework

1 Worksheet B3.5b tests understanding of body temperature control in the context of hypothermia.

2 Worksheet B3.5c presents a set of questions about the control of body temperature in extremely hot conditions.

Points to note

- The term 'feedback control' is introduced in this topic. For some students, it may be appropriate to explain that these are 'negative' feedback mechanisms, where the response is to negate the change and bring it back to normal. There are also positive feedback mechanisms, such as when body temperature gets very high. These make the situation worse by causing the change to increase. In the case of body temperature, it often leads to death.

Route to A*

Students could research the distinction between heat stroke and heat exhaustion, to find out the symptoms of each and why the body responds as it does in those conditions.

Answers to Student Book questions

Answers to B3 3.5 can be found on p.206

B3 3.6 Controlling blood glucose

Link to the Specification

B3.3.3a The blood glucose concentration of the body is monitored and controlled by the pancreas. The pancreas produces the hormone insulin, which allows the glucose to move from the blood into the cells.

B3.3.3b A second hormone, glucagon, is produced in the pancreas when blood glucose levels fall. This causes glycogen to be converted into glucose and be released into the blood.

B3.3.3c Type 1 diabetes is a disease in which a person's blood glucose concentration may rise to a high level because the pancreas does not produce enough of the hormone insulin.

B3 3.6 Controlling blood glucose

Learning objectives

- describe how blood glucose concentration is monitored and controlled
- analyse the role of hormones in the control of blood glucose concentration
- explain what diabetes is and some of the ways it can be treated.

Eating foods that contain lots of sugar or starch soon raises the blood glucose concentration.

Taking it further

When glucose is taken into liver and muscle cells it is converted to glycogen, which is a large carbohydrate, rather like starch. It is insoluble and does not affect the osmotic balance of the cell, so it is a good storage molecule. When blood glucose concentration falls, and glucagon is released, glycogen is quickly converted to glucose and released into the blood.

Glucose in the blood

When you **digest** starchy or sugary foods, they are broken down to simple sugars, mostly glucose, and absorbed into your blood. If all the glucose stayed in your blood it would be dangerous as it causes water to move out of cells by osmosis. The body has to take glucose out of the blood so it can be used for respiration or stored until it is needed.

Normal blood glucose concentration varies throughout the day, but it is kept within limits by another feedback control mechanism in the body. This mechanism is monitored and controlled by the **pancreas**, a digestive organ situated behind the liver.

Controlling blood glucose

If the blood glucose concentration gets too high, the pancreas releases a **hormone** called **insulin**, see Figure 1. Insulin circulates in the blood and causes cells, particularly in the liver and muscles, to take glucose out of the blood. Insulin release into the blood decreases as blood glucose concentration comes back down to normal.

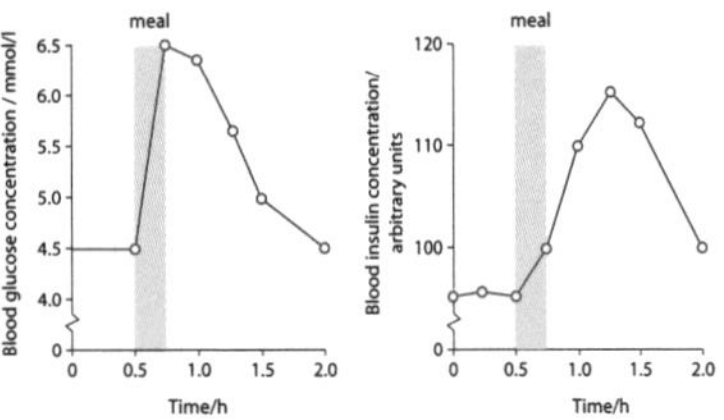

Figure 1 Changes in concentration of blood glucose (left) and insulin (right) after a meal.

If blood glucose concentration drops too low, for example during vigorous exercise, another hormone, called **glucagon**, is released from the pancreas. Glucagon stimulates liver cells to release stored glucose into the blood so that blood glucose concentration rises again.

Diabetes and blood glucose concentration

Some people cannot control their blood glucose concentration properly. We say they have a disease called **diabetes**. Symptoms of diabetes include excreting glucose in urine, unusual thirst and lack of energy. If blood glucose concentration stays high, it can lead to coma and even death, so it is essential that it is brought back down again.

A simple and quick test for diabetes is to check for glucose in the urine using Clinistix. The diagnosis is then checked more thoroughly using a glucose tolerance test. In this test, the patient is given a glucose drink, and then samples of blood are tested for blood glucose concentration to see how quickly the glucose is controlled.

216

Science skills

A patient was given 50 g of glucose to drink at time 0. Blood glucose concentration was measured at half-hourly intervals and compared with results from a healthy person and a person who was severely diabetic.

Table 1 Glucose tolerance test results.

Time/hours	Blood glucose concentration / mg/1000 cm^3		
	healthy person	severely diabetic	patient
0.0	92	247	108
0.5	124	262	159
1.0	145	323	212
1.5	118	304	150
2.0	95	278	129

a Explain the changes in the patient's results over time.

b From the results, do you think the patient is diabetic? Explain your answer.

Practical

To test for glucose in the urine, dip a stick into the urine to wet it completely and wait for the colour on the stick to develop. The colour is compared with a chart to indicate how much glucose is present.

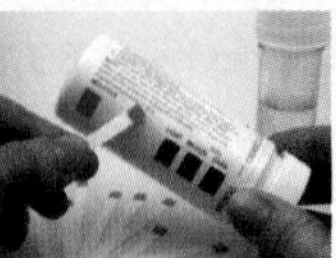

Clinistix to test for glucose in urine.

Types of diabetes

There are different causes of diabetes and they are treated in different ways. In **type 1 diabetes**, the pancreas produces no insulin at all, so blood glucose concentration can rise to dangerous levels after eating. Treatment requires injections of insulin, balanced with a healthy, controlled diet and exercise, to keep blood glucose concentration within a safe range.

Examiner feedback

For the exam you need to know about the causes, symptoms and treatment of type 1 diabetes, but you do not need to know about type 2 diabetes.

Questions

1 Compare the role of the hormones insulin and glucagon in keeping blood glucose concentration within limits in a healthy person.
2 Before a patient is given a glucose tolerance test, they must not eat or drink anything other than water for several hours. Why is this?
3 Explain why the presence of glucose in the urine can be used to diagnose diabetes.
4 Draw a feedback diagram like the one in lesson B3 3.5 to show how blood glucose concentration is kept within limits in a healthy person.
5 Explain why a Clinistix test is followed with a glucose tolerance test to confirm diabetes.
6 Explain in detail why exercise affects blood glucose concentration.
7 Explain fully what diabetes is and why it must be treated.
8 Explain as fully as you can the shape of the graphs of blood glucose concentration and insulin concentration in Figure 1. A*

Taking it further

The other main type of diabetes is type 2. In type 2 diabetes, either the pancreas doesn't make enough insulin or the body cells don't respond properly to insulin. For most people, a healthy, controlled diet and aerobic exercise are sufficient treatment. However, some need tablets to help the body make more insulin or respond better to insulin.

The proportion of people who have type 2 diabetes is increasing, and many doctors think this is related to the increase in the proportion of people who are **obese**.

Homeostasis 217

Learning objectives

Most students should be able to:

- describe how blood sugar concentration is monitored and controlled
- analyse the role of hormones in the control of blood sugar concentration
- explain what diabetes is and some of the ways it can be treated.

Some students should also be able to:

- distinguish between correlation and cause in relation to insulin, blood glucose concentration and diabetes. [Ext]

Key points

Blood sugar concentration is monitored and controlled by the pancreas.

Insulin is a hormone released by the pancreas when blood sugar concentration is too high and causes cells to take in glucose.

Glucagon is a hormone released by the pancreas when blood sugar concentration falls too low and causes cells to release glucose into the blood.

Diabetes is a disease in which the body cannot control blood sugar concentration properly.

ActiveTeach Resource: Diabetes: what, why – *Video*
Blood glucose control – *Labelling activity*
Blood glucose levels – *Gap-fill activity*

Lesson activities

Starter

1 Start the lesson by showing students an iced bun. Ask them: 'What will happen to the bun when I eat it? What will the starch and sugar be broken down into? What will happen to these products?' Elicit the fact that the glucose from digestion will cause a rise in your blood glucose concentration.

2 Revise examples of homeostasis covered in the first lesson of chapter 3, and remind students of the control of blood glucose. Ask them to jot down what they know about blood glucose and three things that they need to find out in order to understand how it is controlled in the body. They should compare their notes with a neighbour and select the three most important points. Then take examples from around the class and ask students to select the top three questions to answer in the lesson. The questions could be retained for the plenary.

Diabetes | digest | glucagon | hormone | insulin | pancreas | Type 1 diabetes

Main

1 Glucose in urine If activity B3 3.2a was not carried out in the lesson on kidneys, it would be appropriate to cover it in a limited way here to show the identification of urine from a diabetic and non-diabetic person. Otherwise, ask students to use that knowledge to explain as fully as possible why the presence of glucose in urine is indicative of diabetes. They should also consider why a urine test should be followed up with a blood test for glucose concentration to confirm the diagnosis.

2 B3 3.6a Discovering insulin Refer to sheet in Activity Pack.

3 Variation in blood glucose concentration Students watch the ActiveTeach video. They then sketch graphs to show their understanding of the roles of insulin and glucagon. ActiveTeach also has labelling and gap-fill activities on this topic. [AT]

Plenaries

1 Return to the three questions selected in Starter 2, and give students three minutes to jot down their answers. Take examples from around the class to assess what has been learnt.

2 Ask students to write a question on the role of insulin and glucagon in the control of blood glucose concentration, and to write a mark scheme to go with it. Encourage students to think up questions that are worth more than 4 marks. If time allows, students could try out their questions on one another.

Homework

1 Worksheet B3 3.6b Refer to sheet in Activity Pack.

2 Worksheet B3 3.6c Refer to sheet in Activity Pack.

Points to note

- The specification uses the term blood sugar concentration where blood glucose concentration is more appropriate. The latter term is used throughout these materials for greater accuracy. It is important that students appreciate that this is what the specification means.
- Although the specification says that in Type 1 diabetes the pancreas does not produce enough insulin, the condition is caused by the death of insulin-producing cells in the pancreas and results in no insulin being produced in the body.
- The specification does not require knowledge of Type 2 diabetes, although some students may be aware of it. If they show interest in knowing more, it is important that they distinguish between the causes and treatment for the two types. For additional information these websites may be useful: Diabetes UK and BBC Health – Diabetes.
- Although not required by the specification, this lesson provides opportunities for discussing the difference between correlation and cause which may be appropriate to your students.

Route to A*

To introduce the difference between endocrine and exocrine secretions, students could research the way in which insulin is secreted from the pancreas, to answer the question 'Insulin is a protein – why is it not digested in the digestive system?'

Answers to Student Book questions

Science skills

a Blood glucose concentration increases in the first hour as glucose is absorbed into the blood. This triggers the production of insulin, which in turn causes glucose to be taken out of the blood, so the glucose level decreases.

b The patient is slightly diabetic because the concentrations are always higher than those of a healthy person. However, they are not severely diabetic because their concentrations are much less than those of a severely diabetic person.

Answers

1 Insulin is released when blood glucose concentration increases too much. It stops blood glucose concentration going too high. Glucagon is released when blood glucose concentration decreases too much. It stops blood glucose concentration falling too low.

2 The glucose tolerance test measures glucose concentration in the blood. Food or drink, other than water, contain sugars that could increase blood glucose concentration and make the test values incorrect.

3 Glucose is normally completely reabsorbed in the kidneys, so urine contains no glucose. In diabetes, the glucose concentration in the blood is much higher than normal, so there will be more filtered into the urine than normal. Not all of this glucose can be reabsorbed so some is left in the urine.

4 Flow diagram, or similar, showing two pathways:

Either:

Blood sugar concentration within normal limits – Pancreas detects rise in blood sugar concentration – Insulin released – More glucose taken up by cells – Blood sugar concentration within normal limits.

Or:

Blood sugar concentration within normal limits – Pancreas detects fall in blood sugar concentration – Glucagon released – More glucose released by liver – Blood sugar concentration within normal limits.

5 A Clinistix test only shows that there is glucose in the urine, and there are reasons other than diabetes that could give this result, such as kidney infection. A glucose tolerance test shows whether blood glucose concentration is controlled normally or not.

6 Exercise needs energy for the contraction of muscles. That energy comes from respiration in which glucose is broken down. Glucose is delivered to cells in the blood, so if more glucose is being broken down, blood glucose concentration will fall. The more vigorous the exercise, the more blood glucose concentration will fall.

7 Diabetes is a failure of the body to control blood glucose concentration. It can be caused by the pancreas producing less insulin than normal, or none at all, or by cells not responding to insulin as they do in a healthy person. Diabetes must be treated because a very high concentration of glucose in the blood can cause a coma or even death.

8 The left graph shows that blood glucose concentration increases rapidly during a meal. This is due to digestion of carbohydrates to sugars, which are absorbed in the blood. Blood glucose concentration gradually falls back to the pre-meal value over about two hours. Blood insulin concentration gradually increases during the meal and for about an hour afterwards. This is what brings the blood glucose concentration back down after a meal. The blood insulin concentration decreases after that, as less insulin is released from the pancreas.

B3 3.7 Treating diabetes

Link to the Specification

B3.3.3c Type 1 diabetes is a disease in which a person's blood glucose concentration may rise to a high level because the pancreas does not produce enough of the hormone insulin.

B3.3.3d Type 1 diabetes may be controlled by careful attention to diet, exercise, and by injecting insulin.

How Science Works

SKU: B3.3 bullet point 2: Evaluate modern methods of treating diabetes.

B3 3.7 Treating diabetes

Learning objectives

- describe different methods of treating diabetes
- explain the effect of different methods of treating diabetes on patients
- evaluate modern methods for treating diabetes.

Insulin is injected just below the skin, for example in the stomach or thigh, and diffuses into blood vessels.

The effects of diabetes

The problems with diabetes are not just extreme swings in blood glucose concentration. Over many years, poor control of blood glucose can cause damage to small blood vessels all over the body. In the eyes, this damage can lead to a form of blindness. Diabetes can also cause kidney damage. Up to one-third of patients may need a kidney transplant after suffering years of diabetes.

The better blood glucose concentration is controlled, the less damage is caused.

Controlling blood glucose

In addition to exercise and a healthy diet, patients with type 1 diabetes need treatment with insulin. Insulin is usually injected because it is a protein and would therefore be broken down in digestion if taken by mouth.

Different forms of insulin are used: some are fast acting and injected just before every meal; others are slow acting and injected once a day. Many patients use a combination of slow-acting insulin to produce a background level of insulin all day and fast-acting insulin to control the rapid change in blood glucose concentration after a meal. This produces control that is more like the body's own process.

Some diabetics now use **insulin pumps**, which continually supply insulin just under the skin. Most of the time this is at a background level, but the dose is easily increased at mealtimes.

Science skills The results in Table 1 come from a survey of 272 diabetic patients who used either an insulin pump or multiple daily injections to control blood glucose concentration.

Table 1 Comparison of insulin pump with multiple insulin injections.

Measure	Insulin pump (continual delivery)	Multiple insulin injections
mean blood glucose concentration / mmol/l	7.45	7.67
fluctuation in blood glucose concentration / mmol/l	±3.9	±4.3

a Normal blood glucose concentration varies between about 4 and 8 mmol/l. Which method gave the best control of blood glucose? Explain your answer.

Each method of treating diabetes has problems, and some problems will affect some patients more than others. In the UK, patients can only be given a pump if they pass certain criteria that suggest they will get greater benefit using a pump than using injections.

US golfer Kelly Kuehne is a diabetic who wears an insulin pump on her waist. This photo shows her in the 1999 Women's US Open Golf Championship.

218

Table 2 Advantages and disadvantages of different methods of treating diabetes with insulin.

Method	Advantages	Disadvantages
multiple insulin injections	• discreet: injection syringe or pen can be carried around in a bag and used in privacy • equipment is cheaper	• greater chance of extreme high or low blood glucose concentration • uses more insulin each day than pump
insulin pump	• better control of blood glucose concentration • uses less insulin per day	• must be worn almost all the time • equipment more expensive

Measuring the insulin dose

Before insulin is injected, the correct **dose** must be calculated. The dose will depend on the concentration of blood glucose, and how it is expected to change in the next hour or so, such as at a mealtime. So diabetics have to take a blood test every time they need an injection. This can now be done quickly and simply using a pinprick of blood measured with a blood glucose meter.

Using a blood glucose meter is easy, even with children.

Science in action

Scientists are developing automatic blood glucose meters combined with an insulin pump that can be implanted below the skin, so that the process is completely automatic and discreet.

b Explain the advantages of a completely automatic monitoring and delivery system.

c Suggest a disadvantage of a completely automated system.

Questions

1 Explain why insulin cannot be taken in tablet form.
2 In the US, patients have to pay for much of their medication. What impact do you think this may have on the number of diabetics using an insulin pump? Explain your answer.
3 Explain the importance of having a simple system for testing blood for glucose.
4 Explain why doctors use criteria to help decide who gets which treatment.
5 Explain how a mixed treatment of injections of fast-acting and slow-acting insulin controls blood glucose more like the natural way than treatment using just one form of insulin.
6 In a study of insulin pumps, one teenage girl who spent a lot of time on the beach with her friends chose to go back to injections. Suggest why she preferred injections.
7 Explain fully why blood glucose concentration must be measured before an insulin dose is given. Include the effect of exercise and food in your answer.

Route to A*

When comparing different treatments for type I diabetes, remember to explain their advantages and disadvantages fully in terms of keeping blood glucose concentrations as closely within the normal range as possible. It is the extremes of blood glucose concentration that cause damage to cells, and the nearer to normal blood glucose concentrations can be maintained, the more healthy the patient is likely to remain.

Homeostasis 219

Learning objectives

Most students should be able to:

- describe different methods of treating diabetes
- explain the effect of different methods of treating diabetes on patients
- evaluate modern methods for treating diabetes.

Some students should also be able to:

- explain fully the process for evaluating which treatment methods should be provided to patients for free. [Ext]

Key points

Diabetes may be treated in different ways depending on the type of diabetes the patient has.

Different methods of treating diabetes have different disadvantages.

The best method for treating a patient must be decided using criteria that indicate which treatment works best for different types of diabetes.

Lesson activities

Starter

1 Write the word *insulin* on the board and ask students to suggest related words and how they should be linked to create a mind map on the topic. This could be revisited in the plenary to add any new learning and correct any errors.

2 Explain to students that Type 1 diabetes used to be called juvenile-onset diabetes because it usually starts when a person is young. Tell them to imagine a doctor is coming to visit to explain the condition to them, and ask them to suggest a question that they would like answered by the doctor. Take a selection of questions from around the class, and then ask students to arrange them into groups of similar questions and to produce three key questions that need answering. Keep these for the plenary.

Main

1 Worksheet B3 3.7a Creating assessment criteria Refer to sheet in Activity Pack.'

2 Type 1 diabetes treatments Ask students to research the range of treatments available for Type 1 diabetes at Diabetes and insulin delivery devices and also NHS Diabetes. They should evaluate each of the treatments they find, identifying advantages and disadvantages, and suggesting which type of patient each treatment would suit best.

3 Evaluating a new treatment Using the example of the control trials on Worksheet B3 3.7a, ask students to work in groups to decide the best way to set up a study to evaluate a new treatment, such as the insulin pump. This is a challenging extension of a 'fair test' because it includes ethical issues of not increasing health risks for patients, as well as practical issues of not being able to control for many factors. Getting reliable data on which to base conclusions will include choices such as sample size, controlling for as many lifestyle factors as possible, and preparing patients so they are all at the same starting point. Students could carry out research on how clinical trials are set up to support their choices.

Plenaries

1 Return to the three key questions for the doctor that were selected in Starter 2. Give students three minutes to answer the questions, then take a selection of answers until you feel all the main points of the lesson have been covered.

2 Ask students to write questions for a crossword on homeostasis, including the maintenance of water balance by the kidneys, maintenance of core body temperature and blood glucose control with insulin. Give students three minutes to write as many questions as they can, then take a selection from around the class and ask other students to answer them.

Homework

1 Worksheet B3 3.7b contains questions that evaluate the treatment of diabetes using different injection regimes.

2 Ask students to imagine that they have a friend who has been newly diagnosed with Type 1 diabetes. Ask them to write a message to their friend to help them understand what is happening to them, and the choices they may be offered in the range of treatment. They need to consider the importance of diet and exercise, as well as the method of insulin delivery.

Points to note

- Treatments for Type 1 diabetes only are considered in this lesson. If students wish to know more about treatment of Type 2 diabetes, they can find further information from Diabetes UK and BBC Health – Diabetes.

Route to A*

Ask students to research the use of stem cell therapy for the treatment of Type 1 diabetes. They should identify the advantages and disadvantages of this kind of treatment, and explain what technical challenges still need to be resolved before the treatment could be considered on the NHS.

Answers to Student Book questions

Science skills

a The insulin pump gave the best control, because the mean value plus fluctuations were more within the normal range than with injections.

b A completely automatic system could respond continuously to changes in blood glucose concentration, in the same way as the pancreas. This reduces the chances of extreme highs or lows, which can damage health in the short or long term.

c A disadvantage would be that patient would not regularly check their blood glucose concentration, as they do in the current treatments, so if anything went wrong with the equipment they might not realise until it was too late and damage was done to their body.

Answers

1 Insulin is digested in the gut, so if taken by mouth it does not reach the blood where it is needed.

2 It is likely that a smaller proportion of US diabetic patients will use the insulin pump because it is more expensive than the syringes.

3 Anyone can carry out a simple glucose test, rather than needing a medically trained person all the time. The test also needs to be easy for use with children, who are less likely to tolerate something that is complicated or time-consuming.

4 Criteria are used to judge which treatment is most suitable. They need to be used with all patients to make sure they get the best treatment for their particular type of diabetes.

5 One slow-acting insulin injection a day provides a single blood insulin concentration through the whole day. Several fast-acting insulin injections gives peaks of insulin concentration that deal with glucose absorbed from meals. However, it means that there may be very low concentrations of insulin in the blood between meals. In a healthy person, insulin is never completely cleared from the blood, and extra is released as food is digested. So the combination of fast and slow-acting injections is nearer to the normal situation.

6 An insulin pump needs to be worn all the time because it delivers insulin continuously. On the beach, the girl may have been wearing a swimsuit/bikini, which would make the pump visible. She might have not liked everyone knowing that she was diabetic. With injections she could carry the syringes in her bag and use them discreetly so nobody would know.

7 Blood glucose concentration varies with many factors, including food and exercise. If glucose concentration gets too high or too low, it can cause health problems. Insulin causes cells to take up glucose from the blood. Measuring the blood glucose concentration before using insulin helps the patient to see what the background glucose level is. Calculating the impact of a meal or exercise helps the patient work out the right dose of insulin to keep blood glucose concentration within safe levels.

ISA practice: rates of transpiration

In the Student Book, each ISA practice is contained on one double-page spread. However, you can, if you prefer, use the sheets provided in the Teacher and Technician Planning Pack and the Activity Pack to more closely mirror the experience of a real ISA which would then take place over several lessons and/or as homework.

Link to the specification

3.2 How Science Works

Observing phenomena can lead to the start of an investigation, experiment or survey. Careful observation is necessary before deciding which variables are the most important.

3.6 Controlled assessment

Scientific investigations often seek to identify links between two or more variables. [B4.1.1, B4.3.1.]

Scientists need to ensure repeatability, reproducibility and validity in evidence. [B4.3.3]

There is a link between the type of graph used and the type of variable represented. [B4.4.2]

In evaluating a whole investigation the repeatability, reproducibility and validity of the data obtained must be considered. [B4.5.2]

The patterns and relationships observed in data represent the behaviour of the variables in an investigation. However, it is necessary to look at patterns and relationships between variables with the limitations of the data in mind in order to draw conclusions. [B4.5.3, B4.5.4]

ISA practice: rates of transpiration

A number of factors affect the rate of transpiration. If the rate of transpiration is too high, plants may wilt.

A horticulturist has asked students to investigate the effect of wind on the rate of transpiration. The horticulturist's hypothesis is that the air movement will affect the rate of transpiration.

Section 1

1 Write a hypothesis about how you think wind affects the rate of transpiration. Use information from your knowledge of physical processes, such as evaporation, to explain why you made this hypothesis. *(3 marks)*

2 Describe how you could carry out an investigation into this factor.
You should include:
- the equipment that you could use
- how you would use the equipment
- the measurements that you would make
- how you would make it a fair test.

You may include a labelled diagram to help you to explain the method.
In this question you will be assessed on using good English, organising information clearly and using specialist terms where appropriate. *(6 marks)*

3 Think about the possible hazards in the investigation.
(a) Describe one hazard that you think may be present in the investigation. *(1 mark)*
(b) Identify the risk associated with the hazard that you have described, and say what control measures you could use to reduce the risk. *(2 marks)*

4 Design a table that you could use to record all the data you would obtain during the planned investigation. *(2 marks)*

Total for Section 1: 14 marks

Section 2

A groups of students, Study Group 1, carried out an investigation into the hypothesis. They used an electric fan to simulate wind. They measured the mass of a plant shoot in different 'wind' speeds for thirty minutes. Their results are shown in Figure 1.

Zero
Wind speed 1 m/s: mass 75.6 g
Wind speed 2 m/s: mass 76.3 g
Wind speed 3 m/s: mass 75.1 g
Wind speed 4 m/s: mass 75.4 g

After 10 minutes
Wind speed 1 m/s: mass 75.5 g
Wind speed 2 m/s: mass 76.0 g
Wind speed 3 m/s: mass 74.8 g
Wind speed 4 m/s: mass 74.9 g

After 20 minutes
Wind speed 1 m/s: mass 75.3 g
Wind speed 2 m/s: mass 75.7 g
Wind speed 3 m/s: mass 74.4 g
Wind speed 4 m/s: mass 74.3 g

After 30 minutes
Wind speed 1 m/s: mass 75.1 g
Wind speed 2 m/s: mass 75.5 g
Wind speed 3 m/s: mass 74.0 g
Wind speed 4 m/s: mass 73.8 g

Figure 1 Study Group 1's results.

5 (a) Plot a graph of these results. *(4 marks)*
(b) What conclusion can you make from the investigation about a link between air movement and the rate of transpiration? You should use any pattern that you can see in the results to support your conclusion. *(3 marks)*
(c) Look at your hypothesis, the answer to question 1. Do the results support your hypothesis? Explain your answer. You should quote some figures from the data in your explanation. *(3 marks)*

Here are the results of three more studies.

Below are the results from three other study groups.

Figure 2 shows the results from Study Group 2, a second group of students.

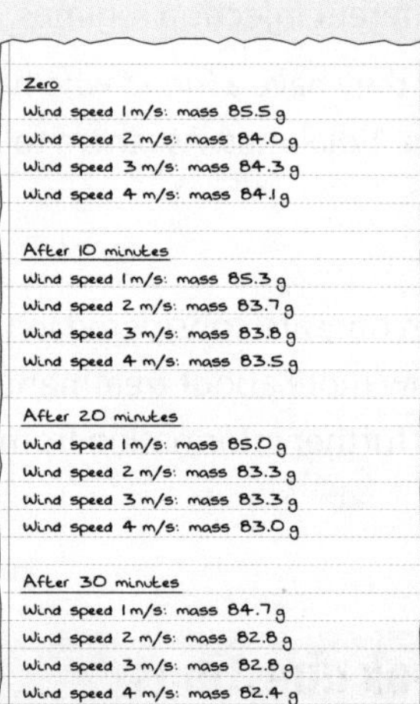
Zero
Wind speed 1 m/s: mass 85.5 g
Wind speed 2 m/s: mass 84.0 g
Wind speed 3 m/s: mass 84.3 g
Wind speed 4 m/s: mass 84.1 g

After 10 minutes
Wind speed 1 m/s: mass 85.3 g
Wind speed 2 m/s: mass 83.7 g
Wind speed 3 m/s: mass 83.8 g
Wind speed 4 m/s: mass 83.5 g

After 20 minutes
Wind speed 1 m/s: mass 85.0 g
Wind speed 2 m/s: mass 83.3 g
Wind speed 3 m/s: mass 83.3 g
Wind speed 4 m/s: mass 83.0 g

After 30 minutes
Wind speed 1 m/s: mass 84.7 g
Wind speed 2 m/s: mass 82.8 g
Wind speed 3 m/s: mass 82.8 g
Wind speed 4 m/s: mass 82.4 g

Figure 2 Study Group 2's results.

Table 1 shows the results from Study Group 3. This group of students studied the effect of a different factor on the rate of transpiration.

Table 1 Results from Study Group 3.

Humidity (%)	Transpiration rate/ arbitrary units
20	26.0
40	21.0
50	16.5
60	11.0
70	9.5

Study Group 4 was a group of researchers, who looked on the internet and found a graph (Figure 3) showing the effect of a third factor on the rate of transpiration.

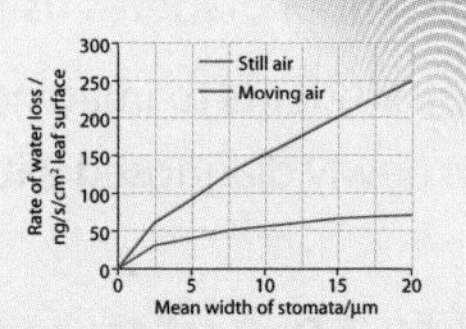

Figure 3 Graph showing the effects of another factor on transpiration.

6 (a) Draw a sketch graph of the results from Study Group 2. *(3 marks)*
(b) Look at the results from Study Groups 2 and 3. Does the data support the conclusion you drew in answer to question 5(c)? Give the reasons for your answer. *(3 marks)*
(c) The data contain only a limited amount of information. What other information or data would you need in order to be more certain whether or not the hypothesis is correct?
Explain the reason for your answer. *(3 marks)*
(d) Look at the results from Study Group 4. Compare it with the data from Study Group 1. Explain how far Study Group 4's results support or do not support your answer to question 5(b). You should use examples from Study Group 4 and Study Group 1. *(3 marks)*

7 (a) Compare the results of Study Group 1 with Study Group 2. Do you think that the results for Study Group 1 are *reproducible*?
Explain the reason for your answer. *(3 marks)*
(b) Explain how Study Group 1 could use results from other groups in the class to obtain a more *accurate* answer. *(3 marks)*

8 Suggest how ideas from the original investigation and the other studies could be used by the horticulturist to reduce the risk of his plants wilting. *(3 marks)*

Total for Section 2: 31 marks

Total for the ISA: 45 marks

Learning objectives

Most students should be able to:
- make observations and develop into a hypothesis
- identify the independent and dependent variables in the hypothesis
- obtain some data to process
- produce a graph or bar chart from the data obtained
- identify any trends that may be present in the data
- relate that trend to their hypothesis.

Some students should also be able to:
- make a risk assessment of their chosen method, with suitable control measures
- examine the evidence obtained to establish its repeatability and /or reproducibility.

anomalous result calibration control measure hazard hypothesis mean observation prediction range repeatable reproducible research theory uncertainties (errors): random systematic zero validity variables: control categoric continuous dependent independent

Key points

Investigations should be designed so that patterns and relationships between variables can be identified.
It is important to ensure repeatability, reproducibility and validity in evidence when designing and evaluating investigations.
The choice of graph used depends upon the type of variable represented.
When drawing conclusions, the limitations of the data must be kept in mind.

Lesson activities

Starter

1 Pre-prepare a plant by placing it in a plastic bag that is tied round its stem, so that condensation occurs inside the plastic bag just before the lesson starts. (Putting it in a fridge for an hour works well.) Ask students to describe the plant and the plastic bag. Ask them to explain why there is so much condensation on the bag. They should produce the idea that the plant has transpired water from its leaves.

Main

1 Researching and planning Students need to research, using at least two different sources, a way of investigating rates of transpiration and develop a hypothesis. Suggest a suitable context, e.g. determining how the volume of water required to irrigate plants varies according to wind conditions. Please refer to the **B3 ISA practice 1 Teacher and technician sheet**.

2 Students can complete their research/notes for homework. They need to be aware of the likely risks and how to control them. See the **B3 ISA practice 1 Student research notes sheet**.

3 Ask two students to read their notes on one of the points. Get the class to decide whose notes are best, with a reason. Repeat until all the points are covered.

4 Give students the **B3 ISA practice 1 Section 1 paper**.

5 In a following lesson students set up their investigation and record and process their results. Students can work in groups to obtain the data. If several groups have used the same method they may wish to pool results and obtain a mean. Please refer to the **B3 ISA practice 1 Student practical sheet**.

6 Students should process the data individually in **controlled** conditions. A bar chart or graph should be plotted and the trend of the graph/bar chart identified and a conclusion made.

7 The conclusion should be compared with their hypothesis to identity if their hypothesis has been confirmed or denied.

Plenaries

1 Students discuss sources of possible errors and ways to overcome them.

2 Give students the **B3 ISA practice 1 Section 2 paper**.

Homework

After the practical, ask students to write brief notes about ways in which they could improve their investigation. They should mention how to reduce errors and what further data or information they would need to confirm their conclusion.

Points to note

- With able students simply outline the points they need to cover. You should adjust delivery to match the time that it takes to obtain meaningful results.
- Students should describe a complex relationship between the independent variable and the dependent variable.

Route to A*

Students' risk assessment should include sensible risks, with a clear indication of the likelihood of the hazard occurring and how to sensibly control the risk.

Depending on how closely you wish to mirror the real ISA experience all three parts can be done in class or some can be done for homework. You should adjust delivery to match the time that it takes to obtain meaningful results.

Answers to Student Book questions

6 **(a)** Both axes labelled. (1) A suitable curve/line drawn. (1) Indication (arrow or numbers) of direction of increase in value of axes. (1)

(b) The student states that data in Study 1 strongly supports the original hypothesis and quotes some data from tables that supports this. (1)

Critical appraisal of data to include data for Study Groups 2 and 3 show the same pattern, although there are significant differences in some of the masses. (1)

A statement is made that indicates that the candidate realises that Study 2 is inappropriate, because the investigation does not involve a change of air movement.

N.B. If Study 2 has been used inappropriately at any point during the student's answer then one mark should be deducted as the data is irrelevant in this context. (1)

(c) Suggests at least one other piece of information that would be needed to form a firm conclusion. The reason for the need for this other information is clearly stated. (3)

(d) Comment that Study 4 was much more accurate because it measured water loss in $ng\ s^{-1}\ cm^{-2}$.

Comment that the graph only uses two wind speeds.

Comment that the investigation also measured stomatal width. (3)

For the full mark scheme, see the Teacher and Technician Planning Pack.

B3 4.1 Human activities produce waste

Link to the Specification

B3.4.1a Rapid growth in the human population and an increase in the standard of living means that increasingly more waste is produced. Unless waste is properly handled, more pollution will be caused.

B3.4.1b Waste may pollute:

- water, with sewage, fertiliser or toxic chemicals
- air, with smoke and gases such as sulfur dioxide, which contributes to acid rain
- land, with toxic chemicals such as pesticides and herbicides, which may be washed from the land into waterways.

B3.4.1c Humans reduce the amount of land available for other animals and plants by building, quarrying, farming and dumping waste.

How Science Works

SKU: B3.4 bullet point 1: Analyse and interpret scientific data concerning environmental issues.

CA: B4.4.2a Drawing tables; B4.4.2b Drawing charts and graphs; B4.5.4a Writing a conclusion, based on evidence that relates correctly to known facts; B4.5.4d Evaluating methods of data collection.

B3 4.1 Human activities produce waste

Learning objectives

- describe how the human population is growing and explain why increasing amounts of waste are being produced from human activity
- analyse how increased waste may pollute different areas of the environment.

The downside of increased living standards and human population growth

The March 2010 world population estimate is over 6.8 billion. Six thousand years ago the population of the world was about 0.2 billion. People lived in small groups and most of the world was unaffected by human activities.

Many people in the UK have money to spend on non-essential goods and services. Shopping to replace items like televisions and mobile telephones with the latest technology, or furniture and clothes with the latest styles, generates waste and uses up the world's resources. Manufacturing, transport and packaging all contribute to more waste. Our standard of living is increasing but this increases demands on raw materials to build better roads, houses, schools and hospitals.

Science skills

Look at Figure 1.

a Describe how the world's population changed between 1750 and 2000.

b What percentage of the estimated world population in 2050 will live in less developed countries?

c Suggest reasons why the populations of less developed countries are rising faster than those of more developed countries.

Figure 1 Graph of world population estimates from 1750 to 2150.

Household waste: recycle, reuse, incinerate or bury

Some waste can be recycled and used to make new products so we don't use more raw materials. However, it costs money and uses energy to collect and sort all the waste before it can be recycled.

In 2008–09, household waste accounted for 89% of local authorities' waste collection. However, the proportion of household waste recycled, reused or composted continued to increase between 1996 and 2008 in England (see Figure 2). The government has given local authorities recycling targets to meet.

Most household waste is dumped in landfill sites. As buried waste decays, it produces methane gas. This can be piped away and used to heat homes and offices, or burned to produce heat for generating electricity. Toxic liquids can also be released from landfill sites and may pollute water. The amount of rubbish dumped in landfill tips has decreased in recent years.

The new generation of refuse incinerators removes toxic chemicals and small particles from the smoke and fumes produced by burning. Most modern incinerators are 'energy from waste' plants, which use the heat from incineration to generate electricity. The ash from incinerators must be disposed of safely, or it can cause land or water pollution.

Figure 2 Household waste and recycling in England 1996–97 to 2008–09.

Preventing pollution

Unless the waste we produce is properly handled, it may pollute water. Sewage from our homes and industries, fertiliser used in gardens and on farms, and toxic chemicals from landfill and industry can end up polluting water. Whole ecosystems are affected and take many years to recover.

The air may be polluted by smoke or by gases such as sulfur dioxide (SO_2). Sulfur dioxide is a waste product from some power stations, from industrial processes and from vehicles that use fossil fuels. Some scientists have predicted that global SO_2 emissions will reach a peak around 2020, as developing countries, driven by rapid economic development, increase their use of fossil fuel. Sulfur dioxide contributes to acid rain, which can damage forests and freshwater organisms.

Modern farming practices often involve the use of large amounts of chemicals, including **pesticides** and **herbicides**. Some of these chemicals end up in the soil. Some break down quickly into less harmful chemicals, but others may last and harm animals and plants in the soil for many years. These chemicals may also be washed from land into water, and so cause water pollution.

Less space for wildlife

The land used for building cities and other human communities previously provided habitats for plants and animals. Building materials such as brick and cement are made from raw materials such as clay and limestone, which are obtained by quarrying. Quarrying can threaten the habitat of rare species. Farming and dumping waste pollutes land that would otherwise be available for wildlife.

Questions

1. Give two reasons why the production of waste from human activities is increasing annually.
2. How can industrial waste pollute the environment?
3. Describe the risk to the environment from chemicals such as herbicides and pesticides.
4. List the human activities that reduce the amount of land available for other living organisms.
5. **(a)** How much of local authorities' waste collection was accounted for by household waste in 2008–09? **(b)** What government action has been taken to reduce this amount?
6. Look at Figure 2. **(a)** During which years was most household waste produced? **(b)** What is the difference between the not recycled, combusted or reused waste in 1996–97 and 2008–09? **(c)** What percentage of household waste in 2008–09 was recycled? **(d)** Describe the trend in the data for amount of recycled, composted and reused waste from 1996 to 2009.
7. Look at Figure 3. **(a)** Tabulate the data for the following types of waste: chemicals, metallic, discarded equipment, animal and plant, and mineral wastes. **(b)** Display the data in a bar chart.
8. Explain the advantages and disadvantages of disposing of refuse by recycling and incinerating refuse.

Science in action

Since 1 February 2010 any shop selling more than 32 kg of portable batteries per year, e.g., supermarkets, newsagents or hardware stores, has to take back used batteries from the public free of charge. This should help to prevent pollution of land and water by toxic chemicals from the batteries.

Polluted waste from copper mining. Many organisms are killed when water becomes polluted.

Figure 3 Human waste comes from many sources.

Learning objectives

Students should be able to:

- explain why increasing amounts of waste are being produced from human activity
- describe how increased waste may pollute different areas of the environment
- list the human activities that reduce the amount of land available for other animals and plants
- explain how an increased standard of living means that increasingly more waste is produced and global SO_2 emissions may not peak until 2020
- describe how agricultural practices can cause pollution and harm wildlife.

Key points

Human population growth and a higher standard of living mean that raw materials are being used up quickly and more waste is being produced than previously, causing more pollution.

Humans are destroying animal and plant habitats by building, quarrying, farming and dumping waste.

Some species are finding it difficult to survive because of pollution to water, air and land.

Acid rain | black bag waste | ecosystems | herbicides | landfill | methane | particulate matter | pesticides | water courses

Lesson activities

Starter

1 Ask students what they have thrown away today. Follow this up by asking if their journey to school created waste, and does growing the food we eat create waste etc.

2 Show students a photograph of new buildings in your local area and of a quarry. Ask them how wildlife is affected by such activities. Discuss the importance students attach to this.

Main

1 B3 4.1a Chemicals in water In this practical activity, students investigate the hydrogen sulfide content of 5 water samples. (~25 mins)

2 B3 4.1b Sulfur dioxide and plants This practical investigation compares the effect of sulfur dioxide on barley and maize seedlings. (~ 45 mins)

Plenaries

1 Put the table below on the white board, with a list of waste products e.g. food, newspapers, packaging, clothes, glass, derelict buildings, old railway lines, old canals, carbon dioxide, sulfur dioxide. Fill in the table with student suggestions.

Type of waste	Reduce	Recycle	Re-use	Other

2 Write **6.8 billion in March 2010** on the white board. Ask the students what this statistic refers to. Go on to discuss the consequences of such a large human population on Earth, inviting contributions from the students, and give them 5 minutes to write their own summary of the human impact on Earth in the current year.

Homework

1 Students research details about the local authority's refuse disposal facilities, and create a spreadsheet to show how much recycling, landfill and incineration of materials goes on.

Points to note

- Student practicals B3 4.1a and B3 4.1b need to be done in a fume cupboard.

Route to A*

1 Students use the Internet to research types of batteries and types of toxic chemicals that can leak from them, and record their findings in a PowerPoint presentation.

2 Students could research two types of pesticide and two types of herbicide, frequently used by growers in the UK, and the measures taken to prevent them being washed from land into water courses.

Answers to Student Book questions

Science skills

a Less developed countries increased slowly until 1920. There is a rapid increase from 1950. More developed countries had a much lower increase from 1750 to 2000.

b ~80-85%.

c Reasons include: a large proportion of the population in developing countries is capable of childbearing; cultural reasons; children contribute to family income; status within society; fewer birth control measures; poor education system.

Answers

1 Population is increasing; higher standard of living.

2 Toxic chemicals and sewage can leak into land or water; sulfur dioxide in smoke can pollute the air.

3 Such chemicals can persist in the soil for many years; they may be washed into water, harming plants and animals.

4 Building; quarrying; farming or dumping waste.

5 **(a)** 89%. **(b)** Local authorities were given recycling targets to meet.

6 **(a)** 2001–03. **(b)** Approximately 130 kg per person per year. **(c)** ~38%. **(d)** There is an increase throughout the period. It is a steady increase up to 2002 and then increases more steeply.

7 **(a)**

Type of waste	Percentage of industrial and commercial waste
chemical	11
metallic	5
discarded equipment	1
animal and plant	9
mineral wastes	20

(b) Bar chart – *x*-axis types of waste, *y*-axis percentage of industrial and commercial waste.

8 Both recycling and incinerating refuse have advantages. Recycling saves raw materials and prevents the need to use land for waste disposal. The heat from incinerating refuse can be used to generate electricity. Disadvantages of recycling include the expense involved in collecting and sorting waste, and the energy used in these processes. As a result of incineration, ash may cause pollution. Installing a new incinerator is very expensive.

B3 4.2 Tropical deforestation and the destruction of peat bogs

Link to the Specification

B3.4.2a Large scale deforestation in tropical areas, for timber and to provide land for agriculture has:

- increased the release of carbon dioxide into the atmosphere (because of burning and the activities of microorganisms)
- reduced the rate at which carbon dioxide is removed from the atmosphere and 'locked up' for many years as wood.

B3.4.2b Loss of forest leads to reduction in biodiversity.

B3.4.2c Deforestation has occurred so that:

- crops can be grown from which biofuels, based on ethanol, can be produced
- there can be increases in cattle and in rice fields to provide more food. These organisms produce methane and this has led to increases in methane in the atmosphere.

B3.4.2d The destruction of peat bogs and other areas of peat releases carbon dioxide into the atmosphere.

How Science Works

CA: B4.4.2c Choosing the most appropriate form of data presentation; B4.5.4a Writing a conclusion based on evidence that relates to known facts; B4.5.4b Using secondary sources; B4.5.4c Identifying extra evidence that is required for a conclusion to be made.

B3 4.2 Tropical deforestation and the destruction of peat bogs

Learning objectives

- describe the effects of large-scale tropical deforestation on the release and removal of carbon dioxide from the atmosphere
- explain the importance of maintaining biodiversity
- give reasons why land has been deforested
- explain how destruction of peat bogs affects carbon dioxide in the atmosphere.

Tropical deforestation

Despite increased awareness of the importance of tropical rainforests, deforestation rates have not slowed down. Timber is extracted and land is made available for agriculture. Figures from the Food and Agriculture Organization of the United Nations (FAO) show that tropical deforestation rates increased by 8.5 per cent between 2000 and 2005.

Trees are plants: they make their food by photosynthesis. They remove carbon dioxide from the atmosphere and combine it with water to make sugars. The sugars are then used to synthesise the plant tissues. Trees are sometimes described as **carbon stores** because carbon (from carbon dioxide) is locked up in wood and other tissues for many years, until it is broken down either during respiration or when the tree dies. Deforestation reduces the number of trees and other forest plants available to take up carbon dioxide. Microorganisms break down parts of trees that are cut down, and release the carbon dioxide into the atmosphere through respiration. Clearing the deforested area to prepare it for another use often includes burning the tree debris and other vegetation. This increases the release of carbon dioxide into the atmosphere.

Deforestation area/ha: 0, 500 000, 1 000 000, 1 500 000, 2 000 000, 2 500 000, 3 000 000, 3 500 000
Country: Brazil, Indonesia, Sudan, Myanmar, Zambia, Tanzania, Nigeria, Zimbabwe, Venezuela, Bolivia, Mexico

Figure 1 Brazil and Indonesia had the world's highest deforestation rates between 2000 and 2005.

Reduction in biodiversity

Tropical rainforests have abundant rainfall all year round and the temperature is warm. High humidity, warmth and sunlight provide ideal growing conditions, so the trees grow very tall. There is also incredible diversity. In any one hectare of tropical forest you may find trees of one hundred different species. Each tree supports many other organisms. Plants, such as orchids and vines, and fungi grow on the trees. Animal species are found either in the tree canopy 40 metres above the ground, or on the relatively clear forest floor.

Over 50 per cent of the species on Earth live in rainforests. These species will be lost, and **biodiversity** will be reduced, if rainforests are cleared. Some of these species might be useful in the future for making medicines. Forty per cent of western **pharmaceuticals** come from natural plant or animal products. Habitats and wildlife are destroyed when rainforest is destroyed, but the forests are home to indigenous people too. They lose their land when rainforest is cut down.

Adding to the atmosphere's carbon dioxide concentration.

Biofuels instead of forests

Crops such as palm oil from Indonesia and Malaysia are grown on land that was previously rainforest. Some oil-powered power stations in the UK use palm oil as a fuel rather than oil from fossil fuel. This is because by 2020, 20 per cent of all energy used in the European Union has to come from renewable sources, and palm oil is a good replacement fuel. Palm oil sells as a fuel at a high price. This has led to some palm oil producers illegally cutting down rainforests to make space for growing more palm oil. Palm oil can be chemically reacted with an alcohol to form biodiesel fuel.

230

Food not trees

Population increases and increased trading in developing countries has led to demand for new farmland to grow more food. In Asia, rainforest has made way for more rice fields. In Brazil, some land has been deforested to provide space and grass for cattle-rearing. In addition to the loss of rainforest, these changes of land use increase methane production. Cattle produce and release methane during digestion. Paddy fields, where rice plants grow in water, produce methane through the rotting of plant material. Methane is a powerful greenhouse gas that has eight times the warming effect of carbon dioxide. Increases in methane production are therefore likely to accelerate climate change.

The rosy periwinkle, a native of Madagascar, provides the main drug for treating childhood leukaemia.

Science skills

Table 1 shows the changes in the amount of methane in the atmosphere between 1989 and 2009.

a Display the data as a graph.

b Describe the trend in the data.

c These data were collected in the southern hemisphere. Suggest how the validity of the data could be improved.

Table 1 Changes in atmospheric methane concentration.

Year	Methane concentration in air/parts per billion
1989	1655
1993	1700
1997	1719
2001	1742
2005	1747
2009	1758

Science in action

After seeing evidence of widespread illegal deforestation by one of its palm oil producers in Indonesia, the Unilever Corporation decided in December 2009 to stop buying palm oil from them.

Are biofuels more important than rainforests?

Peat bogs and compost

Peat bogs provide unique wildlife habitats and are valuable stores of carbon. There is more carbon held in peat bogs globally than in the world's forests. Extraction of peat releases carbon dioxide into the atmosphere. Some UK peatlands are now protected but many in Europe are not.

Questions

1 Describe the ways in which deforestation can increase the amount of carbon dioxide in the atmosphere.

2 'Tropical rainforests are the most diverse habitats on Earth.' Provide three pieces of evidence to support this statement.

3 Explain why a reduction in biodiversity is a cause for concern.

4 Name a biofuel that can be used in place of fossil fuels for electricity generation. How can this fuel be converted to biodiesel?

5 How has agriculture led to an increase in methane in the atmosphere?

6 Name two countries that had high deforestation rates between 2000 and 2005 and suggest two reasons for them allowing this to happen.

7 Suggest three reasons for action taken by the Unilever Corporation in December 2009 in Indonesia.

8 Explain to a new gardener why he should not use peat in his garden. A*

PEAT-FREE
FOR A
GREENER
GARDEN
ACT ON

Figure 2 All garden centres in the UK now stock peat-free composts.

Humans and the environment 231

Learning objectives

Students should be able to:

- describe the effects of large scale tropical deforestation on the release and removal of carbon dioxide from the atmosphere.
- explain the importance of maintaining biodiversity
- give reasons why land has been deforested
- explain how destruction of peat bogs affects carbon dioxide in the atmosphere
- explain why palm oil plantations are growing on deforested land in some parts of the tropics
- explain why there has been an increase in methane in the atmosphere as a result of changing the land use in deforested areas.

Key points

Tropical deforestation increases the release of carbon dioxide into the atmosphere and reduces the rate at which carbon dioxide is removed from the atmosphere.

Loss of forest reduces biodiversity.

Deforested land is used to grow crops for biofuel and to provide more food.

Increase in cattle and rice fields leads to an increase in methane in the atmosphere.

When peat lands are destroyed, carbon dioxide is released into the atmosphere.

Biodiesel | biofuel | canopy | compost | indigenous | paddy fields | peat bogs

Lesson activities

Starter

1 Write the words "Tropical rainforest" on the board and ask students to describe it and the environmental conditions in it. This will give you an opportunity to assess their knowledge so far and to correct any misconceptions.

2 Show the class an aerial photograph of a rainforest and ask the students how/where/why they think deforestation would begin. Suggestions should include the need to build roads; space for heavy equipment to cut down trees and drag the tree trunks to vehicles; and space to provide living accommodation for the loggers.

Main

1 B3 4.2a What's so special about peat? Refer to sheet in Teacher and Technician Pack.

2 'Dying for a biscuit' is a BBC Panorama film about the palm oil industry, lasting for 29 minutes and released in February 2010. Students watch the film and then follow the instructions on **Worksheet B3 4.2b**.

3 Worksheet B3 4.2c provides an opportunity to consolidate new language as the students solve the clues and fill in a word grid.

Plenaries

1 Write 'carbon dioxide stores' in the middle of the whiteboard. Ask the students to give you two natural examples of these and put them on the board. With the students' help add to the diagram to show how carbon dioxide is taken from the atmosphere by plants and released into the atmosphere because of burning and decay by microorganisms.

2 Give students 3 minutes to write down as many reasons as they can for conserving tropical rainforests. Then let the students share each others' contributions.

Homework

1 Worksheet B3 4.2d is a comprehension about the impact of deforestation on soil and indigenous people.

2 Students research peat lands in the UK and Europe and produce a Spreadsheet to show country; area; protection; extraction amounts; destination of peat extracted.

Points to note

- You may need to explain that the rapid process of rotting that occurs in tropical rainforests is caused by microorganisms feeding on the dead biological material.
- High temperatures and high humidity speed up the process of decay – leather sandals and straps can disintegrate in a matter of days.
- Medical cures and the key to improving future crop yields may be present in the genes of organisms that have not yet been discovered, but will become extinct if deforestation continues.
- Genetic diversity in the gene pool of all the species on Earth is essential to protect life on earth from possible catastrophic future events such as meteor impacts or massive sustained volcanic eruptions.
- When roads are cut through rainforests, vegetation, especially trees, near to the roads does not survive.
- When loggers extract a few valuable trees this destroys the local microclimate and the other vegetation in the area dies.
- If rainforest is allowed to recolonise it contains fewer species than the primary rainforest.

Route to A*

1 Students use the Internet to research the location of monitoring stations for methane concentration in the atmosphere and tabulate their findings in a Word document.

2 Students research either:
   a Unilever products and how many of them they and their family use; or
   b Sustainable palm oil production, reporting their findings in a Word document.

Answers to Student Book questions

Science skills

a Line graph, x-axis: year, y-axis: methane concentration. Line of best fit drawn.

b The data show a continuous increase in amount of methane in the atmosphere. The increase slowed down from 2001.

c Collect data from many areas of northern and southern hemispheres.

Answers

1 Burning; effect of microorganisms; less photosynthesis.

2 One hectare of tropical forest may contain trees of one hundred different species. Each tree supports many different species of plants, fungi and animals. Over 50% of the species on Earth live in rainforests.

3 Some of the species that are lost may have been of use in the future. The ecosystem will become unbalanced, which could affect other species too. In some cases the ecosystem could be destroyed completely.

4 Palm oil (or other vegetable oil). Biodiesel made from chemically reacting vegetable oil with an alcohol.

5 Increase in cattle ranching and rice growing: both produce methane.

6 Brazil and Indonesia had high deforestation rates. Increased population and increased trading from these developing countries cause them to continue deforestation.

7 Growing palm trees for oil on illegally deforested land is unacceptable because it reduces biodiversity, releases carbon dioxide into the atmosphere, and it could lead to a boycott of Unilever Corporation products.

8 Peat bogs are unique wildlife habitats. They contain stores of carbon. There is more carbon in peat bogs than in forests globally. Extraction of peat releases carbon dioxide into the atmosphere

B3 4.3 Environmental effects of global warming

Link to the Specification

B3.4.3a Levels of carbon dioxide and methane in the atmosphere are increasing and contribute to 'global warming'. An increase in the Earth's temperature of only a few degrees Celsius:

- may cause big changes in the Earth's climate
- may cause a rise in sea level
- may reduce biodiversity
- may cause changes in migration patterns, e.g. in birds
- may result in changes in the distribution of species.

B3.4.3b Carbon dioxide can be sequestered in oceans, lakes and ponds and this is an important factor in removing carbon dioxide from the atmosphere.

How Science Works

SKU: B3.4 bullet point 1: Analyse and interpret scientific data concerning environmental issues; B3.4 bullet point 2: Evaluate methods used to collect environmental data and consider their validity and reliability as evidence for environmental change.

CA: B4.5.1a Recognising that an opinion might be influenced by factors other than scientific fact; B4.5.1b Identifying scientific evidence that supports an opinion; B4.5.3a Describing the relationship between two variables and deciding whether the relationship is causal or by association; B4.5.4b Using secondary sources; B4.5.4d Evaluating methods of data collection.

B3 4.3 Environmental effects of global warming

Learning objectives

- explain how increases in levels of carbon dioxide and methane in the atmosphere contribute to the enhanced greenhouse effect, known as global warming
- describe how a small increase in the Earth's temperature may cause big climate changes and a rise in sea level
- evaluate methods used to collect environmental data and consider their validity and reliability as evidence for environmental change.

The greenhouse effect

The Earth receives heat from the Sun. Gases in the atmosphere absorb most of this heat. If they didn't, it would be lost back into space. Carbon dioxide and methane are called **greenhouse gases**. They keep the surface of the Earth warmer than it would be without them. This is known as the **greenhouse effect**.

If the amounts of carbon dioxide and methane in the atmosphere increase, this increases the amount of heat reflected back to the Earth's surface. This makes the Earth even warmer. This increased greenhouse effect is known as **global warming**. Global warming is happening, and there is evidence that at least some of it is due to human activities.

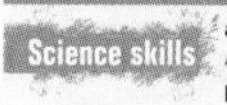

a What was the mean air temperature in Antarctica 14 000 years ago?

b Describe how the carbon dioxide concentration in the atmosphere changed from 18 000 years ago to the present.

c Explain how the data from the graph give evidence that carbon dioxide is a greenhouse gas.

d Explain why the graph does not prove that carbon dioxide is responsible for global warming.

CO_2 concentration/ppm: 180, 220, 260, 300, 340, 380
Temperature variation/°C: −10, −8, −6, −4, −2, 0, 2, 4
Time/thousands of years before present: 18, 16, 14, 12, 10, 8, 6, 4, 2, 0
Temperature
CO_2 concentration

Figure 2 Changes in carbon dioxide levels and global temperature over the last 18 000 years.

Examiner feedback

You will not need to know how the greenhouse effect works for the exam. However, understanding the greenhouse effect helps to explain why changes in greenhouse gas levels can produce climate change.

Summer visitors to the UK may be reduced if temperatures rise.

Climate change modelling and redistribution of species

Scientists use computer models to predict what will happen to the Earth's climate if global warming continues. There are so many different factors to take into account that there is still a lot of disagreement about what will happen. However, most people think that a rise of only a few degrees could change the way that weather patterns form. This could cause higher rainfall and floods in some places. It would also change where different plants and animals could live. A few scientists feel that more reasearch should be done into possible natural explanations for global warming.

The place where any particular type of tree in the northern hemisphere is found is likely to shift northwards.

Climate change would result in extinctions, and a reduction in biodiversity, as plants and animals fail to either migrate or adapt to changing habitats.

Swallows, house martins and cuckoos visit the UK and northern Europe. They come to nest and reproduce in a cooler climate than Africa, where they spend the rest of the year. Geese and swans visit the UK in winter. If the climate warms, all these birds will need to change their migration times and patterns in order to survive.

Rising sea levels and carbon storage

Increasing temperatures are causing glaciers and polar ice caps to melt and release more water into the oceans. Some scientists predict that this could result in a sea level rise of up to *80 metres*. Millions of people live in areas that would be deep underwater if sea levels rose this much.

Some scientists have proposed using carbon storage or **sequestration** as a way of removing CO_2 from the atmosphere. Several proposals have been made for carbon storage in the oceans, such as depositing CO_2 on the ocean floor in 'lakes' at depths of 3000 metres, where CO_2 is denser than water. However, we do not yet have sufficient scientific understanding to be sure that such ocean storage proposals would work.

A scientist examines part of a 3-km ice core drilled from the Antarctic ice cap.

Methods used to collect environmental data

To find out about the climate before 1860, scientists have to rely on 'proxy' records rather than direct measurements with instruments. For example, the width of tree rings is related to temperature. Other techniques that have been used include examining the time of crop harvests and other historical records.

Scientists can obtain more reliable data on past temperatures by taking measurements from ice cores. As the ice was formed, air bubbles were trapped in it. Scientists can analyse the air trapped in these bubbles and so measure carbon dioxide levels in the atmosphere hundreds of thousands of years ago. They can also estimate the temperature of the atmosphere when the bubbles were trapped.

The most recent report on climate change produced by the Intergovernmental Panel on Climate Change (IPCC) uses the output from 18 computer models that produce a range of possible scenarios that might result from climate change. Through the media and in the public mind, these scenarios have become predictions.

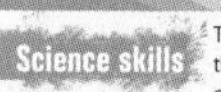

To improve the reliability of evidence for global warming, measurements are repeated, often many times. If other groups of scientists repeat an experiment and get similar results, this makes any conclusions more valid. Reliability and validity apply both to evidence and to projections of future events.

About 10 per cent of Bangladesh would be flooded if the sea level were to rise by one metre.

Questions

1. Name two greenhouse gases.
2. Explain how an increase in greenhouse gases in the atmosphere causes global warming.
3. Why is the greenhouse effect important for life on Earth?
4. Describe how the distribution of species may be affected by global warming. Give examples of species that may be involved.
5. What changes in sea level do some scientists think could result from global warming? What would be the effects of such a change?
6. Discuss how the media, scientists and the general public perceive the IPCC's climate change scenarios.
7. Give three methods that have been used to collect environmental data from before 1860, when records began. Evaluate two methods and consider their validity and reliability.
8. Evaluate the methods used today to produce scenarios that might result from climate change, and consider their validity and reliability.

A*

Learning objectives

Students should be able to:

- explain how increases in levels of carbon dioxide and methane in the atmosphere contribute to enhanced greenhouse effect, known as global warming
- describe how a small increase in the Earth's temperature may cause big climate changes and a rise in sea level
- list the possible effects of these changes on species
- evaluate methods used to collect environmental data
- explain that complex computer models are used by scientists to produce a range of possible scenarios that result from climate change
- describe how global warming may cause a redistribution of species on Earth.

Key points

Large organisms have developed exchange surfaces and transport systems for efficient exchange of materials with the environment.

The effectiveness of an exchange surface is increased by:

- having a large surface area
- being thin, to provide a short diffusion path
- (in animals) having an efficient blood supply
- (in animals) being ventilated.

Greenhouse effect | greenhouse gases | global warming | sequestration

Lesson activities

Starter

1 Write 'Climate Change' on the whiteboard. Then discuss with the students the meaning of the words and how often they hear them in a week. Go on to discuss what contexts the words are heard in; how do the students react to the words? This will give you the opportunity to correct any misapprehensions and judge the students' current understanding of them.

2 Ask each student to write down the names of ten edible plants that grow well in the UK. Then go on to ask the students how they think hotter summers would affect the plants they have named and discuss why.

Main

1 **B3 4.3a Tree rings and climatic conditions** Refer to sheet in Teacher and Technician Planning Pack.

2 **Worksheet B3 4.3b Britain's future 40 °C heatwaves** Refer to sheet in Activity Pack.

3 **Worksheet B3 4.3c** Refer to sheet in Activity Pack.

Plenaries

1 Ask the students what is meant by 'the greenhouse effect'. After revision of the term ask each student to illustrate the concept with a simple well labelled diagram. Collect these in and select the best six to display on the notice board.

2 Ask the students why sea levels are rising and what the predicted sea levels may rise by. Go on to discuss what effects a rise of 20 metres would have on the UK – people, crops and wildlife. Suggest two areas of the world that would be more affected than the UK.

Homework

1 Ask the students to make up a ten question test about the environmental effects of global warming. Each question should have a mark allowance and model answers should be supplied.

2 Students research possible consequences of the greenhouse effect using two wildlife websites, e.g. WWF and RSPB, and put their findings into a Word document.

Points to note

- Global warming is only one aspect of climate change.
- Although it is scientifically unproven that human-produced CO_2 is causing global warming, scientists advocate the precautionary principle while there is time.
- Extinctions are taking place in the 21st century at the fastest rate ever recorded.
- Due to political and economic influences and frequent conferences taking place on the environmental effects of global warming, it is essential to keep abreast of current issues and events related to it.

Route to A*

1 Students investigate climate change sceptics via BBC and CNN websites and produce a PowerPoint presentation of their findings to stimulate a class discussion on the topic.

2 Students type 'Scientific evidence for climate change' into a search engine, then review six websites from the results and summarise their findings in two hundred words.

Answers to Student Book questions

Science skills

a −2 °C.

b Upward trend. Quite steep increase for 5000 years after 18#000 BP (before present). Levelling off for 2000 years and then a sharp increase at 11#000 BP, followed by levelling off and then gradual increase from 3800#BP. Final very steep increase from ~200 years until present.

c CO_2 concentration and temperature follow the same trends on the graph; there is a correlation between them.

d There is no causal link between the variables.

Answers

1 Carbon dioxide; methane. (Water vapour, sulfur dioxide, sulfur trioxide, nitrous oxide and nitric oxide are also greenhouse gases.)

2 An increased amount of heat is reflected back to the Earth's surface, making the Earth warmer.

3 The Earth's temperature would be too extreme for life without it.

4 Tree distribution would move northwards; habitats would be lost, e.g. cool mountains in Scotland; extinctions and reduced biodiversity may result, e.g. loss of ptarmigan/dotterel; may be able to grow olives/grapes in UK; migrating birds may change their path, e.g. cuckoos, swallows.

5 A sea level rise of up to 80#metres. Millions of people would lose their homes and be forced to move to higher ground. Large-scale flooding would cause death by drowning for people and animals.

6 Scientists have produced a range of possible scenarios from 18 computer models. The media have portrayed the scenarios as predictions of climate change. The public perceive the scenarios as predictions because this is how they are presented by the media.

7 Tree rings; harvest records; ice cores. Tree rings and harvest records are not based on direct measurements with instruments relating to temperature or CO_2 in the atmosphere, therefore neither is reliable; ice cores provide reliable and valid evidence.

8 Computer models: there are many factors to take into account and the models can produce varying results. Their reliability and validity are disputed within the scientific community; they cannot be repeated by other scientists. More research is needed into other explanations for climate change.

B3 4.4 Biofuels containing ethanol

Link to the Specification

B3.4.3c Biofuels can be made from natural products by fermentation. Biogas, mainly methane, can be produced by anaerobic fermentation of a wide range of plant products or waste material containing carbohydrates.

How Science Works

SKU: B3.4 bullet point 1: Analyse and interpret scientific data concerning environmental issues.

B3 4.4 Biofuels containing ethanol

Learning objectives

- describe how ethanol-based fuels (biofuels) are produced
- explain that research is increasing the range of plant types and plant waste that can be used as a source of ethanol
- interpret economic and environmental data about fuel production by fermentation and the use of these fuels.

Converting crops to biofuels

Carbohydrate-rich crops such as sugar cane, sugar beet, maize and wheat can be **anaerobically fermented** with microorganisms to form ethanol-based fuels. This is known as bioethanol or biofuel because it is produced from living plant material. Starch in the source crop is converted to glucose (hydrolysed) by the action of carbohydrase enzymes. Yeast is added to ferment the sugars anaerobically to carbon dioxide and ethanol. The ethanol can then be separated by distillation and used as fuel instead of, or in combination with, petrol.

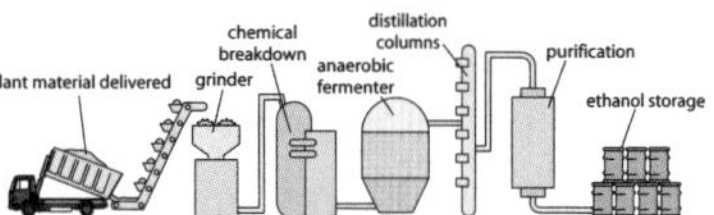

Figure 1 Making bioethanol from plant material. In the fermenter, the plant material is used as food for microorganisms, which produce ethanol as a waste product.

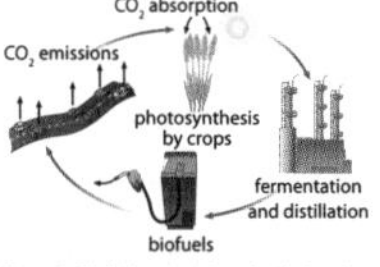

Figure 2 Biofuels emit carbon dioxide, but the plants that they are made from absorb it.

Is ethanol a carbon-neutral fuel?

Ethanol is often described as a 'carbon-friendly' or carbon-neutral fuel. This term is used because the crops grown to make it remove carbon dioxide from the atmosphere as they grow, through photosynthesis. The cars that burn biofuels release carbon dioxide back into the air, but this is only replacing the carbon dioxide that the crops took in. An ideal biofuel produces no net carbon emissions, but in practice bioethanol is not completely carbon neutral. Transport, fertiliser production and processing of the crop to produce ethanol all cause release of carbon dioxide. Biofuels are renewable and do not deplete the Earth's resources. Burning ethanol produces less air pollution than burning petrol.

Using food crops such as wheat, sugar cane and maize to produce bioethanol puts pressure on food prices, causing them to rise, as less land is available to grow food to supply an increasing world population.

Science skills

Gasohol is a mixture of ethanol and petrol. In Brazil it contains 22 per cent ethanol. Table 1 shows the changes in pollutant levels in Brazil for 15 years after the introduction of gasohol. The data show average emissions per car of CO (carbon monoxide), HC (hydrocarbons) and NO (nitrous oxides) in grams per kilometre travelled.

a Why is petrol included in the data?

b Describe the trends in the data.

c Which pollutant shows the greatest percentage decrease since before 1980?

Table 1 Average pollutant emissions after the introduction of gasohol.

Year	Fuel	Pollutant / g/km		
		CO	HC	NO
<1980	petrol	54.0	4.7	1.2
1986	gasohol	22.0	2.0	1.9
	ethanol	16.0	1.6	1.8
1990	gasohol	13.3	1.4	1.4
	ethanol	10.0	1.3	1.2
1995	gasohol	4.7	0.6	0.6
	ethanol	3.2	0.4	0.3

Government directives for renewable energy

By 2020 each European Union (EU) member state must ensure that 10 per cent of total road transport fuels come from renewable energy. Road transport accounts for around 22 per cent of UK carbon dioxide emissions. A world-scale bioethanol facilty in Hull is due to start producing bioethanol in 2010. It will produce 420 million litres of bioethanol each year from UK and EU wheat. Some of the ethanol will be mixed with just 15 per cent petrol to produce a fuel known as E85. 'Flex-fuel' cars have engines that can run on pure ethanol, pure petrol or any mixture of the two. A computer chip analyses the mixture when the tank is filled and adjusts the engine accordingly.

In 2009, flex-fuel vehicles were sold in 18 European countries.

Ethanol obtained from straw and wood

The bar chart in Figure 3 shows the overall carbon dioxide emissions of various fuels used in vehicles. Emissions for each type of fuel can vary, depending how it is produced. However, wood and straw are not used much commercially to produce ethanol. This is because they contain carbohydrate in the form of cellulose, which cannot easily be converted into sugars for fermentation.

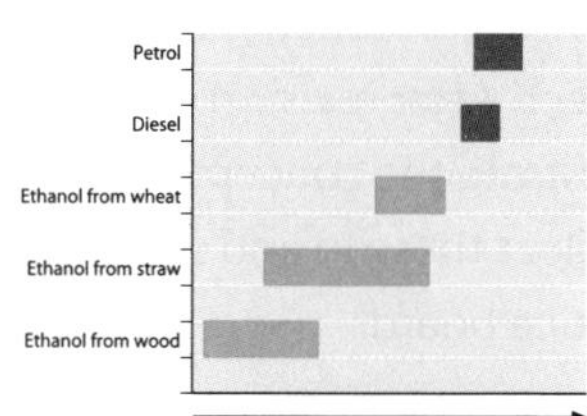

Figure 3 Carbon dioxide emissions from transport fuels.

Questions

1. Explain what is meant by 'biofuels'.
2. **(a)** Describe how ethanol-based fuels are made. **(b)** What are these fuels used for?
3. Explain what is meant by 'carbon-neutral fuels'.
4. Apart from lowering carbon dioxide emissions, give **(a)** two advantages and **(b)** one disadvantage of using biofuels.
5. Explain what gasohol is and how it compares with E85.
6. What is meant by a 'flex-fuel' car and what is the advantage of owning one?
7. Look at Figure 3. **(a)** Which fuel produces the highest carbon dioxide emission? **(b)** Which fuel produces the lowest carbon dioxide emission? **(c)** Which ethanol-based fuel has the highest carbon dioxide emission?
8. Explain how E85 fuels and the gribble worm may help lower the UK's carbon dioxide emissions from transport and why the UK government is encouraging both.

A*

Science in action

In February 2009, researchers at the universities of York and Portsmouth were awarded £2 million as part of the UK's bioenergy research programme. The scientists are working with gribble worms, *Limnoria quadripunctata*, a marine pest that bores through the wood planks of ships and piers. The worm's gut produces enzymes to break down woody cellulose and turn it into energy-rich sugars. Fermentation of the sugars obtained in this way from wood and straw could produce ethanol.

Learning objectives

Students should be able to:

- describe how ethanol-based fuels (biofuels) are produced
- explain that research is increasing the range of plant types and plant waste that can be used as a source of ethanol
- interpret economic and environmental data about fuel production by fermentation and the use of these fuels
- explain why bioethanol is not completely carbon neutral
- describe the advantage of, in the future, being able to use straw and wood as a source for ethanol.

Key points

Ethanol for use as a fuel can be produced from wheat and other crops containing starch.

Carbohydrase enzymes break the starch down into sugars.

Ethanol is produced by fermentation of sugars followed by distillation.

Burning ethanol produces less pollution than burning fossil fuels, and ethanol is a renewable fuel.

ActiveTeach Resource: Biofuels: the fuel of the future? – *Sorting activity*

Anaerobically fermented carbohydrase enzymes

Lesson activities

Starter

1 Write the term 'transport fuels' on the board. Ask students to name some of these fuels. You will probably have petrol, diesel, and perhaps aviation fuel suggested. Add any suggestions to the board and then add 'biofuels'. Invite suggestions as to what this might be.

2 Show students a picture of an early model T Ford car, which was designed to run on ethanol, petrol or kerosene. Before revealing the type of fuel it used ask the students what fuel they think it used.

Main

1 Debate Organise a debate on the motion 'The UK could develop an oil-free economy by 2030'. **Worksheet B3 4.4a** will support this and provide information about Sweden's plans for 2020. (~35 mins)

2 Worksheet B3 4.4b provides the opportunity for students to research and write about running the latest models of E85 cars.

3 Worksheet B3 4.4c Promoting biofuel gives students the opportunity to incorporate information they have researched on the Internet, and some that is supplied, into a poster to promote the use of biofuel.

Plenaries

1 Ask students to draw a concept map to show the origins and advantages of biofuels. Their results will allow you to judge their understanding of the topic. ActiveTeach has a sorting activity on the pros and cons of biofuels. [AT]

2 Ask the students to consider if, when they become car owners, they would expect to own a flex-fuel car or one with some other form of sustainable fuel such as hydrogen.

Homework

1 Students learn about production of ethanol from cane sugar in **Worksheet B3 4.4d Brazil's alcoholic cars.**

2 Students research to find the Environment Agency's position statement on Biofuels for Transport and then make a list of implications for the environment and land use of increasing the amount of crops grown for biofuels.

Points to note

- Bioethanol fuel is 200 proof.
- Economic data relating to production of fuels is related to national situations, e.g. whether a particular country has a desire to be an independent producer of transport fuel, not reliant on oil imports. The situation is political and is in a state of ongoing change.
- Hand in hand with national transport policies are tax incentives or penalties, e.g. less tax on biofuels and flex-fuel cars.
- The price of biofuels and fossil fuels at the pump is very similar.
- Flex-fuel cars and biofuelled cars may cost more to buy than cars consuming fossil fuel, though tax on them is less.
- Lowest carbon emissions are obtained from ethanol produced using lignocellulose from wood and straw, but the technology to do this is not so advanced, at present, as that for using cereals.
- The availability of E85 biofuels in 2010 in the UK is limited, but provision is already in hand to change this in the next decade.

Route to A*

1. Ask students to research Biofuel production and/or availability in their area.
2. Ask students to compare the price of a new petrol/diesel car to one that uses biofuel. Also ask them to research the price at the pump for fossil fuels compared with biofuels.

Answers to Student Book questions

Science skills

a To give a baseline value for pollution.

b All three pollutants decrease over time. The value for ethanol is always lower than that for gasohol.

c CO. ~85%

Answers

1 Fuels that are obtained from carbohydrate-rich crops.

2 **(a)** Hydrolysis of starch in plant material using carbohydrase enzymes, anaerobic fermentation of sugar into ethanol, followed by distillation. **(b)** They are used as transport fuels in motor vehicles instead of petrol.

3 Carbon-neutral fuels are fuels that have no net effect on carbon dioxide levels in the atmosphere.

4 **(a)** Advantages: they are fully renewable; they produce less air pollution. **(b)** Disadvantages: their production may lead to an increase in food prices.

5 Gasohol is a mixture of ethanol and petrol. In Brazil it contains 22% ethanol. In Europe it contains 85% ethanol.

6 A 'flex-fuel' car is one whose engine can run on pure ethanol, pure petrol or any mixture of the two. The advantage is that the cheapest petrol/ethanol source can be used.

7 **(a)** Petrol. **(b)** Ethanol. **(c)** Ethanol from wheat.

8 E85 is a mixture of 85% ethanol and 15% petrol. Ethanol is a carbon-neutral fuel. By 2020 each EU member state must ensure that 10% of road transport fuel comes from renewable energy. Twenty-two per cent of UK carbon dioxide emissions come from road transport. The gribble worm produces enzymes to digest wood and straw. If these digested products are used as a source for ethanol, carbon dioxide emissions will be lowered further and there will be no pressure on food crops.

B3 4.5

Biogas from small-scale anaerobic fermentation

Link to the Specification

B3.4.3c Biofuels can be made from natural products by fermentation. Biogas, mainly methane, can be produced by anaerobic fermentation of a wide range of plant products or waste material containing carbohydrates.

Ideas for practical work

Build a simple biogas generator to collect methane and demonstrate how the methane can be burned as a fuel.

How Science Works

SKU: B3.4 bullet point 4: Evaluate the use of biogas generators.

CA: B4.4.2a Drawing tables.

B3 4.5

Biogas from small-scale anaerobic fermentation

Learning objectives

- explain what biogas is
- describe how biogas can be produced from plant and animal waste by anaerobic fermentation
- evaluate the use of a small-scale biogas generator in a rural setting.

Microorganisms produce fuel

Biogas is produced by anaerobic fermentation of plant material or animal waste, such as manure, sewage sludge and kitchen waste. Microorganisms in the waste break down the waste materials in the anaerobic conditions of the fermenter, to produce biogas.

Biogas can only be produced in this way if the waste contains carbohydrates. Many different types of microorganisms are involved in the breakdown of the waste materials into biogas. The fuel or biogas produced is made up mainly of methane, with some carbon dioxide. Biogas makes an excellent fuel for cooking stoves and furnaces. The scale of biogas production can vary from small-scale household production to large commercial biogas generators.

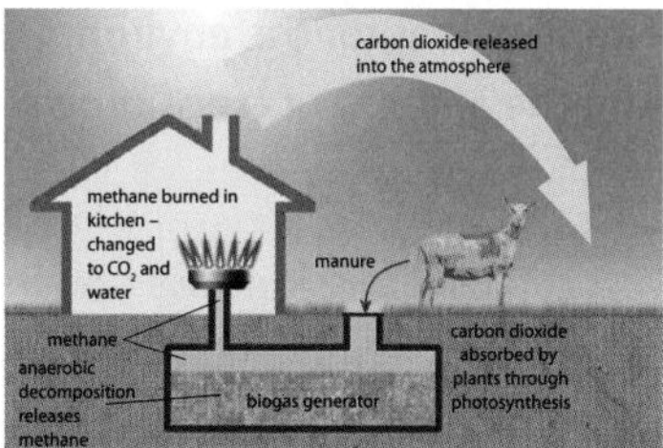

Figure 1 Locally produced biogas can be used for cooking and for heating water.

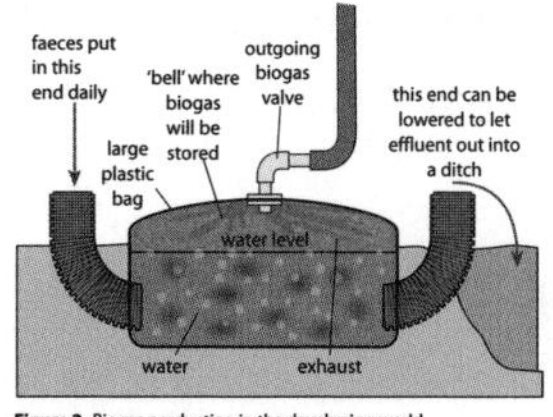

Figure 2 Biogas production in the developing world.

Biogas for families

The simplest types of biogas generators have no moving parts. Figure 2 shows a biogas generator suitable for a small farm in the developing world. A trench about 10 metres long and 1 metre deep is dug in the ground, and a heavy-duty plastic bag is then placed in the trench. The bag is fitted with inlet and outlet pipes and a valve to draw off the gas. To start up the digester, the bag is two-thirds filled with water, and then topped off with the exhaust gases from a car. Then a mixture of water and faeces is fed through the inlet pipe. It takes about 18 kg of faeces per day to provide enough gas for the farmer's needs. The methane produced is released through the valve at the top. The **effluent** is the solid particles and water left after gas production. The solids settle into a sludge that can be used as a crop fertiliser. The effluent can be run off by lowering the outlet pipe into a ditch.

236

Gas is fed directly to the farmer's house, to be used for cooking and/or heating. The gas can also fuel farm machinery.

Disadvantages of having farm-based biogas generators include having to stock and monitor the biogenerator on a daily basis, using land to house the biogenerator and pipework, and the initial set-up costs. Gas pressure may vary when gas is collected in a simple dome or 'bell'.

In addition to biogas production, biogas generators facilitate nutrient recycling, waste treatment and odour control.

Biogas for rural schools

A biogas generator at a school at Myeka in a remote part of South Africa uses human and animal faeces to produce gas for cooking, science experiments and driving an electric generator. The installation consists of two 20 000-litre digesters. These receive the faeces from 16 school toilets. The toilets are arranged in two concentric circles around the digesters. The installation also incorporates two cow-dung inlet ports. The farm animal waste increases the output from the digesters and allows biogas production to continue at weekends and during holidays when the students are not in school.

The installation at Myeka High School delivers an estimated 13 cubic metres of gas daily. This produces 18 kilowatts of power – enough to run the school's computers and electric lighting. To operate efficiently, biodigesters like the one at Myeka need to be located in a warm climate where there is a good supply of water, so that the fermentation rate of the microorganisms is fast.

What a difference biogas makes.

Constructing a biogas generator similar to the one at Myeka.

Biogas can be used to fuel farm machinery, as on this pig farm in Argentina

Questions

1. What is biogas?
2. What materials are needed to produce biogas?
3. What biological process is used to make biogas?
4. **(a)** Suggest two uses of biogas in a farmer's household. **(b)** Suggest how the sludge remaining after fermentation is used on the farm.
5. How would village hygiene be improved by a biodigester?
6. Where is the gas collected in a simple farm-type of biogas generator? Give an advantage and a disadvantage of this type of collection.
7. Make a table to show the factors that influence the rate at which biogas is produced in a small-scale biogas generator. Alongside each factor explain how it will have its effect.
8. Explain how a school in a remote part of South Africa can produce enough electricity for computers and lighting using biogas.

A*

Humans and the environment 237

Learning objectives

Students should be able to:

- explain what biogas is
- describe how biogas can be produced from plant and animal waste by anaerobic fermentation
- evaluate the use of a small-scale biogas generator in a rural setting
- describe the structure of a low tech biogas generator in a third-world village
- explain how a community building such as a school can benefit when a biogas generator is installed.

Key points

Biogas is a mixture of gases consisting mostly of methane and carbon dioxide.

Microorganisms produce biogas by fermentation in anaerobic conditions.

Animal and human faeces are used to feed biogas generators on farms and in villages.

Gas can be piped directly to homes or school, or used to run an electricity generator.

ActiveTeach Resource: Biogas production small scale – *Diagram labelling activity*

Biodigester effluent sewage sludge

Lesson activities

Starter

1 Look at the diagrams and photographs of rural biogas production in developing countries in the Student Book lesson B3 4.5. Ask students how they think the biogas will benefit people in rural communities.

2 Write "Biogas = methane + carbon dioxide" on the white board. Invite the students to tell you what they know about both gases.

Main

1 **Worksheet B3 4.5a** has a series of questions to answer after doing the ActiveTeach labelling activity of a small-scale biogas fermenter. (~20 mins) [AT]

2 **Worksheet B3 4.5b** introduces the installation of an anaerobic digester to produce biogas in Costa Rica, which is shown on YouTube. The video is in two parts, each lasting about 8 minutes. A transcription in English is available on the Biogas Digester webpage. It is easy to fast forward the video through technical parts about connecting valves etc. The value of the video is in showing how low-tech the project is, and the environment in which it is used. Watching the video is followed by Internet research, including reading information from another webpage Bringing biogas to Nepal, to produce an A5 flyer about two countries that are using anaerobically-produced biogas in a rural setting. (~35 mins)

3 **Worksheet B3 4.5c Get clued up on biogas** is a puzzle that revises the material on biogas production. The task of solving each other's puzzles could be held over for the plenary. (~20 mins to create the clues + 5 mins to solve a puzzle)

Plenaries

1 Solving the puzzles created in **Worksheet B3 4.5c** is an ideal activity here.

2 Write this sentence on the board: 'Life in my village with our new biogas fermenter'. Ask students to imagine they are the villagers and to make appropriate comments. Responses can be either written or verbal; students can work individually or in groups of 2 or 3.

Homework

1 Students go to the Biogas Developers website to see how this company are hoping to construct anaerobic digesters (ADs) on farms in the UK. This is linked to a government scheme introduced in 2010 known as the Feed in Tariff Scheme (FITS). Students present their findings in a Word document.

2 Students research to try to find out if the governments of India, Pakistan and Bangladesh encourage biogas generation in rural villages, and then present their findings in a Word document.

Points to note

- Internet searches for information on biogas generators are more productive if the term 'biogas digesters' is used.
- Untreated biogas from rural generators, containing impurities such as hydrogen sulfide, has a low calorific value when combusted.
- Warn the students that the construction of a home-made biogas gas generator is NOT a task for them. The specification has a suggested idea for practical work to build a simple biogas generator, but this is a task only for a teacher/technician to set up for demonstration.

Route to A*

Higher achievers could be asked to write a Word document about the new government FITS scheme (see Homework task 1) and how biogas production and other energy conversion schemes, such as solar panels, relate to it.

Answers to Student Book questions

1 A mixture of mostly methane and carbon dioxide.

2 Plant material or animal waste, such as manure or sewage sludge.

3 Anaerobic fermentation.

4 **(a)** Cooking, lighting or electricity generation. **(b)** As a fertiliser.

5 Animal and human excreta will be used and not left to cause disease; also the village will be less smelly.

6 Gas is collected in a simple dome or bell. This is an advantage as there are no moving parts involved to break down. It is a disadvantage because gas pressure may vary.

7

Factors that influence the rate of biogas production	Effect on production rate
amount of waste added	more raw material produces more gas
amount of water added	water provides the required conditions for fermentation
temperature	within limits, a higher temperature will speed up microbial fermentation
type of waste	the more carbohydrate in the waste, the faster the rate of gas production
amount of microbes in the waste	more microbes increase the rate of decay and gas production

8 The school feeds human and animal faeces into a larger biogas digester. Anaerobic fermentation produces gas that is used to run an electricity generator. A warm climate and a good water supply are needed.

B3 4.6 Generating biogas on a large scale

Link to the Specification

B3.4.3c Biofuels can be made from natural products by fermentation. Biogas, mainly methane, can be produced by anaerobic fermentation of a wide range of plant products or waste material containing carbohydrates.

How Science Works

SKU: B3.4 bullet point 4: evaluate the use of biogas generators.

CA: B4 4.2a Drawing tables; B4 4.2b Drawing charts and graphs.

B3 4.6 Generating biogas on a large scale

Learning objectives

- describe how biogas can be generated from domestic waste
- explain how cooperation between farmers results in the supply of energy to small towns in rural locations
- evaluate the advantages and disadvantages of the design of biogas generators.

Using a city's organic waste for biogas

Biogas can be generated on a large scale from manure and organic waste. Figure 1 shows a scheme that operates in Kristianstad in Sweden using waste from several sources (see data box). The biogas is produced in the digester. Most of the gas is piped to a district heating supply in the town.

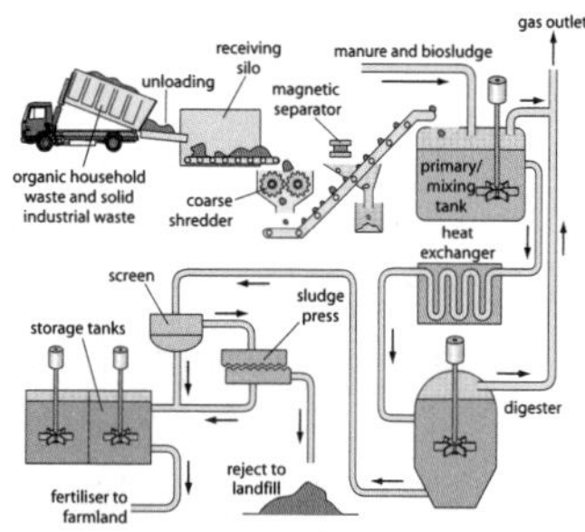

Figure 1 Producing gas from city refuse. The gas is drawn from the primary/mixing tank and the digester.

Science skills Table 1 shows the Swedish biogas digester's annual input, output and energy statistics.

a Calculate the percentage mass of the input material that is converted into biogas.

b Calculate the proportion of the gross biogas production that is needed to heat the plant.

c List the advantages and disadvantages of producing fuel in this way rather than using mains gas.

Table 1 Statistics from biogas digester in Kristianstad in Sweden.

Input/tonnes	
manure	41 200
household waste	3100
abattoir waste	24 600
distillery waste	900
vegetable waste	1400
Output/tonnes	
liquid biofertilliser	67 150
biogas	4000
waste	50
Energy produced/MWh	
gross biogas production	20 000
biogas used to heat plant	2100
biogas sales to district heating plan	17 900
electricity purchased to operate biogas plant	540

238

Farmers produce biogas on an industrial scale

The town of Tillamook Bay in Canada has constructed a biogas plant to process the manure of 10 000 dairy cows.

The digesters are 40 m × 10 m × 4 m in size. Each digester is equipped with heating and insulation.

Canada is not a warm country. The digester needs both insulation and heating to keep the microbes warm enough to quickly ferment the waste.

This installation cost about £1 000 000 to build.

The benefits are:

- it provides enough electricity for 150 average homes
- it produces 23 000 tonnes of high-quality potting soil per year
- It returns 64 million litres of liquid fertiliser per year to farmers' fields.

gas dome, separator, conveyor, digester 1, digester 2, fibre

Figure 2 Cow manure digester at Tillamook Bay.

Maximising biogas production

In a biodigester facility some or all of the features shown in Table 2 may be included in the design of the system.

Table 2 The advatages and disadvantages of various digester features.

Feature	Advantage for system	Disadvantage for system
automatic mixing system in feed tank	speeds up digestion in the fermenter	maintenance and energy costs of mixing equipment
pump to force organic matter into the fermenter	reduces labour and supplies a constant amount of feed to the fermenter	maintenance and energy costs of pump
heating system in the fermenter	speeds up the fermentation rate and biogas production in temperate climates	energy costs, especially during cold seasons
agitation system in the fermenter	speeds up the fermentation rate as microbes and organic matter are in closer contact	high energy costs and potential for agitator breakdown
floating gas holder (drum)	constant gas pressure supplied	expensive and requires intensive maintenance

The more efficient the biogas generator is, the more gas and profit it will make. Some features speed up the fermentation rate, while others help regulate the gas supply and pressure.

Questions

1. Give three sources of organic waste for a city biogas reactor other than manure and household waste.
2. What is most of the gas from the Swedish biogas digester used for?
3. Name two secondary products from the gas production facility supplied by manure.
4. Explain what would happen to the volume of gas output from biogas generators in Sweden and Canada if they were not supplied with heating and insulation.
5. Name two design features of a biodigester facility that help regulate the gas supply and pressure. What are the advantages of these features?
6. If the Tillamook Bay facility was located in the south of France, why would running costs be reduced?
7. Consider the two main types of gas in biogas. Suggest how the waste from a sugar beet factory in Norfolk could optimise growing conditions in the greenhouses of a neighbouring tomato grower.
8. Evaluate the advantages and disadvantages of three design features of biogas generators.

A*

Humans and the environment 239

Learning objectives

Students should be able to:

- describe how biogas can be generated from domestic waste
- explain how co-operation between farmers can supply energy to small towns in rural locations
- evaluate the advantages and disadvantages of the design of biogas generators
- explain the advantages that increasing numbers of anaerobic biogas generators in the UK would bring
- describe how the output from a biogas generator might be affected by climatic conditions.

Key points

Many different sorts of waste can be used to generate biogas.

Initial costs of installing digesters may be high.

The biomass used as a raw material is plentiful and renewable.

In cold climates biogas generators need to be supplied with insulation and heating.

Lesson activities

Starter

1 Go through the flow diagram in Figure 1 in the Student Book and allow students to ask any questions.

2 Log onto the BBC website and enter 'biogas' in the search window. Choose a video clip about biogas, from a current news event, to show to the students.

Main

1 Worksheet B3 4.6a Upgrading biogas generators will allow you to assess students' understanding of the fermentation process. It also provides an opportunity for students to research local biogas generators. (~25 mins)

2 Which biogas generator? Three designs of biogas generators are shown in **worksheet B3 4.6b**. Take time exploring these with students before they construct their table of advantages and disadvantages of each. (~30 mins)

3 Worksheet B3 4.6c Zero-carbon refuse hope requires the students to produce an information leaflet for local householders. (~25 mins)

Plenaries

1 Write "Garden Waste" ↙ ↘ Composting Anaerobic digestion

on the whiteboard. Ask the students to tell you what pros and cons each method of dealing with the waste has for Local Authorities.

2 Return to the information leaflets produced when using **worksheet B3 4.6c**. These can be presented by the students and/or displayed on the noticeboard.

Homework

1 Students write an article, suitable for a British farming magazine, about the biogas production plant in Canada, see lesson 4.6 in the Student Book. The article should include the costs and benefits.

2 Students research to find out what plans US-based Air Products and SITA UK have for using household waste as feedstock for energy-from-waste facilities in the North East of England.

Points to note

- Figure 1 and the table of design features of digesters in the Student Book need to be studied carefully in preparation for the student tasks.
- Biogas generators (ADs) are being planned to be built by an increasing number of local authorities as we go to press.
- Zero-carbon refuse is refuse that does not release carbon dioxide emissions during its disposal.

Route to A*

Students log onto the BBC website and enter 'biogas' in the search window; they write a one hundred word summary, as a Word document, of one of the articles on the page.

Answers to Student Book questions

Science skills

a 5.6%.

b 10.5%.

c Advantages: biogas and liquid fertiliser are produced from waste; pollution of land and water by waste are prevented; the source materials are renewable.

Disadvantages: biogas generator systems are expensive to build; energy costs for transport of waste to the site and heating are high.

Answers

1 Abattoir waste; waste from distilleries; vegetable waste.

2 A district heating supply.

3 Potting soil; liquid fertiliser.

4 The volume would fall because of low temperatures; slowing the rate of fermentation.

5 Pumps to force organic matter into the fermenter. Advantage: reduces labour costs. Floating gas holder. Advantage: supplies gas at a constant pressure.

6 Less need to supply insulation and heating to speed up fermentation as the south of France has a warm climate.

7 Biogas is produced from fermentation of sugar beet waste. It contains carbon dioxide and methane. Carbon dioxide can be supplied to greenhouses for plants to use in photosynthesis. Biogas can be used for heating the greenhouses.

8 Any three features from Table 2, giving one advantage and one disadvantage of each.

B3 4.7

Collecting biogas from landfill and lagoons

Link to the Specification

B3.4.3c Biofuels can be made from natural products by fermentation. Biogas, mainly methane, can be produced by anaerobic fermentation of a wide range of plant products or waste material containing carbohydrates.

How Science Works

SKU: B3.4 bullet point 4: evaluate the use of biogas generators.

CA: B4 4.2b Drawing charts and graphs; B4 5.3a Describe the relationship between two variables.

B3 4.7

Collecting biogas from landfill and lagoons

Learning objectives

- explain how methane from landfill sites can be collected for use as a fuel
- describe how lagoons containing large volumes of animal waste prevent odour problems and supply biogas
- compare biogas output from a variety of farm animals.

In 2008, 57 million tonnes of waste went to landfill in England and Wales.

Science in action

Some local councils have put radiofrequency identification (RFID) chips into wheelie bins to monitor the amount of landfill waste produced by each household. The idea behind the RFID chips is to increase recycling and decrease landfill.

Biogas from landfill sites

Most waste in the UK is still disposed of in landfill sites. Waste is deposited in a section of the site, and compacted. When the section is full, it is covered with soil. The organic waste dumped in such a landfill site will decompose with time. If there is an impervious surface below the waste, the waste will become waterlogged and anaerobic fermentation will occur. This will lead to production of biogas from the waste, mostly methane. This methane will slowly work its way up through the waste and be vented into the atmosphere. If landfill is covered after use, the gas will slowly seep through the earth covering and be released into the atmosphere.

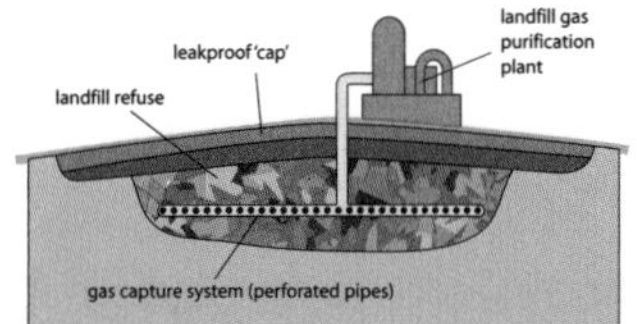

Figure 1 Fuel from rubbish.

Instead of letting methane escape, it can be collected and used as a fuel. Perforated pipes (pipes with holes in) are used to collect the gas. A cover prevents gas escaping into the atmosphere. The production of gas from many landfill sites can continue for around 20–30 years, though there is a gradual reduction after about 10 years.

Biogas from farm lagoons

Farms with large numbers of animals have problems disposing of all the faeces and urine produced. These are often run into large lakes or lagoons and left to decay naturally. The smell can be terrible. However, these lagoons produce biogas, and can be fairly easily adapted to collect it: the lagoon is covered with heavy-duty plastic sheeting to prevent biogas escaping, and tubes are put in to collect the gas. The gas is then used as a fuel on the farm. Biogas lagoons are being built extensively in countries south of the UK, but there are comparatively few in the UK because the climate is too cold.

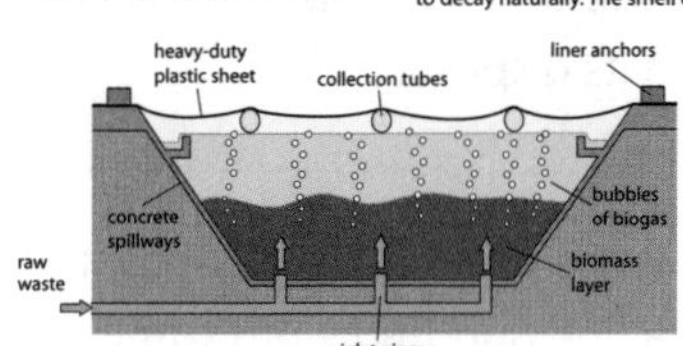

Figure 2 Biogas from an anaerobic lagoon.

240

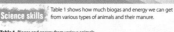

Science skills

Table 1 shows how much biogas and energy we can get from various types of animals and their manure.

Table 1 Biogas and energy from various animals.

	Hen	Pig	Horse	Sheep	Cow	Unit of measurement
mass of each animal	2	70	400	60	500	kg
Manure						
	0.19	5.88	20.40	2.40	43.00	kg per day
	0.085	0.084	0.051	0.040	0.086	kg manure per kg animal per day
Output						
total biogas	0.0167	0.3338	1.62	0.1975	1.24	m^3/day
total power	0.0045	0.0904	0.44	0.0535	0.34	kW
biogas/kg manure	89.43	56.77	79.44	82.28	28.91	litres/kg manure per day
power/kg manure	24.22	15.38	21.51	22.28	7.83	W/kg manure per day
biogas/kg animal	7.60	4.77	4.05	3.29	2.49	litres/kg animal per day
power/kg animal	2.06	1.29	1.10	0.89	0.67	W/kg animal per day

a Display the data for total kg manure per kg animal per day as a bar chart.

b Produce a pie chart to show production of biogas/kg animal as a portion of the total biogas/kg animal from all five animals.

c **(i)** What is the general relationship between biogas/kg animal and the mass of the animal? **(ii)** Are there any anomalies in the relationship you identified in (i)?

Preventing pollution and generating gas.

Examiner feedback

Remember that many different types of microorganism are involved in the production of biogas. These microorganisms are present in the feedstock material from plants and animals.

Science in action

Landfill gas can be hazardous and can cause explosions. To prevent this, the gas used to be burned on site at the top of a flare stack. Land gas purification plants that capture the gas avoid this waste of energy.

Questions

1 Why is it important to stop methane escaping into the atmosphere?
2 How is methane collected from landfill sites for use as a fuel?
3 Explain what an anaerobic lagoon is.
4 Give two advantages of covered lagoons on farms.
5 Using the biogas statistics above, discuss why an egg production unit would benefit from contributing to a biogas generator.

A*

Humans and the environment 241

Learning objectives

Most students should be able to:

- explain how methane from landfill sites can be collected for use as a fuel
- describe how lagoons containing large volumes of animal waste prevent odour problems and supply biogas
- compare biogas output from a variety of farm animals.

Some students should also be able to:

- describe how biomethane is expected to contribute to transport fuels in the future [Ext]
- evaluate landfill as a means of dealing with household waste. [Ext]

Key points

Organic waste in landfill sites is decomposed by microbes producing biogas containing methane.

Methane production from landfill sites can continue for up to 30 years.

Covering landfill waste with a gas-proof cap allows the biogas to be piped away and used as a fuel.

Lakes or lagoons of animal faeces and urine can be used to supply biogas if covered with a strong plastic sheet.

Lesson activities

Starter

1 Tell students that methane generated by rotting vegetation in Lake Eyak in Alaska can be collected in a large balloon as it bubbles up to the surface of the water. The methane can then be set alight. Lake Eyak is in fact acting like a lagoon.

2 Ask students what a landfill site is. Let them suggest why these can be dangerous and elicit the fact that they produce biogas that can cause explosions if not controlled. Write the words 'landfill', 'biogas' and 'hazard' on the board, then add 'biogas flaring' and ask students what this means. Save a copy of what you have written to return to later.

Main

1 Worksheet B3 4.7a Role for biogas in transport is a comprehension with associated tasks, requiring Internet access, about the development of biomethane as a transport fuel. (~35 mins)

2 Smelly lagoons The students write two letters in the tasks required from **worksheet B3 4.7b**. Internet access is required for research. (~35 mins)

3 Worksheet B3 4.7c Sustainable fuels provides a summary of chapters 4.4 to 4.7. The students construct a spider diagram. (~20 mins)

Plenaries

1 Return to your starter activity on landfill. Ask the students how they can add to it now.

2 Write these two statements on the whiteboard: 'Landfill fines of £182.5 million per year likely in the UK in future' and 'Pig and cattle slurry used in lagoons'. Let the students choose one of the topics and work in groups of 2 or 3 for 3 minutes preparing to speak on it for 1 minute. Ask for volunteers to give their presentation.

Homework

1 Students find out the number of landfill sites in a 10-mile radius of their home and school. Note whether they are still receiving rubbish. Mark the sites on a map and display it on the classroom noticeboard or whiteboard.

2 Students research to see if Holland, Belgium, France and Germany have many lagoons for biogas collection, and tabulate their findings in a Word document.

Points to note

- Students' experience of landfill sites will vary but have in mind one or two locations of sites in your area.
- Large covered lagoons are not found in the UK because the climatic temperatures are too cold for most of the year.
- Generally the biogas from lagoons is used to generate electricity and is used on farms.

Route to A*

Students do an Internet search on 'Abbeystead explosion', and find out about a devastating explosion caused by methane in 1984. They produce an A5 Fact Card about the explosion to inform the public about the danger of methane.

Answers to Student Book questions

Science skills

a x axis animals, y axis kg/kg animal per day

b Suitable pie chart, with following percentages: 34.23% – hen; 21.49% – pig; 18.24% – horse; 14.82% – sheep; 11.22% – cow.

c **i** The smaller the mass of the animal the greater is the biogas/kg animal produced. **ii** Horses have a higher biogas/kg production than sheep.

Answers

1. Methane is a greenhouse gas.
2. A cover prevents gas escaping into the atmosphere; perforated pipes collect the gas; the gas is sent to a purification plant.
3. A lake or large tank containing animal urine and faeces.
4. Stops the smell from waste; allows collection of the biogas.
5. Hens produce about the same amount of manure/kg of animal as pigs and cows; the power output from hens is larger than any of the other animals; the biogas per kg manure per day is higher than any of the other animals; egg production units house large numbers of birds; there is a large volume of waste produced; money can be earned from biogas production.

B3 4.8

Protein-rich food from fungus

Link to the Specification

B3.4.4d The fungus *Fusarium* is useful for producing mycoprotein, a protein-rich food suitable for vegetarians. The fungus is grown on glucose syrup, in aerobic conditions, and the biomass is harvested and purified

How Science Works

CA: B4.42a Drawing tables; B4.42b Drawing charts and graphs.

B3 4.8

Protein-rich food from fungus

Learning objectives

- define mycoprotein and recall which fungus produces it
- explain that the biomass of fungal hyphae is the product from the fermenter
- describe the conditions needed to produce mycoprotein
- evaluate mycoprotein as a useful food for vegetarians.

Science in action

Food for the future?

A 500 kg bullock can yield 1 kg of new protein per day; 500 kg of soya beans can yield 40 kg of new protein per day; but 500 kg of microorganisms could yield 50 000 kg of protein per day.

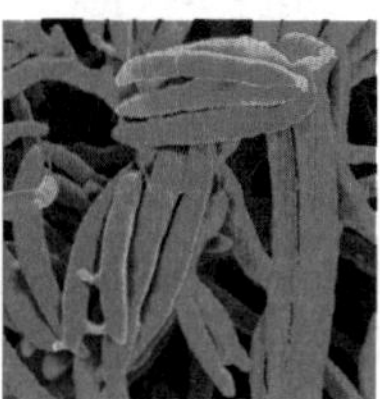

A photomicrograph of the fungus *Fusarium*. Mycoprotein is made from the species *Fusarium venenatum*.

Examiner feedback

Mycoprotein is produced from a micoscopic fungus grown in a fermenter. It is an aerobic process and so cannot be described as a fermentation, which is an anaerobic process.

Fusarium is a soil fungus

The global population is increasing rapidly. This has resulted in increased demand for protein for both people and animals. Using microorganisms as a protein source is one solution to this problem. The fungus *Fusarium venenatum* is used in 50-metre-high fermenters to produce a protein-rich food called mycoprotein. It is suitable for vegetarians because it has no connection whatsoever with animals.

Fusarium lives naturally in the soil, where it feeds on the dead remains of plants and animals. Its fungal body consists of microscopic, narrow, branched, thread-like structures called **hyphae**. These microscopic fungi grow quickly and reproduce, needing relatively little space. In optimum aerobic conditions with a plentiful supply of nutrients, they can double their biomass every five hours.

Growing *Fusarium* in a fermenter

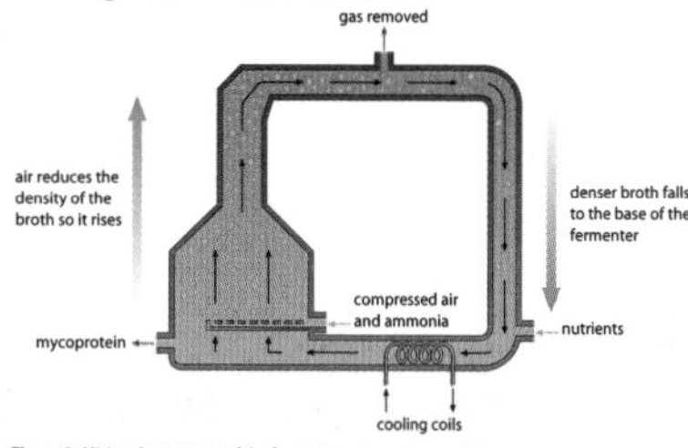

Figure 1 Mixing the contents of the fermenter using compressed air.

Keeping the fungus growing

The contents of the fermenter need to be mixed constantly to keep the fungus growing. However, the fungal hyphae of *Fusarium* are delicate, and a mechanical stirrer would damage them. Instead, a stream of compressed air provides more gentle agitation that protects the fungal hyphae.

The growth process in the fermenter lasts for six weeks. There is a steady input of nutrients into the fermenter during this time to maintain the growth of the fungus. The fungus converts the nutrients into biomass. Starch from potatoes or cereals is used as a source of carbohydrate because it is cheap and so makes the process economical. The starch is treated with enzymes to break it down to glucose before it is added to the fermenter. Ammonia is also added, as a source of nitrogen. The product is the whole fungal body of *Fusarium*, or its biomass.

242

Making food from mycoprotein

After being harvested from the fermenter, the mycoprotein is dried. At this stage it looks similar to pastry but at the microscopic level the harvested hyphae have a similar shape to animal muscle cells. Like muscle, they are made up of microscopic filaments. The fibrous texture of the mycoprotein makes it slightly chewy, similar to meat or fish.

Flavoured, shaped and packaged mycoprotein.

Science skills

a Use the data shown in the bar chart to make a table showing the nutrients in mycoprotein and their weight per 250 g of freshly harvested product.

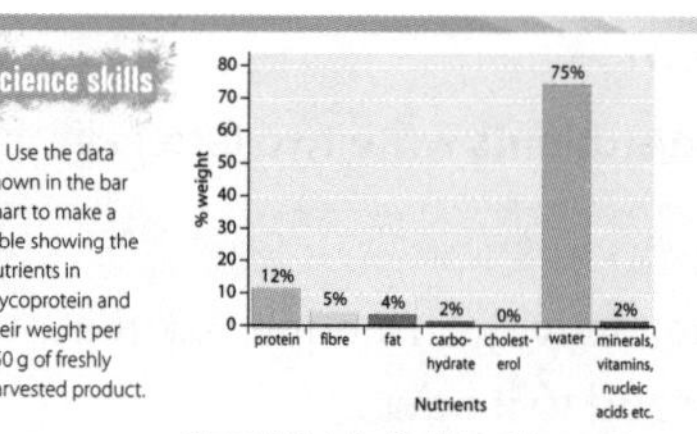

Figure 2 Nutrient value of freshly harvested mycoprotein.

Science skills

Table 1 shows the composition of chicken pieces, beefburgers, and some Quorn products (food made from mycoprotein).

b Evaluate the health issues associated with each of the four products.

c Explain the difference in carbohydrate values for the two animal products.

d Give the percentage of saturated fat in the total oil/fat for each food.

Table 1 Composition of Quorn and other foods.

Per 100 g	Quorn pieces	Chicken pieces	Quorn burgers	Beef burgers
energy/kJ	355.0	621.0	490.0	1192.0
protein/g	12.3	24.8	12.8	15.0
carbohydrate/g	1.8	0.0	5.8	3.5
oil/fat/g	3.2	5.4	4.6	23.8
of which saturates/g	0.6	1.6	2.3	10.0
fibre/g	4.8	0.0	4.1	0.4
sodium/g	0.2	0.1	0.5	0.5

Questions

1 **(a)** Which fungus produces mycoprotein? **(b)** What conditions does the fungus need to grow and reproduce?

2 Give two reasons why compressed air is pumped into the loop fermenter where *Fusarium* is grown.

3 **(a)** Use Figure 1 to explain how heat from the aerobic fermentation is prevented from overheating the fermenter so its temperature is a constant 32 °C. **(b)** Explain what might happen to enzymes if the temperature reached 45 °C.

4 **(a)** Give *two* nutrients that are added to the fermenter. **(b)** Explain why they are added throughout the fermentation process.

5 Explain precisely what the product from the fermentation is.

6 A vegetarian finds it difficult to include enough protein in his diet. Write a fact sheet for him to explain what mycoprotein is, an outline of its production, and three ways that it could be included in his diet.

A*

Humans and the environment 243

Learning objectives

Students should be able to:

- define mycoprotein and recall which fungus produces it
- explain that the biomass of fungal hyphae is the product from the fermenter
- describe the conditions needed to produce mycoprotein
- evaluate mycoprotein as a useful food for vegetarians
- explain why *Fusarium* needs air and ammonia to grow in a fermenter
- describe how the structure of mycoprotein can be compared to animal muscle at a microscopic level.

Key points

The fungus *Fusarium* is used to make food called mycoprotein, which is rich in protein and suitable for vegetarians.

The fungus is grown using glucose from potato or cereal starch, in aerobic conditions, in fermenters.

Ammonia is supplied as a source of nitrogen to help the microbes build proteins.

Lesson activities

Starter

1 Write the word "Mycoprotein" on the whiteboard. Ask the students what they know about it and build up a concept map as they contribute.

2 Hold up an empty packet or an advert for a mycoprotein food (most well-known are Quorn™ products). Divide the class into groups of four and give each group a different Quorn™ product box or cut-out advert. Give each group 5 minutes to write down what they already know about mycoprotein and what they have found out from the prop they have been given. Groups should then report their findings back to the rest of the class.

Main

1 Worksheet B3 4.8a How nutritious is Mycoprotein? allows students to compare nutrients in mycoprotein fillets, beef and lentils. Students can use Microsoft Excel for producing bar charts.

2 Worksheet B3 4.8b Foods produced using microorganisms provides practice in table construction and students learn about the loop fermenter in which mycoprotein is produced.

3 Soya beans and edible fungi Students make a PowerPoint presentation about either soya-based foods or edible mushrooms, detailed in **worksheet B3 4.8c**.

Plenaries

1 Write "Mycoprotein food is suitable for vegetarians" in the centre of the whiteboard. Invite the students to suggest why and build up a spider diagram from their responses.

2 Students watch each others' PowerPoint presentations from the **worksheet B3 4.8c**. Make the link with the microscopic fungus *Fusarium* that produces mycoprotein.

Homework

1 Students use the Internet to find out if mycoprotein is produced in mainland Europe and the USA, and then present their findings in a Word document.

2 Students use the 'What is mycoprotein?' website to look at photographs of Quorn™ production and read some of the statistics or school resources; they then produce a ten bullet point summary card, with the title "This is Quorn™".

Points to note

- The Student Book provides nutrient data for freshly harvested mycoprotein. The activity sheets provide nutrient data for mycoprotein fillets, as they can be bought in a supermarket.
- Fibre, being carbohydrate, is part of the 'carbohydrate total' figures as well as being shown separately.
- The whole fungal biomass is harvested from the fermenter.

Answers to Student Book questions

Science skills

a

Nutrient	Weight/g per 250 g of freshly harvested
Protein	30
Fibre	12.5
Fat	10
Carbohydrate	5
Cholesterol	0
Water	187.5
Minerals, vitamins, nucleic acids, etc.	5

b Quorn products are best for fibre and contain less oil/fat. Chicken pieces contain more protein and less sodium than the others, and contain less saturated fat than Quorn burgers. Beef burgers are by far the least healthy: they contain much more fat and saturated fat.

c Chicken pieces are just chicken meat; beef burgers contain some type of cereal to bulk the meat out.

d

Per 100 g	Quorn pieces	Chicken pieces	Quorn burgers	Beef burgers
Percentage of total fat/oil that is saturated fat	18.7	29.6	50	42

Answers

1 **(a)** *Fusarium venenatum* produces mycoprotein. **(b)** To reproduce and grow, the fungus needs warmth and a plentiful supply of nutrients and oxygen.

2 Compressed air supplies oxygen for respiration; it also gently agitates the culture broth.

3 **(a)** Cooling coils full of cold water take heat away from the fermenter. **(b)** The enzymes will be denatured and stop working.

4 **(a)** Glucose and ammonia are added to the fermenter as nutrients. **(b)** They are added continuously to maintain the growth rate of the fungus.

5 The product of the fermentation is the fungal body or biomass of *Fusarium venenatum*. It is made up of microscopic thread-like hyphae.

6 Factsheet to contain: mycoprotein is a fibrous synthetic food product that is slightly chewy, similar to meat. It is produced by fermentation of the fungus *Fusarium venenatum*. It is suitable for vegetarians because it contains no animal products. It can be flavoured and textured and used in many different recipes. (Provide three menu/recipe examples). It is available in supermarkets, has a high protein and fibre content, a lower fat content than meat, and a low energy content.

B3 4.9 Improving the efficiency of food production

Link to the Specification

B3.4.4a At each stage in a food chain, less material and less energy are contained in the biomass of the organisms. This means that the efficiency of food production can be improved by reducing the number of stages in food chains.

How Science Works

SKU: B3.4 bullet point 5: evaluate the positive and negative effects of managing food production and distribution, and be able to recognise that practical solutions for human needs may require compromise between competing priorities.

CA: B4 4.2a Drawing tables; B4 4.2c Choosing the most appropriate form of presentation; B4 5.1b Identifying scientific evidence that supports an opinion.

B3 4.9 Improving the efficiency of food production

Learning objectives

- explain why biomass and energy decrease at each stage in a food chain
- describe how a fixed area of land could be cultivated to provide food for the maximum number of people
- interpret diagrams showing transfer of biomass and energy along a food chain
- explain how we can improve the efficiency of food production.

Where does our protein come from?

Producing protein food for humans.

Protein is an essential requirement for the maintenance and growth of cells, so we must eat it regularly. What people actually eat depends on where they live and what they can afford. Meat is an excellent protein source, but it is more expensive than plant proteins such as whole grains. The reason is connected with the flow of biomass in food chains.

You will remember from B1 5.1 that there is a loss of biomass at every stage in a food chain. Food production is therefore less efficient when the food we eat is higher up the food chain.

Energy flow in food chains

Plants can only trap a tiny percentage (0.023%) of the energy in the sunlight for photosynthesis. At each stage in a food chain, energy is lost to the atmosphere as heat via respiration. At least 50% of the energy that primary consumers take in is lost as faeces. Animals that move around to search for prey use much of the energy from their food in the muscles, via respiration.

The units for energy flow are kilojoules per square metre per year (kJ/m^2/year).

The data for producers show that of the 7 106 000 kJ/m^2/year of light energy absorbed, only 87 000 kJ/m^2/year was used in photosynthesis.

Of this 87 000 kJ (see Figure 1):

- 50 000 was used by the plants in respiration
- 14 000 was consumed by primary consumers
- 23 000 became detritus when producers died.

Food at lower levels in the food chain will have been produced more efficiently in terms of the energy it has retained.

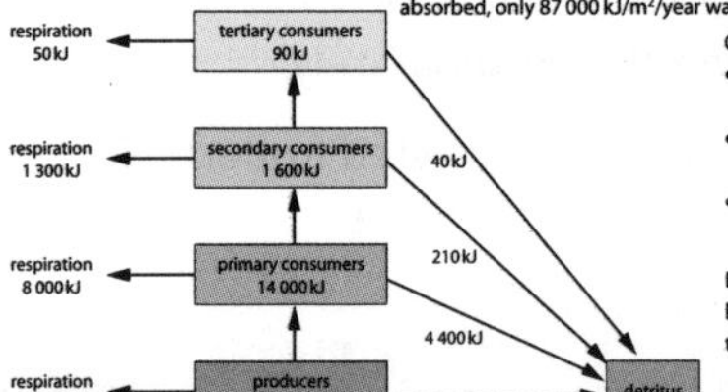

Figure 1 Energy flow in a stream.

Science skills

a Tabulate the information in Figure 2.

b Display the information in another format.

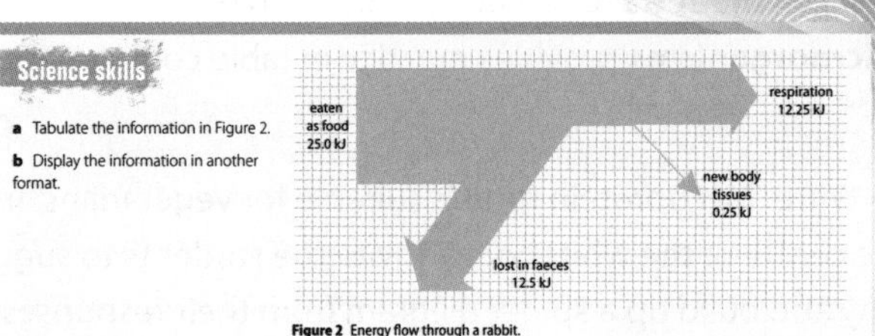

Figure 2 Energy flow through a rabbit.

Cereals or cows?

Energy that is wasted in the food chain does not get into our food. The higher our food is in the food chain, the less efficient the energy transfers to it. By using organisms for food that are low in the food chain, we can improve the efficiency of food production.

Figure 3 shows how many people can be fed from four hectares of land: an area about the size of five football pitches. The land will support 58 more people if they get their protein from soya beans than if their protein comes from beef.

10 acres (5 football pitches) will support:

60 people growing soya

10 people growing maize

24 people growing wheat

2 people rearing cattle

Figure 3 The number of people an area of land can support depends on how it is used.

Questions

1. **(a)** Explain why all animals need protein in their diets. **(b)** Give three different ways that protein from the environment can be harvested.
2. Suggest why it is less expensive to buy a 500 g loaf than it is to buy 500 g of minced beef.
3. Give a reason why predators use a higher proportion of respiratory energy in their muscles, than their prey use in their muscles.
4. Refer to Figure 1. **(a)** Calculate the proportion of energy absorbed by the producers that was used in photosynthesis. **(b)** Calculate the proportion of energy in the producers that was passed on to the primary consumers.
5. In which type of organism was the proportion of energy lost via respiration the highest?
6. Explain what is meant by detritus and how the biomass and energy in it are used.
7. Soya plants are about one-third of the height of maize plants and can be grown more densely than maize plants. Suggest why growing soya on a fixed area of land will feed six times more people than growing maize on the same area of land.
8. Describe energy flows along a food chain and, using this information, suggest how food production can be made more efficient.

A*

Learning objectives

Most students should be able to:

- explain why biomass and energy decrease at each stage in a food chain
- describe how a fixed area of land could be cultivated to provide food for the maximum number of people
- interpret diagrams showing transfer of biomass and energy along a food chain
- explain how we can improve the efficiency of food production.

Some students should also be able to:

- manipulate data for biomass and energy in food chains [Ext]
- explain what detritus is and give examples of detritivores. [Ext]

Key points

All plants and animals are part of a food chain.

At each level in a food chain less material is contained in the biomass of the organisms.

Energy is lost at each level because of waste and respiration; some is lost as heat.

Wasted energy in the food chain means eating meat or fish is not the best or cheapest way for humans to obtain their energy.

ActiveTeach Resource: Improving the efficiency of food production – *Interactive matching activity*

Decomposers	detritivores	phytoplankton	primary consumers
producers	secondary consumers	tertiary consumers	trophic levels

Lesson activities

Starter

1 In groups of 2 or 3 ask students to construct a food chain using the words carnivore, producer and herbivore, and to give a specific example of each. Ask them to add numbers to represent the number of individuals at each stage. This could lead on to giving a definition of biomass and asking the students which stage will have the biggest biomass and which the smallest. Share the information with the rest of the class.

2 Write 'African Wildlife Safari' on the whiteboard. Ask the students to name four types of animals they would expect to see on such a safari. Then go on to elicit the fact that lions (large carnivores) are more difficult to find than antelopes (herbivores) and other grazing animals. Link this to the amount of biomass at each stage in the food chain and let students suggest why this is so.

Main

1 Worksheet B3 4.9a Biomass in food chains provides questions on biomass in food chains. Additionally it gives an introduction to fish farming and the unnatural biomass relationship that this may involve, leading to environmental disadvantages. (~30 mins)

2 Worksheet B3 4.9b Energy loss in a food chain provides an opportunity for students to identify where and how energy is lost from a food chain. (~20 mins)

3 Questions of energy Further questions on energy flow through food chains are presented in **worksheet B3 4.9c**. (~20 mins)

Plenaries

1 'Will the Sunday roast be a thing of the past in 2050?' Write this sentence on the whiteboard and invite students' comments on the statement in view of what they have learned in this spread.

2 Tell the students that you would like them to consider the proposition that 'Meat-free Monday' should become law. Give the students, individually, 3 minutes to write down points in favour or against the proposal, with reasons. Students then share their views with the rest of the class.

3 Class activity: ActiveTeach matching activity 'Improving the efficiency of food production'. [AT]

Homework

1 Students use textbooks or the Internet to research data showing energy flow through an insect such as a grasshopper, locust or honeybee, then present the information as an A5 Fact Card with a diagram to show the energy flow.

2 Students research to find out what percentage of the population are vegetarians in the following countries: UK, USA, India, China, New Zealand, then display the data graphically.

Points to note

- The Student Book lesson begins with general information about loss of biomass and loss of energy at progressively higher levels in food chains.
- Figure 1 and Figure 2 provide numerical data for analysis. Figure 1 shows data for energy flow in a stream.

Route to A*

Students research the cause of the collapse of the salmon fish farming industry off the coast of Chile in 2009.

Answers to Student Book questions

Science skills

a

Type of energy transfer	Energy/kJ
eaten as food	25.0
lost in faeces	12.5
heat loss in respiration	12.25
new body tissues	0.25

b Bar chart with type of energy transfer on x-axis and energy values on y-axis.

Answers

1 **(a)** Protein is needed in animals for the maintenance and growth of cells. **(b)** Growing cereal crops, farming livestock and catching fish are all ways to harvest protein from the environment.

2 Beef is more expensive to produce than wheat flour because cattle are higher up the food chain than wheat plants.

3 Predators need to move around more than prey to find their prey and kill it.

4 **(a)** $\frac{87\,000}{7\,106\,000} = 0.012 = 12\%$. **(b)** $\frac{14\,000}{87\,000} = 0.16 = 16\%$.

5 The secondary consumers lost the greatest proportion of energy via respiration.

6 Detritus is the broken down, solid waste produced by organisms and their dead bodies. The biomass and energy in it are used by organisms that feed on it.

7 Soya plants can trap more light energy than maize plants in a fixed area because they are shorter, can be grown more densely and do not shade each other.

8 Producers trap light energy during photosynthesis and produce sugar. Primary consumers eat the plants and use the energy to build new biomass, and to respire. Some energy is lost through waste. At each stage in the food chain there is less energy present than in the previous level. We can improve the efficiency of food production by feeding from organisms low down in the food chain.

B3 4.10

Intensive animal farming

Link to the Specification

B3.4.4b The efficiency of food production can also be improved by restricting energy loss from food animals by limiting their movement and by controlling the temperature of their surroundings.

How Science Works

SKU: B3.4 bullet point 5: Evaluate the positive and negative effects of managing food production and distribution, and be able to recognise that practical solutions for human needs may require compromise between competing priorities.

B3 4.10 Intensive animal farming

Learning objectives

- describe how energy losses from food animals can be restricted
- evaluate the positive and negative effects of managing food production by factory farming.

Which is the better way of rearing chickens?

Figure 1 Energy flow through a free-range chicken.

Factory farming

At factory farms animals are kept indoors permanently in large numbers. Meat, milk and eggs are the main products of this industry. The aim of factory farming is to produce the most product at the lowest cost. There are risks and benefits to factory farming.

Rearing animals = inefficient food production

Many people like to eat meat, and factory farming supplies it as efficiently as possible. Even so, when you eat plant foods, all the material and energy from the plant goes directly into your body. If the same plant food was fed to an animal, and then the animal was killed and eaten, not all the original material and energy in the plant would be passed to your body. This is why rearing animals is not a very efficient way of producing food. Up to half of the world's harvest is fed to farm animals, while 800 million people go hungry.

Energy flow through mammals and birds

Cattle are primary consumers; they eat grass. The proportion of energy lost via respiration is high in cattle. This is because cattle are mammals. Mammals such as cattle, pigs, sheep and humans maintain a constant body temperature by generating heat inside the body. Keeping the body temperature high and constant needs a lot of energy from food.

Birds keep an even higher constant body temperature than mammals, so chickens and turkeys use an even higher proportion of their food in maintaining a constant body temperature.

Free-range or battery chickens?

Free-range chickens live outdoors for most of the time, where they feed mainly on natural food. Figure 1 shows how much of the energy we supply in food to a free-range chicken is transferred to human food.

Many hens that produce eggs are kept in cages, one above the other. This is battery hen farming. Keeping the hens in cages restricts their movement and so reduces energy loss.

Broiler chickens are reared for meat. Most of them are kept in poultry sheds holding up to 50 000 birds. They are not in cages. Poultry sheds are windowless buildings and have to be lit using artificial light.

Keeping hens in warm sheds reduces the amount of energy from food that they need to use to keep warm. Even so, almost half of the cereal food fed to the hens is not converted into meat or eggs. For factory-farmed chickens it takes 3.6 kg of cereal food to produce 2.0 kg of body mass.

It is generally acknowledged that rearing free-range chickens compared with factory farmed chickens provides the birds with a better standard of animal welfare. There is less disease and injury to the birds. Some consumers prefer to buy free-range poultry products for these reasons and some consumers also think the eggs and chickens taste better. However, free-range poultry products cost more to buy.

Farmers of free-range poultry have less expenditure on sheds and cages for the birds but they need more land to house a large flock of birds. Farming costs are reduced as there are no energy bills for heating and lighting the poultry houses.

Science skills

Table 1 World egg production, past and projected.

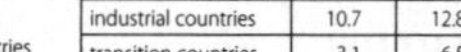

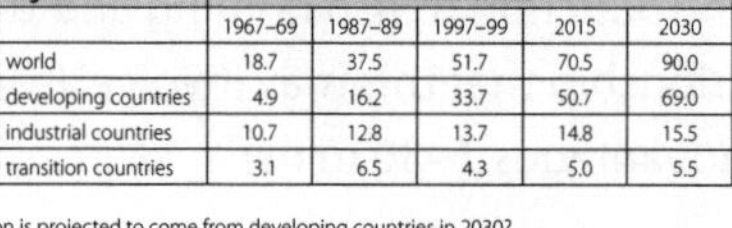

Region	Million tonnes				
	1967–69	1987–89	1997–99	2015	2030
world	18.7	37.5	51.7	70.5	90.0
developing countries	4.9	16.2	33.7	50.7	69.0
industrial countries	10.7	12.8	13.7	14.8	15.5
transition countries	3.1	6.5	4.3	5.0	5.5

a How much increase in egg production is there projected to be in developing countries from 1967 to 2015?

b What percentage of world egg production was in industrial countries between 1967 and 69?

c What percentage of world egg production is projected to come from developing countries in 2030?

Zero-grazing dairy systems

Intensively farmed cows can produce around 10 times their natural milk yield. Choosing certain varieties of cattle and feeding them high-energy and protein food such as grain or food pellets helps produce this higher milk yield. However, this increase in production comes at a cost.

Cattle confined in sheds or outdoor yards stand permanently on concrete floors that are often covered with manure. The cattle often end up lame. Vast quantities of animal waste are produced from factory farms, and this is an important source of greenhouse gas emissions. Water may also be polluted by run-off from manure storage. The food concentrates given to the cattle can also cause problems. The outbreak of BSE in UK cattle in 1984 was linked to food pellets produced from diseased cattle and sheep.

What price cheaper food?

Questions

1. Explain what is meant by 'factory farms', and their aim.
2. Why is rearing animals for food inefficient?
3. Explain how in intensive poultry farms the movement of chickens is reduced and why it makes food production more efficient.
4. Poultry and cattle are kept in warm sheds on factory farms. Explain one advantage and one disadvantage of this for the farmer.
5. Why are there concerns about the spread of infectious diseases in intensive poultry farms?
6. **(a)** A farmer is deciding whether or not to keep battery hens. Make a table to show the advantages and disadvantages to him of farming battery hens. **(b)** Suggest other factors the farmer should think about before making a decision.
7. List two issues involved in factory farming that are of concern to you. Explain your choices.
8. Many people pay extra to buy free-range eggs. Outline an investigation to find if people can taste the difference between eggs from free-range hens and eggs from battery hens. Your investigation should be designed to give reliable results. You should include the independent variable, controls and how to measure the dependant variable.

A*

246

Humans and the environment 247

Learning objectives

Most students should be able to:

- describe how energy losses from food animals can be restricted.
- evaluate the positive and negative effects of managing food production by factory farming.

Some students should also be able to:

- suggest compromises for rearing food animals that are economic and still promote animal welfare [Ext]
- discuss the reasons for probable high increases in meat prices in the next 20 years. [Ext]

Key points

Rearing animals is an energy inefficient method of food production.

There are risks and benefits to factory farming.

Keeping animals warm means that they convert more of their food into meat.

Restricting animals' movement means they convert more of their food into meat.

Lesson activities

Starter

1 Draw a circle 21 cm in diameter on a whiteboard and tell the students that this is the amount of space a chicken gets when it is intensively farmed. Ask the students why a farmer might keep chickens like this.

2 Watch a video clip such as 'Live fast die young' about chicken farming from the Compassion in World Farming web site. Careful monitoring of video content is recommended in order to judge the suitability of it for your students.

Main

1 Worksheet B3 4.10a Chicken farming is an evaluation exercise.

2 Worksheet B3 4.10b Choosing chicken Students are required to interpret data and produce a poster related to chicken rearing.

3 Worksheet B3 4.10c What's on the supermarket shelves? Students write a letter to a supermarket chain about the type of foods they supply.

Plenaries

1 Write the following on the whiteboard: 'chicken burger', 'organic chicken breast', '30-year-old couple without children', 'teenage student'. Ask students to match up the chicken product with the people and write down their reasons for doing this.

2 Use the posters made using **worksheet B3 4.10b** and let the students present them to the class verbally. Alternatively you could display the posters in two groups and ask the students to make a list of the key points they show.

Homework

1 **Worksheet B3 4.10d** provides an opportunity to revise the material from this lesson.

2 Students survey an animal protection website such as World Society for the Protection of Animals (WPSA – Factory farming); and a site regulating intensive farming such as the UK Department for Environment, Food and Rural Affairs (DEFRA). They can read about the DEFRA – 'Five freedoms', a code that forms the basis for assessing cattle welfare on farms. Students prepare a PowerPoint presentation to discuss whether it is possible to farm intensively without compromising animal welfare.

Points to note

- It is important with issues of this type that you do not give a biased view but rather present the evidence and let the students come to their own conclusions about cost/benefits.
- Internet research into the ways animals are kept may present students with distressing images and information; this may need controlling or monitoring.
- You may need to make clear early on the regime under which free-range hens are kept.
- Students from urban areas may be unfamiliar with farms and animal rearing. Some images of these methods would be useful and some are shown in the Student Book.

Route to A*

1 Students research to find out about the digestive system of cattle and why cattle produce so much methane, then write up their research as a Word document.

2 Students research to find the links between shrimp farming, mangroves and increased risk from tsunami damage in Thailand and Indonesia, and present their findings in an A5 fact card.

Answers to Student Book questions

Science skills

a 45.8 million tonnes.

b 57.2%.

c 76.7%.

Answers

1 Factory farms are farms where animals are kept indoors in large numbers. The aim is to produce the highest yield at the lowest cost.

2 Animals use up a lot of the energy in the food they eat, so only a small proportion of the biomass of their food becomes animal biomass.

3 Chickens are either kept in battery cages or crowded together in sheds. Less energy is used for movement, so more energy is available for growth of the chicken.

4 Advantage: the animals use less energy from their food to keep themselves warm, and so more energy is available for growth. Disadvantage: keeping the sheds warm costs money for the fuel.

5 Overcrowding, warmth and dust in poultry sheds are conditions in which disease spreads fast.

6 **(a)**

Advantages	Disadvantages
large numbers of chickens are kept, so more profit	heating costs
small amount of land needed to keep hens on	hygiene costs disposal of large amount of manure
easily fed	food costs
eggs easily collected and more produced	lighting costs higher veterinary bills

(b) Other factors to consider include the lifestyle of the hens; spread of disease; air and water pollution; lower unit selling price for battery-farmed eggs or broiler chickens.

7 Any two, each justified by a reason.

8 Independent variable: free-range or battery eggs; dependent variable: preferred taste, measured on a score card by ticking a numbered box to indicate preference. Controls: eggs cooked in same way, served in same way, e.g. seasoning. Reliability: at least 10 people tested individually, each type of egg presented three times from different sources.

B3 4.11 Fish stocks

Link to the Specification

B3.4.4c Fish stocks in the oceans are declining. It is important to maintain fish stocks at a level where breeding continues or certain species may disappear altogether in some areas. Net size and fishing quotas play an important role in conservation of fish stocks.

How Science Works

SKU: B3.4 bullet point 1: Analyse and interpret scientific data concerning environmental issues; B3.4 bullet point 3: Evaluate the methods being used to feed and provide water to an increasing human population, both in terms of short term and long term effects.

B3 4.11 Fish stocks

Learning objectives

- describe the state of the oceans' fish stocks and the importance of allowing breeding populations to survive
- explain conservation measures such as net size and fishing quotas
- evaluate modern fishing as an example of sustainable food production.

Is the ocean's supply of fish unlimited?

High-protein food from the sea

For thousands of years people living along coasts have harvested fish from the sea. But in recent years, over-harvesting has led to a collapse of fish stocks in many parts of the ocean.

The modern fishing industry can harvest fish extremely efficiently. Sonar can be used to pinpoint whole shoals of fish accurately. Enormous nets or lines are dragged through the oceans, sometimes for many hours. Large factory ships have on-board facilities for processing, packing and freezing fish.

Some spectacular collapses of fisheries have occurred because of overfishing. In 1992 the cod fishery off Newfoundland, Canada collapsed because the population dropped below that needed for sustainable breeding. Cod stocks in the North Sea, to the east of the UK, are also close to collapse.

Science in action

The Convention on International Trade in Endangered Species (CITES) can give protection to fish on the brink of commercial extinction; the bluefin tuna is one such fish. However, at a United Nations conference in Doha in March 2010, governments failed to pass a vote to protect the bluefin tuna. Some countries that voted against protection did so for economic reasons because their fishing fleets catch a high proportion of bluefin tuna. In other countries bluefin tuna is eaten as a delicacy so these consumers did not want the numbers caught to be reduced. Conflicting interests are often involved when trying to conserve an endangered species.

The bluefin tuna is on the brink of extinction.

Science skills

The Food and Agriculture Organization of the United Nations (the FAO) publishes a two-yearly report on the state of the world's fisheries. Fish stocks that are fully exploited are in danger of over-exploitation, at which stage they collapse.

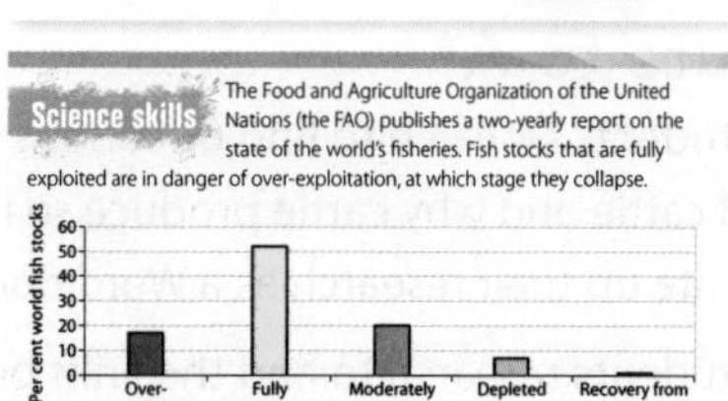

Figure 1 Over-exploited fish stocks are in danger of collapse.

a What percentage of world fish stocks have not been affected by fishing?

b What percentage of world fish stocks are neither over-exploited nor fully exploited?

Using food webs to manage fish stocks

Scientists believe that the complex food web that exists in the ocean must be taken into account if fisheries management is to be successful. **Ecosystem overfishing** is when the balance of the ecosystem is altered due to overfishing. For example, the abundance of large predatory fish such as swordfish, tuna, cod and halibut has declined sharply. Ninety per cent of stocks of these fish have already gone. As a consequence, there is an increase in abundance of their prey. These are small foraging fish such as gurnard, wolf fish and black bream.

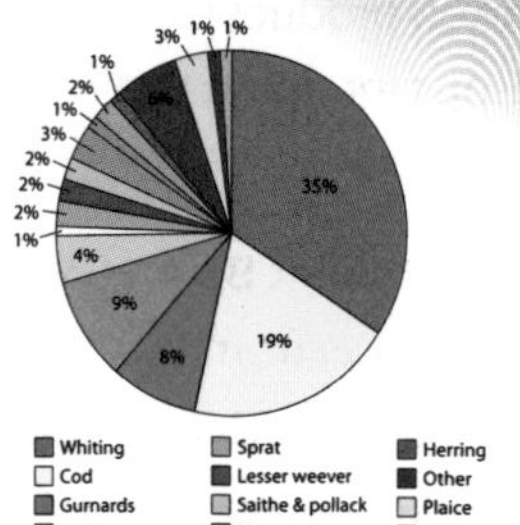

Figure 2 Food that fish in waters around the UK prefer to feed on.

Sustainable fishing

Sustainable fishing means catching a consistent amount of fish over an indefinite period without otherwise damaging the environment. This is the aim of fisheries management organisations. Unless they are fished sustainably, certain species may disappear altogether in some areas. Mature adult populations must be able to produce enough offspring to keep the population stable. Cod reach maturity at about 3–4 years of age, when they are about 50 cm long. The minimum length of cod that can be caught under EU regulations is 35 cm, which is too small for sustainability.

Practical measures that can be taken to maintain fish stocks include:

- controlling net size
- fishing quotas.

A net's mesh size determines what size fish the net will catch. Fish that are smaller than the mesh can pass through. If the mesh size is right, juvenile and immature fish can escape and live to reproduce. EU laws govern the minimum mesh size for specific target fish.

Mesh size controls which fish are caught.

The Common Fisheries Policy (CFP) of the EU sets limits or quotas for each country on the amounts of fish they can catch. Each fishing vessel is given an individual fishing quota for different fish types. These compromises for the fishing industry are imposed to create a basis for a viable fishing industry in the future.

Questions

1. What has caused the collapse of fish stocks in the oceans?
2. Describe what factory ships do.
3. Why do modern fishing vessels use sonar?
4. **(a)** Name a species of fish on the brink of commercial extinction. **(b)** Suggest why the species you mention has not been given protection.
5. Why must ocean food webs be considered in order to manage commercial fisheries successfully?
6. What is the aim of fisheries management organisations?
7. Controlling net size is a conservation measure to protect fish stocks. Explain how it works.
8. Explain what the competing priorities are that require a compromise in the form of fishing quotas.

A*

248

Humans and the environment 249

Learning objectives

Students should be able to:

- describe the state of the oceans' fish stocks and the importance of allowing breeding populations to survive
- explain conservation measures such as net size and fishing quotas
- evaluate modern fishing as an example of sustainable food production
- discuss the compromise that is required between competing priorities, if endangered species, such as Bluefin tuna, are to survive
- analyse data relating to fisheries in different parts of the world.

Key points

The ocean's fish stocks are in decline.

Fish must breed in sufficient quantities if the target species are to survive.

Practical strategies to manage fish stocks and sustain food production include controlling net size and fishing quotas.

Lesson activities

Starter

1 Ask the students to tell you what types of fish they have eaten or seen named on menus or in supermarkets in the last six months. List the suggestions on the whiteboard and then go on to ask where in the world those fish came from. Establish that many fish come from far away and the reasons for this.

2 Write 'Fishing Techniques' on the whiteboard and invite the students to tell you what they know about this. Student experiences will vary greatly depending on your locality, but it will be very helpful if the basic vocabulary is established.

Main

1 Sustainable food production debate Students watch the video 'The death of the oceans?' and use **Worksheet B3 4.11a** to support them in preparing for a class debate. Each student's contribution will be assessed. If time is short written preparation for the debate could be set as a homework task. (~40 minutes)

2 Fishing terms Worksheet B3 4.11b introduces students to some of the terms associated with conserving fish stocks and provides data to display graphically.

3 'What's cod really like?' Worksheet B3 4.11c provides data to display and requires the students to produce a Word document as a fact file sheet about cod.

Plenaries

1 Ask the students if they think they will be able to afford a meal of fish and chips in 2030. Ask both the 'Yes' and 'No' groups the reasons for their choice.

2 Write 'The death of the oceans?' in the middle of the whiteboard. Invite the students to respond and build up a spider diagram with their contributions.

Homework

1 Worksheet B3 4.11d is a word puzzle that provides an opportunity to revise terms associated with this topic.

2 Students use the Internet, e.g. the CEFAS website, to find information about fish egg surveys and produce a PowerPoint presentation of their findings.

3 Students look on the Fisheries Science Partnership part of the CEFAS website to find out about the location of projects in waters around the UK, and produce a poster to display the information they find.

Points to note

- Take time to discuss the meaning of sustainable fishing with the students. The Student Book has a definition.
- For **worksheet B3 4.11a**, 'The death of the oceans?' video was in the Horizon 2010–11 series, shown on BBC 2. It is available on YouTube in four parts. Part 1; Part 2; Part 3; Part 4. Some scientists were gathering data for a census of marine life. The most relevant part runs for approximately 10 minutes and begins about 13 minutes 18 seconds after the start of the programme, finishing about 23 minutes after the start. Advise students to read through the whole sheet of tasks before you play the video. They should be aware that each person's contribution to the debate will be assessed. If time is short, assess some contributions in written form.

Route to A*

Higher achievers could investigate the change in materials used to make fishing nets in the 1960s and evaluate the contribution this might have made to the collapse of cod stocks off Newfoundland in 1992.

Answers to Student Book questions

Science skills

a Approx. 3%

b 27–31%.

Answers

1 Over-harvesting of fish has caused fish stocks to collapse.

2 Factory ships are giant ships that process and package enormous numbers of fish on board.

3 To locate fish shoals.

4 **(a)** e.g. Bluefin tuna. **(b)** Student response, e.g. stock levels unknown; no fishing controls imposed.

5 Fishing for one species may affect prey, predators and competition from other species.

6 The aim is to achieve sustainable fishing by catching a consistent amount of fish over an indefinite period without reducing fish stocks or damaging the environment.

7 Juvenile fish can pass through the net and live to reproduce and help maintain stocks.

8 Fishermen need to make a living by catching fish; over-fishing leads to collapse of fish stocks and can cause extinction of species; quotas are set and net sizes controlled to protect species and allow sustainable fishing.

B3 4.12 Feeding the world

Link to the Specification

B3.4 Humans rely on ecosystems for food, water and shelter.

B3.4.4 Food production.

How Science Works

SKU: B3.4 bullet point 1: Analyse and interpret scientific data concerning environmental issues; B3.4 bullet point 3: Evaluate the methods being used to feed and provide water to an increasing human population, both in terms of short term and long term effects; B3.4 bullet point 5: Evaluate the positive and negative effects of managing food production and distribution, and be able to recognise that practical solutions for human needs may require compromise between competing priorities.

B3 4.12 Feeding the world

Learning objectives

- evaluate methods being used to secure a global food supply
- describe the solutions being employed to provide the daily water needs of the global population
- assess the implications of food miles.

Agriculture, water and food security

The United Nations Food and Agriculture Organization (FAO) published the following statistics relating to the global supply of food and water.

- The daily drinking water requirement per person is 2–4 litres, but it takes 2000–5000 litres of water to produce one person's daily food.
- It takes 1000–3000 litres of water to produce one kilogram of rice and 13 000–15 000 litres to produce one kilogram of grain-fed beef.
- Over the period 2010–2050, the world's water supply will have to support agriculture to feed an extra 2.7 billion people.

A billion people in the world today are malnourished, while in more developed countries over-consumption is creating a global crisis of obesity. The aim of the FAO is to achieve food security for every household. A household is considered food secure when its occupants do not live in hunger or fear of starvation.

a Tabulate and display the data on the map in graphical form for the following countries: UK, South Africa, India, Australia, Chile and USA.

b Suggest two reasons for the uneven consumption of food worldwide

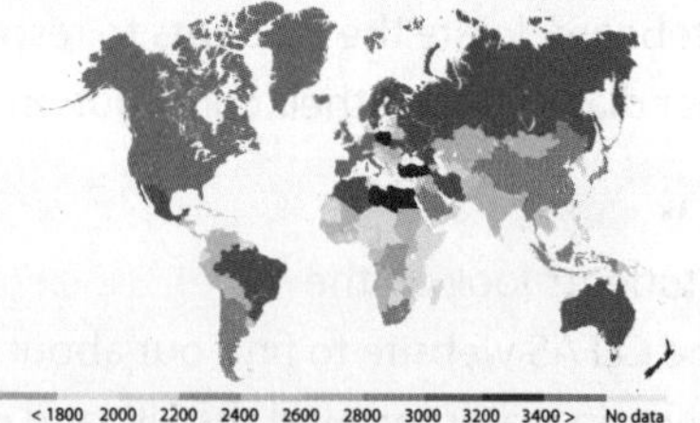

Figure 1 World food consumption 2001–2003.

Solutions to reduce global hunger

The United Nations World Food Programme (WFP) provides food assistance to save lives in disasters and emergency situations. In 2010, an earthquake devastated Haiti and there were severe floods in Pakistan. In Haiti, part of the emergency response consisted of distributing food aid with the goal of feeding children first. WFP also has training and education programmes to help poor people and communities become self-reliant and produce their own food.

The long-term solution to food security must involve the growth of more **staple crops**. These are crops such as cereals, the seeds of which can be kept all year round to provide energy and protein. This may require a conversion from growth of vegetables like carrots or leafy vegetables to cereals. It may also require more land for crop use in developed countries, for example amenity or national park land.

GM crops are widespread in America. In Europe many countries have banned their growth.

One way to increase yields of staple food may be to use genetically modified or GM crops. To date more than 39 million hectares of GM crops have been grown worldwide. Scientists have concerns about the potential effects of GM crops on human health, the environment and biological diversity.

Are the world's taps running dry?

The world's six billion people are using 54 per cent of all the accessible freshwater contained in rivers, lakes and underground **aquifers**. This is putting great pressure on the natural systems that recycle and replenish water supplies. The world cannot increase its supply of fresh water, but we can change the way we use it. For instance, management of water in agriculture should be improved. About 20 per cent of all crop land is irrigated. This irrigation accounts for 60 per cent of world water use. Drip irrigation and low-pressure sprinklers use far less water than conventional irrigation. If these techniques were widely adopted this would reduce water waste.

Irrigation needs careful management.

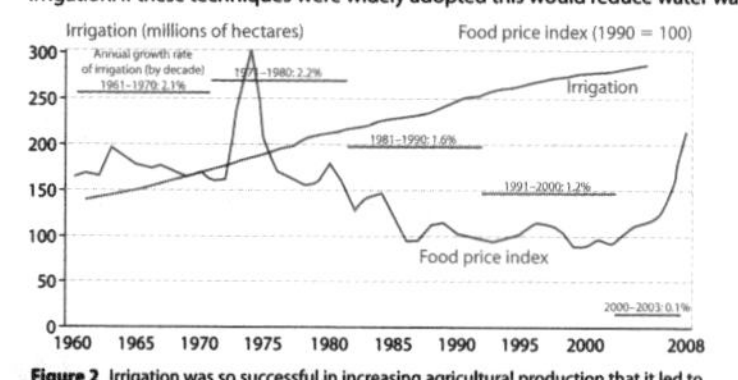

Figure 2 Irrigation was so successful in increasing agricultural production that it led to a 30-year decline in food prices.

Are food miles fair miles?

Developed countries import food from around the world to fill the supermarket shelves. **Food miles** are the distance food is transported from the place it is grown until it reaches the consumer. Some people have expressed concern about the carbon emissions produced when food is transported large distances. They argue that consumers in developed nations should avoid buying green beans from Peru or winter strawberries from Kenya.

However, the economy of less economically developed nations often relies heavily on food exports. If consumers boycott their goods, the livelihoods of farmers in those countries may be threatened.

Figure 3 The World Food Programme logo.

Questions

1. Explain what is meant by food security.
2. Give an example of where the WFP has supplied food aid and the types of food supplied.
3. How much more water is needed to produce one kilogram of beef than one kilogram of rice?
4. **(a)** How may GM crops be advantageous to world food supply? **(b)** Give two concerns that some scientists have about the potential effects of GM crops.
5. **(a)** How is water used extensively in agriculture and how could its use be better managed? **(b)** Look at Figure 2. **(i)** What was the increase in irrigation between 1970 and 2000? **(ii)** What was the difference in the price index between 1970 and 2000?
6. List three natural types of fresh water stores on Earth.
7. Evaluate the implications of using the term 'food miles' to make consumers aware of energy used to transport food we buy.
8. Discuss the options available to increase the world supply of staple crops by 2050.

A*

250

Humans and the environment 251

Learning objectives

Most students should be able to:

- evaluate methods being used to secure a global food supply
- describe the solutions being employed to provide the daily water needs of the global population
- assess the implications of food miles.

Some students should also be able to:

- explain what the FAO's (United Nations Food and Agriculture Organisation) aim is for every household worldwide [Ext]
- suggest strategies to prevent wasting the supply of fresh water. [Ext]

Key points

The human population is growing and making increasing demands on food and water supplies.

Short-term solutions to relieve hunger include food aid in emergency situations.

Long-term solutions to food security must involve greater production of staple food crops, and may include a role for GM foods.

Management of freshwater supplies must be improved, especially its use in agriculture.

Global food distribution is one factor affecting the environmental impact of food supply.

Aquifers | food miles | staple crops

Lesson activities

Starter

1 Ask the students to write down how much water a day they use. Discuss what the water is used for and write a list of suggestions. If the students have not mentioned water used in manufacturing and growing food etc. add these to the lists.

2 Show the BBC Learning Zone video clip 'World water supply'. Lasts for 1 minute 26 seconds.

Main

1 **World Food Production Worksheet B3 4.12a** is a comprehension and related questions on this subject.

2 **Water supply** Students use **Worksheet B3 4.12b** to support them in producing an information leaflet or puzzle about water needs and water supply.

3 **Fairer food miles** are explored in **worksheet B3 4.12c.**

Plenaries

1 Tell the students that Tilapia fish from Zimbabwe are available on the shelves of British supermarkets. Point out how poor and hungry the people of Zimbabwe are. There is little food available in their shops. Ask the students what positive outcomes they can suggest for the people of Zimbabwe from this situation. Hopefully they will suggest raised incomes for some families and safer working conditions. Show students the Channel 4 video clip 'What goes in your basket?' about UK imports of Tilapia fish from Zimbabwe. Several of the issues in the Student Book are well illustrated. The clip required is 26 mins 50 s after the start and it lasts approximately 8 minutes. Be aware that the earlier part of the programme includes scenes of butchery.

2 Use the puzzles and/or information leaflets produced using **Worksheet B3 4.12b**. Individual students can present their work or their work can be displayed on a notice board or table. Choose a couple of challenging puzzles for class use.

Homework

1 Students choose a case study from the UNESCO World Water Assessment Programme, WWAP – Case Studies and then produce a summary of it as a Word document.

2 Students research to find out which GM crops are grown in Europe and where GM crops are grown in the UK.

Points to note

- Take time to help students assimilate the statistics in the first paragraph in lesson B3 4.12 of the Student Book.
- Sensitivity to cultural, personal and religious preferences for food will be needed.
- A downloaded copy of the World Food Programme logo would be useful to show/display and discuss.

Route to A*

1 Students research the United Nation's Food and Agriculture Organisation Special Programme for Food Security, then produce a one hundred word summary of its aims as a Word document.

2 The World Food Programme (WFP) is the United Nations' food aid branch. Students research to find five facts about the WFP, then produce an A5 information flyer about it and download the WFP logo to add to their flyer.

Answers to Student Book questions

Science skills

a Suitable table and graph.

b Economic differences between countries; climate differences; differences in soil quality.

Answers

1 Food security is where the occupants of a household do not live in hunger or fear of starvation.

2 For example, Chile, Haiti. Cereals like rice are supplied.

3 About five times more water is needed to produce beef than rice.

4 **(a)** GM crops could increase yields and make agriculture more sustainable. **(b)** The effects on human health, the environment and biodiversity are concerns.

5 **(a)** Water is used in irrigation. It could be better managed by drip irrigation and low-pressure sprinklers. **(b) (i)** Approx. +100 million hectares. **(ii)** A decrease of approx. 90.

6 Rivers, lakes and underground aquifers.

7 Besides energy used in transport, food production may involve energy used for heating greenhouses, which may give the wrong impression of energy efficiency. The economies of some less economically developed countries depend on growing and exporting food, as do the livelihoods of the farmers.

8 GM foods can be grown, although concerns about the use of these exist; (answer should give one named concern). Conversion of other crops to cereals is another option, as are more land use for crops, increased number of small farmer systems in developing countries, and more efficient irrigation.

ISA practice: how does temperature affect fermentation?

In the Student Book, each ISA practice is contained on one double-page spread. However, you can, if you prefer, use the sheets provided in the Teacher and Technician Planning Pack and the Activity Pack to more closely mirror the experience of a real ISA which would then take place over several lessons and/or as homework.

Link to the specification

3.2 How Science Works

Observing phenomena can lead to the start of an investigation, experiment or survey. Careful observation is necessary before deciding which variables are the most important.

3.6 Controlled assessment

Scientific investigations often seek to identify links between two or more variables. [B4.1.1, B4.3.1.]

Scientists need to ensure repeatability, reproducibility and validity in evidence. [B4.3.3]

There is a link between the type of graph used and the type of variable represented. [B4.4.2]

In evaluating a whole investigation the repeatability, reproducibility and validity of the data obtained must be considered. [B4.5.2]

The patterns and relationships observed in data represent the behaviour of the variables in an investigation. However, it is necessary to look at patterns and relationships between variables with the limitations of the data in mind in order to draw conclusions. [B4.5.3, B4.5.4]

ISA practice: how does temperature affect fermentation?

A bread company has found a new yeast, and wants to investigate the fermentation of the yeast at different temperatures.

Section 1

1 Write a hypothesis about the fermentation at different temperatures for a yeast. Use information from your knowledge of fermentation to explain why you made this hypothesis. *(3 marks)*

2 Describe how you are going to do your investigation.
You should include:
- the equipment that you are going to use
- how you will use the equipment
- the measurements that you are going to make
- a risk assessment
- how you will make it a fair test.

You may include a labelled diagram to help you to explain your method.

In this question you will be assessed on using good English, organising information clearly and using specialist terms where appropriate. *(9 marks)*

3 Design a table that you could use to record all the data you would obtain during the planned investigation. *(2 marks)*

Total for Section 1: 14 marks

Section 2

Study Group 1 was a group of students who carried out an investigation into the hypothesis. They used several different temperatures of yeast and sugar solution. Figure 1 shows their results.

At 18°C the volume of CO_2 produced was 12 cm^3
At 23°C the volume of CO_2 produced was 16 cm^3
At 28°C the volume of CO_2 produced was 21 cm^3
At 33°C the volume of CO_2 produced was 25.5 cm^3
At 38°C the volume of CO_2 produced was 30 cm^3
At 43°C the volume of CO_2 produced was 35 cm^3

Figure 1 Study Group 1's results.

4 (a) Plot a graph of these results. *(4 marks)*
(b) What conclusion can you draw from the investigation about a link between temperature and the rate of fermentation? You should use any pattern that you can see in the results to support your conclusion. *(3 marks)*
(c) Do the results support the hypothesis you put forward in answer to question 1? Explain your answer. You should quote some figures from the data in your explanation. *(3 marks)*

Below are the results from three more study groups.

Study Group 2 was a second group of students who carried out a similar investigation. They used different temperatures. Figure 2 shows their results.

At 20°C the volume of CO_2 produced was 15 cm^3
At 30°C the volume of CO_2 produced was 23 cm^3
At 40°C the volume of CO_2 produced was 32 cm^3
At 50°C the volume of CO_2 produced was 29 cm^3
At 60°C the volume of CO_2 produced was 18 cm^3

Figure 2 Study Group 2's results.

Study Group 3 was a third group of students. They decided that they wanted to know what happened throughout the experiment, not just at the end. Table 1 shows their results.

Table 1 Results from Study Group 3.

Time after first gas released/min	Volume of gas collected/cm^3		
	18 °C	22 °C	26 °C
0	0	0	0
2	1	2	3
4	2	5	12
6	4	13	20
8	7	20	28
10	10	28	36
12	17	35	41

Study Group 4 were a group of scientists working for the bread company. They measured the loss in mass of the yeast and sugar solution at different temperatures. Instead of using just 100 cm^3 of sugar solution they used 1000 cm^3, and left the experiment for 1 hour. Their results are shown in Table 2, and plotted as a graph in Figure 3.

Table 2 Study Group 4's results.

Time / min	Loss in mass/grams			
	20 °C	30 °C	40 °C	45 °C
0	0	0	0	0
10	21	32	45	34
20	42	66	90	59
30	64	94	130	75
40	84	119	136	76
50	102	136	137	77
60	118	137	138	78

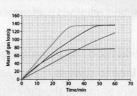

Figure 3 Graph of results from Study Group 4.

5 (a) Draw a sketch graph of the results from Study Group 2. *(3 marks)*
(b) Look at the results from Study Groups 2 and 3. Does the data support the conclusion you reached about the investigation in question 5(b)? Give reasons for your answer. *(3 marks)*
(c) The data contain only a limited amount of information. What other information or data would you need in order to be more certain whether or not the hypothesis is correct?
Explain the reason for your answer. *(3 marks)*
(d) Look at Study Group 4's results. Compare them with the data from Study Group 1. Explain how far the data support or do not support your answer to question 5(b). You should use examples from Study Group 4's results and from Study Group 1. *(3 marks)*

6 (a) Compare the results of Study Group 1 with Study Group 2. Do you think that the results for Study Group 1 are *reproducible*?
Explain the reason for your answer. *(3 marks)*
(b) Explain how Study Group 1 could use results from other groups in the class to obtain a more *accurate* answer. *(3 marks)*

7 Suggest how ideas from the original investigation and the other studies could be used by the bread company to decide the best temperature at which to ferment the bread (let it rise) and the optimum time for fermentation. *(3 marks)*

Total for Section 2: 31 marks

Total for the ISA: 45 marks

Learning objectives

Most students should be able to:
- make observations and develop into a hypothesis
- identify the independent and dependent variables in the hypothesis
- obtain some data to process
- produce a graph or bar chart from the data obtained
- identify any trends that may be present in the data
- relate that trend to their hypothesis.

Some students should also be able to:
- make a risk assessment of their chosen method, with suitable control measures
- examine the evidence obtained to establish its repeatability and /or reproducibility.

anomalous result calibration control measure hazard hypothesis mean observation prediction range repeatable reproducible research theory uncertainties (errors): random systematic zero validity variables: control categoric continuous dependent independent

Key points

Investigations should be designed so that patterns and relationships between variables can be identified.

It is important to ensure repeatability, reproducibility and validity in evidence when designing and evaluating investigations.

The choice of graph used depends upon the type of variable represented.

When drawing conclusions, the limitations of the data must be kept in mind.

Lesson activities

Starter

1 Show students a loaf of bread and a boiling tube/flask of fermenting yeast mixture. Ask them to describe the link between the two, and how they could make the yeast work quicker to make the bread rise (prove) faster.

Main

1 Researching and planning Students need to research, using at least two different sources, a way of investigating how temperature affects fermentation and develop a hypothesis. Suggest a suitable context, e.g. baking bread, fermenting beer, etc. Please refer to the **B3 ISA practice 3 Teacher and technician sheet.**

2 Students can complete their research/notes for homework. They need to be aware of the likely risks and how to control them. See the **B3 ISA practice 2 Student research notes sheet.**

3 Ask two students to read their notes on one of the points. Get the class to decide whose notes are best, with a reason. Repeat until all the points are covered.

4 Give students the **B3 ISA practice 3 Section 1 paper.**

5 In a following lesson students set up their investigation and record and process their results. Students can work in groups to obtain the data. If several groups have used the same method they may wish to pool results and obtain a mean. Please refer to the **B3 ISA practice 3 Student practical sheet.**

6 Students should process the data individually in **controlled** conditions. A bar chart or graph should be plotted and the trend of the graph/bar chart identified and a conclusion made.

7 The conclusion should be compared with their hypothesis to identity if their hypothesis has been confirmed or denied.

Plenaries

1 Students discuss sources of possible errors and ways to overcome them.

2 Give students the **B3 ISA practice 3 Section 2 paper.**

Homework

After the practical, ask students to write brief notes about ways in which they could improve their investigation. They should mention how to reduce errors and what further data or information they would need to confirm their conclusion.

Points to note

- With able students simply outline the points they need to cover. You should adjust delivery to match the time that it takes to obtain meaningful results.
- Students should describe a complex relationship between the independent variable and the dependent variable.

Route to A*

Students' risk assessment should include sensible risks, with a clear indication of the likelihood of the hazard occurring and how to sensibly control the risk.

Depending on how closely you wish to mirror the real ISA experience all three parts can be done in class or some can be done for homework. You should adjust delivery to match the time that it takes to obtain meaningful results.

Ask students to critically evaluate their data and explain that the findings are only valid within the range of the independent variable, whose range may be quite limited.

Answers to Student Book questions

5 **(a)** Both axes labelled. (1) A suitable curve/line drawn. (1) Indication (arrow or numbers) of direction of increase in value of axes. (1)

(b) The student states that overall the data supports the original hypothesis and quotes some data from tables that supports this. There is an appreciation that there is some conflicting evidence. (1)

Critical appraisal of data to include:

- Study 3 does support the hypothesis.
- Study Group 3 has used very small range of temperatures.
- Study 2 at low temperatures confirms the hypothesis.
- Study 2 at higher temperature doesn't confirm the hypothesis.
- From Study 2 it appears that the quickest fermentation occurs at about 40 °C. (2)

(c) Suggests at least one other piece of information that would be needed to form a firm conclusion. The reason for the need for this other information is clearly stated. (3)

(d) Comment that the data supports the hypothesis at lower temperatures. Increasing the temperature does increase the rate of loss of mass. Above 40 °C, the fermentation does not work as well, giving less of a loss of mass than at 20 °C after an hour. Uses data extensively to support the answer. (3)

For the full mark scheme, see the Teacher and Technician Planning Pack.

Answers

B1 4.3 (Continued from page 45 of Teacher Book)

Science skills

a Place equal numbers of marked banded and unbanded snails in an area of long grass and an area of open ground of similar colour (e.g. brown snails on brown earth). Leave for a few days, then return to see how many marked snails of each kind can be recovered alive. If camouflage is the key adaptation, then there should be more banded snails in the long grass and more unbanded snails in the open area. Also check to see if there are any shells predated by birds – you would expect to see more empty shells of banded snails in open land and plain shells in long grass areas. Possible improvements include a snail-proof barrier open on top around each plot, an experiment in which birds are presented with snails on different backgrounds, or a third plot with one sort of snail only, in equal quantities of marked and unmarked, to test whether the markings themselves are more noticeable to birds.

Answers

1 The yield (mass of seeds produced) increases up to a density of about 200 seeds sown per m^2, after which it decreases.

2 It is camouflaged against snow so that their prey doesn't notice them getting close – it is an ambush predator, and can't run for long.

3 **(a)** Predators can easily see and hear the robins. **(b)** They warn competing robins to keep away, so that the robin has enough food to feed its young.

4 Some examples are:

Resource	Example	Adaptation
food	lion	strong to fight off other animals
light	plants on rainforest floor	red-backed leaves to collect more light
water	cactus	large root system to gather as much water as possible
mate	stag	strong and with antlers for fighting
territory	robin	sings and fights to scare off other robins

5 To warn potential predators that they are poisonous – the blue stands out against the green of the plants. Young animals need to learn what is good to eat. They should quickly learn that bright colours are 'bad' food and so avoid blue frogs in future.

6 **(a)** It is an advantage because if he has the best feathers/gives the best display, the females will mate with him instead of with other males. **(b)** Males with the best display must have genes that make them strong and healthy, so the young that the females produce from mating with them will be more likely to be strong and healthy.

7 Poppy seeds must be present in the ground that has been cleared. Clearance of other plants gives the poppy seeds space and resources to germinate and grow into new plants. At the end of the year the plants scatter their seeds and die. The following year there are other plants growing in the ground. The poppy seeds cannot compete with the other plants so they don't germinate.

8 Competition for light occurs where there is heavy shade, as with bluebells in deciduous woodland and plants with red backs to their leaves in tropical rainforests. Competition for water and nutrients (dissolved in water) could occur wherever plants are too close together, as in the planted crop, or where water is short, such as with cacti and marram grass, which have deep roots to catch as much water as possible.

9 The advantage to the hoverfly is that it doesn't have to use energy to make a sting; however, predators, such as birds, will avoid trying to eat it because they think it is a wasp. There is no advantage to the wasp; and if there are more hoverflies than wasps, predators may get the impression that yellow/black striped insects are safe to eat and will start eating wasps as well as hoverflies. Then it will be no advantage to the hoverflies either. So numbers of hoverflies visible to predators must be less than numbers of wasps.

 (Continued from page 129 of Teacher Book)

Science skills

Round × wrinkled seed:

a All round seed.

b Using R for round and r for wrinkled (other suitable letters accepted):

Parents	RR × rr
Gametes	all R all r
First generation	all Rr (round seed)
Body cells	Rr × Rr
Gametes	Rr × Rr RR Rr Rr rr
Second generation:	3 round : 1 wrinkled

c Theoretical is 3 : 1 round to wrinkled, or 75% round. Actual is 3.33 : 1 or 76.9%, so a little high, but quite close to the theoretical value.

Tall × dwarf stem:

a All tall.

b Using T for tall and t for dwarf (other suitable letters accepted):

Parents	TT × tt
Gametes	all T all t
First generation	all Tt (round seed)
Body cells	Tt × Tt
Gametes	Tt × Tt TT Tt Tt tt
Second generation:	3 tall : 1 dwarf

c Theoretical is 3 : 1 tall to dwarf, or 75% tall. Actual is 2.84 : 1 or 74.0%, which is fairly close to the theoretical value.

Answers

1 A dominant allele produces its form of the characteristic even if only one of the pair of chromosomes carries that allele. A recessive allele only produces its form of the characteristic when both chromosomes of the pair carry that allele.

2 Fifty per cent, because two combinations out of four produce boys.

3 Fifty per cent, because the chance of having a boy or girl is the same each time/is not affected by previous children.

4 Using F for purple flower allele and f for white flower allele (any suitable letters can be used as an alternative, but must be defined).

		First parent	
		F	F
Second parent	f	Ff	Ff
	f	Ff	Ff

100% purple, 0% white.

5

		First parent	
		F	f
Second parent	f	Ff	ff
	f	Ff	ff

50% purple, 50% white.

6 A cross between purple- and white-flowered plants produces only purple flowers, which could be one outcome of the blended inheritance idea. But a cross between the offspring from that first cross produces plants with only white or purple flowers, proving that there has been no blending.

7 Creating pure-breeding parents helped to make sure that each cross was repeatable and that results could be reliably compared. Making the crosses by hand and preventing further crosses made sure that the offspring were from the crosses he was investigating and not random crosses with plants of other characteristics. Repeating the experiments many times helps to average out random errors.

B3 3.5 (Continued from page 171 of Teacher Book)

Science skills

a Heat production increases during activity as more respiration is carried out in muscles to produce contraction; some of that energy is converted to heat energy. Heat production decreases as exercise ends because the muscles have stopped contracting, and the body slowly returns to the state it was in before exercise.

b Increased blood flow nearer to the skin surface where heat energy can more easily be transferred to the surroundings. Increased sweat flow on to the skin surface where its evaporation takes heat energy away from the skin surface.

Practical

c The controlled variable would be the external temperature. You would need different places at different temperatures, and leave the person in that temperature for a short while, so their body adjusted to it, before taking skin temperature.

Answers

1 Most of the man's body is much warmer than the air surrounding it.

2 The warmest areas are around the head, heart and lungs; the coolest areas are the extremities.

3 The rate of cell reactions is controlled by enzymes. Many enzymes in the human body work best at around 37 °C. Maintaining a core body temperature of around 37 °C means that reactions in the major organs of the body controlled by these enzymes can work most efficiently.

4 Flow diagram, or similar, showing two pathways:

Either:

Core body temperature of 37 °C – Receptors in brain and skin detect temperature increase – Thermoregulatory centre in brain instructs body mechanisms to increase heat loss – Core body temperature of 37 °C.

Or:

Core body temperature of 37 °C – Receptors in brain and skin detect temperature decrease – Thermoregulatory centre in brain instructs body mechanisms to decrease heat loss and increase heat generation from shivering – Core body temperature of 37 °C.

5 When you get hot, receptors monitoring the temperature of blood flowing through the brain and in the skin detect an increase in body temperature. The thermoregulatory centre of the brain responds by instructing the blood vessels supplying the skin capillaries to dilate. This increases blood flow to the skin surface. The redness of the blood shows through the skin, so you look pink.

6

Part of body	Temperature too high	Temperature too low
blood vessels supplying the skin capillaries	dilate to increase blood flow	constrict to keep more blood flow deeper in body
sweat production	increases, releasing watery sweat onto skin surface where it evaporates	reduces, so less watery sweat is produced
muscles	no effect	shiver, releasing heat energy from respiration
body hair	lies flat to allow faster heat exchange from body to air	stand upright to create still layer of air that insulates, reducing rate of heat loss

7 The investigation would need a range of activity levels, e.g. different speeds on an exercise machine or speeds of walking/running. Activity level is the controlled variable. Skin temperature, the measured variable, could be measured using thermistors. All other variables, e.g. the person doing the activity, air temperature, humidity, should be kept the same as far as possible. Between each measurement, the person doing the activity will need time to recover completely and for their body temperature to fall. Repeating measurements with the same person for each level of activity will help to increase the reliability of the results. Repeating the whole investigation with one or more other test subjects will check if the results can be applied generally or are specific to one person.

8 The thermoregulatory centre in the brain monitors the temperature of the body. It also controls core body temperature by adjusting heat loss and gain by the body. The thermoregulatory centre receives responses from receptors in the skin and in blood flowing through the brain. If body temperature is too high, it instructs the blood vessels supplying the capillaries in the skin to dilate and allow more blood nearer to the skin surface. This allows heat to be transferred to the air more easily. The centre also instructs the sweat glands to produce watery sweat, which flows out on to the skin and evaporates, reducing skin surface temperature.

If core body temperature is too low, the thermoregulatory centre instructs the blood vessels supplying skin capillaries to constrict, reducing blood flow near the skin, and reduces the production of watery sweat so less heat is lost. Muscles also start to shiver to generate heat released by respiration.